THE RELIGIOUS ORIGINS OF THE FRENCH REVOLUTION

THE
RELIGIOUS
ORIGINS OF THE
FRENCH
REVOLUTION

From Calvin to the Civil Constitution,

1560–1791

Dale K. Van Kley

Yale University Press   New Haven and London

Designed by James J. Johnson and set in Fournier
Roman types by The Composing Room of Michigan,
Inc., Grand Rapids, Michigan.
Printed in the United States of America by Edwards
Brothers, Inc., Ann Arbor, Michigan.

A catalogue record for this book is available from the
British Library.

The paper in this book meets the guidelines
for permanence and durability of the Committee
on Production Guidelines for Book Longevity
of the Council on Library Resources.

Library of Congress Cataloging-in-Publication Data

Van Kley, Dale K., 1941–
    The religious origins of the French Revolution :
from Calvin to the civil constitution, 1560–1791 /
Dale K. Van Kley.
        p.   cm.
    Includes bibliographical references and index.
    ISBN 0-300-06478-0 (alk. paper)

    1. France—History—Revolution, 1789–1799—
Religious aspects.   2. Christianity and politics—
History.   3. France—Church history—18th century.
4. Secularism—France—History—18th century.
5. Church and state—France—History— 18th century.
I. Title.
DC158.2.V36   1996
944.04–dc20   95-47072
                                                    CIP

10 9 8 7 6 5 4 3 2 1

Contents

Acknowledgments

This book has in some sense been in the making ever since, as a frustrated student of the German Reformation, I stumbled into Stanley Mellon's Yale University graduate seminar on Restoration and July Monarchy France and wrote my seminar paper on Lamennais and the birth of liberal Catholicism. Having won me over to French history, Mellon later raised no objection to my dropping back to the eighteenth century. The French eighteenth century was at least closer to the sixteenth century and, though not German, also allowed me to indulge an interest in religion in the "age of reason" originally aroused by the reading of Carl Becker's *The Heavenly City of the Eighteenth-Century Philosophers* and Robert Palmer's *Catholics and Unbelievers in Eighteenth-Century France*. The "cunning of reason" eventually had it that Palmer himself came to preside over the last stages of my dissertation. But I had not gone to Calvin College as an undergraduate or returned there to teach for nothing. And so it was only a matter of time before I would try to renew contact with the sixteenth century in an effort to have my French eighteenth century and my reformation too. That, in a very few words, is the history of this book.

It goes without saying that in the course of these thirty and some years I have incurred a staggering indebtedness to foundations, to academic institutions, and to people, and I can only hope to acknowledge the most recent debts here. The greatest of these is to The Pew Charitable Trusts, specifically its Evangelical Scholars' Program, which relieved me of much of an otherwise heavy undergraduate teaching load during the years 1991 to 1994 and allowed me to break the logjam of scholarly commitments, of which this book was the chief. Without that help this book would never have happened. With some additional help from the American Council of Learned Societies, the Evangelical Scholarly Initiative also took me and part of my family back to Paris for the summer of 1993, when I did some remedial research on the 1720s and 1730s in the Bibliothèque Mazarine, the Bastille Archives, and the Bibliothèque de Port-Royal. As usual, Mlle. Odette Barenne gave me the run of the Bibliothèque de Port-Royal, allowing me an unmediated access to the Le Paige Collection, the single richest source for eighteenth-century political and religious history in all of France.

The writing of this book actually began, however, in January 1990 at the National Humanities Center in Research Triangle Park, North Carolina, where the benign administration of Robert Connor and Kent Mullikin and the friendship of my fellow fellow Melvin Richter created an ideal ambiance for taking inventory of my ideas and putting pen to paper. Or rather the writing did not begin until that January, since the bicentennial commemoration of the French Revolution, at best a mixed blessing for French historians, somehow consumed my first four or five months at the Center. I nonetheless left the Humanities Center with drafts of five of the book's six chapters, incomplete and imperfect though they were. Research specifically geared toward a book like this takes me back even further, to 1983–84 at the Newberry Library in Chicago and its splendid and still underused French Revolution Collection, where an NEH Fellowship supported my family for ten months, and then in Paris, where a Fulbright-Hayes grant sustained us for the three summer months. I did not then formally propose, much less promise, to write a book, although essays tantamount to one have since come from the research done that year. But I know that Dr. Richard Brown, then head of the Newberry's Research and Education Department, ardently hoped for a book, and I am happy at long last to be able to deliver one. Last but not least, I am indebted to a Calvin College sabbatical and Faculty Research Fellowship that took me to Paris during the winter of 1987, when I did the pivotal research on the 1770s linking my earlier research on eighteenth-century French Jansenism with the patriot movement of the prerevolutionary decades.

My indebtedness to professional colleagues and friends is just as extensive, if harder to define. Although it is not likely that he knows it, the suggestion that I write a book like this one first came from Keith Michael Baker, who, conversing with me in 1984 about a book I had just published on the mixed religious and political controversies in mid-eighteenth-century France, observed that those controversies were peculiarly damaging to an absolutist political order that had originally justified itself by its ability to resolve and transcend such conflicts in the sixteenth century. As it all too frequently happens, it was hard not to wonder why it had not occurred to me to say something in print so obviously true and to the point, and so I resolved to do so some time in the future. That resolve was fortified by François Furet, who, reacting in 1990 to what became Chapter 5, admonished me to give more weight in my analyses to absolutism's role in shaping the religious configuration of early-modern France. Frequent and sometimes maddening conversations with Lionel Rothkrug in the latter 1980s always left me with the probably salutary impression that there was much more potential significance to the evidence before me than met the eye—or at least my eye. Although he might well maintain that impression, Rothkrug's often penetrating instincts and insights left their mark on the book's overall argument at a number of crucial junctures. It was at Orest Ranum's urging that I tried to sharpen and reinforce the book's definitions of competing ecclesiologies and articulate the implications that they held for the whole political order. And David Avrom Bell, like Ranum a reader for Yale University Press, went beyond every conceivable call of duty in critiquing the manuscript. Often stating my arguments more clearly than I myself had, his many helpful suggestions improved the focus and organization of some of the chapters. He also all but walked me through the introduction, paragraph by paragraph.

     Many other friends and colleagues read and critiqued the manuscript or at least parts of it. The list includes Gail Bossenga of the University of Kansas, Yann Fauchois of the Bibliothèque nationale, Rita Hermon-Belot of the EHESS in Paris, Jeanine Olsen of Rhode Island College, Thomas Kaiser of the University of Arkansas at Little Rock, Marianne Robins of the Calvin History Department, James Smither of Grand Valley State University, Susan Rosa of the University of Wisconsin-Milwaukee, and John Woodbridge of Trinity Evangelical Seminary. Jane Haney, the Calvin History Department's ontological secretary—that is, one than which no greater can be conceived—detected innumerable typos and cheerfully bore the burden of imposing a consistent style on the manuscript, while Dan Heaton, Yale University Press's manuscript editor, did a superb job of both curtailing my occasionally rococo sentences and drawing out my more elliptical thoughts. Together these readers saved me from more mistakes than I would like to remember and from no small number of stylistic infelicities. Mine alone, of course, is the cross of those that remain.

     Throughout the past twelve hectic years my colleagues in the History Department of Calvin College have been most supportive of my scholarship, taking a lively interest in its results and putting up with my frequent leaves of absence. In a real sense, this book is the Calvin History Department's as a whole. Calvin's administration has invariably allowed me to take these leaves and generously supplemented the grants I received, making them affordable for my family as a whole. To the considerable extent that my family was a part of this project, they cheerfully and frequently uprooted themselves to spend time in parts unknown and far from home. And when, as it also happened, my family could not be a very integral part of the project, they stoically put up with my physical absences while away and my just as frequent mental absences while at home. I am deeply indebted to their patience and forbearance. To my wife Sandra, my daughters Annique and Kristen, and my son Erik, my most heartfelt thanks. This book is dedicated to you.

Abbreviations

Introduction

TO SUGGEST THAT THE FRENCH REVOLUTION HAD RELI-
gious origins, and that the religion in question was mainly Catholic Christianity, may seem deliberatively provocative if not outrageous. What revolution before the Bolshevik Revolution of 1917 was more anti-Christian than the French Revolution of 1789? Even in its initial and most moderate phase the French Revolution deprived the Catholic Church of the tithe, nationalized its property, and ended its corporate independence, unilaterally redrew ecclesiastical boundaries, all but abolished the regular clergy, demoted the secular clergy to the status of elected and salaried state servants, and persecuted clergymen who refused to swear loyalty to these and other peremptorily imposed "reforms." During the Revolution's later and more radical phases, revolutionaries imprisoned or massacred many clergy, hounded many more into hiding or exile, "persuaded" still others to renounce their "superstitious" profession, rewrote the Christian calendar and changed Christian place-names, destroyed or defaced Christian iconography, cut down church towers and melted down church bells, and rechristened—or de-christened—churches themselves as "temples of reason" or of some "Supreme Being." How could a revolution that invented "dechristianization" have had Christian origins?

Yet the claim for Christian origins is no more remote than that of the more traditional pretenders to influence in a revolution that virtually refused to acknowledge origins of any sort. For the French Revolution was the first revolution proudly to proclaim its novelty and to condemn most of the immediate past—the "feudal" noble and "despotic" royal pasts, to be sure, but eventually the "superstitious" and "fanatical" Christian past as well. So unless the French Revolution be regarded as absolutely sui generis, it cannot be taken at its word on that or any similar score. Just as eighteenth-century atheism itself presupposed and to that extent perpetuated the theism it denied, so even dechristianization at least presupposed Christianity and might have obscured its debt to it by its very spectacularity.[1] And if, as it has been recently argued, the French Revolution's notions of national sovereignty and individual rights were dialectically indebted to Old Regime absolutism and privilege, it would seem hardly more paradoxical to suggest, for example, that the Revolution's political declarations mediated meaning derived from the profession of faith, that its conception of law might have carried connotations of dogma, that its many "scissions" recapitulated the experience of schism, or that revolutionary "regeneration" owed something to the Christian doctrine by that name.[2] The many political credos, catechisms, professions of faith, pater nosters, votive masses, and litanies that appeared in the titles of revolutionary pamphlets attest to the massive weight of Christian liturgical and doctrinal forms in the making of revolutionary political culture.

The longer-term falling out between the Revolution and the Catholic Church, moreover, gave all sides a vested interest in denying religious origins— except, perhaps, for the ultra-Catholic contention that it had Protestant ones. The parting of the paths between the Catholic Church and the Revolution had no sooner begun than some of those in favor of the Revolution's ecclesiastical legislation proudly invoked the authority of the eighteenth-century's anti-Christian philosophes, while some Catholics both inside and outside of the revolutionary assemblies accusingly pointed to the same Enlightenment as inspiring the policies of their political opponents. That contentious tendency only increased as the Revolution grew more radical. Whatever else may have divided them, just about all the revolutionaries were at one in their reluctance to acknowledge intellectual ancestry in what they denounced as superstition. And by the time the Revolution was over Catholics were similarly reluctant to acknowledge complicity in an upheaval that had culminated in dechristianization. The work of obfuscation did not stop there, for the Revolution foisted its version of an exclusively "enlightened" ancestry on nineteenth-century French politics and historiography, as a Catholic Right and a liberal Left generally overpowered all voices in between and disagreed about everything, with one exception: both conceptualized the history and the future of the Revolution and Catholicism in terms of mutual exclusion.

1. Alan Charles Kors, *Atheism in France, 1650–1729* (Princeton, N.J., 1990).

2. David D. Bien, "Old Regime Origins of Democratic Liberty," in *The French Idea of Freedom: The Old Regime and the Declaration of Rights of 1789*, ed. Dale Van Kley (Stanford, Calif., 1994), pp. 23–71; and François Furet, "The Revolution Is Over," in *Interpreting the French Revolution*, trans. Elborg Forster (Cambridge, 1981), pp. 1–79.

That the Revolution owed nothing to Catholicism is as plausible as that it owed nothing to France. For to be French was to be Catholic until the very eve of the Revolution: the Catholic sacrament of baptism functioned as a certificate of citizenship for native-born Frenchmen, while acceptance of Catholicism was a prerequisite for the naturalization of foreigners.[3] For all of France's twenty-seven million subjects and throughout the length of the prerevolutionary eighteenth century the Catholic calendar and church bells continued to order time, and Catholic churches and other edifices dominated space. As measured by such indexes as the provision for requiem masses or sacred burial and the invocations to Christ in last wills and testaments, "baroque" Catholic observance perhaps peaked in France in the first third of the eighteenth century and held its own for a while thereafter.[4] This identity of France and Catholicity was hardly compromised by the existence of forty or fifty thousand Jews who waited until the Revolution for citizenship, or by a half a million or so Calvinists or Huguenots who obtained a minimal civil status in 1788 after a hundred years of official nonexistence. Nor for that matter was it aggressively challenged by philosophes, most of whom found it impossible to imagine a France formally separated from the church. On the contrary, philosophes underwent baptism in the church, the few who married solemnized their marriages as a Catholic sacrament, and most ended their days receiving the last rites of Catholicity.

It is true that French philosophes were in the forefront of the eighteenth-century European Enlightenment, that the French variant of enlightenment was far more anti-Christian than others in Europe, and that its campaign against the "infamous" Christian "thing" could not but compromise France's identity as a Catholic kingdom in the long run. Beginning in 1750 Diderot's and d'Alembert's *Encyclopedia* undermined Christian belief with a system of sly cross-references like the entry *anthropophages,* which turned out to be about cannibals and referred the reader to *eucharist* and *communion;* the whole rationale of the work disenfranchised faith as a source of knowledge, putting *knowledge of God* in a category with *divination* and *black magic.*[5] At the same time Voltaire overtly ridiculed just about all Christian beliefs except in God and the golden rule, and the baron d'Holbach went still further, anonymously preaching atheism even to Voltaire's chagrin. Yet the capacity of Voltaire's *Philosophical Dictionary* or d'Holbach's

3. On the history of citizenship in France before the Revolution see Charlotte C. Wells, *Law and Citizenship in Early Modern France* (Baltimore, 1994).

4. Michel Vovelle, *Piété baroque et déchristianisation en Provence au dix-huitième siècle: Les attitudes devant la mort d'après les clauses des testaments* (Paris, 1973), p. 610; and Pierre Chaunu, *La mort à Paris: XVIe, XVIIe, XVIIIe siècles* (Paris, 1978), pp. 432–56.

5. Diderot and d'Alembert, *Encyclopédie, ou dictionnaire des sciences et des métiers, par une société de gens de lettres,* 36 vols. (Geneva, 1777–79), 2:742; and Robert Darnton, "Philosophers Trim the Tree of Knowledge: The Epistemological Strategy of the *Encyclopédie*," in *The Great Cat Massacre and Other Episodes in French Cultural History* (New York, 1984), pp 200–201.

Christianity Exposed to shock their readers presupposed a large residue of belief on the part of even most literate Frenchmen who, even if they had absorbed much of the Enlightenment's terrestrial outlook, remained for the most part unaware of any tension between secular lights and the basic tenets of Christian faith. The many Catholics who joined Masonic lodges in the prerevolutionary decades did not think of Catholicism and Freemasonry as incompatible. Even philosophes remained more Christian—even more Catholic—than they knew they were. When, as he often did, Voltaire invidiously contrasted the consensus achieved by natural philosophers to the many disputes and schisms dividing Christians—"there are no sects among geometricians, he repeatedly chided"—he unwittingly damned Christianity by means of an apologetical topos long employed by Catholics against Protestants.[6] Catholicism's unity, universality, and perpetuity—so went the argument—were the infallible marks or *notae* of truth, while the Protestantism's divisions and "variations" were by themselves evidence of error, quite apart from any examination of the beliefs in question.[7]

Not only did eighteenth-century Catholicism continue to make headway against Protestant "heresy" by means of this and other arguments—and with a little help from the French monarchy—but, with its ranks replenished and upgraded by the Catholic Reformation's seminary and new congregations like Saint-Sulpice and the Oratory, the Catholic Church held its own even against that monarchy. In the midst of the wreckage of once self-governing corps and corporations and at a time when "ten nobles could not get together to confer on any subject without the king's express permission," the church alone, as Alexis de Tocqueville pointed out, retained its financial independence and corporate autonomy intact, supported by the mandatory tithe and income from its own seigneurial property.[8] Although the church's periodical contributions to the monarchy were not really the voluntary "free gifts" that their name suggested, the financial negotiations with the monarchy that they necessitated kept the Gallican clergy's periodical General Assemblies and interim agencies in good working order—good enough at least to win occasional concessions in royal religious policy in return for its financial outlays. And although the church's "spiritual" jurisdiction suffered some losses against the secular justice administered by the royal courts, the church maintained its separate ecclesiastical courts or *officialités* until the very end of the Old Regime. Despite the suppression of the Jesuits and the closing of their

6. Voltaire, *secte*, in *Dictionnaire philosophique, comprenant les 118 articles parus sous ce titre du vivant de Voltaire avec leurs suppléments parus dans les Questions sur l'Encyclopédie*, ed. Raymond Naves, Garnier series (Paris, 1967), p. 385. See also *tolérance*, p. 406.

7. Susan Rosa, "Il était possible aussi que cette conversion fût sincère": Turenne's Conversion in Context," in *FHS* 18 (Spring 1994):632–66.

8. Alexis de Tocqueville, *L'ancien régime et la Révolution française* in *OC*, ed. J.-P. Mayer (Paris, 1951–91), vol. 2, pt. 1:170.

colleges in 1762, moreover, education remained an almost exclusively clerical affair in Old Regime France, from the Sorbonne in Paris to the humblest priestly tutor in the countryside. Despite the steady growth of royal administration in the eighteenth century, the parish priest and his Sunday homily remained the monarchy's only reliable mouthpiece for communicating with all of its twenty-seven million subjects. And whatever the ups and downs of the Gallican church's doings with the Bourbon monarchy in the eighteenth century, Catholicism continued to give that monarchy its identity to the very end. When, in June 1791, Louis XVI tried unsuccessfully to remove himself physically from France, he did so in defense of Tridentine Catholicism.

Churchmen were also everywhere and conspicuous. Following the example of Louis XIII, who ruled with the help of the cardinals Richelieu and Mazarin, the monarchy of Louis XV and Louis XVI entrusted major ministerial responsibility to clergymen on at least four occasions: to Guillaume Dubois from 1716 to 1723, to André-Hercule de Fleury from 1726 to 1743, to Joachim-François de Pierre, abbé de Bernis, from 1757 to 1758, and to Loménie de Brienne from 1787 to 1788. If judged by the presence of clerics on the membership lists of learned academies or by the number of publications whose authors were churchmen, learned culture remained a clerical culture to a degree out of all proportion to the clergy's percentage of the population. Churchmen or former students of theology at the Sorbonne—the abbé Etienne Bonnet de Condillac, the abbé Gabriel Bonnet de Mably, André Morellet, the abbé Guillaume-Thomas Raynal, and Anne-Robert Turgot—were conspicuous in the ranks of the philosophes themselves, while just about all lay philosophes could count clergy or very pious believers among their closest relatives. Diderot's younger brother was a priest, Condorcet's uncle was successively bishop of Lisieux and of Auxerre, Voltaire's older brother dabbled in miracles and apocalyptic signs and wonders, and D'Alembert's uncle was Pierre-Guérin, the cardinal de Tencin, and his mother an ex-nun. Even the early Revolution owed some of its crucial successes to priests, most notably those who defected from the First Order in enough numbers to embolden the Third Estate to proclaim itself the National Assembly in June 1789. And the abbé Emmanuel-Joseph Sieyès, author of the most famous pamphlet of the whole Revolution, was a curate under the Bishop of Chartres.

That priests and curates were willing to break ranks with their bishops and the rest of the First Order is evidence of division within the French Catholic Church. Although in 1789 that division seemed to be mainly about power and position within the ecclesiastical hierarchy, it had assumed religious and theological form earlier in the century, pitting austere disciples of Saint Augustine, repeatedly condemned as Jansenists by the papacy, against much of the episcopal hierarchy and the influential Society of Jesus—Jesuits—supported by the monarchy. In retrospect it is easy to see that that division seriously weakened the eighteenth-century Gallican church, enabling the likes of Voltaire to point to doctrinal division as evidence of mutual ignorance and belying Catholic claims to unity in the face of Protestant dissent. Yet the church had weathered internal controversy before, and, in the short run at least, it is not surprising that the Gallican church should have thought itself strong enough to bear the heat of intra-Catholic combat under the sun of the High Enlightenment. Religious controversy kept the church and doctrinal issues conspicuously on the pages of eighteenth-century newsprint and even generating newsprint of its own in the form of the clandestine Jansenist weekly called the *Nouvelles ecclésiasiques (Ecclesiastical News)* and an anti-Jansenist periodical reply. Sacred and secular being as insepar-able as they were, the controversy spilled over and occupied public space, at least until 1770; the boundaries of church and state being as porous as they were, much of the ecclesiastical reflection generated by that controversy was also reflection about the state. Indeed, the controversy over the condemnation of Jansenism in eighteenth-century France may have been the last great religious controversy in western Europe that was at the same time a major affair of state. At one of its high points in 1728 the Jansenist weekly thumbed its nose at authority in both church and state, while police observers, frustrated by their inability to penetrate the news sheet's clandestinity, regularly estimated Jansenist effectives at three-fourths of the population of some of the same Parisian quarters that would abound in revolutionary sans culottes sixty-five years later. That century-long dissention within the Catholic Church, then, suggests that such religious origins as the French Revolution may have had were not simple or one-directional, that they may have been a factor in the formation of both counterrevolutionary and revolutionary ideology.

If so, France would have been far from unique in the Europe of the age of democratic revolutions. For elsewhere in Europe the transition from confessional conflict to political ideology was clear enough. Another strain of Catholic Reformism (also called Jansenism) was current elsewhere in western Catholic Europe, particularly in Austria, Italy, and Spain, and it, too, encountered a militant propapal Catholicism; these rivals acted as religious bridges to "liberal" and "conservative" political ideologies, respectively.[9] These Catholic cases have Protestant counterparts in the well-documented role of Presbyterian and Congregationalist Dissent or Non-Conformity, along with a resurgent High-Church Anglicanism in the making of English political radicalism and conservatism.[10] So pervasive were religion and religious forms of argumentation in eighteenth-century England that J. C. D. Clark has been able to make a plausible if much disputed case for the

9. See Dale Van Kley, "Piety and Politics in the Century of Lights," in the new *Cambridge History of Eighteenth-Century Political Thought* (Cambridge, forthcoming).

10. On the religious origins of English radicalism see James Bradley, *Religion, Revolution, and English Radicalism: Non-Conformity in Eighteenth-Century Politics and Society* (Cambridge, 1990).

persistence of an English "old regime" until the parliamentary reform of 1832.[11] And although the Protestant Germanies might seem to be an exception to this patterns as to so many others, enough evidence has accumulated surrounding Lutheran Pietism's midwifery in the making of nineteenth-century German nationalism to invite some comparison, say, to Jansenism's role in the Italian Risorgimento or in Spanish nationalist resistance to the Napoleonic occupation.[12] What is clearly different about France in the eighteenth century is the presence of an enlightenment sufficiently anti-Catholic—indeed, anti-Christian—in tone as to make for a third force in contrast to the gradual shading of the cause of lights into that of religious dissent elsewhere in Europe. But that difference should not be permitted to obscure other obvious similarities between France and the rest of Europe.

Another feature unique to France is that, whereas elsewhere in Catholic Europe as in Protestant Prussia the cause of religious dissent allied itself with "enlightened" monarchs against ecclesiastical establishments, in France as in seventeenth-century England religious dissent found secular institutional support *against* a monarchy that allied itself with an ecclesiastical establishment. For in France religious dissent took refuge in the royal law courts, or parlements, especially the Parlement of Paris, which were manned by judges or magistrates ennobled by inheritable ownership of their judicial offices. The result is that the religious history of eighteenth-century France is entwined in that of constitutional contestation between the parlements and Bourbon absolutism—entwined in political history, that is, even more than elsewhere on the European continent. Any attempt to find religious origins of the French Revolution must therefore remain close to political ground, even at the risk of having to rehabilitate political origins almost as obscured by the Revolution and Counterrevolution as are the religious origins. For revolutionaries were just as loath to recognize any indebtedness to Old Regime parlements as to Catholicism, while the postrevolutionary parlementary nobility was similarly reluctant to acknowledge complicity in the origins of a revolution that destroyed the parlements and abolished titles of nobility.

Even if, finally, one holds that the eighteenth century was a religiously tepid century and that "real" belief was in abeyance—the vitality of "belief" is of course notoriously elusive and hard to verify—it remains the case that the eighteenth century does not exhaust the search for the Revolution's origins, which on any reasonable reading must be taken back to the sixteenth century, the rise of absolutism, and the beginning of what Tocqueville thought of as the "old regime" in France. For it was then that, caught in the crossfire of a religious civil war that

---

11. J. C. D. Clark, *English Society, 1688–1832: Ideology, Social Structure, and Political Practice during the Ancien Regime* (Cambridge, 1985).

12. G. Kaiser, *Pietismus und Patriotismus im Literarischen Deutschland* (Wiesbaden, 1961); Maurice Vaussard, *Jansénsime et gallicanisme aux origines du Risorgimento* (Paris, 1959); and Richard Herr, *The Eighteenth-Century Revolution in Spain* (Princeton, N.J., 1959).

pitted the forces of Protestant reform against an ever more militant Catholicism, the French monarchy reinvented itself as a religious as well as a political institution that, while it raised the monarchy above the confessional fray in the short run, made it uniquely vulnerable to religious criticism in the longer run. It was as a reconstructed religious institution that the monarchy came under renewed religious as well as "enlightened" attack in the eighteenth century. What outright religious civil war failed to fell in the sixteenth century, religious controversy in an era of public opinion effectively undid in the century of lights. Hence the book's starting point in 1560 and its attempt to think of the religious origins of the Revolution in the longer term.

That much said about religious origins and political context, it is not possible to read the Voltaires and the Diderots out of the French eighteenth century or to pretend that their Enlightenment had nothing to do with the origins of the French Revolution. If religious origins there were, these could not have remained unaffected by the Enlightenment or the Enlightenment by them. On the one hand, religious conflict helped politicize and to some degree even Catholicize the French Enlightenment; on the other hand, contact with an Enlightenment context conceptually radicalized and secularized both sides of the religious conflict, aiding and abetting its transition to ideological conflict. Hence, finally, the book's partial engagement with secular political ideology and ideological origins as well. If it does not also address itself to the subject of social and economic origins, it is not due to the opinion that the Revolution had no such origins or that they are irrelevant to religion but rather to the conviction that enough is enough, that sufficient unto this book is the evil thereof. What might be said by way of further clarification is that the book pretends neither to be *the* history of the Revolution's religious origins nor to replace the many existing treatments of its ideological origins. Much less does it pretend to be a total explanation of why the Revolution occurred. On the religious front, this book hardly touches on the post-1685 Huguenot diaspora—the subject of a very different book—while on the ideological front it leaves large tracts of the Enlightenment in the shade. What it is, then, is a look at the ideological origins of the French Revolution in long-term religious perspective, with close attention to the political conjuncture.

Readers familiar with the Old Regime and its historiographical scene will recognize this book as not unrelated to others that I have written on the interplay between politics, religion, and ideology in eighteenth-century France, namely *The Jansenists and the Expulsion of the Jesuits from France, 1757–1765,* which appeared in 1975, and *The Damiens Affair and the Unraveling of the Old Regime, 1750–1770,* published in 1984.[13] A straightforward monograph, the first of these books argued

---

13. Dale Van Kley, *The Jansenists and the Expulsion of the Jesuits from France, 1757–1765* (New Haven, Conn., 1975); and *The Damiens Affair and the Unraveling of the Old Regime, 1750–1770* (Princeton, N.J., 1984).

that Jansenists, not philosophes, engineered an event long thought of as one of the first political successes of the Enlightenment in France, while the second, a more ambitious enterprise, used an unemployed domestic servant's physical assault on King Louis XV in 1757 as a narrative springboard to demonstrate the centrality of religious and ecclesiastical conflicts in the breakdown of the Old Regime and the ideological origins of the French Revolution. Although research for the present book began as an attempt to complete that argument by extending it to the French Revolution itself, the discipline of writing several preliminary essays on the admittedly more secular politics of the prerevolutionary period gave rise to the sober realization that they did not together amount to a book, or at least not a very coherent book about *religious* origins; and that these, if they were to hold their own in the ideologically heterogeneous decades immediately preceding the Revolution, would have to make up in time for what they would inevitably lose in space. The project hence gradually took on the proportions of a much more synthetic study, one that would span the whole French eighteenth century and root its religious conflicts in the religious civil wars of the sixteenth century.

That a book about the religious origins of the French Revolution can be projected at all is due in part to a prior revolution in the historiography of the Revolution. It is no longer fresh news that the 1970s and 1980s witnessed an assault on the Marxian socioeconomic account of the Revolution as a political upheaval whereby a capitalistic bourgeoisie displaced a "feudal" aristocracy in political power. That Marxian paradigm's fall from a certitude into a problem is by now a fait accompli; although this book presupposes it, it does not propose to belabor it. To say that much is not to say that the French Revolution had no economic and social origins—what revolution does not?—nor even that it had no bourgeois origins, but rather that those origins are in need of reformulation.[14] But the demise of the Marxian explanation has at least had the salutary effect of freeing prerevolutionary politics and thought from functional subservience to socio-economic "substructures" and raising them to the status of independent agents in their own right, making political and intellectual origins of the French Revolution possible. Historians of thought and politics have reacted accordingly. Thus William Doyle, a political historian, has responded with his largely political "origins" of the French Revolution; Keith Baker, an intellectual historian, has come forward with an intellectual "inventing" of the French Revolution; while Roger Chartier, an historian of cultural practices in the French mode, has set out in search of the Revolution's "cultural origins."[15] But if politics and ideology, why not politics and religion? And if political culture, why not political theology?

14. See Colin Jones, "Bourgeois Revolution Revivified: 1789 and Social Change," in *Rewriting the French Revolution: The Andrew Browning Lectures 1789*, ed. Colin Lucas (Oxford, 1991), 69–118.

15. William Doyle, *The Origins of the French Revolution* (Oxford, 1980); Keith M. Baker, *Inventing the French Revolution: Essays on French Political Culture in the Eighteenth Century* (Cambridge, 1990); and

The words *religion* and *ideology* have already cropped up frequently enough to warrant cursory comment. The Calvinist confessional tradition on which I have been nurtured has always refused to regard religious activity as distinct from other dimensions of life, holding that all of life is ultimately religious. That view accounts in part for Calvinism's complicity in the secularization of the West since the sixteenth century, for to hold that everything is religious is in the long run perilously close to holding that nothing is. Unsubtly interpreted, it can lead to reductionistic distortion fully the equal if opposite to the more recent forms of socioeconomic reductionism. Yet that view harbors the insight that, whether or not it be defined in terms of transcendence, religious experience transcends society and is capable of permeating all other aspects of experience, including social and economic ones.[16] The burden of that tradition hence militates against Emile Durkheim's definition of religion as the veneration of the "sacred"—that is, society transfigured—and toward Max Weber's of religion as capable of independent agency, apt to create political, social—even economic—"logics" that may take on lives of their own. If religions have most often sacralized the social order, they have also sometimes undermined and transformed it—something seemingly impossible on Durkheimian premises. And yet, for purposes of Old Regime religious history, the two views are perhaps less opposed than complementary, Durkheim's being more appropriate to what will be called devout Catholicism and Weber's to Calvinism and eighteenth-century Jansenism.[17]

However it be defined, ideology obviously differs from religion in its disinvestment in transcendence and conscious focus on the sociopolitical order. Yet, as I hope to show in this book, ideologies have on the one hand drawn generously from religions both for their languages and general orientations. On the other hand, as in the case of early conservatism, they have sometimes made the role of religion in society their primary object of concern. This book is in part about such a gradual, almost imperceptible, transition from religion to ideology without thereby meaning to imply that there is anything irreversible about this process, that ideology has ever replaced or can replace religion in the quest for ultimate meaning. Like religion, however, ideology is as apt to construct social reality as to reflect it. The attention lavished here on language in the descriptions of religious and ideological phenomena is a measure of my sympathy for Clifford Geertz's definition of ideologies as "maps of problematic social reality and ma-

Roger Chartier, *The Cultural Origins of the French Revolution,* trans. Lydia G. Cochrane (Durham, N.C., 1991).

16. Marcel Gauchet has brilliantly restated and expanded Weber's general viewpoint in *Le désenchantement du monde: Une histoire politique de la religion* (Paris, 1985).

17. Durkheim himself seemed to have doubts about Protestantism as exemplifying belief in the sacred. See *The Elementary Forms of the Religious Life: A Study in Religious Sociology,* trans. Joseph Ward Swain (London, 1915), p. 41.

trices for the creation of collective conscience."[18] It is not intended, however, to mean that language entirely constitutes social or political reality.

Sociologists of religion have stated parts of this book's argument about the transition from religion to revolution in more peremptory and less contingent form.[19] But it falls to the historian to show that such transitions are not effected by impersonal forces acting on human societies, but rather represent the largely unintended consequence of conflict and contestation within human societies. In the case of France, the Old Regime was not taken from without, nor did any party to its many conflicts and contestations ever aspire to do much more than to define, refine, or restore. If secularizing force there was, it was that released by the internal splitting up of the Old Regime and Catholicism by unpredictable human agents and a thousand conflicts between them. Hence the book's attention to these human agents and their many conflicts and contestations, many of which will seem most remote from a revolution that changed the terms of human conflict once and for all. Lest the multitude of those agents and the vagaries of their conflicts produce the effect of a maze with no obvious exit, however, it may be prudent to state the book's argument in outline at the outset.

The book starts with what has been called royal religion, which, assimilating aspects of Catholicism, endowed the French monarchy with reliquary sanctity, thaumaturgical prowess, and an immortal as well as mortal body. From opposite directions—so the argument proceeds—both sixteenth-century Calvinism and the ultra-Catholic League or Holy Union assaulted this monarchy and its embryonic absolutism, Calvinism on the grounds that the monarchy was in effect too religious, the League because the monarch was not religious enough. When in the person of Henri IV the Bourbon monarchy survived these politico-confessional challenges, it sought to become an alternative focus of religious veneration and to place itself securely above the confessional fray. And as it waxed in strength as divine-right absolutism, the monarchy exacted a slow revenge against its erstwhile confessional tormenters. On the one hand, it persecuted Protestants as well as Protestant-like tendencies within French Catholicism. On the other, it politically emasculated the judicial corporations and the lower or second order of the Catholic clergy—the two chief constituencies, as it happens, of the sixteenth-century League.

But this persecutory policy went too far, the argument continues, and backfired badly when applied to French and Flemish Catholic disciples of Saint Augustine—"Jansenists." It is therefore a central thesis of this book that, for a half-

18. Clifford Geertz, "Ideology as a Cultural System," in *The Interpretation of Cultures* (New York, 1973), p. 220.

19. Well before Gauchet's *Le désenchantement du monde*, Peter Berger's *The Sacred Canopy* (Garden City, N.Y., 1967) made a sociologically elegant argument for the importance of the Judeo-Christian religious outlook in the secularization of the West.

century or more, what marched under the banner of Jansenism somehow united some of the biblical, doctrinal, and presbyterian ecclesiastical tendencies of the Protestant Reformation with the apologetical miracles and some of the chief social constituencies of the Catholic League—marched, that is, at the head of conceptual and even social baggage that brought together all that was most politically subversive about *both* sides of the sixteenth-century religious divide. Whether explicitly or not, therefore, Jansenism could not avoid flinging a religious gauntlet in the face of divine-right monarchy, which of course responded by way of direct persecution and by soliciting a series of papal condemnations culminating in the constitution or bull called *Unigenitus* in 1713.

It is hence another of the book's central tenets that the French eighteenth century was as much a century of religious controversy as that of lights and that, from the outset, this controversy undermined absolute monarchy. For the papal and royal condemnation of Jansenism pitted some of the chief casualties of seventeenth-century absolutism—the cause of divine grace, an antihierarchical church, and the priests and parlements who tended to defend these causes—against absolutism's chief beneficiaries—the cause of the human will, of a hierarchical church, and the bishops and Jesuits who championed these causes—in a series of mixed religious and political controversies that dominated the French domestic scene until 1770. At the height of these set-tos in the 1750s, the Bourbon monarchy's vacillation provoked the formation or reformation of a Jesuitical and episcopal *parti dévot* ("devout" or "pious" party) on the monarchy's right in some respects reminiscent of the Catholic League, while some Jansenist energies channeled themselves into a political *parti janséniste* and developed a closer resemblance to Protestantism. The result was that the mid-eighteenth century replayed, albeit in a minor key, the religious-political conflict of the sixteenth century. So a third tenet is that, quite apart from the French Enlightenment, these Jansenist-related controversies brought Bourbon absolutism to its knees, undermining its last and best justification, which was to have imposed religious peace and to have successfully transcended the confessional fray. By the mid-eighteenth century all the legislative and religious symbols of Louis Quatorzian divine-right absolutism—the Jesuit confessor at court, the Edict of Fontainebleau ending toleration of Protestants, even the papal bull *Unigenitus* condemning Jansenism—were all but dead letters. At the same time, heretofore authoritative definitions of Bourbon absolutism came undone, dividing strands of absolutist ideology against each other. If royal absolutism were to have survived this debacle, it would have had to reinvent itself in new, perhaps more frankly utilitarian and enlightened terms.

So much for the destruction of sacral absolutism. The more constructive half of the argument concentrates on the period from 1770 to 1790, and tries to show how the secularized legacies of both sides of the eighteenth century's religious and political controversies contributed dialectically to the formation of revolutionary ideology. On the one hand, a self-conscious *parti patriote* took shape in opposition to Chancellor Maupeou's attempt to purge and reform the parlements in 1771. Although it recruited much of its membership from the pre-Maupeou parti janséniste and prolonged the life of that party, it also attracted non-Jansenist members in some numbers and began to adopt elements of enlightened thought, particularly from the natural law tradition and Rousseauism. On the other hand, part of the parti dévot merged its identity with the pro-Maupeou "ministerial party" and similarly helped itself to other strains of the Enlightenment, notably physiocracy and other aspects of the Rousseauian message. These two parties persisted long enough to have opened the prerevolutionary debate of 1787–89, a debate that, under the pressure of events, ended in their synthesis into revolutionary ideology in 1789.

The last two chapters nonetheless try to complicate this simple picture in such a way as to account for the formation of counterrevolutionary as well as revolutionary ideology. For neither the patriot nor ministerial party remained entirely intact during the last decade of the Old Regime. Some "patriots" remained primarily loyal to the parlements' antidespotic constitutionalism–some of them even to the parlements–while others more obviously Jansenist and interested in ecclesiastical reform went their own way, sometimes trying to interest the monarchy in this cause. When in June 1789 these two clerical and constitutional strands rejoined with revolutionary force, the resultant synthesis left elements of both behind, potential recruits for counterrevolutionay forces. On the ministerial side, it was mainly latter-day philosophes who appropriated the old parti dévot's unitary absolutist ideology–an ideology that readily made the transition from king to "nation" in 1789–while the devout episcopal rank and file, the monarchy's traditional allies in absolutism, distanced themselves from the monarchy until the National Assembly brandished its ecclesiastical reforms in 1790. When, in reaction to this revolutionary reorganization of the French Catholic Church, they belatedly came to the monarchy's defense, it was already too late to save royal absolutism, with the result that a resurgent "devout" ideology only hastened the constitutional monarchy's demise and entered into the making of an ideological Right. The composite character of revolutionary ideology and its constitutional legislation, finally, contributed to the Revolution's instability, while the polarization over the Revolution's ecclesiastical legislation accounts for why a Revolution with so many religious–even Christian–origins, became the first revolution to undertake dechristianization.

Although it was an attempt to destroy Christianity rather than to reform it, revolutionary dechristianization bore an uncanny resemblance to the Calvinist iconoclasm of the French Reformation more than two centuries earlier. The French Reformation, then, is an appropriate place to begin.

CHAPTER 1

From Calvin to Quesnel

THAT THE FRENCH MONARCHY DID NOT FINALLY THROW IN
its lot with the Protestant Reformation of the sixteenth century may seem somewhat puzzling. Although the Concordat of Bologne, negotiated by Pope Leo X
and François I on the eve of Martin Luther's initial protest, gave the French
monarchy control over episcopal nominations and curtailed the amount of revenue leaving France for Rome, thereby removing some of the material considerations that were soon to tempt many German princes away from the Roman fold,
embracing the Reformation would nonetheless have filled this "new monarchy's"
coffers with the proceeds of ecclesiastical and monastic property, enabling it to
further the work of state centralization and better to prosecute its chronic wars
against rival dynasties. From François I's time until the mid-eighteenth century
these dynastic wars would have been domestically easier to justify as a Protestant
monarchy than as a Catholic one, since they typically aligned France with other
Protestant states against the militantly Catholic Habsburgs. The particular form
in which France experienced the Reformation, namely Calvinism, was as French
as it was anything else, and perhaps only needed a little royal help in order to put
down deeper roots than it did. Indeed, by 1560 it seemed as though the momentum
of the Calvinist movement might carry everything before it, monarchy and all.
Yet choose against the Reformation that monarchy did, at first very tentatively,
then ever more decisively. By the end of 1572 Charles IX's complicity in the
massacre of thousands of Protestants on Saint Bartholomew's Day and the days
following made the Valois monarchy and Calvinism all but incompatible in
France. The last chance for a French Protestant monarchy disappeared when the

15

heretofore Protestant Henri de Navarre found it necessary to convert to Catholicism in order to become King Henri IV, even if he never uttered the cynical saying so often attributed to him, that Paris "is worth a mass."[1]

So irrevocable was this choice that, confronted in the seventeenth century with some Protestant-like religious sensibilities wearing a far more Catholic face in the form of Jansenism, the monarchy reacted much more promptly than it had against Protestantism in the sixteenth century, even though Jansenism, like Protestantism, seemed to represent many of the monarchy's best interests. For not only was Jansenism both French and Catholic, it also eventually associated itself with the parlements, which had done more to extend royal authority at the expense of rival feudal or ecclesiastical jurisdictions than had any other institution until then. Yet so decisively did Henri IV's grandson Louis XIV move against Jansenism that he voluntarily confounded it with Protestantism, literally razing Jansenism's spiritual home, the abbaye of Port-Royal, a couple of decades after razing the remaining Protestant "temples" in France.

Why these confessional choices? Why especially the decision against Jansenism? For if association with Catholicism on its own terms eventually enabled the French monarchy to present itself as a focus of something like religious devotion above and beyond the Calvinist-Catholic clash, thus justifying the divine-right monarchy of the seventeenth century, it also committed that monarchy to the defense of a pre-Reformation Catholicism increasingly unacceptable to many literate Frenchmen, making any challenge to the Catholic Church into one against the state and thereby provoking religious opposition to the monarchy itself. That is what had already happened in the case of the Protestant Reformation, and it would happen again with Jansenism.

Royal Religion in the Wars of Religion

The most obvious factor limiting the monarchy's range of religious options was that, as an institution, it was far from religiously neutral. For in France the monarchy was itself an object of something like religious veneration, the sacramental center of *la religion royale*. Because this royal religion did not exactly coincide and at best overlapped with a Catholicism that at times—during the investiture conflict, for example—had challenged it in essential ways, the monarchy's religious preferences were perforce dictated by reason of their compatibility or incompatibility with its own cultic identity. The roots of this royal

---

1. On the origins of this remark, see Michael Wolfe, *The Conversion of Henri IV: Politics, Power, and Religious Belief in Early-Modern France* (Cambridge, Mass., 1993), p. 1. A good case for the sincerity of Henry IV's conversion is made by Thierry Wannegffelen, "Des Chrétiens entre Rome et Genève" (doctoral thesis, Université de Paris I, 1994), pp. 160–91.

religion lay deep in the pagan past, on the Germanic side in the notion of a kingly family or *reges criniti* descended from Woden and from which kings had to be chosen, and on the classical side in the gradual divinization of emperors during late Roman antiquity. Early Frankish kings had deftly exploited both traditions, being at once Germanic chieftains and the agents of declining imperial authority. The conversion of Clovis around A.D. 500 did not so much displace as Christianize these traditions, a process that culminated when Pope Stephen II crossed the Alps to legitimate Pepin the Short's seizure of the Frankish kingship by anointing him king in 754. Because the precedent Stephen invoked was the anointing of the first Old Testament kings by the prophet Samuel, the anointing of Pepin transformed him and his successors into *L'Oint du Seigneur* (the Lord's Anointed), the successors of kings David and Solomon—and, through the same line, into successors of Christ as well.[2] Charlemagne may or may not have thought of himself as Christlike or as a partly divine person, a *gemina persona*, but he most certainly acted the role of agent or vicar of Christ and effective head of Christendom, convening and presiding over local church councils, taking a hand in the formulation of Christian doctrine, and forcibly "converting" Arian Germans and pagan Saxons to Nicene orthodoxy.[3] The title of Roman Emperor, revived for his benefit by Pope Leo III in 800, continued the confusion between classical and Christian as well as Germanic precedents.

Count Hughes Capet's usurpation of the Western kingship in 987 dealt the coup de grâce to Carolingian legitimacy and therefore to any possibility of imperial pretensions in France, while the Gregorian reform movement of the eleventh and twelfth centuries vested the quality of "vicar of Christ" once and for all in the papacy.[4] But Robert II, "the Pious," Capet's successor as King of France, compensated for both losses by miraculously curing the sick, a power which his Capetian successors honed to the disease of scrofula and attributed to the episcopal anointing or consecration that, since the late ninth century, had come to accompany the coronation ceremony.[5] And while Germanic emperors staked their sacrosanctity in spectacular confrontations with the reforming papacy, Louis VI and Louis VII less obtrusively enhanced theirs in cooperation with Rome by putting themselves at the head of the hitherto papal and episcopal "peace move-

2. Fritz Kern, *Kingship and Law in the Middle Ages*, trans. S. B. Chrimes (Oxford, 1968), pp. 5–68.

3. Ernst Kantorowicz, *The King's Two Bodies: A Study in Mediaeval Political Theology* (Princeton, N.J., 1957), pp. 42–86; and H. X. Arquillière, *L'Augustinisme politique: Essai sur la formation des théories politiques du moyen âge* (Paris, 1955), pp. 154–69 and passim.

4. Robert Fawtier, *The Capetian Kings of France: Monarchy and Nation, 987–1328*, trans. Lionel Butler and R. J. Adam (London, 1968), pp. 79–95; and R. W. Southern, *Western Society and the Church in the Middle Ages*, Pelican History of the Church, vol. 2 (Harmondsworth, England, 1970), pp. 104–5.

5. Marc Bloch, *The Royal Touch: Sacred Monarchy and Scrofula in England and France*, trans. J. E. Anderson (London, 1973), pp. 12–21, 28–48.

ment," both in France and on crusade.[6] For at the prompting of Suger, abbé de Saint-Denis near Paris, these two kings effected a virtual identification between the Capetian kingship and the memory and relics of that saint, the missionary martyr to Gaul confused with Denis the Areopagite, thereby appropriating for their benefit, as Lionel Rothkrug has argued, an upward displacement of indigenous reliquary sanctity and helping to produce a saint of their own in the person of Louis IX.[7] This royal relation to the peace movement also came to occupy a prominent place in the consecration and coronation ceremony, swearing as the king did "to preserve the true peace for the church of God." That ceremony, meanwhile, assumed the aspect of an elaborate liturgical rite, tantamount to an eighth sacrament—a kind of hybrid of baptism and ordination—that made its royal recipient an "exterior bishop" as well as a king and hence able, like priests, to take communion in both forms.[8]

The sanctity of the king extended by degrees to the kingdom. The myth that the oil used to baptize Clovis had been sent to Saint Remigius by the Holy Spirit in the form of a dove and had survived in the safekeeping of the abbey of Saint-Remy spread from its origin in Reims to Paris under royal sponsorship in the thirteenth century and became the central motif in what one historian has called the "thirteenth-century reconceiving of the kingship."[9] The use of this oil for the royal consecration not only suggested that the kings of France were secular successors of Christ but featured their subjects in the role of a chosen people, singled out by God for special attention. The myth that the Capetian arms, the *fleurs de lys*, had been given by an angel to Clovis's wife on the eve of his consecration as a sign of God's special care for France also attached itself to the monarchy in the thirteenth century, as did the myth of the divine origin of the abbey of Saint-Denis's red and yellow silk banner or *oriflamme*. At a more learned level the jurists, too, made their contribution at about the same time, transferring the notion of the church as a mystical body *(corpus mysticum)* to the French realm, conceived as a *corpus reipublicae mysticum,* and casting the king as the head of the body politic in a way analogous to Christ's position as head of the church. Enough sanctity had accumulated in France by the thirteenth century for a pope to concede that France was a "holy kingdom," and for a French cleric to declare, even against the papacy, that "he who carries on war against the King [of France], works against the whole

6. Georges Duby, *Le dimanche de Bouvines: 27 juillet 1214,* Trente journées qui ont fait la France series (Paris, 1973), pp. 75–99.

7. Lionel Rothkrug, *Religious Practices and Collective Perceptions: Hidden Homologies in the Renaissance and Reformation,* special issue of *Historical Reflections / Réflexions historiques* 7 (Spring 1980), pp. 30–31.

8. Richard Jackson, *Vive le Roi: A History of the French Coronation from Charles V to Charles X* (Chapel Hill, N.C., 1984), pp. 26–34, 203–6.

9. Ibid., p. 32.

Church, against the Catholic doctrine, against Holiness and Justice, and against the Holy Land."[10]

Far from damaging this royal religion, the Hundred Years' War seemed in the end only to enhance it. At the apex of the social pyramid, Charles V's response to the disastrous Treaty of Brétigni was to augment the liturgy of the royal consecration ceremony with prayers that underscored the divine origins of the Valois kingship and God's protective relation to France.[11] And near its base, the realm's recovery of northern France in the fifteenth century remains impossible to recount without reference to the peasant maid from Domrémy whose faith in her divine mission to restore God's kingdom to its rightful Valois vassal and the "royal blood" galvanized the uncrowned dauphin Charles into action against the English, even if it finally fell short of the crusade that she had in mind. Although in other respects it was unimpeachably Catholic, Jeanne d'Arc's current of inspiration ran directly from the "God of heaven" and angelic "voices" to the king and his subordinates, bypassing the bishops except for their mandatory role in the consecration and coronation at Reims. What the English put on trial in her person in Rouen was not just Jeanne's religion, but royal religion.[12] Indeed, where the affairs of the church were directly concerned, this quasi-independent sanctity later enabled the same Charles VII to act as virtual head of the French Catholic Church and to promulgate its "liberties" against the papacy in one of Gallicanism's classic statements, the Pragmatic Sanction of Bourges, in 1438.[13]

It was at this time and against this background that jurists gradually abandoned the analogy of the king as head of the body politic in favor of a fiction that better expressed the idea of the immortality of the realm in contrast to the mortality of individual kings. With conceptual help, again, from originally ecclesiastical concepts—that of a fictive person or a corporation that never died because its members forever renewed themselves, and an abiding *dignitas* that an office impressed upon its successive occupants—French jurists elaborated the concept of the king's two bodies: the one a natural body that died like others, the other the crown or body politic, which, like angels, was sempiternal.[14] This juridical distinction was acted out, as it were, and ever more elaborately displayed in the Renaissance royal funeral ceremonies from Charles VI's in 1422 to Henri IV's in

10. Kantorowicz, *The King's Two Bodies*, p. 254, and in general pp. 193–272. The quotation in Latin reads: "Igitur qui contra regem [Franciae] invehitur, laborat contra totam ecclesiam, contra sanctitatem et justitiam et terram sanctam."

11. Jackson, *Vive le Roi*, pp. 26–31.

12. Régine Pernoud, *Jeanne d'Arc par elle-même et par ses témoins* (Paris, 1962), pp. 52–57.

13. Charles Petit-Dutaillis, *Charles VII, Louis XI, et les premières années de Charles VII*, vol. 4, 2d part, *Histoire de France illustrée depuis les origines jusqu'à la Révolution*, ed. Ernest Lavisse (Paris, 1911), pp. 261–74.

14. Kantorowicz, *The King's Two Bodies*.

1610. Expressed in part in the difference between the mourning march as the royal cortege approached Paris and a triumphal march after its entry into the capital, the distinction attained clearer expression with the separation between the coffin bearing the mortal king's remains and the lifelike effigy of the king representing the immortal dignity, accompanied by the red-robed presidents of the Parlement of Paris representing royal justice, which also did not die. The distinction also found expression at the moment of burial in the abbey church of Saint-Denis with the couplet, "The king is dead. Long live the king!" *(Le roi est mort. Vive le roi!)*[15]

On the one hand, this juridical distinction would seem to have detracted from the king's sacrosanctity and secularized his person, transferring his quasi-divinity to the immortal crown and the emerging concept of the state. And there can be little doubt that to the degree that the distinction between the two bodies was thought of as a separation, such would have been the effect. On the other hand, the distinction hardly excludes—and perhaps even invites—the mortal king's being thought of as incarnating the sempiternal kingdom, in which case whatever Christlike qualities might have been lost by the analogy of head to body would have been more than regained by analogy to the mystery of the incarnation. The juridical distinction between the two bodies did not prevent the contemporary jurist Charles de Grassaille from holding that the king of France was not only the "vicar of Christ in his kingdom" but "just like, in fact, a God in bodily form"; and the historian of the "king's two bodies," Ernst Kantorowicz himself, referred to the juridical notion as a "new secularized version of the hypostatic union."[16] Nor, for that matter, was all analogy to Christ's relation to his church abandoned, for Renaissance jurists also had recourse to the metaphor of Christ's marriage to his church in order to express the inalienability of the royal domain conceived of as the realm's dowry to the king.[17]

The royal funeral ceremony also invites comparison to the central mystery of Catholic Christianity, namely the Mass, especially in fully developed form at the end of the reign of François I.[18] Just as the Mass ritually reenacted the death

15. Ralph E. Giesey, *The Royal Funeral Ceremonies in Renaissance France* (Geneva, 1960).

16. Charles de Grassaille, *Regalium Franciae, Libri Duo: Juro Omnia et Dignitates Christianissimi Galliae Regis Continentes* (Lyon, 1535), as quoted in Louis Marin, "The Body-of-Power and Incarnation at Port Royal and in Pascal, or Of the Figurability of the Political Absolute," in *Fragments for a History of the Human Body,* ed. Michel Feher, 3 vols. (New York, 1990), 1:4; and Donald R. Kelley, *Foundations of Modern Historical Scholarship: Language, Law, and History in the French Renaissance* (New York, 1970), p. 197. See also Kantorowicz, *The King's Two Bodies,* p. 445, and in general pp. 273–450.

17. Grassaille, *Regalium Franciae,* p. 217; and Jackson, *Vive Le Roi!* pp. 85–93.

18. While admitting the aptness of this analogy, Alain Bourreau denies that any such belief ever took hold, maintaining that the "the body of the sovereign remains constantly and hopelessly simple." But besides the argument's dependence on the mere absence of evidence, this denial can only be sustained at the price of dismissing the whole corpus of sixteenth- and seventeenth-century rhetoric as "mere rhetoric." See his *Le simple corps du roi: L'impossible sacralité des souverains français, XVe–XVIIIe siècle* (Paris, 1988), p. 23, and in general pp. 1–31.

and resurrection of Christ on the cross, so did the royal funeral ceremony ritually enact the death and resurrection of the kingdom, most poignantly at the moment of the ritual lowering and raising of the banner and sword of France and the crying of the formula, "the king is dead; long live the king!" followed by a meal for the dead king's household. Was the king's body any more lowly than the elements of bread and wine that became the body and blood of Christ? Although it may be speculative to suggest, with Lionel Rothkrug, that these funerary processions joined French subjects with the "crown made flesh," just as the Mass joined the faithful with the body of Christ, there can be little doubt that the notion of the body politic as a corpus mysticum retained some of the sacramental connotations derived from the time when the terms had actually denoted Christ's resurrected body.[19] Combining the heretofore separate *corpus christi* procession with those devoted to Sainte Geneviève and Saint Denis, Parisian processions against heresy in the sixteenth century provocatively associated the monarchy with the consecrated host, the one in 1568 juxtaposing the host not only to the king, in this case Charles IX, but also to the symbols of monarchy, namely the hand of justice, the scepter, and the crown.[20]

To sacral monarchy's many Germanic and Christian accretions, the sixteenth century added Renaissance humanism and a revived interest in Roman law, and with it an interest in the king as bearer of *imperium:* the prince's exclusive right to command and to lay down law. This new conception of monarchy's defining attribute implied a distinction between legislation and the administration of justice quite foreign to medieval kingship. The distinction appeared in ceremonial form in King François I's revival or invention of the *lit de justice* assembly (literally, bed of justice), a royal forum that he used to promulgate constitutional law in the presence of the Parlement of Paris, princes of the blood, and officers of the realm.[21] It also took printed form in the juristic invention of the "Romanist thesis," which featured Frankish kings and their Capetian successors as inheritors

19. Lionel Rothkrug, *Religious Practices and Collective Perceptions,* pp. 32–33; and "From Sanctity and Heresy to Virtue and Corruption: The Ideological Backgrounds to the French Revolution," paper presented in session entitled "Mort et vertu sous l'Ancien régime et la Révolution / Modes of Death and Ideologies of Virtue in the Ancien Regime and the Revolution" in the thirty-second annual meeting of the Society for French Historical Studies, Québec City, 21 March 1986, p. 8.

20. Barbara Diefendorf, *Beneath the Cross: Catholics and Huguenots in Sixteenth-Century Paris* (Oxford, 1991), p. 44, and in general 38–48. See also Denis Crouzet, *Les guerriers de Dieu: La violence au temps des troubles de religion,* (Seyssel, 1990), 2:53–62.

21. Sarah Hanley, *The Lit de Justice of the Kings of France: Constitutional Ideology in Legend, Ritual, and Discourse* (Princeton, N.J., 1983), pp. 1–143. Hanley's thesis that François invented this kind of assembly, which was without any real medieval precedents, has been subject to much criticism, notably Elizabeth A. R. Brown's and Richard C. Famiglietti's *The Lit de Justice: Semantics, Ceremonial, and the Parlement of Paris, 1300–1600* (Sigmaringen, Germany, 1994), but I accept Hanely's contention that François I tried to use the *lit de justice* assembly to distinguish between the king's unique constitutional capacity and the Parlement's ordinary sessions, which were limited to "private" justice.

of Roman imperial authority and therefore the natural adversaries of all "feudal" – and constitutional–limitations. The emphasis on legislation even took legislative form proper with the addition of the phrase "for such is our good pleasure" *(car tel est notre bon plaisir)* at the conclusion or royal edicts and declarations.[22] Behind these formulas there stood François I's new monarchy and its administrative innovations: the concentration of policy making in the king's *Conseil étoit* (Privy Council) and the amalgamation of hitherto distinct ordinary and extraordinary revenues in the royal treasury.[23] Encapsulated by the new royal quality of majesty, these conceptual and practical changes pointed, if not to absolutism, at least to a novel view of kingship as creator as well as mediator.

By the sixteenth century, then, the cult of the French monarchy had acquired critical mass, as it were, and had become so inextricably entwined in miracles, relics, and saints, and most recently divine majesty, that any religious "reform" that reserved majesty for God alone, regarded Christ's passion as an unrepeatable event, minimized the miraculous and put Christians "on guard against wonder-workers," regarded relics and images as so many manifestations of "idolatry" and "superstition"–and those of Saint Denis in particular as a "lie"–was obviously asking the monarchy to redefine itself in radical ways.[24] And that was precisely the case of Calvinism. There could have been nothing politically neutral, for example, in Calvin's restriction of the term *majesté* to God, his declaration that "it was to [God] *alone* that all majesty belongs," and his condemnation of all statues and images "as so many reproaches to [God's] majesty," because it was precisely in the 1550s that *majesty* (meaning something like sovereignty) replaced *dignity* as the most important of the French monarchy's juridical attributes.[25] Nor could the French monarchy have been very far from his mind when, maintaining

22. Quentin Skinner, *The Age of the Reformation*, vol. 2 of his *The Foundations of Modern Political Thought* (Cambridge, 1982), pp. 254–67; William Farr Church, *Constitutional Thought in Sixteenth-Century France: A Study in the Evolution of Ideas* (New York, 1969), pp. 43–73; 179–94; and Julian H. Franklin, *Jean Bodin and the Sixteenth-Century Revolution in the Methodology of Law and History* (New York, 1963), pp. 6–37.

23. R. J. Knecht, *Francis I* (Cambridge, 1982), pp. 13–32, 117–31, 344–61; and John H. M. Salmon, *Society in Crisis: France in the Sixteenth Century* (New York, 1975), pp. 13–91.

24. For references to Saint Denis, see Jean Calvin, *Advertissement très utile du grand proffit qui reviendroit à la Chrestienté, s'il se faisoit inventoire de tous les corps sainctz, et reliques, qui sont tant en Italie, qu'en France, Allemaingne, Hespaigne, et autres* (Geneva, 1543) and reprinted in *La vraie piété: Divers traités de Jean Calvin et confession de foi de Guillaume Farel*, eds. Irena Backus and Claire Chimelli, "Histoire et société" no. 12 (Geneva, 1986), p. 195. On miracles, see *Institution de la religion chrestienne*, ed. Jean-Daniel Benoit, 4 vols. (Paris, 1957), "Au roy de France tres chrestien, François premier de ce nom, son prince et souverain seigneur," 1:35 and 4:474. See also Calvin's comments on Mark 16:17 in *Commentaires de Iehan Calvin sur la concordance ou harmonie composée de trois evangelistes, ascavoir S. Matthieu, S. Marc, et S. Luc, dict les Actes des apostres* (n.p., 1561), 606–7.

25. Ralph Giesey, "The King Imagined," *The Political Culture of the Old Regime*, vol. 1 of *The French Revolution and the Creation of Modern Political Culture*, ed. Keith M. Baker (Oxford, 1988), pp. 41–59.

that "God is deprived of his honor . . . if all that is proper to his divinity is not left to reside in him alone," he excoriated the "superstition" of "surrounding [God] with a multitude of little gods, among whom his virtue is shared . . . and the glory of his divinity is dissipated."[26]

Politically apropos as well, perhaps, is Calvin's critique of the Catholic Mass and his own theology of the Eucharist. Calvin notoriously objected to the doctrine that the substance of the bread and wine became the body and blood of Jesus Christ while their "accidental" qualities remained the same—the doctrine of transubstantiation, in short—as blasphemous, idolatrous, and superstitious: blasphemous because it tended to replicate or at least reapply Christ's unique sacrifice for sinners and to substitute the priest for Christ; idolatrous and superstitious because it encouraged worship of the bread and wine, or sacramental signs, as though they were Christ himself, the person signified. If, for Calvin, the sacrament of the Eucharist communicated Christ's body and blood to believers—and it did—it was not by turning the bread and wine into Christ's body and blood, but by means otherwise mysterious. He also insisted that both the bread and the wine be given to the whole community, including the laity, lest the eucharistic mystery be divided. What was not very mysterious in Calvin's theology was his quite rationalistic if not proto-Cartesian insistence that qua man the God-Man's body was no more than any other body capable of being in two places at the same time, that since the ascension it occupied specified space at the right hand of God, and that it could not therefore be in the eucharistic elements as well. Calvin's eucharistic theology, in other words, surgically separated Christ's body from the sacramental elements, secularized these latter, and turned them over to the whole Christian community.

Was the analogy between Christ's body and the eucharistic elements on the one hand and the king's "immortal" body and mortal person on the other clear enough for an attack on the one to have been felt as an attack on the other? Even if this suggestion is to push the relation too far, it remains the case that the French monarchy was in general too implicated in sacramental conceptions not to have taken an attack on the Mass very personally. Lest it not be taken personally, the proto-Calvinist reformers who placarded attacks on the Mass in France in 1534 took pains to affix, for example, a placard on François I's bedchamber door at the château of Amboise. In response, as has been noted, the processions organized against Calvinist heresy in Paris thereafter provocatively associated the monarch and monarchy with the consecrated host, uniting corpus Christi processions with those devoted to Saint Denis and Saint Geneviève.

But quite apart from the Calvinist critique of the Mass and well in advance of the development of its political casuistry of contract and revolt, the Calvinist

---

26. Jean Calvin, *Institution de la religion chrestienne*, 1:114. See also pp. 120–21.

denigration of images, relics, and the miraculous made for a politically subversive force in France. As early as on the occasion of the famous affair of the placards, the monarchy—indeed, François I in person—characteristically responded with a religious procession through Paris bristling with relics and images of the saints, Christ, and the Virgin Mary.[27] Even if it had been possible—as was emphatically not the case—to distinguish cleanly between Catholic and royal relics and remains in France, Calvinist iconoclasts in the 1560s cannot be credited with having tried very hard. They ravaged the tomb of Louis XI at Cléry, burned the heart of François II at Orléans, exhumed the body of Jeanne de France at Bourges, and desecrated the tombs of the Bourbons at Vendôme.[28] When they defiled consecrated hosts, felled statues of the saints and the Virgin, and smashed stained-glass windows, Calvinist iconoclastic crowds in Capetian France implicitly struck at symbols of the monarchy along with those of Catholicism. The incompatibility of Calvinist iconoclasm and the denigration of the miraculous with French royal religion is perhaps nowhere more poignantly dramatized than in the spectacles of Henri of Navarre abjuring his "heresy" near the relics of Saint Denis, or of King Henri IV duly touching for scrofula in Paris shortly after his coronation and consecration ceremony at Chartres, which made do with the oil of Saint Martin of Tours if not with that in the Holy Vial at Reims.

Adding to the force of Calvinism's subversive potential was its system of church governance consisting of elected presbyters—that is, of elected pastors and lay elders *(anciens)*. Four centuries have so domesticated this "presbyterian" polity in Protestant countries as to make it hard to imagine how the systematic introduction of the elective principle and lay participation shocked a world dominated by hierarchy and everywhere peopled by clerics. "Hierarchy" was an "improper name," held Calvin, because the Scriptures interpreted with the aid of the Holy Spirit "wanted to make sure that, where the government of the church was concerned, no one imagine any principality or domination."[29] It is true that neither Calvin nor sixteenth-century French Calvinists directly transferred this antihierarchical polity to the state, although Calvin's insistence on the independence of the church along with the power of excommunication directly threatened any lay magistracy in a confessional state. But it was simply not possible to confine the Calvinist polity's antihierarchical implications to the church alone in a society where church and state were coterminous and similarly hierarchical and where, especially in France, the monarchy's power lay largely in its control over bishops in a hierarchical church. The antimonarchical implications of Presby-

27. H. Lemonnier, *Les guerres d'Italie: La France sous Charles VIII, Louis XII et François I*, in *Histoire de France illustrée*, vol. 5, 1st part, p. 378; and, more recently, Crouzet, *Guerriers de Dieu*, 1:756–62.

28. J.-H. Mariéjol, *La réforme et la ligue; L'édit de Nantes, 1559–1598*, in *Histoire de France illustrée*, vol. 6, 1st part, pp. 64–65.

29. Calvin, *Institution de la religion chrestienne*, 4:76.

terian polity did not escape Calvin's own pen, as when he wrote that "even if it were good and useful . . . that the whole world be ruled by a monarchy, which itself is very false, I nonetheless do not admit that the same ought also to hold for the church," which, he added, has "Jesus Christ alone as its head." At work in this ecclesiology was the same heightened sense of the incommensurate majesty of God, a majesty better honored in a polity in which mere ministerial "men made of earth" were tempted to usurp none of it, "reserving to Christ alone the honor and the name of chief."[30]

Far from passively accepting Calvin's or Geneva's dictates, the French Reformed churches further radicalized this ecclesiology, abandoning even Calvin's limited toleration for the term *bishop* and elaborating the first nonepiscopal polity in the church's history. "We believe that all true pastors, wherever they may be, have the same authority and equal power under one head, the sole sovereign and universal bishop Jesus Christ; and that for that reason no church may aspire to any domination or lordship *(seigneurie)* over one another," proclaimed the Paris synod's "confession of faith" in 1559.[31] That radical congregationalism did not prevent the French Reformed churches from elaborating a system of provincial and national synods, despite the protests of the logician Pierre de La Rame and others. Yet so great was the fear of "hierarchy" and "domination" in all their forms that the synods neither allowed for the election of presidents for longer than the duration of a single synod nor appointed intermediate committees to ensure continuity from one synod to the next. That in the absence of a sympathetic magistracy the French Reformed churches developed without much internal interference from that magistracy only increased the Calvinist polity's tendency toward independence from the state, and hence its potential threat to the state.

Along with its well-known insistence on a theologically literate laity and emphasis on the written word, Calvinism's implicit challenge to the Valois monarchy was undoubtedly one of the factors limiting its social recruitment. The movement symptomatically put down its deepest social roots among well-to-do merchants and the most skilled and newest crafts—segments of the population, in other words, that were relatively unbeholden to the monarchy. Chief among the more Protestant-prone craftsmen seem to have been goldsmiths, printers, booksellers, the more skilled clothworkers like hosiers, and painters.[32] Although these

---

30. Ibid., 4:113. See also pp. 14–15, 55, 76.

31. Cited in Glenn S. Sunshine, "From French Protestantism to the French Reformed Churches: The Development of Huguenot Ecclesiastical Institutions, 1559–1598" (Ph.D. diss., University of Wisconsin, 1992), p. 58. It is to Sunshine (p. 114) that I owe the characterization of this polity as the "first nonepiscopal, non-hierarchical synodical system in church history."

32. Philip Benedict, *Rouen during the Wars of Religion* (Cambridge, 1981), pp. 71–82; Natalie Zemon Davis, "The Rites of Violence," in *Society and Culture in Modern France: Eight Essays by Natalie Zemon Davis* (Stanford, Calif., 1975), pp. 177–78; and Emile Léonard, *Le Protestant français* (Paris, 1953), p. 45.

crafts were organized as guilds, sixteenth-century guilds remained more or less independent of the monarchy and had not quite become the corporate adjuncts of royal fiscality and office holding that Louis XIV and his famous controller general Jean-Baptiste Colbert later made them. For those portions of the landed nobility, concentrated largely in the south and west, who initially embraced it, Calvinism became at once a badge of independence and a means of maintaining it. And except for some cities in the south, parts of which became an all but independent Protestant confederation from 1573 until after Navarre's accession as Henri IV, Calvinism did *not* greatly attract the nobility of the robe and lesser royal officialdom—lawyers, attorneys, and judges in presidial and prevotal courts— despite some initial flirtation with the movement on the part of parlementary magistrates in Paris.[33] The "lesser magistrates" whom French Calvinist political theory eventually called upon to resist Valois "tyranny" were not the magistrates of the sovereign courts but municipal officers in towns that had already adopted the Protestant reform.[34]

That theory began to appear with the religious civil wars, although French Protestantism's most classic utterances waited until after Saint Bartholomew's Day 1572 in Paris and its sequels in the provinces. At once goading them into action yet sobering them into a realization of their minority status in France, this event prompted French Calvinists to recast their hitherto "covenantal" and some- what sectarian justifications for active political resistance in broader and more secular terms, a trend already evident in parts of the second dialogue of the *Wake- Up Call for Frenchmen* published on the morrow of the massacre.[35] One such approach was the jurist François Hotman's attempt in his *Francogallia* to rewrite the French past as a history of representative institutions beginning with the Merovingian Public Council, which, according to Hotman, had once legislated on behalf of the Franco-Gaulic "nation," elected the kings, and closely controlled them in war as in peace. That Hotman had completed the work in manuscript before Saint Bartholomew's Day 1572 is evident in that it hardly addressed the

33. On these aspects of Calvinism's social recruitment, see Janine Garrisson-Estèbe, *Protestants du Midi* (Toulouse, 1980); and her chapter in *Histoire des Protestants en France*, ed. Robert Mandrou et al. (Toulouse, 1977), p. 61; and Denis Richet, "Aspects socio-culturels des conflits religieux à Paris dans la seconde moitié du XVI siècle," in his *De la Réforme à la Révolution: Etudes sur la France moderne* (Paris, 1991), pp. 30–31.

34. Ralph E. Giesey, "The Monarchomach Triumvirs: Hotman, Beza and Mornay," *Bibliothèque d'humanisme et Renaissance* 32 (1970):46–47.

35. [Etienne de La Boétie, Johann Fischart, Bernard Jobin, Thomas Sampson, and others], *Le reveille-matin des François, et de leurs voisins. Composé par Eusèbe Philadelphe cosmopolite, en forme de dialogue*, 2 parts (Edinburgh, 1574), 2:76–93, as analyzed by Robert M. Kingdon, *Myths about Saint Bartholomew's Day Massacres, 1572–1576* (Cambridge, 1988), pp. 70–87. This attribution of authorship is also Kingdon's.

question of what recourse Calvinists were to have, since Hotman regarded the existing Estates General as a sorry deformation of a pristine Public Council. The principle of national sovereignty is nonetheless contained in *Francogallia* in embryo, even if its exercise is restricted to the political elites. By making its version of the French constitutional past the pristine and normative one, the book undermined the legitimacy of successive French presents, of which the sixteenth century was only the first. However little it may have helped Protestants at that time, its thesis of a pristine Franco-Gallic constitution helped justify the Fronde in the seventeenth century and parlementary and Jansenist resistance in the eighteenth century, while its critique of such royalist formulas as "such is our good pleasure" served as ammunition against absolutism until the end of the Old Regime.[36]

Although not entirely eschewing the strategy of historical legitimation, the tactic taken by the other two "monarchomach triumvirs," Théodore de Bèze and Philippe Du Plessis-Mornay, was at once more theoretical and practical. The theory consisted in part in such principles as equity, natural reason, and the law of nature as expressed in Roman Law, most notably the right to self-defense and the duty of tutors toward minors and their property. As practically applied by de Bèze in his *The Right of Magistrates over Their Subjects*, the right of self-defense entitled such "lesser magistrates" as municipal officers to resist a king's "tyranny" in the absence of the infrequent meetings of the Estates General.[37] And as applied by Du Plessis-Mornay in his more famous *A Defense of Liberty Against Tyrants*, the principle that public power was ultimately the property of the whole people while the king only administered it cast the king in the role of principal tutor, the realm's chief officers in the role of associate tutors, and the people in that of the minor. The corollary was that if the king served his own interests to the detriment of the minor's, it fell to the delegate of the Estates General—and in their absence to the chief officers of the Crown—to resist or to discipline him, even to depose him if necessary.[38]

The same distinction between property and its administration also undergirded both authors' occasional recourse to the late medieval conciliarist doctrine that granted ultimate doctrinal authority to the general council in preference to the pope. Reasoning by analogy, both de Bèze and Mornay declared the Estates or

36. François Hotman, *Francogallia*, ed. and trans. Ralph E. Giesey and John H. M. Salmon (Cambridge, 1972), p. 345. On Hotman and his *Francogallia* see also Donald R. Kelley, *François Hotman: A Revolutionary's Ideal* (Princeton, N.J., 1973), pp. 227–63.

37. [Théodore de Bèze], *Le droit des magistrats sur leurs subjets*, ed. Robert Kingdon, Les classiques de la pensée politique series (Geneva, 1971), pp. 10, 24, 29–31, 44–45, 47–49, 52.

38. [Philippe Du Plessis-Mornay], *Vindiciae contra Tyrannos, or, Concerning the Legitimate Power of a Prince Over the People, and of the People Over a Prince*, ed. George Garnett (Cambridge, 1994), pp. 49–50, 82–86, 89–91, 165–70.

realm to be similarly superior to the king, and hence as capable of deposing a tyrannical king as the council a heretical pope.[39] And in thus distinguishing between the kingdom or its people and the king, de Bèze and Du Plessis-Mornay also distinguished between the king's two bodies, a distinction that Du Plessis-Mornay pulled apart to the point of outright opposition. For him, it was the "laws of well-ordered states" that were quasi-divine and the commonwealth that was "immortal," while, as for the prince, it was vain "to expect divine attributes in a nature so frail and so subject to imperfections."[40]

The eligibility of the Protestant Henri de Navarre to the French throne after the death of childless Henry III's last brother, the duc d'Alençon, in 1584, pragmatically pointed Calvinist political thought in a more royalist direction, and led to a virtual reversal of Calvinist and Catholic positions.[41] For the prospect of a "heretical" accession to the throne also touched off the verbal violence and political radicalism of the militantly Catholic *Sainte Union*, or Holy League, which seized power in numbers of cities, including Paris itself, between Henri III's assassination of the duc and cardinal de Guise in December 1588 and Navarre's accession as Henri IV in 1594.

This militantly Catholic Holy League was able at once to release and politicize the compressed energy of an apocalyptic and expiatory religious sensibility that Denis Crouzet described as unbearably taut with "tension toward the sacred." Scandalized by Protestant heresy and courtly debauchery and traumatized by periodic pestilence and astrological portents, this sensibility sought palpable intimacy with the sacred and ritual purification from Protestant pollution. In starkest contrast with Calvinism, which regarded God and his Word alone as sacred and subordinated evil to divine providence, Leaguelike Catholicism's sense of the sacred and sacrilegious was at once immanent and imminent, seeing Protestants as the harbingers of the anti-Christ and good Catholics as God's warriors. Images, relics, miracles, astrological signs, above all the consecrated host—all of them regarded as superstitious by Calvinism—these not only bore witness to the sacred but were themselves manifestations of the divine. In white-clad, cross-bearing processions organized around the consecrated host, these Catholic "warriors of God" aspired to forge themselves into a mystical body ready to replicate the passion of Christ, while in ritual violence against Protes-

---

39. [De Bèze], *Du droit des magistrats sur leurs subjets*, pp. 52–53; and [Du Plessis-Mornay], *Vindiciae contra Tyrannos*, pp. 47–48, 160, 163–65. On the monarchomachs' dependence on conciliar thought, see Skinner, *The Age of the Reformation*, pp. 113–34, 189–348.

40. [Du Plessis-Mornay], *Vindiciae contra Tyrannos*, pp. 89, 98, 154–55.

41. Myrian Yardeni, "French Calvinist Political Thought, 1534–1715," in *International Calvinism, 1541–1715*, ed. Menna Prestwich, (Oxford, 1985), pp. 315–37; and Roland Mousnier, *L'assassinat d'Henri IV: Le problème du tyrannicide et l'affermissement de la monarchie absolue*, Trente journées qui ont fait la France series (Paris, 1964), pp. 71–90.

tants—and eventually against kings—they sought to avenge an offended holiness and achieve reconciliation with God. Although the anti-Protestant violence culminating in Saint Bartholemew's Day 1572 gave way to a more introspective, penitential mysticism in the decade that followed, enough sacral tension and holy dread remained combustible to burst into the paroxysm of the Holy League that culminated in the assassination of the "tyrant" Henri III by the Dominican monk Jacques Clément in 1589.[42]

The Holy League's spiritual sensibility was therefore hardly antimonarchical in any iconoclastic sense. On the contrary, its lachrymose sermonry, spectacular processions, penitential piety, reliquary religiosity, and mystical politics—all of these traits sat easily enough in the company of "royal religion." Although directed against the person of the king, the League's habit of swearing oaths in the conspicuous presence of clerics recreated a sacral community in the absence of a sacred head and replicated the ceremony of royal coronations at a lower level. In spite of its insistence upon "democratic" electoral procedures, the League's quarrel was initially less with the monarchy's fledgling absolutism than with its reluctance to subordinate its interests to those of the "faith," in particular to the Catholic crusade against the heretical Huguenots. What it sought in these electoral procedures was less democracy than a civic unanimity, lest that body social be any less unitary than the king's had been. Indeed, the monarchy that the League dreamed of was a priestly monarchy, embodied by a new Melchizedek of Salem or *rex versus et sacerdos,* which it thought it had found for a while in Navarre's cousin, the cardinal de Bourbon, proclaimed Charles X in 1589.

The League's political subversiveness therefore lay less with the monarchy as such than with the persons of the monarch and his favorites at court: the hopelessly high standards of exemplary piety to which it held Catholic princes and the immense vilification to which it subjected those—the "debauched" Henry III, the "heretical" Henry IV—who in its opinion failed to measure up to these standards. The League's threat to the French monarchy, in still other words, consisted above all in a sort of political Donatism—a tendency to allow the moral deficiencies of the king's mortal body and its entourage to invalidate the sacral efficacy of his office.[43] Although overflowing with "moral revulsion against the Valois state," the League's preaching in Angers, Nantes and Rennes analyzed by Robert Harding directed the lay faithful's righteous wrath against "the personnel

42. Crouzet, *Guerriers de Dieu.* See also the same author's "Recherches sur les processions blanches, 1583–1584," *Histoire, Economie, Société* 4 (1982):511–63; and "La représentation du temps à l'époque de la Ligue: '*Le clouaque et esgoust des immondices des autres (siècles) passez,*'" *Revue historique* 270 (1983):297–388.

43. On the vilification of Henry III in the pamphlets of the League and its relation to the royal touch, see David A Bell, "Unmasking a King: The Political Uses of Popular Literature Under the French Catholic League," *Sixteenth Century Journal* 20 (1989):371–86.

of the state, not the form of the state . . . and against churchmen, not the church,"
and at most proposed to "hand the sword to the *menu people* but not the sceptre."[44]
Whereas Calvinism's iconoclastic riot directed its ire by definition against *things*
that symbolized the objectionable features of the institutions of the sixteenth-
century church and state, Leaguelike Catholicism's preferred form of violence
symptomatically bore down on heretical *persons,* supposing that their physical
removal would purify church and state.[45] What real radicalism it contained was,
unlike Protestantism's, more social than political, a consequence of the extension
of its political Donatism to the nobility and the magistracy. "Nobility in general is
based on the subject of virtue acquired by oneself alone as opposed to that
acquired from others; and the title of noblesse ought to be personal and not
hereditary, such that he who is not virtuous cannot be noble," declared the zealous
Manant to the noble Maheustre in the anonymous *Dialogue Between the Maheustre
and the Manant,* one of the League's last and most authentic utterances in 1593.[46]
That ethic was potentially corrosive of a hereditary nobility, to say nothing of a
venal magistracy.[47]

The League's politically Donatist tendency to subordinate institutions to
persons even affected its contribution to the political theory of tyrannicide and
revolt. It is of course true that while it suited their purposes between 1584 and
1594, League preachers and publicists like Jean Boucher and Guillaume Rose
rivaled the political radicalism of their Protestant adversaries by vesting sovereignty in the entire Catholic community—or at least the oath-taking Catholic
community—and in making kings elective by and accountable to the Estates
General. It is also true that, in doing so, they exploited the same Roman, patristic,
and scholastic sources as had the Protestants, sometimes shamelessly plagiarizing
Protestant monarchomach literature, Boucher, for example, borrowing from Du
Plessis-Mornay's *Vindiciae* and George Buchannan's *The Right of the Kingdom of
Scotland.*[48] Putting theory into practice, Leaguish delegates to the Estates General
went so far as to try to elect a king to their liking in the still League-controlled

44. Robert Harding, "Revolution and Reform in the Holy League: Angers, Rennes, Nantes," *JMH*
53 (Sept. 1981):413–14.

45. Zemon Davis, "The Rites of Violence," pp. 173–76.

46. [François Cromé], *Dialogue d'entre le maheustre et le manant,* ed. Peter Ascoli (Geneva, 1977),
p. 189.

47. Although in his introduction to the *Dialogue* Peter Ascoli attacks Myriam Yardeni, Roland
Mousnier, and others for anachronistically attributing an antiaristocratic social conscience to the League
[see Myriam Yardeni, *La conscience nationale en France pendant les guerres de religion* (Louvain, 1971),
p. 255], the point of view taken here is to regard antinoble utterances such as the "manant's" quite
seriously, but as that of a small minority and as a function of an intensely religious conscience.

48. Frederick Baumgartner, *Radical Reactionaries: The Political Thought of the French Catholic
League* (Geneva, 1976), pp. 114, 131, 138–39, 157, 226. On the political thought of George Buchannan and
the dependency of League publicists on Protestant political thought, see Skinner, *The Age of the Reformation,* 338–48.

Paris of 1593. Yet the League left its characteristic tracks in even this largely derivative terrain by adding the king's Catholicity to the realm's "fundamental" laws and by reviving the thesis of the papacy's "indirect" temporal power to depose tyrannical—and perforce heretical—kings in deadly combination with scholastic casuistry's justification of the assassination of tyrants. Whether judged so by pope or Sorbonne, a heretical or excommunicate king was by definition the most heinous type of tyrant and hence adjudicative, in the most surgical version of this casuisty, by the first assassin's knife. Unlike their Protestant predecessors, who also countenanced tyrannicide, the League's publicists typically named the kings they had in mind—Henri de Valois, Henri de Navarre—while lesser leaguers put theory into practice.[49] If, as Crouzet insists, Jacques Clément was not indebted to this casuistry when he laid Henri III low in 1589, it is arguably otherwise in the case of Jean Chastel, who tried unsuccessfully to assassinate Henri IV in 1594, as well as in that of François Ravaillac, who finally succeeded in 1610.[50]

The mainly limited and reformist character of the League's political and ecclesiastical agenda was undoubtedly reinforced by a social constituency that, in contrast to Protestantism's, was structurally attached to both the monarchy and the Catholic Church. With the exceptions of Paris and Dijon, where the League's seizure of power assumed the aspect of a social conflict pitting lesser judicial and municipal officers (barristers, attorneys, and the like) against the high magistracy of the sovereign courts, the League's most conspicuous social constituents were parish priests, members of the regular clergy (notably Jesuits, Dominicans, and Franciscans) and the whole community of royal judicial officers, *including* a fair percentage of magistrates from the sovereign courts. Among other social groups the League similarly appealed to the older and less skilled artisans and workers like butchers and bakers as opposed to goldsmiths and printers.[51] The League also seems to have attracted women more successfully than Calvinism, despite the Reformed Church's new place for women as wives of pastors.[52]

---

49. Baumgartner, *Radical Reactionaries*, pp. 127–28, 132–40, 155–56, 225–26.

50. On Clément's assassination of Henri III, see Denis Crouzet, "La ligue et le tyrannicide de 1589: Une expérience mystique?" a paper delivered at the annual meeting of the Society for French Historical Studies in Québec City in April 1986 and cited with the permission of the author. On the case of Ravaillac in particular and the theory of tyrannicide in general, see Mousnier, *L'assassinat d'Henri IV*, pp. 47–90.

51. Zemon Davis, "The Rites of Violence"; Benedict, *Rouen during the Wars of Religion*, pp. 83–94; John M. H. Salmon, "The Paris Sixteen, 1589–1594: The Social Analysis of a Revolutionary Movement," *JMH* 44 (1972):540–76. On the rather exceptional situation in Dijon and Paris, see Richet, "Aspects socio-culturels des conflits religieux à Paris," pp. 35–38; Elie Barnavi, *Le parti de Dieu: Etude sociale et politique des chefs de la Ligue parisienne, 1585–1594* (Brussels, n.d.), esp. pp. 25–53, 137–48, 215–38; and H. Drouot, *Mayenne et la Bourgogne, 1587–1596*, 2 vols. (Paris, 1936), esp. 1:160–62, 334–52.

52. Benedict, *Rouen during the Wars of Religion*, pp. 86–88; and Natalie Zemon Davis, "City Women and Religious Change," *Society and Culture in Early-Modern France*, pp. 65–95.

Aspects of Absolutism

However politically radical the Catholic League had become or sincerely Protestant Henry may once have been, the French monarchy's opportunity to choose Protestantism—if such opportunity had ever existed—had long passed by the 1590s. The confessional options available to the monarchy hence consisted in a choice between competitive Catholicisms. The zealotry of the Holy Union—what was already being called the *parti des dévots* (party of the devout)—entailed the extermination of "heresy" in France and a pro-Catholic Habsburg policy in Europe. A more *politique* or Gallican Catholicism—called that of *bons françois* (good Frenchmen)—invited the pursuit of the monarchy's dynastic interests in both France and Europe to the detriment of its Catholic identity and relations with the papacy. Yet a third option—and the one actually taken—consisted of an uneasy compromise between these two. Balancing a vigorous assertion of the crown's religious, even specifically Catholic, identity on the one hand, and its dynastic interests both in France and in Europe on the other, this compromise made up part of the posture of Bourbon absolutism.[53]

As employed here, the term *absolutism* will refer primarily to the increase in claims to power made by the monarchy and its apologists and only secondarily to the institutionalization of those claims. Central to those claims is Jean Bodin's famous definition of *sovereignty* as an "absolute and perpetual power" as well as an "indivisible thing," a power capable of "laying down law to all in general and each in particular" without the consent of anyone above, below, or outside it save God alone.[54] It is therefore appropriate that Bodin himself should have been only a reluctant leaguer, for the tone of his *Six Books of the Republic*, published in 1576, which in so many ways charted the course of the Bourbon monarchy, is decidedly politique, almost as alien to the Holy League's integral Catholicism as it was to Protestant monarchomach constitutionalism. As translated and expanded upon by royal apologists—and imperfectly implemented by the monarchy itself—the elements of Bodin's definition took the form of a heightened accent on the king's legislative will as opposed to his justice, on succession to the throne by virtue of dynastic blood-right as opposed to constitutional law, and the studious demotion of competing institutions like the parlements and the Estates General. In principle, absolute monarchy remained different from "despotic" or "seigneurial" monarchy by being limited by divine, natural, and constitutional law. In practice, as

53. On the character of the politico-religious debate after the assassination of Henry IV, see Denis Richet, "La polémique politique en France de 1612 à 1615," in Roger Chartier and Denis Richer, *Représentation et vouloir politique: Autour des Etats généraux de 1614*, Editions de l'Ecole des hautes études en sciences sociales (France, 1982), pp. 151–95.

54. Jean Bodin, *Les six livres de la république de J. Bodin, Angevin. Ensemble une apologie de René Herpin* (Paris, 1583), pp. 122, 221–22, 254.

numbers of recent studies have underscored, Bourbon absolutism was never entirely able to institutionalize its claims to undivided power, even at its height under Louis XIV, although its successes were more salient in religious affairs than in others.[55]

By itself, however, Bodin's definition of sovereignty is incomplete as a characterization of absolutism because it is insufficiently religious. For Bodin's elegant definition, William Church has shown, coalesced during the latter six-teenth and early seventeenth century with a resacralization–even further diviniza-tion–of the French monarchy that, though foreign to Bodin's book, arose sim-ilarly in reaction to the wars of religion.[56] By 1625 the Bishop of Chartres, Léonore d'Estampes, ventured the opinion that "there is no one who does not hold and believe that [the King of France] is in no way mortal but instead something very like the Deity and similar to him"; while just a few years later the future academician Guez de Balzac commended the Roman practice of emperor worship as worthy of emulation, maintaining that Louis XIII in particular was so saintly that he had never lost the innocence vouchsafed to him by baptism.[57] Far from representing a secularization of French political thinking, Church has ar-gued, Richelieu's notorious politics of "reason of state" presupposed this diviniza-tion, and made sense in the cardinal-minister's own mind only on the assumption of France's special relation to God and the sacrosanctity of French kingship.[58]

Whatever else it may have been, then, Bourbon absolutism was a defensive response to the French religious civil wars. It represented an attempt to raise the monarchy securely above and beyond the confessional fray, to immunize the royal "conscience" against judgment by priests and pastors alike, and to make the monarchy a rival of the church as mediator of its subjects' relation to God.[59] In order to do that, however, the Bourbon monarchy had first and foremost to come to terms with the conciliar aspects of the Gallican tradition, which had lent themselves to subversive effect by both Calvinist and Catholic participants in the wars of religion. That reckoning hence took the form of sponsoring a redefinition

---

55. I refer to such studies as William Beik's *Absolutism and Society in Seventeenth-Century France: State Power and Provincial Aristocracy in Languedoc* (Cambridge, 1985); Roger Mettam's *Power and Faction in Louis XIV's France* (Oxford, 1980); Sharon Kettering's *Patrons, Brokers, and Clients in Seventeenth-Century France* (Oxford, 1983); and of course Russell Major's authoritative and voluminous studies of the Estates General.

56. Among the *politique* publicists who combined Bodin's definition of sovereignty with Gallica-nism's conception of semidivine kingship are Jean Duret, François Grimaudet, Pierre Grégoire, and Adam Blackwood. For their contribution to the seventeenth-century notion of divine-right kingship see Church, *Constitutional Thought in Sixteenth-Century France*, pp. 43–271. See also John Figgis, *The Divine Right of Kings*, 2d ed. (Cambridge, 1922), pp. 126–36.

57. William Farr Church, *Richelieu and Reason of State* (Princeton, N.J., 1972), pp. 145, 252.

58. Ibid., passim.

59. Wolfe, *The Conversion of Henri IV*, pp. 157–58, 190–91.

of the Gallican tradition, culminating in the famous Declaration by the General Assembly of the Gallican Clergy in 1682.[60]

As elaborated in the late Middle Ages by royal jurists and Sorbonne theologians in reaction to the papacy's claims to temporal dominion, Gallicanism upheld both the temporal independence of the monarchy and the spiritual independence of the Gallican Church in their respective relations with the papacy. The Gallican Church's independence meant, among other things, an adherence to the Council of Constance's assertion that the church as a whole, as represented by a general council, was superior to the pope in the formulation of dogma, as well as to the assertion of the Gallican Church's particular rights to judge doctrine concurrently with Rome and to retain its own canonical usages. And the monarchy's independence meant a rejection of the papal or ultramontanist claim to direct temporal lordship over emperors or kings as enunciated, for example, in Boniface VIII's bull *Unam sanctam* in 1302, or even the claim to indirect temporal power by reason of the papacy's spiritual power to punish sin. Part of Gallicanism's answer to a spiritual power's temporal pretensions, as we have noted, had been to "spiritualize" French kingship. But no matter how sacrosanct and however close was the mortal king to the immortal body, liturgical kingship in the Gallican imagination had not generally aspired to more than an assimilated sacerdotal or saintly status—a type of Christ in no greater sense than bishops were types of Christ—and had therefore never exempted individual kings from the temporal consequences of unabsolved sin. The possibility of a deservedly excommunicate king was no more to be denied than that of a heretical priest or pope.

What Gallican theologians defended was rather the right of the Gallican Church to concur in any papal sentence of excommunication against a king, as well as the right of the coterminous French nation "to draw out and enforce whatever temporal implications—the loss of kingship, for example—that a sentence of excommunication might entail. Indeed, on the subject of the popular origin of political power, such early sixteenth-century Sorbonne theologians as Jacques Almain and John Major were quite explicit: the community only delegated the "exercise" or "use" of its political power while always retaining its "property" and "ownership"; if a king abused his "ministry," he could always be deposed and replaced by another.[61]

Participants in the sixteenth-century French wars of religion had justified

---

60. The following analysis of late-medieval Gallicanism and the changes it underwent in the crucible of the sixteenth-century wars of religion is highly dependent on Victor Martin's classic studies, namely *Le gallicanisme politique et le clergé de France* (Paris, 1929); and *Les origines du gallicanisme*, 2 vols. (Paris, 1939).

61. On the character of traditional Gallicanism, see Martin, *Le gallicanism politique et le clergé de France*, pp. 25–40. On the political thought of Jacques Almain and John Major in particular, see Skinner, *The Age of Reformation*, pp. 113–34.

both revolt and assassination in precisely such Gallican terms. Even on the Calvinist side, de Bèze and Du Plessis-Mornay had relied strategically if not massively on conciliar theory in attempting to "vindicate" the Huguenots' right to armed resistance to the Valois "tyrants." Since it was "settled" among the "saner sort of those who call themselves Roman Catholics that the universal Council is above the pope, even to the point of being able to depose him . . . in cases of heresy," so "it follows," De Bèze had argued, "either that Kings have more authority than popes, and that heresy is a lesser crime than Tyranny, or that people have just as much power over Kings become tyrants as a Council over a heretical pope."[62] And the Gallican component loomed at least as large in the Catholic League's casuistry of political revolt and assassination, since it relied on the intervention of the Gallican Church. To be sure, some League theorists like Jean Boucher were more ultramontanist than Gallican. But such League manifestos as the anonymous *De justa reipublicanae authoritate (On the Just Authority of a Republic)* did just as well without any ultramontanist premises at all, and even Boucher restated his thesis in more Gallican terms in his *Apologie pour Jean Chastel (Apology for Jean Chastel)*, which he published in exile in 1595. It was not the pope, after all, but the Sorbonne which on 7 January 1589 had formally absolved Frenchmen of their obedience to the much maligned Henri III, justifying both the League's revolt and Jacques Clément's physical assault in 1589. And though Pope Sixtus V both excommunicated Henri de Navarre and declared him disbarred from the French kingship, it was the League-controlled Estates General of 1593 that, in accordance with "old" Gallican theory, premised its action on that excommunication and contemplated the election of another king.[63]

The conceptual task facing politiques, as Catholics loyal to the cause of the Bourbon dynasty were pejoratively called, was therefore to seal off these chinks in the monarchy's Gallican armor, to make the monarchy invulnerable to both revolt by the Protestants' "inferior magistrates" and assassination by the League's priestly preachers and monks. That new suit of armor was the proposition that the French king was accountable to God alone. It already appeared in all syllables in the last decades of the sixteenth century in the works of politique publicists who combined it with Bodin's novel definition of sovereignty.[64] But it did not officially surface until the Third Estate demanded that it be recognized as a "fundamental law of the realm" by the Estates General of 1614. Drafted by a parlementary barrister named Antoine Arnauld—a prophetic touch!—the proposition specified that "as [the king] is recognized as Sovereign in his State, not holding his Crown from anyone but God, there is no Power on earth, whether Spiritual or Temporal,

62. [De Bèze], *Du droit des magistrats sur leurs subjets*, pp. 52–53.
63. Baumgartner, *Radical Reactionaries*, pp. 103–5, 114–22, 145–65, 222–29.
64. Church, *Constitutional Thought in the Sixteenth Century*, pp. 243–71.

which has the least right over his realm, such as would take it away from the sacred persons of our Kings," and went on to anathematize the admissibility of any deposition or assassination.[65]

The proposition did not become a fundamental law at that time due to the resistance of the nobility and the clergy. The cardinal du Perron, the main spokesman for the clergy's delegation, found it outrageous that a French king might have the right to convert, say, to Mohammedanism without fear of deposition or resistance. And Louis XIII and Richelieu prevented the Sorbonne and the Parlement of Paris from condemning the Jesuit Antonio Santarelli's *Tractatus de Haeresi . . . et de Potestate Romani Pontificis in his delictis puniendis (Treatise on Heresy . . . and the Power of the Roman Pontif in Punishing Sin)* in defense of the papacy's temporal power some twelve years later.[66] That proposition then lay dormant for the remainder of Louis XIII's reign, only to rear its head anew—and with royal backing this time—when the young Louis XIV prevailed upon the Sorbonne to brandish it momentarily in 1663 as a maneuver in one of the king's earliest skirmishes with the papacy. But it attained the status of political orthodoxy only when the Sun King clashed with Pope Innocent XI in 1682 over his regalian rights to the revenues of vacant bishoprics and prevailed upon an extraordinary assembly of the Gallican Clergy—and a somewhat reluctant Bishop Bossuet—to enshrine it as the first of "his" church's four liberties in 1682.[67] Henceforth something like fundamental law and an article of faith in France, the proposition of royal accountability to God alone raised the king above his bishops and even the pope, since the Gallican Declaration's other articles still held the pope accountable to the church. Whereas medieval kingship had tended to assimilate kingship to priesthood and pointed to Christ as man-god, divine-right monarchy as it emerged from the religious-civil wars tended more directly toward the divinization of the king, or the state as personified by the king.[68] Continuing to draw, however, on selected elements of Catholicism, this Gallic variant of divine-right monarchy was far from religiously neutral, as both docile Protestants and Jansenists were soon to learn at their cost. At the same time, what the General Assembly enacted in 1682 represented royal policy as much as if not more than

65. Cited in Mariéjol, *Henri IV et Louis XIII*, pp. 164–65. For the relatively recent discovery that it was Antoine Arnauld who drafted the proposition, see Denis Richet, "La monarchie au travail sur elle-même?" in *De la Réforme à la Révolution*, p. 437.

66. On Cardinal Du Perron's speech see Michael Hayden, *France and the Estates General of 1614* (London, 1974), pp. 139–40. On the Santarelli controversy see Church, *Richelieu and Reason of State*, pp. 157–61; and Martin, *La gallicanisme politique et la clergé de France*, pp. 168–244.

67. Aimé-Georges Martimort, *Le gallicanisme de Bossuet* (Paris, 1953). In his *Les assemblées du clergé de 1670 à 1693* (Rome, 1972), Pierre Blet has nuanced Martimort's overall emphasis on the royal initiative in the Declaration of 1682 by showing that by that date the Gallican bishops were not declaring anything that they did not really believe.

68. Richet, "La monarchie au travail sur elle-même," p 440.

episcopal policy. For the stock of Gallicanism's conciliar tenets tended to rise or fall in tandem with the monarchy's need for them as a weapon in its relations with the papacy.[69]

Yet the vagaries of monarchical policy do not mean that divine right, as defined by the Gallican Declaration's first article, ever ceased to be an integral tenet of royal orthodoxy. Much has occasionally been made of Louis XIV's disavowal of the declaration in the course of liquidating the *régale* controversy with Innocent XI in 1693. But that disavowal concerned the more traditionally Gallican—that is, the episcopal and conciliar—parts of the declaration more than the proposition of the king's accountability to God alone, which the French monarchy in fact reiterated on every obvious occasion thereafter, even as late as on the eve of the French Revolution. And so far as the conciliar tradition and the independence of the Gallican Clergy are concerned, these Gallican tenets were in some sense already the casualties of the General Assembly of 1682, to which the disavowal of 1693 only added the coup de grâce. For an episcopacy as closely tied to the monarchy as were the French bishops to Louis XIV in 1682, "independence" had meaning in relation to the papacy alone. The Declaration of 1682 had quite simply redefined the Gallican bishops as partners in absolutism. And for a monarchy as sure of its episcopacy as was Louis XIV in 1693, the threat of papal ultramontanism receded in comparison to that posed by the republican implications of conciliar Gallicanism itself. It was already with a certain "embarrassment," according to Martimort, that French readers encountered the thesis of the popular origin of the king's purely representative power in the treatises by the old Sorbonnists Jacques Almain and John Major when a Parisian bookseller reprinted them along with the complete works of Jean Gerson in 1606; at the height of his conflict with Louis XIV, Pope Innocent XI himself malignly pointed out to the king's ambassador that "if councils were superior to the popes whose power comes from God, then the Estates General would have leave to press the same claim against kings."[70] Allied with the Jansenism that Louis XIV was then trying to suppress, that kind of Gallican challenge seemed to be materializing again in the 1690s. Hence Louis XIV's rapprochement with the papacy, whose help he needed against Jansenism; hence also his growing estrangement from the Parlement of Paris, whose rearguard actions in defense of integral Gallicanism stood in the way of his offensive against Jansenism.

If as an absolute sovereign the Bourbon monarchy sought to displace the subversive aspects of Gallicanism common to both Protestantism and the League, as an indivisible one it aspired to eliminate what remained of the infrastructure of

---

69. Martimort, *Le gallicanisme de Bossuet,* pp. 363–497. It is true that Martimort's argument has been challenged by Blet in his *Les assemblées du clergé et Louis XIV de 1670 à 1693.*

70. Martimort, *Le gallicanisme de Bossuet,* p. 50; and Blet, *Les assemblées du clergé et Louis XIV de 1670 à 1693,* p. 396.

each of these parties. This was above all true of the remaining separatist Protestant estate in France. For that is close to the legal status enjoyed by French Protestants under Henry IV's Edict of Nantes, promulgated in 1598. The edict granted Protestants freedom of public worship in areas of their numerical strength (mainly the south and west) as well as in specified places elsewhere in France, access to all royal offices in the kingdom, and the right to be tried by biconfessional chambers *(chambres de l'édit)* in all the sovereign courts. Two even more important letters or *brevets* assigned crown revenues for the payment of Protestant pastors and the upkeep of some fifty military garrisons in Huguenot strongholds in western and southern France.

It was the pious Louis XIII, "the Just," who, getting the better of another of many princes' revolts in 1620, seized the occasion to lead his army to Navarre and Béarn, there to honor his father's unfulfilled commitment to restore Catholic worship and secularized ecclesiastical property in these previously Protestant domains. The result was the resumption of the sixteenth-century's chronic civil wars of religion, culminating in Cardinal Richelieu's spectacular siege of La Rochelle in 1628 and the collapse of Protestant military power in southern France a year later. Depriving them of just about all their fortifications and garrisons, Richelieu's Peace of Alès (or of Grace) nonetheless maintained the religious and civil toleration of the Edict of Nantes—and ironically freed Richelieu to pursue the monarchy's dynastic interests on the side of threatened Protestantism in the Empire and in defiance of much of Catholic opinion, even in France.[71] The midcentury civil war known as the Fronde gave the Huguenots some temporary respite, but it was fatal for them in the longer run because it tended to associate them anew with the English and "republican" sedition by reason of the Puritan revolution simultaneously taking place across the Channel.[72] And although these had often stood the Huguenots in good stead in the past, the Bourbon dynasty's anti-Habsburg interests—in this case Louis XIV's imperial aspirations in the Germanies—sounded the death knell to civil as well as religious toleration when the Sun King formally revoked the Edict of Nantes with the Edict of Fontainebleau in 1685. For the coincidence of the accession of the Catholic—and pro-French—James II as King of England and an unprecedented *entente* between German Protestants and their Catholic Habsburg emperor in the face of a revived Turkish threat in the east conspired to make Louis XIV's imperial ambitions seem momentarily more attainable in the role of avenger of Catholic orthodoxy every-

71. On the liquidation of the Protestant "estate" in the South, see A. D. Lublinskaya, *French Absolutism: The Crucial Phase, 1620–1629,* trans. Brian Pierce (Cambridge, 1968), pp. 146–219.

72. Elisabeth Labrousse, *"Une foi, une loi, un roi?" Essai sur la révocation de l'édit de Nantes,* no. 7, Histoire et société series (Geneva and Paris, 1985), pp. 39–44. On the subject of the revocation, see also Janine Garrisson-Estèbe's *L'édit de Nantes et sa révocation: Histoire d'une intolérance* (Paris, 1985).

where in Europe than in the traditional one of protector of Protestants in the Empire.[73]

Louis XIII and Louis XIV doubtlessly also strove to realize the old medieval ideal of "one faith, one law, one king," updated by Bodin as true sovereignty's indivisible nature. Given the forced hypocrisy of many of the newly converted Huguenots who remained in France after the revocation of the Edict of Nantes, it is evident that Louis XIV's concern for indivisibility extended to the domain of conscience, disallowing even the division between the interior conviction and exterior conformity that Reinhard Koselleck, in a classic thesis, thought characteristic of the "absolutist compromise."[74] For the same drama, as we shall soon see, was simultaneously being played out by the French Jansenists, similarly forbidden to maintain an attitude of "respectful silence" vis-a-vis the factual side of the papal condemnation of Augustinian doctrine. Even more than in the case of Jansenism, moreover, Louis XIV's treatment of Protestantism represented *royal* religious policy. For while the Edict of Fontainebleau finally answered the French episcopacy's swelling litany of anti-Protestant complaint voiced on the occasion of every meeting of its General Assembly, it apparently proved something of a disappointment to Pope Innocent XI, at least in the longer run. In one blow the revocation dashed the hopes that he and Emperor Leopold II had placed in ten years of ecumenical negotiations between Royas y Spinola, Bishop of Tina, and the German Lutheran states, in view of a new general council that would end the religious schism in the Empire. Nor, in spite of all the official rejoicing, was the revocation entirely to the liking of those bishops—Bossuet of Meaux, for example— who had been involved in these negotiations, or others, like Etienne Le Camus of Grenoble, who had taken a more irenical tack toward Huguenots in their dioceses.[75]

In contrast to the Protestant estate, the legacy of the Catholic League was much closer to the monarchy's religious identity, and the threat that it represented was hence more difficult to identify and dispel. Whereas what remained of the Protestant estate was all too confined and contracting, post-League French Catholicism was diffuse and expanding. The proliferation of new secular and religious orders like the Oratory and Ursulines, the reform of the secular clergy

73. Jean Orcibal, *Louis XIV et les protestants* (Paris, 1951), pp. 81–158.

74. Reinhart Koselleck, *Kritik und Krise: Eine Studie zur Pathogenese der bürgerlichen Welt* (Fribourg, 1959).

75. This interpretation of the Edict of Fontainebleau relies heavily on Jean Orcibal's *Louis XIV et les Protestants*, pp. 81–158. Orcibal's version of Pope Innocent's reaction to the revocation of the Edict of Nantes has sustained a challenge, it is true, in Pierre Blet's "Les papes et la Révocation" in *La Révocation de l'Edit de Nantes et la protestantisme français en 1685: Actes du colloque de Paris, 15–19 octobre 1985*, ed. Roger Zuber and Laurent Theis (Paris. 1986), pp. 263–80.

effected by seminaries in the wake of the Council of Trent, the burgeoning of Baroque Catholic piety under the inspiration of "devout" humanism and Mediterranean mysticism—all these got their start in the latter sixteenth century and went into the making of the French Catholic "century of saints." By the death of Henri IV this flowering of French Catholicism had attained enough momentum to have produced an informal political lobby in the form of the *parti dévot*, and that devout or pious party exercised enough clout at court to have been in part responsible for the sharp reversals in French domestic and foreign policy during the regency of the Queen Mother Marie de Medici and the brief ministry of Charles-Albert, duc de Luynes. The policies that the parti dévot stood for were the continuation of the offensive against Huguenot heresy, increased charity toward an overtaxed French peasantry, and at least benign neutrality toward the Habsburg crusade against Protestantism elsewhere in Europe. Its chief accomplishments during these years were the forcible restitution of Catholic property and worship in Navarre and Béarn, the marriage of the young Louis XIII to Anne d'Autriche, daughter of Spain's Philip III, and France's virtual abandonment of her Protestant allies in Europe on the eve of the Thirty Years' War. Yet even at its height the influence of the parti dévot went only so far, and it took a turn for the worse after the rise of the anti-Habsburg Richelieu as first minister. It sustained something like shipwreck on 10 November 1630, the "day of dupes," when Richelieu dissipated a "devout" cabal organized around the queen mother to replace him, and Louis XIII sent the party's lay leader, the chancellor Michel de Marillac, to his death on Paris's public execution block in the place de Grève.[76]

One "devout" organization that survived this debacle was the shadowy Company of the Holy Sacrament, founded in the late 1620s by Henri de Lévis, duc de Ventadour. Like the committees of the League, this clandestine company grouped pious laymen like Ventadour and the master of requests René II de Voyer d'Argenson with zealous clerics, some of whom—Pierre Olier and Saint-Vincent de Paul, for example—became leading figures in the French Counter-Reformation. And like the committees of the League, it too preferred semiclandestinity and indirect action through the intermediacy of existing institutions, such as municipal governments, the parlements, and of course the church. The company also resembled the Holy Union in its goal of promoting Catholic orthodoxy, piety, and social action: the continuing campaign against Huguenots, the adoration of the Eucharist, the work of foreign missions, the reformation of morals, and of course charitable activity on behalf of the poor and the sick. The Parisian General Hospital and the Foreign Missions were among its institutional legacies. But the company's very clandestinity and continuing advocacy of a pro-Habsburg Catho-

---

76. Victor L. Tapié, *La France de Louis XIII et de Richelieu* (Paris, 1967), pp. 53–230.

lic foreign policy made it suspect to Louis XIV, who finally suppressed it in 1666.[77]

More conspicuous but less vulnerable was the situation of the parish priests and their auxiliaries—the so-called second order of the clergy. Although subordinate to bishops they were also indispensable, being the only agents of sacramental grace for the vast majority of French Catholics. It is they who had constituted the clerical backbone of the Catholic League both in Paris and provincial cities in the 1590s. Parisian parish priests had moreover put on another impressive display of political and confessional insubordination, as we shall soon note, just as Louis XIV reached his majority and in the wake of the Fronde.[78]

The monarchy could neither eliminate them nor even purge them, because it did not control the distribution of parish benefices as it did episcopal ones. But it contrived to increase its indirect influence over them at the end of the century by permitting its episcopal partners in absolutism to redefine the entire second order as their humble and obedient servants. The Edict of 1695, obtained from Louis XIV in return for the General Assembly's generous contribution to his war effort, granted the Gallican bishops the sole right to authorize nonbeneficed priests to preach, administer the sacraments, or to hear confessions—in effect depriving parish priests of the right to appoint their own auxiliaries—as well as the exclusive power to confer the *visa* that qualified candidates for sacerdotal offices. Hard on the heals of this edict came the royal Declaration of 15 December 1698, which gave bishops the discretionary right to send their priests to seminaries for three-month disciplinary stays and to use the king's extrajudicial *lettres de cachet* (sealed or secret orders) for indefinite incarceration in cases of continued insubordination. In 1700, finally, the General Assembly of the Gallican Clergy deprived delegates of the second order of any deliberative voice in its proceedings, even though these delegates were not typically parish priests but rather *vicaires* (curates) already well on their way to the episcopacy.[79] Together these measures redefined the parish curé as a dependent agent of episcopal authority, even as it underscored the episcopacy's own identification with the crown. Indirectly strengthening the monarchy's control over the parish clergy, particularly in Paris, the Edict of 1695

---

77. On the Company of the Holy Sacrament see Raoul Allier, *La cabale des dévots, 1627–1666* (Paris, 1902); René Taveneaux, *Le catholicisme dans la France classique, 1610–1715*, 2 vols. paginated continuously (Paris, 1980), pp. 225–34; and Alain Tallon, *La Compaqnie du Saint Sacrament* (Paris, 1990).

78. See Richard M. Golden, *The Godly Rebellion: Parisian Curés and the Religious Fronde, 1652–1662* (Chapel Hill, N.C., 1981).

79. Edmond Préclin, *Les jansénistes du dix-huitième siècle et la Constitution civile du clergé: Le développement du richérisme, sa propagation dans le bas clergé* (Paris, 1929), pp. 28–34; and Robert Kreiser, *Miracles, Convulsions, and Ecclesiastical Politics in Early Eighteenth Century Paris* (Princeton, N.J., 1978), pp. 22–26.

concluded a centuries-long decline of parochial autonomy that had begun with the defeat of the Parisian League in 1594.

Their association with the League and the parti dévot not only predisposed the monarchy against devout companions and curés but was also a factor in its hostility toward such "constitutional" institutions as the Estates General and the parlements. The Estates General, it is true, had initially found some favor among Protestant pamphleteers, who did not thereby endear themselves to the monarchy either. But there were never enough Protestants to be able to use let alone remake this medieval institution, which, when it finally challenged the monarchy, did so as an instrument of the Catholic League. For not content with enthusiastically valorizing the Estates General, the League's adherents had also translated theory into action, all but controlling the agenda of the Estates convened by Henri III in Blois in 1576 and 1588 and nearly electing a king in the Paris Estates of 1593. And although not obviously associated with the demand for the convocation of the Estates in 1614, devout voices had made themselves heard within the clergy and succeeded in vetoing the Third Estate's proposition in favor of the temporal independence of the king.[80]

Except in some provincial cities like Rouen, the League had been somewhat less successful with the parlements. In the Parisian center, the Sixteen's military governor Bussy-Leclerc purged an insufficiently zealous Parlement of Paris on 16 January 1589 and executed its first president Barnabé Brisson, along with two other magistrates, on 15 November 1591. It was also the Parlement's judgment (the famous *arrêt* Jean Lemaître) in favor of the Salic Law that helped ward off the possibility of a Spanish Habsburg succession to the still vacant French throne in the summer of 1593. Still, the resistance of the Parlement of Paris to Henri III's forced loans, as well as other fiscal measures, had been decisive from 1580 forward—a necessary condition, arguably, for the League's later successes in Paris. And if barristers, attorneys, and clerks count as part of the Parlement's personnel, then the judicial community, along with parish priests and monks, stands out as one of the Parisian League's two chief social constituencies. Absolutism had therefore a score or two to settle with the Estates General and the parlements; an indivisible sovereignty in any case precluded any sharing of royal legislative authority.

Of the two institutions, the Estates General was the more easily dispensed with. Consisting of the "natural" or well-born delegates of the clergy, nobility, and the third estate, something resembling the Estates had met for the first time at Philip the Fair's behest in 1302 and intermittently by royal convocation during the following two centuries. At their most effective, as in 1357, delegates to the Estates General might bargain for royal assent to their electoral constituents' petitions or

---

80. Roland Mousnier, *L'assassinat d'Henri IV,* pp. 260–64.

doléances for redress of grievances in return for consenting to the king's request for extraordinary subsidies. But the monarchy usually contrived to renege on these promises, and more often to circumvent the Estates altogether by negotiating with each province individually. For the Estates General remained hamstrung not only by divisions between the three orders but by the diversity of the realm's disparate parts and parcels. Even the right to consent to extraordinary subsidies— their main power—was all but lost after 1440 when the Estates allowed Charles VII to raise a standing militia and a permanent tax to maintain it. By the sixteenth century the only force that might have filled the Estates General's all too heterogeneous sails and given them some constitutional direction was religious passion, a passion that, in Catholic form, indeed resulted in four meetings between 1562 and 1595. Yet despite a real attempt on the part of the League-dominated Estates of Blois in 1576 and 1588 to place the monarchy under their tutelage, their final attempt to do so adjourned empty-handed in 1593. Under pressure from the Bourbon princes the young Louis XIII and his regent, Marie de Medici, convoked the Estates for a last time in 1614 and, taking advantage of the divisions between the orders, dismissed them sine die, in effect until May 1789.

The parlements were not so easily dismissed, because they were the chief royal or "sovereign" law courts within their several jurisdictions—the crown of the king's judicial system with subaltern bases in the local bailiwick, seneschal, and prevotal courts. In the late Middle Ages, French kingship represented nothing if not eternal justice, symbolized by the bright red robes worn exclusively by the Parlement's presidents in royal funerary processions.[81] So long as the French kingship defined itself in primarily judicial terms, no king could reign without parlements; and even when the monarchy began to assume a more administrative aspect in the sixteenth century, the parlements kept pace by taking on important administrative functions. Armed since the fifteenth century with the rights—or duties—of transcribing or "registering" all royal edicts and declarations in its judicial registers, and of "remonstrating" against these laws in case of perceived incompatibilities with received law, the parlements considered themselves co-guardians of the French constitution and had often acted on this assumption by opposing the monarchy's legislative initiatives, particularly in defense of the "liberties" of the Gallican Church against Louis XI's and François I's concordats with the papacy. Whatever its relationship with the Estates General—this remained unclear throughout the period—it was at least clear that the Parlement of Paris was an important constitutional check on the monarchy's "good pleasure."[82]

But François I's use of the lit de justice assembly, as Sarah Hanley has shown, frontally challenged the constitutional attributes of the Parlement of Paris by

81. Giesey, *The Royal Funerary Ceremony in Renaissance France,* pp. 51–61.
82. J. H. Shennan, *The Parlement of Paris* (Ithaca, N.Y., 1968), pp. 152–87.

ceremonially underscoring the king's legislative capacity as superior to the Parlement's purely judicial one. And despite the weakness of the monarchy under the last Valois kings, the religious wars did nothing to arrest the erosion of the Parlement's constitutional role. On the one hand the Parlement lost no time in purging "Nicodemites" or covert Calvinists from its ranks, and ineffectively pressed the monarchy for strong action against "heresy." Thus in 1563 Charles IX took the occasion of parlementary resistance to one of his many short-lived edicts of religious toleration of Huguenots to devalorize the Parlement of Paris by holding a constitutional lit de justice assembly in the Parlement of Rouen. On the other hand the Parlement remained too politique, or loyal to the Valois and then Bourbon dynasties, to throw in its whole lot with the League. Not even the League's purge of parlementary personnel, and the Parlement's docility thereafter, did anything to allay the League's distrust, which culminated in the execution of the Parlement's first president in 1591.[83] The Parlement's association with the League was close enough to merit some monarchical enmity but not close enough to have derived any political force from the League's religious zeal.

The right granted by Henry IV in 1604 to transmit their already purchased judicial offices to their posterity failed to strengthen the hand of the Parisian magistrates. To be sure, the prohibitive cost of reimbursing the price of these inherited offices would later make it difficult for the eighteenth-century monarchy to break parlementary resistance to its policies. But in the seventeenth century, on the contrary, the threat to rescind this still recent concession was a powerful bargaining lever in the monarchy's relations with the Parlement.[84] Familial transmission of judicial office, moreover, made it conceptually more difficult to oppose the monarchy's absolutist tendencies, because the *parlementaires* thereby acquired a stake in the principle of automatic biological succession that the Bourbon kings were then trying to accredit at the expense of constitutional succession. Nor did the Parlement's attempt to take the place of the defunct Estates General in constitutional thought—its claim, for example, to be as old as the monarchy—advance the Parlement's constitutional cause very much.[85] However effective that initially precarious claim was in giving the Parlement the semblance of independent authority in the eighteenth century, it did nothing to prevent the vertiginous rise in royal taxes and the proliferation of nonvenal administrative personnel under Louis XIII, both largely consequent upon France's participation in the Thirty Years' War. The agents in question, in part administrators and in part *commissaires* (judicial commissioners) among whom figured the provincial inten-

83. Hanley, *The Lit de Justice of the Kings of France*, pp. 48–101; and A. Labigre, *La révolution des curés* (Paris, 1980), pp. 173, 220–21.

84. Roland Mousnier, *La vénalité des offices sous Henri IV et Louis XIII* (Paris, 1971), pp. 223–308, 579–663.

85. Hanley, *The Lit de Justice and the Kings of France*, pp. 273–315.

dants, began to usurp the functions of venal judicial officers like the *trésoriers* (treasurers) who were akin to the parlementaires themselves. These developments threatened even the Parlement's judicial functions to the extent that the litigation between commissioners and officers either bypassed the parlements entirely or sustained "evocation" to the *Conseil d'état* (Council of State, or Royal Council), where an increasingly administrative monarchy might act as judge and party in its own cause.[86]

The consequently strained relations between monarchy and sovereign courts showed up, in the reign of Louis XIII, in the novel and ever more frequent use of the lit de justice assembly for the forcible registration of fiscal measures; in the ceremonial demotion of magistrates in relation to ministers and princes of the blood; in increasing numbers of extrajudicial imprisonments and exiles of parlementary councillors; and in the ever more peremptory tone taken by the king and his ministers in their dealings with the Parlement. Relations reached a nadir in 1632 when, in a lit de justice assembly, the king downgraded the magistrates' opinions to consultative status after those of the first minister and the princes of the blood; and Louis "the Just" lectured First President Le Jay that "you have been established only to judge between Master Peter and Master John . . . and, if you continue [to meddle in other matters], I will cut your nails so close that it will hurt you."[87] In his last lit de justice assembly in 1641, he promulgated an edict that, vaunting the benefits of "absolute authority" and still deploring the "disorders of the League," restricted the use of remonstrances to the government's fiscal declarations and forbade them altogether in edicts and declarations "regarding the government of the State."[88]

The Parlement of Paris's resistance to an ever more administrative and fiscally oriented monarchy eventually touched off the revolt known as the Fronde during the regency government of Ann of Austria and Cardinal Jules Mazarin in 1648. The usual waves of popular antifiscal and antiseigneurial revolt, further stirred by princely fishing in troubled waters, soon engulfed the specifically parlementary contribution to the Fronde, more thoroughly obscuring the few constitutional issues than in the League and Huguenot revolts a half-century earlier. With French Protestantism already politically senescent and Jansenism still in its infancy, the Fronde remained largely devoid of the religious passion

---

86. Roland Mousnier, "Le Conseil du roi de la mort de Henri IV au gouvernement personnel de Louis XIV" and "Etat et commissaire: Recherches sur la création des intendants des provinces," in *La plume, la faucille, et le marteau: Institutions et société en France du moyen âge à la Révolution,* Collection hier (Paris, 1970), pp. 141–213; and Richard Bonney, *Political Change in France under Richelieu and Mazarin, 1624–1661* (Oxford, 1978), passim.

87. Mariéjol, *Henry IV et Louis XIII,* p. 395; and Hanley, *The Lit de Justice and the Kings of France,* pp. 281–306.

88. Mariéjol, *Henri IV et Louis XIII,* pp. 398–99.

simultaneously energizing the Puritan Revolution across the English Channel. The Fronde's five thousand pamphlets or *mazarinades* directed against the Italian-born cardinal-minister Jules Mazarin displayed neither the passion nor the political principle of French pamphleteering in the sixteenth or eighteenth centuries. To a greater extent than polemical pamphlets in either of these centuries, the mazarinades were exercises in what Christian Jouhaud has aptly characterized as a kind of political "thought in action," functioning as instruments in the competition for power between the Fronde's "great actors" like the prince de Condé and Paul de Gondi, not excluding Mazarin himself.[89]

That much said by way of damnation, the reform proposals of the Parisian courts meeting in the Chambre de Saint-Louis in May–June 1648 stated the "constitutional" case against extrajudicial arrests, unregistered taxes, unverified administrative commissions, and "bloodsucking" fiscal contractors or *partisans* in ways that would not be forgotten. Proparlementary pamphlets, especially Louis Machon's *Les véritables maximes du gouvernement de la France (The True Maxims of the French Government)*, brought the historical-constitutional argument of François Hotman's *Francogallia* up to date by substituting the Parlement of Paris for the now defunct Estates General in the role of the inheritor of Frankish national assemblies, or what Machon renamed the *Judicium Francorum.* "The Parlement represents that assembly, is the same Authority," and is "just as ancient as the Crown," Machon maintained. It followed for Machon that "it is a fundamental law that no taxes can be levied on the king's subjects . . . without the consent of the Parlement, which represents the general assent of the people," and that—in words that would echo as late as in the 1730s—"it is in that place alone that the king makes law and contracts with his people."[90] Similarly it was to the Parlement of Paris that Jean Beaudeau, the marquis de Clanleu, addressed his monarchomach-like dictum that "as soon as a king abuses his power . . . and contravenes his duty, he ceases to be the king and his subjects to be subjects"; while an anonymous *Epilogue,* following Du Plessis-Mornay, laid it down that "the rulers of the people . . . ought not to be considered otherwise than are tutors

89. Christian Jouhaud, *Mazarinades: La Fronde des mots* (Paris, 1985), p. 93–94. Jouhaud's deflationary conclusions, it is true, are in tension with those in Paul Rice Doolin's still useful *The Fronde* (Cambridge, Mass., 1935), and have recently sustained a challenge in Hubert Carrier's *La Presse de la fronde: Les mazarinades,* vol. 1, *La conquête de l'opinion* (Geneva, 1989), esp. pp. 219–72, 396–420. Carrier deems some of the *mazarinades* more "radical" and revolutionary, as well as more reflective of "public opinion," than Jouhaud does. More recently, Jeffrey K. Sawyer's *Printed Poison: Pamphlet Propaganda, Faction Politics, and the Public Sphere in Early Seventeenth-Century France* (Berkeley, Calif., 1990), has also made a case for the pertinence of the pamphlet to "public opinion" in the seventeenth century.

90. [Louis Machon], *Les véritables maximes du gouvernement de la France, justifiées par l'ordre des temps, depuis l'établissement de la monarchie jusques à présent: Servant de réponse au prétendu arrest de cassation du Conseil du 18 janvier 1652.* (Paris, 1652), in *La Fronde, contestation démocratique et misère paysanne: 52 mazarinades,* 2 vols, ed. Hubert Carrier (Paris, 1982), 1:8, 12.

to their pupils."[91] Maintaining that the notion of "absolute power" was "incompatible with our mores, whether Christian or French," the same author quite accurately recalled that the apologists of "absolute authority" had written as they did, "some to reform the first Huguenots, who wanted to change the State into a Republic, the others to oppose the assassinations and pernicious maxims of the League," and that they all, notably Jean Bodin, "threw themselves to the other extremity, attributing more power to princes than is expedient for them to have, even for their own security."[92]

But for the remainder of the seventeenth century the Fronde proved as disastrous for the cause of parlementary constitutionalism as it had for Huguenots. With no religious issues to galvanize them or ennoble their sundry causes, the all too separate parlementary, princely, disgruntled noble, and clerical frondes canceled each other out, enabling royal absolutism to present itself as the only alternative to anarchy.[93] Thus was Louis XIV, "the God-Given," empowered to carry the absolutist argument to its logical if not empirical conclusion. Without doubt, as Albert Hamscher has reminded us, many of the Parlement's constitutional gains survived the remainder of Cardinal Mazarin's ministry and the morning years of the Sun King's personal reign.[94] But Louis XIV's first wars made short shrift of that constitutional legacy, and by means of a series of severe edicts culminating in that of 1673, he limited the right to deliberate on public affairs to the older and always more amenable magistrates of the Parlement's *Grand' chambre* and permitted these magistrates to remonstrate in the name of their company only after the formality of registration. So cavalier did he become in his relations with the Parlement of Paris that, if he did not actually appear in one of his last lit de justice assemblies in riding boots, he might as well have; and so docile did the Parlement become that he held no lit de justice assembly at all during the last forty years of his reign.[95]

The decline of occasional "official" or "constitutional" pageantry to the benefit of the continuous social ceremony of the court of Versailles is perhaps the most subtle yet pertinent aspect of absolutism, having to do with the "perpetual" part of Bodin's definition of sovereignty and the reconstitution of royal religion after the desacralizing blows of the sixteenth century. For Bodin's little noticed

91. [Jean Beaudeau, marquis de Clanleu], *Lettre d'avis à messieurs du parlement de Paris, escrite par un provincial* (Paris, 1649), p. 28, and *Epilogue, ou dernier appareil du bon citoyen, sur les misères publiques* (n.p., 1649), in *La Fronde, contestation démocratique et misère paysanne*, 1:7.

92. *Epilogue*, pp. 9–10.

93. This is the point of Ernst Kossman's brilliantly metaphorical characterization of the Fronde as the falling apart of France's "baroque" constitution in *La Fronde* (Leiden, 1954).

94. Albert Hamscher, *The Parlement of Paris After the Fronde, 1653–1673* (Pittsburgh, 1976). For a similarly nuanced view of the results of the Fronde, see A. Lloyd Moote, *The Revolt of the Judges: The Parlement of Paris and the Fronde* (Princeton, N.J., 1971), pp. 368–76.

95. Hanley, *The Lit de Justice and the Kings of France*, pp. 321–28.

emphasis upon sovereignty's perpetuity defended the Valois and then Bourbon dynasties against claims by both Leaguish and Protestant publicists that the monarchy had been and ought again to be elective, as well as the League polemicists' challenge to the legitimacy of Henri of Navarre's succession after the extinction of the Valois line. "For it is certain that the king never dies, as they say," was Bodin's explanation of how French royal sovereignty was perpetual, "because as soon as one has died, the closest male of his stock is seized by the Realm *(saisi du Royaume),* and in possession of it before being crowned."[96] This formula was nothing if not precarious, arbitrarily substituting "king" for "royal authority" in a saying that had circulated widely during the previous couple of decades. Moreover, it legitimated what had hitherto only been the practice of dating a king's reign immediately from the death of his predecessor, a practice first imposed in 1270 by the contingency of Louis IX's death on crusade. Before then reigns had not been dated until after the ceremonies of consecration and coronation, which contained several electoral gestures.[97]

Bodin's judicial legitimation of automatic biological succession did not wait long to assume ceremonial form, showing up as early as in the studied deemphasis of electoral elements in Henri IV's consecration and coronation at Chartres in 1594. And though probably unplanned, taking place only twelve hours after the assassination of Henri IV in 1610, the ceremonial improvisation whereby a prematurely crowned boy-king Louis XIII presided over a lit de justice assembly well before either his father's funeral or his coronation at Reims set an important precedent—the reigns of Louis XIV and Louis XV similarly began with regency governments—and underscored the automatic and nonconsensual character of dynastic succession. This new ceremonial emphasis on instantaneous biological dynastic succession also had the effect of downplaying those public ceremonies that featured the king in official or state-related capacities.[98] Henri IV's funeral was the last to display an "eternal" or official effigy juxtaposed to the king's actual body, while Louis XIV, as previously noted, dispensed with the lit de justice assembly as well as royal entries *(entrées)* into cities during the last forty years of his reign.

What tended to take the place of these civic ceremonies was of course court ceremonial, which, especially in the case of Louis XIV's Versailles, quite literally made all of the king's functions into official functions and his least idiosyncracy into an affair of state. The result was a total conflation of official with private time—or of immortal with mortal time—carrying with it the complete congruence

96. Jean Bodin, *Les six livres de la république,* p. 166.
97. Ralph E. Giesey, *The Royal Funeral Ceremony in Renaissance France,* pp. 177–92; and "The King Imagined," pp. 50–51. See also Hanley, *The Lit de Justice and the Kings of France,* pp. 178–79.
98. Hanley, *The Lit de Justice and the Kings of France,* pp. 231–53.

of the king's hitherto distinguishable "two bodies."[99] Whether this result should be thought of as the state or the king himself—probably the former—is moot because along with this personalization of power went the impersonal routinization of power having to do with the transition from judicial to administrative monarchy that was symbolized by the Royal Council at Versailles and the royal commissioner in the provinces.[100]

The two tendencies—divinization and bureaucratization—are both evident in the rhetorical exaltation of the monarchy that flourished at high noon of the Sun King's reign. If, for Bishop Bossuet, no one including even bishops carried "the majesty of God more clearly imprinted, than kings," it was in part because "they had only to move their lips and immediately everything moves from one extremity to the other." The king, thought Bossuet, had "even received from God, by the practice of state affairs, . . . a certain penetration as though he divines," citing as an example the ability to "penetrate the most secret plans" and to "pluck out his enemies from the extremities of the world." It goes without saying that Louis Quatorzian absolutism's invention of the standing army and the provincial intendant powerfully aided Bossuet's imagination—helped him in fact to imagine God, rather than the other way around. Kings "were gods": thus Bossuet, going still further. And lest one be reassured by the warning that kings "would die like men," Bossuet hastened to add that "[they] were gods anyway, even though they die." To specify as Bossuet also did that kings were "gods of flesh and blood" was to confound the king's two bodies, and compromise the traditional distinction maintained elsewhere in the same sermon, between the "man who dies" and the "king who dies not."[101]

The Jesuits and the Parti Dévot

It was in the vicinity of absolutism's "crucial phase," in A. Lublinskaya's phrase, just as it was taking shape under the administrations of the cardinal-ministers Richelieu and Mazarin, that the monarchy confronted another confessional conflict, this one within Catholicism itself, pitting Augustinians against Molinists, so-

99. Geisey, "The King Imagined," pp. 54–58; and Norbert Elias, *The Court Society*, trans. Edmund Jephcott (New York, n.d.), pp. 78–145.

100. On these developments, see Richard Bonney, *Political Change in France under Richelieu and Mazarin*, pp. 1–213; and Michel Antoine, "La Monarchie absolue," in *The Political Culture of the Old Regime*, vol. 1 of *The French Revolution and the Creation of Modern Political Culture*, ed. Keith M. Baker (Oxford, 1988), 1:9–15.

101. Jacques-Bénigne Bossuet, *Sermon pour le dimanche des rameaux prêché devant les rois sur les devoirs des rois* in *Oeuvres de Bossuet, évêque de Meaux*, eds. abbés Hemey d'Aubertine and Caron, 42 vols. (Versailles, 1815–19), 13:352–54. See also of course Bossuet's *Politique tirée des propres paroles de l'Ecriture sainte*, ed. Jacques Le brun (Geneva, 1967), passim.

called Jansenists against members and partisans of the Society or Company of Jesus.[102] Choose the monarchy must and choose it did, acting much more decisively and consistently than it did vis-à-vis Calvinism a century earlier. Still, the givens of that decision did not clearly run in one direction to the exclusion of the other and may be worth pondering a little, if only by way of introducing this story's main protagonists.

It may seem surprising, then, that the monarchy chose in favor of the Society of Jesus. Recruited by the converted Spanish knight Ignatius Loyola, the original "companions of Jesus," as they styled themselves, had won papal recognition as a new quasi-religious order in 1540, in part by swearing an unprecedented fourth vow of obedience to the papacy in addition to the standard ones of chastity, poverty, and obedience to their immediate superiors. That feature in particular defined the Jesuits as ultramontanists—partisans of papal infallibility—from the very outset, and that at a time when ultramontanism was far from representing a Catholic consensus, least of all in Gallican France. It was as champions of the thesis of papal infallibility that such Jesuits as Diego Laynez distinguished themselves as early as the Council of Trent.

Although less unanimously, the Jesuits also tended to affirm temporal ultramontanism: that is, to defend the thesis of ultimate papal power over the temporal affairs otherwise governed by earthly princes and emperors. The thesis of direct papal power—that the papacy had delegated temporal power to kings and potentates while retaining the exercise of spiritual power in its own hands—had of course fallen upon hard times since the late Middle Ages, but the thesis of indirect power still rallied many adherents. As formulated by the Italian Jesuit Roberto Bellarmino in 1604, the papacy legitimately exercised indirect temporal authority "by reason of sin," that is, in temporal consequence of the spiritual sentence of excommunication incurred by a ruler at the hands of his papal pastor. In religiously divided sixteenth-century France, such theories had not remained in books, as we have noted. In League-held Paris, for example, the Jesuit Père Comolet had publicly prayed for the assassination of the heretical Henri of Navarre. As late as 1626, the Parlement of Paris and the Sorbonne tried to condemn the thesis of indirect power as it appeared in the Italian Jesuit Santarelli's *Tractatus de Haeresi*.[103]

Yet in 1626 Richelieu intervened with the Sorbonne and the Parlement on behalf of the Jesuits, who by that date had become fixed features at the royal court.[104] Why? In part the Jesuits' success at court resulted from the society's

102. Lublinskaya, *French Absolutism: The Crucial Phase.*

103. Martin, *Le gallicanisme politique et le clergé de France*, pp. 26–28; and Aristide Douarche, *L'université de Paris et les jésuites* (Paris, 1888), pp. 101–2.

104. Church, *Richelieu and Reason of State*, pp. 157–61; and Martin, *Le gallicanisme politique et le clergé de France*, pp. 169–71, 242–44.

considered policy of literally courting the court—or rather the order's self-conscious policy of wooing the elites culminating in court society. Acting on Loyola's advice in the society's constitutions "to retain the benevolence of . . . the temporal rulers and noble and powerful persons whose favor or disfavor does much toward opening or closing the gate to the service of God," Jesuit preachers generally bypassed the countryside in favor of urban-based noble and bourgeois elites, who, if things proceeded according to plan, became sponsors and benefactors of the rapidly multiplying and soon renowned Jesuit colleges in France.[105] These colleges in turn specialized in the education of the elites, becoming the standard schools of the French nobility by the end of the seventeenth century. For their part, these elites were doubtlessly attracted to a religious society whose conspicuously hierarchical and monarchical structure, culminating in the professed fathers and the powerful general at Rome, reflected the hierarchical society at large and their privileged places within it. And both they and the royal court found themselves attracted to Jesuit educators' cultivation of classical letters and their preachers' Ciceronian sermonry.[106] For at their best, as in the case of Edmond Auger, Jesuit sermons were artful exercises in classical rhetoric and hence humanistic in the curricular sense.[107] That humanism, moreover, had been most at home among urban elites and princely courts since the beginning of the Renaissance in Italy. Finally, the Jesuits were also a missionary order, and classically lettered missionaries were eventually to make ideal agents of a colonizing monarchy's attempt to spread French civilization in North America.

The Jesuits' humanism was civic or active rather than contemplative, taking the world as their cloister and committing themselves to a service-oriented or public apostolate. This emphasis on activity, in combination with the society's cultivation of rhetoric and missionary zeal, produced a humanism of a more philosophical stripe, expressing itself as a bias in favor of the human condition generally and especially in defense of the free human will. This bent received further encouragement as a result of the Jesuits' apologetical efforts against Protestantism—another of their specialties—and in reaction to the denial of the free will implicit in the doctrine of justification by faith alone. In theological parlance the Jesuits displayed neo-Pelagian tendencies: that is, they tended to minimize human corruption and the natural effects of the first man's fall, stressing rather humanity's residual goodness and its still intact freedom of will. For the Jesuit Louis Richéome, for example, writing under Henri IV, the human body's mobile hand was "a true portrait of free will and a truly seigneurial liberty," which "not

105. Quoted in Lynn Martin, *The Jesuit Mind: The Mentality of an Elite in Early-Modern France* (Ithaca, N.Y., 1988), p. 15.

106. Marc Fumaroli, *L'âge de l'éloquence: Rhétorique et "res litteraria" de la Réforme au seuil de l'époque classique* (Geneva, 1980), pp. 427–92, 587–660.

107. L. Martin, *The Jesuit Mind*, pp. 4, 14–15.

even God forces" lest he "destroy his [own] image and make the will no will at all." By means of this divine faculty, Richéome optimistically argued, human nature might "become ever more wise and perfect, without terminus or end." Indeed, even the remains of original sin were only so many occasions for the "virtuous" to "be tested" and spurs for the honorable to win greater "glory." "A noble and brave heart gets bored," he thought, "if it does not have some reason to exercise itself."[108]

These neo-Pelagian tendencies assumed a fixed theological form in the hands of the Spanish Jesuit Luis Molina, who published his treatise entitled *De concordia liberi arbitrii cum gratiae donis (Concerning the Concord of the Free Will with the Gift of Grace)* in 1588.[109] Without contesting the Christian doctrines of humankind's original sin and consequent fall, Molina nonetheless minimized their consequences. Human nature did not as a result become totally corrupt or "concupiscent," but simply found itself bereft of God's supernatural gifts, such as eternal life. Human nature as such—above all its freedom to choose for good or evil—remained essentially intact. And in order to supplement free will and compensate for the loss of eternal life, God dispensed to each person on every occasion a "sufficient" grace, which, together with the individual's free choice to use it, would enable him or her to overcome temptation, to observe all the commandments, and—with, to be sure, the help of the church's sacraments for the sins actually committed—eventually to merit eternal life. Instead of Luther's or Calvin's grace by faith alone and unmerited election, Molina then held to a merely sufficient grace and a kind of divine prescience: God simply foresaw the meritorious or offensive acts that people would freely choose to commit and rewarded them accordingly.[110]

But late sixteenth- and early seventeenth-century *humanisme dévot* (devout humanism), to use Henri Brémond's happy phrase, was far too diffuse to have been contained within the Society of Jesus. Besides the Jesuits themselves, the religious outlook in question found important institutional bastions in the religious order of the Visitation of Saint François de Sales and Jeanne de Chantal, the Franciscan Order's Capuchin affiliates, and Pierre Olier's seminary and priestly congregation of Saint-Sulpice. Devout humanism was also more amorphous than Molina's neoscholastic formulations would suggest. "A theology, a doctrine, to be sure," in Brémond's definition, but "affective" and "oriented toward practice," devout humanism was above all a religious sensibility, a sort of nontheoretical

108. Louis Richéome, *Adieu de l'âme dévote laissant le corps* (Rouen, 1605), pp. 97–99, 105–6, 165–70; as quoted in Henri Brémond, *Histoire littéraire du sentiment religieux en France depuis la fin des guerres de religion jusqu'à nos jours*, 11 vols. (Paris, 1916–33), 1:54–55, 58.

109. Luis Molina, *De concordia liberi arbitrii cum gratiae donis, divina praescientia, providentia, praedestinatione et reprobatione* (Lisbon, 1588).

110. On Molina and Molinism, see F. Stegemüller, *Geschichte des Molinismus* (Münster, 1935); and Nigel Abercrombie, *Origins of Jansenism* (Oxford, 1936).

"Christian optimism," which readily recognized the divine everywhere in nature and most especially in human nature.[111] This outlook held not only for human reason but also for the will—indeed, even for physical beauties and the passions. The devout humanistic universe was therefore one in which, as the Jesuit Pierre Le Moyne put it, "the inferior beauties are as the degrees by which it is necessary for human love to ascend foot by foot until it arrives at the enjoyment of sovereign beauty," and in which, in the Dominican Laurent Bénard's words, "the body was a means for the spirit, the spirit for virtue, virtue for grace, and grace for glory."[112] Devout space was hence a plenum filled with audible and sensible emanations of the divine, and devout time was a continuum punctuated with the miraculous testifying to the possibility of spiritual progress—or at least refuting the thesis of inevitable regression from a pristine and patristic past. The effect was a continuous natural and spiritual hierarchy in which even the lowliest of objects and events played legitimate roles as props for popular piety and even the proudest of temporal "grandeurs" might be rendered an acceptable sacrifice to God.[113]

Grandeur, glory, hierarchy—that these were the "virtues" of the seventeenth-century royal court goes a long way toward explaining the profound affinity between the Jesuits in particular and the courts of Louis XIII and Louis XIV. The Jesuits may indeed have been similar to Calvinists in dedicating themselves to the "honor and glory of God," but for the Jesuits, glory and honor did not remain confined to the heavens but rather cascaded downward onto the heads of kings and noblemen, making the social hierarchy a reflection of the divine. Nor was majesty an exclusively divine possession as it was for Calvin; there were many intermediate majesties—the majesty of worship, the majesty of the consecrated host, and of course the majesty of the king—all of them pointing toward God's. The Jesuits' defense of free will against Jansenist grace also went with the grain of a would-be absolute monarchy inclined to define itself as legislative will at the expense of distributive justice. Devout humanist spirituality was hence not only compatible with but, in Catholic France, a necessary religious buttress for the notion of the divine right of kings.

But divine right also spelled Richelieu's *raison d'état*, including dynastic war on the side of the Protestant Dutch and Swedes; and the king's honor and majesty had their quite human undersides in the form of his mortal body's chronic sexual infidelities. As the king's ordinary confessors, however, Jesuits proved themselves men for these royal seasons as well. For one of the moral consequences of Molinism's optimistic assessment of human nature's capacity for virtue was a relatively benign attitude toward its inevitable off-seasons. To compensate for moral lapses was the point of the church's sacraments—penance and the Eucharist

111. Brémond, *Histoire littéraire du sentiment religieux en France*, 1:17.
112. Ibid., 1:371, 378.
113. Ibid., 2:120.

in particular—and the Jesuits soon made advocacy of very frequent confession and communion one of the hallmarks of their devotional style. As to the interior dispositions prerequisite to penance, the Jesuits typically insisted only on fear of divine punishment; and by way of satisfaction, a largely exterior conformity to the Decalogue. Aside from a few spectacular lapses into penitential rigorism, in other words, seventeenth-century Jesuits at court espoused "attritionism" (mere fear of hell's pains) against the more rigorous "contritionist" position, which insisted on pure love or "charity" as a prerequisite to absolution. Undergirding this peniten- tial theology and practice was devout humanism's intrinsic externality and conse- quent tendency to think of sin as sins in the plural, consisting in so many discrete and discernible lapses or acts. But this penitential theology also conveniently served the interests of—was indeed indispensable to—a Catholic body politic chronically in need of absolution by reason of both politics and the body.

But how then did French Jesuits square their oath of obedience with, say, their acquiescence in the Bourbon dynasty's pursuit of "reason of state?" How, in other words, did they reconcile their much maligned ultramontanism with the French monarchy's version of Gallicanism? The answer seems to be that they effected some sort of compromise between the ecclesiastical and temporal aspects of ultramontanism and Gallicanism and that, while eschewing canonical and conciliar Gallicanism, they gradually accepted the newer "political" Gallicanism: namely, the principle of royal accountability to God alone. As early as 1610, in the wake of Ravaillac's assassination of Henri IV, Pierre Coton went on record as thinking that kings were "the children and sucklings of God, or rather . . . His living image," and in 1626 he disavowed Santarelli's statement of "indirect power," declaring himself ready to shed blood in defense of the truth that "Their Majesties answer independently to God." Coton's Gallican proclivities gained converts among his colleagues with Richelieu's encouragement, only to become even more pronounced under Louis XIV. In the *régale* controversy with the papacy, Louis XIV's Jesuit confessor François de La Chaise quite openly sided with his king and frankly declared to his general in Rome that, in all but dogmatic matters, he would sooner obey the king than the pope. By the eighteenth century, according to Pierre Blet, a good many if not all French Jesuits had accepted the conclusion that, as one of them put it, "the first part of the Declaration [of 1682] presents no problem for anyone not blinded by ultramontanist opinions."[114] Papal infallibilists the French Jesuits may have always at heart remained, and enthusias- tic conciliarists they never became. By 1695 Louis XIV himself, as we have seen,

114. Pierre Blet, S.J., "Jésuites gallicans au dix-septième siècle? A propos de l'ouvrage du P. Guitton sur le P. de La Chaize," *Archivum Historicum Societatis Jesu* 29 (1960):55–82. For quotations from Pierre Coton's *Lettre déclaratoire à la Reine mère du Roy et régente en France* (Paris, 1610), pp. 7–8, as well as from his declaration of 1626, see pp. 61–62; for the quotations from La Chaize and Robillard d'Avrigny, pp. 78, 80.

was willing enough to abandon the conciliar aspect of the Gallican legacy. But it was otherwise with the principle of the entire temporal independence of the French crown, and on that article French Jesuits quite simply sacrificed papal indirect power on the altar of royal divine right.

So domesticated and Gallican did French Jesuits become that a renewed, court-based parti dévot briefly appeared apart from and effectively to the "right" of them during the last decade and a half of the seventeenth century. United by an ardent piety—and perhaps common hostility to the politically powerful Le Tellier family—this group coalesced around the figure of the duc de Bourgogne, next in line to the throne after the *grand dauphin*, and included Louis XIV's trusted adviser the duc de Chevreuse and the director of the Royal Council of Finance, the duc de Beauvilliers. The group's key figure, however, was François de Salignac de La Mothe Fénelon, who was the spiritual director of the king's former mistress and new wife Madame de Maintenon, before becoming preceptor of the royal children—and hence the duc de Bourgogne's tutor—in 1689. It was for Bourgogne's edification that, after his father had died and he himself had become the heir apparent, Fénelon later penned his well-known novelistic critique of Louis Quatorzian absolutism called *Télémaque*.

The spirituality that in part held this court group together bore a distinctively mystical cast; and in Fénelon's case, that spirituality consisted of one long quest for what he called "pure love" for God and for the eradication of self-love or *amour propre*. At first glance that quest would seem to have been very Augustinian and therefore spiritually akin to what was then being called Jansenism. Look again, however, because for one thing Fénelon's quest took place entirely within the domain of the conscious and voluntary. "I ask only for what is voluntary," Fénelon reassured the penitent, speaking of the many seemingly involuntary relapses into anxious self-concern along the way toward pure love.[115] Although reliant on divine grace, progress toward pure love also valorized the role of the human free will, for "you will always be free in God," Fénelon again promised, "provided you do not imagine that you have lost your liberty."[116] For another thing, the grace that finally prevailed when self-love relinquished its hold and pure love took over was hardly distinguishable from the divine itself because in pure love, Fénelon insisted, the penitent's heart "expands without limits, so that it becomes immense; with nothing restricting it, it fulfills the [divine] promise and becomes, in due proportion, the same thing with God himself."[117] Indeed, pure love is attained precisely at the point where grace dissolves into the divine, where

115. François de Salignac de La Mothe Fénelon, "De la simplicité" in *Oeuvres complètes*, 10 vols. (Paris, 1810), 4:217. On *"pur amour"* in general, see "Sur le pur amour," ibid., 4:32–53.

116. "Sur l'abandon à Dieu," ibid., 4:238.

117. "Des opérations intérieures de Dieu pour ramener l'homme à sa vraie fin, pour laquelle il nous a creés," ibid., 4:197.

grace ceases to be a "gift" that the "self" possesses and becomes instead inseparable from its source in the divine. Fénelon's spirituality therefore optimistically
held out the promise of union with the divine, and as such perpetuated a more
mystical variant of seventeenth-century "devout humanism," which itself took
root in the sixteenth-century League. Symptomatically, Fénelon's favorite theological references were not to Saint Augustine or even to Thomas Aquinas but to
François de Sales, author of an *Introduction à la vie dévote (Introduction to the
Devout Life)*, and to the mystic Saint Theresa. Fénelon's own "devout" lineage
was unimpeachable, going back to his uncle Antoine de Salignac, marquis de La
Motte Fénelon, who had been a member of the Company of the Holy Sacrament
earlier in the century.[118]

   That mystical spirituality eventually got Fénelon into trouble, not because it
was inherently very unorthodox but because it led him to a spiritual collaboration
with one Madame Guyon, whose own mystical effusions were less doctrinally
disciplined than his. Introduced to Fénelon in 1688, Jeanne-Marie Bouvier de La
Motte enjoyed the confidence of the group for a while, including that of Madame
de Maintenon, who introduced her and her writings to the aristocratic convent of
Saint-Cyr. But Guyon had some formidable enemies as well, among them François de Harlay de Chanvallon, Archbishop of Paris. Chanvallon tried to cast
doubts on her orthodoxy by associating her spirituality with the recently condemned Molinos heresy, which held that mystical union with God exempted those
so favored from the standards of ordinary morality. Alarmed, Maintenon took
steps to distance herself and Saint-Cyr from Guyon and tried to persuade Fénelon
to follow her. But when he instead undertook Guyon's defense, Maintenon and
Louis XIV unleashed Bishop Bossuet on them both, leading to Fénelon's exile
from court to his bishopric in Cambrai in 1697, as well as papal condemnation of
parts of his defense of the mystical tradition in 1699.

   The Bishop of Cambrai did not manifest any opposition to absolutism until a
decade or more later, when the duc de Bourgogne had become the dauphin and
Louis Quatorzian absolutism had run afoul of the War of the Spanish Succession.
Yet that opposition, when it developed, implicated the same kernal group as
before—Beauvillier and Chevreuse—and it is hard not to see in its character a
political extension of Fénelon's mysticism, a kind of new *cabale des dévots*.[119] As in

---

118. Lionel Rothkrug, *Opposition to Louis XIV: the Political and Social Origins of the French
Enlightenment* (Princeton, N.J., 1965), p. 64.
   119. It is of course possible to hold that Fénelon's spirituality was unrelated to his opposition to
absolutism. Stressing the amount of time—about fifteen years—that elapsed between Fénelon's involvement in the Quietist movement and his political activity as part of the group around the duc de Bourgogne,
Denis Richet has taken this position in his "Fénelon contre Bossuet: La querelle du quiétisme," in his *De la
réforme à la Révolution*, pp. 119–39. The position taken here is more similar to that of Lionel Rothkrug in
Opposition to Louis XIV, pp. 234–98.

the case of the old parti dévot's opposition to Richelieu, Fénelon's group opposed the Bourbon policy of dynastic war, even if prosecuted in part against Protestants, as well as courtly waste and "luxury," even if now concentrated outside sinful Paris at Versailles. What was also new to the latter seventeenth century was that war and luxury had become more explicitly associated with each other as parts of the state policy called mercantilism, for which the manufacture and export of artisinal luxuries were among the ordinary means in the state's pursuit of economic advantage, and war was the continuation of the same pursuit by other means. Against that policy Fénelon therefore opposed the humanistic principles of peace and the unity of all humankind—the human race, Fénelon held, constituted a single family—and particular preferences for agriculture and free trade. Among the sources of eighteenth-century physiocracy or the party of economists, Rothkrug has pointed out, is this late-seventeenth-century "devout" opposition to Louis Quatorzian absolutism and mercantilism, or what Rothkrug himself has called "Christian agrarianism."[120]

All of these themes are clearly expressed in *Télémaque*, Fénelon's novel which recounts the adventures and misadventures of the young prince by that name as he travels the Mediterranean in the company of his god-guide Mentor in quest of his father and king of Ithaca, the Homeric hero of Ulysses. Louis XIV's pursuit of conquest and magnificence, Fénelon implied, was the pursuit of "false glory," the political counterpart to concupiscent amour propre. Fénelon's strictures against "false glory" optimistically presupposed the possibility of true glory, or something like political pure love. Like pure love, Fénelon's true glory took the form of a rigorous denial of the self, if not in relation to God at least in relation to the prince's subjects. The future king Télémaque's odyssey across the Mediterranean is, among other things, a sort of political pilgrim's progress—and reversal of the original *Odyssey*—whereby he sheds himself in turn of attachment to things, emotions and passions, and finally his own self-esteem so that, by the time Mentor finally ascends and reveals herself as Minerva, he has almost sorrowfully resigned himself to a life of selfless dedication to the material and moral welfare of his future Ithacan subjects. Of course this Mentor has all along been Minerva—god of wisdom, the classical pantheon's nearest relative to a god of peace who can make "Mars himself afraid"—with the result that, like Fénelon's penitent, Télémaque has himself become all but one with "that infinite and immutable light" from which "our spirits . . . arise only to return and lose themselves."[121] Fénelon's political ideal hence remained like the old parti dévot's, a virtuous monarchy following Fénelon's advice to "fear the gods" and to seek disinterested counsel but unprotected from degenerating into tyranny in the absence of these virtues.[122]

120. Rothkrug, *Opposition to Louis XIV*, pp. 234–98.
121. Fénelon, *Les aventures de Télémaque, fils d'Ulysse*, in *OC*, 8:79.
122. Ibid., p. 500.

But kings like Télémaque themselves possessed "I know not what of the divine." This saying is more familiar as Fénelon's contemporary and adversary Bossuet's, but it is Fénelon's as well. The difference is that Fénelon's *"je ne sais quoi de divin"* takes hold of Télémaque's heart only as he takes to heart Mentor's advice and the obligations of virtuous kingship. "When royalty is used to satisfy oneself," Télémaque is told in the Underworld, "it is a monstrous tyranny; when, however, it is assumed in order to fulfill one's desires and lead an innumerable people as a father leads his children, it is a staggering servitude demanding a heroic penance."[123] In other words, the same tendencies toward political Donatism evident in the Catholic League and the original parti dévot resurfaced in the case of Fénelon, Chevreuse, and Beauvillier's "devout" opposition to Louis XIV. By Fénelon's lights, the Sun King had about him something of the divine only to the degree that he abandoned the pursuit of "vain glory" and ruled as a Christian prince.

That Louis XIV ever perceived these political implications is improbable. No political principle was explicitly at issue—except, perhaps, Gallicanism—at the time of Fénelon's fall from royal grace in 1697 or papal condemnation two years later. The papal condemnation, it is true, again represents royal rather than papal ecclesiastical policy, for Innocent XII had been personally partial toward the mystical tradition that Fénelon defended in his *Maximes des saints*. But Innocent was clearly not unhappy about Bourbon cooperation in driving another nail into the coffin of conciliar Gallicanism. This latest manifestation of devout political opposition, for its part, disappeared with the death of the new dauphin in 1712, having survived his father by only a year. Yet no seventeenth-century book was reprinted in the following century as often as was Fénelon's *Télémaque*.

Jansenism

Just as superficially surprising as that the monarchy chose in favor of Jesuits is that it chose against Jansenists. Unlike the Society of Jesus, which had been founded by a Spaniard, Jansenism was unimpeachably French—or at least French and Flemish, arising simultaneously in northern France and the southern Netherlands. Jansenists' acceptance of Gallicanism was moreover eventually wholehearted, in contrast to French Jesuits' belated and selective appropriation of that tradition. And unlike the equally French Calvinists, Jansenists never separated from the Catholic Church; no sin would be more heinous in their eyes than that of schism. But the seemingly natural alliance between Jansenists and the Bourbon monarchy was never to be; indeed, it took much less time for this to become apparent that it had in the case of Calvinism.

The pejorative term *Jansenism*—which Jansenists themselves never acknowl-

123. Ibid., p. 383.

edged—took its name from the seventeenth-century Flemish theologian Cornelius Jansen, or Jansenius, who spent his mature years at the University of Louvain and died as Bishop of Ypres in 1638. His most controversial legacy was a bulky manuscript entitled *Augustinus,* which, published posthumously in 1641, sought to restate in systematic form the theology of the fifth-century saint and bishop Augustine of Hippo, especially as bearing on the agitated questions of divine grace and free will. *Augustinus* was the offspring of a lifelong interest in the reform of the Catholic Church that Jansen shared with one Duvergier de Hauranne, with whom he had studied in Paris and spent the years from 1611 to 1616 reading patristic theology at Duvergier's home in Bayonne. Better known as Saint-Cyran, of which he became the abbé in 1620, Duvergier de Hauranne for his part eventually emerged as the spiritual director of the reformed Cistercian convent of Port-Royal near Paris, where he experimented with a rigorous penitential theology stereotyped by the practice of deferring the Eucharist until after an interior renewal or "conversion" had taken place. After going their separate ways in 1616, the two progenitors of Jansenism maintained their friendship by means of correspondence. As the years passed a common project of ecclesiastical and theological reform took shape in their minds, assuming the mysterious code word *Pilmot*.[124]

An interest in the reform of the church, a more rigorous penitential theology—such tendencies were banal in counterreformational France and hardly distinguished what was not yet called Jansenism from, say, the purification of Catholic theology and the reform of the priesthood undertaken by Pierre de Bérulle and his disciples in his newly formed order of secular priests called the Oratory. A friend of Bérulle as well as of Saint Vincent de Paul, Saint-Cyran at most amplified themes common to a "French school" of Catholic counterreformational spirituality to which French Jesuits were largely deaf, and whose apologetical approach was to recover and recatholicize the authentically Christocentric elements in the Protestant Reformation, the better to isolate and expose the schismatic residue.[125] What ruthlessly clarified this creative confusion and divided French Catholics into two sharply defined and mutually hostile camps was the controversy over Jansen's *Augustinus* in the 1640s. This controversy began in earnest when the French theologian-philosopher—and son of the author of the Third Estate's proposition in 1614—Antoine Arnauld spelled out his deceased master Saint Cyran's penitential theology in *La fréquente communion (On Frequent Communion)* and then undertook the defense of *Augustinus* itself in reaction to

---

124. Jean Orcibal, *Jansénius d'Ypres, 1585–1638* (Paris, 1989), esp. pp. 95–125. For a more purely doctrinal perspective see also Abercrombie, *The Origins of Jansenism;* and John Kevin Hargreaves, "Cornelius Jansen and the Origins of Jansenism" (Ph.D. diss., Brandeis University, 1974).

125. Jean Orcibal, *Jean Duvergier de Hauranne, abbé de Saint-Cyran et son temps, 1581–1638* (Louvain, 1947), passim. See also the same author's *La spiritualité de Saint-Cyran avec ses écrits de piété inédits* (Paris, 1962), pp. 1–135.

attacks by Notre Dame's theologal Isaac Habert and the Jesuit theologian Jacques Sirmond. Because six sisters at Port-Royal, including the abbess Angélique, were also Arnauld's biological sisters who had come under Saint-Cyran's influence when he was their spiritual director, and because others of Antoine's friends and Saint-Cyran's converts, like the barrister Antoine Lemaistre, had taken up residence in the abbey's vicinity as ascetic "solitaries," both the abbey and its friends found themselves caught up in the enveloping controversy.[126]

There was much indeed to quarrel about. For where the Jesuits' Molinism nuanced and shaded the differences between created and fallen human nature, Jansenism accented humankind's pristine perfection and original innocence, the better to underscore the catastrophe of the original sin of disobedient pride and the ensuing fall. Hence Jansenism's "tragic vision" of humankind's resultant concupiscent state, that is, its utter alienation from a partially "hidden God" and native inability to relate—or dilate—to Him as opposed to imploding in amour propre or self-love. So while in Molinism a merely sufficient grace enabled the believer to resist temptation and avoid sin, Jansenism insisted upon the need for an "efficacious grace," which would pluck a chosen few from among the concupiscent mass, reorient their desires or "delectations" toward God, and enable them to enact works of charity, that is, acts inspired by love for God. What this tragic scenario implied, in sharp contrast again to Molinism, was some form of denial of a free human will, along with the formidable doctrine of predestination of the elect to salvation—and of the nonelect to damnation. To Molinism's "Christian optimism" on the subject of human nature and somewhat humanistic version of Christianity as a whole, Jansenism hence opposed a most tragic vision of the human situation and an Augustinian rendering of Christianity full of the starkest, almost lunar contrasts.[127]

As it hardened in reaction to continuing polemical exchange, papal condemnation, and combined royal and episcopal persecution, Jansenism's opposition to Molinism developed in liturgical, sacramental, and moral directions. Against the Jesuits' preference for Latin and elites, Port-Royal's director Le Maître de Sacy began to translate the Bible into French, and Pascal appealed to literate lay opinion against the ecclesiastical hierarchy.[128] Later on, Jansenists translated the Mass and divine office as well as the whole Bible and routinely invoked the laity's support in

126. Louis Cognet, Le jansénisme, Que sais-je series (Paris, 1964), pp. 35–61; Alexander Sedgwick, Jansenism in Seventeenth-Century France: Voices in the Wilderness (Charlottsville, Va., 1977), pp. 47–106; and Augustin Gazier, Histoire générale du mouvement janséniste depuis ses origines jusqu'à nos jours, 2 vols. (Paris, 1924), 1:38–112.

127. In addition to the works cited above, this characterization owes much to Lucien Goldmann's Le dieu caché: Etudes sur la vision tragique dans les Pensées de Pascal et dans le théatre de Racine, Bibliothèque des idées series (Paris, 1955), pp. 1–94.

128. On Jansenism and the translation of the Bible, see Bernard Chedozeau, "Les traductions de la Bible, le jansénisme et la Révolution," in Jansénisme et révolution: Actes du colloque de Versailles tenu au

the "good cause." Against the Jesuits' advocacy of frequent communion, Arnauld after Saint-Cyran counseled the deferral of communion. Eventually Jansenism produced priests too humble to celebrate Mass and penitents who went years without communion. Against Jesuitical attritionism Jansenists insisted upon contrition lest penance become a sacrilege. The insistence that one's every action be "charitably" related to God became a Jansenist devotional mainstay. And against Molinistic probabalism, or the notion that between two probable moral opinions, the least probable might be followed, Jansenists opposed a rigorous tutiorism, maintaining that God's moral law admitted of no probable exceptions or diminutions. It was against Molinism's casual confessional casuistry that Pascal deployed his most mordant wit in the *Provincial Letters*.[129]

These doctrinal, moral, and liturgical emphases made Jansenists vulnerable to the charges of renewing Calvinist "heresies," and so it is not surprising that most of the "messieurs" of Port-Royal—Arnauld, Pierre Nicole, Blaise Pascal—should eventually have sought to prove their Catholicism by opening a second front against Calvinism. Unlike Calvin's, their predestination, Pascal for example argued, was authentically Catholic and Augustinian: necessitated, that is, by Adam's freely willed original sin rather than by God's eternal decrees. More important was the difference that Jansenists correctly detected between Calvinism's "irresistible grace" and their own quite Augustinian "efficacious grace," which neither could be taken for granted, once received, nor dispensed its recipients from "meriting" their salvation by means of works worthy of contrition.[130] For the first generation of Jansenists developed no counterparts to Martin Luther's doctrine of justification by faith alone nor to the uniquely Calvinist doctrine of the perseverance of the saints. As evidenced by Saint Peter when he denied Christ thrice, Antoine Arnauld's God might at any moment withdraw efficacious grace from the "just," causing them to "fall" *(échoir)* into concupiscence.[131] Deriving no comfort from the doctrine of election and beseiged by Pascalian "distractions" and "diversions" susceptible of causing a fall from grace, Jansenism, unlike Calvinism, issued into no frank sanctification of secular activity or the human institutions that were its product. Far from any "this-worldly asceticism," Jansenist "conversions" not infrequently resulted in the withdrawal from secular vocations

---

Palais des congrès les 13 et 14 octobre 1789, ed. Catherine Maire, *Chroniques de Port-Royal* 39 (Paris, 1990), pp. 219–28.

129. Jean Mesnard, *Pascal*, 2d ed., Connaissance des lettres series (Paris, 1962), pp. 66–97; and Walter E. Rex, *Pascal's Provincial Letters: An Introduction* (London, 1977).

130. Blaise Pascal, *Ecrits sur la grâce*, in Louis Lafuma, ed. *OC* (Paris, 1963), p. 314, 327–35. Jean La Porte's *La doctrine de la grâce chez Arnauld* (Paris, 1922) and his later *La morale d'après Arnauld* (Paris, 1952), are the clearest secondary treatments of the doctrinal differences between pristine Jansenism and Calvinist Protestantism.

131. Antoine Arnauld, *Le renversement de la morale de Jésus Christ, par les erreurs des Calvinistes, touchant la justification*, in his *OC*, 42 vols. (Lausanne, 1775–83), vol. 13, passim.

and a quite other-worldly asceticism: a renowned mathematician, Pascal quit mathematics—or tried to; a rising and already stellar barrister, Antoine Lemaistre left the law; a well established councillor in the Parlement of Normandy, Thomas Du Fossé sold his charge; and all took up life as solitaries around the abbey of Port-Royal-des-Champs.

These biographical about-faces are symptomatic of a religious sensibility that, in contrast even to Calvinism, to say nothing of Molinism, articulated itself as a series of antitheses between incommensurate orders: between humankind's original grandeur and its misery after the fall; between the resultant state of concupiscence and the order of charity by grace; between the purity of the apostolic and patristic church and its corruption in latter days—in fine, between the order of fallen creation and a hidden and righteous God. The radicalism of Pascal's *Pensées* consists precisely in the systematic destruction of all links between these orders, save of course for the miracle of divine grace—or for the miracle *tout court*.[132] Because, unlike Calvinism and more Leaguelike in this respect, Jansenists relished their relics and spectacular miracles and came to look to them for consolation amidst their otherwise lost cause, from the time of the "miracle of the Holy Thorn," which cured Pascal's niece of a fistula in the eye in 1656, to the thaumaturgical miracles around the tomb of the deacon Pâris in the 1720s and 1730s.[133] And because the miracle occurred in history and was itself a historical event, history too gave Jansenists a limited look at an otherwise hidden God, being a theatre of grace full of "figures" of Christ for the "pure and humble of heart," who could alone discern its signs. Pascal all too successfully passed on his interest in figures, prophecies, and miracles to his eighteenth-century spiritual descendants, who were to be among that century's most prolific historians and commentators on the contemporary event.[134]

Yet those few glimpses of grace hardly attenuated Jansenism's all-or-nothing religious temperament, which, as the Franciscan François de Bonal put it in 1655, tended to regard "nothing [as] virtuous if it is not heroic, nothing [as] Christian if it is not miraculous, nothing [as] tolerable if it is not inimitable." Jansenists, he complained, "find only the immense to be big."[135] Not immense and therefore not very big—therein may lie pristine Jansenism's problem with the French monarchy. That is to say that, at its most radical, Jansenism's implicit

132. The study that best encapsulates this radical aspect of Jansenism is perhaps Paul Bénichou's *Les morales du grand siècle*, Bibliothèque des idées series (Paris, 1948), esp. pp. 14–51, 97–130. On Pascal's politics see also Etienne Demahis's still useful *La pensée politique de Pascal* (Saint-Amand, 1931).

133. René Taveneaux, *La vie quotidienne des jansénistes aux XVIIe et XVIIIe siècles* (Paris, 1973), pp. 179–200. Note also Pascal's considerable section on miracles in his *Pensées* in *OC*, pp. 606–16.

134. For Pascal on "figures" and "prophéties" see *Pensées* in *OC*, pp. 532–36, 542–46, 548–49, 556–66, 569–74.

135. François Bonal, *Le Chrétien du temps*, 3: introduction to paragraph 24, and quoted in Brémond, *Histoire du sentiment religieux en France*, 1:400–401.

challenge to divine-right absolutism lay, like Calvinism's, in a tendency to de-sanctify everything between conscience and God, to limit divinity to God alone. If, as Marcel Gauchet has argued, there exists a "law of human emancipation by way of divine affirmation" to the effect that, the more transcendent the conception of God, the freer people become, then Jansenism carried with it an implicit message of political emancipation, no matter how orthodox the explicit utterances of individual Jansenists' on the subject of the superiority of monarchical govern-ment and obedience to political sovereigns.[136] Pascal again best articulated Janse-nism's unique mixture of explicit obedience with implicit subversion when he denied any intrinsic value or respect to the "greats" of this world, granting a mechanical obedience to the rights of sheer force but defining as tyranny any force that demanded esteem or tried to dominate conscience.[137] Or, to put it another way, Jansenism may illustrate another of Marcel Gauchet's laws to the effect that, to the degree that any political power asserts its own autonomy in relation to the heavens above—arguably French absolutism's case after 1682—it invites a secu-larizing demystification from below.[138]

That much said, it remains true that Jansenism's political challenge to divine-right monarchy remained largely latent for most of the seventeenth cen-tury, and that one combs through Jansenists' printed and explicitly political utterances in vain for anything more seditious than, say, "the great" Arnauld's preachments of passive disobedience in the case of commands contrary to con-science.[139] To preach docility in the face of persecution by the established powers was of course another way for defensive Jansenists to have distinguished them-selves as Catholics from the sometime seditious Calvinists. Yet this initial differ-ence in political comportment between the two groups was more than merely tactical and had to do with the pessimistically total tenor of Jansenist political opposition. Although Jansenist bishops indeed opposed "superstitious" reli-giosity in their dioceses, a full-fledged Jansenist iconoclasm is hard to imagine, at least for the seventeenth century, as is any other Huguenot-like forms of active political resistance. For these presupposed what Jansenist all-or-nothingness tended to deny: some sort of "reformed" temporal alternative to absolutism, such as Calvinist Geneva's "covenantal" community. It was only after the Fronde that such distinguished *frondeurs* as the duc de La Rochefoucauld or Madame de Longueville found themselves attracted to Jansenism.[140] Pascal spoke for them as

136. Marcel Gauchet, *Le désenchantement du monde: Une histoire politique de la religion* (Paris, 1985), p. 53.

137. Blaise Pascal, "Trois discours sur la condition des grands" in *OC*, pp. 366–68. On Pascal's—and Port-Royal's—implicitly subversive "discourse" on kingship, see Louis Marin, "The Body of Power and the Incarnation at Port-Royal and in Pascal," pp. 421–47.

138. Marcel Gauchet, *La Révolution des droits de l'homme* (Paris, 1989), pp. 14–35.

139. J.-A.-G. Tans, "Les idées politiques des jansénistes," *Neophilogus* 40 (Jan. 1956):1–18.

140. René Taveneaux, *Jansénisme et politique*, Collection U series (Paris, 1965), pp. 7–29.

well as for Jansenism when, not too much later, he pessimistically wrote that, "unable to fortify justice, we have justified force."[141]

When it eventually occurred, a more active form of Jansenist political opposition was paradoxically dependent upon a certain attenuation or blurring of Jansenism's most radical political Augustinianism. When it developed, moreover, that attenuation resulted in part from alliances with other groups in French society and a partial assimilation of their varied agendas. And those marriages of political convenience with other constituencies were in turn consummated in consequence of absolutism's relentless persecution of the movement.

For even more than the suppression of Protestantism in the sixteenth century, the persecution of Jansenism represented royal policy. It was Cardinal Richelieu's decision to imprison Saint-Cyran in the château of Vincennes as early as 1638, as it was on Richelieu's posthumous orders that Notre Dame's cathedral lecturer, Isaac Habert, began to preach against Jansen's *Augustinus* in Paris in a series of Advent sermons in 1642. If the papal condemnation of the five infamous propositions supposedly extracted from *Augustinus* cannot be laid precisely at the monarchy's door, the initiative having again come from Habert and other Molinist allies in the Sorbonne and episcopacy, Cardinal-Minister Mazarin's request in the name of the young Louis XIV to Pope Innocent X that he judge the issue against the defenders of Jansen could have been no small factor in the origin of the first papal bull against Jansenism: *Cum occasione*, fulminated in 1653. And when the Sorbonne expelled Antoine Arnauld from its ranks in 1655, it did so in the intimidating presence of Chancellor Antoine Séguier, acting as the executor of Mazarin's ecclesiastical policy.[142]

The persecution only intensified when Louis XIV personally took over the conduct of royal policy after the death of Mazarin in 1661. It was at the Sun King's own insistence that a docile General Assembly of the Gallican Clergy ordered the sisters of Port-Royal to sign Mazarin's hitherto unused Formulary, which, reinforced in the meanwhile by Pope Alexander VII's bull *Ad sacram*, specifically attributed the condemned propositions to *Augustinus* and more or less disallowed any distinction between a heretical and a possibly orthodox sense that they might bear. After having exhausted all the resources of Arnauld's casuisty, the sisters in the end refused to sign the Formulary of Alexander VII, which became the cross of both the abbey and the solitaries' pedagogically experimental "little schools" *(petites écoles)*. And when, after the ten-year Peace of Clement IX, the persecution resumed in 1679, it was again Louis XIV who first acted, this time in disregard of papal policy, which had meanwhile allowed the sisters to sign with the proviso of

141. Blaise Pascal, *Pensées*, in *OC*, p. 509.

142. In addition to the works by Cognet, Gazier, and Sedgwick cited above, see Albert de Meyer, *Les premières controverses jansénistes en Frances, 1640–1649* (Louvain, 1917); and Lucien Ceyssens, "Les cinq propositions de Jansenius à Rome," *Revue d'histoire ecclésiastique* 60 (1971):149–501, 821–68.

"respectful silence" concerning the attribution of heretical intent to Jansen. But in 1705 the Sun King had his way with the papacy too, extracting from Pope Clement XI the bull *Vineam domini* forbidding the distinction between fact *(fait)* and right *(droit)*—and in effect allowing him to proceed with the physical destruction of the abbey in 1709. And it was finally Louis XIV who, asking Pope Clement XI to condemn more than one hundred propositions from the Oratorian Pasquier Quesnel's *Réflexions morales sur le Nouveau Testament (Moral Reflections on the New Testament)*, obtained the anti-Jansenist bull to end all bulls, the so-called constitution *Unigenitus*, which condemned precisely a hundred and one of them in 1713.[143]

Why? Were Richelieu, Mazarin, Louis XIV, or even their Jesuit confessors such perspicacious readers of Jansenist texts that they detected the profound incompatibility between the Jansenist religious temperament and divine-right absolutism that historians and literary critics have detected more recently? Probably not. But if so, might they not also have sensed that, left to its own devices, Jansenist dissent would probably never have gone beyond an attitude of "respectful silence," in which case the monarchy's best policy would have been to let proverbially sleeping dogs lie? This indomitable Jansenist conscience indeed stubbornly maintained its right to "respectful silence" in the face of the Formulary, but only regarding the empirical fact of Jansenism and not where the principle of the heresy of the five propositions was concerned. Did, then, that conscience's refusal to agree that five dubious propositions were to be found in a three-volume treatise, written in Latin by a Flemish theologian, pose so great a threat to Louis Quatorzian absolutism as to justify so sustained a deployment of force? From the religious point of view of divine-right absolutism—and in the light of Louis XIV's simultaneous treatment of French Protestantism—the answer must be some kind of yes. But it may make this yes—and royal policy in general—a little clearer to attend more closely to some of the political connotations surrounding Jansenism's first manifestations in France.

Jansenism and Absolutism

French absolutism's first encounter with Jansen's "Jansenism" first came in the form of a book entitled *Mars Gallicus*, which appeared in 1635.[144] Its author was indeed Cornelius Jansen, a subject of the Spanish Habsburgs, its point of view that of a counterreformational or devout Catholic critical of France's recent entry into the Thirty Years' War on the side of the Calvinist Dutch and Lutheran Germans

143. Cognet, *Le jansénisme*, pp. 62–99; Gazier, *Histoire générale du mouvement janséniste*, 1:113–251; and Sedgwick, *Jansenism in Seventeenth-Century France*, pp. 107–192.

144. *Mars Gallicus, seu de justitia armorum et feodorum regis Galliae* (Louvain, 1635).

against the Spanish and Austrian Habsburgs—and so against the very real prospect of the Catholic reconquest of Europe.[145] It was in the Brussels *Grand' Place*, the center of the capital of the Spanish Netherlands, where French heralds had announced France's formal declaration of war earlier the same year.

The threat that *Mars Gallicus* represented to Richelieu was not a "foreign" one alone, for its militantly Catholic point of view had won the support of an important constituency in France in the form of Chancellor Michel de Marillac's parti dévot, within which the cardinal de Bérulle and the abbé de Saint-Cyran were both conspicuous. The parti dévot had been a powerful force in the regency government of Marie de Medici following the assassination of Henry IV, as has been noted, and Richelieu had only with difficulty risen to power over its objections. In alliance with Marie, Louis XIII's mother, the parti dévot had come close to unseating Richelieu from his still precarious position in the Day of Dupes, 10 November 1630. In connection with the queen Anne d'Autriche, the sister of the governor of the Spanish Netherlands, elements of the parti dévot again indirectly threatened Richelieu's power in 1637, when Louis XIII's Jesuit confessor Nicolas Caussin troubled the king's conscience on account of Richelieu's "sinful" alliance with Protestant powers against Catholic Habsburgs in the Thirty Years' War. Richelieu managed to dispatch the troublesome Jesuit to greener pastoral pastures in far-off Brittany, but "contritionism" continued to haunt him when Louis XIII encountered the same rigorous penitential theology in the Oratorian theologian Claude Séguenot's treatise on virginity. In this case Richelieu was able to trace the doctrine to Jansen's friend Saint-Cyran, resulting in Saint-Cyran's imprisonment in 1638.[146]

While Jansen's and Saint-Cyran's opinions and associations thus far recalled the Catholic League and its political offspring in France, namely the parti dévot, both the devotional practice of penitence without the Eucharist and the theological direction of the infamous five propositions supposedly extracted from Jansen's *Augustinus* recalled the challenge of French Protestantism. It is true that the five propositions are in fact not to be found in Jansen's book, and represent a very prejudicial summation by Molinistic readers. There is no reason to suppose the Jansenists to have been insincere in regarding them as heretical, or at least as susceptible of a heretical sense. Still, they pointed incontestably in the direction of Jansenism's religious sensibilities and represented conclusions that might be drawn from Augustinian premises. Writing against Calvinists in the 1670s, Antoine Arnauld did not take issue with the first four propositions laid down by the Calvinist Synod that met in Dordrecht in 1618—19, directing all of his fire against the doctrine of the perseverance of the saints. What matters in any case is French

145. Orcibal, *Jansénius d'Ypres*, pp. 223—43.
146. Orcibal, *Jean Duvergier de Hauranne, abbé de Saint-Cyran et son temps*, pp. 519—94.

absolutism's perception of a new form of Calvinism—sharpened, needless to say, by many contemporary accusations to that effect—seeing that the threat from French Calvinism itself was still alive if not very well in 1642.

It had been only fifteen years earlier, after all, that French Protestants had revolted with English help, ironically distracting Richelieu from a pro-Protestant policy in the Empire and necessitating the costly siege of La Rochelle and other fortified towns in the south. Although Protestants lost their fortifications, garrisons, and other privileges in the resultant Peace of Alès, the threat of a Huguenot revolt in alliance with a Protestant England remained very much alive in the mind of Mazarin during the Fronde because the "revolution of the saints" in the 1640s had seemed to leave England more zealously Protestant than ever before. The association of French Protestants with the Puritan commonwealth is undoubtedly one of the factors in the rapid deteriorization of their position after the Fronde. The connection between these two and Jansenism in turn seemed obvious enough for the Jesuit François Hallier to assure Mazarin, the queen mother, and Louis XIV in a sermon that Jansenists had promised Oliver Cromwell six thousand soldiers to help him invade France and become their protector.[147] And in fact some of the Fronde's most eloquent and independent mazarinades, like Arnauld d'Andilly's *The Unvarnished Truth* and the Parisian curé Jean Rousse's *A Response to a Pressing Question,* came from Jansenist pens.[148]

It was in part due to its suspected role in the Fronde revolt that Louis XIV resolved to extirpate Jansenism from the moment that he personally assumed control of the government in 1661. That same year marked the end of the third or religious Fronde of the Parisian curés. That revolt, running from 1652 to 1661, took place after the parlementary and princely frondes had spent their force, and thanks to the research of Richard Golden, we now know that Jansenist curés played the most prominent part. That Fronde took the form of the unswerving allegiance of Parisian curés to their archbishop-designate, Jean-François Paul de Gondi, later Cardinal de Retz. Their loyalty defied the will of Mazarin, who arrested Gondi in 1652 and later tried to declare his see vacant because of his conspicuous role in the earlier frondes from 1648 to 1652. The curés were attracted to Retz because he symbolized the independent authority of the secular clergy— the more conveniently so because his absence the whole time, first as Mazarin's

---

147. Golden, *The Godly Rebellion*, p. 130.

148. [Robert Arnauld d'Andilly], *La vérité toute nue, ou advis sincère et désintéressé sur les véritables causes des maux de l'Estat, et les moyens d'y apporter remède* (Paris, 1652); and [Jean Rousse], *Décision sur la question du temps, à la reyne régente* (Paris, 1649). On attributions of authorship, see Carrier, "Port-Royal et la Fronde: Deux mazarinades inconnues d'Arnauld d'Andilly," *Revue d'histoire littéraire de la France* 75 (1975):3–29; and the introduction to the same author's *La Fronde: Contestation démocratique et misère paysanne,* 2:2. On Arnauld d'Andilly's pamphlet in particular, and on Jansenism's relatively independent voice in the Fronde in general, see Jouhaud's *La fronde des mots*, pp. 174–83.

prisoner and then as political refugee in Rome, allowed the curés to enhance their own corporate authority under the pretense of defending the distant archbishop's. Under the cover of the conveniently absent archbishop's authority, in other words, Parisian curés defended their own authority over their parishes against the encroachments of the regular clergy, especially Jesuits, as well as against Mazarin's government, with whom the Jesuits were in league. What attracted these curés to Jansenism, in contrast, was its simultaneous counteroffensive against the Jesuits' "lax" moral theology—Arnauld, Nicole, and Pascal in fact wrote seven of the curés' public *Letters* against this moral theology in the 1650s—and noisy defense of the secular against the regular clergy.[149]

For this, too, was a feature of Jansenism, despite the movement's close association with the abbey of Port Royal. From the time of Saint-Cyran's defense of the authority of the episcopacy against English Jesuits in 1632 and Jansen's own metamorphosis into a bishop in the same year, Jansenism had sided with the episcopacy's older and more patristic priestly authority against the upstart regulars.[150] Although early Jansenists were more concerned with bishops than with simple priests, priestly authority implied simple priests as well as bishops: witness Edmond Richer, the fiercely Gallican and proto-Jansenist syndic of the Sorbonne, whose defense of episcopal authority against Jesuits and ultramontanists in 1611 already wooed former *ligueur* Paris curés by featuring them as the direct successors of Christ's seventy-two disciples mentioned in Luke 10 and as the bishops' partners in the governance of the diocese.[151] Richer's ecclesiology would soon become part and parcel of the Jansenist movement. Although it obviously differed from Calvinist Presbyterianism by raising the status of priests within the hierarchy rather than substituting pastors and laymen for the hierarchy, "Richerism" readily lent itself to suspicions of crypto-Calvinism in that it located ultimate spiritual authority in the whole church, including the laity, who in turn delegated it to their ministers, just as Calvin following the conciliarists had done earlier and Protestant polemicist Pierre Jurieu would again do in debate with Bossuet in 1677.[152] More important than Richer or Richerism in the preparation of the former ligueur priests for Jansenism, however, was probably Pierre de Bérulle's Oratory, a congregation of secular priests that was devoted specifically to the restoration of the priests' sacerdotal dignity against regulars and that, doubling as

149. See Louis Lafuma's introduction to the *Factum pour les curés de Paris contre un livre intitulé Apologie pour les Casuistes contre les calomnies des jansénistes et contre ceux qui l'ont imposé, imprimé et débité,* in *OC,* p. 471.

150. Orcibal, *Jean Duvergier de Hauranne, abbé de Saint-Cyran et son temps,* pp. 334–75.

151. Monique Cottret, "Edmond Richer, 1539–1631: Le politique et le sacré" in *L'état baroque: Regards sur la pensée politique de la France du premier XVIIe siècle,* ed. Henry Méchoulan (Paris, 1985), pp. 62–77.

152. Pierre Jurieu, *Traité de la puissance de l'église* (Quevilly, 1677), as cited in Yardeni, "French Calvinist Political Thought, 1534–1715," pp. 333–34.

a teaching order, began to run afoul of the Jesuits as early as the 1630s. By the 1650s, in any case, the remarkable "conversion" of the Parisian curés from ligueur and Jesuit-tainted ultramontanism to a kind of Gallicanism and moral Jansenism was just about complete.[153] Of sixty-eight Parisian curés who attended the extraordinary assemblies studied by Golden during the religious Fronde, about fifty-six were Jansenists or sympathetic to Jansenism while only twelve were clearly anti-Jansenist.[154]

Or was the ideological distance traversed since the 1590s so very great as the curés' Jansenism would suggest? In fact, the comportment and associations of the curés during the religious Fronde must have reinforced Jansenism's Janus-like aspect, somehow reminiscent of both Protestantism and the Catholic League. On the one hand, the Jansenist Augustinian theology and anti-Jesuitism of the curés recalled Calvinist doctrine and Puritan anti-Jesuitism, while the diocesan assemblies of both, as well as their assertion of independence as spiritual governors of their respective parishes, suggested a kind of clerical presbyterianism. On the other hand, the curés also looked for help from the papacy, which supported Retz's claims to his archiepiscopal see and hosted him in Rome, waiting impatiently for Retz to excommunicate Mazarin and the king or, better yet, to impose an interdict on the archdiocese. They also gave voice to their hopes for a victory by the *frondeur* prince Condé's Spanish army against Cardinal Mazarin and the king, tried fitfully to concert measures with curés in other cities, in particular Rouen, and derived consolation from such reliquary miracles as that of the Holy Thorn. Now all of this and more seemed to hark back to the comportment of the Parisian curés during the League. Not even their Gallican recourse to the Sorbonne to condemn the Jesuits' moral casuistry or their appeal to Jean Gerson's authority in defense of their right to constitute themselves as a separate ecclesial order were entirely free from Leaguish associations. Had not both authorities been successfully appealed to by priestly partisans of the League?[155] Indicative of the suspicious perception of Jansenist curés as latter-day Leaguers is the celebrated controller-general Colbert's charge in 1657 that the "Jansenist friends of the Cardinal de Retz . . . are deeply involved and carry along the *dévots.*"[156]

A series of stern *arrêts du conseil* (orders in council) issued during the summer of 1659 finally obliged the Parisian curés to put an end to their monthly diocesan assemblies from which they had staged their religious Fronde. The ecclesial counterpart to the edicts that were shortly to silence the Parlement of Paris, these orders prepared the way for the Edict of 1695, which completed the subjection of the curés to the bishops. What little remained on the surface of the

153. Ibid.
154. Golden, *The Godly Rebellion*, pp. 143–51.
155. Ibid., for appeal to Gerson p. 72; and for petition to Sorbonne, pp. 87–91.
156. Ibid., p. 130.

religious Fronde after 1659 went underground in 1662 when Retz deserted his Jansenist allies by resigning his Parisian see, exposing them to a rigorous round of Louis Quatorzian persecution of a piece with that of Port-Royal. The religious Fronde nonetheless revealed that Jansenism had captured the former League's clerical constituency, which despite the demise of 1662 would eventually survive the Sun King and prove troublesome again in reaction to *Unigenitus*. Can the same be said of the main protagonists of the earliest Fronde who had also become one of the casualties of absolutism—the magistrates and barristers, that is, of the Parlement and lesser Parisian courts?

Much has been made of the social connections between the milieu of the "robe" (shorthand for judicial milieu, including both noble and commoner barristers) and Jansenism at the time of the Fronde. One hypothesis calls attention to the perfect "fit" between Jansenists' "tragic vision" of themselves in a hopelessly fallen world and the equally tragic social situation of venal royal officers financially beholden to a monarchy in the process of displacing them with newer commissioners and a reorganized Royal Council.[157] An equally plausible hypothesis might stress the proximity between Jansenism's conception of truth as factual, biblical and patristic, susceptible to corruption but not improvement, and the judicial milieu's predilection for ancient precedents and abiding fundamental law. But while it may be true that the "first" Jansenism drew its recruits disproportionately from robe or officer families—Arnauld, Pascal, Thomas, Nicole, Bagnols, to name just a few—it does not follow that the robe was disproportionately Jansenist, or that the Parlement of Paris in particular harbored very many Jansenists. In that Parlement at the time of the Fronde, only the Bignon, Briquet, Le Nain, and Robert families seem to have been devotedly Jansenist, and their influence was hardly overwhelming.[158] And although it is again true that the Parlement's ingrained Gallicanism opposed the registration of the anti-Jansenist bull *Cum occasione,* the Parlement's very lay version of Gallicanism was without qualms about a lay court's trial of the Archbishop of Paris, and hence directly opposed the more ecclesiastical version of Gallicanism—if it was even that— professed by the Parisian curés during the religious Fronde.

This Gallican gap between Parisian curés and Parlement at the time of the Fronde suggests that, to the degree that the mutual attraction between Jansenism and parlementary personnel depended on the gravity of Gallicanism, conditions

157. Lucien Goldmann, *Le dieu caché,* pp. 115–56.
158. Ibid.; and Bruno Neveu, "Un parlementaire parisien érudit et janséniste: Jean Le Nain (1609–1698)," *Paris et Ile de France: Mémoires,* 17–18 (1965–66):191–230; Robert Mandrou, "Tragique XVII siècle à propos de travaux récents," *Annales* (Apr.–June 1957):105–13; and Albert Hamscher, "The Parlement of Paris and the Social Interpretation of Early French Jansenism," *Catholic Historical Review* 63 (July 1977):192–410. See also Taveneaux, *Jansénisme et politique,* pp. 19–22.

for that attraction were mainly absent for much of the remainder of the seventeenth century. Jansenists, for their part, were far from unanimously Gallican: Jansen himself was unabashedly ultramontanist, while Saint-Cyran's Gallicanism was at best episcopal and would probably have balked at any secular court's infringement of the church's jurisdiction. "The great" Arnauld and Pasquier Quesnel later approved of the General Assembly's 1682 Gallican Declaration, it is true, but the two Jansenist bishops of Pamiers and Alet conspicuously sided with Pope Innocent XI against Louis XIV in the régale conflict that provoked that same declaration. Yet just three or four years later bishops who were Jansenist or sympathetic to Jansenism—Le Camus of Grenoble, Percin de Montgaillard of Saint-Pons—were conspicuous among the very few voices critical of Louis XIV's Edict of Fontainebleau against Protestants, thereby calling attention to Jansenism's subversive association with the legacies of both ultramontanist League and Protestant Reformation, as well as underscoring the movement's penchant for independence vis-à-vis secular authority whether royal or parlementary.[159] It was only after Jansenism had entirely given up on both the papacy and Louis XIV's purged episcopacy that it was ready to embrace the Parlement's brand of lay Gallicanism and to sacrifice its commitment to ecclesiastical independence.

Meanwhile, the Parlement of Paris stood obligingly aside while Louis XIV proceeded against Port-Royal in the 1660s and again after 1680. For the Sun King was scrupulous about Gallican niceties, covering his actions with the Gallican episcopacy's authority while keeping the papacy at arm's length. That policy changed in the late 1690s after Louis XIV resolved his outstanding quarrels with the papacy and solicited its intervention against Fénelon's mysticism, as well as on two occasions against Jansenism. Another mark of the monarchy's growing distance from an aspect of Gallicanism is the Edict of 1695, which besides extending episcopal authority over the priesthood, also reinforced episcopal jurisdiction vis-à-vis the parlements. In reaction to the papal bulls and their ultramontanist formulas, the Parlement of Paris's attorney general Henri d'Aguesseau began a rearguard defense of traditional Gallicanism, "king's man" though he was, and the Parlement as a whole started to stiffen its resistance behind him.[160] The personnel of Louis XIV's Parlement of Paris has not benefited from the same prosopographical attention lavished on Louis XV's. Yet it is clear enough that the chief members of the Parlement's early eighteenth-century *parti janséniste* (Janse-

---

159. Sedgwick, *Jansenism in Seventeenth-Century France*, pp. 174–80; Orcibal, *Louis XIV et les protestants*, pp. 132–33.

160. Henri-François d'Aguesseau, *Réquisitoire pour l'enregistrement de la bulle contre le livre des maximes des saints*, in *OC*, ed. M. Pardessus, 16 vols. (Paris, 1819), 1:261–65. D'Aguesseau required that the bull be registered only with a "modification salutaire" that disallowed several ultramontanist clauses, notably that which claimed that the bull "est émanée du propre movement de sa Sainteté."

nist party) acquired their offices during the setting two and a half decades of the Sun King's reign.[161] The ranks of the magisterial parti janséniste found themselves reinforced by numbers of would-be priests who, refusing to sign the Formulary of Alexander VII, instead entered the Parlement's Order of Barristers. As it turns out, moreover, it was Jansenist barristers who in large measure created this "order," which like the magisterial parti janséniste took shape between the years 1690 and 1710.[162]

Toward Unigenitus

Theological Augustinianism, forgotten aspects of late-medieval Gallicanism, the cause of the Parlement of Paris and its putative place in the French "constitution" – these were to be eighteenth-century Jansenism's chief conceptual elements. As it happens, these were also the elements that absolutism had discarded as useless in the course of its conceptual elaboration in the seventeenth century. To some degree, that fit even holds for social groups, because the magistrates, barristers, curés, and the upper and literate echelons of the artisinate who were to make up eighteenth-century Jansenism's social rank and file had also been casualties of absolutism, some as Protestants and others as Leaguers. Eventually enrolling under its banners many of the conceptual and social casualties of absolutism, eighteenth-century Jansenism could hence hardly avoid becoming a critical commentary on absolutism. As much the accumulated effect of persecution as it was originally the occasion for it, eighteenth-century Jansenism turned upon its persecutors in a slow but inexorable war of attrition. Yet Jansenism was more than an accumulation of lost causes and aggrieved groups. Even in its most political form it never lost its religious identity, making it all the more devastating as a critique of absolutism, inasmuch as absolutism itself was a kind of religion and hence most vulnerable to deconstruction on its own terms.

Like Jansenism, the cause of integral absolutism also attracted some social

---

161. For example, Louis-Basile Carré de Montgeron, in 1711; Alexandre-Julien Clément, in 1711; Marc-Jacques Fermé, 1708; Claude-François Fornier de Montigny, in 1707; Charles-Bertrand Le Clerc de Lesseville, in 1711; Nicolas-Jérôme de Pâris, in 1717; René Pucelle, in 1684; Louis Robert, in 1691; Jean-Baptiste Maximilien Titon, in 1717; Philippe Thomé, in 1713; Nicolas Vrévin, in 1691. Of that generation of magisterial Jansenists, only René-François Boutin, Pierre Guillebaut, and Jean-François Ogier d'Enonville entered the Parlement after 1720. This summary survey is of course based on the prosopographical information in François Bluche's invaluable *L'origine des magistrats du parlement de Paris*, vols 5–6 of the *Mémoires* published by the Fédération des sociétés historiques et archéologiques de Paris et de l'Ile-de-France (Paris, 1956). For an analysis of the parlementary parti janséniste around 1730, see Peter Campbell, "The Conduct of Politics in the Time of the Cardinal de Fleury" (Ph.D. diss., University of London, 1983), pp. 322–43.

162. On the subject of Jansenist *avocats* and the Order of Barristers see David Avrom Bell, *Lawyers and Citizens: The Making of a Political Elite in Old Regime France* (Oxford, 1994), pp. 1–128.

constituents more than others: the royal commissioners *(commis)* and, perhaps a certain courtier nobility; some religious orders or congregations such as that of Saint-Sulpice, the Capuchins, and above all the Jesuits; the overwhelming majority of France's obedient and faithful bishops; and some humbler layers of the laity, like weavers, masons, and shoemakers, who clung to the visual trappings of baroque piety and enrolled in force in the Jesuits' Marian congregations until their demise in 1760.[163] Absolutism's ensigns were the Declaration of 1672 against parlementary remonstrances; the Gallican Declaration of 1682, or at least its first article; the Edict of 1695 on behalf of bishops against curés and royal courts of law; and the Edict of Fontainebleau against Huguenots, soon to reinforced by that of 1724. But in the eighteenth century it was to be another religious symbol that above all rallied absolutism's allies and maintained—even reinforced—its religious identity: namely the "constitution" *Unigenitus* against Jansenism.[164]

Solicited by Louis XIV against the Oratorian Pasquier Quesnel's book *Réflexions morales sur le Nouveau Testament* as the ultimate solution to the Jansenist problem, this papal bull indeed aimed its first seventy or so anathemas against the related doctrines of efficacious grace and the two mutually exclusive "delectations," charity or concupiscence, as well as the practice of deferred absolution and the insistence on contrition for the sacrament of penance. Characteristically Jansenist, all these practices and preachments had sustained censorship before. Hitherto uncensored, however, were eight propositions in favor of laypersons' reading Scripture in the vernacular as well as advocating their participation in the Catholic liturgy.[165] In condemning these propositions now, the bull called attention to one of Jansenism's most striking similarities to Calvinism and condemned a distinguished Catholic generation's ecumenical effort to meet Protestantism liturgically halfway. Another eighteen or so of the censored propositions defined the church in essentially invisible and antihierarchical terms: it consisted of all the "saints," the "just" and "elect" in communion with Christ, instead of, say, the episcopal hierarchy united with the pope.[166] The condemnation of these propositions took explicit aim at Jansenism's Richerist exaltation of parish priests within the hierarchy as well as its tendencies toward laicism, and implicitly associated both with Protestant Presbyterianism. To the extent that the propositions were also antipapal, the bull's condemnation of them also aimed at Gallicanism, as did the censure of the infamous ninety-first proposition that "the fear of an unjust excommunication ought never to deter us from doing our duty." Might popes again excommunicate French kings, the Parlement's *gens du roi* were to ask, and prevent their fearful subject from obeying them?

163. Louis Chatellier, *L'Europe des dévots* (Paris, 1987), pp. 73–83, 238–53.
164. For the text of *Unigenitus*, see Gazier, *Histoire générale du mouvement janséniste*, 2:303–41.
165. Ibid., propositions 79–86, pp. 326–27.
166. Ibid., propositions 72–78, 90–100, pp. 324–25, 328–32.

Upon receiving the bull Louis XIV convened an extraordinary assembly of mainly nonresident bishops and virtually ordered them to accept it. Although a few bishops did so purely and simply, most accompanied their acceptance with pastoral explanations and qualifications, while the Archbishop of Paris, Antoine, cardinal de Noailles, led seven other bishops in a remarkable refusal to accept it without papal explanations that were never forthcoming.[167] Having failed in his attempt to obtain the unanimous and unqualified acceptance of even a handpicked group of otherwise docile bishops, Louis XIV next faced the Parlement of Paris's gens du roi, who predictably objected to the bishops' lack of unanimity as well as to the bull's frontal assault upon the Gallican tradition. Although not theologians, these magistrates ominously shared the impression of some of the bishops that the bull had condemned propositions innocent in themselves, almost word-for-word translations of the New Testament or patristic sources. D'Aguesseau's virgin reaction to a first reading was that the bull ought to be deposited at the *greffe* of the Parlement, "there to remain as a durable proof of and an eternal monument to the fallibility of the pope." To be sure, the gens du roi and the Parlement of Paris were still sufficiently intimidated by the aging king to register the bull in 1714, with the proviso that the registration be "without prejudice to the liberties of the Gallican Church, rights, and preeminence of the Crown"—and by implication to the bishops' own written explanations and qualifications of the bull.[168]

At least two hundred books and pamphlets against the bull were published in 1714; a thousand more, most of them against the bull, would appear by 1730. Louis XIV died in 1715, and the Parlement quashed his will, which had tried to legitimize the king's bastard sons and to entrust them with the regency government for the six-year-old Louis XV. In return for this favor, the dead king's nephew and new regent, Philip, duc d'Orléans, restored the Parlement's right to remonstrate before registering new edicts and declarations.[169] For a few years he also charted a less certain course in religious policy, emboldening four Jansenist bishops to appeal in 1717 against *Unigenitus* to a "future general council" and three-quarters of the Paris clergy, Archbishop Noailles at their head, to follow them. But these Jansenist bishops were already a small minority within the episcopacy, most of whom accepted the bull. For at roughly the same time the Parlement of Paris, which welcomed the appeal, also began to entertain appeals by parish priests interdicted for their opposition to *Unigenitus* by bishops more enthusiastic about this bull than the Archbishop of Paris. The century of *Unigenitus* had begun.

167. Pierre Blet, *Le clergé de France, Louis XIV, et le Saint Siège* (Vatican, 1989), pp. 429–603. See also Jacques M. Gres-Gayer, "The *Unigenitus* of Clement IX: A Fresh Look at the Issues," *Catholic Historical Review* 49 (June 1988):259–82.

168. Henri-François d'Aguesseau, *Fragment inédit des mémoires du chancelier Daguesseau*, ed. Augustin Gazier (Paris, 1920), passim. The quotation is from p. 11.

169. Michel Antoine, *Louis XV* (Paris, 1989), pp. 30–38.

CHAPTER 2

✦‑➤‑➤‑➤‑➤‑➤‑➤‑◄‑◄‑◄‑◄‑◄‑◄‑➤

The Century of *Unigenitus*

THE EIGHTEENTH CENTURY WAS OF COURSE A CENTURY OF "lights," or the Enlightenment, and one of the first of its many literary lights appeared not long after the bull *Unigenitus,* in 1721, in the form of the baron de Montesquieu's *Persian Letters.* In these spirited letters and elsewhere Montesquieu set the tone for philosophes who followed him by taking a detached, Olympian view toward the issues dividing Jansenists and Jesuits, wishing a pox on both their houses. Although his own view of the nature of natural justice and human liberty of action were not far from those defended by Molinists, he could make sport of the ignorant zealotry of the defenders of *Unigenitus* in the 101st Persian letter—a mocking commemoration of the 101 propositions from Quesnel's *Réflexions morales* that the bull had condemned.[1] "The Jesuits," he was later to say, "defended a good cause in Molinism by some very evil means."[2] And although he obviously sympathized with Jansenists as ecclesial constitutionalists and as opponents of the politics of "despotism," he felt "animated against those doctors who represent God as someone who makes a tyrannical use of his power, who puts it to work in a way in which we would not act ourselves, for fear of offending him."[3] No book he had ever read, he was later to say, fell so far below its reputation as Quesnel's *Réflexions morales.* And although in very different ways, both Jansenism and

---

1. Charles-Louis de Secondat, baron de Montesquieu, *Lettres persanes,* Lettre CI, in *OC,* ed. Roger Caillois, 2 vols. (Paris, 1949–51), 1:280. For examples of Montesquieu's views on liberty of action and human responsibility, see letters LVII and LXIX, 1:215, 239.

2. Montesquieu, *Mes pensées,* no. 1326, in *OC,* 1:1320.

3. Montesquieu, *Lettres persanes,* Lettre LXXXIII, *OC,* 1:256–57.

Jesuitical Molinism fell well short of Montesquieu's ideal religion of "charity and humanity."[4]

His own *Persian Letters,* however, rendered reluctant homage to the eighteenth century as the century of *Unigenitus* as well as of lights, and to the damage that a mere seven or eight years of controversy about it had already done to royal religion in France. The king of France is a "great magician," Montesquieu had the Persian traveler Usbek write from Paris in his twenty-fourth letter. This king went "so far as to make [his subjects] believe that he can cure them of all kinds of diseases by touching them, so great is his force and power over their minds." This not very reverent reference to the royal touch was followed by the Persian's description of an even greater magician called the pope, who, "two years ago, sent [the king] an important writing called the Constitution *[Unigenitus],* and wanted to oblige both him and his subjects to believe everything it contained, on pain of the severest penalties." The pope succeeded vis-à-vis the king, Usbek went on, but the king failed to convince all of his subjects, especially the women, "some of whom revolted and said that they did not want to believe anything that was in that writing." The consequence of the king's pursuit of these rebels, the next paragraphs suggested, was that while King Louis XIV laid down the law for his foreign enemies, he made little headway against "an innumerable host of invisible enemies right around him."[5] Whether Montesquieu meant to assert any relationship between a religious controversy and the decline of a royal religion to which his own incredulity bore eloquent witness is far from clear. But by saying that the bearer of the royal touch had subordinated his own wonder-working powers to those of the pope for the sake of the authority of *Unigenitus,* the letter strongly hints as much.

By 1750 the French monarchy seemed to have weathered the worst of the Jansenist controversy, just as it had the Protestant one a century and a half earlier. Although the years immediately following the fulmination of *Unigenitus* remained religiously fecund ones for the Jansenist movement, its theological vitality—even its capacity to maintain its own numbers—eventually succumbed to a renewed policy of persecution begun by the cardinal-minister André-Hercule de Fleury in the 1720s. For that policy effectively shut down Jansenism's foyers of theological reflection, purged its remaining centers of monastic and clerical recruitment, and fragmented the movement into several distinct factions.

Yet the monarchy's victory over Jansenism proved a phyrric one, as events after Fleury's death soon showed. The monarchy may have ended Jansenism's theological—even religious—vitality, but its transformation into a judicial phe-

---

4. On charity and humanity, see ibid., Lettre XLVI, 1:194; on Quesnel, *Mes pensées,* no. 901, 1:1247.

5. Montesquieu, *Lettres persanes,* lettre XXIV, *OC,* 1:165–67.

nomenon reinforced the late sixteenth-century alliance between the judicial milieu and the lower clergy. The monarchy may have suppressed Jansenist miracles and deprived parishioners of their favorite priests, but at the cost of alienating large segments of the Parisian populace that had been the staunchest support of sacral monarchy in the trials of the late sixteenth century. The monarchy may have aspired to silence the loquacious movement by means of new and reinforced censorship laws, but it did not succeed in this endeavor, instead further metasticizing the movement into the voice of public opinion. And in its effort, finally, to cast out the devil of Jansenism, the monarchy inadvertently raised up the Beelzebub of a revived Leaguelike parti dévot that not only gave an otherwise moribund Jansenism a plausible enemy but posed a religious threat to the monarchy of a different sort. By making a papal bull into a central symbol of its authority, the French monarchy sustained collateral damage from both the religious loyalty and the opposition that that symbol provoked.

A Metaphor for Absolutism

That the defense of Augustinian "truth" against *Unigenitus* was from the outset a precocious critique of absolutism became apparent on the very morrow of the bull, as its opponents and defenders staked out their respective positions. This critique is especially clear in the pages of a pamphlet and a book published in 1714 and 1716, respectively: Vivien de La Borde's *On the Testimony of Truth* and Nicolas Le Gros's two-volume *On the Downfall of the Liberties of the Gallican Church*.[6]

Admitting that the papacy and the majority of bishops had unequivocally condemned the truth, La Borde set out to explain how the Catholic Church might remain the church in spite of that fact, or how, in other words, the "elect" or "true" church might continue to discern the "light" of truth within the larger church amidst the "shadows" cast by *Unigenitus*. For just as Christ's glory went unperceived except by the true Israelites whose "simple, righteous and pure hearts waited for the redemption of Israel," so now Christ's "humble and timid truth . . . hardly dare[d] raise its voice," and went unheard except by the "pure of heart." Such indeed, even under the best of circumstances, was the infallible voice or "testimony" promised by Christ to his church: not one "so strong and powerful as to be impossible to miss it," but such as to be heard only by those endowed with a "pure heart" *(coeur droit)*.[7]

But how? If a numerical majority of pastors reliably articulated the voice of

6. Vivien de La Borde, *Du témoignage de la vérité* (n.p., 1714); and Nicolas Le Gros, *Du renversement des libertés de l'église gallicane*, 2 vols. (n.p., 1716).

7. La Borde, *Du témoignage de la vérité*, pp. 16–17, 25–26, 151–53.

the church "in times of liberty," when all the canons had been scrupulously followed, how was it to be heard in times of oppression and "violence," when fear encouraged "prevarication"? By listening to the still small voice of the smaller number, answered La Borde, enlisting Jansenist penitential theology in an ecclesiology that anticipated Jean-Jacques Rousseau's later quest for the "general will." Because in that case the concupiscent "passions," "vile interest," "fear"—egotistical amour propre, in a word—could always be counted upon to produce a majority, while the few "upright hearts" alone would remain faithful to the truth. This faithful remnant would be consoled and fortified by the "public outcry" of the "lay faithful," who, even though they were not pastoral "judges of the faith," were valid "witnesses" to it and who, innocent of material interest, were all the more steadfast in defense of the truth. Or at least some of them—enough of them in any case to prevent the voice of truth from being lost in the din of prevarication. For La Borde's final criterion of truth was nothing less than unanimity—"the unanimous testimony rendered by the entire body of the [lay] faithful"—failing which a faithful remnant and its "public outcry" might still prevent *Unigenitus* from being mistaken for a law of the faith.[8]

La Borde's paradoxical apology for the smaller number in the name of unanimity was in part an apology for parish priests or the clerical second order, but only implicitly so. Far more explicit was his ecclesial laicism. To be sure, La Borde distinguished sharply between the clergy and the lay faithful: pastors were "judges of the faith" while the lay faithful were only its "witnesses." Yet this distinction all but disintegrated on contact with a radical if mainly implicit Gallicanism that entrusted Christ's keys of spiritual authority neither to the bishops nor to the pope, but instead to the "entire body of the faithful" including the lay faithful. It also disintegrated as a result of La Borde's peculiarly passive conception of judging, which was not much different from the act of witnessing. Hence La Borde's bishops had "no [other] authority . . . than that of representing and judicially declaring the testimony of their churches," nor any "apart from the avowal of the faithful." "Judges without doubt, but not legislators," La Borde declared, the bishops' authority "reduced itself to the judicial declaration of the law of the faith."[9]

Along with his laicism, then, this judicial language also strongly colored La Borde's ecclesiology, even his conception of the faith. For the faith itself in La Borde's simile was "something like a law subsisting in every corporate nation, or that society of men we call the . . . Church." If, then, the Catholic Church was like a nation, its bishops the nation's judges, and its faith the nation's public law, were not the assembled bishops also something like France's Parlement of Paris, espe-

8. Ibid., pp. 68–69, 83, 96–97. See also pp. 107–8, 220.
9. Ibid., p. 78, 93–94.

cially since La Borde specified elsewhere that the nation's "public magistracy was in some sense the précis of the nation?"[10] So close was La Borde's assimilation of episcopacy to magistracy that it virtually invited that lay magistracy to intervene by default in the affairs of the church should the bishops themselves fail in their duty. And if, to run the simile backward, the bishops only represented their respective churches, and only judicially attested to the law of faith implicit in the hearts of the lay faithful, then did not the nation's magistrates legitimately represent that nation, as well as to attest to and defend that public law, even against the king if necessary?

Evidence that such political implications were not unique to La Borde, that they belonged to post-*Unigenitus* Jansenism more generally, was their even more explicit statement in the Remois canon Nicolas Le Gros's *Du renversement des libertés de l'église gallicane,* which appeared just two years later, in 1716. But while La Borde's ecclesiology opposed the lay witness and the law court to the clergy and its spiritual jurisdiction, Le Gros's pitted priest and parish against episcopacy and diocese. And while La Borde threatened the monarchy with the revolt of the judges, Le Gros looked forward to the restoration of the Estates General.

Le Gros's Catholic Church, like La Borde's, spoke infallibly only when it spoke unanimously. "It is to unanimity, to concert, to charity, to goals arrived at by consensus that Jesus Christ promised his assistance and to which he attached his sovereign authority." Not as content as La Borde with code words like *pastor,* Le Gros also spelled out more clearly than had the Oratorian how the criterion of unanimity enhanced the status of parish priests. Following Jean Gerson and Edmond Richer, Le Gros laid it down that curés "were the successors of the seventy-two disciples whom Jesus Christ himself had commissioned in addition to the apostles, receiving immediately from him their jurisdiction." Bishops were therefore obliged to consult with their curés at every turn in diocesan synods.[11] And although Le Gros drew a sharper distinction than had La Borde between pastoral judges and lay witnesses, Le Gros too hankered nostalgically after the "ardor which the faithful witnessed in all [doctrinal] questions" of Christian antiquity, and acknowledged that when "even Catholic prelates are motivated by political interest to authorize decretals [like *Unigenitus*], . . . the simpler and freer laypeople, speaking out more clearly, can protest against the prevaricators."[12] Even if he did not explain it, Le Gros too allowed for the role of the public outcry.

That degree of overlap between the two was inevitable because they shared— Le Gros much more explicitly than La Borde—a radical version of Gallicanism

10. Ibid., pp. 81–82, 147. See also pp. 78, 88–89.

11. Le Gros, *Du renversement des libertés de l'église gallicane,* 1:171–72, 192, 327. On Le Gros's sources, see Edmond Préclin, *Les jansénistes du dix-huitième siècle et la Constitution civile du clergé: Le développement du richérisme, sa propagation dans le bas clergé, 1713–1791* (Paris, 1929), p. 63.

12. Le Gros, *Du renversement des libertés de l'église gallicane,* 1:230–31, 235.

that the largely royal and episcopal Gallicanism of the Declaration of 1682 had temporarily eclipsed. Explicating the famous passage in Scripture which has Jesus entrusting the keys of his kingdom to the Apostle Peter, Le Gros insisted, as La Borde had, that "it is not only to the corps of pastors which Saint Peter [metaphorically] represents as being the first pastor; it is also to the corps composed of both pastors and simple faithful [laypersons] of which he is equally a metaphor, seeing that he is at once a Christian and an apostle."[13] Like any good Jansenist, Le Gros appealed to the authority of the "holy Doctor," Saint Augustine, to legitimate this interpretation of Scripture, but it was in fact the far more explicit scholastic definitions and arguments of the late medieval "theologians of Paris"– Jean Gerson, Jacques Almain, John Major–who were dictating the Remois canon's discursive *démarche*. Distinguishing, with these Sorbonne-school conciliarists, between the "basis" *(fonds)*, "property," and the "principal and radical authority" of the church's spiritual power on the one hand; and its "usage," "exercise," and "ministry" on the other, Le Gros specified that "spiritual power" was radically and fundamentally the property of the entire church, including the lay faithful, who then entrusted its usage to its pastors or ministers.[14]

To be sure, Le Gros laid it down in good Gallican terms that the faithful were only the conduit by which the pastors received their sacerdotal powers, and that these originated in Christ alone. Yet this distinction between divine origin and institutional means hardly removed the republican edges of Le Gros's ecclesiology. "The authority of the church is in this regard little different from the temporal jurisdiction of a Republic," Le Gros held. "For those who have written about republics"–he cited Jacques Almain and Roberto Bellarmino–"agree that the power of life and death . . . belong in property to the corps of the republic, even though [that power] be exercised by one or by many who act, ordain, judge, and punish in [the republic's] name." Drawing the parallel between the two polities further, Le Gros maintained that "just as the entire republic consents through those who govern it, so in effect the entire church consents by its pastors," explicitly in the case of ecumenical councils, implicitly in the case of "more obscure matters." These matters included excommunications, resulting in the conclusion that "the faithful laypeople [implicitly] consent in more than one manner in the just excommunications fulminated by a pastor," as well as in the corollary–the ninety-first proposition condemned by *Unigenitus*–that unjust or arbitrary excommunications need not prevent them from doing their duties.[15]

Among the duties that both Quesnel and Le Gros had in mind was the obligation of subjects to obey their sovereigns. But what Le Gros gave to the king

13. Ibid., 1:336–37.
14. Ibid., 1:318–19, 336–37.
15. Ibid., pp. 343–44, 395–96.

with his right hand he took away with his left by making it clear that by republic he meant any well-ordered state, including the French monarchy. Wielding the comparison of the Catholic Church to the monarchy with the effect of a boomerang, Le Gros concluded that temporal authority like spiritual authority "is more essentially attached to the society than to the chief *(chef)* who governs it." Implicitly recalling, moreover, the distinction between the king's two bodies, Le Gros specified that "the persons who exercise [temporal authority] die and are replaced by others, while the [political] corps does not die." Lest his readers suspect that he was making an exception of monarchies, Le Gros let it be known that "even in hereditary monarchies the kings are always ministers of God and the republic no matter how absolute their power." And lest his remarks about monarchies be taken to exclude France, Le Gros made it clear that in France royal orders in council became law "only in virtue of the *arrêt* of the Parlement of Paris and other parlements which together . . . are like the Estates [General] always assembled."[16]

For Le Gros writing in 1716 the conclusion followed that, because the Parlement of Paris had registered *Unigenitus* only under duress and had moreover disavowed that registration after Louis XIV's death, the bull was not an enforceable law of state and opposition to it was not a crime.[17] But in order to reach that conclusion Le Gros had to combine a theological critique of *Unigenitus* with the revival of radical Gallicanism and a theory of the Estates General's ultimate superiority. Like La Borde's, Le Gros's critique of *Unigenitus* culminated in a critique of absolute monarchy.

That critique did not go unperceived by the era's orthodox or Molinist anti-Jansenists, with the result that, even during the vacillatory regency, a defense of the bull *Unigenitus* was already tantamount to a defense of absolute monarchy. This pattern is most clearly exemplified in the works of Jean-Joseph Languet de Villeneuve de Gergy, Bishop of Soissons before becoming Archbishop of Sens. The author of three "warnings . . . to those in his diocese who have declared themselves appellants of the constitution *Unigenitus*," he was perhaps the chief scourge of Jansenists in the first half of the eighteenth century.

In a cause not noted for the theological substance or rhetorical candor of its French defenders, who usually contented themselves with simple appeals to papal or royal authority, Languet de Gergy stands out for having taken the bull resolutely, as it were, by the horns.[18] Gladly would he have defended the condemnation of each and every one of the 101 propositions extracted from Quesnel's book;

16. Ibid., pp. 238–39, 343–45.

17. Ibid., 476–78, 510–11.

18. On the defense of *Unigenitus* in the Sorbonne see Jacques M. Gres-Gayer, *Théologie et pouvoir en Sorbonne: La faculté de théologie de Paris et la bulle Unigenitus, 1714–1721* (Paris, 1991), p. 94.

and in the absence of the urgently requested papal explanations, he would willingly have provided ones of his own. Did the bull's multiple anathemas, for example, lack any precise objects because the document failed to apply any of its many condemnatory qualifications—heretical, bordering on heretical, captious, offensive to pious ears, etc.—to any of the condemned propositions in particular? No, replied the Bishop of Soissons, because the bull's "object was to believe that, among these propositions, some were heretical, others erroneous, still others temerarious, etc., and that all were dangerous and pernicious." Besides, he added, the Council of Constance had already condemned the teachings of Jan Hus in this unspecific way, and the heresiarch Martin Luther alone had so far objected to it.[19] Again, did *Unigenitus* condemn propositions that lent themselves to innocent interpretations, or that were virtual paraphrases of patristic sources? So much the worse for innocent expressions and patristic sources, the bishop disarmingly retorted, because as the guardian of the truth the Catholic Church was also "the mistress of the language used to enunciate the Truth, putting that language in the scales, weighing expressions, introducing new words, proscribing others as need be, . . . [sometimes] sacrificing innocent expressions in the interests of the faith, [as well as] the usage of certain terms employed by the Holy Fathers, when the perversity of heretics have made these terms dangerous." Anyway, he went on, "it is the Church which is our rule, and not Saint Augustine." Did the bull, finally, censure nearly word-for-word translations of the Vulgate New Testament? If so—Languet de Gergy did not concede that it did—then the church was only exercising its right under certain circumstances "to interdict in whole or in part the reading of the Sacred Text to the common laity," and so by implication some of the passages translated and commented on by Quesnel. To say, as had Quesnel, that it was always and everywhere meet for all persons to read Scripture was to reiterate "an insane pretension of Calvinists" that had been rightly condemned by *Unigenitus*.[20]

Languet was more convincing on the subject of typically Jansenist propositions about divine election, efficacious grace, charity and fear, and penitence and absolution. It sufficed for the condemned propositions to be at least false, he explained, that their logical "contradictories" be true, a contradictory being a particular negation or affirmation of a universal proposition. Thus, for example, the true contradictory of Quesnel's condemned proposition that there was "no grace except by Faith" was the proposition that "*some* [prevenient] kinds of grace

19. Jean-Joseph Languet de Gergy, Bishop of Soissons, *Lettre pastorale de Monseigneur Jean-Joseph Languet évêque de Soissons, aux ecclésiastiques de son diocèse* (Reims, 1719), pp. 20–23.

20. Languet de Gergy, *Première instruction pastorale contenant le premier avertissement de Monseigneur l'évêque de Soissons à ceux qui dans son diocèse se sont déclarés appellans de la constitution Unigenitus* (n.p., 1719): on terms and expressions, p. 40; on the church and Saint Augustine, p. 25; and on the reading of Scripture, pp. 11–12.

are *sometimes* given in advance of faith"—a proposition that Languet evidently thought true.[21] Languet's logic effectively isolated the all-or-nothing character of Jansenism's religious sensibility and also rhetorically underscored its most obvious similarities to doctrinal Protestantism. But the Bishop of Soissons devoted only one of his five pastoral "warnings" and "letters" to refuting Jansenist doctrine. By far the greater bulk of his polemical energy went into excoriating Jansenist "disobedience" of *Unigenitus* and justification of ecclesiastical "presbyterianism."[22] For in defiance of the "absolute obedience without examination" rightfully required of the lay faithful by the church as well as the state, the Jansenists had taught "indocility, preference for one's own ideas *(lumières)*, curiosity, pride, love of disputation, and reasonings without end." In consequence, the bishop charged, the Jansenists' appeal had "taught simple people, women, nuns, and artisans to be theologians of Grace, to cite Saint Augustine, to accuse the Pope, to badmouth the Bishops, and to find fault with their Mandamuses and their Decisions."[23] And in the course of doing all that, the Jansenists had renewed "the ecclesiogical extravagances of William of Ockham, John Calvin, and Edmond Richer."[24]

All of these accusations, of course, begged the question of how to define the church and to recognize its authority, to which the Bishop of Soissons had ready answers. Although like La Borde and Le Gros he occasionally used the term *pastors*, Languet's church consisted in the supposed successors of Christ and his apostles, or in other words the pope and the bishops. Although still recognizably Gallican, his church was decidedly "not a Republic but a Monarchical State," to which he a little reluctantly added a "mixture of Aristocracy." Languet allowed that the bishops always had and still should consult with their cathedral and parish clergies, but he quickly added that "consultation is neither an essential condition whose absence would annul the Bishop's Decision, nor a sure sign by which to judge of its validity." Bishops alone, this bishop made clear, were true "Judges of the Faith." Even clearer was the division of labor between pastors and their lay "flocks." The lay faithful's submission to their pastors was to be as absolute as subjects' to their sovereign; "docility," "simplicity," and "obedience" were to be their lot. Far from voicing, then, the decisive witness in times of doctrinal controversy and division, Languet's lay faithful had only to look to the "greater number of Bishops throughout the universe united to the Holy See." And far from

---

21. Ibid., pp. 32–33.

22. Languet de Gergy, *Lettre pastorale*, p. 6.

23. Languet de Gergy, *[Troisième] instruction pastorale, contenant un troisième avertissement de Monseigneur l'évêque de Soissons à ceux qui dans son diocèse se sont déclarés appellans de la constitution Unigenitus* (n.p., 1719): on obedience and indocility, p. 15; on the task of searching for the truth, pp. 13, 27; and on women and laymen as theologians, p. 94.

24. Languet de Gergy, *Lettre pastorale*, p. 9.

inflicting the faithful with a "laborious and difficult search," finding the truth was only a matter of looking and counting.[25]

Armed with such blunt definitions and criteria, it was not hard for Languet de Gergy to demolish the Jansenists' defensive and shifting ecclesiology. Were only general church councils infallible, as some Jansenist pamphlets maintained? In that case—also the position, Languet recalled, of the Calvinist pastor Jean Claude—Christ lied when he promised to be with his church at all times, since church councils could meet only sometimes, and all the papal decisions tacitly accepted by the dispersed church would be invalid unless subsequently ratified by councils. If acceptance of papal decisions by the dispersed bishops were sufficient, was a unanimous acceptance required, as other Jansenist pamphlets maintained? In that case a small number of heretical bishops might always invalidate an ecclesial decision against them and, like Languet's few contemporary Jansenist bishops, lay claim to a monopoly of truth to the exclusion of the church universal. But was not Truth more likely to be found on the side of the smaller number in times of persecution and oppression, as La Borde had maintained? The argument proved too much, even for Jansenists, the bishop retorted, since it proved that Albigensians, Waldensians, and Huguenots had also defended the Truth in times of undeniable oppression and persecution. Should not then the magisterium listen to the whole church, including parish priests and the plaintive "hue and cry of the people" invoked by La Borde? Heretics and most especially Calvinists have always fortified themselves with the "clamors" of the "mutinous." And besides, Languet added, the "cry of the people" was not really singular much less unanimous, some of it being directed against Jansenist bishops. Was then the coeur droit of the "elect" to be the ultimate arbiter, as La Borde in places seemed to suggest? "Where are we, my dear Brothers, and what religion do we profess?" cried the bishop, out of sorts. "Behold the exact blasphemy uttered by Pastor Jean Claude in his debate with Bishop Bossuet, and that horrified that good prelate."[26]

Having lain siege to La Borde's lay outworks, Languet bore down on Le Gros's Gallican citadel: namely, as he restated it, the proposition that although "the Pope and the Bishops indeed exercised the [sacerdotal] ministry, they only held the property of it [conjointly] with the people, and in no greater measure than with the merest woman." Contenting himself with the refutation that this "Protestant" principle transformed Christ's "monarchical" church into a "Republic," the Bishop of Soissons hastened to underscore its political ramifications.[27] "Once

25. Ibid.: on church as monarchy, p. 4; on obligation for bishops to consult with the cathedral or parish clergy, pp. 67, 72; on absolute obedience owed by laypeople to bishops, pp. 38, 58; on majority of bishops with pope as infallible, pp. 14–15, 89.

26. Ibid.: on church councils and unanimity, pp. 14–15; on the criterion of the *cri du peuple*, p. 31; on the principle of the *coeur droit*, p. 34; and on Jean Claude's debate with Bossuet, p. 33.

27. Ibid., pp. 43, 47.

infallibility is attributed to the voice of the people, with the pope and the bishops subordinated to it, the temporal power of kings will with as little ceremony be subordinated to this same Tribunal, which is supposedly assisted directly by God and is the Repository of every kind of power. Also," he continued, "these writers have no more respected the Power of Kings than they have of Bishops; and they have dared to argue that temporal power as well as spiritual power resides in the entire Corps, inasmuch as the people are a part of it and are the possessors of its property. . . . It is thus," he concluded, quoting the relevant passages from La Borde and Le Gros, "that they play court to the people by giving them rights that they do not possess; all then belongs to the people; everything comes from God via the people; everything is the ministry of the people; the Church, Monarchy, Republic—everything is confounded by these reformers because they must do so lest the Constitution *[Unigenitus]* triumph by the suffrage of the Bishops."[28]

Thus did the Bishop of Soissons extract and publicize the political corollaries of the premises of his Jansenist foes, corollaries that might have lain latent and unperceived under less polemical pressure. So, too, did *Unigenitus* function as a metaphor for the French monarchy in the parlance of the bull's defenders and critics alike.

Some Events

The religious policy of the duc d'Orléans's regency government was at first conciliatory if not favorable to Jansenists. Orléans appointed the Archbishop of Paris, Antoine de Noailles, to the head of the new advisory *Conseil de conscience* (Ecclesiastical Council), where he kept company with Chancellor d'Aguesseau, the abbé Antoine Dorsanne, and the parlementary councillor René Pucelle—all of them, like Noailles, highly critical of *Unigenitus*. Bypassing the Jesuits for the first time since Henri IV, the regent appointed an ardent Gallican, the ecclesiastical historian and abbé Claude Fleury, as the young Louis XV's confessor, and went so far as to exile Louis XIV's former confessor Michel Le Tellier from the royal court. Encouraged by these signs, the Sorbonne elected a Jansenist syndic, Hyacinthe Ravachet, under whose aegis the faculty rescinded its allegedly forced acceptance of *Unigenitus,* as did the theological faculties of the universities of Nantes and Reims.[29] From the pope himself the regent tried to extract some "explanations" of *Unigenitus* and from his bishops a conciliatory "corps of doctrine" that he hoped would satisfy the Jansenist bishops and Sorbonne theologians without alienating either the papacy or the numerous acceptant or constitutionary

---

28. Ibid., pp. 51–52.
29. On the Sorbonne and *Unigenitus* see Gres-Gayer, *Théologie et pouvoir en Sorbonne.*

bishops who had unreservedly received the controversial bull.[30] But when Clement XI and the constitutionary bishops remained obdurate, four impatient Jansenist bishops—Colbert of Montpellier, De Langle of Boulogne, La Brou of Mirepoix, and Soanen of Senez—undertook their famous pilgrimage to the Sorbonne, where on 5 March 1717 they formally appealed *Unigenitus* to an ecumenical council. By March 1719 this appeal had won the adhesion of the theological faculties of the universities of Paris, Nantes, and Reims, several religious congregations, the cathedral clergy of Notre Dame de Paris, the cardinal-archbishop Antoine de Noailles, and three fourths of his diocese's 450 curés—all told, about one-tenth of the Catholic clergy of France. The regent's increasingly heavy-handed attempts at "accommodation" provoked a less massively subscribed "re-appeal" in 1720.[31]

In Paris, the presence of an archbishop favorable to Jansenism and hostile to Jesuits proved even more fertile for the development of parochial activity than had the absence of an archbishop during the religious Fronde some sixty years earlier. Even before his own ecumenical appeal—and as a means, perhaps, to prompt it—a collective witness or *témoignage* signed by 270 Parisian priests informed Noailles that, "pastors by divine right" laboring "under a Chief who knows not that spirit of domination so foreign to the mind of Christ, . . . we confidently give to ourselves . . . the quality of [Christ's] seventy-two disciples, and render according to our Order the witness that the Truth expects from us."[32] The Jansenist theologians Laurent Boursier and Lefebvre d'Eubonne's *Defense of the Paris Curés* and an anonymous *Dissertation on the Rights of the Curés* made the same point in the same year.[33] The point to laying claim to this biblical ancestry in Luke 10:2 was of course to prove that curés were not beholden for their sacerdotal powers to their bishops, and might therefore render an independent witness to the faith. And while the point might seem superfluous in Paris so long as Archbishop Noailles remained sympathetic to the appeal, it was otherwise in dioceses such as Mailly's Reims and Languet de Gergy's Soissons, where appellant priests were on the defensive and had already appealed their superiors' mandamuses to a sympathetic Parlement of Paris.

30. Georges Hardy, *Le cardinal de Fleury et le mouvement janséniste* (Paris, 1925), pp. 1–29; and Jean Carreyre, *Le jansénisme durant le Régence*, 3 vols. (Louvain, 1932), vol. 1.

31. Gabriel-Nicolas Nivelle, *Le cri de la foi, ou recueil des différents témoignages rendus par plusieurs facultés, chapitres, curés, communautés ecclésiastiques et réguliers au sujet de la Constitution Unigenitus*, 3 vols. (n.p., 1719). See also Marie-José Michel, "Clergé et pastorale jansénistes à Paris, 1669–1730," *RHMC* 27 (Apr.–June 1979):177–97.

32. *Le témoignage de MM. les curés du diocèse de Paris à son éminence Monseigneur le cardinal de Noailles* (n.p., 1771), pp. 2–3, as quoted in Carreyre, *Le jansénisme durant la Régence*, 1:124.

33. [Laurent Boursier and Lefebvre d'Eaubonne], *Apologie des curés du diocèse de Paris* (n.p., 1717); *Dissertation sur le droit des curés* (n.p., 1717). See also Du Saussoy, *La vérité rendue sensible à tout le monde*, 2 vols. (n.p., 1719); and Edmond Préclin, *Les jansénistes du dix-huitième siècle*, pp. 77–83.

The appellants needed all the help they could get because, coincident with the Declaration of 1724, which codified and hardened all the legislation against Protestants since the revocation of the Edict of Nantes, a new round of persecution began to afflict them in the 1720s. Whatever assurances the regent may initially have given to opponents of *Unigenitus* about a change in the monarchy's religious policies, he could not fail in the end to perceive that, like the Edict of Fontainebleau, *Unigenitus* had become a symbol of royal authority, and that opposition to the bull perforce posed a greater challenge to absolutism than the papacy or the reputedly ultramontanist Jesuits. Besides, the regent needed at least the papacy's benevolent neutrality in his government's brief war against Spain in 1718. Finally registered in a lit de justice assembly by a reluctant Parlement of Paris, the duc d'Orléans's accommodation of 1720 annulled the ecumenical appeals of 1717–19; and the more vulnerable of those who reappealed later the same year found themselves summarily exiled by lettres de cachet.[34] When in 1723 the ailing Claude Fleury resigned his position as the young king's confessor, Claude-Bertrand Taschereau de Linières, a Jesuit, took his place despite Archbishop Noailles's opposition. "Thus . . . have the Jesuits had the last laugh at his expense," noted the barrister Mathieu Marais in his diary, "and the [new] confessor will not fail to insinuate respect for the Pope and the Constitution *[Unigenitus]*."[35]

About the same time a royal declaration renewed the lapsed requirement for all candidates for academic degrees and ecclesiastical benefices to sign Pope Alexander VII's formulary condemning the five propositions reputedly extracted from Jansen's *Augustinus*. The principal promotor of this new anti-Jansenist campaign was the Bishop of Fréjus—and the king's tutor—André-Hercule de Fleury, who since 1720 had presided over the Council of Conscience, renamed the Ecclesiastical Committee.[36] This committee, which controlled episcopal appointments, now also seated the cardinals Rohan and de Bissy, some of France's most ardent constitutional bishops, prompting Marais to predict in 1720 that "we shall soon see the credit of the Jesuits rise higher than ever, and the triumph of their adversaries, which lasted just a few years, turn into dishonor and confusion."[37]

The regent's death in 1723 increased Fleury's influence over the young king during the brief first ministry of the duc de Bourbon. Bourbon's fall from royal

34. On the regency government's reversion to an anti-Jansenist ecclesiastical policy, see Carreyre, *Le jansénisme durant la Régence*, especially vol. 2, *La politique antijanséniste du Régent, 1718–1723*.

35. Mathieu Marais, *Journal et mémoires de Mathieu Marais avocat au parlement de Paris, 1715–1737*, ed. M. de Lescure, 4 vols. (Paris, 1863), 2:305–6. See also Edmond-Jean-François Barbier, *Chronique de la Régence et du règne de Louis XV (1718–1763), ou Journal de Barbier* (henceforth *Journal*), 8 vols. (Paris, 1857), 1:209–23.

36. On Fleury's ministry see in general Hardy, *Le cardinal de Fleury et le mouvement janséniste*; and Peter Campbell, "The Conduct of Politics in France in the Time of the Cardinal de Fleury" (Ph.D. diss., University of London, 1983).

37. Marais, *Journal et mémoires*, 1:486.

favor in June 1726 represented a victory for Fleury, who virtually ruled France with the king's consent as a kind of informal first minister in the years that followed. The strict application of the formulary of Alexander VII, plus Fleury's control over ecclesiastical appointments or what was called the *feuille des bénéfices*, would have eventually purged the clergy and the universities of most Jansenists in any case. But because that method was too slow for the eighty-year-old Fleury, his infamous cascade of about forty thousand lettres de cachet began descending on the heads of appellant individuals and institutions alike.[38] In dioceses with constitutionary bishops, recalcitrant members of parish and cathedral clergies found themselves almost immediately interdicted or summarily exiled, whether they held benefices or not. Appellants in dioceses with Jansenist bishops were temporarily more secure, except for the notorious case of Senez, where the appellant bishop Jean Soanen fell prey to an interdiction by the provincial Council of Embrun as early as 1727.[39] The controversy surrounding that council was the first episode in a growing religious and political crisis that culminated in the early 1730s.

But Paris presented the greatest challenge to Fleury's persecutory prowess, which initially took the form of wearing down the octogenarian archbishop Noailles's waning resistance to the authority of *Unigenitus*. The doddering archbishop finally died after retracting his appeal in 1728, making way for Charles-Gaspard-Guillaume de Vintimille, Fleury's handpicked successor over the capital see, and also for a constitutionary open season on the diocese's still largely Jansenist clergy.[40] With its personnel either purged or intimidated, the archiepiscopal court or officialité and the cathedral chapter registered the bull in quick succession, followed by the Sorbonne, from which Fleury, its new provisor, proceeded to expel about a hundred doctors by reason of their reappeal against *Unigenitus* or their protestations against the Council of Embrun.[41] Just as serious for the future of Jansenism's intellectual vitality and clerical recruitment was the closing or gutting of less obvious foyers of theological reflection. Fleury summarily replaced the Jansenist principal and regents of the College of Sainte-Barbe with priestly products of the Seminary of Saint-Sulpice, while he simply closed the doors of the Oratorian—and heavily Jansenist—Seminary of Saint-Magloire. Similarly nonirenic tactics were employed to obtain the submission to *Unigenitus* of such notoriously Jansenist religious congregations as the Benedictines of Saint-Maur and Saint-Vanne: that is, by systematic disenfranchisement of all appellant

38. For the estimate of forty thousand lettres de cachet see Cécile Gazier, *Histoire de la Société et de la Bibliothèque de Port-Royal* (Paris, 1966), p. 9.

39. Augustin Gazier, *Histoire générale du mouvement janséniste*, 2 vols. (Paris, 1924), 2:1–24.

40. *Nouvelles ecclésiastiques, ou mémoires pour servir à l'histoire de la constitution Unigenitus* (henceforth *NE*), 3d ed. (Utrecht, 1728–1803), 28 Oct.–3 Dec. 1728, pp. 219–23, 245–50.

41. *NE* 6–16 Dec. 1729, pp. 207–11, 216–21; and 21 Dec. 1730, p. 265.

members, after which the purged general assemblies duly rescinded the congregation's appeal.[42]

Hardest hit were Paris's parish priests, three-quarters of whom had appealed *Unigenitus*. The new archbishop began moderately, using the Edict of 1695 to deprive thirty nonbeneficed priests of the right to catechise, preach, or hear confessions. Paris's feisty beneficed clergy, who did not take lightly to this episcopal challenge to their right to appoint their own clerical subordinates, responded with illicit corporate conferences reminiscent of those employed during the religious Fronde, and with a series of consultations, requests, and letters that, deploring the bull and the "blind and lax" penitential theology of the Jesuits, gave vent to their Richerist pretensions at parochial autonomy. Vintimille then retaliated with the king's authorization, this time revoking the powers of about sixty priests and suspending five beneficed curés—those of Saint-Barthélemy, Mont-Valérien, Saint-Médard, Saint-Etienne-du-Mont, and La Vilette—from their functions.[43] The conflict continued to escalate, later centering on supposedly thaumaturgical miracles on behalf of Jansenist Truth and the archbishop's refusal to acknowledge them. At the conflict's apogee, the curés collectively remonstrated to the king and individually refused to publicize the archbishop's mandamuses and pastoral instructions, while Vintimille for his part continued to interdict and exile priests on all sides, eventually disabling about three hundred of them.[44]

Richerism, Figurism, and Miracles

Victimized by Vintimille's assault on the appellant priests in Paris and its counterparts elsewhere in France, Jansenists compensated for their political powerlessness with doctrinal audacity. In their thought about the church, that audacity took the form of a radical Gallicanism or Richerism evident in exemplary form in the anonymous *Memorandum on the Rights of the Second Order*, which appeared in 1733. Its author was in fact Nicolas Le Gros, the same Le Gros who had written *Du renversement des libertés de l'église gallicane* in 1717, and his *Mémoire* testifies to the distance traversed since that time. While the Le Gros of *Du renversement* wrote as a Remois canon, the Le Gros of the *Mémoire* wrote as an exile in the Nether-

42. On these developments, see in general Hardy, *Le cardinal de Fleury et le mouvement janséniste*, pp. 173–78; and B. Robert Kreiser, *Miracles, Convulsions, and Ecclesiastical Politics in Early Eighteenth-Century Paris* (Princeton, N.J., 1978), pp. 59–65. On the closing of Saint-Magloire, *NE* 28 Nov. 1729, p. 205; and on purging of Sainte-Barbe, ibid., 26 Oct. 1730, pp. 225–32; on acceptance of *Unigenitus* by Benedictines of Saint-Vanne, ibid., 26 May 1730, p. 105; and by Saint-Maur, ibid., 29 June 1730, 138–40.

43. On the interdiction of confessors see *NE* 2 Apr. 1730, pp. 61–70; on destitution of five curés, ibid., 9 Oct. 1730 and 17 Nov. 1730, pp. 218–19, 243–44; and on their replacements, ibid., 21 Dec. 1730, pp. 266–67.

44. Hardy, *Le cardinal de Fleury et le mouvement janséniste*, pp. 78–85; and Kreiser, *Miracles, Convulsions, and Ecclesiastical Politics*, pp. 115–39.

lands. And whereas the Le Gros of *Du renversement* had defended the Gallican clergy and tradition against *Unigenitus* and Rome, the Le Gros of the *Mémoire* defended appellant priests and even the lay faithful against the "Gallican" bishops. More than in *Du renversement*, then, Le Gros appealed to the lay and clerical witness so dear to La Borde; indeed, Le Gros's *Mémoire* represents a synthesis between his own radical or conciliar Gallicanism and La Borde's laicism.[45]

The *Mémoire* began conservatively enough by admitting that bishops alone were both "judges" and "witnesses" to the faith, while priests and laypeople were at best witnesses to it. That is to say that, successor though he was of the seventy-two disciples sent out by Christ to preach, the priest might only "ascertain and report on what is believed and has always been believed," while the bishop and bishop alone also "decides by the law of the faith what ought to be believed."[46] Yet just about everything else in the *Mémoire* seems to subvert and undermine this basic distinction, as well as the portrait of the bishop as someone who might legitimately "menace" and "anathematize." The engine of this exercise in deconstruction was a principle and a practice: the practice, that of Christian antiquity, when the term *priest* had been used to designate priests and bishops alike; the principle, that the sacrament of ordination conferred the same sacerdotal power to bind and to loose on priest and bishop alike, the main difference being the extent of canonical jurisdiction. Once introduced about a quarter of the way through the *Mémoire*, this principle and putative practice provoked consequences that all but buried the original distinction between bishop and priest.[47]

On the one hand, it turned out that in Le Gros's vocabulary episcopal judging was not different from witnessing after all. Even while away from his diocese attending a national or ecumenical council, a bishop represented only his own church and could "judge" only according to its "witness." "It is by means of [her bishop] that this church judges, but it is for her, with her, and conformably to the faith she professes, and to the counsels she has given him, that he ought to judge."[48] When at home, the bishop was if anything even more bound to the witness of his clergy, for what kind of judge—here came the inevitable judicial analogy—judged without "listening to the parties, to the barristers, to the witnesses, or the gens du roi on the cases that come before them?" Thus the case for diocesan synods and a regular "concert in government," without which, far from the "spirit of peace, charity, humility, and wisdom that ought to animate all pastors," the bishop would display a "spirit of domination" more appropriate to

45. On the authorship of this pamphlet and its relation to the earlier Le Gros as well as to La Borde's ecclesiology, see Préclin's always helpful *Les jansénistes du dix-huitième siècle*, pp. 138–41.

46. [Nicolas Le Gros], *Mémoire sur les droits du second ordre du clergé: Avec la tradition qui prouve les droits du second ordre* ("en France," 1733), pp. 3, 8.

47. Ibid., p. 20.

48. Ibid., pp. 30–31.

an "absolute government," even a "despotism."[49] On the other hand, the seemingly passive role of witnessing proved susceptible in Le Gros's vocabulary of no
little activity of its own, including that of actively protesting against episcopal
decisions and pastoral instructions. For "if the Bishop fails in his duty, it is for the
priest to raise his voice, whether in place of [the bishop's] if he keeps silent, or
against [the bishop's] if he combats the truth." As Le Gros's *Mémoire* proceeded,
priests increasingly peopled his ecumenical councils as judges as much as did
bishops, since "Scripture does not appear to restrict the authority to judge doctrine
to [bishops alone]." To the contrary, curés had sometimes governed whole dioceses in the absence of bishops, notably, Le Gros perversely recalled, in post-
Fronde Paris in the absence of the cardinal de Retz.[50]

Like the Parisian curés, Le Gros drew less inspiration from Edmond Richer
than from Jean Gerson and the late medieval "doctors of Paris." (Indeed, the term
Richerism is something of a misnomer for the ecclesiology in question: the
Nantese priest Nicolas Travers, whose monumental *Legitimate Powers of the First
and Second Orders* Edmond Préclin considered exemplary in the genre, failed to
cite Richer in more than seven hundred pages, taking his cues instead, as did Le
Gros, from "Pierre d'Ailly, [Jean] Gerson, Jean Major, and the old Theologians
of Paris.")[51] And, as in his earlier *Le renversement*, Le Gros's use of the conciliar
legacy in the *Mémoire* was not restricted to the church and was not without
antiabsolutist point or implication. For Jehovah's anger in response to Israel's
request for a king was "figurative," explained Le Gros, "and gives us to understand that one of the greatest evils for the church—and the source of all others—
would be to witness the substitution of an absolutist government for that of the
judges who governed in common according to the holy Canons."[52] That those
judges might still be secular judges as well as clerical ones Le Gros made clear by
calling for a lay witness to the faith in case of priestly prevarication, that of the
secular magistrates in the first place but of "even the people" in the event that the
magistrates failed in their duty.[53] And if, as Le Gros well knew, the monarchy was
on the side of the prevaricating bishops, he hardly needed to specify that the
priests, magistrates, and people had to oppose the king as well.

Alas, not even judicial allies would prove very helpful until after 1750, by
which time Le Gros himself had died. In the absence of effective protection from

49. For judicial analogy, ibid., pp. 24–25; for description of ideal governance of church as opposed
to "despotism," ibid., pp. 36, 78–79.

50. On priests' active witness see ibid., pp. 23, 44; on priests as judges in ecumenical councils, etc.,
ibid., pp. 60, 70; for reference to Fronde, ibid., p. 73.

51. Ibid., pp. 13–15; Nicolas Travers, *Les pouvoirs légitimes du premier et du second ordre, dans
l'administration des sacremens, et le gouvernement de l'église* ("en France," 1744), p. 306. See also pp. 301,
387–91.

52. [Le Gros], *Mémoire sur les droits,* p. 79.

53. Ibid., p. 23.

either the parlements or Richerist ecclesiology, Jansenist curés consoled themselves with a theology that, assimilating that ecclesiology, featured themselves and
their lay parishioners as a faithful remnant of witnesses to Christian truth in a
period of prophesied trouble, obscurity, and defection by the "Gentiles." In part a
hermeneutics of biblical prophecy, figurism, as this theology was known, held that
Holy Scripture had foretold this period of *Unigenitus*-engendered apostasy, nowhere more clearly than in Saint Paul's eleventh chapter to the Romans, which
also prophesied that this apostasy would precede the return of the prophet Elijah
and the massive conversion of the Jews to Christianity. This conversion would be
followed not by the return of Christ and his thousand-year reign as in Puritan
millenial eschatology but by a period of unprecedented expansion of Christianity.
Only after a final apostasy would Christ return and the apocalypse occur. Meanwhile, Christ's promise never to abandon his church meant not that the ecclesial
hierarchy or even the majority of its members would always remain faithful to the
Truth, but only that the church would always contain a visible witness to the truth,
be it that of a persecuted minority during transitional "times of trouble." It was
this theology of witness that underlay La Borde's témoignage and that made some
sense of the otherwise impractical appeal of *Unigenitus* to a general council in
1717. As one of the architects of both this theology and the appeal, the abbé Le
Sesne de Ménilles d'Etemare, explained in his memoirs, "It was not essential for
[Christ's] promises to the Church that there be an appeal. What was alone
essential is that the Church contain opponents of the Constitution *[Unigenitus]*."[54]

Although elaborated by a small and quasi-conspiratorial group of theologians–d'Etemare, Jacques-Joseph Duguet, Laurent-François Boursier–closely
associated with the Oratorian Seminary of Saint-Magloire, this figuratist theology of faithful witness to truth in "troubled and obscure times" did not effect so
sharp a break with classic Jansenism as has been commonly supposed, as any
careful reading of Arnauld's preface to his *La fréquente communion* or Pascal's
reflections on "figures" in his *Pensées* will reveal. For figurism remained above all
a theology of grace. The chief elements of continuity are the catastrophic conception of the fall into sin, the consequent hiddenness of God, and the valorization of
human history as the scene and medium of grace. At the center of this history lay,
of course, the Christic mysteries of the incarnation and atonement. But in contrast
to the more optimistic Bérulle and his orthodox Oratorian disciples for whom

54. Quoted in Catherine-Laurence Maire, "L'église et la nation: Du dépôt de la vérité au dépôt des
lois. La trajectoire janséniste au XVIIIe siècle," *Annales* 46 (Sept.–Oct. 1991):1177–1205. I am much
indebted to the work of Maire on the subject of figurism as well as on the convulsionary phenomenon. See
also her *Les convulsionaires de Saint-Médard: Miracles, convulsions et propheties à Paris au XVIII siècle*,
Collection Archives (Paris, 1981). Figurism's founding treatise was arguably Jacques-Joseph Duguet's
Règles pour l'intelligence des Ecritures (Paris, 1716), but one of its clearest expositions is Jean-Baptiste de
Fourquevaux's *Introduction abrégé à l'intelligence des prophéties de l'Ecriture, par l'usage qu'en fait Saint Paul
dans l'Epitre aux Romains* (n.p., 1731).

these mysteries exemplified the timeless relations between Christ and God the Father, Jansenists as Augustinians saw them as the historical forms or sensible figures of grace to which fallen believers were limited. And while in contrast to equally Augustinian Protestants, for whom divine hiddenness spelled an invisible church and the opacity of history's vicissitudes, Jansenists as Catholics tied a visible church and its witness to these very vicissitudes. The result was a conception of grace that, as periodically manifested in history, at once enlightened the pure of heart and blinded the hard of heart, as well as a conception of the church as the body of Christ that found itself condemned—or rather predestined—indefinitely to reenact or "refigure" the world's rejection of Christ in historical time.[55]

This theology was obviously well adapted to the Jansenists' situation as a persecuted minority within a church from which, as Catholics, they refused to regard themselves as excommunicated. But that adaption did not prevent figurism from attaining wide and even popular diffusion or from affecting everything it touched. Not only did figurism employ the conciliar appeal for its own purposes but, as is evident in the case of Le Gros, it reoriented the Richerist tradition, using the clerical second order and its putative rights as means to further the witness to truth despite episcopal apostasy and despotism. Figurism also inflected the articulation of parlementary constitutionalism. La Borde's *Du témoignage de la vérité*, for example, bore precocious witness not only to the judicial world's imprint on Jansenist theology but also prefigured that theology's reciprocal ability to recast the secular role of magistrates and barristers as faithful witnesses to constitutional truth. But figurism, as La Borde's treatise shows, featured a prominent role for laypeople in doctrinal disputes as well. For if to render a "judgment of authority in matters of faith" was the prerogative of the clergy alone, as the abbé d'Etemare explained, the right to give a "judgment of discernment"—that is, a witness to the faith—belonged to "all the lay faithful" without exception.[56] Giving ample scope to the witness of laypeople, figurism also attached cosmic importance to the secular event. Although figuratist millenialism was less precise than Puritanism's about time, prudently postponing Christ's second coming into an indefinite future, it was for that reason better adapted to the eighteenth century's more open-ended sense of time. Its immediate impact motivated Jansenists to become the century's journalistic commentators par excellence on the news of the day—what contemporaries called *les affaires du temps*. In the longer run and in secularized form, figurism may well have issued into the hermeneutics of the revolutionary event or *journée*, which would similarly be a day of grace for the pure of heart and of judgment for those who were not.

55. This paragraph owes much to Ephraim Louis Radner's "A Pneumatological Investigation of the Miracles of Saint-Médard and their Rejection" (Ph.D. diss., Yale University, 1994).

56. Quoted in Maire, "L'église et la nation," 1181–82. D'Etemare's still manuscript "Souvenirs" are located in the Bibliothèque municipale de Troyes, Ms. 2170.

In the 1720s and 1730s the Saint-Magloire theological bureau's attempt to create a lay witness and to interpret events took the form of hundreds of books and pamphlets that, like the famous *Hexaples,* translated the terms of the theological debate into accessible French and invited the lay faithful to judge—or at least witness—for themselves. It was in view of furthering that oppositional lay witness that some of these same appellant theologians—Boursier, d'Etemare, Poncet des Essarts—masterminded the publication of the eight-page periodical called *Nouvelles ecclésiastiques, ou mémoires pour servir à l'histoire de la bulle Unigenitus (Ecclesiastical News, or Memoirs Toward the History of the Bull Unigenitus)* in the wake of Bishop Soanen's condemnation by the Council of Embrun in 1727. Well adapted to the "times of trouble and obscurity" that it chronicled, the *Nouvelles ecclésiastiques* was a precocious model of clandestine publication, impudently thumbing its nose at the Edict of 1723, which had just codified and reinforced the monarchy's efforts to control the press.[57] The journal's editorial directorate structured itself in parallel distributional chains, all of them descending from a single principal author-editor through multiple correspondents and printers down to peddlers at street level. The result was that the breaking of one chain by the police would leave the others unaffected, and that a minute's tardiness on the part of any one human link in a given chain would immediately alert the next link to an impending arrest and the need to repair to a designated refuge. The scheme was successful, for the occasional arrest of small-fries, as the curé of Saint-Gervais reportedly explained to Cardinal Noailles, served only to "pique the [public's] curiosity without remedying the evil, seeing that the *Nouvelles* still always appears."[58] A precursor of consistently ideological—even revolutionary—journalism, the *Nouvelles ecclésiastiques* was in 1728 also perforce political news, and artfully wove diverse and anecdotal evidence into a seamless indictment of despotism in both church and state.[59]

Invoking a lay witness and eliciting a "public outcry" were also forms of appealing to public opinion. Although it is as a tour de force of clandestine publication that the Jansenist weekly has attracted the bulk of historical attention, the journal is perhaps even more noteworthy as a pioneering venture in adversarial journalism. To be sure, the quest for the beginnings of "public opinion" in absolutist France, whether as a political force or a rhetorical appeal, has been an elusive one. In one form or another these beginnings must surely be sought in the sixteenth-century religious reformations and the simultaneous appearance of print culture. So far as French Jansenism is concerned, that appeal may be said to

57. For full bibliographical data see note 40.
58. BA: AB, Ms. 10159, fols. 32, 26–27, Jan. 1729.
59. Françoise Bontoux, "Paris janséniste au dix-huitième siècle: Les *Nouvelles ecclésiastiques, Mémoires de la Fédération des sociétés historiques et archéologiques de Paris et de l'Ile de France* 7 (1955), 205–20. See also Barbier, *Journal,* 2:211, 231.

have begun the day that Pascal penned his first provincial letter after his friend Antoine Arnauld lost his case in the Sorbonne. At roughly the same time that the *Nouvelles ecclésiastiques* first appeared, moreover, both the marquis d'Argenson and the abbé de Saint-Pierre were busily trying to rethink the legitimations of Bourbon absolutism so as to make it more open to—even dependent upon—something like enlightened public opinion.[60]

Yet there is nothing either before or at the time quite so explicit or programmatic as the *Nouvelles ecclésiastiques'* call to arms in its inaugural issue on 1 January 1728. Whereas the "ordinary lay faithful," explained the anonymous editors, may heretofore have thought that the disputes about *Unigenitus* "concerned only opposing schools of thought better left to Theologians to fight over and unbecoming for simple laypeople to take part in," the Council of Embrun's recent condemnation of the Bishop of Senez had dramatically changed all that. "In such circumstances," asked the editors, "how could one do better than to find a means by which to place the facts [of this case] before the eyes of the Public?" Whence "this little writing entitled the *Nouvelles ecclésiastiques,*" they continued, which proposed "to bring back [to the side of] the Appellants any number of persons prejudiced against them in good faith, to excite the multitude now submerged in insensitivity to the afflictions of the church, and to make everybody attentive to the events that ought to interest them." The editors were prepared, they said, "to be accused of lying, etc.," but "the Public, to which we now defer the cause of the Appellants (all the other Tribunals having been closed to them) will [surely] judge in our favor, and be convinced of our sincerity by the evidence of facts that only deceitfulness can deny."[61]

This systematic appeal to the public was anything but merely formal or abstract. On the one hand, the *Nouvelles ecclésiastiques* dramatically directed its putative "public" toward those people and institutions it was supposed to endorse and pitted it against those it was to oppose. Among those so honored were the barristers and magistrates of the Parlement of Paris. The *Nouvelles ecclésiastiques* not only printed some of the barristers' legal consultations and magistrates' remonstrances but named the names of its magisterial heroes in the parlementary debates, sometimes to the considerable chagrin of those named but always to the detriment of absolutist politics.[62] Among the vilified were the Jesuits and the Paris general lieutenant of police René Hérault de Fontaine. Their vain attempts to

60. On the French monarchy's relation to public opinion during the Regency, see Thomas Kaiser, "The Abbé de Saint-Pierre, Public Opinion, and the Reconstruction of the French monarchy," *JMH* 55 (Dec. 1983):618–43; and "Money, Despotism, and Public Opinion in Early Eighteenth-Century France: John Law and the Debate on Royal Credit," *JMH* 63 (Mar. 1991):1–28.

61. *NE* 1 Jan. 1728, p. 2.

62. For evidence of the unhappiness of magistrates at having their opinions and actions in the Parlement publicized by the Jansenist journal, see BA: AB, Ms. 10170, fol. 309, undated.

penetrate the secret of the publication of the *Nouvelles ecclésiastiques* provided no end of copy for the hunted journal, which meticulously pilloried them in its pages. On the other hand, the *Nouvelles ecclésiastiques,* as Arlette Farge has recently urged, put faces on the "public" and words into its mouth. A domestic servant, for example, arrested and interrogated by Hérault for being in communication with some Jansenist priests in the Seminary of Saint-Magloire, "responded to everything," according to the journal, "according to his conscience, while Monsieur Hérault found out nothing from him, except perhaps that even the lowliest stations harbor sincere and Christian souls whose fidelity is a match for the most odious inquisition."[63] When a poor wagoner from Rouen named Martin Baudrier was arrested and put on display in Paris's place de Grève for having helped distribute one of the Jansenist pastoral instructions of Bishop Soanen of Senez, the *Nouvelles ecclésiastiques* devoted an entire issue to the incident, doting on the details of the scene in the place de Grève, naming Baudrier "the first martyr of the constitution *[Unigenitus],*" and recording the reactions of the sympathetic "menu peuple."[64]

The *Nouvelles ecclésiastiques* also found—indeed, even created—its own public. When in May 1732, according to a police observer, the recently appointed curé of the profoundly Jansenist parish of Saint-Jacques-du-Haut-Pas tried to read Archbishop Vintimille's mandamus against the *Nouvelles ecclésiastiques* at the time of his homily, the entire congregation stumbled noisily out of the church, leaving the curé to listen to himself. Amplifying the effect, the *Nouvelles ecclésiastiques* did not miss the opportunity to publicize the incident, along with similar ones in the parishes of Saint-Benoît, Saint-Médard, Saint-Etienne-du-Mont, Saint-Jacques-de-la-Boucherie, and still others.[65] A low price of about six sols per issue and a relatively high circulation of about six thousand copies explain in part how the journal found is way into the hands of so many parishioners in Saint-Jacques-du-Haut-Pas and elsewhere.[66]

But the printed word was far from the only means of figuratist communication. Open conferences held in such seminaries and colleges as Saint-Magloire and Sainte-Barbe spread the figuratist good news to Jansenist curés, who in turn employed figuratist catechists and occasional preachers in their parish churches. Amid the crush of contemporary police reports testifying to the extent and intensity of popular Jansenism, the fear and resentment by Parisians of being deprived of their appellant priests and curés stands out as a key component. "All are saying as usual"—so reads such a report dated 28 July 1729—"that to all

63. *NE* 14 Dec. 1729, p. 215.
64. Ibid., 27 Feb. 1730, pp. 41–44.
65. BA: AB, Ms. 10161, fol. 272, 12 May 1732. See also *NE* 21 May 1732, pp. 97–100.
66. Bontoux, "Paris janséniste au XVIIIe siècle," pp. 219–20.

appearances Cardinal Fleury is intent on provoking an uprising in the capital of the realm, and they suppose that that will happen if he carries out his designs against the curés of Paris, seeing, they add, that three-fourths of the inhabitants of this city are Jansenists without knowing it, and will readily sacrifice themselves for their pastors." As to Vintimille, the new archbishop of Paris, Parisians thought that "he will be well advised to avoid getting involved in the affairs of the constitution [Unigenitus] when he gets here," reported the same agent a couple of weeks later, "because for as little as he might wish to pester the appellants, Jansenists . . . will pop up from beneath the paving stones–the expression they use to indicate that three-quarters of Paris are infected with that doctrine." Although obviously bourgeois "principal parishioners" figure prominently on the rare occasions that the omnipresent and anonymous "they" are specified in these reports, charcoal burners, street porters, stevedores, port hands, water carriers, "mesdames the herringwives" and other "dregs of the people" also put in appearances. It was charcoal burners from the port de la Grève, for example, who went to the archiepiscopal residence to tell Vintimille that "if he tried to vex their curé he would have to deal with them."[67]

It was one such appellant clergyman, the deacon François de Pâris, whose death in the parish of Saint-Médard and burial in the parish church cemetery gave rise to his popular canonization and the infamous rash of thaumaturgical miracles at the site of his tomb in the same years that witnessed the birth of the *Nouvelles ecclésiastiques*. These thaumaturgical miracles began innocently enough, as local residents clutched at the hair, toenails, clothes, furniture–any relic of a neighbor who had died "in the odor of sanctity" after having lived a life of charitable devotion and ascetic self-denial. For Jansenist observers of these miraculous events, the deacon's identity as an appellant made his posthumous miracles so many witnesses to truth and figures of grace, which, even if–or especially be-cause–they failed to convince the ecclesiastical hierarchy, separated the pure from the hard of heart and refigured Christ's rejection by the Jewish scribes and Pharisees. But even "the greater number," according to a police observer, re-garded the thaumaturgical miracles "as a prodigy and as evidence that God is manifesting himself overtly in favor of the appellants of the bull *Unigenitus*."[68] No doubt many artisans internalized this meaning and became Jansenists of sorts, as evidenced by the prayers on behalf of the "troubled" church uttered by many of them while seeking cures. It was the miracles of Saint-Médard at least as much as the *Nouvelles ecclésiastiques* and the identification of parishioners with their exiled

---

67. Quotation from BA: AB, Ms. 10160, fol. 130, 13 Oct. 1729. See also ibid., fols. 93, 110, 26 and 31 Oct. 1729; and Ms. 10158, fols. 237–38, 248, 25 and 29 Oct. 1728.

68. BA: AB, Ms. 10163, fol. 262, 18 June 1733.

and interdicted curés that gave the appellant cause a genuinely popular constituency.[69]

But as the miracles proliferated and the merely curious became a crowd, the phenomenon took a bizarre turn in the autumn of 1731. A partially lame abbé named Bescherand arrived in Paris from his native Montpellier and settled into a schedule of twice-daily pilgrimages to the cemetery, where, far from getting cured, he experienced spasmodic writhings and theatrical levitations accompanied by groaning, shrieking, and occasional foaming at the mouth. These convulsions, as they were soon called, proved contagious for many, becoming in the end an end in themselves and rivaling thaumaturgical miracles at the center of the cemetery. The convulsions also gave the monarchy a plausible reason for closing the cemetery, after which the convulsions moved to closed seances indoors, where they grouped mainly lay "brothers" and "sisters," some of whom experienced involuntary muscular convulsions while others administered help ("secours") in the form of blows ("coups") to counteract them.[70] Not even the convulsionary phase of the Saint-Médard episode, however, erased the signature of figurist theology. For within the widely diffused system of figurist meaning, the convulsive movements symbolized or figured the true church and the truth in a period of apostasy, the blows represented the persecutions that these endured, while the apparent invulnerability of the convulsed persons to the blows they received *prefigured* the eventual triumph of the truth. As this scheme suggests, the convulsionary phenomenon was not without prophetic and apocalyptic overtones made more explicit by verbal discourses that often accompanied or sometimes took the place of bodily convulsions. Often uttered by illiterate artisans, many of them women, and recorded by curés or barristers, these discourses typically railed against *Unigenitus*, lamented the interdiction of appellant curés, bewailed the apostasy of the hierarchical church, described the sins of "Gentility," and sometimes prophesied the destruction of "Babylon," the return of the prophet Elijah, and the conversion of the Jews.[71]

No amount of scholarship is likely entirely to dissipate the opprobrium that came to cover the Saint-Médard miracles and their convulsionary sequels. They committed the unpardonable offense of occurring in Paris just as the rising sun of the French Enlightenment began to dispel belief in the miraculous and trust in "enthusiasm"—and of scandalizing a young poet and graduate of the Jesuit Col-

69. Maire, *Les convulsionnaires de Saint-Médard*, pp. 1–99; and Daniel Vidal, *Miracles et convulsions jansénistes au XVIIIe siècle: Le mal et sa connaissance* (Paris, 1987), pp. 1–182. For the political and ecclesiastical context of the affair, Kreiser's *Miracles, Convulsions, and Ecclesiastical Politics* remains essential.

70. Kreiser, *Miracles, Convulsions, and Ecclesiastical Politics*, pp. 140–275.

71. By far the best analysis of the convulsionary phenomenon from the inside is Maire's *Les convulsionaires de Saint-Médard*, pp. 103–250, on which this analysis is mainly dependent.

lege of Louis-Le-Grand named Voltaire, whose own brother was a devotee of Pâris's posthumous miracles. Thereafter the Saint-Médard episode stood permanently between Jansenism and the French Enlightenment, disrupting the kind of gradual transition from religious dissent to Newtonian lights so typical of the radical Whiggish Opposition in Georgian England, of the alliance between Lutheran Pietism and the early *Aufklärung* in the Germanies, and of what was alternately called Jansenism and *luces* in Spain.[72] The parting of the paths between Jansenism and the early Enlightenment is visible in the memoirs of the barrister Mathieu Marais. Until the late 1720s, he somehow managed to admire the "excellent" Pierre Bayle and the "consummate" Voltaire while being quite partial toward Jansenism, regarding the Jansenist cause as that of "the faith and the truth," and expecting the first miracles to convert Voltaire. But as the political crisis deepened and the miracles multiplied and gave way to convulsions, this balancing act became harder for Marais, as he refused to sign his Jansenist colleagues' consultations, described the convulsions irreverently, and found Voltaire guilty of Jansenism as well as atheism.[73]

Not even the Enlightenment's bias, however, should obscure the sense in which the Saint-Médard affair threw down the gauntlet at the feet of the absolute monarchy and its dependent episcopacy. In a manner reminiscent not in this instance of antisacral Protestantism but of the sixteenth-century Catholic Parisian League—and with a similar social constituency—these thaumaturgical and reliquary miracles in defense of an appeal against a symbol of absolutism implicitly challenged French kingship's knack at getting monarchical mileage from the miraculous.[74] Even Leaguelike penitential processions were undertaken. One of the first appellant miracles, that of Madame La Fosse in 1725, occurred in a procession of the Holy Sacrament that had been consecrated and borne by the appellant curé of Saint-Barthélemy; when they first heard of it, both the *jansénisant* barrister Marais and his anti-Jansenist colleague Edmond-Jean-François Barbier thought that the miracle would serve to "confound the Protestants."[75] Not taking the challenge lightly, the monarchy closed the cemetery of Saint-Médard in January 1732, but the king's opposition did not prevent processions from "contin-

72. Dale Van Kley, "Piety and Politics in the Century of Lights," in the new *Cambridge History of Eighteenth-Century Political Thought* (Cambridge, forthcoming).

73. Marais, *Journal et mémoires*. On the Jansenist cause, 1:503; on "excellent" Bayle, 3:30, 371; on Voltaire, 3:89, 4:332.

74. Lionel Rothkrug, "From Sanctity and Heresy to Virtue and Corruption: The Ideological Backgrounds to the French Revolution," paper presented at a session entitled "Mort et vertu sous l'Ancien Régime et la Révolution / Modes of Death and Ideologies of Virtue in the Ancien Regime and the Revolution" for the thirty-second annual meeting of the Society for French Historical Studies in Québec City, 21 Mar. 1986.

75. The quotation is from Marais, *Journal et mémoires*, 3:192; see also Barbier, *Journal*, 1:390–92, 404.

ually taking place along the route to that church nor that church from being always filled with persons devoted to M. de Pâris."[76]

Coming after the closing of the Jansenist seminaries and colleges, the closing of the cemetery of Saint-Médard nonetheless spelled the defeat of figurism as theology and the beginning of the end of clerical Jansenism as such. The convulsionary movement itself split into numbers of sects while Jansenist theologians for their part publicly disagreed on the subject; Bidal d'Asfeld, Gabriel Nivelle, and Nicolas Petitpied repudiated the whole phenomenon against Boursier, d'Etemare, and the editors of the *Nouvelles ecclésiastiques* who defended parts of it.[77] The hard-pressed Jansenist cause could ill afford these internal divisions, which Cardinal Fleury did not fail to exploit, going so far as to subsidize the writings of Petitpied and the anticonvulsionary party. These and other divisions within the Jansenist ranks also lent plausibility to the accusation of crypto-Protestantism, reflecting as they did the Catholic image of Protestantism as a series of self-invalidating schisms and variations. So, too, for that matter, did the convulsions themselves. For the phenomenon of convulsive muscular movements accompanied by prophetic discourse on the part of laypeople in an antiabsolutist cause bore at least a superficial resemblance to the prophetic utterances of the Protestant Camisards of the Cevennes, who, just a few decades earlier, had accompanied their armed revolt with prophecies of the imminent restoration of Protestant worship or, failing that, the end of the world.[78] The similarity was not lost on some Parisians. "It is said that there is a new sedition or uprising in the Sevennes [sic] for reasons of religion," a police observer reported Parisians as saying in 1728, "and that a party has been formed to come to the aid of the Jansenists."[79] To the extent that Jansenist reaction to Fleury's persecution might have actually made the movement more Protestant, the figurist venture would have failed in its principal aim of defining a place for Jansenism within Catholicism.

Toward Protestantism

Convulsions and Camisards may have been the most recent association linking Jansenism and Calvinism in the collective memory of Parisians in the late 1720s and early 1730s, but it was far from the most traumatic. As a largely Jansenist Paris lost the protection of Cardinal Noailles and as the possibility of persecution by Fleury and Noailles's successor loomed ever larger, memories flew back to the

76. BA: AB, Ms. 10161, fol. 68, 30 Jan. 1732.

77. Kreiser, *Miracles, Convulsions, and Ecclesiastical Politics,* pp. 341–51.

78. Philippe Joutard, *La légende des camisards: Une sensibilité au passé* (Paris, 1977), pp. 1–48; and *Les camisards,* Collection Archives (Paris, 1976).

79. BA: AB, Ms. 10158, fols. 266–67, 4 Nov. 1728.

seventeenth and even sixteenth centuries and the wars of religion–with this difference, however, that it would be most Parisians and their curés, mainstays of sacral monarchy in the sixteenth century, who would be the objects of any "second Saint Bartholomew's Day," such as a Jesuit reportedly called for in 1728.[80] Thus did Jansenism maintain its Janus-like character, its curious capacity to evoke the ghosts of both Protestantism and the Catholic League.

No sooner, for example, had Noailles officially accepted *Unigenitus* in the autumn of 1728 than rumors began to circulate that if Paris's appellant curés did not accept it too, "they will be declared schismatic and chased from the realm as was once done to the Protestants."[81] In the spring and summer of 1729 the conflict between the constitutionary bishop of Orléans and his Jansenist curés and parishioners echoed in Paris in the form of the rumor that "all the wars of religion have begun in the city of Orléans under the past reigns" and that, even if things did not come to that, the affair "would do more damage to the [Catholic] religion than Calvinism did at its beginning."[82] By the height of the religious and political crisis in 1732, Parisian rumors were associating Jansenism and Protestantism even more closely, saying that the appellant curés and their parishioners "have the Protestants in their party, Lutheran as well as Calvinist, and that if [the government] puts the iron to the fire against them (these are the terms that are used), the war will be much worse than those that Louis XIV fought to extirpate heresy from his Realm."[83]

The references to heresy and to damage done to Catholicism do not indicate a global hostility to Protestantism on the part of Parisian opinion. On the contrary, many of the remarks recorded by Lieutenant General Herault's agents in the streets hint at a certain appropriation of the tragic history of French Protestantism by popular Parisian Jansenism, which, perhaps persuaded by the experience of persecution, pointed toward Jansenist-Protestant entente. In a sense, such a rapprochement was scripted after *Unigenitus* made it objectively more difficult for Jansenists to have their Jansenism and their Catholicism too. For whereas Arnauld and Nicole and their immediate successors had plausibly argued that the papal bull *Cum occasione* had not condemned authentically Jansenist doctrines taken from Jansen's *Augustinus,* that very Catholic tactic rang less true after *Unigenitus* had condemned clearly Jansenist doctrines articulated in language verifiably extracted from Quesnel's *Réflexions morales*–had condemned, by Jansenist reckoning, the truth itself. Although no such rapprochement took place on a political level until the 1750s, some of the propos recorded by the police paralleled developments

80. BA: AB, Ms. 10158, fols. 135–36, 1 Sept. 1728.
81. BA: AB, Ms. 10158, fol. 292, 15 Nov. 1728.
82. BA: AB, Ms. 10159, fols. 100, 272, 3 Apr. and 9 Aug. 1729.
83. BA: AB, Ms. 10161, fol. 254, 3–4 May 1732.

internal to Jansenism that, visible in controversies pitting Jansenists against other Jansenists, are hard to interpret otherwise than in a Protestantizing sense.

One such contemporary controversy had to do with the proper proportions of "fear" and "confidence" in the penitent's progress toward salvation.[84] In the background of this controversy lay the Calvinist doctrines that one was justified by faith alone and that one so justified necessarily persevered to the end. As rigidly defined by the reformed Synod of Dordrecht in 1618, these doctrines struck Catholics schooled in the Tridentine doctrine of justification as a recipe for the most unjustified presumption and unmerited confidence. And far from distancing themselves from other Catholics in this polemic, Jansenists like Antoine Arnauld and Pierre Nicole had taken the lead in it, in the process proving the "orthodoxy" of their own Augustinianism against their Jesuit nemeses. The clinching argument of Arnauld's nine hundred–page polemic against the decisions of Dordrecht was that the Calvinist doctrine of the perseverance of the saints undermined fear and gave rise to a "false assurance" of salvation, proving that the "supposed Reformation of the Calvinists, far from being a work of the Holy Spirit, can only be regarded as the work of the demon."[85]

In the light of this legacy, the mere fact of controversy on the subject within the eighteenth-century Jansenist theological community is significant. That that development spelled a step in a Protestant direction is amply borne out by the appearance of Pavie de Fourquevaux's *Treatise on Confidence* in 1731, no matter its protestations to the contrary. To be sure, Fourquevaux denied the possibility of any "perfect assurance of our election and our salvation, as the Calvinists pretend"; neither the Scriptures nor Catholic tradition, he thought, vouchsafed total confidence during the penitent's lifetime. Then, too, Fourquevaux retained the reference to Catholic "virtues": a modicum of confidence was commendable because it was akin to hope, which was itself a Christian virtue. That much said, confidence was for Fourquevaux the source and ongoing sustenance of all other virtues, including the "charity" so beloved by Jansenists, because without confidence all the other virtues collapsed, revealing themselves not to have been virtues at all. In lyrical language reminiscent of Luther's *On the Freedom of the Christian Man*, Fourquevaux virtually conflated confidence with faith, not only by occa-

---

84. This intra-Jansenist debate about *crainte* and *confiance* has not, to the best of my knowledge, been the object of any sustained study, even among those devoted to eighteenth-century Jansenism. The debate also seems to have escaped Jean Delumeau's attention in his magisterial studies of *peur*, *péché*, and *sécurité* in the West. See his *La peur en Occident, XIVe–XVIIIe siècle* (Paris, 1978); *Le péché et la peur: La culpabilisation en Occident, XIIIe–XVIIIe siècle* (Paris, 1983); and *Rassurer et protéger: Le sentiment de sécurité dans l'Occident d'autrefois* (Paris, 1989).

85. Antoine Arnauld, *Le renversement de la morale de Jésus-Christ par les erreurs des Calvinistes, touchant la justification*, in *OC*, 42 vols. (Lausanne, 1775–83), 13:645. See also Pierre Nicole, "De la crainte de Dieu," in *Essais de morale, contenus en divers traités sur plusieurs devoirs importants*, 3 vols. (Paris, 1715), 1:114–50.

sionally using the terms interchangeably but by making it clear that, although commanded, confidence was also a gift of God and an effect of his grace. To base confidence of salvation on evidence of virtues already acquired was, for Fourquevaux, to put the effect before the cause; nor would he permit the believer to hope—or even to fear—except from the perspective of one of the elect. And in comparison with confidence in election, fear of damnation was a paltry thing, destined to decline in proportion as confidence grew. If it was not devoid of a certain "utility," it was also "neither properly speaking commanded nor given; rather, we are left with it," coming as it did from our "proper selves." And what came from ourselves, Fourquevaux specified, was "not from God."[86]

Fourquevaux's doctrine strayed too far from the straight and narrow preached by Arnauld and Nicole to go unchallenged by some Jansenists, one of whom, a certain M. Pichard, a canon of Saint-Aignan in Orléans, denounced its tendencies in 1734 to the eminent appellant theologian Nicolas Petitpied.[87] Living in exile in the Netherlands at the time, Petitpied was clearly out of the circuit of the figuratist "theological bureau" in Paris—that is, Boursier, d'Etemare, and Co.—for whom Fourquevaux had spoken all along. So when confronted by a proposition supposedly extracted from Fourquevaux's book—namely that "fear is as opposed to confidence, as cupidity is to charity"—he felt obliged to condemn it as "false, dangerous, and erroneous" without further qualification. Fear and confidence, he responded, were both virtues on a level with each other, which, far from being "enemies," needed and presupposed each other "as two weights in the same scale."[88] Pressed hard, however, in exchanges with d'Etemare, Fourquevaux, and others after the publication of his first letter, Petitpied began to retreat from this position of equilibrium, making concession after concession to "confidence."[89] By 1735 Petitpied was expressing himself more or less to the satisfaction of the Paris theological bureau, whether he knew it or not.[90] Meanwhile, a certain François de Paule Mariette had taken up cudgels in the controversy, attacking d'Etemare and Fourquevaux and defending Petitpied's first utterances on the subject if not his last. At stake for Mariette was not only the authority of Arnauld and Nicole but the statute of fear as a virtue of any kind.[91] Like Petitpied in his first published

86. Pavie de Fourquevaux, *Traité de la confiance chrétienne ou l'usage légitime des vérités de la grace* (n.p., 1731), p. 26.

87. [Nicolas Petitpied], *Lettre de M. P[etipied] à M. P[ichard], chanoine de Saint-Aignan à Orléans] sur la crainte et la confinace* (n.p., 1734). The authorship of the pamphlet and identity of the correspondent is supplied by Adrien Le Paige in BPR, CLP, Ms. 452, no. 1.

88. [Petitpied], *Lettre sur la crainte et la confiance*, pp. 6–8, 11.

89. [Nicolas Petitpied], *IIe lettre de Monsieur Xxx sur la crainte et la confiance* (n.p., 1734), p. 2; *IVe lettre* (n.p., 1734), pp. 30–31; *Ve lettre* (n.p., 1734), pp. 6–7; and *VIe lettre* (n.p., 1734), pp. 20–21.

90. See Louis-Adrien Le Paige's note to this effect in BPR, CLP, Ms. 543, no. 1.

91. [François de Paule Mariette], *Examen d'un écrit qui a pour titre: Eclaircissements sur la crainte servile et la crainte filiale selon les principes de Saint Augustin et de Saint Thomas* (n.p., 1734), p. 26.

letter, Mariette also thought that confidence had to find justification for its existence in the actual increase in the works of charity, not just in faith in the promises of God.

These assertions brought the Paris Jansenist theological bureau back into the fray, culminating with Laurent Boursier's three *Letters on Christian Hope,* published in 1739. Despite its initial homage to fear as "good in itself," "useful," and "salutary," the first of Boursier's three letters defended Fourquevaux's treatise against Mariette's "new system," adding greater theological precision to Fourquevaux's arguments while blaming Mariette for the confusion between faith and hope.[92] From the thought of God's "supreme majesty," on the one hand, Boursier derived the quasi-Calvinist comfort of being among the elect to whom God vouchsafed the gift of hope while delegating to charity the role of providing some additional "marks" of salvation. And from a consideration of God's "infinite mercy" as displayed in the crucifixion, on the other hand, he also derived confidence that spoke directly to the heart, whose independent testimony in the matter he defended against Mariette's accusations of "enthusiasm." "Let us listen to our heart; let us listen attentively to its voice," he cried in accents that anticipated Rousseau's. "Does it not cry out of its own accord? Is it not possible to hear it?" Boursier did not go out of his way to explain the difference between this testimony of the heart and the inner testimony of the Holy Spirit that Arnauld had so excoriated when appealed to by Calvinists.[93]

But even if Boursier's and d'Etemare's many qualifications be deemed sufficient to distinguish their position from Calvinist confidence, their emphasis was all on the side of confidence and against fear—a far cry, in any case, from the emphases of Arnauld and Nicole. Moreover, the Paris theological bureau carried the day in this internecine controversy. As early as 1734, when the *Nouvelles ecclésiastiques* devoted an article to the subject, just about everyone—Boursier, d'Etemare, Fourquevaux, Guiltauld, Le Gros, the *Nouvelles ecclésiastiques,* even Petitpied himself—were in the corner of confidence, while Mariette alone defended fear.[94] The extent to which the debate went in favor of the proponents of confidence amply confirms Jean Delumeau's contention that the eighteenth century witnessed a "decline of insecurity."[95] And to the extent that the Jansenist theological community had become more "confident," it also became a little more Calvinist, at least by the standards of its own understanding of Calvinist theology.

As it happened, the controversy over confidence and fear intersected with another within the Jansenist camp that similarly compromised the authority of seventeenth-century predecessors, notably Pierre Nicole. This controversy en-

---

92. [Laurent Boursier], *Lettre sur l'espérance et la confiance chrétienne* (n.p., 1739), p. 5.
93. Ibid., pp. 20, 127.
94. Ibid., pp. 20, 127.
95. Delumeau, *Rassurer et protéger,* pp. 477–568.

gaged not theology but Jansenist ecclesiology and pitted the likes of Boursier and d'Etemare against Jansenist controversialists even more Protestant than they. Like the controversy over fear and confidence, this one began with the publication of a pamphlet, the anonymous *Letter to M[onsieur] Nicole*, which appeared in 1726.[96]

Written in fact by Louis de Bonnaire, in 1726 still a doctor of theology in the Sorbonne, the public letter took Nicole posthumously to task for having invoked the principle of the "greatest visible authority"—that is, the authority of the Roman Catholic hierarchy—in the heat of controversy with Protestants like Jean Claude and their appeal to *sola scriptura*, the authority of Scriptures alone. Worse yet, thought Bonnaire, Nicole had stuck by this principle in moments of calm, as when writing his *Essais de morale* and in interpreting Scripture as in his exegesis of Matthew 23:1–3, in which Jesus, having described the scribes and the Pharisees as sitting "in Moses' seat," then enjoined his disciples and other Jews to do as the Pharisees preached but not as they acted. The burden of Nicole's very anti-Protestant exegesis of this passage had stressed that Jesus had *not* advised the Jews to follow the Pharisees only insofar as their preachments conformed to the Scriptures because that would have obliged the Jewish laity to an independent examination of Scripture that was quite beyond them. Rather, according to Nicole, Christ had instructively enjoined the Jews to follow the Pharisees in all they taught insofar as it conformed to the teaching clearly authorized by the magisterium of Moses, or the Synagogue. The implication was that Christians should follow their clergy insofar as their teaching conformed to that of the magisterium of Christ, or in other words to the Catholic Church.

It was this tortuous exegesis that Bonnaire fell upon in his *Lettre à M. Nicole*. First, since Jesus' advice was to follow the Pharisees' preachments but not their practice, his words, Bonnaire argued, clearly concerned their moral conduct and not matters of belief. Second, Nicole's argument supposed a distinction between the scribes and Pharisees on the one hand and the Jewish magisterium on the other, a distinction that Bonnaire denied. What was the Jewish magisterium, Bonnaire asked, if not the scribes and Pharisees who sat "in Moses' seat?" If, however, as Nicole's definition of the Catholic magisterium as the *whole* church suggested, his distinction was really between what was taught by only some of the Pharisees as opposed to what was unanimously taught by all of them, then the knowledge of that unanimity would have entailed lifetimes of travel and comparison on the part of those Jews who sincerely sought the truth. And because such advice was even harder to follow, in Bonnaire's opinion, than to compare the Pharisees' teachings to the Scriptures then extant, that, Bonnaire concluded, is what Jesus was asking his disciples and the Jewish people generally to do, even as

96. On this pamphlet and its attribution to Louis de Bonnaire, see Préclin, *Les jansénistes du dix-huitième siècle*, pp. 167–69.

he himself constantly appealed to Scripture in his disputes with the Pharisees. "That condition is not expressed," Bonnaire admitted, "but it is evident that Jesus supposes it."[97] From there it was but a short step for Bonnaire to conclude that that is what even lay Catholics ought to do in the contemporary controversies about *Unigenitus,* despite the notorious obscurity of parts of the Scriptures. Those obscurities, he argued, did not concern the principal articles of the Catholic faith, nor were the faithful without the aid of the tradition's commentary on the obscurities in question. And if it were objected that it was then the tradition authorized by the church and not the Scriptures that prevailed, "I respond," Bonnaire wrote, "that whatever means is used to fix the meaning of the Scriptures, that means will not thereby become the real rule of faith; [on the contrary,] that rule will still be the Scriptures themselves understood in this determined sense."[98]

Like Fourquevaux's *Traité de la confiance,* Bonnaire's land mine lay around for a while before exploding into internecine controversy in the early 1730s. What made it necessary to engage its argument sooner or later was the terrible Languet de Gergy's discovery and use of it in debate with the Jansenist bishop Joachim Colbert of Montpellier.[99] Already in 1726 Abbé d'Etemare felt obliged to mention it, admitting that if the author had really intended to argue that Christians, like Jews, knew no other rule than that of the Scriptures, "then it is visible that that is heresy itself, or rather the principle of all the heresies of the sixteenth century, which tried to place the text of Scripture alone in the place of the authority of the Church."[100] But then a lull intervened, and it was not until 1733 that d'Etemare undertook a refutation in good order—and launched the accusation of Protestantism in all syllables. "Such is your doctrine, Monsieur, and I do not hesitate to ask you if you are a Catholic, and to summon you as much as I can to explain in what your doctrine differs from that of the Protestants."[101]

So far, perhaps, so good. But for d'Etemare and his colleagues the difficulty lay not with showing how Bonnaire's logic led to Protestantism—that was easy enough—but with showing how they themselves could contrive to cling to Nicole's principle of the "greatest visible authority" without at the same time condemning themselves: how, in other words, they were to remain a minority in

97. [Louis de Bonnaire], *Lettre à M. Nicole sur son principe de la plus grande autorité visible dont il fait la vraie règle de la foi* (n.p., 1726), p. 2, but in general pp. 1–10.

98. Ibid., p. 10.

99. Languet de Gergy, *Lettre de Monseigneur l'évêque de Soissons, à Monseigneur l'évêque de Montpellier, en réponse aux deux lettres de ce prélat qui ont paru en mars 1727, communiqués aux ecclésiastiques du diocèse de Soissons pour leur instruction* (Paris, 1727), p. 12.

100. [Le Sesne de Ménilles d'Etemare], *Lettre à un théologien, dans laquelle, après avoir posé pour principe, que la voix de l'église se fait entendre en tout tems, on recherche comment elle se fait entendre dans le tems de trouble et de partage* (n.p., 1726), p. 1.

101. [Le Sesne de Ménilles d'Etemare], *Première lettre à l'auteur de la lettre à M. Nicole, où en réfutant les erreurs de cet auteur on établit la vraye règle de foi* (n.p., 1727 [1733]), p. 17.

opposition to the papacy and the majority of the bishops and yet remain orthodox Catholics too, even in their doctrine of the church. And it was not possible to do either in turn without again exposing the fragile skeleton of their ecclesiology of the "small number's" salutary witness in times of "trouble and obscurity"—the ecclesiology, in a word, that had been in process since the advent of *Unigenitus* and first adumbrated in La Borde's *Du témoignage de la vérité*. Thus did it fall to d'Etemare to explain, this time with some crucial help from Colbert of Montpellier, how the "greatest visible authority" also included the witness of all of Christian antiquity as well as all those who testified to that witness, including of course the clerical second order and even the simplest lay faithful; and how, even if a minority, the combined hue and cry of disenfranchised priests and lay faithful in times of "trouble and obscurity" effectively invalidated the authority of a judgment like *Unigenitus,* which needed unanimous acceptance to become binding.[102] But in the course of showing how even the "least woman" might easily recognize on which side lay the truth in times of "division and obscurity"—how it was at once both respectful toward the church and simpler than examining Scripture for herself—d'Etemare had to appeal in the last resort to the "true and simple heart" *(coeur droit et simple)* of the elect, who would know doctrinal deviation when they saw it.[103] How this testimony of the elect's true and simple heart differed in kind from Calvinism's interior testimony of the Holy Spirit, d'Etemare no more explained to Bonnaire than had Boursier to Mariette.

But the most dramatic evidence of Protestant-like tendencies within the Jansenist movement current in 1730 occurs not in theology or ecclesiology but in the elusive domain of religious sensibilities. This evidence was particularly clear in Jansenism's steadily growing hostility to ornate and baroque Catholicism, a hostility that, as recorded at least by police observers in the streets, is hard to distinguish from classically Calvinist characterizations of Catholicism as idolatry and superstition.

In response, for example, to the news that appellant curés might be excluded from the indulgences connected with the papal jubilee of 1728, various "others" reported that these curés said that they "gave as much credence to the indulgences . . . as they did to the constitution *Unigenitus,* and that they and their parishioners were happy to do without the supposed graces that His Holiness believed himself entitled to dispense, because they served only to induce men to profane what is sacred in the [Christian] religion." The news about a book that had denounced the Jesuits' "lax" ethics to a European congress in 1728 elicited the judgment that

102. [Le Sesne de Ménilles d'Etemare], *Seconde lettre à l'auteur de la lettre à M. Nicole* (n.p., 1727 [1733]), on second order and lay faithful, p. 4; on witness of antiquity, pp. 26–27; on consent of whole church, pp. 34–35.

103. On example of "least woman," ibid., p. 18; on "right and simple heart," *Première lettre à l'auteur de la lettre à M. Nicole,* p. 36.

"what gives umbrage to Protestants is the multitude of monks and ecclesiastics in the Roman Church, that it is they who are the authors of a thousand *momeries* and even idolatries committed by common Christians and even by some from more distinguished [social] stations, who believe that after burning a candle in front of a stone or marble statue they have done the best action possible to do." The queen's visit to Notre Dame in October 1728 to perform a novena in order to give birth to a dauphin provoked a plethora of adverse comments, among them that "novenas, indulgences, pilgrimages, and other devotions of the sort are nothing but human inventions, that God is even offended by them, because they direct a cult to creatures that is due to God alone, . . . and that the queen herself would have done better to stay at Versailles and pray there than to come to Paris amidst such to-do and fracas *(avec si grand appareil)*, because nothing more closely resembles paganism than such feasts and festivities."[104] A mardi gras procession orchestrated in 1732 by the Molinist curé of Saint-Sulpice—and the brother of Languet de Gergy—gave rise to the complaint that the procession bore "the aspect of a pagan feast rather than that of a [Christian] gesture of piety."[105] And sermons delivered on the occasion of the feast of the Assumption of the Virgin Mary in 1741 prompted the opinion that "the church has in general pushed the cult of the Virgin too far, that it is false that she was ever taken up body and soul to heaven by angels, because the tradition never mentions it, to say nothing of the apostles who were present at the time of her death."[106]

That these sorts of propos represent Jansenist rather than, say, protophilosophical incredulity is clear not only because the police knew very well how to distinguish between the two but also because they typically came attached to other propos whose Jansenist provenance is unmistakable. In 1741, to take a single example among hundreds, the police reported on a lament by unspecified "others" that "religion is disfigured, that everything consists of ceremonies having more relation to those of pagans than those owed to the true God." That discourse was concluded, however, according to the same report, by "saying that such is the fruit that the constitution *Unigenitus* has engendered since it has appeared, and that if some legitimate authority does not finally destroy it roots and all, religion itself will disappear."[107]

Judicial Jansenism

The "legitimate authority" in question could only have been the Parlement of Paris, just as the "they" and "others" whose "sayings" the police observers

104. BA: AB, Ms. 10158, fol. 6, 6–7 Jan. 1728; fol. 138, 3 Sept. 1728; fol. 183, 4 Oct. 1728.

105. BA: AB, Ms. 10161, fol. 348.

106. BA: AB, Ms. 10168, fol. 275, 15–16 Aug. 1741.

107. BA: AB, Ms. 10168, fol. 241, 22–23 May 1741. For some examples of reports on protophilosophical unbelief, see those on one abbé Bouchard and his preachments in the Luxembourg Gardens

reported was probably a largely lay and judicial public. Although priests and friars were certainly among those quoted, the clergy tended to cross paths with the police observers mainly in the Luxembourg Gardens and to leave clear traces of their identity in the reports that the police wrote. The other areas most frequented by the police on the prowl for *dires*—the café de Maugis and the Palais de justice—were more heavily inhabited by barristers and the attorneys.[108] However circumstantial, that social bias in police reporting reflects an overall shift in Jansenism's leadership from the seminaries, priories, and parishes to the Palais de justice. By 1730 if not earlier it is possible to identify a full-fledged, self-conscious parti janséniste within and around the Parlement of Paris. And however Protestant-like that milieu's street-level religious reactions, its public diction was to be neither Protestant nor even distinctively religious but rather legal. As translated by that milieu, Jansenism was to become ever more judicial.

Among the mainly noble magistrates who were the Parlement's only judges, that parti janséniste's most obvious if not most politically active members were the deceased deacon Pâris's brother Jérôme and the convulsionary Carré de Montgeron. More important were the eloquent abbé René Pucelle and Pierre Guillebault, both of them touted by the *Nouvelles ecclésiastiques* for their adamant "sentiments against the bull"; as well as Nicolas Le Clerc de Lesseville and Nicolas de Vrévin, the former praised by the Jansenist journal for his "humble" and "sweet" piety, the latter for "intrepid" defense of the "truth." Nine or ten others merited less effusive but still telltale praise from the *Nouvelles ecclésiastiques,* including Alexandre-Julien Clément de Feillet, Marc-Jacques Fermé, and the convulsionary Jean-Baptiste-Maximilien Titon. Although always a minority in the Parlement, Jansenists consistently exerted political leverage all out of proportion to their numerical strength. Peter Campbell's recent analysis of parlementary politics during the ministry of Cardinal Fleury has shown how, by construing episcopal or ministerial acts as threats to the Parlement's judicial competence, this eloquent minority of Jansenist judges was so often able to talk a majority of their colleagues into adopting essentially Jansenist causes as the Parlement's own.[109]

---

to the effect that all religions were equally "human" and therefore acceptable, in Ms. 10158, fols. 151, 281, 12 Sept. and 10 Nov. 1728.

108. The café de Maugis in the rue Saint-Séverin was singled out for an anonymous denunciation in a letter to the Paris lieutenant general of police "tant par un motif de religion, que par l'interest public." The letter called it a "grande assemblée d'avocats, procureurs, libraires et nouvellistes, qui y montrent et lisent toutes sortes de libelles diffamatoires, [et] on y parle hautement de toutes sortes d'affaires d'Etat." See BA: AB, Ms. 10170, fol. 4.

109. Peter Campbell, "The Conduct of Politics in France in the Time of the Cardinal de Fleury," pp. 322–43; and Maire, "L'église et la nation," p. 1190. Other magistrates mentioned by the *NE* are René-François Boutin, Claude-François Fornier de Montagny, Jean-François Ogier d'Enonville, Louis Robert, Lefevre de Saint-Hilaire, and Philippe Thomé.

This magisterial parti janséniste was able to fortify itself with the vast historical, ecclesiastical, and judicial erudition of the even more numerous Jansenist *avocats* or barristers, who virtually created the Parisian Order of Barristers in the two or three decades spanning the end of the seventeenth century and the beginning of the eighteenth. Possessing no venal offices and hence no royal statutes, this peculiar order was not a royal corps in the ordinary sense of that term, freeing its members of direct royal or even parlementary supervision and allowing the liberty of occasionally "striking" or ceasing their indispensable functions, most often in support of the Parlement of Paris but sometimes against it. For the late 1720s and early 1730s, David Bell has identified a "hard core" of about twenty-four barristers, including Jacques-Charles Aubry, François de Mairamberg, and Claude-Joseph Prévost, who dominated the order by means of controlling the *tableau* or annual membership roll and shouting down opposition in the open assemblies.[110] After 1730 the order of barristers similarly escaped the tightened requirement to sign the anti-Jansenist Formulary of Alexander VII that so effectively cut off Jansenist recruitment in other orders and professions, allowing would-be Jansenist clerics like Claude Mey and Christophe Coudrette to find an outlet for their frustrated zeal in the law and enabling Jansenists to maintain their hold on the order well into the century's middle decades.

Another breach allowed the barristers to publish legal consultations without prior royal censorship so long as they bore so much as a single barrister's name.[111] It was this breach that enabled Jansenist barristers to deploy their legal language against the bull in public case after case, beginning with one that came hard on the heels of Louis XIV's death in 1715. Pitting six Jansenist clergymen against their archbishop, who had recently suspended them, this case galvanized a Parisian public both audible and visible in the galleries to which the Jansenist barristers appealed over the heads of the judges. Not content with this public's applause, the barristers published their memoirs as fast as printers could obtain copies of them. The case also allowed these barristers to develop their radically Gallican conception of the church as a purely spiritual, free, and persuasive space in sharp contrast to the state's coercive power, which, they argued, was supposed to protect this

110. For the role of Jansenism in the development of the Order of Barristers in general see David Avrom Bell, *Lawyers and Citizens: The Making of a Political Elite* (Oxford, 1994), pp. 41–105; for his analysis of the "hard core" of Jansenist barristers, see as well his "Des stratégies d'opposition sous Louis XV: L'affaire des avocats, 1730–31," in *Histoire, économie, et société* 9 (1990):567–90, but esp. n. 31. Among the better known in this 1730 "hard core" besides Aubry, Mairamberg, and Prévost were Claude Berroyer, Henri Cochin, Clément-Charles de La Verdy, Nicolas de La Vigne, Henri Duhamel, Philippe Guillet de Blaru, Jean-Louis de Prunay, Georges Le Roy, Georges-Claude Le Roi, Pierre Le Roy de Vallières, Claude-Nicolas L'Herminier, Alexis-François Normant, Pierre-Salomon Pothouin, and Nicolas-Claude Visinier.

111. Sarah Maza, "Le tribunal de la nation: Les mémoires judiciaires et l'opinion publique à la fin de l'ancien régime," *Annales* 42 (Jan.–Feb. 1987):73–90, esp. p. 77.

freedom. "We are not slaves," intoned Louis Chevallier in 1715. "We do not live under the yoke of blind obedience. We are the children of a free woman [the church] and we hold this freedom from our divine master."[112] The monarchy's putative role of protector did not prevent its coercive power from suffering by contrast to this freedom. Because the same case, moreover, had been allowed to come before the Parlement of Paris only over the literally dead body of Louis XIV, who had originally reassigned it to the Royal Council, barristers like Claude-Joseph Prévost took the occasion to revive the long dormant distinction between the king's mortal and sempiternal bodies to the advantage of the Parlement. Unlike the "king's own person," Prévost pointed out, the High Court "did not die," and that High Court Prévost defined as "the Parlement of Paris, true Parlement of the Kingdom of France, Court of Peers, august Tribunal, born with the state, and whose founding is connected with and adjacent to the Monarchy itself."[113]

These arguments and accompanying judicial diction took more memorable form in the consultations and memoirs produced by the protracted political crisis following the deposition of Jean Soanen, the Jansenist Bishop of Senez, by a provincial church council in Embrun in 1727: above all, the consultation signed by fifty barristers in support of the Bishop of Senez against that council, and François de Mairamberg's memoir on behalf of three Jansenist clerics against the Bishop of Orléans in 1730. These publications reached a wider public as well, finding further amplification in the *Nouvelles ecclésiastiques,* which arose in reaction to the "brigandage of Embrun" and which pronounced the consultation of 1727 against it to be "a masterpiece in its genre, enough by itself to immortalize the barrister [Jacques-Charles Aubry] regarded with good reason as its principal author," and one of the main vehicles mobilizing support for a cause in which the "Public had taken only a mediocre and cool interest until then."[114]

The price paid by the Jansenist cause for that and similar successes was the gradual displacement of its center from theology to ecclesiology and public law and its articulation in ever more judicial language. Thus the barristers' Jansenism more typically took the discreet form of telltale definitions, distinctions, and a certain diction. Occupying pride of place among the definitions was again that of the church, which, echoing Quesnel quoting Saint Bernard, possessed "a government of humility, of tenderness, and of charity, diametrically opposed to arbitrary despotism."[115] The "domination of Temporal princes" was altogether foreign to

112. Cited in Bell, *Lawyers and Citizens,* p. 77. For a description of the whole affair, see pp. 76–80.

113. Claude-Joseph Prévost, *Mémoire pour les trois docteurs et curez de Reims, au sujet des poursuites contre eux faites pour raison de la Constitution Unigenitus* (Paris, 1716), pp. 7, 10, as cited in Bell, *Lawyers and Citizens,* p. 78.

114. *NE* 19 Dec. 1739, pp. 197–98, where it is specified that Aubry had help from the Jansenist theologian Abbé Boursier.

115. *Consultation de messieurs les avocats du parlement de Paris, au sujet du jugement rendu à Embrun contre M. l'évêque de Senez* (Paris, 1728), p. 32. See also p. 15.

the church, in the barristers' view, for "Jesus Christ himself told his apostles"—and by clear implication their episcopal successors—that while "the Gentile princes dominated each other, . . . it shall not be so among you." Far from a temporal prince, therefore, who commanded in an "absolute manner," the church's pastors acknowledged Jesus Christ as their "only king and monarch," which meant that "they bore a much greater resemblance to magistrates as interpreters and protectors of the laws laid down by Christ's sovereign authority than to princes who at their whim could abrogate old laws and establish new ones."[116] The barristers' assimilation of pastors to royal judges had other implications as well, among them that just as the king communicated his judicial authority to his whole parlement and not to the first president only, so Christ communicated his spiritual authority directly to the "Church universal" and not to the pope alone. For the barristers, then, this universal church clearly meant the clerical second order and "even Laypeople" as much as the bishops.[117] The judicial analogy further implied that, like these parlementary magistrates, the church's pastors should subject every papal pronouncement or decision—notably *Unigenitus*—to a "serious discussion" and a "juridical examination," which, in the church's case, ought to continue until a "clear, free, decisive, and unanimous acceptance" had emerged.[118]

Even more radical in its way was François de Mairamberg's memoir of 1730. For while the consultation of 1727 maintained that the church's authority was "purely spiritual," Mairamberg's spelled out how little that spiritual authority meant. With surgical distinctions that recalled the radical conciliarism of Robert Ockham and Marsilius of Padua, Mairamberg denied the church any "role for constraint," allowing only "the way of persuasion"—at most "the fear of the loss of one's soul and of eternal penalties."[119] Whatever "exterior jurisdiction and constraint" the church held by virtue of "concessions from and conventions with" the state, the state necessarily retained the right "to examine the judgments of these ecclesiastical tribunals, and to restrict them to the rules to which they are bound as well as to the determined boundaries of their competence." Even in apparently spiritual matters, in other words, "exterior" sentences were vulnerable

116. Ibid., p. 15. The biblical reference is to the book of Matthew, 20:25–28. See *Biblia Sacra Vulgata,* evangelium secundum Mattheum, 2:1556.

117. The Royal Council singled out this participatory ecclesiology in its condemnation of the consultation. See *Arrest du Conseil d'estat du roy . . . par lequel le roy ordonne la suppression de l'écrit qui a pour titre, Consultation de MM. les avocats . . . Du 5 juillet 1728* (Paris, 1728), in BPR, CLP, Ms. 437, no. 20, pp. 3–4.

118. *Consultation . . . au sujet du jugement rendu à Embrun,* pp. 21–22.

119. *Mémoire pour les sieurs Samson, curé d'Olivet, Couet, curé de Parroi, Gauchet, chanoine de Jargeau, diocèse d'Orléans . . . contre Monsieur l'évêque d'Orléans . . . Délibéré à Paris le 27 juillet 1730* (Paris, 1730), BPR, CLP, Ms. 449, unnumbered, p. 2. For similar principles in Marsilius of Padua, see *The Defender of the Peace,* trans. Alan Gewirth (New York, 1956), pp. 108–26.

to secular judicial review.[120] And while Aubry's consultation in defense of the Bishop of Senez had conceded that absolute and independent temporal power belonged to the king, Mairamberg's memoir all but took it away.[121] For the memoir's occasional concessions to absolutist orthodoxy were undermined by the argument that, because the parlements contained both lay and clerical councillors, they "possessed the representative character of public authority" and for that reason the right to "reform" acts of ecclesiastical as well as of secular jurisdictions. "Representative" of what? The memoir's next sentence, which called the parlements the "sovereign tribunal of the nation," seemed to suggest that they represented the nation as well as the king. That the memoir at least posited the nation as an entity apart from the king and able to treat with him as an equal partner was the clear implication of its definition of laws: namely that of "veritable conventions between those who govern and those who are governed."[122] Its initial definition of the king as a "chief" was moreover the consultation's only recourse to the term *king*, where it was further undermined by being juxtaposed to a description of the parlements as "the Senate of the Nation." Elsewhere the memoir referred only to the "state," "nation," "public authority," "sovereign authority," "temporal power," and "secular authority."

If this were not political heterodoxy enough, the Royal Council's public condemnation of the memoir discerned still more. Already a "criminal exercise" to have based the Parlement's judicial competence on the "vain title" of "Senate of the nation," it was "a temerity even more inexcusable" to have called the king its mere "chief." The term *chief* may have been innocent enough in the minds of the barristers in the relative Eden of 1730, but its culpabilization at the hands of the Royal Council at that time charged it with subversive meaning that no royal grace was able subsequently to undo. Indeed, the memoir, to believe the royal council, had "attributed the whole administration of justice to the nation"; while a reference to ordinances promulgated by the Estates General revealed an intention to assert the superiority of such ordinances to all royal ones. The council also accused the barristers of asserting that no one stood above the Parlement's arrêts. And the memoir's definition of laws as "conventions between governors and the governed" would be "inadmissible even in Republics and absolutely intolerable in a monarchy," charged the council, "since in divesting the Sovereign of his most

120. *Mémoire pour les sieurs Samson . . . contre . . . l'évêque d'Orléans*, pp. 2–3. For the origin of the maxim that the church is in the state, not the state in the church, see Saint Optatus, Bishop of Mileve, *S. Optati milevitani libri VII*, ed. Carolus Ziwsa (Prague, 1893), p. 74, l. 3: "non respublica in ecclesia, sed ecclesia in respublica."

121. On François de Mairamberg's authorship of the consultation and the story of its publication, see Bell, *Lawyers and Citizens*, pp. 91–93.

122. *Mémoire pour les sieurs Samson . . . contre . . . l'évêque d'Orléans*, pp. 1–2.

august quality, which is that of legislator, [the memoir] reduces him . . . to receiving the law from those to whom he should be giving it."[123]

The barristers, it is true, disavowed this antiabsolutist reading of the memoir's reference to "conventions between governors and the governed"—and with all the better reason, it might be added, in that the phrase had been Mairamberg's alone and not that of the other signers, who had not seen the memoir before it went to press. They also held that the phrase's context limited its application to relations between church and state. Another possible gloss on that text, however, appeared two years later in the form of a pamphlet entitled *Judicium Francorum*, which was an updating and reworking of a pamphlet that first appeared during the Fronde.[124] Almost certainly published with the connivance of Jansenist barristers, the *Judicium Francorum* maintained that the Parlement of Paris was the successor of the ancient Frankish assemblies that everyone had been obliged to attend and where "all the laws were made," with the consequence that, although the "the person of the king" was "holy and sacred" enough, the soul of the royalty lay in the Parlement, "where sovereignty was principally to be found."[125] The Parlement dutifully condemned the pamphlet August 1732, in part to mollify provincial parlements that took offense at finding themselves demoted vis-à-vis the Parlement of Paris.[126]

Devout Catholicism

Yet no number of Jansenists in the Parlement of Paris and the bar could by themselves have effected the juncture between these judicial institutions, their peculiar brand of Gallicanism, the appellant press, the Parisian curés, and even some of the popular constituents of antiroyal miracles—the whole antiabsolutist agenda, in short, galvanized by the bull *Unigenitus*. For that to happen, it took not only Cardinal de Fleury's moderate and mainly political defense of *Unigenitus* as a symbol of absolutism but also "devout" Catholics who believed as fervently in the bull as did Jansenists in the condemned propositions, and who preached a far more

123. *Arrest du Conseil d'estat du roy, rendu au sujet d'un écrit intitulé: Mémoire pour les sieurs Samson . . . contre . . . l'évêque d'Orléans. Du 30 octobre 1730.* (Paris, 1730), in BPR, CLP, Ms. 449, unnumbered, pp. 1–3.

124. The Frondish pamphlet in question is [Louis Machon], *Les véritables maximes du gouvernement de la France* (Paris, 1752), reprinted in *La Fronde, contestation démocratique et misère paysanne: 52 Mazarinades,* ed. Hubert Carrier, 2 vols. (Paris, 1982), 1:paginated separately.

125. *Mémoire touchant l'origine et l'autorité du parlement de France, et appellé Judicium Francorum* (n.p., n.d.), pp. 1–2. On probable Jansenist complicity in the publication of this pamphlet, see Barbier, *Journal,* 2:325–26.

126. Such, at least, was the explanation given for the Parlement's condemnation by Parisian *nouvellistes* who were for the most part sympathetic to the pamphlet. See BA: AB, Ms. 10162, fols. 82–83, 5–6 Aug. 1732.

draconian enforcement of it than even Fleury was willing to contemplate. For while Jansenists may have in some respects been growing more Protestant, a revived and militantly anti-Jansenist parti dévot was taking shape to the right of the cardinal-minister and in some sense becoming more Catholic than the pope.

In the episcopacy, this parti dévot was led by Languet de Gergy, Bishop of Soissons before being promoted to the diocese of Sens; Etienne de La Fare, Bishop of Laon; Pierre-Guérin de Tencin, architect of the Council of Embrun; ex-Jesuit Henri-Xavier Belsunce, Bishop of Marseilles; ex-Jesuit Pierre Lafitau, Bishop of Sisteron; Louis-Gaston Fleuriau, Bishop of Orléans; as well as, of course, some Jesuits themselves, prominent among them Dominique Colonnia and Louis Patouillet, coauthors of a polemical dictionary of Jansenist books and pamphlets.[127] Although there was no lay parti dévot at the royal court in the 1720s and early 1730s, the clerical dévots could count upon the sympathy of Phélypeaux La Vrillière, comte de Saint-Florentin, secretary of state in charge of the provinces; the "pious" Armand de Béthune, duc de Charost and captain of the king's guards; Fleuriau d'Armenonville, keeper of the seals until his death in 1728 and brother of a Jesuit and adamantly anti-Jansenist Bishop of Orléans; and Hérault de Fontaine, lieutenant general of police, whose "bitter zeal" against Jansenists provided endless copy for the *Nouvelles ecclésiastiques* and whom even the anti-Jansenist Barbier thought excessively beholden to the Jesuits. But devout sentiment had no permanent foothold at court until the new queen Marie Leszczynska brought the products of a highly devout upbringing with her from her family home in Alsace.[128]

What Marie Leszczynska bought with her when she joined the French royal household in 1725 is what had become the affective heart of devout religiosity: the cultic devotion to the Sacred Heart of Jesus. The immediate origins of this special devotion lay in the latter seventeenth century with the theology of the Norman Oratorian Jean Eudes and the revelations of the Visitandine nun Marguerite-Marie Alacoque at the convent of Paray-le-Monial near Autun. As conceived by Jean Eudes, devotion to the heart of Jesus was primarily veneration of the interior dispositions of Jesus, above all his love for God the Father. As such the devotion was in a line with Berullian theology's Christocentric and theocentric emphases—the abasement of the human self vis-à-vis the "grandeurs" of Jesus and the "majesty" of God—and was to that extent not incompatible with Jansenism. Indeed, the imagery of the heart of Jesus figures prominently in the literature of

127. Dominique de Colonia and Louis Patouillet, *Bibliothèque janséniste, ou catalogue des principaux livres jansénistes, ou suspects de jansénisme, qui ont paru depuis le commencement de cette hérésie*, 2d ed. (n.p., 1731).

128. On Charost, see Claude-Louis Hector, duc de Villars, *Mémoires du maréchal de Villars, publié d'après le manuscrit original, par la société de l'histoire de France*, ed. the marquis de Vogüé, 6 vols. (Paris, 1884–1904), 5:343, 360; and Barbier, *Journal*, 2:233. On Hérault see *NE*, table, "Herault, lieutenant de police à Paris," 1:608–18.

early Jansenism.[129] But, in Henri Brémond's persuasive analysis, this Oratorian devotional strain intersected with the devotion that issued from Jesus's visitations to Marguerite Alacoque at Paray-le-Monial, a devotion that highlighted a more literal than metaphorical divine heart and a decidedly more human than metaphysical love. The devotion that emerged from this juncture hence drew liberally from Salesian and devout humanist as well as Berullian sources. Marie Alacoque's religious order was one that Saint François de Sales had founded; and her chief spiritual mentors were the Jesuits Claude de La Colombière and Jean Croiset. By 1730 devotion to the Sacred Heart had clearly become a "devout" affair. For by then the Society of Jesus had adopted the new devotion as its own, becoming its chief advocates in the quest for papal approval. The first French bishop aggressively to promote the devotion was the ex-Jesuit Belsunce of Marseilles, who invoked the Sacred Heart's help against the last major outbreak of smallpox in Europe in the early 1720s.[130]

That devout humanism's typically affective and palpable sensibility had also come to prevail in the new devotion is evident in Languet de Gergy's *Life of the Venerable Mother Marguerite-Marie*, which burst upon the attention of the Parisian public in 1729 with "more scandal than edification," according to Marais. For in this spiritual biography the Bishop of Soissons unblushingly displayed Alacoque's most affective descriptions of her many encounters with her "divine husband" and "sweet master."[131] On the day of their "spiritual engagement," for example, Jesus gave Alacoque to understand that he wished her to "savor what was sweetest in the suavity of the caresses of his love." These attentions were so "excessive" and "ravishing" that Alacoque was "often beside herself" and the "subject of a very strange confusion." In the first of her visitations, Jesus revealed to her the "marvels of his love and the inexplicable secrets of his sacred heart," then took her heart and placed it within his wounded side before replacing it all aflame, there "to consume her until the last moment of her life."[132] At Jesus' request, Alacoque responded to this and other such "graces" in the form of the new devotion conceived of as "an honorable reparation" *(amende honorable)* and "a precious bouquet offered to the divine heart" which, introduced by her to the monastery's novices, taught them "to savor consolations and delights unknown to

129. Louis Cognet, "Le jansénisme et le Sacré-Coeur," *Etudes carmélitaines* 29 (1950):234–53.

130. J. Bainvel, "Sacré Coeur de Jésus, dévotion au," in *Dictionnaire de théologie catholique*, 12 vols., ed. A. Vacant, E. Mangenet, and E. Amann (Paris, 1903–48), 3:271–351; and Henri Brémond, *Histoire du sentiment religieux en France depuis la fin des guerres de religion jusqu'à nos jours*, 11 vols. (Paris, 1916–33), 3:583–671.

131. Jean-Joseph Languet de Gergy, *La vie de la vénérable mère Marguerite-Marie, religieuse de la Visitation de Sainte Marie du monastère de Paray-le-Monial en Charolais, morte en odeur de sainteté en 1690*, ed. Léon Gauthey (Paris, 1890). The reference to the book's dubious reception by the Parisian public is from Marais, *Journal et lettres*, 4:87.

132. Languet de Gergy, *La vie de la vénérable mère Marguerite-Marie*, pp. 115–16, 220–21.

them until then."[133] The contrast between this baroque spirituality and Jansenist austerity could not have been sharper. Comparing Languet's *Life* to the Jesuit Isaac Berruyer's contemporary attempt to rewrite the Old Testament as a novel, the *Nouvelles ecclésiastiques* found the bishop's style to be perhaps "more romantic than episcopal" and speculated that "*mondains* in the habit of reading novels and other profane books will not find themselves out of their element in this one."[134]

To be sure, Alacoque's discipleship was far from the bed of roses that such passages by themselves suggest. Not only did Alacoque carry Christ's cross but she endeavored in some sense "to attach myself with him to it, in order to keep him faithful company and participate in his sufferings and opprobrium." Thus, much of her spiritual pilgrimage was in Languet's rendering a litany of humiliation, temptation, and torment in an attempt to annihilate herself in a "holocaust" of disinterested love for Christ.[135] So while the biography's ample "suavities" and "douceurs" recall the devotional delights of François de Sales, the "immolation" of self is more similar to Fénelon's contemporaneous quest for the mystic experience of utterly disinterested "pure love."[136]

Still, it was a most hierarchical sort of humility that culminated in Alacoque's becoming something like Christ's coredemptrix in the work of salvation, whereby she played the same propitiatory role for sin vis-à-vis Christ as Christ did vis-à-vis the Father—one in any case that was bound to offend Jansenist religious sensibilities, as was much else in Languet's biography.[137] Christ frequently complained to Alacoque, for example, that his blood was so "uselessly lavished on so many souls." In spite of this blood and Alacoque's ardent prayers, people remained in the last analysis the "arbiters" of their own salvation.[138] Not even Jansenist sacramental and liturgical sensibilities were spared. Jesus enjoined very frequent communion on Alacoque, who in turn tried to inspire Paray's novices with the same desire, predicting misfortune for "those who, on the pretext of a respectful fear or the need for a longer preparation, postpone their approach to the holy table." And God first addressed Alacoque in Latin even though she understood only French.[139]

The partisan "subtext" of Languet's biography extended to politics as well, for its language was laden with absolutist overtones. In what Languet quoted from Alacoque's writings, she habitually described Jesus as her "absolute master" or

133. Ibid., pp. 241–42, 327.

134. *NE* 1 Jan. 1730, p. 2.

135. Languet de Gergy, *La vie de la vénérable mère Marguerite-Marie*, pp. 282, 297.

136. On *suavités, douceurs,* and *pur amour* see ibid., pp. 131, 167, 209, 361–62. François de Sales and Jeanne de Chantal themselves appear to Alacoque on pp. 410–13

137. On Alacoque's redemptive role see ibid., pp. 281–82, 306–13, 401–13.

138. Ibid., pp. 306, 395–96.

139. Ibid., pp. 112, 227, 384, 389–90.

"sovereign master" and herself as his "slave."[140] Repeatedly playing on the register of "for such is our good pleasure" *(car tel est notre bon plaisir)*, with which all royal declarations ended, Languet had Alacoque's mother superior enjoin her "to desire only that . . . the good pleasure of God reign in you sovereignly," while he had Jesus himself repeatedly tell her that obedience was his favorite virtue, that he wanted it to be such as to prefer her superior's orders to his own should the two conflict.[141] In his own characteristic vocabulary Languet lauded Alacoque's obedience for being "absolute" and "blind," adding that it was this virtue that guaranteed that her revelations were authentic.[142] It was hardly inappropriate, then, that Alacoque had prophesied that the new devotion would some day triumph at the French royal court, urging Louis XIV to add the Sacred Heart to the Bourbon dynasty's arms in 1688, or that Languet himself dedicated his biography to the new queen in 1729.[143] The political implications of this emphasis on obedience were not lost on the *Nouvelles ecclésiastiques,* which devoted the last and longest installment of its review to Languet's "chimerical duty of blind obedience."[144]

A similar combination of absolutist political reflexes and devout religious sensibilities declared themselves among episcopal firebrands like Belsunce of Marseilles, La Fare of Laon, or Tencin of Embrun, most clearly during the political crisis of 1730–33 and especially in reaction to the judicial memoir of 1730. The political reflexes of these devout bishops tended toward an absolutism more absolute than the king's, an ultramontanism more papal that the pope's, and a "sacred union" between these two. The memoir of 1730, charged Tencin, "trampled on the sentiments and duties of both Catholics and Subjects" and simultaneously assaulted the Church of God and the Majesty of Kings." On the one hand, "the Bishops and their judgments are outraged with a haughtiness that would have made Calvin and Luther blush before they had consummated their defection," while on the other "the authority of the Sovereign himself is overturned." These political reflexes typically came accompanied by persecutory sighs and apocalyptic cries. "On what unhappy days have we fallen?", bemoaned the Archbishop of Embrun. "What dreadful signs of things to come?"[145] Like Tencin,

---

140. Ibid., pp. 81, 268, 283.

141. On Christ's "good pleasure" see ibid., p. 275, but also pp. 130–31, 174, 362; on Christ's injunction of "blind obedience" see esp. pp. 124–25.

142. Ibid., pp. 142–44, but also pp. 32, 114, 132, 355, 381–82.

143. Ibid., "A la reine," pp. 1–4. On the political connotations of the devotion to the Sacred Heart in 1670s and 1680s, see Jacques Le Brun, "Politics and Spirituality: The Devotion to the Sacred Heart," trans. John Griffiths, in *The Concrete Christian Life,* ed. Christian Duquoc, 69 in *Concilium* series (New York, 1971), pp. 29–43.

144. *NE* 16 Jan. 1730, pp. 9–11.

145. Pierre Guérin de Tencin, Archbishop of Embrun, *Mandement de Monseigneur l'archévêque prince d'Embrun portant condamnation d'un écrit signé par 40 avocats, et intitulé* . . . (Embrun, 1731), in BPR, CLP, Ms. 449, pp. 2–3.

La Fare of Laon also thought that he labored in most lamentable times. "What times, my dear brothers, has the savior reserved for us?", he asked his flock shortly after the appearance Mairamberg's memoir of 1730. "And if Jesus Christ were to appear today on earth, would he find any faith?" In what condition in particular would he find France, "which has always been one of the strongest ramparts of the Christian religion, and where heresy never set foot without being immediately annihilated." What Christ would find, in La Fare's estimation, was a "sad spectacle" indeed: the papacy's pronouncements "despised," the episcopal authority "trampled underfoot," charity "extinguished in all hearts," the heretics' calumny "triumphant," and the "supposed *beaux esprits* swimming in their thoughts."[146]

La Fare and Tencin did not neglect the occasion of their conflicts with the parlements and Jansenist barristers to trumpet their orthodox royalism. To believe them the king had no more loyal allies than they. "Who, the appellants or us," challenged Tencin, "have explained themselves more clearly and forthrightly . . . about the absolute and indispensable obedience owed by all Orders of the Realm to the King, about the King's right to be the sole Legislator and Sovereign Judge in his States, able at his pleasure to restrict or expand the Jurisdiction which it has pleased him to give to the different Tribunals of the Realm?"[147] He himself, he had no doubt; nor did La Fare, ever animated for his part by such righteous "indignation at the sight of any penchant toward disobedience by others [to the king] that we could not have felt more cut to the quick than if it had been directed against ourselves."[148] The trouble was that the Bourbon monarchy was not the only authority to which La Fare and his like were inclined to be obedient. For they felt just as beholden to the other author of the bull *Unigenitus,* namely the papacy, whose authority had once been thought all but incompatible with the monarchy's in Gallican France and was still in tension with the tenets of conciliar Gallicanism. Although in general it would not be until midcentury that episcopal firebrands began to put discernible distance between themselves and the Gallican Declaration of 1682, La Fare occasionally came close to outright ultramontanism in the 1730s. "But are the liberties of the Gallican Church, the Rights of the Crown, and our usages compromised by the constitution *Unigenitus?*" La Fare asked his diocesans in his mandamus of 13 November. "May God never permit, my brothers, that our liberties ever close the doors of this Realm to the Holy Decrees

---

146. Etienne-Joseph de La Fare, *Mandement de Monseigneur l'évêque duc de Laon, second pair de France, comte d'Ainsy, etc., sur la soumission due à la constitution Unigenitus, sur la fidélité indispensable des sujets envers leur Souverain, et sur les droits sacréz de l'épiscopat* (Laon, 1730), pp. 3–4.

147. Pierre Guérin de Tencin, *Mandement de Monseigneur l'archévêque prince d'Embrun, contre un écrit intitulé: Lettre de M. l'ancien évêque d'Apt* . . . (n.p., 1731), p. 5.

148. Etienne-Joseph de La Fare, *Instruction pastorale de Monseigneur l'évêque duc de Laon, second pair de France, comte d'Ainsy etc., contre les réquisitoires de M. Gilbert de Voisins, avocat général, au sujet de son mandement et de sa lettre pastorale, et de l'instruction pastorale de M. l'archévêque de Paris qu'il a adopté* (Laon, 1731), in BPR, CLP, Ms. 449, pp. 19–20.

that the Holy See judges apropos to send us," was his answer. The Gallican liberties "would be as pernicious as they are useful, if they are ever opposed to anything more than to some attack on our usages or the Rights of the Crown." Because, for the monarchy, these rights amounted to "being obeyed and to being accountable only to God," Unigenitus did not threaten them.[149]

La Fare's attempt to hide behind royal authority would not do, however, as Gilbert de Voisins was quick to point out, because what his line of reasoning skipped over was that the superiority of general councils over papal pronouncements as well as the Gallican Church's right to judge doctrine concurrently with Rome also figured among the Gallican liberties. What the appellants were denying is that the Gallican Church had ever so judged in the case of Unigenitus, and what they were appealing to was precisely a general council. Nowhere was the cleavage dating from the 1690s between Gallicanism's royal and conciliar tenets more evident than in this bishop's subterfuges. That these episcopal subterfuges might issue into a "devout" challenge to royal authority was apparent elsewhere in the mandamus, where La Fare, taking issue with judicial Jansenism's definition of ecclesiastical power as purely "persuasive" and interior, held that the church possessed a jurisdiction that was exterior, coercive, and quite independent of the king's. This jurisdiction, according to La Fare, also possessed "legislative power, which always entails that of making itself obeyed by canonical penalties."[150] An independent, exterior, coercive jurisdiction with the power to legislate might possibly legislate and coerce in opposition to royal authority.

What form that devout disobedience might take became likewise apparent as soon as royal authority, having defined Unigenitus as a "judgment of the universal church in the matter of doctrine" in March 1730, began to balk at that definition's canonical consequences as some bishops began to construe them in the months that followed. That began to happen as early as 22 July 1731, when Cardinal Fleury, in a circular letter to the Gallican bishops, maintained that Unigenitus fell short of being a "rule of faith"—a denomination apparently given to it by a Roman synod in 1725—meaning in plainer words that the bishops should not go so far as to refuse the sacraments or sacred burial to appellants or other opponents of the bull. Just about all the pro-Unigenitus stalwarts at the time, notably the bishops of Arles, Embrun, Laon, and Marseilles, fairly stumbled over each other in their zeal to put their disobedience in writing, using the phrase "rule of faith" and appealing to the Roman Council's authority as well as their own as spelled out in the Edict of 1695.[151] It is this brittle and impolitic vindication of episcopal and papal jurisdic-

---

149. Etienne-Joseph de La Fare, *Mandement de Monseigneur l'évêque duc de Laon . . . sur la soumission due à la constitution Unigenitus . . .* , pp. 15–16.

150. Ibid., pp. 17–20.

151. See, for example, Henri-Xavier Belsunce, Bishop of Marseilles, *Lettre pastorale de Monseigneur l'évêque de Marseilles, à l'occasion de l'arrêt du Conseil d'état du roy, pour faire cesser toutes disputes et*

tion, as manifested in the controversy over refusal of sacraments, that was to deal such mortal blows to royal and episcopal authority in the 1750s and 1760s.

In the long run, then, the chief danger posed by these ultraenthusiasts of *Unigenitus* for the monarchy was that, thinking it insufficiently zealous on behalf of the altar, they would come to oppose the monarchy from the religious right. But even in the shorter run their imprudent zeal on behalf of *Unigenitus* was dangerously *impolitic.* "With regard to your project of excommunicating everyone reluctant to receive the constitution *[Unigenitus]*, I think you can hardly be too circumspect," Fleury warned La Fare in 1730, trying in vain to convince him that a Jansenist did not lurk behind each and every confessional. Tiredly admonishing the irrepressible La Fare on another occasion, Fleury reminded him that "it is not enough to have zeal, which you know must be tempered by prudence."[152] The ever present danger for Fleury and the monarchy was that La Fare and his ilk would resort to jurisdictional acts that made an *éclat*–a public refusal of sacraments or the publication of inflammatory mandamuses like the ones against the Mairamberg's memoir–that would backfire in the form of judicial counterattack.

That counterattack in turn typically took the form of the *appel comme d'abus* or an "appeal in case of abuse": a judicial appeal of an ecclesial act or judgment to the royal courts, whether by the aggrieved parties or by a parlement's own *procureur général* acting as public prosecutor, on the grounds that some sort of procedural abuse had been committed by the offending bishop or his episcopal court *(officialité).* To be sure, ecclesiastical courts were in principle independent of secular ones; they judged misdemeanors committed by clerics as well as spiritual offenses committed by laypersons, and they judged conjointly with royal courts in so-called "mixed" secular-spiritual cases. But one of the implications of Gallicanism, especially as construed by the parlements, was that the king–and consequently his courts–were ultimately the source of all justice in the realm, with the result that French ecclesiastical courts were not free to violate the provisions of their own canon law as approved in France, much less to interpret it in a manner, say, contradictory to the Gallican "liberties" themselves.

Hence the appel comme d'abus, which allowed the parlements or even the subaltern secular courts to correct on appeal various "abuses" of ecclesiastical justice; hence also the importance of the appel comme d'abus in the steady erosion of ecclesiastical justice to the benefit of royal justice since the later Middle Ages. That even in the monarchy's estimation this erosion had proceeded too far,

contestations au sujet de la constitution Unigenitus (Marseilles, n.d.), p. 1; Pierre-Guérin de Tencin, *Mandement de l'archévêque prince d'Embrun, contre un écrit intitulé: Lettre de M. l'ancien évêque d'Apt,* (n.p., 1731), p. 3; and Etienne-Joseph de La Fare, *Lettre de Monseigneur l'évêque de Laon à Monseigneur le cardinal de Fleury* (n.p., 1731), p. 4.

152. AN: AP 257 (Maurepas papers): Ms. 14 I, fol. 75, Fleury to La Fare, Issy, 22 Dec. 1730; Ms. 14 II, fol. 120, Fleury to La Fare, Marly, 12 Feb. 1733; and fol. 134, Fleury to La Fare, Versailles, 27 Dec. 1733.

threatening its ability to maintain the crucial "balance" between the Gallican Church and the secular courts, is evidenced by Louis XIV's Edict of 1695, which, besides reinforcing episcopal jurisdiction over the curés, also tried to shore up the bishops' eroding spiritual jurisdiction by limiting the appel comme d'abus. But that did not prevent the parlements, especially their Jansenist magistrates, from seeing the crown's interest very differently and from defending the legacy of 1682 against that of 1695. And that meant seizing every occasion to invoke the appel comme d'abus.

The Political Crisis of 1730–33

The "rights" of Jansenist curés, the deacon Pâris's posthumous miracles, the figuratist "news" of the *Nouvelles ecclésiastiques,* judicial Jansenism, the zeal and high-handedness of constitutionary bishops, and the Parlement of Paris's appel comme d'abus—these added up to more than the sum of their parts when they converged in a political crisis, which is what happened in 1730–33. While the elements of it have been considered piecemeal and separately, this crisis is worth recounting as such, not only to show how these elements came together, but because, as Jeffrey Merrick has argued, it is a revelatory dispute over words, illustrating how the Old Regime establishment might rupture from the inside. Although barristers, magistrates, curés, bishops, and the Royal Council all appealed to still universally venerated traditions and institutions, their wrangling over the meanings of these traditions and institutions revealed the existence of not one old regime but many, and that attempts at clarification only underscored their incompatibility.[153]

The political crisis of 1730–33 began with a zealous vindication of episcopal authority that provoked a defensive appel comme d'abus—to be specific, the interdiction by the Bishop of Orléans of three priests from their functions because they had refused to read his mandamus against the famous legal consultation against the Council of Embrun, and the subsequent appeal by these priests for justice to the bailiwick of Orléans, which was under the jurisdiction of the Parlement of Paris. In order to be judged, the appeal had first to be validated or "received" by the Parlement, whether by the procureur général's plea or at the initiative of one of the councillors. All of Fleury's diplomacy after the appeal came to his attention was initially devoted to dissuading the procureur général Guillaume-François Joly de Fleury and the first president Antoine Portail from

153. Jeffrey Merrick, "'Disputes over Words' and Constitutional Conflict in France, 1730–1732," *FHS* 14 (Fall 1986):497–520. See also David Bell, "Des stratégies d'opposition sous Louis XV: L'affaire des avocats, 1730–31"; Campbell, "The Conduct of Politics in France in the Time of the Cardinal de Fleury, 1723–1743," pp. 293–384; and of course Hardy, *Le cardinal de Fleury et le mouvement janséniste,* pp. 147–291, all of which recount the crisis from different perspectives.

allowing the appeal to obtain that validation, and to devising instead some way to settle the conflict out of court. But to suspend the priests' appeal was not to prevent it from pending both literally and figuratively, a sword of Damocles ready to drop at any moment.

By the end of the winter, however, Fleury felt strong enough to attempt a structural solution to the problem of the appeal and problems like it: a new royal declaration that would fortify once and for all the status of *Unigenitus* as a "law of church and state" and disallow all appeals having to do with it. This declaration, dated 24 March 1730, also declared the bull to be "a judgment of the universal church in the matter of doctrine," reiterated the requirement to sign Pope Alexander VII's Formulary for all candidates to benefices, and prescribed silence on all parties to the dispute over *Unigenitus,* threatening them with exemplary punishments for violations of this silence, except for bishops as pastors of their flocks. Forcibly registered by Fleury and Chancellor d'Aguesseau in a lit de justice assembly on 3 April, the declaration provoked the abbé Pucelle to say that it had in effect declared the king "a Vassal of the Pope" and the "venerable *vieillard*" Le Clerc de Lesseville to implore the king on bended knee. All in vain, these pathetic gestures and rhetoric, because d'Aguesseau declared this declaration to have been registered anyway, and because lettres de cachet prevented Portail from allowing the Parlement's various judicial chambers to reassemble in order to deliberate on the lit de justice assembly in the weeks that followed.[154] The uneasy calm did not last because, exempted from the silence otherwise ordered by the Declaration of March 1730, the bishops soon made themselves heard. Invoking the letter of the Edict of 1695, the June meeting of the quinquennial General Assembly of the Gallican Clergy, which since 1695 no longer contained any curé delegates, loudly remonstrated against the appel comme d'abus in the case of the curés of Orléans and reminded the king in the closing address by Rousseau de La Parisière, Bishop of Nîmes, that his reign rested on "catholicity." Duly remonstrated, the king in council "evoked" or removed the curés' case from the Parlement's purview in October. These events were in turn enough to reanimate the Parlement of Paris, which, goaded by Pucelle, remonstrated against the Bishop of Nîmes's speech and the evocation of the curés' appeal, as well as against the earlier prohibition to deliberate about the Declaration of 1730 and the lit de justice assembly in which it had been forcibly registered.

Back in the bar, meanwhile, copyright considerations forced François de Mairamberg to rewrite an earlier 1718 judicial memoir that he had originally intended to republish in support of the three Orléans priests and their appeal against their bishop. Unable to consult the original memoir's cosigners because

---

154. *NE* 5 Apr. 1730, p. 74. The Jansenist weekly contended that the royal declaration had won only 40 of 250 of the Parlement's votes.

they were already on vacation, he allowed the printer to publish the rewritten memoir, which began circulating in October.[155] The memoir was a blockbuster, as we have seen, prompting the Royal Council to condemn it and to demand that the barristers retract it as well as to sign an absolutist confession of political faith. But while their contrition may have mollified the monarchy, it left the bishops unavenged, provoking incendiary mandamuses from La Fare and Tencin and even from the more moderate Vintimille, who described some of the memoir's statements about the church and spiritual jurisdiction as heretical. Vintimille's pastoral letter in turn prompted the Parlement to appeal it comme d'abus on 5 March. Fleury and the King's Council then tried to play a mediating role with a judgment or arrêt, which, acknowledging that the church possessed the "exterior apparatus of a public tribunal," also extended the injunction of silence on the subject of *Unigenitus* to the bishops. But this measure failed to satisfy the bishops, who insisted that the arrêt acknowledge that the church had a jurisdiction pure and simple, and that the Council quash the Parlement's appel comme d'abus. A circular letter from the Royal Council to the bishops satisfied them on the first count, and another conciliar arrêt dated 30 July 1731, allowing the distribution of Vintimille's mandamus, was a gesture toward satisfying them on the second. That arrêt, however, touched off a three-month strike by the Parisian barristers, outraged that the arrêt had apparently vindicated Vintimille's accusation that they were heretics.

The Royal Council at first responded punitively to this strike—the first of its kind—exiling ten of the "agitators" to different towns in August. But a conciliatory exegesis of the archbishop's charge of heresy finally enabled the Council to negotiate the end of the strike, just in time for the Parlement of Paris's return from its annual autumnal recess in November 1731. And none too soon, either, because Fleury needed a truce with the barristers, war being again imminent with the magistrates. For meanwhile a separate but related affair, again involving the Bishop of Orléans, had resulted in another appel comme d'abus, a parlementary injunction, the Council's annulment of this injunction, and three successive sets of rebuffed remonstrances, culminating in the Parlement's attempt to lay down its own version of the Gallican liberties just before its scheduled recess beginning on 7 September 1731. Enunciating the "heretical" principle recently laid down in the barristers' consultation, to the effect that the church was totally accountable to the king—"and, in case of abuse, to his court"—the Parlement's announcement would have reaped an episcopal whirlwind had not Fleury annulled it and literally had it erased from the Parlement's registers before its publication. But he well knew that in place of the episcopal whirlwind he would face a parlementary one as soon as the magistrates returned from their recess and reviewed their altered registers.

155. Bell, *Lawyers and Citizens*, pp. 91–93.

So the parlementary return or *rentrée* began with an anguished impasse between the assembled councillors bent on discussing the erasure of their arrêt of 7 September and a first president duty-bound by sealed royal orders to prevent this discussion. When, on 29 November, the Parlement deigned to open and peruse the content of another such sealed royal order, they unanimously took to their carriages and, on the abbé Pucelle's urging, went to Marly to raise Fleury's "blockade" of the king, only to find when they got there that the forewarned royal court had moved elsewhere, leaving the magistrates with nothing to do except to take the road back to Paris.

But just as the Parlement, repeatedly rebuffed, seemed inclined to return to obedience, its confrontation with Fleury over this new appel comme d'abus coalesced with two others pitting Archbishop Vintimille against the Parisian curés, supported by their pious parishioners, apropos of the Jansenist *Nouvelles ecclésiastiques* and the Saint Médard miracles. A first archiepiscopal mandamus condemning three hagiographical biographies of the deacon Pâris prompted the councillor Jérôme de Pâris to interject an appel comme d'abus in defense of his deceased brother's defamed memory, while a second mandamus, threatening anyone caught reading the *Nouvelles ecclésiastiques* with excommunication, made the mistake of describing *Unigenitus* as having been "received by the whole church." Thinking themselves members of the universal church, yet knowing that they had not received the bull, twenty-one curés refused to read the archbishop's mandamus to their congregations, and when Vintimille threatened them with interdiction they appealed the mandamus comme d'abus to the Parlement. Left to its own devices the Parlement would almost certainly have acted on these appeals, but it was again prevented from doing so by the King's Council, which on 3 May 1732 ordered the magistrates not to meddle with the miracles; still other conciliar and verbal orders forbade them to entertain any appeals "concerning the church." The outspoken Pucelle found himself exiled to his Benedictine abbey in the Nièvre, and the Jansenist councillor Jean-Baptiste Titon incarcerated first in the royal château at Vincennes, then in the fortress in Ham.[156] Thus excluded from the world of real action, the magistrates compensated with melodramatic scenes and pathetic gestures.

When on 16 May, First President Portail reported to the Parlement's assembled chambers on his failed mission to the king at Compiègne and suggested remonstrances on the subject of their two missing colleagues, most of the councillors, including several from the normally conservative Grand' chambre, silently filed out of the Palais de justice and imitated the barristers by going on judicial strike. Resuming their functions on 23 May after being ordered to do so by

---

156. On Titon's Jansenism see ibid., p. 272, where he is described as "quite a Jansenist" and an "important protector of M. de Pâris."

a lettre de cachet, the assembled chambers formally appealed Vintimille's mandamus against the Jansenist news sheet comme d'abus, and this despite the refusal
of the procureur général Joly de Fleury to request such an appeal and in defiance
of repeated royal orders to the contrary. When on 15 June the royal council
arrested four more Jansenist councillors and then annulled the Parlement's appeal
on the sixteenth, just about the whole Parlement submitted their resignations in
what struck the memoirist and barrister Antoine-Alexandre Barbier as "the greatest event yet seen since the beginning of the monarchy."[157] The threat of outright
confiscation of their venal offices and consequent loss of noble status soon
brought them back to the Palais de justice, however, where the ministry confronted them with a disciplinary declaration that would have made all royal
declarations enforceable with or without the Parlement's remonstrances and
would have undone all the gains made by the Parlement under the regency of the
duc d'Orléans.

The first lit de justice assembly ever held at the royal château of Versailles
forcibly registered this declaration but failed to overawe the magistrates, who
responded with the now disallowed remonstrances, assembled chambers, and
another judicial strike; whereupon the royal council exiled 139 parlementaires to
unpleasant places in France, there to spend their two-month judicial recess that
began on 7 September. The crisis continued apace until the scheduled return in
early November, when, in need of the Parlement's financial cooperation for what
would be the War of the Polish Succession, Fleury recalled the exiled magistrates
and, on the Parlement's "humble" plea, suspended the disciplinary Declaration of
18 August 1732.

Thus the judicial crisis of 1730–33, which established the script followed by
the many others like it in the 1750s and 1760s. This archetypical crisis differs from
the later ones, however, in that the linked causes of absolutism, episcopacy, and
Unigenitus emerged more or less triumphant in 1732, only a little worse for the
wear. It is true that by imposing and then rescinding the disciplinary Declaration
of 18 August, Fleury seemed to have retreated from his most advanced position;
and his policy toward the Parlement and the clergy was evenhanded enough for a
while to confuse Parisian opinion and enrage firebrands like La Fare. Still, Fleury
contrived to get the magistrates to acquiesce in the Declaration of March 1730,
declaring Unigenitus a law of church and state—the real bone of contention. He
was also later able to empty his ample quiver of lettres de cachet against the
remaining Jansenists in the priesthood and religious orders, as well as to complete
his purge of the University of Paris by disenfranchising another eighty doctors
from the faculty of arts in 1739.[158] Dividing and conquering, Fleury also cleverly

157. Barbier, *Journal*, 2:297.
158. Hardy, *Le cardinal de Fleury et le mouvement janséniste*, pp. 323–36; and *NE* 12 Aug. 23–Sept.
1739, pp. 125–52.

exploited the divisions within the Jansenist community apropos of the convulsionary movement, going so far as to subsidize such "moderate" Jansenist critiques of the convulsions as Nicolas Petitpied's *Consultation des trente sur les convulsions (Consultation of Thirty Concerning Convulsions)* and to allow the Parlement to concern itself with the matter, resulting in a hostile inquest into the convulsionary phenomenon in 1735. Fleury thereby not only exacerbated the divisions with the Jansenist movement already in its religious "agony," but also permitted the Parlement temporarily to alienate an important segment of its own popular support.[159]

Indeed, the environs of 1730 mark the high tide of absolutism, at least so far as its legislative pretensions and religious self-definition are concerned. The Declaration of 24 March 1730, which enshrined *Unigenitus* as a law of both church and state, took its place alongside the Declaration of 14 May 1724, which codified and strengthened all the seventeenth-century statutes against "the so-called reformed religion" and "newly converted" Catholics. Reinforcing the fiction that there were no more Protestants in France, the new declaration made Catholic priests parties and judges in their own cause by giving them sole right to attest to the "catholicity" of suspected Protestants, failing which their marriages were reputed as concubinages, their children as illegitimate, and adult Protestants themselves subject to deportation, galley labor, or death, depending on whether they were women, men, or pastors.[160] And reinforcing the declarations concerning both Jansenism and Protestantism, in a sense, was the Edict of 1723, known as the Printers' and Booksellers' Code *(Code de la librairie)*, which similarly codified and fortified the monarchy's many legislative attempts at control over the printed word that had begun with the Protestant Reformation.[161]

Yet Fleury's gains in the crisis of 1730–33 came at the cost of considerable longer-run liabilities. Fleury's Declaration of March 1730 may have finally enshrined the place of *Unigenitus* as a law of church and state alongside the Edict of Fontainebleau. But by also having *Unigenitus* declared a "judgment of the universal church in the matter of doctrine," Fleury encouraged zealously constitutionary bishops to proceed as though appellants were heretics, while by warning that the bull was not a "rule of faith," Fleury encouraged the parlements to proceed as

---

159. Kreiser, *Miracles, Convulsions, and Ecclesiastical Politics,* pp. 324–51; and Maire, *Les convulsionnaires de Saint-Médard,* pp. 153–79; also Joseph Dédieu, "L'agonie du jansénisme, 1715–1790: Essai de bio-bibliographie," *Revue d'histoire de l'église de France* 14 (1928):161–214, from which the term *agonie* is taken.

160. Henri Carré, *Louis XV, 1715–1774,* vol. 8, 2d part, *Histoire de France illustrée depuis les origines jusqu'à la Révolution,* ed. Ernest Lavisse (Paris, 1911), pp. 84–86; Joseph Dédieu, *Histoire politique des Protestants français* (Paris, 1925), 1, chap. 2; and Geoffrey Adams, *The Huguenots and French Public Opinion, 1685–1787* (Waterloo, Ont., 1992), p. 40.

161. Henri-Jean Martin, "La direction des lettres," in *Histoire de l'édition française,* 2 vol., ed. Roger Chartier and Henri-Jean Martin (Paris, 1990), 2:73–87.

though these bishops were troublemakers. In the short run Fleury was able to keep devout episcopal firebrands in check and prevent the wholesale refusal of sacraments. But not before bishops like La Fare had sounded the constitutionary tocsin, articulating an ideology that would survive to haunt the monarchy when a cardinal-bishop was no longer there to dispel it. Fleury may well have crushed Jansenism as a clerical and theological force while humiliating the Parlement of Paris, its ally. But not before protestantizing Jansenism as well as effecting its juncture with the Parlement, producing a judicial Jansenism that would do far more damage to episcopacy and monarchy than either Jansenism or the parlements had ever separately done. Finally, Fleury may even have crushed Jansenism as a popular movement. But not before compromising the monarchy's prestige with a public that had been its chief mainstay in the sixteenth century, eventually making Louis XV as unpopular in Paris as ever Henri III had been. This last development, the monarchy's fall in Parisian public opinion, calls for some further comment.

Public Opinion and the Monarchy

Although the potential threat to the monarchy posed by judicial Jansenism and devout Catholicism in the 1730s may be obvious enough, assessing the real damage done to the monarch or the monarchy by the Jansenist controversy in public opinion is another matter. Taking the pulse of public opinion is an elusive business in the best of circumstances; in the 1720s and 1730s the phenomenon of public opinion was embryonic and the available sources are few and suspect. One of the best such sources, the police reports of Parisian street and café gossip compiled for the lieutenant general of police, has recently been scrutinized by Arlette Farge, who has underscored their problematical nature as texts. In complicity with the circulation of manuscript news sheets, these reports were part of an effort to influence public opinion as well as to read it. Yet even Farge has noted the exceptional character of those written during the height of religious turmoil from 1728 to 1733, when popular opinion took on a "new face" and acquired "political sense," and jaded agents were taken aback.[162] "Be assured, Monsieur," a police spy warned the lieutenant general in 1728, commenting on his own text, "that the bile spread throughout these memoirs is conformed to the mind of the Public, which is just about universally infected with Jansenism, and that I have had no more part in them than that of a faithful amanuensis who believes it his duty to record what is being said, and who cannot without danger dissimulate what people

---

162. Arlette Farge, *Dire et mal dire: L'opinion publique au XVIIIe siècle* (Paris, 1992), p. 45, and in general pp. 37–81.

are thinking."[163] Weighted though they are toward Parisian opinion—and Parisian Jansenist opinion at that—these reports are valuable evidence of public opinion.

What emerges very clearly from these reports is that articulate Parisian opinion never held the young Louis XV in high regard, quite apart from his performance in the Jansenist controversy. As early as 1724 a police reporter noted that Parisians "continue to talk about the dissipations *(plaisirs)* and the limitations of this young monarch, of whom they foresee nothing good."[164] At various points in the roughly twenty years spanned by these police reports the king was thought to have been a debaucher of men, a pastrymaker, and a cheesemaker—none of them very royal occupations—as well as an ungracious gamester, a reckless hunter, and a melancholic "imbecile" when not distracted by these or other activities—none of them very royal qualities. Well before the government's first experiment in freeing grain prices in the 1760s, Parisians suspected that they "had a grain merchant for their king"; long before the children's kidnapping riot of 1750, they suspected him of arranging for the kidnapping of children.[165] But most of all the king was thought to be lazy and irresponsible, "given over to pleasures and the hunt," and incapable of asserting himself vis-à-vis Cardinal Fleury and other ministers to whom he had abnegated all governmental responsibility. Although, as Thomas Kaiser points out, the young king's handlers tried to market him as Louis the Pacific, Parisians promptly renamed him Louis the Hunter.[166] And although the hope persisted during this period that if Fleury ever died the king would finally come into his own, reign by himself, and make all things right, skeptics were never lacking to warn "that the king is naturally stupid and timid, that it is natural for His Majesty to follow the prejudices of his childhood, and those suggested to him by his preceptor [Fleury]."[167]

How if at all, then, did the Jansenist controversy affect this body of adverse opinion about the king, especially during the tumultuous years from 1728 to 1733? However fragile and difficult to interpret, the evidence suggests that the religious controversy began or at least hastened the transformation of criticism of the monarch into a more structural critique of the monarchy, and that in three ways.

First and foremost, the religious controversy activated Jansenism's Calvinist-like tendency to locate majesty in a transcendent God at the expense of everything below, not excepting the king. To say, for example, as unnamed "others" were reported to have said in 1728, that Cardinal Fleury "will never find

163. BA: AB, Ms. 10158, fol. 245, 27 Oct. 1728.
164. BA: AB, Ms. 10155, fol. 17, 29 Nov. 1724.
165. BA: AB, Ms. 10163, fol. 196, 2–3 May 1733; and Ms. 10168, fols. 292–94, 13–14 Aug. 1741.
166. Thomas Kaiser, "Louis *le Bien Aimé* and the Rhetoric of the Royal Body," manuscript cited with the author's permission.
167. BA: AB, Ms. 10161, fols. 171–72, 4 Apr. 1732.

grace before God, because he [has] abandoned the interests of divine majesty for that of terrestrial majesty" was to criticize Fleury, but was more profoundly to demote the monarchy by virtue of an invidious contrast between divine and human majesty. It was this invidious contrast that lay behind the chronic criticism directed against the baroque pomp and circumstance connected with the religion of the monarchy, not only on the occasion of the queen's visit to Notre Dame in 1728, but in regard to official praise for the king or public rejoicings ordered after recovery from his frequent illnesses. In part this sort of criticism was personal, as when some said that there was "little desire to rejoice when there was so little reason to be content with the king's religious policies." Yet some of it was structural, as when "others say that there is a sort of malediction on God's part on the occasion of these rejoicings, that there is always someone killed, proving that God does not approve of them."[168] This kind of reaction to the baroque and court-confined monarchy was one of a kind with Jansenist reactions to baroque piety generally and tended to demote the king to the status of a mortal like others.

The religious damage to a religiously defined monarch is most apparent in popular reaction to the monarchy's opposition to the veneration of the deacon Pâris and the closing of the cemetery of Saint-Médard. "All-powerful though he was, the king had no right to suppress the news of the marvels of God," the Parisian "they" were said to have said, in reference to the deacon's thaumaturgical miracles. Praising the sainthood of the abbé, "others went further, maintaining that one might doubt the divinity of God if the divine majesty did not reward those who had followed in the [His] footsteps . . . with apparent signs [of their sainthood] after their death, . . . and that those [like the king] who combat his . . . miracles are enemies of the truth, and the partisans of paganism and impiety."[169] Such partisans, it went without saying, were mortal as well as immoral. That, of course, was the profound meaning of the famous quatrain reportedly placarded onto the cemetery wall and noted by a police observer on 14 February 1732:

> By order of the king
> It is forbidden to the Divinity
> To perform any more miracles
> In this vicinity.[170]

It was likewise the sense of a less inspired but more pointed bit of doggerel, to the effect that if the king did not side with the "party of grace," he would no longer be king by the "grace of God."[171]

168. BA: AB, Ms. 10158, fol. 254, 1 Nov. 1728; fols. 286–87, 12 Nov. 1728.

169. BA: AB, Ms. 10161, fol. 32, 10 Jan. 1732; fol. 243, 2–3 May 1732.

170. BA: AB, Ms. 10161, fol. 106, 14 Feb. 1732.

171. BA: AB, Ms. 10161, fol. 403, "Nouvelles publiques, depuis le dimanche 29 juin 1733 jusques à samedi 5 juillet."

A second adverse effect of the religious controversy on public opinion toward the monarchy lay in the damage it did to the Jesuits and the episcopacy. Louis XIV had so closely associated both Jesuits and bishops with the monarchy that they had become its defensive outworks, with the result that they could have hardly have sustained major attacks in public opinion without collateral damage to the monarchy itself. Largely Jansenist and persecuted for their Jansenism, Parisian curés and other secular priests may have survived the religious crisis of the late 1720s and early 1730s with only minor cuts and bruises in public opinion, but bishops and Jesuits were major casualties. People "also declaim as usual against the bishops as partisans of the constitution [Unigenitus]," repetitiously reported a police agent in 1732, adding that the same people "do not hesitate to say that [these bishops] are men without religion, who ask no more than that they have enough to satisfy their passions, saying in a word that these prelates do not believe in God."[172] Individual bishops, especially constitutionary ones, fared worse: Languet de Gergy was a common "scoundrel," and La Fare had "a soul as corrupt as his body, which, they say, is filled with flour and furthermore afflicted with an infamous disease *(mal immonde)*."[173] As for the Jesuits who were typically seen as the evil geniuses behind Fleury's persecutory policies, numerous were the reported wishes that the parlements expel them from France, failing which that their houses be burned to the ground. Reporting on a civil suit tried in the subaltern Parisian court called the *Châtelet* pitting the natural inheritors against the Jesuits for possession of some valuable paintings bequeathed to them by a pious donor, police reporters found it simply "impossible to describe the indecent joy of the public," or at least that part of it present in the Palais de justice when the decision was announced: "ecstatic clapping of hands and praise for the judges who had ruled against the society," and "a thousand names as injurious as they were scandalous" at the expense of those Jesuits so unfortunate to be there.[174] In sum, "it can be assuredly stated that the public is extremely biased against the bishops and the Jesuits," reported a police agent, in perhaps the understatement of the 1730s.[175]

The popular hostility directed against bishops and Jesuits was far too massive and intense, and bishops and Jesuits were far too closely identified with the Bourbon monarchy, for that monarchy to have escaped some institutional damage. The argument successfully deployed against the Jesuits by the Jansenist barrister Aubry in the case of the contested paintings—and, with minor modifica-

172. BA: AB, Ms. 10162, fols. 231–32, 15 Aug. 1732.
173. BA: AB, Ms. 10158, fol. 195, 9 Oct. 1728; and Ms. 10162, fol. 58, 27 July 1732. See also *NE* 30 July 1729, p. 136.
174. BA: AB, Ms. 10159, fol. 250, 15 July 1729; and fol. 273, 9 Aug. 1729. See also *NE* 30 July 1729, p. 136.
175. BA: AB, Ms. 10161, fols. 315–16, 29 May 1733.

tions, used in the 1760s to dissolve the order—worked in part because of the "monarchical" or top-down authority structure of the Jesuits' constitutions. Aubry's point was that no monarchy was big enough to harbor another one within its borders, but the police observer, who was close to the scene of verbal action and reaction, took the argument as critical of monarchy itself. Commenting on Fleury's policy of "giving a portion of royal authority to each of the king's bishops," some said, according to this report, "that whatever authority that the prince might give to such people, it will only result . . . in making His Majesty and the said bishops contemptible alike." And if local opposition to bishops like Languet de Gergy was "entirely republican," in the reported opinion of Parisians in 1732, might not opposition to the monarchy that enforced the authority of the likes of Languet have been similarly construed?[176]

These various propos point to the beginnings of a structural opposition to and critique of Bourbon absolutism that resonated in the Parisian streets and cafés as well as in legal consultations and figuratist treatises. "And they say that should the king uphold everything that is likely to emanate from his authority against the Jansenists, His Majesty will not be able to prevent the inhabitants of Paris from revolting against that authority," a police agent reported in 1729.[177] To such characteristically Jansenist justifications for disobedience, these Parisian propos added a tendency to denigrate the purely personal authority of the king to the benefit of immutable law or a putative public authority, especially after the intervention of the Parlement of Paris in the controversy in 1732. "The greater number convince themselves that the court [of Parlement] will prevail and that everything it demands will be conceded, failing which the king will risk losing the crown," an agent reported in June 1732, "to which they add that if the [other] parlements follow the example of those of Paris and Rennes, the king's power will amount to very little."[178] It is hard to gainsay the subversiveness of some of these reported propos, as for example one that had "some going so far as to assert that if the state continues to be governed as it has been for a while longer, the king will lose all his authority" and, adding that this opinion was held by the "most sensible people," predicted that "it may well happen that this monarchy will fall, and that the Realm will be governed like a republic."[179]

What is characteristically Jansenist about these utterances is the focus on the monarchy's immortal body to the detriment of its mortal incumbent. "Some go even further," reported the police observer in 1733, "and say that however power-

176. For comment about monarchy and bishops, BA: AB, Ms. 10161, fol. 253, 3–4 Nov. 1732; for description of opposition to Languet de Gergy, fol. 224, 25 Apr. 1732.
177. BA: AB, Ms. 10159, fols. 277–78, 13 Aug. 1729. See also Ms. 10160, fol. 18, 14 Oct. 1729.
178. BA: AB, Ms. 10161, fol. 353, 14 June 1732. For a similar report, see fol. 292, 18 May 1732.
179. BA: AB, Ms. 10161, fols. 1–2, 3 July 1732.

ful they may be, the kings of France cannot alienate or destroy the laws of the Realm, much less the liberties of the Gallican Church, because, they add, the said liberties are the finest attribute of the French Crown which the kings are not the masters to destroy."[180] But as to the king's mortal body, Jansenists like Calvinists earlier tended to leave it alone, even if vulnerable and exposed. To the not inconsiderable stock of scurrilities on the subject of Louis XV's person the typical Jansenist "seditious saying" added little or nothing, not even holding the king's many sexual infidelities against him when these became a regular feature of courtly life as the 1730s gave way to the 1740s. On the contrary, even at the height of the religious crisis of 1732 the perennial Parisian "they" held that "it would be desirable if the king were to fall in love, because, they say, that might distract him from the blind love that His Majesty has for Cardinal Fleury."[181] It is as though the conviction that all human activity was sinful if unredeemed by efficacious grace deterred the Jansenists from harping on this or that individual sin, especially where the king was concerned, lest such moral vigilance add to his already sufficient biases against them.

When on Easter 1740 police observers witnessed the first public reaction to the king's failure to touch for scrofula, they reported that Parisians referred to the touch as a royal right, a "right, they said in jest, that His Majesty [seems inclined to] allow to lapse." The language of "right" seems typical of judicial Jansenists; and if the right in question were, as they put it, to be "prescribed," the beneficiary they had in mind was probably the deacon Pâris.[182] But judicial Jansenist opinion had nothing to do with the reason for the loss of the royal touch, namely Louis's failure to confess and receive absolution, itself the result of his Jesuit confessors' uncharacteristic rigor. So Montesquieu's quip in 1719 that the king had subordinated his miraculous powers to the pope for the sake of *Unigenitus* turned out to be more prophetic than he could have known. And when later on in that decade Louis began to encounter heavy criticism for his moral misconduct, that criticism, too, tended to come from the parti dévot and the Jesuits, and not from the Jansenists, who continued to pit a judicial monarchy against the actual monarch in their typically institutional way.

If in the last analysis none of this popular criticism was fatal to the monarch or the monarchy in the 1730s or 1740s—if, even if only for a brief moment, Louis XV could still become Louis the Beloved in 1744—it was in part because Cardinal Fleury continued to act as first minister and bore most of the brunt of popular wrath. Even in the 1740s it remained possible for "some" to hope that if Fleury

180. BA: AB, Ms. 10163, fol. 222, 20 May 1733.
181. BA: AB, Ms. 10161, fol. 46, 18 June 1732.
182. BA: AB, Ms. 10167, fol. 88, 26–27 Apr. 1740.

continued to persecute Jansenists on all sides, it was because "God was evidently using His Eminence to purify his elect, but that there will come a time when the branches will be thrown into the fire, after which those who are now in opposition will enjoy peace, holding that as soon as the said Eminence is gone, the affairs of the church will change their visage."[183] Things indeed were to change after Fleury's disappearance in 1743, but not, alas, the way Parisian appellant opinion had hoped they would.

183. BA: AB, Ms. 10168, fol. 38, 15–16 June 1741.

CHAPTER 3

The Siege of Sacral Absolutism

IN JUNE 1749 ONE CHARLES COFFIN FELL DANGEROUSLY ILL and, fearing death, requested the viaticum—the Eucharist given, along with extreme unction, to a dying communicant—from the curé of his parish of Saint-Etienne-du-Mont in Paris. No very obvious obstacle stood in the way of honoring his request. Poet, rhetorician, and liturgist, Coffin had been principal of the College of Beauvais before becoming rector of the University of Paris and remained fondly remembered in both capacities. At the request of Archbishop Vintimille he had composed numbers of hymns for the Parisian breviary, including one entitled "On Jordan's Banks," which is still sung to the music of Michael Pretorius as a Christmas carol today. But Coffin had also been an opponent and appellant of the bull *Unigenitus,* and excluded as such from the university by Cardinal Fleury in 1739. So when called for by Coffin his curé, named Bouëttin, asked him to show a *billet de confession* (certificate of confession) proving that he had last confessed to an "orthodox" priest—that is, one who had accepted *Unigenitus.* When Coffin refused to produce the required certificate, the curé, acting on instructions from Paris's new archbishop, left Coffin to his own devices, namely to die without receiving the last sacramental rites of Catholicism. The incident provoked outrage on the part of many Parisians, who showed their sympathy with Coffin by following the funeral cortege on 22 June. It also provoked the beginning of the great controversy over refusal of sacraments, which dominated—even constituted—French domestic politics throughout the 1750s.[1]

This need not have been so. For in spite of the crisis of 1730–32 and a few after-tremors in 1739–40, French absolutism, as we have seen, seemed to emerge triumphant from this new *Unigenitus*-related round of religious "wars," just as it had from the old ones. A worthy successor of Richelieu and Mazarin, Cardinal-Minister Fleury had generally succeeded after 1732 in keeping parlements and bishops from each other's throats and devout firebrands and Jansenist reappellants in their respective places. For the latter, those places very often continued to be exile in the Netherlands, the Bastille, or monastic "prisons"—and increasingly the cemetery, as an aging generation of appellants failed to pass on the torch of "truth" to a new one. Its means of recruitment cut off by Fleury, Jansenism all but disappeared from the episcopacy, steadily dwindled in the priesthood, and found itself ever more quarantined in the judiciary. And as the century passed its midpoint, even Jansenism's hold on Parisian public opinion encountered worthy challengers in the persons of "enlightened" philosophes whose rehabilitation of human nature made light of penitential pessimism and whose first political instincts were to damn all confessional antagonists.

It was nonetheless at the "century of light's" high noon, during the decades of the 1750s and 1760s, that *Unigenitus*-related conflict in the form of the controversy over refusal of sacraments delivered to both the monarchy and the episcopacy its most telling blows. To be sure, the religious controversy did not do its worst unassisted. What was perceived as an ignominious peace with England and Austria in 1748, the loss of both an Indian and an American empire in the Seven Years' War in 1763, the monarchy's disastrous experimentation with freeing the grain trade beginning in 1763, and the monarchy's resultant fiscal dependence on both the parlements and the episcopacy—these wreaked havoc in their own right besides functioning as necessary conditions for the kind of damage that the religious controversy did. Yet the monarchy's failure to get the better of a religious and political controversy of its own making, albeit with roots in the sixteenth century, undermined Bourbon absolutism's first and best reason for existence, invalidating it as nothing else could have done. The degree and kind of desacralization sustained by the French monarchy in the course of this controversy represented religious damage that only rival religions could have done. Directly attributable to the controversy over *Unigenitus* as well is the monarchy's loss of pivotal position as supreme arbiter among the Old Regime's contending corps and corporations, reflected in the parlements' clear triumph in 1757 over an

1. L.-G. Michaud, *Biographie universelle, ancienne et moderne*, 83 vols. (Paris, 1811–53), 9:185–86; *Nouvelles ecclésiastiques, ou mémoires pour servir à l'histoire de la constitution Unigenitus* (henceforth *NE*), 3d ed. (Utrecht, 1728–1803), 10 July 1749, pp. 109–11.

episcopacy even more discredited than the monarchy. Symptomatic of the demise of French absolutism in the 1750s and 1760s is the crumbling of several of its legislative pillars: the Edict of Fontainebleau, the Gallican Declaration of 1682, and the Edict of 1695. How that happened is the subject of this chapter and the next.

The Demise of the Symbols of Absolutism

When "his" Mazarin, Cardinal Fleury, died in 1743, Louis XV resolved to do what he said he would but did not do in 1726: imitate his "great" predecessor by governing the realm without the help of a principal minister. Although it is not clear who if anyone could have taken Fleury's place, it is at least clear that Louis the Great's royal act was a hard one to follow and that Louis the Beloved was not up to it. The permanent pageantry that had grown up around Louis XIV at Versailles had so personalized the monarchy—had so collapsed the king's mortal and sempiternal bodies, to use Kantorowicz's terminology again—that the monarchy now required its occupant's personality to be an entirely public one. Louis XV's recent and largely sympathetic biographers, most notably Michel Antoine, have convincingly argued that Louis XV was intelligent and reasonably diligent about state business, but they have also conceded that he was a shy and almost pathologically private person.[2] Alternately assuming the appearance of haughty remoteness and glacial indifference, the king's public demeanor baffled contemporaries, who soon ran short of plausible explanations for his "taciturnity" and apparent "cruelty."[3] At the same time the impersonal bureaucratization of absolutism as described as well by Michel Antoine continued apace, as the judicial office of chancellor became ever more ceremonial in comparison to the removable secretaries of state, the once brash commissioner *(commissaire)* lost ground to the newer functionary or *commis,* decisions debated in royal councils gave way to administrative orders *(arrêts du conseil),* and the courts remonstrated in vain against the growth of administrative law and the judicial immunity of governmental agents.[4]

The simultaneous bureaucratization and privatization of the monarchy produced disconcerting results during the reign of Louis XV. On the one hand, the apparatus of conciliar government as bequeathed by Louis XIV continued to

---

2. Michel Antoine, *Le Conseil du roi sous le règne de Louis XV* (Geneva, 1970), pp. 598–627; and *Louis XV* (Paris, 1989), pp. 162–67, 405–56.

3. Edmond-Jean-François Barbier, *Chronique de la Régence et du règne de Louis XV (1718–1763), ou Journal de Barbier* (henceforth *Journal*), 8 vols. (Paris, 1857), 1:257–58, 260.

4. Antoine, *Le conseil du roi sous le règne de Louis XV,* pp. 329–431; and his "La monarchie absolue" in *The Political Culture of the Old Regime,* ed. Keith M. Baker, vol. 1 of *The French Revolution and the Creation of Modern Political Culture* (Oxford, 1988), pp. 3–24.

function as before: the Council of State *(Conseil d'un haut)* debated and decided issues of foreign policy, and the Council of Dispatches *(Conseil des dépêches)* did the same for the most important domestic issues. Indeed, Louis XV almost always abided by the majority vote in these councils. And to his chief ministers, called secretaries of state and the controller-general of finance, Louis XV gave unprecedented independence, creating the effect of three or four "first ministers" instead of one. Behind their backs, however, and outside the councils, a diffident king pursued his private or "secret" policies with the help of such outside advice as the prince de Conti's and with foreign agents and the apparently bisexual chevalier d'Eon. Yet these secret foreign and domestic royal policies did not prevent the king from occasionally reasserting his public authority in spectacular and seemingly arbitrary ways, most often by "disgracing" and exiling his chief ministers when their policies proved disastrous or drifted too far afield from his own.[5] The effect of this style of royal leadership was a chronic incoherence extending from the very center to the farthest peripheries.

To the degree that the recent conflation of the two royal bodies survived these developments, it did so only in the minds of the parti dévot. Yet any such conflation of the king's proverbial two bodies only made it more vulnerable to controversy about the sacraments. For if, as Roger Chartier has argued, the king's person became at once a sign and the thing signified—both a representation of the monarchy and the monarchy itself—it bore an evident similarity to the eucharistic sacrament that was also at once a sign of Christ's body and that body itself. And to the degree that it became analogous to that sacrament, the royal body was bound to suffer politicization—even desacralization—by performing badly in a controversy that tended to politicize and desacralize the sacraments themselves.[6] And there is no want of evidence, as we shall see, that for portions of the Parisian population something like that took place.

For judicial Jansenists, in contrast, the same developments served only to widen the space between the two royal bodies that the revival of the lit de justice assembly after 1715 had helped them resurrect. So long as Fleury lived and governed in the king's name, judicial Jansenists could hold the distinction between the king's two bodies in reserve, as it were, and do battle with royal policy in the name of the misguided king against his evil chief minister. Thus, in the most melodramatic moments of the crisis of 1730–32, did the president de Lesseville throw himself at the king's feet, and the abbé Pucelle propose to "lift the siege" of the king, both of them acting on the supposition that the real or "private" king

5. Martin Mansergh, "The Revolution of 1771, or the Exile of the Parlement of Paris" (Ph.D. diss., Oxford University, 1973), pp. 1–12.

6. Roger Chartier, *The Cultural Origins of the French Revolution*, trans. Lydia G. Cochrane, Bicenntenial Reflections on the French Revolution (Durham, N.C., 1991), pp. 128–35.

would agree with his magistrates if left to his own untutored devices. After Fleury's death, however, as a supposedly governing but inaccessible king retreated behind many ministers and the anonymity of his councils, judicial Jansenists had increasingly to deploy the distinction between a mortal and immortal king without abandoning the even older one between the king and his evil ministers. Thus, in 1751 did the parlementary councillor Drouin de Vandeuil appeal to the king's "eternal and as it were immutable will" while, outside the Parlement's assembled chambers, other magistrates and barristers routinely speculated about and often successfully acted on their assumptions about the mortal king's real will, as opposed to that publicly imposed on him by this or that minister or the Royal Council.[7] In combination the two distinctions enlarged the space for opposition to take hold—so much so that the contestatory politics of the 1750s and 1760s may be thought of as the last chapter in an old politics of the king's two bodies. In despair in 1760 at the widespread contempt for royal authority based on the conviction that the king knew nothing about the orders that emanated in his name, the first president of the rambunctious Parlement of Normandy confided to Chancellor Lamoignon his ardent wish "that the king would destroy this general error, that he would show himself, that he would act, that he might finally make it clear that he is the master," as though such a show of force would not have immediately motivated an even more overt opposition to the king's merely mortal and momentary whim.[8]

The ministry of episcopal appointments—the feuille des bénéfices—was perhaps the first governmental function to be adversely affected by the king's "personal" government. Fleury's replacement in charge of appointments to benefices, the *Théatin* monk and former Bishop of Mirepoix Jean-François Boyer, became a linchpin of the royal court's reemerging parti dévot. Not only did he continue Fleury's policy of seeing to it that no new Jansenists replaced dying ones in the episcopacy—the policy did not always work, of course—he went well beyond Fleury's policy by appointing new bishops whose enthusiasm for *Unigenitus* as well as their own spiritual jurisdiction knew no bounds. It was impolitic enough, for example, to have appointed such ardent constitutionary firebrands as Poncet de La Rivière, Montmorency de Laval, and Caritat de Condorcet as bishops to the former Jansenist refuges of Troyes, Orléans, and Auxerre, respectively. But to have brought the incendiary Christophe de Beaumont du Repaire as Vintimille's successor at the head of the still combustible Parisian see was a blunder that Fleury would never have made. Nor, thanks to the ongoing purge of the priesthood, did the parti dévot now lack a considerable constituency in the clerical second order—

7. "Journal de Rolland d'Erceville" in AN: AB XIX, Ms. 3336/2, fols. 32–33, 18 May 1751.
8. AN: 154 AP II (archives de Tocqueville, fonds Lamoignon), Ms. 45, no. 14, Armand-Thomas Hué de Miromesnil to Chancellor Lamoignon de Blancmesnil, 29 June 1960.

even in Paris, and even in the solidly Jansenist parishes like Saint-Etienne-du-Mont and Saint-Jacques-du-Haut-Pas. The parti dévot's Parisian strongholds, however, remained the Jesuits' church and professed residence in the rue Saint-Antoine, the parish and seminary of Saint-Sulpice, and of course the archiepiscopal residence at Notre Dame.

Meanwhile, the number of like-minded zealots at the royal court had increased to the point of constituting a veritable parti dévot, to which episcopal zealots could turn for support. Besides the inevitable Jesuit confessors and court preachers like Henri Griffet and prelates or former prelates like the cardinal de Tencin and Boyer himself, this courtly parti dévot now included much of the royal family, including the neglected queen Marie Lezczynska, the king's pious daughters or *mesdames de France,* and the king's oldest son Louis-Auguste, all of them under the devout influence of the Jesuits and the duc de La Vauguyon, governor of the royal children. After 1750 the dauphin was also able to represent the parti dévot within the king's councils, as did the new chancellor—and intimate of the dauphin—Lamoignon de Blancmesnil, and such ministers as the comte de Saint-Florentin, Henri-Léonard Bertin, and especially the comte d'Argenson. Assuming the direction of the ministry of war and the supervision of Paris after the fall of the comte de Maurepas in 1749, d'Argenson became, in Michel Antoine's words, "one of the oracles of the queen's circle" as well as the champion of the clergy's case in the controversies over the taxation of clerical property and the refusal of sacraments to Jansenists.[9] Held together by hatred not only of Jansenists but of the king's new mistress Jeanne-Antoinette Poisson d'Etioles (later madame de Pompadour), the court parti dévot could exercise influence over Parisian opinion by way of the confessionals and pulpits of the Parisian priests with whom Vintimille had replaced Jansenist ones.

Not that Jansenist priests had altogether disappeared from Paris. Appellant curés or ones at least sympathetic to Jansenism remained in cases where, as in the parish of Saint-Gervais, their "revolt" against archiepiscopal authority had not been too "characterized," or exceptional cases where, as in Saint-Paul, the curé was not dependent on the Archbishop of Paris. And of course the genuinely Jansenist parishes like Saint-Etienne-du-Mont or Saint-Séverin maintained nests of nonbeneficed and unrepentantly appellant priests, most of whom had long lost archiepiscopal approval to act as auxiliary preachers, confessors, or catechism teachers. By the 1750s Jansenism had been all but purged from the ranks of the episcopacy, except for rare cases like those of François de Fitz-James, Languet de Gergy's replacement in the see of Soissons, and Malvin de Montazet of Lyon, both of whom developed their *jansénisant* proclivities only after their appointments. Even more than in the 1720s and 1730s, therefore, it was from the judicial

9. Michel Antoine, *Louis XV* (Paris, 1989), pp. 626–27.

milieu, especially the Parlement of Paris, that the parti janséniste recruited its leadership. If, in Paris, the decades of the 1750s and 1760s could boast no Jansenist oratory as eloquent as the abbé Pucelle's, they produced a second generation of Jansenists if not as numerous at least as effective as the previous one. For the generation of the Regency had nothing to teach such parlementary councillors as Clément de Feillet, the abbé Chauvelin, Guillaume Lambert, Laverdy de Nizaret, Henri de Revol, Robert de Saint-Vincent, Rolland de Challerange, among others, about the art of maneuvering the whole Parlement into a defense of irreducibly Jansenist causes against the constitutionary episcopacy and the Royal Council by means of tying them to the issues of the Parlement's jurisdiction or the Gallican liberties.[10] Nor did the Parisian Order of Barristers fail to reproduce—in some cases literally—a second generation of eighteenth-century Jansenists, as Aubry junior took the place of Aubry senior, Le Paige junior carried on after Le Paige senior, and Pothouin junior continued in the ways of Pothouin senior. Although Jean-Baptiste Gerbier's Jansenism was only a pale reflection of his father's, he acquired an international reputation as a courtroom orator, while the canonistic prowess of Gabriel-Nicolas Maultrot, the abbé Claude Mey, Piales, and Texier was easily the equal of signers of the famous consultations of 1727 and 1730.

Indeed, the quartermaster general of the Parisian parti janséniste from the 1750s until the very eve of the French Revolution was a nonpleading or consultative barrister, namely Louis-Adrien Le Paige. Convulsionary, figuratist theologian, specialist in canon law, and proparlementary pamphleteer and adviser, Le Paige still incorporated all of the sundry strands of the Jansenist movement that had otherwise begun to unravel after 1730. In 1756 a prince of the royal blood, Louis-François de Bourbon, prince de Conti, appointed Le Paige as his personal librarian and judicial bailiff *(bailli)* of the Temple of the Order of Malta, of which the prince was the lay prior, thereby giving Le Paige Conti's protection and the judicial invulnerability of the Temple's precincts as well as augmenting his already considerable political influence. From that fortified redoubt Le Paige squared off against another barrister, one Jacob-Nicolas Moreau, who, though a son of an exiled Jansenist professor and once himself a "good little Jansenist," deserted the "party" in the 1750s and achieved the position of titular historiographer of the king, the royal minister Henri-Léonard Bertin's right-hand man, and the courtly parti dévot's lay éminence grise. Since both Le Paige and Moreau were not only anonymous pamphleteers but in fact the authors of many public pronouncements that purported to emanate from much higher authorities—parlementary arrêts and remonstrances and royal responses to these remonstrances—many

---

10. Peter Robert Campbell, "The Conduct of Politics in France in the Time of the Cardinal de Fleury, 1723–1743" (Ph.D. diss., Queen Mary College, University of London, 1983), esp. pp. 293–396.

of the exchanges of the 1750s and 1760s between the parlements and the monarchy can be read as a debate between these two judicial representatives of the parti janséniste and the royalist wing of the parti dévot.

After the relatively quiet 1740s, during which the War of the Austrian Succession succeeded in distracting the national attention, another round of Jansenist-related public controversy and institutional confrontation broke out around 1750. It was then that the new Archbishop of Paris Christophe de Beaumont and several other like-minded colleagues systematized within their dioceses, perhaps with Louis XV's initial and ill-considered encouragement, the heretofore scattered practice of refusing the last sacraments—the viaticum and extreme unction—to appellants and otherwise "notorious" opponents of *Unigenitus*. The ensuing refusal-of-sacraments controversy is also known as the certificates of confession quarrel because of Christophe de Beaumont's attempt to require of all deathbed penitents a written billet de confession attesting to their having been confessed by a priest who had formally accepted the controversial bull. Such a certificate was not without precedent, having been principally required as a way of monitoring laypeople taking Easter communion outside their own parishes. Christophe de Beaumont's main purpose in using it, however, was to disrupt the functioning of a kind of Jansenist church within the Gallican Church in which nonbeneficed and sometimes interdicted priests confessed each other as well as laypersons who thereby escaped the control of their ecclesiastical ordinaries. (Indeed, one of the chief aims of the Jansenists' adoption of Richerist ecclesiology was precisely to legitimate this practice.) But the refusal-of-sacraments controversy went on even after the Archbishop of Paris discontinued the practice of certificates of confession, because all that a priest had to do was to ask a moribund penitent for the name of his or her confessor or, more directly, to accept the bull *Unigenitus,* in order to achieve the same effect.

Already the despair of Voltaire the historian as well as the philosophe, the controversy over refusal of sacraments has been the extreme unction of just about every attempt at clear, much less engaging, exposition. For all but Jansenist martyrologies it is a singularly unedifying not to say lugubrious story, reeking more of the stench of death than the "odor of sanctity," as though one were literally witnessing the death of French Catholicism itself under the hot glare of a hostile Enlightenment. Yet just as much if not more than philosophes' disdain for the Catholic sacramental system, this controversy was central to the changes that France was then undergoing. Because what that controversy was witness to was the traumatic intersection between the formation of rival ideological-political parties within absolutist space on the one side, and Catholicism in its ultimate capacity to reconcile the living to death on the other. In a polity where citizenship was still coincident with Catholicity, that intersection was bound to wreak havoc with a Catholic monarchy and even with Catholicism as such.[11] Even "un-enlightened" contemporaries seemed confusedly aware of the stakes in what was happening. When early on in his career the curé of Saint-Etienne-du-Mont tried to refuse the sacraments to a reputed Jansenist in 1732 and Archbishop Vintimille, though no friend of Jansenists, intervened on the person's behalf, Parisians appreciated Vintimille's demarche but added, according a police observer, that "the constitution [Unigenitus] will entirely destroy religion."[12] Yet it was that curé's comportment that became episcopal policy under Vintimille's successor Christophe de Beaumont.

What makes the story moreover so tortuous is that it is not only about whether Jansenists were true Catholics and therefore entitled to the church's sacraments but also about the controverted boundaries between the state's tempo-ral and the church's spiritual jurisdictions, as well as between the Parlement's constitutional and the monarchy's sovereign authority.[13] The story's main plot is also inextricably entwined with several subplots. One of them concerns Christophe de Beaumont's attempt, with royal help, to wrest control of the Paris General Hospital (l'Hôpital général) from the Parlement of Paris so that, continu-ing the work of Cardinal Fleury, he could purge its ecclesiastical staff of still more Jansenists. Because they were under the Parlement of Paris's general control and often administered by Jansenist barristers, the Hôpital général and its many subsidiaries—Bicêtre for men, the Salpêtrière for women, the Quinze-Vingts for the blind—had survived the brunt of Fleury's purges and continued to function as refuges for Jansenist clerics.[14]

Another related story has to do with the jurisdictional rivalry between the Parlement of Paris and a rival royal court of more recent origin called the Grand conseil, which was much more compliant than the Parlement in matters of royal religious policy and hence a possible replacement for it in times of trouble. The crisis point in this rivalry came in 1756, when the Parlement of Paris invited the realm's princes and peers to attend its constitutional deliberations concerning the status of the Grand conseil, adding the issue of whether the Parlement was really the only Court of Peers to the many and already sufficiently explosive others.[15]

11. For a helpful theoretical analysis of an analogous controversy in a very different time and place, see Clifford Geertz's "Ritual and Social Change: A Javanese Example," in his *The Interpretation of Cultures* (New York, 1973), pp. 142–69.

12. BA: AB, Ms. 10161, fol. 74, 2 June 1732.

13. For a remarkably clear and successful attempt to tell this story, see Jeffrey Merrick's *The Desacralization of the French Monarchy in the Eighteenth Century* (Baton Rouge, La., 1990), esp. pp. 78–104.

14. Legier Desgranges, *Madame de Moysan et l'extravagante affaire de l'Hôpital générale, 1749–1758* (Paris, 1954).

15. Jean Egret, *Louis XV et l'opposition parlementaire, 1715–1774* (Paris, 1970), pp. 72–76; Jules Flammermont, *Remontrances du parlement de Paris au XVIIIe siècle*, 3 vols. (Geneva, 1978), 2:22–102; and,

Unlike in 1730–32, moreover, some of the provincial parlements began to remonstrate on behalf of the Parlement of Paris as well as to solicit Paris's support in their own particular quarrels with the Royal Council or the local bishops, making it all but impossible to disentangle Parisian from provincial politics. In addition to being chronic, finally, the controversy was also occasionally acute. By the time it was over in 1758, it had produced one mass resignation of magisterial offices and two exilings of magistrates, not to mention three judicial strikes, all of them seconded by the Order of Barristers.

The refusal-of-sacraments controversy pitted the parlements against the monarchy as well as the episcopacy because the monarchy at first tended to support the constitutionary episcopacy's new sacramental policy. Or at least the King's Council opposed the Parlement of Paris's opposition to this policy—the Parlement's profane violation, it was thought, of the church's spiritual authority—annulling most of the Parlement's legal efforts to guarantee dying Jansenists the last sacraments. To an extent, royal religious policy was inevitable. *Unigenitus* was, after all, a symbol of royal as well as episcopal and papal authority; its status as such was clearer than ever after the monarchy had risked all on its behalf in 1730. The constitutionary bishops, moreover, were only enforcing the bull's authority, or so it seemed; the magistrates most active in opposing these bishops were clearly members of the Parlement's parti janséniste. Although the Royal Council displayed some signs of second thoughts, reflecting internal divisions and perhaps a recollection that Fleury's policy had not been one-sidedly "devout," the Council continued to pursue a mainly pro-episcopal policy in the controversy, culminating in the exile of the Parlement's personnel to nine different towns in France on 8–9 May 1753.

Typical of the refusal of sacraments to appellant priests during this period is the case of the abbé Ignace Le Mere, an ex-Oratorian priest and translator of Greek patristic texts, who fell ill in the spring of 1752 and demanded extreme unction from the curé of the heavily Jansenist parish of Saint-Etienne-du-Mont, the same Bouëttin who had already figured infamously in Coffin's ordeal. Acting on orders from the Archbishop of Paris, both Bouëttin and the curate or *vicaire*, one Brunet, insisted that Le Mere first formally accept the bull *Unigenitus*, produce a certificate of confession, or at least name the priest who had been acting as his confessor—obviously not Bouëttin. When Le Mere rebuffed the demand of the curé and vicaire, he was refused extreme unction and accused of acting on the "principle of the Calvinists," giving him recourse to judicial summons. Five successive summons failed to moderate Bouëttin's and Brunet's "schismatic" behavior, but they effectively brought Le Mere's case to the attention of the

more recently, Julian Swann, "Parlement, Politics, and the *Parti Janséniste:* The *Grand Conseil* Affair, 1755–56," *FH* 6 (1992):435–61.

Parlement of Paris, where the councillor Claude-Etienne Blondeau persuaded the assembled chambers to take it up on 23 March 1752. Not even the Parlement's intervention prevented Le Mere from dying without the last sacraments five days later, by which time his case had become an affair of state, embroiling the Parlement with both the episcopacy and the king.[16]

The case turned out to be typical for the Parlement of Paris as well, because it provided the occasion for hammering out the procedures it subsequently followed. Having interrogated Bouëttin, the Parlement at first contented itself with forbidding him to renew the "scandal" in question and enjoining him to behave "charitably" toward all his parishioners, while inviting the Archbishop of Paris to come to Le Mere's spiritual aid. Alas, these rhetorical concessions to the church's spiritual autonomy did not prevent the Royal Council from annulling this relatively moderate judgment, and neither Christophe de Beaumont nor Bouëttin administered the last sacraments to the moribund Le Mere. The Parlement then sent its two public prosecutors or gens du roi to plead with the king that he personally intervene on Le Mere's behalf, whereupon the king promised to do so. But when Le Mere finally died without the sacraments anyway, the Parlement ordered the arrest of Bouëttin for his criminal conduct as a "disturber of the public peace," sending the curé into hiding. And when the King's Council annulled this sentence also, the Parlement laid it down as a general rule that it henceforth meant not only to forbid ecclesiastics from publicly refusing the sacraments to anyone by reason of failure to produce a certificate of confession, to name one's confessor, or to refuse to accept *Unigenitus*—entailing the right to punish in cases of the infraction of this prohibition—but also to enjoin them to "to conform themselves in the exterior administration of the sacraments to the canons and regulations authorized in the realm"—in franker words, to administer the sacraments.[17] The Royal Council's predictable annulment of this ruling of 18 April did not deter the Parlement from acting on it when other such cases arose, and its persistence in this matter is what provoked its fifteen-month-long exile from Paris beginning in May 1753.

However inconvenient and costly for them, this exile did not bring the magistracy to its knees, much less its parti janséniste, in large measure because a loyal lawyers' strike foiled the ministry's attempt to set up a substitute Royal Chamber *(Chambre royale)* to administer justice in the Parlement's stead, and in part because some of the provincial parlements, most notably those at Rouen and Rennes, continued to prosecute sacrament-refusing priests as best they could. The long exile therefore ended when, abandoning the forum of the royal Conseil des

16. *NE* 17 Apr. 1753, pp. 61–64.

17. BN: CJF, Ms. 1487, fols. 71–107. For the text of the arrêt of 18 Apr. 1752, see Flammermont, *Remontrances,* 1:498. For an extended and accurate, if biased, description of the affair, see *NE* 17 Apr. 1753, pp. 61–64.

dépêches, Louis XV sought out the advice of the prince de Conti, brought the Parlement back to Paris in September 1754, and persuaded it to register the so-called Declaration of Silence dated 2 September 1754. This declaration represented a complete reversal of royal religious policy; under the pretense of imposing silence on the constitutionary clergy—and by construing "schismatic" acts as violations of "silence"—it allowed the parlements to order that the last sacraments be administered to dying appellants, if not in so many words at least in effect, and to prosecute curés as "disturbers of the public peace" if they disobeyed. The Declaration of Silence's unspoken but clearly understood proviso was that the Parlement would leave the bishops to the discretion of the king, who duly exiled the likes of Christophe de Beaumont, Montmorency de Laval, and Poncet de La Rivière to their diocesan residences or, in extreme cases, to their familial properties elsewhere in France.

The case that defined the terms of royal-parlementary cooperation during this brief period is that of a fifty-two-year-old laundress named Marie-Gabriel Lallement, who, endowed "with a piety long renowned in her parish" of Saint-Etienne-du-Mont, fell dangerously ill in late November 1754.[18] That renown was enough to make her piety suspect in the eyes of the parish's vicaire and two *portes-Dieu*, who performed the curial functions in the absence of the now exiled Bouëttin. These priests refused to bring her the viaticum or administer extreme unction unless she produced a certificate of confession or divulged the identity of her confessor. Lallement and her family had recourse to judicial summons, while all of the parish's three priests, acting on orders by the archbishop, continued their refusal. When this stance persisted in the face of the Parlement's inimitably indirect order to administer extreme unction, the Parlement decreed the arrest of the three priests, who for their part took to hiding. At the same time the Parlement sent its secretary to Christophe de Beaumont to "invite" him to "cause the scandal to cease" and to "destroy . . . the allegations tending to impute it to him"; the archbishop responded that this spiritual matter was none of the Parlement's judicial business. At this point the king exiled the archbishop to his residence outside Paris, while the Parlement sentenced the priests to be exiled from the realm as "disturbers of the public peace."[19] Meanwhile it was not until a well known Jansenist priest simply resident in the parish obeyed the parlementary summons that poor Lallement received the viaticum in time to die.[20]

That Lallement was someone whom Barbier described as "a washer-woman living on the place Maubert, . . . a sister or daughter of a coppersmith," does not make her case untypical either, whether as an adherent to the Jansenist cause or as

18. *NE* 16 Jan. 1755, p. 9. See this whole issue for a convenient description of the affair.
19. *Arrest de la cour de parlement. Du 3 février 1755* (Paris, 1755), in AN: AD, Ms. 11, fol. 128.
20. Ibid., pp. 9–12; and BN: CJF, Ms. 1487, fols. 183–91.

an object of a refusal of sacraments.[21] Of the eight or so cases of refusals in the parish of Saint-Etienne-du-Mont between 1749, when the controversy began, and 1758, when it began to die down, six involved laypersons of whom half—Coffin's cousin Elisabeth, a certain démoiselle Breton, and Lallement herself—were women. This is not the place to undertake a history of Jansenist feminism, but it is worth pointing out in passing that Jansenism combined the access to the printed word offered to women by Protestantism with the religious space provided for women by the Catholic Reformation. Thus women played a conspicuous role in Jansenism from its beginnings in Port-Royal to its transformation into the "patriot" movement against Chancellor Maupeou in the early 1770s; likewise, antifeminism was a leitmotif of devout opposition to Jansenism from the seventeenth century to its partial transformation into a defense of absolutism, also apropos of the Maupeou ministry in the 1770s.[22] Astride the centers of the two histories lies the eighty-third proposition condemned by *Unigenitus* from Quesnel's *Réflexions morales:* "It is an illusion to imagine that the knowledge of religious mysteries ought not be communicated to this sex by means of reading the Holy books," and further, "it is not from the simplicity of women but from the prideful science of men that heresies have been born."[23]

It is perhaps also the high visibility of humble laypeople of either gender as apparent objects of priestly persecution that accounts in part for the continued popularity of the Jansenist cause and the parlements, at least in Paris. Lallement's encounter with death came to the sacramental conclusion it did to the "great joy of the people," according to the marquis d'Argenson. More obviously biased although usually very accurate, the *Nouvelles ecclésiastiques* concurred that Lallement had received the last rites from a Jansenist priest "amidst a great concourse of people, who applauded in a marked though modest manner," adding that a voice in that appreciative multitude was heard to say, "it is our good king who had the sacraments given to the sick woman."[24]

What compromised the terms of this brief reconciliation between a mainly proparlementary Parisian public and the king was the Parlement of Paris's noisy appeal against *Unigenitus* itself, if not again to a general council at least comme d'abus, in the course of judging a particularly ugly case involving Jansenist

21. Barbier, *Journal*, 6:75–85.

22. On the subject of women in the "patriot" movement and antifeminism in the pamphlet defense of Maupeou's reforms, see Shanti Marie Singham, " 'A Conspiracy of Twenty Million Frenchmen': Public Opinion, Patriotism, and the Assault on Absolutism during the Maupeou Years, 1770–1775" (Ph.D. diss., Princeton University, 1991).

23. Augustin Gazier, *Histoire générale du mouvement janséniste, depuis ses origines jusqu'à nos jours,* 2 vols. (Paris, 1924), 2:326–27.

24. *NE* 16 Jan. 1755, p. 11–12; and René-Louis de Voyer, marquis d'Argenson, *Journal et mémoires du marquis d'Argenson,* ed. E.-J.-B. Rathery, 9 vols. (Paris, 1859–67), 2–5 Dec. 1754, 8:375–76, 379–80.

canons against their cathedral chapter in Orléans in mid-March 1755.[25] What finally ended this half-year period of parlementary-royal cooperation was not only this frontal attack on what was still a symbol of royal authority—and what was also a clear violation of the spirit if not the letter of the Declaration of Silence— but also the king's bad conscience about his chief court's apparent violation of the church's spiritual jurisdiction, combined with his own need for the clergy's fiscal contributions to France's efforts in what would be the Seven Years' War.[26]

The spring of 1756 hence introduced a confusing third phase in the course of the controversy, marked by a spectacular falling out between the king and Conti, the reemergence of the King's Council and elements of the parti dévot in the making of sacramental policy, and the monarchy's renewed but tentative search for a middle way between the episcopal zealots and the judicial parti janséniste. What this search meant in practice was an attempt to articulate a royal declaration that would put into words what had been the de facto religious policy of the cardinal de Fleury: to uphold the respect due to the bull *Unigenitus* as a law of church and state without going so far as to call it a rule of faith, to minimize if not exclude any intervention by the secular courts in the public administration of the sacraments while somehow restraining the zealotry of the clerical firebrands, to maintain the respective jurisdictions of state and church and the subordination of curés to bishops—in a word, to reconcile the Edict of 1695 with the Gallican Declaration of 1682, as well as with the respect due to the papacy with the traditions of the French monarchy.

That policy failed. In effect, no royal declaration could do with words in the 1750s what only a person, a more prestigious monarchy, and a securer fiscal situation had been able to do in the 1730s. Although Louis XV eventually obtained Pope Benedict's authorization for saying that *Unigenitus* was not a rule of faith— and by implication that not all opponents of the bull were heretics and unworthy of the sacraments—the papacy under Benedict XIV was the least of the French monarchy's religious problems.[27] For that provision as well as other parts of the declaration predictably stoked the righteous ire of Christophe de Beaumont at the head of the episcopal parti dévot. The declaration sat even less well with the Parlement of Paris because it disallowed secular injunctions to administer the

---

25. Flammermont, *Remontances,* 2:4; and Barbier, *Journal,* 6:143–46.

26. For a fuller treatment of this confusing phase of the controversy, see Dale K. Van Kley, *The Damiens Affair and the Unraveling of the Old Regime, 1750–1770* (Princeton, N.J., 1984), pp. 133–49.

27. For the duc de Choiseul's negotiations that led to Benedict XIV's *Ex Omnibus,* see Maurice Boutry, *Choiseul à Rome, 1754–1757: Lettres et mémoires inédites* (Paris, 1898), pp. 4–218; and for the text of *Ex Omnibus* see ibid., 320–27, or *Collection des procès-verbaux des assemblées générales du clergé de France, depuis l'année 1560 jusqu'à présent, redigée par ordre des matières,* 9 vols. (Paris, 1778), vol. 8, part 1, no. 5, pp. 274–78. On the interpretation of *Ex Omnibus* see [Louis-Adrien Le Paige], *Observations sur les Actes de l'Assemblée du clergé de France de 1765* (n.p., n.d.), pp. 182–209.

sacraments. Accompanied by an edict reducing the number of parlementary offices and a disciplinary declaration similar to the one Fleury had brandished and then withdrawn in 1732, the declaration on *Unigenitus* was the real reason for the lit de justice assembly held on 13 December 1756, a forcible registration that provoked the resignation by most of the magistrates, a move supported by a barristers' strike in the days that followed. That collective resignation in turn prompted an unemployed domestic servant who had formerly served some Parisian magistrates, one Robert-François Damiens, to return from Arras and speak up for his former masters as well as the "good priests" of Paris by "touching" the king—that is, by wounding him with a penknife—at Versailles on 5 January 1757. There followed the exile of sixteen of the resigned magistrates, including the hard core of the parti janséniste; the highly politicized trial of Damiens by the few magistrates who had not resigned, along with the princes and peers of the realm; and his gory execution on 28 March 1757. Meanwhile a new war with England had broken out, augmenting the government's need for parlementary registration of new taxes, though hardly ending the zealots' war against dying appellants at home. So when, in September, the king rescinded his magistrates' resignations and reconvened them in Paris, it was to announce his pardon of the sixteen exiled magistrates, to postpone the execution of the disciplinary declaration sine die, and to permit the Parlement to register the declaration about *Unigenitus* "conformably with the canons received in the realm, and with the laws and ordinances"—that is, the canons and laws that, in the magistrates' opinion, permitted them to enjoin priests to administer the church's sacraments to opponents of the bull.[28]

And that is what the parlements did. For those so disposed persisted in ordering priests to administer the sacraments to opponents of *Unigenitus* and exiled them hither and yon if they refused. Between 1758 and 1763, within the parishes of Paris alone, the Parlement itself or the Châtelet acting in its stead instituted criminal proceedings in at least fifteen instances against curés, vicaires, or portes-Dieu who refused to administer the sacraments to appellants or to celebrate services for the repose of their souls.[29] In the parish of Saint-Nicolas-des-Champs, for example, the Parlement ordered the curé Jacques de L'Ecluse—he was also one of Christophe de Beaumont's grands vicaires—to administer the

28. The king's responses of 29 Aug. and 1 Sept. 1757 are in BN, CJF 336, file 3614 (1), fols. 211–12, 227; along with the *Arrest de la cour de parlement du 5 septembre 1757*, and the Parlement's *arrêté* and the king's response concerning the sixteen arrested magistrates on the same date (fols. 238–40). The king's response of 1 Sept. 1757 is also in Flammermont, *Remontrances*, 2:167–69. On the question of how to interpret the king's response and the Parlement's registration of it, see Le Paige's note in BPR: CLP, Ms. 547, no. 168; *NE* 22 Oct. 1757, p. 174; and Barbier, *Journal*, 6:576–77, 581.

29. That is at least the number of such cases that left traces in the BN's Joly de Fleury Collection. A full inventory of the registers or minutes of the Parlement of Paris and the Châtelet would undoubtedly turn up more.

viaticum to a moribund appellant priest after the latter vainly summoned the curé to do so in April 1758. Rather than obeying the Parlement's order, L'Ecluse disappeared, furniture and all, whereupon the Parlement proceeded in similar fashion against the first vicaire, the third vicaire, and the porte-Dieu, all of whom likewise took flight. Meanwhile the sick priest's nephew, who was also a priest, came to his uncle's rescue by administering the viaticum before his death. At about the same time, one of the parish's vicaires, the abbé Bonnet, refused to administer the sacraments to a woman who would not produce a certificate of confession or name her confessor. When the Parlement proceeded against Bonnet, he too disappeared from the parish. Finally, on 17 January 1759, the Parlement completed its contumacious procedures against these priests, banishing all five from the realm for life. And lest it leave any stone unturned, the Parlement later drove out the parish's sole surviving beneficed clergyman when he followed his colleagues' example by refusing the viaticum to yet another appellant priest resident in the parish.[30]

Although this reconciliation of the king with his Parlement was to be ephemeral—it came to an end in 1770—it was of more than temporary significance because the specifically Jansenist victory in the refusal-of-sacraments controversy extended well beyond that issue to nearly all the outstanding areas of religious and political contestation, and in ways that were never entirely undone. The new minister François-Joachim de Pierre, abbé de Bernis, transferred bishops like Montmorency de Laval and Poncet de La Rivière to other sees and exiled Christophe de Beaumont to his ancestral estate in Périgord. Back in Paris, the Parlement, or rather its parti janséniste, succeeded in reopening the parish church of Saint-Médard for the anniversary of the deacon Pâris's death as well as for his namesake Saint Francis's feast day, allowing the deacon's still numerous devotees to gather there and sympathetic priests to say mass. Elsewhere in Paris, the parlementary parti janséniste virtually administered the numerous parish churches with the help of cooperative lay churchwardens.[31] In 1758 the Parlement reobtained control over the contested Hôpital général and publicly vindicated the memory of Port-Royal by condemning a Jesuit's book which updated Jean Filleau's seventeenth-century accusation that the first Jansenists had plotted the destruction of Catholicism in France. Beginning in 1758 the Parisian police all but

---

30. The raw documentation for this whole affair may be found in the BN: CJF, Ms. 1569, fols. 306–14, 345, and 389; and Ms. 1570, fols. 7–9. See also *Arrest de la cour de parlement du 17 janvier 1759* (Paris, 1759). Another account may be consulted in *NE* 14 Aug. 1758, pp. 133–35; and 31 July 1759, pp. 126–27.

31. On the crucial and politically educational role of the lay charchwardens in the administration of Paris's parishes, see David Garrioch, "Parish Politics, Jansenism, and the Paris Middle Classes in the Eighteenth Century," *FH* 8 (1994):403–19.

called off their search for the elusive *Nouvelles ecclésiastiques*, which in turn trumpeted all of these developments.[32]

Indeed, what happened after 1757 represented nothing less than the demise of the bull *Unigenitus* and the Declaration of 1730 that had enshrined it as a law of church and state. The anonymous author of the ironic pamphlet entitled *Funeral Oration for the Most High, Most Mighty, and Most Holy Princess, the Bull Unigenitus* was only a little premature, writing as he did in the wake of the Parlement's ruling of 18 April 1752 forbidding the refusal of sacraments to anyone by reason of opposition to *Unigenitus*.[33] Although the ruling was formally annulled by the King's Council toward the end of the same year, it took effect when the Parlement finally registered the king's Declaration of 10 December 1756 "conformably to the canons received and authorized in the realm, to the laws and ordinances, . . . and to the usages and maxims whose observation is necessary to uphold the king's authority and his sovereign justice." For those laws and maxims, as the *Nouvelles ecclésiastiques* took care to point out, included the ruling of 18 April 1752, which forbade public refusals of sacraments on account of opposition to *Unigenitus*, as well as that of 18 March 1755, which appealed the execution of the bull comme d'abus.[34] There is no doubt that curés opposed to *Unigenitus* continued to bear the brunt of episcopal persecution from time to time, but this persecution was henceforth piecemeal, the work of this or that bishop, who could no longer count on the support of the crown if these initiatives came to the attention of the courts.

That was in turn so because the Edict of 1695 was another casualty of the crisis of 1757, which damaged it in at least two areas. First, by successfully prosecuting and exiling curés who obeyed their bishops in the matter of the refusal of sacraments and by requisitioning merely resident priests to perform their functions in their stead, the parlements undermined the subordination of parish curés to their episcopal superiors. And second, by asserting its judicial control over so "spiritual" a domain as the public distribution of the sacraments, the parlements breached the edict's crucial provisions that divided spiritual from secular authority and thereby protected the church from the royal courts.[35] The

---

32. Ibid. See also the *Déclaration du roi, qui révoque l'arrêt du Conseil du 20 novembre 1751 et les lettres-patentes du 28 janvier 1752; ordonne en conséquence qu'on se règle à l'avenir, pour tout ce qui concerne l'administration de l'Hôpital général de Paris . . . comme avant l'année 1749. Donné à Versailles le 15 mars 1758*, in BPR: CLP, Ms. 547, no. 276; as well as *Arrest de la cour de parlement, qui condamne un libelle intitulé: La réalité du projet de Bourg-Fontaine, démontré par l'exécution*, in BN: Mss. Fr., Ms. 22093 (170), p. 3.

33. *Oraison funèbre de la très-haute, très-puissante et très-sainte princesse la bulle Unigenitus, prononcée dans l'église métropolitaine de Sxxx, par M. l'évêque de Mxxx, le premier septembre 1752* (n.p., n.d.).

34. *Arrest de la cour de parlement. Du 5 décembre 1757* in BN: CJF, Ms. 336, fol. 3614 (1); *NE* 21 Oct. 1757, p. 174.

35. The provisions in question are articles 30 and 34. Article 30 accorded jurisdiction over and judgment of doctrine to the bishops and archbishops and enjoined the parlements not only to defer to the

potential consequences of these two violations became precociously apparent in 1756 when, in order to justify having had recourse to the curé of a neighboring parish to administer the last sacraments to a Jansenist, the Parlement of Paris laid down the principle that "all Pastors were co-responsible for the debt of the sacred ministry" and that "the division of [ecclesiastical] boundaries is only a matter of ecclesiastical and civil law, whereas the exercise of spiritual functions derives from divine law."[36] "Adieu to territorial rights and the episcopal orders," commented d'Argenson.[37] Thirty-five years later the National Assembly would not need any other principles in order to justify redrawing France's ecclesiastical boundaries and replacing a "refractory" clergy with a "constitutional" one. The only reason that this assault on the Edict of 1695 did not have the effect that it might have had before the French Revolution is that by 1757 the lower clergy had been largely purged of Jansenists except in dioceses protected by sympathetic bishops, like Malvin de Montazet's Lyonnais or Charles de Caylus's Auxerrois, where they did not have to appeal the actions of their bishops to the royal courts. All the same, the Parlement's control over the parishes of Paris had become so great by the end of the 1760s that when in 1769 Christophe de Beaumont wanted to purge the anti-Jansenist parish of Saint-Sulpice of just one inconveniently Jansenist archdeacon, he felt obliged to consult with the notoriously Jansenist canons Claude Mey and Gabriel-Nicolas Maultrot, who advised him that he would do well not to think about it.[38]

The Edict of 1695, the bull *Unigenitus,* the Declaration of 1730–these legislative monuments could not have fallen without damage to the prestige of the monarchy, symbolic as they were of post-Protestant French absolutism, of the way in which the seventeenth-century monarchy had religiously defined itself. The rubble of these monuments was there for all to see. Nor was the damage symbolic alone: although in 1732 the monarchy had emerged from its confronta-

---

prelates in this matter but also to give them whatever help they needed in the execution of censures and other ecclesiastical judgments. Only in the case of a "scandal" occasioned by the "publication of the said doctrine" were the royal courts to intervene. Even more to the point, Article 34 accorded "jurisdiction over cases concerning the sacraments, religious vows, the divine office, ecclesiastical discipline, and other purely spiritual matters" to the judges of the church and enjoined the royal judges and "even our courts of parlement" to leave such cases with the ecclesiastical courts and even to send them there except in the event of an appeal comme d'abus. For the full text of these provisions see Léon Mention, *Documents relatifs aux rapports du clergé avec la royauté,* 2 vols. (Paris 1893–1903), 1:114–50. See also Philippe Godard, *La querelle des refus de sacrements, 1730–1735* (Paris, 1937), p. 146.

    36. The case was that of M. Feu, curé of Saint-Gervais, who obeyed the Parlement's summons to administer the viaticum to Jean-François Gritte Cocquelin. Cocquelin, a priest resident in the neighboring parish of Sainte-Marguerite, himself had earlier cooperated with the Parlement of Paris by administering the sacraments to reputed Jansenists. The quotation is from *NE* 17 Apr. 1756, p. 63. See also BN: CJF, Ms. 1568, fols. 221, 248–49, 330–34.

    37. D'Argenson, *Journal et mémoires,* 2 Feb. 1755, 8:428.

    38. BN: CJF, Ms. 1570, fol. 327.

tion with the magistracy and barristers with its reputation tarnished but its religious legislation intact, in 1757 it all but abandoned that religious agenda and the episcopacy with it to the discretion of the parlements. In doing so, the monarchy also lost its pivotal or arbitral position vis-à-vis the church and the royal courts, the clergy and the magistracy—that is to say vis-à-vis the realm's two major and most powerful corps. The immediate result was that for the rest of the 1750s and 1760s the parlements did pretty much as they pleased in religious policy in return for cooperation with the monarchy in financing the Seven Years' War. It is true that the monarchy took its revenge in 1771, when Chancellor Maupeou purged or suppressed most of the parlements and broke the proud independence of the Parisian barristers. But to purge or suppress one of the realm's chief corps was not the same as regaining an arbitral position vis-à-vis the corps. On the contrary, not only did the old parlements return after Louis XV's death but they tended thereafter, as we shall see, to make common cause with the episcopacy against the monarchy. Further, they compensated for their no longer credible claim to represent the people by rehabilitating the constitutional role of the long defunct Estates General, despite this institution's association with Protestantism and the League.

What in part made that subsequent development possible was that the French monarchy's anti-Protestant legislation, too, emerged from the 1750s somewhat the worse for the wear. For at roughly the same time that the Edict of 1695 sustained its most signal reverses and *Unigenitus* became the object of satirical funeral orations, two important pieces of that legislation—Louis XIV's Edict of Fontainebleau, ending toleration of Protestants, and the Declaration of 1724, which had further criminalized them—fell upon hard times, both at their point of origin in Paris and at the point of their greatest application in Languedoc. Also visible in both places are the traces of the prince de Conti, who, perhaps remembering his sixteenth-century Protestant Bourbon ancestors, initiated contacts with the Protestant community in Languedoc while at the same time, in the spirit of his more recent seventeenth-century frondish ancestors, he drew closer to Jansenist parlementaires like Le Paige and Murard.

As told by John Woodbridge, the story of Conti's involvement with the Protestants began with a Protestant officer in his regiment named Jean-Louis Le Cointe, whom Conti used to establish informal contact with the leader of the Languedocian Protestants, the pastor Paul Rabaut.[39] These contacts led to secretive conversations between Conti and Rabaut in July–August 1755 in Paris in an

39. John Woodbridge, *Revolt in Prerevolutionary France: The Prince de Conti's Conspiracy against Louis XV, 1755–1757* (Baltimore, 1994), passim. A few older works allude to the episode, most notably Edmond Hughes, "Un épisode de l'histoire du protestantisme français," in *BSHPF* 26 (1877):289–303, 337–50, esp. p. 297.

abandoned hôtel on the quai of the Seine: Conti offered to champion the Protestant cause of civil and religious toleration vis-à-vis the king, while Rabaut was to obtain the ratification of these demands by the Huguenot community in both north and south. These plans came to nothing. Conti got nowhere with his Bourbon cousin, who was unwilling to take on Saint-Florentin and the court's parti dévot, while Rabaut ran into the opposition of well-to-do urban and northern Protestants, fearful of provoking a Catholic backlash by asking for religious as well as civil toleration. Instead of ending at that point, however, Conti's relations with the Protestants turned ever more "seditious" as his relations with the king worsened, culminating in instructions to Rabaut to ask the elders and his fellow pastors at the Synod of May 1756 how many men they could afford to arm. By that time Conti held in his hands the elements of a potential alliance of religious malcontents consisting—whether these constituents were aware of each other or not—of parlementary Jansenists at war with the monarchy in the refusal-of-sacraments controversy and Languedocian Protestants chafing at their continuing civil and religious nonexistence, and all this, finally, just as France was embarking on a war neatly pitting Europe's chief Catholic powers against Protestant Prussia and England.

Thereafter the plot thickens to the point of occasional knots of impenetrability. Whether, for example, Conti himself was ever in contact with the ministry of William Pitt apropos of plans for an English descent on the French coast near Rochefort in coordination with a Huguenot uprising is less than certain, although Conti could have had access to the Pitt ministry through a certain Theobald Taaffe, an Irish agent arrested and interrogated in the Bastille in 1758 despite being protected by Conti.[40] Even less clear is what Conti's ultimate intentions might have been with regard to the French monarchy, even without such an English connection. Though ambiguous, however, the evidence on the English side indeed suggests that the channel fleet's expedition to the French coast off Rochefort in the autumn of 1757 had been undertaken in anticipation of an uprising by southern Huguenots, who not unnaturally looked to the English for protection in a war that pitted Protestant against Catholic states. And although the descent on Rochefort did not succeed—the English fleet's lateness would have botched any planned coordination with a Huguenot rising—the evidence on the French side is that of a considerable effort at military repression in Languedoc undertaken by the intendant de Tourny and the maréchal de Thomond in anticipation of some such Huguenot uprising. A few years later, in 1760, the most rambunctious of the Protestant pastors who had been in contact with Conti, Jean-Louis Gibert, led a

40. Woodbridge, *Revolt in Prerevolutionary France,* pp. 90–93; and BA: AB, Ms. 12022, fols. 64–69, 109–10.

group of Huguenots to South Carolina by way of Ireland in what was to be the last significant exodus of Protestants from postrevocation France.[41]

But whether attributable to the threat of Conti's ephemeral alliance or to the Seven Years' War generally, a royal policy of de facto toleration did not wait until 1760. Although the execution of the pastor François Rochette and the Protestant merchant Jean Calas in 1762 served as spectacular examples of intolerance, providing gist for Voltaire's philosophical mill against religious "fanaticism" or "the infamous thing," both occurred in ultra-Catholic Toulouse and represented regional variation rather than royal policy. For Versailles, on the contrary, the latter 1750s seem to have been decisive for the beginnings of a policy of nonenforcement of the Edict of Fontainebleau and the Declaration of 1724, as indeed the same years were decisive in the nonenforcement of the bull *Unigenitus* and the Declaration of 1730.[42] The two developments ought therefore to be seen as parts of a larger pattern, as signifying the beginning of the end of French absolutism's efforts to enforce conformity between its own religious identity and that of the realm. That much, in sum, was the opinion of the General Assembly of the Gallican Clergy, which began to remonstrate against the nonenforcement of the Edict of Fontainebleau as well as the legislation on behalf of *Unigenitus* in 1760. "This great work [the Edict of Fontainebleau] was nearing its perfection when some unfortunate events interrupted the enforcement of the laws that your predecessors as well as you yourself, Sire, had enacted on the subject of [Protestant] religionists," remonstrated the General Assembly to Louis XV that year. "Since that moment, just about all the barriers opposed to Calvinism have been successively breached."[43] The General Assembly moreover reiterated these complaints, with apparent good reason, on every available occasion until its last meeting in 1788.

At roughly the same time, Jansenists metamorphosed into advocates of civil if not religious toleration of Protestants.[44] However different from the stance of

41. Daniel Robert, "La fin du 'désert héroïqé': Pourquois Jean-Louis Gibert a-t-il émigré (1761–63)?" *BSHPF* 6th series, 28, (Oct.–Dec. 1951):238–47; and Jon Butler, *The Huguenots in America: A Refugee People in New World Society* (Cambridge, Mass., 1983), p. 218.

42. Burdette C. Poland, *Protestantism and the French Revolution* (Princeton, N.J., 1957), pp. 67–69; Geoffrey Adams, *The Huguenots and French Public Opinion* (Waterloo, Ont.), p. 43.

43. *Procès verbaux des assemblées générales du clergé de France*, vol. 8, part 1, no. 6, p. 294.

44. On the Jansenist campaign for civil toleration of Protestants see Jeffrey Merrick, *The Desacralization of the French Monarchy in the Eighteenth Century* (Baton Rouge, La., 1990), pp. 135–64; Adams, *The Huguenots and French Opinion*, pp. 231–63; but above all the works of Charles H. O'Brien, "Jansenists on Civil Toleration in Mid-Eighteenth-Century France" *Theologische Zeitschrift* 37 (1981):71–93; "Jansenists and Civil Toleration of Protestants in France, 1775–1778: Lepaige, Guidi, and Robert de Saint-Vincent," in *La tolérance civile*, ed. Roland Crahay (Brussels, 1982), pp. 183–99; "The Jansenist Campaign for Toleration of Protestants in Eighteenth-Century France: Sacred or Secular?" *JHI* 46 (1985):523–38; and "New Light on the Mouton-Natoire Case (1768): Freedom of Conscience and the Role of the Jansenists," *JCS* 27 (1985):65–82.

seventeenth-century Jansenists like Arnauld and Nicole, who had tried to demonstrate their Catholic orthodoxy by refuting Protestants more compellingly than their Molinistic opponents, this new and more irenic stance had been prepared, as has been noted, by developments in eighteenth-century Jansenist theology and ecclesiology as well as by the slow evolution of the movement's religious sensibility. Still, it was not until 1756 that Jean-Pierre Ripert de Monclar, the quite Jansenist procureur général of the Parlement of Aix, went to press with his *Theological and Political Memoir on the Protestants' Clandestine Marriages in France,* followed shortly by Gabriel Maultrot's and the abbé Jacques Tailhé's *Questions on Toleration* published, appropriately, in Geneva in 1758.[45] Whatever his attitude earlier may have been, Le Paige lent the campaign his pen in the 1760s, arguing eloquently for civil toleration of Protestants in the pages of the *Nouvelles ecclésiastiques* on the occasion of the controversy surrounding the philosophe Jean-François Marmontel's play *Belissaire* in 1768.[46] The cause of civil toleration remained a leitmotif in Jansenist literature in the 1770s and 1780s, as we shall see, until Robert de Saint-Vincent tried to persuade the Parlement of Paris to take up the matter in 1787 and then steered Louis XVI's Edict of Toleration through the gauntlet of registration the following year.

But that is to get too far ahead of the story. The most immediate use that the parlementary parti janséniste made of its victory in the controversy over refusal of sacraments was not to aid the Protestants but to strike the ultimate blow against their old enemy the Society of Jesus—another conspicuous symbol of Bourbon absolutism. Beginning in the latter 1750s with obscure trials in the consular courts of Marseilles and Paris, this offensive against the Jesuits continued until 1766, by which time even the confessors and preachers had disappeared from the royal court. Its crucial moment, however, came on 6 August 1761, when, appealing the Jesuits' constitutions and "formulas of vows" comme d'abus, the Parlement of Paris forbade further recruitment to the society and closed its colleges after a short delay.

The Seven Years' War, it is true, came to the aid of the parti janséniste against the Jesuits even more dramatically than it did in the case of the refusal-of-sacraments controversy. For it was the English navy's seizure of several vessels bearing merchandise on its way to Marseilles from the French Jesuit mission on the Caribbean island of Martinique that put the last nail in the declining fortunes

45. Jean-Pierre-François de Ripert de Monclar, *Mémoire théologique et politique au sujet des mariages clandestins des protestans en France* (n.p., 1755); Gabriel-Nicolas Maultrot and Jacques Tailhé, *Questions sur la tolérance, où l'on examine si les maximes de la persécution ne sont pas contraires au droit des gens, à la religion, à la morale, à l'intérêt du souverain et du clergé* (Geneva, 1758), republished as *Essai sur la tolérance chrétienne* ("en France," 1760). On Ripert de Monclar as Jansenist see the anonymous *Lettre d'un gentilhomme du diocèse d'Apt à M. Xxxx* (n.p., n.d.), published in 1774 on the occasion of Ripert de Monclar's death.

46. On Le Paige's authorship of these pages, see his letter to the abbé Clément de Bizon, treasurer of the cathedral of Auxerre, in BPR: CLP, Ms. 579, no. 1.

of the père de La Valette, head of that mission, as it was La Valette's financial misfortunes that caused the bankruptcy of his chief creditors in France, the house of Lioncy and Gouffre based in Marseilles. Having first sued the Jesuits' West Indian Missions to no decisive financial effect, Lioncy and Gouffre and some of their creditors then sued the whole Society of Jesus in France and obtained a favorable verdict from the consular court of Paris in 1760. The French Jesuits foolishly appealed this verdict to the Grand' chambre of the Parlement of Paris. There their numerous enemies not only upheld it but succeeded in widening the case into a challenge to the Jesuits' very right to exist in France, demanding to see their heretofore unexamined and unapproved constitutions.

It is also true that these enemies pursued their case against the Jesuits with the help of the benevolent neutrality both of the king's titled mistress Madame de Pompadour, perhaps resentful of the continued denial of absolution by her court confessors, and of the secretary for war and foreign affairs Etienne-François, duc de Choiseul, happy to throw the Jesuits to the parlements in return for cooperation on the fiscal front. At the very least, their neutrality counteracted the efforts of the courtly parti dévot led by the dauphin and Chancellor Lamoignon to save the Jesuits by "reforming" them—the aim of an abortive royal edict that the Parlement of Paris circumvented with the help of the provincial parlements in the spring of 1762. At the most, Choiseul's secret encouragement may have prompted the Parlement's parti janséniste to transform the case against La Valette into the trial of the Jesuits in the first place. In any case it was surely with his and Pompadour's approval that Louis XV reluctantly put the seal of royal approval on the parlements' action against the Jesuits with the Edict of November 1764, which dissolved the Jesuits' society while allowing them to live as "particulars" within the realm.[47]

In all other respects, however, the case against the Jesuits was the work of the Parlement of Paris's parti janséniste, who saw the event in apocalyptic terms, fraught with figuratist meaning. It was the Jansenist barrister Charlemagne Lalourcé, for example, who conducted the case of the Jesuits' creditors in its earliest stages, and Le Paige and his canonist colleague Christophe Coudrette who took over when the trial became that of the Jesuits themselves.[48] In the public sphere of parlementary action, it was the Jansenist magistrates Henri-Philippe Chauvelin who inspired the Parlement's order that the Jesuits submit their constitutions for examination, the councillors Clément de Feillet and Guillaume Lambert who found another copy of these constitutions when the King's Council

47. *Edit du roi, concernant la Société des jésuites, donné à Versailles au mois de novembre 1764* (Paris, 1764).

48. See the obituaries of Charlemagne Lalourcé in *NE* 27 June 1768, pp. 100–101; and Christophe Coudrette, ibid., 12 Dec. 1774, pp.197–200.

demanded the one that the Jesuits had delivered, and Laverdy de Nizaret who carried the case against these constitutions and the Jesuits' "corrupt doctrine" in the decisive session of 6 August 1761. The crucial role of Jansenists in the affair extends even to some of the provinces, especially Rouen, where the councillor Thomas Du Fossé, the grand nephew of a famous Port-Royal "solitary" by the same name, pushed through the first definitive judgment against the Jesuits, thereby crippling the chancellor's attempt to reform them in cooperation with moderate magistrates in Paris.[49] The one spectacular exception to this rule for Paris would seem to be the president Durey de Meinières, quasi-philosophic dabbler in science and the arts, who at a crucial juncture overruled Le Paige's advice of slow strangulation of the Jesuits' society in favor of the more surgical procedure actually followed.[50] But Durey de Meinières was a close friend of Le Paige's and collaborator with him in erudite projects, and he had recently married the pious Madame Bellot, the widow of a deceased Jansenist barrister.[51]

Although the event naturally invites comparison to the expulsion of the Jesuits in Portugal a few years earlier and from Spain and the Kingdom of Naples a few years later, the initiative came from "below" and in Jansenist form in France, in contrast to clearly royal and vaguely "enlightened" Catholic impulses elsewhere. If Louis XV acquiesced in his parlements' religious policy more readily in the 1760s than in 1757, that was mainly because the parlements' offensive against the Jesuits represented the conclusion of premises more reluctantly conceded in 1757. To say, as did Louis XV to Choiseul, that he had gone along with the dissolution "for the sake of the peace of my realm" but "against my will" was not a very enthusiastic endorsement of his parlements' actions.[52] In no sense, then, did

49. Olivier Chaline has recently denied the existence of a parti janséniste in the Parlement of Rouen in "Les infortunes de la fidélité, le procureur, le roi et les Normands," forthcoming. Be that as it may—the matter remains far from settled—that thesis hardly detracts from the crucial role of Thomas Du Fossé, who did nothing in turn without consulting Le Paige in Paris.

50. Durey de Meinières's winning strategy is outlined in a letter to Le Paige in BPR, LP 582, no. 97. In Dale Van Kley, *The Jansenists and the Expulsion of the Jesuits from France, 1757–1765* (New Haven, Conn., 1975), p. 127, n. 51), I speculated that the author of the unsigned letter was the councillor Laverdy although it was not in his handwriting, since it was l'Averdy who implemented the stategy in question on the floor of the Parlement. The handwriting, I thought, could have been that of a copyist. One difficulty with that hypothesis was, however, that the author of the letter addressed Le Paige as "mon chèr Le Paige" (my dear Le Paige), while l'Averdy never addressed Le Paige in these familiar terms in any of the letters identifiably his. The one magistrate who did consistently address Le Paige in this way was Le Paige's erudite friend and collaborator in the research for the *Lettres historiques sur les fonctions essentielles du Parlement, sur le droit des pairs, et sur les loix fondamentaux du royaume,* 2 vols. (n.p., 1753–54), namely Durey de Meinières. A subsequent look at that manuscript letter in comparison with others signed by Durey de Meinières has confirmed that it is indeed in that magistrate's handwriting.

51. Her first husband had just begun to attract the favorable notice of *NE* for his legal contribution to Jansenist causes when he died, apparently prematurely. See *NE* 9 October 1755, pp. 161–62.

52. Quoted in the père de Ravignan, *Clément XIII et Clément XIV,* 2 vols. (Paris, 1854), 1:135.

the dissolution of the Jesuits in France represent royal religious policy as it did in Portugal, Spain, or the Kingdom of Naples. What happened to the Jesuits in France was also more radical even if more genteel than in Spain and Portugal because, instead of physically expelling Jesuits for having fallen short of their society's standards, the parlements dissolved the society itself as "impious" and confiscated its property on the grounds that it belonged ultimately to the nation, thus setting another precedent for what the National Assembly did to the Gallican Church less than thirty years later.[53]

The dissolution of the Jesuits' society also represented another defeat for the episcopacy as well as for the monarchy. French bishops, as closely identified with the monarchy as the Jesuits since the reign of Louis XIV, had long ceased to resent them as many curés still did for their papal privileges and relative independence as "regulars" vis-à-vis the bishops' ordinary or secular jurisdiction. What was at stake for the bishops in 1762 was spiritual authority as such, which the parlements had transgressed the more fragrantly by dissolving the Society of Jesus as both despotic and impious, in contrast to expelling it as simply incompatible with the Gallican liberties and other fundamental laws of the realm.[54] So when Louis XV formally solicited the Gallican bishops' opinion on the usefulness of the Jesuits in an extraordinary meeting of the General Assembly in 1762, its approval of the institute was all but unanimous. The few jansénisant bishops, like Fitz-James of Soissons, were spectacular exceptions that proved the rule.[55]

When in a last act of bravado, the General Assembly of the Gallican Clergy promulgated a set of *Acts* laying down its own version of the proper boundaries between sacerdoce and empire, it remonstrated on behalf of the Jesuits as well as against the nonenforcement of *Unigenitus* and the Edict of Fontainebleau.[56] Although it was only an after-tremor after the seismic *Unigenitus*-related quakes of 1727–32 and 1750–62, the ensuing controversy over the 1765 Assembly's *Acts* had the effect of underscoring the extent of the bishops' defeat. As usual, the Parle-

53. *Arrest de la cour de parlement du 6 août 1762* (Paris, 1762), p. 1–2; The *arrêt* is also in Pierre-Paul Alexandre Gilbert de Voisins, *Procédure contre l'institut et les constitutions des jésuites, suivie au parlement de Paris sur l'appel comme d'abus, interjetté par le procureur général du roi, recueillie par un membre du parlement et publié par M. Gilbert de Voisins, membre de la Chambre des députés* (Paris, 1823).

54. AN: K, Ms. 1371, no. 3, "Remontrances du clergé concernant les voeux des jésuites que plusieurs parlemens ont entrepris d'annuller," fols. 11–13; and no. 6, "Très humbles et très respectueuses remontrances des agens généraux du clergé de France," fols. 1–5.

55. AN: K, Ms. 1361, no. 1A, "Procès-verbal de l'assemblée extraordinaire des évêques en 1761," esp. fols. 10–16. See also no. 1C for the "Avis particuliers de M. le cardinal de Choiseul et M. l'évêque de Soissons," who dissented from the opinion of the majority of their colleagues in the assembly. Some of these and other episcopal reactions are reprinted in Ravignan's *Clément XIII et Clément XIV*, 2:196–277.

56. *Actes de l'Assemblée générale du clergé de France sur la religion, extraits du procès-verbal de ladite assemblée, tenue à Paris, par permission du roi, au couvent des Grands-Augustins, en mil sept cent soixante-cinq* (Paris, 1765).

ment's parti janséniste—in this case, Guillaume Lambert, with the juristic help of Adrien Le Paige—engineered the high court's condemnation of these *Acts*.[57] And although the Royal Council, which was in need of the General Assembly's fiscal contribution, obligingly annulled the Parlement's condemnation, this annulment did not prevent the Parlement from enforcing the administration of the last sacraments to a Jansenist nun in Saint-Cloud—under the noses of the scandalized bishops—and of having the last word vis-à-vis the monarchy in the form of the published remonstrances of 30–31 August 1766, drafted by Robert de Saint-Vincent.[58] Worse yet, as we shall see, this controversy provoked the appearance of some of the most virulent pamphlets against the clergy as a privileged order that the Old Regime would ever see, including those published on the eve of the Revolution.

The demise of symbols as central to Bourbon absolutism as *Unigenitus*, the Declaration of 1730, the Edict of Fontainebleau, the Edict of 1695, and the Society of Jesus does not exhaust the damage sustained by the French monarchy during another two decades of *Unigenitus*-related confrontations. Evidence about the prestige of kingship is elusive, fragile, and not infrequently ambiguous. Yet there is much to suggest that, for portions of both the "political nation" and the "people," the decades of the 1750s and 1760s were decades of extensive damage to the medieval base of sacral kingship, to say nothing of its seventeenth-century "absolutist" outcroppings. To the debatable extent that such damage was done, it was done in a manner reminiscent of the very sixteenth-century wars that had justified Bourbon absolutism in the first place. Indeed, some of this evidence may be read as the revenge of the wars of religion.

The Wars of Religion Remembered and Revisited

Given these sixteenth-century homologies, it is hardly surprising that contemporaries should have been confusedly aware of them. If the abbé Mably remained virtually alone in the 1750s in frankly thinking that "civil war is a sometimes a great good," even applying that dictum to the political fermentation that resulted from the "doctrines of Luther and Calvin," many relived the wars of religion in their fears and collective imagination, very much as they had begun to do in the late 1720s and 1730s.[59]

Perhaps most traumatized by the resemblance between the events of his own

57. BPR: CLP, Ms. 562, no. 29, note by Le Paige "pour la cour après la lecture rapide des actes qu'on m'avoit fait passer ad hoc"; and no. 31, memoir by Guillaume Lambert. See also *NE* 6 November 1766, pp. 183–84; 30 June 1766, p. 21; and 9 December 1767, p. 197.

58. Flammermont, *Remontrances*, 2:638; on Robert de Saint-Vincent's authorship of these remonstrances, see his "mémoires," p. 413.

59. Gabriel Bonnet de Mably, *Les droits et les devoirs du citoyen*, pp. 221, 280.

century and those of the sixteenth was the marquis d'Argenson, who in 1752 detected "the onset of a League," specifying that any attempt to find a middle way between "what are called Jansenists these days" and the ardent constitutionaries would be "fatal in such a delicate affair, and would give to the sceptre every kind of resemblance to that wielded by Henri III vis-à-vis the League."[60] Adrien Le Paige agreed. Reacting in 1754 to an anonymously published critique of the Châtelet's loyalty to the exiled Parlement of Paris, for example, Le Paige regarded it as the "manifesto" of a clerical "league," its many episcopal endorsements evidence of a full-blown conspiracy against the state or at least the parlements.[61] And pleading in early December 1756 with his patron prince de Conti to intercede with the king and try to head off the coming lit de justice assembly, Le Paige called the attention of the king's cousin to the similarity of France's dilemma in 1756 to that obtaining in the 1580s. "We have here the same situation, the same audacity in the clergy, the same League on the part of false zealots, the same instability and . . . weakness on the part of the king." Just as Henri III was "sometimes for the clergy, sometimes for the Parlement, and sometimes in between," but "finally found himself forced to choose for the League he so abhorred," so it was to be feared that in pursuing the same vacillatory course, Louis XV would come to the same unfortunate end, namely "to die at the hands of the League itself."[62] If Le Paige had known that his patron was in contact at that moment with Protestants in Languedoc, seditiously curious about how many men their synod could equip with arms, these structural similarities may have struck him as more two-sided than they did. And when, less than a year later, someone indeed thrust a knife blade between Louis XV's ribs on a cold January day, others besides Le Paige were willing to point accusing fingers in the same dévot direction. Christophe de Beaumont, to believe the Troyen barrister Jean Grosley, was the "chief" of this new league, a sort of latter-day Jean Boucher, whose recent pastoral instruction had given "the first signal of combat" to a new would-be Jacques Clément or Jean Chastel.[63] That the rump Parlement of Paris sentenced Damiens to endure the same horrible execution as had the assassin of Henri IV in 1610 was no exercise in pointless anachronism. The point was to say that Damiens was cut from the same Jesuitical and Leaguish cloth as had been Clément, Chastel, and François Ravaillac. And just as the first expulsion of the Jesuits followed hard upon Jean

---

60. D'Argenson, *Journal et mémoires* (13 and 24 April 1752), 7:184. See also p. 204 and April 1755, 8:483.

61. [Louis-Adrien Le Paige], *Mémoires sur un nouvel écrit contre le parlement, intitulé: Observations sur le refus que fait le Châtelet de reconnoître la Chambre royale* (n.p., n.d.), p. 1.

62. BPR: CLP, Ms. 547, no. 3, "Première mémoire ou lettre de moi à mr. le prince de conti, 9 décembre 1756."

63. [Jean-Pierre Grosley], *Lettre d'un patriote, où l'on rapporte les faits qui prouvent que l'attentat commis sur la vie du roi a des complices, et la manière dont on instruit son procès* (n.p., [1757]), p. 4.

Chastel's unsuccessful attempt on Henri IV's life in 1595, so the Parlement of Paris lost no time in proceeding a second time against the Society of Jesus after Damiens's apparent attempt on Louis XV's life in 1757. The trial's close proximity to the Damiens affair was hardly coincidental, preceded as it was by such pamphlets as the anonymous *Jesuits Guilty of Leze Majesty, Both in Theory and in Practice* and the abbé Christophe Coudrette's *General History* of the Society, which featured chapters on how the Jesuits had been "the heart of the League," had engaged in "conspiracies against Henri III and Henri IV," and how, having been "guilty of a new assassination of Henri IV, they were finally expelled from the Realm."[64] A few years later the Jansenist historian Louis-Pierre Anquetil hardened the association between the mid-eighteenth century and the ultra-Catholic sixteenth century with his three-volume *Spirit of the League.*[65]

If on the other side the episcopal strategists of the parti dévot seemed a little less sure than their Jansenist and parlementary adversaries that they were reliving the sixteenth-century wars of religion, it was only because they were occasionally convinced that the eighteenth century was even harder on true religion than the sixteenth had been. Most often they compared their many tribulations at the hands of The Most Christian King and the parlements to those of the early church fathers, persecuted as they had been by a combination of pagans, heretics, and well-meaning but misled emperors. Still, when the Bishop of Saint-Pons rhetorically asked his parishioners in 1756, "What century do we live in, my dear brothers?" the sixteenth century was surely a candidate for the correct answer. Detecting, like Le Paige, a new "league" in the making, Saint-Pons made it clear that the one he imagined was Protestant-like, "formed against the Church and her ministers." Or perhaps it was less a league than a "conjuration" like that of Amboise, in which Protestants had tried to kidnap King Francis II; this one, however, "concluded against the adorable Body of Jesus Christ [himself], the better to surrender him hand and foot to his most cruel enemies." These new Protestants were also conspiring to use "ruse and artifice in order to establish their morality of despair."[66] As such this obviously Jansenist conspiracy was akin to the one simultaneously being formed by "furious enemies" against Poncet de La Rivière, Bishop of Troyes; his ultimate recourse was to implore the help of the Virgin Mary, always "happily terrible against heresies," as well as to establish an

---

64. *Les jésuites criminels de lèse-majesté, dans la théroie et dans la pratique* (The Hague, 1758); and [Christophe Coudrette and Adrien Le Paige], *Histoire générale de la naissance et des progrès de la compagnie de Jésus, et l'analyse de ses constitutions,* 4 vols., new ed. (Amsterdam, 1761), 1: chapter 8, "Les Jésuites sont l'âme de la Ligue: Leurs conjurations contre Henri III et contre Henri IV," pp. 196–215; and chapter 10, "Les jésuites coupables d'un nouvel assassinat d'Henri IV sont enfin chassés du Royaume," pp. 215–37.

65. Louis-Pierre Anquetil, *L'esprit de la Ligue, ou l'histoire politique des troubles de France, pendant les XVIe et XVIIe siècles,* 3 vols. (Paris, 1767).

66. *Mandement de Monseigneur l'évêque de Saint-Pons,* pp. 2–3, in BN: Mss. Fr., 22093 (90).

octave of prayer in honor of her immaculate conception, which, along with her scapulary and rosary, had recently sustained an iconoclastic attack in his diocese.[67]

Surrounded by French Protestants though he was, the Bishop of Montauban's sixteenth century was English rather than French. In a mandamus that was at once "insane and fanatical," according to the marquis d'Argenson, the bishop compared the Parlement of Paris to the Parliament of England which, in renouncing the "true faith and Catholic unity," prepared the way for England's subsequent history of "rivers of blood."[68] Only a little less hysterical, Christophe de Beaumont, too, saw good reason to fear the repetition of the English sixteenth century, what with the "degrading *(avilissement)* of its clergy" by an English Parliament which he agreed was all too similar to the eighteenth-century French parlements. Or if it was the ghosts of French Huguenots who haunted him, they were rather those of the seventeenth century like "[Pierre] Jurieu and his ilk," whose "doctrine" concerning the proper relations between church and state had suddenly "become dominant in our provinces."[69]

Although these traumatic memories of religious civil war undoubtedly made their own contribution to reality, that reality was similar enough to the sixteenth century, memory or no memory. Jansenism was in some respects becoming more like Protestantism, an ultra-Catholic and ultramontanist parti dévot had arisen in reaction, and the monarchy maneuvered between them with increasingly desacralizing effect.

One of the chief agents of desacralization was Jansenist-Gallican jurisprudence in the refusal-of-sacraments controversy. Under the influence of this jurisprudence, the Parlement of Paris as early as 1751 abandoned the appeal comme d'abus in favor of the royal courts' purely secular criminal procedure; whereas the former entailed a civil appeal of an ecclesiastical judgment or procedure, the latter allowed the royal courts to enjoin priests directly to administer the sacraments. The crucial premise in this jurisprudence was that the public refusal of sacraments to someone who was not nominally excommunicated was a public defamation of that person's reputation and as such a "royal" or "privileged" case adjudicable by the royal courts alone. Although the appel comme d'abus was premised upon the French king's quasi-sacral qualities as "the Lord's anointed," "exterior bishop," "the eldest son of the church," and "protector of the canons," all of which entitled the kings' judges to see to it that the church abided by her own laws or canons and

---

67. *Mandement de Monseigneur l'évêque de Troyes. Du 22 novembre 1756*, pp. 9–14, in BN: Mss. Fr., 22093 (115).

68. D'Argenson, *Journal et mémoires* (28 Oct. 1753), 8:148.

69. Christophe de Beaumont du Repaire, *Mandement de Monseigneur l'archévêque de Paris, touchant l'autorité de l'église, l'enseignement de la foi, l'administration des sacremens, la soumission due à la constitution Unigenitus, portant défense de lire plusieurs écrits* (Paris, 1756), p. 25.

to allow appeals in cases of procedural abuse; the Jansenist advocates of criminal procedure prevailed upon the king's quality as political magistrate to argue that his judges might punish unjust public refusals of sacraments as gratuitous defamations of personal and familial reputations and as disturbances of the public peace. What was new here was the emphasis on the king as a purely secular political magistrate. The effect was to enlarge the domain of what the king (meaning his judges, or the state) might do in this profane capacity at the expense of his power as sacred personage.[70] It may seem ironic to encounter such juristic casuistry on the part of disciples of Saint-Cyran and the author of a treatise critical of *La fréquent communion,* although an argument not unlike this one can already be found in the "great" Arnauld's two published letters to the duc de Liancourt, who in 1655 was refused communion by a vicaire in the parish of Saint-Sulpice.[71] Yet this argument only took to the point of "Protestant" distortion the already Jansenist tendency to distinguish sharply between the exterior and public aspects of religion on the one hand, and the interior and invisible domain of religious conscience *(for intérieur)* on the other. As Jeffrey Merrick has persuasively argued, the refusal-of-sacraments controversy, and this Jansenist jurisprudence especially, contributed enormously to the privatization of religious sentiment in eighteenth-century France.[72] And although contingent circumstances played their part in its elaboration—the need, for example, to circumvent the time-consuming appel comme d'abus lest the moribund appellants die without the last sacraments—this jurisprudence also represents the working out of Jansenism's long inherent tendency to desacralize everything between God and the individual conscience, divine-right monarchy not excepted.

The same choice between invoking the king as quasi-sacred outside bishop or as secular political magistrate presented itself in the concurrent debate about civil toleration of Protestants. The Protestant "problem" as it confronted the French government in the 1750s was how to legalize Protestant marriages and legitimize the resultant children. By the terms of the Edict of Fontainebleau, reinforced by that of 1724, such marriages were so many concubinages and such children bastards unless solemnized by the Catholic sacraments of marriage and baptism. One tack, urged by the parlement's former procureur général Guillaume-François Joly de Fleury in 1751, was to act on the two edicts' fictitious

70. For an exceptionally clear and forceful exposition of this jurisprudence, see Le Paige's memoir for the prince de Conti in BPR: CLP, Ms. 537, no. 90. But as the next chapter will show, this jurisprudence is pervasively argued in the published literature of the period.

71. Antoine Arnauld, *Première lettre de M. Arnauld docteur de Sorbonne à une personne de condition: Sur se qui s'est arrivé depuis peu, dans une paroisse de Paris, à un seigneur de la cour;* and *Seconde lettre de M. Arnauld docteur de Sorbonne à un duc et pair, pour servir de réponse à plusieurs écrits qui ont été publiés contre sa première lettre,* in *OC,* 43 vols. (Lausanne, 1775–83), 19:311–558.

72. Jeffrey Merrick, *The Desacralization of the French Monarchy in the Eighteenth Century,* pp. 95–96.

assumption that all Protestants had been converted to Catholicism and, again prevailing upon king's sacral quality as enforcer of the church's canons, to enjoin Catholic priests to administer these sacraments to Protestants as though they were good Catholics, with no indiscreet questions asked. To the extent that it was followed—occasionally it was—that tack exactly paralleled the use of the *appel comme d'abus* in sacramental litigation vis-à-vis Jansenists, who of course insisted upon their impeccable Catholicity. But against that approach was the one proposed in 1755 by Ripert de Monclar, the quite Jansenist *procureur général* of the Parlement of Aix-en-Provence, who argued that marriage's status as a natural-law contract antedated and took precedence over its solemnization as a sacrament, so that the king as secular political magistrate might have his judges simply register Protestant marriages and births, and the Protestants, for their part, might have their marriages and their Protestantism too. This argument in favor of civil toleration, precisely paralleling the approach taken by the parlements under the influence of Jansenist jurisprudence in the refusal-of-sacraments controversy, similarly tended to separate citizenship from Catholicity and became a hallmark of Jansenist argumentation on the subject from the mid-1750s until the Revolution.[73]

Indeed, despite a marked tendency to smooth the sharp doctrinal edges of Augustinianism with the application of a little Thomism, mid-eighteenth-century Jansenism continued to take on the Protestant hue already evident earlier in the century. After its expulsion from the cemetery of Saint-Médard, for example, the convulsionary movement became a private, congregational, and ever more lay phenomenon. During the same period what remained of theological and clerical Jansenism hardened its opposition to such Jesuitical or "baroque" devotional practices as the use of the rosary, stigmatizing them as "mechanical" and "superstitious."[74] Although seventeenth-century Jansenists had had frequent recourse to the sacramental metaphor of the sacred heart of Jesus, their eighteenth-century successors directed some of their most withering scorn against the now papally sanctioned cult or devotion of the sacred heart as excessively affective, corporeal, and quintessentially Jesuitical.[75] And judicial Jansenism spread the news of the refusal-of-sacraments controversy not only by means of the *Nouvelles ecclésiastiques* and clandestinely published pamphlets but, increasingly, by means of French-language periodicals of the Netherlands-based Huguenot diaspora, such as the Leyden *Gazette*. It is all but certain that these periodicals received much of

73. Ibid., pp. 149–51.

74. Although for a somewhat later period, the only systematic attention given to this development is Michel Albaric's "Regard des jansénistes sur l'église de France de 1780–1789 d'après les *Nouvelles ecclésiastiques*," in *Jansénisme et Révolution, Chroniques de Port-Royal*, ed. Catherine Maire, (Paris, 1990), 39:72. What is true of the 1780s, however, holds just as well for the century's middle decades.

75. Louis Cognet, "Les jansénistes et le Sacré Coeur," *Etudes carmélitaines* 29 (1950):234–53.

their copy from Jansenist sources in Paris via the Jansenist refuge in the schismatic diocese of Utrecht.[76]

But French Catholicism's contribution to the desacralization of the monarchy was not as lopsidedly Jansenist as this analysis might suggest. The eighteenth-century parti dévot contributed equally if oppositely, in the process reverting to some of its sixteenth-century ancestral forms to the detriment of its more recent past. Against Jansenist jurisprudence, for example, which insisted upon the rights of the king—meaning his judges—in sacramental litigation as a purely lay political magistrate, the parti dévot similarly underscored the king's identity as a layman, the better to deny him any voice over the public dispensation of the sacraments. That was the position of Christophe de Beaumont, as well as of the cardinal de Soubise, who set the tone for the episcopal members of a special commission appointed by Louis XV to advise him on sacramental litigation at the height of the controversy in 1752.[77] Although in part responsible for the registration of the declaration that made *Unigenitus* a law of church and state in 1730, the former procureur général Joly de Fleury became so frustrated with these churchmen in the commission's meetings that he was driven to the conclusion that they and many of their colleagues were simply less Gallican than in 1682, that their pronounced ultramontanism renewed contact with that of the original parti dévot.[78] The effect of this episcopal zealotry was to cripple royal religious policy at the center. In his correspondence with the elder Joly de Fleury, Louis XV's secretary for foreign affairs, Antoine-Louis Rouillé, repeatedly referred to "his majesty's scruples and fear of infringing on ecclesiastical [that is, spiritual] jurisdiction."[79]

It was the same religious scruples that in part prevented Louis XV from confessing and taking communion—and being in a state to touch for scrofula. Intermittent in the 1730s, Louis XV's lapses in touching for the "king's disease" became chronic from the 1740s until the end of his reign. The confessional sources of this inability were of course the king's adulterous liaisons, first with the three De Nesle sisters; next with Jeanne-Antoinette Poisson, Madame d'Etiolles, whom he elevated to the marquisate of Pompadour in 1745; and then with a bewildering series of women of more modest social origins, culminating with Jeanne Becu, the so-called duchesse Du Barry, in the late 1760s and early 1770s. Louis XV himself

76. D. Carroll Joynes, "The *Gazette de Leyde:* The Opposition Press and French Politics, 1750–1757," in *Press and Politics in Pre-Revolutionary France* ed. Jack R. Censer and Jeremy D. Popkin (Berkeley, Calif., 1987), pp. 133–69.

77. AN: AP, 177mi (chartrier de Tocqueville, fonds Lamoignon), Ms. 75, no. 12, memoir by the cardinal de Soubise, 1752.

78. BN: CJF, Ms. 1493, fols. 156–60, letters from the elder Joly de Fleury to Antoine-Louis Rouillé, 8 and 10 Sept. 1752.

79. BN: CJF, Ms. 1494, fols. 215–16, Antoine-Louis Rouillé to the elder Joly de Fleury, 22 Apr. 1753; and fol. 243, same to same, 14 Oct. 1752.

apologetically explained his inability to Ferdinand of Parma in 1769: "At my coronation I acquired the gift of being able to be the instrument of God's grace for the curing of scrofula, but for this I must be in a state of grace myself, and it had been some time since this has happened."[80] As to why he was not in a state of grace, the abbé de Bernis, secretary for foreign affairs in 1758, explained in his memoirs that "the King is religious. He has followed only the most severe counsels for his interior conduct, and has preferred to abstain from the sacraments rather than to profane them."[81] What is curious about these "severe counsels" is that they came not from the Jansenists but from the king's Jesuit confessors, successively Taschereau de Linières, Sylvain Perusseau, and Philippe Desmarets; their penitential severity broke an unofficial "attritional" contract between their society and the French crown from the reign of the *vert gallant* Henry IV, or at least from that of Louis XIII and Richelieu's confrontation with Nicolas Caussin as royal confessor. The fact that the rigorous Desmaret went so far as to refuse absolution to both the king and the marquise de Pompadour so long as she stayed at court, even though she had long ceased to be the king's mistress, may well have been a factor in Pompadour's and the king's relative indifference in the face of the parlements' offensive against the Jesuits in the 1760s.

Far from being personal idiosyncracies, moreover, the moral rigorism of these confessors represented some general tendencies among eighteenth-century Jesuits, at least in France. In spite of the scandal caused by the Jesuit Jean Pichon's published refutation of Antoine Arnauld and defense of accommodating casuistry in 1745—amply exploited by the *Nouvelles ecclésiastiques* during the next several decades—few Jansenists would have disavowed the penitential theology displayed in the published sermons of such Jesuit court preachers as Henri Griffet and the brothers Charles and Claude-Frey de Neuville.[82]

To be sure, the eighteenth-century Jesuit court preachers duly distanced themselves from Jansenist penitential theology and practice, or what they took to be such, namely its confessional perfectionism and eucharistic parsimony. It was on this score as well as for having rejected *Unigenitus,* after all, that thousands of priests had found themselves interdicted by their superiors and exiled by lettres de cachet. So while it was bad enough, complained Pierre-Claude Frey de Neuville, that the eighteenth century had experienced more than its fair share of "voluntary and considered profanation" of the Eucharist—the influence of philosophical unbelief, no doubt—"it was reserved to our own century to accredit, to authorize,

---

80. Louis XV to Ferdinand of Parma, 29 July 1769, in *Lettres à l'enfant Ferdinand de Parme,* ed. Philippe Amiguet (Paris, 1938), p. 135, as quoted and translated by Jeffrey W. Merrick, *The Desacralization of the French Monarchy in the Eighteenth-Century,* p. 20.

81. Quoted in Antoine, *Louis XV,* p. 432.

82. Jean Pichon, *L'esprit de Jésus-Christ et de l'église sur la fréquente communion, par Jean Pichon* (Paris, 1745).

to consecrate as it were a voluntary withdrawal from the sacraments . . . under the cover of a hypocritical respect for our most holy mysteries, a sorrow over the decline of discipline, a nostalgia for the severity of the ancient canons"—a Jansenist remedy perhaps worse than the corruption it was supposed to counter.[83] For Neuville's ex-colleague Pierre-François Lafitau, who left the Society to become Bishop of Sisteron, it sufficed to be in a state of grace—that is, "to be exempt from all mortal sin and all affection for mortal sin"—to be fit to take communion, and "to say or to think the contrary [was] to confound . . . counsels with . . . precepts, to imagine a heretical pretext in order to abolish entirely the usage of the sacraments, and to insinuate that not even at Easter despite the precepts of the church, nor even at death's door despite the desperate needs of the dying . . . does anyone have the right to take communion, because strictly speaking no pure creature merits such an honor."[84] Henri Griffet, the king's "ordinary" Jesuit preacher, similarly asserted that although it might be "a shame that human imperfection obliges us to scale down such an otherwise laudable standard," it sufficed after all to be in a state of grace, and he warned his hearers against the contrary pronouncements of some theologians—he need hardly have said which—lest "the usage of the sacraments be abolished, years pass without anyone approaching the holy table, the precepts of the church be violated, and people be reputed holier and more perfect than others for having violated them."[85]

Having said that much, however, these Jesuits proceeded to lay down conditions for communion that would have satisfied all but the most rigorous Jansenists and would most surely have disqualified Louis XV—and did—to say nothing of Madame de Pompadour. In an Easter Day sermon that both may have heard—his published sermons were "dedicated to the king"—Neuville maintained that the only valid biblical model for the "spiritual resurrection" required of the sinner before taking pascal communion was the resurrection of Christ himself. Just as Christ had left his tomb after his resurrection, never to return, so the converted sinner was obliged to "leave the sojourn and scene of sin," including "a dangerous liaison that is not entirely broken," or "a fund *(fonds)* of indolence, laziness, caprice, and bad moods, that is not absolutely disciplined by work and regularity." Just as Christ's resurrection had been permanent, so the sinner's "spiritual resurrection should be nothing less than real, solid, and similar to Jesus Christ's." And just as Christ's resurrection had been public, so the sinner's must be "fully as known, fully as public, fully incontestable as the spiritual death had been," especially in the case of "the high and mighty of this earth" whose sins had

83. Pierre-Claude Frey de Neuville, *Sermons du père Pierre-Claude-Frey de Neuville, l'aîné, dédié au roi*, 2 vols. (Rouen, 1778), 2:56.

84. Jean-Pierre Lafitau, *Sermons de Lafitau, évêque de Sisteron*, 4 vols. (Lyon, 1752), 3:342–43.

85. Henri Griffet, *Sermons pour l'avent, le carême, et les principaux fêtes de l'année, prêchés par R. Père H. Griffet, prédicateur ordinaire de Sa Majesté Très-Catholique*, 4 vols. (Liège, 1773), 3:116–17.

perforce assumed the proportions of a "public scandal."[86] While Neuville urged the example of Christ on the king, Lafitau held up that of Mary Magdalene for his mistress. For in one day this woman whose nickname had been "sinneress" had left a youth of "voluptuousness," "libertinage," and "luxury" for a whole lifetime of penance, not only confessing her sins but going "so far as to break all contact with those who might be able to ruin [her] with their bad habits and morals, so far as to remove herself from all occasions in which modesty might find itself endangered."[87] Nor was any lesser penance required for pascal communion, because for anyone to take communion who had not, say, "broken that criminal liaison" was "to betray the God-Man with a Judas-like kiss . . . and to nail [Christ] to one's heart as the executioners nailed him to the cross."[88]

Not to be outdone, Griffet also insisted that the "qualities of a veritable penitence . . . consisted in a complete renouncement of sin along with all that had . . . led to it, in a sincere and persevering resolution to love God with . . . a love superior to all inclinations of flesh and blood," and to hold sin in "such perfect detestation and sovereign hatred . . . that one would prefer to die than to commit it."[89] As the king's "ordinary" preacher, Griffet had the greatest opportunity to impress these rigorous confessional standards on the king directly, and if he did not entirely succeed, it was not for want of trying. In a sermon "On Saintliness," for example, delivered in the king's presence after the War of the Austrian Succession but before the disasters of the Seven Years' War, Griffet congratulated Louis XV for having "beaten in person the puissant and bellicose [English] Insularies" in the battles of Fontenoy and Laufeldt, and even more for having "preferred a title that expressed his [subjects'] love for you to one that would recall the terror of your power and the disgrace of your enemies." Yet both were "vain and fleeting" glories, in Griffet's opinion, in comparison "to the felicity of the saints that the gospel proposes to Your Majesty as the recompense to which kings themselves are obliged to aspire." All Christians are called to sainthood, Griffet held, but none more peremptorily than kings because, while "sainthood was respectable enough in the least of men, it is always heroic on the part of Sovereigns."[90]

As it happened, of course, Griffet and his colleagues were only partly persuasive. For while they may have convinced Louis XV not to "profane" the

---

86. Neuville, "Sermon pour la fête de pasques," *Sermons,* 2:61–64, 67, 79, 81. For equally pointed and rigorous advice see also "Sermon pour l'amour de Dieu," ibid., 1:171; and "Sermon sur la rechüte," ibid., 1:311–12.

87. Lafitau, "Sermon pour le vendredi de la semaine du carême, sur la pénitence de Madeleine," *Sermons,* 3:294–95; 307–8.

88. "Sermon pour le dimanche des rameaux, sur la communion paschale," ibid., 3:368, 372.

89. Griffet, "Sermon pour le quatrième dimanche de l'Avent, sur la confession," *Sermons,* 1:146; and "Sermon pour le jour de la Fête-Dieu, sur la communion," ibid., 3:135.

90. "Sermon pour le jour de la Toussaint, sur la sainteté," ibid., 1:21–22.

Eucharist, they most surely did not persuade him to become a second Saint Louis. For the death-scare confession and absolution on the occasion of Damiens's assault on him in 1757 resulted in an even more scandalous relapse in the years that followed. The king's half-conversion had devastating consequences, the devout contribution to the desacralization of the monarchy. On the one hand, moral indignation over the king's sexual misconduct became a leitmotif in the parti dévot's oppositional stance from midcentury on, centering on the outraged virtue of the queen Marie Leszczynska and her daughters, all of whom were devotees of the Sacred Heart of Jesus and of Jesuitical piety generally. To the degree that the parti dévot's moral indignation was a factor in the personal vilification of the king—and it was, as we shall soon see—its moral opposition recalled the "political Donatism" of the sixteenth-century Catholic Holy Union and the nature of its political and religious opposition to the Henri III and Henri of Navarre. On the other hand, that same moralism prevented Louis XV from touching for scrofula during the last thirty-five years of his reign. This long dearth of the royal miracle, comparable in length to Louis XIV's boycott of the lit de justice assembly during the last forty years of his reign, perhaps contributed as much to the desacralization of the French monarchy as anything that the parti janséniste had done.

The Popular Desacralization of the Clergy

If the refusal-of-sacraments controversy and its sequels in the 1760s tended to desacralize the monarchy at the level of judicial and penitential discourse, that tendency was even more pronounced in popular opinion. For Louis XV, this desacralizing effect was both direct and indirect, as the king sustained no little damage by ricochet from the clergy. So associated was the monarchy with the clergy, especially the episcopacy, that the desacralization of the monarchy is hardly thinkable without that of the clergy. It was they, as in the 1720s and 1730s, who occupied the front lines of the confrontation over refusal of sacraments and who, in public opinion, bore the heat of the desacralizing day. As in the 1720s and 1730s as well, this damage affected the episcopacy in the first instance, but more than at that time, the refusal-of-sacraments controversy distributed that damage to the clergy as a whole. "The people are up in arms against priests," reported d'Argenson in 1755, "and those who appear in the streets in clerical garb have reason to fear for their lives."[91] In the 1750s and 1760s as in the crisis of 1730–32, the damage to the clergy took the form of anticlericalism. But in the 1750s more than in the earlier period, that anticlericalism began to shade off into popular irreligion, into forms of hostility to Catholicism if not to Christianity as such. Warning the Archbishop of Rouen against the effects of the worsening "schism,"

91. D'Argenson, *Journal et mémoires* (20 Mar. 1755), p. 453.

the senior Joly de Fleury, who had been procureur général during the crisis-filled years from 1727 to 1733, gave voice to the new "evils that are to be feared, above all seeing that the bulk of the people who still have some Religion have turned against their bishops apropos of the refusal of sacraments and the certificates of confession, that unbelievers are being confirmed in their unbelief, and that the present divisions are swelling the numbers of their followers."[92] The role of Jansenist-related conflicts in the rise of popular unbelief is sufficiently adjacent to that of Jansenism itself to merit parenthetical comment because French historians have often pointed to Jansenist rigor as a prime agent in eighteenth-century "dechristianization." Jansenism's penitential rigor, as well as strictures against pre-Christian "superstitions," alienated parishioners from the sacraments—or so the argument goes—while its excessively exalted view of the priesthood discouraged ordinations, thus making whole areas dependent on priests from the outside.[93] But this argument is difficult to evaluate for several reasons. Where, as in Paris, appellant priests encountered a receptive laity, Jansenism undoubtedly distanced that laity from some of the external forms of "baroque" Catholic piety in ways that we have seen recorded by police agents in the late 1720s and 1730s. Although it may be evidence of the interiorization of piety, that religious sensibility is no more tantamount to dechristianization than is the comparable Protestant one. The Parisian police, moreover, knew very well how to distinguish it from forms of unbelief precociously apparent here and there at the same time. Because the indices used by Michel Vovelle to chart dechristianization in his celebrated study of wills in eighteenth-century Provence are of the same sort—bequests for requiem masses, sacred as opposed to secular burial, etc.—the evidence is similarly suspect in those areas where Jansenism was strong.[94] The evidence for dechristianization is admittedly stronger for rural areas, where rigorous appellant priests imposed penitential abstention from communion on a reluctant peasantry, as perhaps in Jean Soanen's Senez. Yet even such places produced lay villagers who, while embracing the Revolution, knew how to defend their Catholicism against revolutionary dechristianization, as in the dioceses of Auxerre and Sens, recently studied by Suzanne Desan.[95] In no place, however—

92. BN: CJF, Ms. 1493, fols. 144–45, Joly de Fleury to Rouillé, 28 Oct. 1752.

93. For example, Alphonse Dupront, *Du sacré: Croisades et pèlerinages, images et language* (Paris, 1987), pp. 422–24; Dominique Dinet, "Le jansénisme et les origines de la déchristianisation au XVIIIe siècle: L'example des pays de l'Yonne," in *Du jansénisme à la laïcité: Le jansénisme et les origines de la déchristianisation*, ed. Léo Hamon (Auxerre, 1987): pp. 1–33; and Roger Chartier, *The Cultural Origins of the French Revolution*, pp. 104–5.

94. Michel Vovelle, *Piété baroque et déchristianisation en Provence au dix-huitième siècle: Les attitudes devant la mort d'après les clauses des testaments* (Paris, 1973), esp. pp. 593–613.

95. Suzanne Desan, *Reclaiming the Sacred: Lay Religion and Popular Politics in Revolutionary France* (Ithaca, N.Y., 1990). See also Jean-Pierre Rocher, "L'évolution politique et religieuse du département de l'Yonne pendant la Révolution," in *Du jansénisme à la laïcité*, pp. 89–109.

and this is the main point to be made here—were Jansenist priests allowed to ply their pastorates uncontested, and as a result the putative effects of their penitential rigor are virtually indistinguishable from those of the Jansenist controversy, which like all controversies produced effects unintended by either side. The crucial decades in Vovelle's quantitative timetable for dechristianization, the late 1720s and early 1730s and those after 1750, correspond to high points of the Jansenist controversy, not to Jansenism as such. And such qualitative evidence as is available suggests that where genuine unbelief is concerned, it was the controversy that was most decisive.

Spectacular evidence to that effect is at hand in the interrogations and carefully recorded remarks of the king's regicidal assailant, Robert-François Damiens. The evidence is indeed suspiciously spectacular—perhaps too good to be true—because, as a domestic servant in close contact with both parlementary and clerical masters, he had also been uncommonly close to the conflicts of his day and, even among domestic servants, had gained a well-deserved reputation for eccentricity. It was not every day, after all, that someone tried physically to "touch" the king. Yet it is not every day, either, that such a wealth of evidence comes to light on the religious and political attitudes of a barely literate representative of the eighteenth-century "people"; if it is in some sense too good to be true, it is also too good to ignore. However eccentric he may have been, moreover, the world from which he suddenly burst in 1757 is not an unfamiliar one. Although his family was by no means Jansenist, his older brother, a wool carder in Saint-Omer in Artois, had fallen in with his curé's opposition to *Unigenitus* and had lined his humble hovel with bound theological and catechetical books.[96] And like another brother and so many others, Damiens had tried to make his living in domestic service in Paris, where, with a wife and daughter, he had lived surrounded by interdicted Jansenist priests and laundress devotees of the Deacon Pâris in the cloister of Saint-Etienne-des-Grès in the parish of Saint-Etienne-du-Mont.[97] If Damiens had been established there as early as 1730, his disaffection might have taken a more pious turn than it did.

But 1752 was not 1732, as Joly de Fleury noted, and things had in the meanwhile gone from bad to worse. So while Damiens indeed detested the Jesuits and constitutionary bishops, especially the Archbishop of Paris, saying that "the Jesuits and Monsieur the Archbishop were the cause of the downfall of the realm, and that if he were the master, he would expel the Jesuits within twenty-four

96. BN: CJF, Ms. 2068, fols. 104–5, interrogation of Antoine-Joseph Damiens by Vanden Driesche at Saint-Omer, 13 Jan. 1757; and fol. 92, interrogation by Pierre Chenon, 13 Jan. See also fol. 78, procès-verbal by Pierre Chenon, 11–13 Jan., a list of A.-J. Damiens's possessions; and BN: CJF, Ms. 2069, fols. 280–81, a list of his books.

97. BA: AB, Ms. 10202, file on year 1754, report of a police observer on popular frequentation of parish church of Saint-Médard, 5 May 1754.

hours," he also sometimes directed his animus against all priests, frequently speaking "badly of priests" generally, according to his wife, and complaining in his trial about "the trouble he remarked in the priests."[98] Although at times he tried to distinguish the "best priests" from bad ones, those in particular who had been refused the sacraments despite "praying to God every day in the Church from morning until night," he spoke badly even of his brother's Jansenist curé while visiting in Saint-Omer, calling him a "fucking (ffoutu]) curé" and "another one of your dévots."[99] And where Jansenists were typically reluctant to take communion lest they take it unworthily, Damiens, according to his own testimony, had stopped participating in the sacraments altogether around "three or four years ago [1752–1753], since the broils involving the Archbishop."[100] Another domestic servant who had worked with Damiens in the early 1750s remembered that on one occasion, when she had noted a crucifix in the Sainte-Geneviève passage near the church of Saint-Etienne-du-Mont, "he responded as an atheist who does not believe anything."[101]

Does Damiens's abandonment of confession and communion in reaction to the refusal-of-sacraments controversy help explain the gradual abandonment of this and other gestures of Catholicism both in Paris and elsewhere in France from 1750s on?[102] The absence of Parisian parish records—victims of the anticlerical riots of 1832—makes it more difficult to answer this question, although the marquis d'Argenson would have had no doubt. He noted that in his own parish of Sainte-Eustache the consumption of Easter communion hosts had declined by half in 1753, continuing a trend of the previous couple of years, and that comparable declines had been reported by priests in the parishes of Saint-Côme and Saint-Sulpice, and he attributed this "loss of religion in France" not to "English philosophy," which had "made converts of only a hundred or so philosophes," but rather to the "hatred felt toward priests which runs to excess these days. These ministers of religion hardly dare show themselves in the streets for being hooted down," he continued, "and all of that comes from the bull Unigenitus, along with the exile of the Parlement."[103] But if even in the best of all archival worlds it would not be possible to test the close relationship d'Argenson saw between the rise of "unbe-

---

98. On Jesuits and the archbishop, BN: CJF, Ms. 2070, fol. 158, "Extrait de ce que le Prisonnier a dit et qui a paru meriter attention, aux douze sergents de regiment des gardes françoises chargés de le garder à vüe"; on priests, Pièces originales et procédures du procès fait à Robert-François Damiens, tant en la prévôté de l'Hôtel qu'en la cour de parlement, hereafter PO (Paris, 1757), interrogation of 17 Mar. 1757, no. 29, p. 331.

99. PO, interrogation of 28 Mar. p. 402; BN: CJF, Ms. 2068, fol. 91, interrogation of Antoine-Joseph Damiens by Commissioner Chenon at Saint-Omer, 13 Jan. 1757.

100. PO, interrogation of 26 Mar., no. 159, p. 380; and of 28 Mar., p. 402.

101. BN, JF 2070, fols. 183–84, deposition by Marguerite Lafaye.

102. Pierre Chaunu, La mort à Paris, XVIe, XVIIe, XVIIIe siècles (Paris, 1978), pp. 432–65; and Michel Vovelle, Piété baroque et déchristianisation en Provence, pp. 594–614.

103. D'Argenson, Journal et mémoires (6 and 18 May 1753), 8:12, 35.

lief" and the refusal-of-sacraments controversy, it is quite possible to corroborate the growing "hatred of priests" he noted in connection with that controversy. And in this respect the case of Damiens was far from unique.

A worthy successor of Vintimille in this respect as in others, Christophe de Beaumont continued to bear much of the brunt of this popular hostility, as is evident in comments overheard by a police observer on the occasion of the funeral and burial of the abbé Ignace Le Mere. Le Mere had died denied the last sacraments, and the officer heard mourners say that the Parlement had been too lenient in its treatment of Bouëttin, the curé who had denied Le Mere, and that it should also have tried the Archbishop of Paris, whose orders the curé had only obeyed. "In acting this way," many reportedly said, "more than five hundred thousand citizens would have accompanied the Parlement to Versailles and supported its representations to the king, who was ignorant of the vexations which his most faithful subjects are made to suffer." Less than a month later the archbishop had reason to complain that, leaving the cathedral of Notre Dame with his chapter at the head of a canonization procession, he encountered a group of book peddlers affectedly distributing the Parlement of Paris's arrêt of 18 April 1752 against *Unigenitus* to the accompaniment of "immoderate discourses," seconded by those of a crowd of "common women" who were also "expressing themselves in the most imprudent terms."[104] The Jesuits, too, continued to be prime objects of hatred. In May 1752 a wall placard showed up near their residence in the rue Saint-Antoine warning them that if they persisted in "setting fires everywhere you will not be spared, neither your houses nor yourselves, by a fire which will consume you entirely and universally."[105] At the time of Damiens's trial Le Paige recorded that the Jesuits were so suspected for their complicity that there was something like an "uprising against them in Paris," with insults in the streets and a threat of arson against their residence, and the evidence bears him out.[106] Writing from the Bastille on 11 January 1757, the Jesuit confessor-in-residence told a friend that he preferred to remain inside not only because of the cold but "for fear of being called a Ravaillac in the streets, or perhaps even being treated as such by some unruly populace."[107] At about the same time several anonymous billets appeared, one in Thomas Herissant's bookstore and another in the Palais de justice, calling for the burning of the Jesuit residence in Paris.[108] The threat was real enough for orders

104. AN: AB XIX, Ms. 3192, dossier 7, file 3, reports of an "observateur de police," 29 Mar. and 27 Apr. 1752.

105. BN: CJF, Ms. 1566, fols. 85–86.

106. BPR: CLP, Ms. 549, note by Le Paige to himself, unnumbered.

107. François Ravaisson, *Archives de la Bastille*, 18 vols. (Paris, 1886–1904), 16:436, "Le P. Jésuite à l'abbé Xxx," 11 Jan. 1757.

108. AN: Y, Ms. 11475 (Commissioner Doublon), Jan. 1757; and BN: CJF, Ms. 2070, fol. 123, labeled by the procureur général as a "billet contre les Jésuites trouvé dans le Palais et qui m'a été remis."

to have been issued on 14 January "to redouble the vigilance and attention apropos of the houses of the Jesuits, against which a certain public appears enraged," and for Le Paige to have thought that such a fire had actually been set.[109] And of course the popular joy that accompanied the Jesuits' own trial a few years later is well known.

As in Damiens's case, however, this popular hostility began to border on hatred for the priesthood generally, reflecting in part the episcopal purge of appellant priests and their replacement by the likes of Bouëttin. The same police observer listening in on Le Mere's funeral, which had attracted a crowd of "six or seven hundred persons of all sorts and estates," noted that the "populace" cried that Bouëttin "would do well to hide himself, that if he were to show himself they would do well to stone him like a wretch," and that, if it came to a trial, "each would gladly serve as his hangman." The only reason Le Mere had been refused the sacraments in death, they thought, was that "he had lived well and so had condemned by his conduct many wretched ecclesiastics who live loose lives."[110] Sometimes this hostility went beyond words, as it did in the case of the chevalier de Valibouze, a retired Irish army officer who had given his last years to service to the poor, yet found himself denied extreme unction by two priests in the parish of Saint-Etienne-du-Mont on the night of 2–3 February 1755. When it became clear that the two priests were not going to minister to Valibouze, a "great quantity of people" who had gathered at the scene, according to the *Nouvelles ecclésiastiques*, began to "yell loudly at the two priests, who could not escape, and it took a great deal of prudence to calm this tumult." When a third priest named Dubois from the parish of Saint-Eustache happened by and took it upon himself to say that it was necessary to "obey the bishops" and that he for his part would never minister to someone without a certificate of confession, "these words fired up the people to an inexpressible degree, and it took a redoubled prudence to prevent an uprising"; the two priests barely escaped with their lives.[111] The parish of Saint-Nicolas-des-Champs witnessed a similar scene on 18 May 1758, when, in the absence of the already exiled curé, the vicaire Bonnet refused the viaticum to an aged woman named Vaillant. "That adventure caused a lot of emotion in the quarter and wound up amassing quite a crowd," reported the police inspector Poussot to the lieutenant of police Berryer.[112]

The latter reads: "Tant que nous aurons les Jésuites en France le parlement et le peuple seront malheureux puisque le roy ne veut pas s'en defaire il faut les brulé [sic] dans leur maison."

109. BA: AB, Ms. 10181, note by Duval, 14 Jan. 1757, at Versailles.

110. AN: AB XIX, Ms. 3192, dossier 6, file 3, 29 Mar. 1752. The estimate of six or seven hundred people at the burial comes from the procureur général's substitute Boullenois, who was himself a Jansenist. See BN: CJF, Ms. 1487, fol. 81, Boullenois to Guillaume-François Joly de Fleury, 30 Mar. 1752.

111. *NE* 24 Apr. 1755, p. 68; coroborated by *Extrait des registres de parlement. Du 14 mai 1755* (Paris, 1755), in BN: CJF, Ms. 1567, fols. 143–44, which sentenced Dubois to perpetual galley labor for "tending to incite a popular emotion."

112. BN: CJF, Ms. 1569, fols. 389, 396–97, Poussot to lieutenant general and procureur général, 22 May 1758.

A small rash of physical attacks against priests left their marks on police blotters around 1757 very much like the ones d'Argenson and others describe, and it is difficult not to interpret it as directed against priests as priests. In January 1757 the police were searching for two workers who stabbed a Carmelite prior while walking on the rue des Prouvaires in the early evening.[113] On 8 February 1757 the Paris watchmen *(guet)* came to the aid of a priest named La Grive, porte-Dieu of the parish church of Saint-Marguerite in the faubourg Saint-Antoine, who had them arrest a journeyman carpenter named Jacques Reynard for having "insulted" him on his way back from taking the sacraments to a sick parishioner. On 25 March 1757 the police commissioner Rolland had the Paris Watch conduct a "woman without refuge" named Dorothée de La Chaise to the Châtelet prison for having insulted the curé of Saint-Benoît in the church. But the most pointed of these incidents involved a porte-Dieu named Mathieu Flint from the same parish, who found himself beaten and stabbed by two men, one of whom had lured him from the church with the request to administer extreme unction to a dying woman in a street nearby. Only his loud cries saved his life, he reported, forcing them to take flight and preventing them from "consummating their crime."[114] "The irritation of moods is acute," noted Le Paige, writing about the same time. He recorded an incident involving an abbé who, returning from supper, met a soldier who beat him with a cane and drew his sword after greeting him with the words, "there's one of those ecclesiastics who kill our kings." This abbé saved himself only by knocking violently on the first available door.[115]

All of these incidents, it is true, involved proparlementary crowds or individuals in opposition to Jesuits, Christophe de Beaumont, and the constitutionary curés and priests that he and Vintimille had installed. But to recount only such episodes would be to leave a misleading picture of politicization in Paris, to say nothing of the provinces where opinion sometimes took the side of the constitutionary curés against the "heretical" Jansenists. And although most Parisians seem to have sided with the Parlement against the constitutionary clergy, that overall majority sometimes bowed to local majorities or at least vociferous minorities on the other side, depending on parish and circumstances. What the Parlement had effected during the 1750s and 1760s, after all, fell little short of a counterpurge of the Parisian priesthood. That painful process was bound to have alienated some segments of opinion, not only because some of the exiled curés had enjoyed the affection of their parishioners but because replacements were hard to come by and in some cases less than ideal.

113. BN: CJF, Ms. 2070, fols. 118–20, Moreau to procureur général, 12 Jan. 1757.

114. For the curé of Saint-Benoît's case, see AN: AP, 177mi, Ms. 118, no. 79, 25 Mar. 1757; for La Grive's case, no. 37, 8 Feb. 1757; for Flint's ordeal, Ms. 108, no. 10, Moreau to Chancellor Lamoignon, 9 Mar. 1758.

115. BPR: CLP, Ms. 549, note by Le Paige, unnumbered.

A single example must suffice, one that took place in the parish of Saint-Nicolas-des-Champs, deep on the populous right bank but well away from the popularly Jansenist quarters. There, as we have noted, the Parlement of Paris had cleaned out the entire beneficed clergy by 1759—a total of six priests, headed by the parish curé Jacques de L'Ecluse—leaving divine services in the hands of the merely resident clergy that the Parlement requisitioned for the purpose. As it happened, however, l'Ecluse had been both very wealthy and very generous with his wealth, and although the parish churchwardens tried hard to take up the slack, they simply could not match their former curé's Molinistic largesse. The result was that, according to Inspector Poussot, the curé was "very much missed," and "some quite honest people" thought that, in refusing the last sacraments to the appellant Willemsens, he had fallen victim to a deliberately set trap.[116] It probably did not help matters, though, that the Parlement of Paris, in alliance with the Jansenist lay churchwardens, was resolved to be as chary with its charity as God was with efficacious grace, favoring the "honest poor" to the exclusion of "those given to wine or to debauchery; the full-time lazy, the foul-mouthed, and all those of bad life and morals; as well as all those who neglect to send their children to school, to catechism, and other kinds of instruction." The references to catechism and school were not idle threats, either: whereas under the former curé's direction the parish charity schools had allowed (in Boullenois's starchy terms) "the little people to send their children . . . not to instruct them but to get rid of them," the sober churchwardens undertook to reform these schools root and branch, imposing on them 562 volumes of mainly Jansenist catechetical and devotional works, headed by the French New Testament, Bishop Colbert's *Catéchisme de Montpellier*, and Pasquier Quesnel's *Jésus-Christ pénitent*. Soon, Boullenois reported, the parish "little people" were "whining a lot and saying that if they still had their curé, none of this would have happened to them."[117]

The full implications of the priestly purge for the parish charity schools did not unfold until the mid-1760s, but the general direction of events was clear enough right away to make sense of an "insult" sustained in 1758 by the abbé de Willemsens, the one parish priest who had obeyed the Parlement's orders to administer the last sacraments to his dying uncle. As chaplain of the parish's lay-controlled Confraternity of the Holy Sacrament, Willemsens was entitled to beg for alms in the parish church, and as he was doing so just a month or so after coming to his uncle's aid, three women, led by a certain Elisabeth Chauvin, a launderess living on the rue du Temple, accosted Willemsens. Chauvin put her

116. BN: CJF, Ms. 1569, fols. 346–47, Poussot to procureur général, 8 May 1758.

117. BN: CJF, Ms. 1570, fols. 68–69; 92–93, Brière, acting curé of the parish to procureur général; 98, note by Boullenois, one of the "substitutes" of the procureur général, 10 Oct. 1765; fols. 86–91, *Arrêt de la cour de parlement, servant de règlement pour les pauvres de la paroisse de Saint-Nicolas-des-Champs à Paris;* fols. 83–84, list of books and their prices for the charity schools compiled by the churchwardens in 1765.

hands over her eyes while shouting "Shame! Shame! Shame! *(Hou! Hou! Hou!)*
How dare you present yourself here?" When reproached by Willemsens for
"insulting a minister of the Lord," Chauvin shot back, "*You,* a minister of the
Lord?" Willemsens may have had the last word, enjoining Chauvin at least "to
respect the Holy Sacrament" present in church even if she did not respect him, but
he then had to confront numbers of the poor who maintained that the offerings he
had collected belonged by rights to them.[118] Willemsens lodged a formal complaint against Chauvin and two other women, resulting in a trial in the Châtelet
and a sentence of public reprimand *(blâme)* and a three-livre fine.[119] Chauvin's
hostility, it is true, was hardly disinterested; she had been a recipient of L'Ecluse's
largesse and was related to the abbé Dubertrand, one of the vicaires exiled by the
Parlement for his role in the Willemsens affair. But that she nonetheless spoke for
many more people than herself is evident from an anonymous letter sent to a
barrister involved in the case, demanding the return "of our curé and his clergy"
and threatening that "there are enough of us to make plenty of trouble *(pour nous
soulever)* without getting tired until you cease to afflict us." And the Châtelet's
royal procureur Moreau was concerned enough about "tempers being near the
boiling point" in the Saint-Martin neighborhood to take extraordinary precautions against demonstrations of popular wrath on 29 March 1759, the day that
Chauvin's sentence was to be placarded on the walls and carrefours of the
quarter.[120]

    None of this should be taken to mean, however, that these refusals of
sacraments themselves had not also provoked lasting hostility against the clergy,
even in the parish of Saint-Nicolas-des Champs. Not only had the refusal of
extreme unction to the woman Vaillant caused "much emotion in the quarter,"
according to Poussot, but even those who thought L'Ecluse had been a "good
pastor, and assiduous," allowed that he had been "wrong" to do what he did, "for
those sorts of quarrels in the church can only result in harm."[121] One kind of harm
was that it was not until nearly a decade later that the parish of Saint-Nicolas-des-
Champs got a new curé, provided for by the parish's patron, the prior of the
monastery of Saint-Martin-des-Champs in cooperation with the Parlement of

---

118. *NE* 31 July 1759, p. 127.

119. BN: CJF, Ms. 1569, fols. 353–58; and *Sentence rendue en la chambre criminelle du Châtelet de
Paris, qui condamne Elizabeth Chauvin, fille ouvrière en linge, au blâme, pour avoir insulté un prêtre quetant dans
l'église. Extrait des registres du greffe criminel du Châtelet de Paris. Du 23 mars 1759* (Paris, 1759), in AN: AD,
Ms. 11, fol. 92.

120. BN: CJF, Ms. 1569, fols. 359–60, Poussot to procureur général, 6 June 1758; fol. 380, anonymous letter to one Desomme, an avocat, undated; and fol. 419, Moreau to same, 28 Mar. 1759. The full
letter reads: "C'est pour vous avertir que l'on ait a nous rendre notre Curé et son clergé il y a 8 mois qu'ils
sont en captivité nous voulons les ravoir et nous sommes assez pour nous soulever sans nous lasser jusqu'à
ce que l'on cesse de nous affliger."

121. BN: CJF, Ms. 1569, fol. 325, Poussot to procureur général, 24 Apr. 1758.

Paris, and reluctantly agreed to by the archbishop, who tried unsuccessfully to make the appointment provisional. That the new curé, Jean-Etienne Parent, came from a parlementary family and consulted with the Parlement at every turn did not spare him some unpleasant encounters with parishioners still smarting from the refusal-of-sacraments controversy. Writing in frustration to the procureur général in 1769, Parent reported an incident with a certain Sieur Babaud du Mail, a clerk in the Parlement of Paris, who had asked one of the parish priests to bring the sacraments to his grandmother. Asked by the priest and Parent in turn to say whether his grandmother had confessed to a parish priest, or for that matter to anyone at all, a belligerent Babaud persistently responded that "he had nothing to respond." When Parent went to visit the grandmother in question after mass, he found a woman in perfectly good health who had indeed confessed to a priest and who was minded to "receive the good Lord" not then but the next morning. Asked why her grandson could not at least have said as much, she said she did not know. "The conduct that I have followed since being at the head of this parish ought to be a sure guarantee of my intentions . . . to keep the peace," wrote the distraught Parent to the procureur général 31 May 1769. "But for goodness's sake, Monseigneur, please honor me with your protection when such malintentioned people as Babaud come to demand the sacraments while holding forth in a manner so contrary to the principles accepted in the Church and State."[122]

And so it was with Parent and his colleagues: damned if they did and damned if they did not. If ever there were an episode that put priests in this terrestrial hell, it was the refusal-of-sacraments controversy where it raged most fiercely: Aix, Auxerre, Orléans, Troyes, but above all Paris. If they obeyed their bishops and refused the sacraments, they had to flee, prosecuted by the parlements as criminal "disturbers of the public peace." If they obeyed the parlements and administered the sacraments, they were able to stay at the expense of functioning as priests, interdicted as they would be by their bishops. The priests faced a similar dilemma vis-à-vis their parishioners, purveyors of their most pertinent "public opinion(s)." If they obeyed their bishops, they were agents of episcopal and ministerial "despotism," ministers of authority rather than of charity and Jesus Christ. If on the contrary they obeyed the parlements, they became agents of the judicial state and risked losing their sacral status in the eyes of such parishioners as Elisabeth Chauvin. Although these different opinions involved different constituencies, they tended to blur into each other over time and, as in the case of Damiens, produce more than the sum total of their anticlerical parts. "I hold all your feast days and ceremonies in abomination," began a placard found on the door of the church of Saint-Eustache on 15 May 1760. And although the next lines made it clear that the inspiration was ultimately Jansenist—"because you have renounced the truth to adore the constitution *Unigenitus,*" and so on—the sacrilegious exordium outdistanced any and all of its anticlerical reasons.[123]

The monarchical and episcopal purge of the Jansenist priesthood, followed by the refusal-of-sacraments controversy and the parlementary counterpurge—these developments go a long way toward explaining why, despite some crucial mutual cooperation between priests and the early French Revolution, French priests could play nothing like the role in that upheaval as they had played in the municipal "revolutions" of the late sixteenth century, or even in the Fronde. Even during the summer of 1789, when memories of the curés' crucial contributions to the revolutionary cause were still fresh, the cry *a bas la calotte*—down with the skullcap emblematic of the priesthood—could be heard in many of the formerly Jansenist Parisian parishes, and Etienne Parent in particular sustained an anticlerical siege of his residence in Saint-Nicolas-des-Champs. That popular anticlericalism in turn goes a long way in explaining why the French Revolution eventually turned as anti-Christian as it did.

The Popular Desacralization of the Monarchy

The fallout from the *Unigenitus*-related confrontations of the mid-eighteenth century affected the French monarchy more directly in popular opinion than had those of the 1720s and 1730s, in part because as of 1743 Louis XV acted as his own first minister, making it more difficult to distinguish between the king's good intentions and the evil advice of his ministers. At times, it must have seemed to close observers that the most generous construction that could be placed on the king's policy was that he simply knew not what he did. In a letter to family members in Saint-Omer, for example, Damiens's younger brother Louis, also a domestic servant in Paris, gave a perfectly lucid and accurate account of the whole sacramental controversy from the case of Le Mere to the time of his writing, noting that "the king, solicited by the archbishop and his confessor, took the side of the Ecclesiastics in such wise that in the measure that the Parlement took up these sorts of cases, the king quashed and annulled them *without examining whether that was in his interest or not.*"[124]

At a deeper level, however, no monarchy so sacramentally conceived could hope to emerge whole and entire from the crossfire of a controversy that politi-

---

123. BN: CJF, Ms. 1567, fols. 210–11. The full text reads, "J'ai toutes vos festes / et vos cérémonies / en abomination / parce que vous avez / renoncé à la vérité / pour adorer la constitution / *Unigenitus* / Impies que vous autorisés / en prechant et pratiquant / les Impiétés de foi."

124. BN: CJF, Ms. 2069, fols. 264–65, Louis Damiens to Antoine-Joseph Damiens at Saint-Omer, Paris, 7 Apr. 1753. Emphasis mine.

cized and in some sense desacralized the sacraments themselves. The resultant *religious* damage sustained by Louis XV and the Bourbon monarchy recalls that effected by the religious civil wars of the sixteenth century at the expense of Henri III and the Valois dynasty. In the eighteenth century as on that occasion, this damage is less dramatically apparent in sermons, books, and pamphlets than in wall placards, songs, and furtive seditious utterances *(mauvais propos* or *mauvais discours)* tracked down by the police or recorded by literate memoirists. These mauvais propos came most spectacularly to the surface in the wake of Robert-François Damiens's apparent attempt to assassinate Louis XV in 1757.

It is of course true that the affair churned them up, as it were, and that they did not exactly rise spontaneously to the surface. Because the police and the prosecutors were on the lookout for mauvais discours, they not unnaturally found them, in some sense even made them happen: some citizens took to denouncing others as guilty of mauvais propos as a way of settling scores with hostile neighbors. Even if all such charges could be taken at face value, the dossiers compiled by the procureur général and the police were unlike anything anybody had put together either earlier or later in the century, making it difficult to draw comparative conclusions. So what conclusions can be drawn about the image of the monarch and the monarchy in the mid-eighteenth century on the basis of information so suspect in its origin and unique in its genre?[125]

It is also true that mauvais discours against the king and the monarchy were anything but new in 1757. The transformation of Louis XV from the "pacific" king of the early 1720s or the "beloved" king during his brush with death at Metz in 1744 into the debauched "despot" of the 1770s was a long time in the making and certainly did not wait for the set-to over refusal of sacraments to get under way. To the king's perceived "laziness" and "taciturnity" in the late 1720s and the gratuitous "cruelty" and "barbarity" of the 1730s, the 1740s added the "debauchery" of his adulterous relations with Jeanne Poisson, Madame de Pompadour, hard on the petticoats of the de Nesle sisters, and the "dishonor" of the Treaty of Aix-la-Chapelle concluding the war with England and Austria in 1748, especially the arrest and exile of the Stuart pretender Charles Edward in consequence of that treaty the same year.[126] "How dare you arrogate to yourself the name of "Be-

125. Arlette Farge's *Dire et mal dire: L'opinion publique au XVIIIe siècle* (Paris, 1992), pp. 240–58, esp. p. 256, has recently raised these questions, which implicitly challenge some hypotheses advanced in my *The Damiens Affair* concerning the importance of the year 1757 in the history of the king's relation with his subjects. Farge's research has certainly revealed that this deterioration began earlier than I suspected it did at the time of writing *The Damiens Affair*—she locates it at the juncture 1728–32—but as to the monarchy's religious policies in general and anti-Jansenist policy in particular there seems to be no compelling reason to revise the judgment that the 1750s were decisive.

126. See above all Thomas Kaiser, "Louis *le Bien-Aimé* and the Rhetoric of the Royal Body," in *Constructing the Body in the Seventeenth and Eighteenth Centuries,* ed. Kathryn Norberg, Sara Melzer, and

loved," asked a scurrilous quatraine in 1749, after detailing some prophetic reasons for revising that epitaph:

> "If we loved you for awhile,
>
> that's before we knew you were vile.
>
> It's the better to abhor you that there are still some French.
>
> And if we see your statue rise,
>
> We will live to see its demise.
>
> By and by a tyrant must die without even a single wench."[127]

And it was during the "children's kidnapping" riot in late April and May 1750 that a police spy heard someone say that the fishwives of Paris would do well to go to Versailles, "grab the king by the hair," and "pluck out the eyes from his head."[128] Nor, any more than in the sixteenth century, did religious and moral accusations ever displace others, such as that the king taxed his subjects too heavily and failed to see to it that they had enough bread.[129]

But if these precedents demonstrate that the mauvais propos was not altogether new to 1757 and the Damiens affair, they also lend a certain credibility to the evidence compiled by the Joly de Fleury brothers on that occasion and thereafter. Nor, for that matter, are Damiens's judges the only ones who collected this information. Much of it was tracked down and sent to the two prosecutors by the same Parisian police who reported on "seditious utterances" earlier in the century, making much of what is to be found in the Joly de Fleury collection a part of a fairly continuous series stretching back to the 1720s. If it is possible to draw some conclusions from the earlier evidence, it seems equally possible to do so for that compiled in 1757. Such as it is, then, that evidence suggests the 1750s marked a considerable aggravation in the sorts of seditions propos directed at Louis XV, which differed from earlier ones in some important respects.

Anne Melbor (Berkeley, Calif., forthcoming); and "Madame de Pompadour and the Theatres of Power," *FHS* 19 (forthcoming), both cited here in manuscript with the permission of the author. See also Farge, *Dire et mal dire*, pp. 40, 102–5, 115–16, 151–67, 225–39; and Bernard and Monique Cottret, "Les chansons du mal-aimé: Raison d'état et rumeur publique (1748–1750)," in *Histoire sociale, sensibilités collectives et mentalités: Mélanges Robert Mandrou* (Paris, 1985): pp. 303–15.

127. Quoted in Bernard and Monique Cottret, "Les chansons du mal-aimé," p. 313. The original, which I have translated *very* freely, reads: "Si tu fus quelque temps l'objet de notre amour / Tes vices n'etaient pas encore dans tout leur jour. / . . . Et c'est pour t'abhorer qu'il reste des Français; / Aujourd'hui on t'élève en vain une statue, / A ta mort je la vois par le peuple abattue. / . . . Un tyran à la mort n'a plus de courtisans."

128. AN: X2b, Ms. 1367, first interrogation of Severd dit Parisien, 9 June 1750; and "addition d'information," 12 June, testimony of Marguerite Benoist, 13 June 1750.

129. On the bread and the origin of the sinister rumor that the king was party to a "famine pact" to profit from artificially high prices, see Steven L. Kaplan's magisterial *Bread, Politics, and Political Economy in the Reign of Louis XV*, 2 vols. (The Hague, 1976).

First, these seditious remarks show that the refusal-of-sacraments controversy had welded the disparate complaints against the king into a whole and given
them religious resonance. This held even—perhaps above all—for the deprivation
of the eucharistic sacraments and the lack of affordable bread, because bread was
literally involved in either case and the king was held ultimately responsible for
access to both. Numbers of witnesses associated the two. Commenting on the
premature death of the "pious" duc d'Orléans in 1752, numbers of Jansenist
ecclesiastics, according to a police observer, maintained "that God had taken the
prince from this world in order to spare him the chagrin of further witnessing the
horrors that the government tolerated, both in the church and among the people
who have no bread, that the prince experienced the greatest grief on being unable
to remedy all these woes, having been forced to retire from the [king's] council
because the advice of the wicked always prevailed over his." For a brief moment
after the recall of the Parlement in September, it seemed as though the king might
finally score in the opinion of his Parisian and pro-Jansenist subjects. "It is our
good king who had the sacraments given to the sick woman," a voice was heard to
say above the applauding crown on the occasion of the forced administration of
the last sacraments to the Lallement woman in September 1754, and the marquis
d'Argenson noted at the same time that "the king is adored by his people by the
side he is more and more taking [in the quarrel] between the clergy and parlement." But that interlude was short-lived, with the result that, writing in the wake
of Damiens's coup, d'Argenson again noted that the people's "tempers are too
frayed by religion and misery."[130] When, after 1757, the Parlement of Paris again
successfully implemented its sacramental policy, it was the Parlement and not the
king who got the credit.

In his responses to his judges' questions, Damiens himself typically linked
the mundane and religious, bread and the sacraments. Asked initially by his judges
why he had wounded the king, he responded that he wished to call the king's
attention to the misery of the people, to the fact that "three-fourths of the people
are perishing." Yet he subsumed this consideration under a "principle of religion,"
by which he perhaps simply meant a basic sense of justice or equity that would
have prevented the misery of the people. But "religion" also meant, he explained
to his judges, that "one ought not to refuse the sacraments to people who live holy
lives and who pray to God in church every day from morning till night"—a clear
reference to the refusal-of-sacraments controversy from the Jansenist perspective.[131] Damiens moreover held the king responsible for both forms of popular
deprivation. And because the king was obviously involved in the policy that

130. *NE* 16 Jan. 1755, pp. 9–12; and d'Argenson (26 Sept. 1754) 8:348; and 5 Dec. 1754, 8:379.
131. *PO*, 1st interrogation at Versailles, nos. 11–12, p. 46; 6th interrogation at Versailles, no. 158,
p. 103; interrogation of 18 Jan. 1757, nos. 135–36, p. 131; of 29 Jan. nos. 320–21; and of 26 Mar., p. 402.

deprived his lay subjects of the last sacraments, the linkage effected at this time between sacraments and bread prepared the way for a conspiratorial view of the king's involvement in the "famine pact" in the 1760s.

The seditious discourse of the 1750s also fortified the religious link between the refusal of sacraments on the one side and the king's adulterous liaisons on the other. However much some people may have loathed the king's flings with the three de Nesle sisters and Jeanne Poisson before the 1750s, especially when pursued while on military campaign, the affairs had not been the object of very articulate or concentrated *religious* indignation, in part because Jansenist opinion had its hands more than full with royal religious policy, while devout opinion was reluctant to preach too loudly so long as royal policy remained more or less in its favor. Even so, when in 1745 the police tracked down the author and printer of a novel entitled *Tanastès*, a moralistic allegory of the king's recent adventures with Madame de Châteauroux and Jeanne Poisson, their leads took them perilously near the court nobility and its parti dévot. It was bad enough that the author, one Marie-Madeleine Bonafon, was the princesse de Montauban's chambermaid and governess of her daughter. But it was worse that her collaborator and liaison with the printer was a certain Mazelin, a valet to Madame de La Lande, who in turn served the dauphin and mesdames de France. And while Bonafon paid for her indiscretion with two years in the Bastille followed by more years in a convent, Mazelin seems to have survived the affair unpunished.[132]

After the "dishonorable" peace of Aix-La-Chapelle and the monarchy's attempt to impose the "twentieth" tax *(vingtième)* on the clergy in 1749, the parti dévot's censorship of and complicity in the public criticism of the king's sexual misconduct grew more direct, merging with criticism of royal policy in these new areas. In 1749, for example, the Parisian police's search for the authors and distributors of some verses critical of the king's recent disgrace of the comte de Maurepas—himself implicated in the composition of verses against Pompadour—began in quarters devout enough: the Jesuit college of Louis-le-Grand, where one François Bonis, the tutor of a pensionary there, was arrested. Bonis, who claimed merely to have copied the verses, pointed accusingly at others, who, when arrested, denounced still others, who denounced others in turn. Yet none of these leads took the police outside "devout" precincts, despite Bonis's claim that the verses "had been made by Jansenists."[133] By the time the police finally snared a

---

132. BA: AB, Ms. 11582, esp. nos. 20–21, a summary of the affair; and nos. 115–16, the third and decisive interrogation of Bonafon by the Paris police lieutenant Feydeau de Marville on 9 Oct. 1745. For a good analysis of *Tanastés* see Lisa Jane Graham, "If the King Only Knew: Popular Politics and Absolutism in the Reign of Louis XV" (Ph.D. diss., Johns Hopkins University, 1994), pp. 109–32.

133. BA: AB, Ms. 11690, nos. 46–47, interrogation of François Bonis by Miché de Rochebrune, 4 July 1749.

probable author, namely the abbé Sigorgne of the college du Plessis, a total of at least nine clerics had implicated themselves, along with the ambiance of the various postpurge, *Unigenitus*-oriented colleges of the University of Paris, not to mention the very un-Jansenist Seminary of Saint-Nicolas-du-Chardonnet. The number of scurrilous verses had also multiplied along the way, in the end including several against the twentieth tax and in criticism of Louis's unchivalric arrest of Prince Charles Edward, the "devout" Stuart pretender to the English throne.[134] Hardly thrown off course by Bonis's clumsy attempt to blame Jansenists, the police warily worked around Christophe de Beaumont, noting that "it is principally around his flock that all of this revolves."[135]

That flock grew even less docile after royal policy began to distance itself from the parti dévot in the refusal-of-sacraments controversy and the trial of the Jesuits. By the mid 1750s the police themselves were spying on the Archbishop of Paris, while the braying of his flock, broadly defined, went up several decibels and affected segments of popular opinion in the process. Thereafter the king—and the monarchy—had to contend not only with Jansenist and parlementary "seditious sayings" but with "devout" ones as well; and however different they were in inspiration and direction, they blurred together over time into a common damning religious indictment.

On the one side, a mauvais propos of judicial Jansenist derivation typically subjected the king to the Parlement while excoriating the Jesuits and the episcopacy. "Without the Parlement there is no king," reportedly opined a certain Sieur Le Blanc, according to a witness, because "the Parlement existed before any royalty," adding that the Jesuits should be "burned and hung," without specifying in what order. While on his way from Arras to Paris, one Sieur Letourneaux, an attorney's clerk studying law in Paris, was reported to have loudly praised the prince de Conti "for having contributed to the recall of the Parlement" in September 1754 and to have blamed "the clergy and above all the Jesuits" for causing all "the troubles that agitate the state."[136] Closer to the religious content of the Parlement's set-to with the king was the comment proffered by a master forger named Hérault to his curé in December 1756: the king, he said, "had done well to

134. BA: AB, Ms. 11690, nos. 150–51, a convenient summary of all those arrested and the "satirical verses" they admitted to having copied and transmitted. One of these (no. 89), uniting complaints about the vingtième, the king's sexual liasons, and the arrest of Prince Charles Edward, reads as follows: "Sans crime on peut trahir sa foi / chasser son ami de chez soi / du prochain corrompre la femme / piller, voler n'est plus infâme / jouir à la fois des trois soeurs / n'est plus contre les bons moeurs / de faire ces metamorphoses / nos ayeux n'avoient pas l'esprit / et nous attendons un édit / qui permettra toutes ces choses.

135. BA: AB, Ms. 11690, no. 51, Duval to d'Hémery, 5 July 1749.

136. BN: CJF, Ms. 2070, fols. 50–51.

say that *Unigenitus* was not a rule of faith" in his declaration registered in the lit de justice assembly of 13 December 1756, but so far as the disciplinary edict against the Parlement was concerned, he thought that the "king would have to take back *(dédire)* quite a few things."[137] "No Parlement, no king," similarly maintained one Jean Aveque, adding for his part that "Cromwell was one of the great men of his century who never wanted to assume the title of king but [preferred] that of protector of England, with which he had the power to lay low the head of the king."

Nor was the mauvais propos of this Parisian journeyman hatter the only one to refer to Protestants. The same Le Blanc who thought that the Parlement preceded royalty also reportedly opined that the king behaved badly in "not following the counsels of the prince de Conti," and that for his part Conti "would do well to retire to Languedoc, where there were plenty of [Protestant] malcontents ready to take his side." And while uttering imprecations against the few magistrates—"a band of robbers"—who had not submitted their resignations after the lit de justice assembly on 13 December 1756, the Parisian locksmith Chaumet also wished "that the Protestants would take up arms and join the enemies [of France] in order to dethrone the king."[138] Such mauvais propos, although not without basis in contemporary reality—particularly in Conti's increasingly suspect relations with Paul Rabaut and the Protestants of Languedoc—eerily echoed the sixteenth-century wars of religion, as well as the complicity of the princely house of Condé. Like the Protestant challenge of the sixteenth century, the parlementary and Jansenist seditious sayings of the mid-eighteenth century tended to spare the person of the monarch while subordinating him to an institutional "immortal body" in the form of the Parlement of Paris if not the Estates General.

But it remained for the contemporary "devout" seditious saying, on the other side, to renew the Leaguish attacks on the king's moral—and mortal—person. Evidence that a given seditious saying has "devout" or Jesuitical derivation includes, apart from open espousal of the cause of *Unigenitus,* favorable references to the queen Marie Leszczynska, the king's sisters mesdames de France, the dauphin Louis-Auguste de France, as well as the Jesuits themselves—the center of the courtly parti dévot, in a word—to the detriment of the king and his mistresses, especially Pompadour. Vaguely devout in inspiration, for example, were the drunken imprecations of one Pierre Liebert, a beer and tobacco retailer established

137. AN: Y, Ms. 15816, police commissioner Miché de Rochebrune, interrogation of Sr. Jean-François Le Vacher, a tonsured cleric, on 17 Aug. 1758.

138. AN: Y, Ms. 15813 (Commissioner Miché de Rochebrune), "Déclaration de Jean Persy et de Louis-Christophe Larquois de Courboissy, au sujet des discours séditieux imputés au nommé Le Blanc. Du 1 mars 1757"; and "Déclaration d'André Aubryé dit Aubry, de Philippe Bery, d'Antoine Percheron, de l'abbé Yun et de la femme Fossier au sujet des discours séditieux imputés au nommé Chaumet, des 18, 19, 20, et 23 mars 1757."

on the Isle de la Cité, who opined in October 1757 that the king was a *Jean Foutre* and that, while the queen was blameless, "the rest were all *B[ougres]* (buggers), good to be hanged."[139] Just as virulent and more visibly devout were the utterances of a destitute vinedresser named Pierre Thomas, arrested in 1757 near Orléans for predicting that because the king had "given his soul to the devil by exiling several bishops," he would die before Easter at the hands of the queen, the dauphin, and other unspecified "high and mighty" *(grands)*. Unmistakably devout are the deranged ravings by Michel Le Roy, the son of a bailiff *(huissier)* from Dreux, who in 1759 began publicly demanding that Louis XV "make a general confession," "convert himself," and "kick out Madame de Pompadour." As though he had come straight from one of Neuville's or Griffet's sermons, Le Roy insisted that the king's conversion "would not be sincere" if he approached the sacraments "without kicking her out." Before being locked up at Pontorson, he repeatedly threatened to go to Versailles in person in order personally to "see to the conversion of the king."[140]

In the case of such regicidal seditious sayings, the devout memory of the sixteenth century was also sometimes explicit. Complaining, for example, on 5 January that France was governed "by two whores *(p[utains])*"—obviously the king's titled as well as unofficial mistresses—and that the king himself was a "bugger," the veteran soldier Jean Le Clerc predicted that the same fate would befall Louis XV as befell his ancestors, presumably Henri III and Henri IV. These names were named in all syllables in an anonymous letter exhibiting some devout traits, which was postmarked from Lyons in March 1757 and received by the procureur général Joly de Fleury. Complaining of the scarcity of bread, the lack of work, and above all the twentieth tax—a tax particularly anathema to the clergy, of course—this barely literate correspondent accused Louis "the Fifteenth by name" of being more an "enemy of religion than the Most Christian King," a representative of the "false branch of the Bourbon family"; the letter warned that the king would soon be "struck down by the same sword as [had felled] the defunct Henri III and Henri IV" if he failed to walk in the footsteps of his immediate predecessors, who [had] reigned in peace with the people."[141] And

---

139. BA: AB, Ms. 11967, nos. 126–31, 157–64, "Déclarations des nommés Arnoult, Castel, Garré et Duchesne, au sujet des discours affreux tenus par le nommé Liebert, le 7 octobre 1757"; no. 171, curé of Saint-Landry to the lieutenant of police Berryer, 22 Nov. 1757.

140. On Thomas's case, see BN: CJF, Ms. 2076, fol. 35, Née de Charmois to procureur général, 10 Apr. 1757. For Le Roy's case, ibid., fols. 68–69, Le Veillard to procureur général, Dreux, 26 Apr. 1759. See also fol. 70, Saint-Florentin to procureur général.

141. For Le Clerc's case, BN: CJF, Ms. 2072, fols. 122–23, depositions by François Gorgu, 7 and 25 Feb. 1757; and for the anonymous letter, fols. 298–99, letter dated 22 Mar. 1757 from Lyon and addressed to procureur général.

from Abbéville in 1757 came a report that a Jesuit had said that "there are still Ravaillacs around."[142]

That denunciation proved difficult to verify, but the ex-Jesuit Jacques Ringuet paid with his neck for having said in Cambrai in 1762 that "only prostitution *(putanisme)* could have destroyed the order of Jesus"—a clear enough reference to Madame de Pompadour—and for having bragged that he had been "present when the king was wounded by Damiens."[143] As this example indicates, the suppression of the Jesuits in 1762–64 spawned another spate of devout regicidal utterances, prompting a certain Arnould, for example, to speculate that "if there were two eyes the less in France, the Jesuits would soon be reestablished"—a reference to the dauphin's notorious sympathies for the Jesuits; a certain Renard, a cabaret keeper in Reims, observed in 1765 that "the dauphin was very sick, and that for her part she preferred the death of the king to that of the dauphin because if the latter were king he would restore the Jesuits in France."[144]

What religion and politics still usually divided, Damiens himself more typically united. Most of Damiens's remarks and responses during his long trial, it is true, pointed in a parlementary and Jansenist direction: he said, for example, that he had attacked the king "because His Majesty had not listened to the remonstrances of his Parlement," that he had originally resolved to do so at the "time of the first refusals [of sacraments] by the Archbishop [of Paris]," and that "if he were in charge, he would expel the Jesuits within twenty-four hours."[145] That Damiens himself had worked as a lackey for some of the more radical parlementary magistrates and especially admired Clément de Feillet in part accounts for these judicial Jansenist echoes. At the same time it was not for nothing that Damiens had also worked at the Jesuit college of Louis-le-Grand and briefly served a very devout Sorbonne professor named Le Corgne de Launay. The act itself of having tried to "touch" the king, and of announcing the intention of dying

142. BN: CJF, Ms. 2075, fol. 85, original denunciation to procureur général by Bacler, *commis aux aydes* at Abbéville, 15 Jan. 1757; and fol. 88, an investigatory memoir dated 13 Feb. See also *PO*, "précis historique," p. xxix.

143. BN: CJF, Ms. 780, fol. 262; and *Arrest de la cour de parlement, qui condamne Jacques Ringuet, prêtre du diocèse de Cambray, à faire amende honorable . . . et à être pendu en place de Grève, pour avoir tenu des propos séditieux contre le roi, le parlement et l'état* (Paris, 1762), in fol. 293.

144. BN: CJF, Ms. 2076, fols. 262–63, Poulain to procureur général, Provins, 22 Oct. 1764; and CJF, Ms. 2077, fols. 121–22, "Copie de la dénonciation faite au procureur du roi du bailliage royal et siège présidial de Reims le 19 décembre 1765"; fols. 123–24, Marlot, procureur du roi to procureur général, 21 Dec. 1765; fol. 125, Bertin to procureur général, 24 Dec. 1765.

145. *PO*, interrogation of 18 Jan. 1757, no. 137, p. 131; and BN: CJF, Ms. 2070, fol. 158, "extrait de ce que le prisonnier a dit et qui a paru mériter attention, aux douze sergents du régiment des gardes françaises chargés à le garder à vüe."

a martyr's death "like Jesus Christ amidst pain and torments"—these gestures connote a devout, even Leaguish quarrel with the king.[146]

Together, finally, the seditious discourse of the 1750s attests to the popular desacralization of the monarchy effected by the refusal-of-sacraments controversy.[147] Although overtly respecting the king's person, the profound tendency of judicial Jansenism's political thought and action was so to identify the Parlement and the nation—so to valorize, in other words, the king's immortal body of state at the expense of his mortal and personal body—as to desacralize it, making it vulnerable to abuse and even attack. Finding this body immoral as well as mortal, the parti dévot then fell upon it, faulting it for vices that were tolerated on the part of Henri IV or Louis XIV—although not, significantly, Henri III—and that in spite of a Catholic alliance with Habsburg Austria against Protestant England and Prussia that would have edified the late sixteenth- or early seventeenth-century parti dévot.

Having done its worst, this religious assault on a sacral kingship left the king's body to the still more scurrilous—and not especially religious—attacks described by Robert Darnton for the 1770s, but not even those attacks were without precedents in the 1750s.[148] These precedents constituted a third kind of "seditious saying," which, deriving neither from judicial Jansenist nor from devout sources, blasphemously mocked the king's sacral quality or reclaimed it in favor of Damiens—and by implication the people—as indeed Damiens had implicitly done when he ventured to "touch" the king rather than to be touched by him. In Damiens's place, a deserter and apprentice tanner named François Bellier de La Chauvellais reportedly said in a cabaret near Château-Gontier, he "would have stuck his knife into the heart of the sacred bugger (in speaking of the sacred person of the His Majesty)"; the king was a "bugger" and a *"f[outu] gueux"*—tramp—in the opinion of an out-of-work cloth shearer in Reims named Joseph Le Cocq, who

146. On service to Le Corgne de Launay, *PO*, interrogation of 25 Jan. nos. 198–202, pp. 136–37; nos. 264–65, p. 141; and nos. 267–68, p. 142. On "touching" the king, ibid., 1st interrogation at Versailles, 5 Jan. 1757, no. 2, p. 44; interrogation of 18 Jan., no. 144, p. 132; 17 Mar., nos. 19, 22, 26, pp. 330–32; 26 Mar., nos. 171–73, p. 381. On dying like Jesus Christ, ibid., "addition d'information," depositions by Jean Bonot, Louis-Joseph Chouet, and the frère Simon-Joseph Duparcq, 7 Feb., pp. 186–88; and "recollement," 23 Feb., pp. 263–64.

147. Roger Chartier (*The Cultural Origins of the French Revolution*, pp. 120–22) has challenged the thesis that the 1750s witnessed the desacralization of the monarchy, in part on the grounds that Paris was not all of France. But to acknowledge that Paris was in this as in many other respects well in advance of the rest of France, and would moreover remain so until 1789, does not to my mind affect this thesis very directly. What might more effectively test it would be to try to measure changes in popular perception of the monarchy in areas directly affected by the refusal-of sacraments-controversy—Auxerre or Troyes, for example—in comparison with others that were not.

148. Robert Darnton, *The Forbidden Best-Sellers of Pre-Revolutionary France* (New York, 1995).

loudly blamed "Louis the fifteenth by name" as "the cause of his misery."[149] In a more positively sacral vein, a day laborer named Filassier, working in the vineyards near Argenteuil, reportedly opined that Damiens was a "saint" and "martyr," who "appeared daily at the place de Grève demanding vengeance for his execution"; and the domestic servant named Paumier, drinking in a Paris cabaret, held that "Damiens ought to be a great saint in Paradise," or at least that "if Damiens suffered his torments patiently, he is a saint."[150]

Very little in these midcentury seditious sayings, it might be observed, owed anything very directly to print culture. It sufficed for most of these "bad mouths" (mauvaises langues)—as indeed it had for Damiens—to have been near to the scene of political and religious action to derive meaning from that action. Nor do they seem to have owed very much to specifically enlightened print culture. The only arrested mauvaise langue in the 1750s or 1760s to have clearly invoked the name of a philosophe articulated the religious and political meaning of that influence in terms that were very ambiguous, to lay the least. Accused in 1759 of having plotted to kill the king, Auguste Tavernier, a ne'er-do-well son of Pâris de Marmontel's porter, claimed that reading Voltaire had reinforced his sentiments of "religion, honor, and fidelity."[151] To some degree that state of affairs would undoubtedly change in the 1770s and 1780s. For unlike Frenchmen in the sixteenth century, those alienated from both church and sacral monarchy by unedifying religious controversy found a secular alternative in the form of the Enlightenment in which to express that alienation. It is perhaps fitting, then, that Voltaire's name was invoked only by Tavernier, who was one of the six remaining prisoners of the Bastille liberated in 1789 by a Revolution that would lay claim to the ideological parentage of this philosophe, among others.

Before that happened, however, literate magistrates, barristers, ecclesiastics, and men of letters also reacted to the religious and political conflicts of the 1750s and 1760s. Their more refined typographical reactions, combined with appeals to public opinion, took apart divine-right absolutism in advance of the Enlightenment in some of the same ways as did the seditious sayings, but in some very different ones as well.

---

149. BN: CJF, Ms. 2072, fols. 233–34, deposition by Gabriel Bienvenu, 5 June 1757; and Ms. 2073, fols. 182–84. 190, interrogations administered by Reaucourt, assessor in the Reims constabulary, and Jacques Savé, lieutenant of the constabulary, on 22–23 Apr.

150. BN: CJF, Ms. 2073, fols. 227–28; and Ravaisson, *Archives de la Bastille*, 17:138–41.

151. Ravaisson, *Archives de la Bastille*, 17:365, Tavernier to the maréchal de Belle-Isle, 4 July 1759.

CHAPTER 4

+-+>-+>-+>-+>-+><+-<+-<+-<+-<+-<+-+>

The Conceptual Dismantling

of Sacral Absolutism

THE EARLY 1750S ARE INDELIBLY ASSOCIATED WITH SOME OF
the maturing French Enlightenment's first political utterances, among them Denis
Diderot's article on political authority in the first volume of his and d'Alembert's
Encyclopedia. Along with the scandal caused by the Sorbonne's acceptance of the
abbé Jean-Martin de Prades's "enlightened" thesis, it was that article that drew
hostile attention to the fledgling enterprise, nearly causing its suppression in 1752.
The same year also witnessed the publication of the abbé Mey's and Gabriel-
Nicolas Maultrot's two-volume *Apologie de tous les jugements (Apology for All the
[Parlement's] Verdicts)* and the following year that of the Parlement's "great"
remonstrances of 9 April 1753, of which Mey was also in part the author. These
works made the Parlement an object of the ministry's hostile attention, causing a
political crisis that came close to culminating in the suppression of the Parlement
of Paris in 1753. Although most contemporaries probably thought that the crisis
that provoked Mey's works was more important than the one surrounding Diderot's *Encyclopedia,* there is no use in appealing the verdict of history, which has
deemed Diderot's works the more significant. Yet some of what Diderot's article
on political authority signified to his contemporaries would remain hidden today
unless read against the backdrop of the tectonic shifts in political thought—even in
political culture—to which works like Mey's and the Parlement's more transpar-
ently attest.

By 1765, as we have seen, the declaration emasculating the parlementary
remonstrance had long been rescinded; the Edict of Fontainebleau, ending toleration of Protestants, was in de facto abeyance; the Edict of 1695 on behalf of the

episcopacy against both parish priests and parlements had been breached at several points; the Jesuit confessor and preacher had disappeared from the royal court; and the monarchy itself had lost much of its sacrosanctity. But the mid-eighteenth century's religious politics of contestation did more than simply rerun the sixteenth century's religious civil wars in reverse—more, that is, than simply to topple the legislative trophies of the French monarchy's reckonings with its sixteenth-century religious and political nemeses. They also scrambled the monarchy's positive redefinition of itself as an absolutism in alliance with the episcopacy, unanswerable to either its lay subjects or to the church in any form. That is to say that the shifts in religious politics also undid the Gallican Declaration of 1682.

The Gallican Declaration proclaimed the absolute independence of the monarchy from both the nation and the church, whether in papal or conciliar form. By 1765, however, judicial Jansenism had theoretically resubjected the monarchy to a lay national constitutionalism, while the parti dévot, although continuing to defend absolutism in relation to lay subjects, had remembered and reasserted some old limits of obedience in relation to the church. Proclaiming the ecumenical council's superiority to the pope, the Gallican Declaration had also proclaimed the independence of the French Catholic Church from the papacy as well as assuming its spiritual independence from the state. By 1765, however, judicial Jansenism had theoretically subordinated that church to laymen and the state in parlementary form, while in reaction to this radical lay Gallicanism a part of the episcopal parti dévot simply took refuge in ultramontanism. Where the absolutism of the Gallican Declaration had asymmetrically coupled a monarchical state with an aristocratic church, twenty additional years of *Unigenitus*-related controversies undid this conceptual alliance, pitting judicial Jansenism's constitutional monarchy, in control of a democratically structured church, against the parti dévot's absolute lay monarchy, in tension with a monarchically structured or ultramontanist church.

Like the Edict of Fontainebleau and the Edict of 1695, the undoing of the Gallican Declaration of 1682 was the work of the events of the 1750s and 1760s. These events took shape in a matrix of discourse in the form of at least a thousand books, pamphlets, published remonstrances and arrêts, and a periodical press led by the clandestine *Nouvelles ecclésiastiques* and such French-language newspapers printed by the Huguenot diaspora in Holland as the *Gazette de Leyde*.[1] Political action being inseparable from discourse, this discourse, it goes without saying, played a role of the first order in talking France out of absolutism's other chief

---

1. Jeremy Popkin, *News and Politics in the Age of the Revolution: Jean Luzac's Gazette de Leyde* (Ithaca, N.Y., 1989); and D. Carroll Joynes, "The *Gazette de Leyde:* The Opposition Press and French Politics, 1750–1757," in *Press and Politics in Pre-Revolutionary France*, ed. Jeremy Popkin and Jack Censer (Berkeley, Calif., 1987), pp. 133–69.

legislative symbols as well. In the case of the Gallican Declaration, however, its demise is clearly visible in discourse alone. Hence its separate treatment here.

To the extent that print culture and discourse at once effected and clearly revealed the unraveling of the Gallican consensus, the argument encounters another influential "private-public" paradigm: not, in this case, the hoary one of the king's public versus a personal body, but that of the emergence of a new public space in mid-eighteenth-century France. Brilliantly formulated by the German political philosopher Jürgen Habermas, this thesis holds that mercantile capitalism and the administrative monarchy to which it gave rise called into being a new bourgeoisie consisting of professors, writers, civil servants, and entrepreneurs. What was economically and politically new about this bourgeoisie was that, unlike the citizens of the ancient polis, its claim to citizenship was an extension of a private bourgeois family, rigorously separated from the workplace or "means of production." Based, then, on that private familial sector—itself a product, of course, of modern capitalism—and such notions as "humanity" that it made possible, this new bourgeoisie invented "public opinion," which in turn subjected first culture and then administrative absolutism to a rational critique, having meanwhile become politically oriented. The medium of that culture was at first conversation and the cultured salon, but eventually the bourgeoisie took over print culture and especially the periodical press as its medium par excellence. In France, it was the eighteenth century, especially the 1750s and 1760s, that witnessed the emergence of this new bourgeois "public space," along with its main midwives, the philosophes.[2]

Whether the French bourgeoisie was very entrepreneurial, and whether the Enlightenment was very bourgeois, are questions that have been amply agitated elsewhere in recent decades. They may perhaps be benignly neglected here. But whether, as Habermas and others have argued, the 1750s and 1760s were decisive for the formation of—or appeals to—public opinion is a contention more germane to the argument developed here and should be subject to at least a word of caution. Taking advantage, as we have noted, of a loophole in royal censorship that allowed barristers to publish virtually anything in the form of a judicial memoir or consultation, Jansenist barristers had created a highly politicized "public space" close to the center of the monarchy, including explicit appeals to the "public" and its "citizens," as early as the 1720s and 1730s.[3] The Parlement's magistrates, for their part, began to publicize and distribute their (in principle) secret remon-

2. Jürgen Habermas, *L'espace public: Archéologie de la publicité comme dimension constitutive de la société bourgeoise*, trans. Marc de Launay (Paris, 1986), pp. 1–112.

3. That is one of the principal conclusions to emerge from David Bell's *Lawyers and Citizens: The Making of a Political Elite in Old Regime France* (Oxford, 1994). See also Sarah Maza, "Le tribunal de la nation: Les mémoires judiciaires et l'opinion publique à la fin de l'ancien régime," *Annales* (Jan.–Feb. 1987):73–90.

strances to the king during the same tempestuous period. The approximately fifteen hundred books and pamphlets against *Unigenitus* and in defense of the Truth and its miracles, which appeared in the vernacular from 1713 to 1730, were not addressed to theologians alone. As for the periodical press, the *Nouvelles ecclésiastiques,* unmentioned by Habermas, inaugurated its seventy-year career as a clandestine weekly in 1728, with an explicit appeal to "the Public." As much as an ecumenical council, if not more, the Jansenist case was already an appeal to a lay literate public opinion.

Important as these precedents were, they are not invoked in order to deny that the 1750s and 1760s may have represented something like a quantum leap in appeals to the public and to public opinion. Very likely they did, perhaps even with the effect that the form as well as the subjects of French political contestation "broke out of the absolutist mold," in Keith Baker's words.[4] Surely there is something emblematic about the secret advice sent Versailles in 1760 by Jacob-Nicolas Moreau, then first president of the Parlement of Besançon, to the effect that the monarchy should abandon scruples and plead its case against the parlements in the public forum. "It is useless to object that the king should not plead against his subjects," he argued. "For the last ten years the king has not pleaded while from all quarters everybody pleads against him. And thus has he lost his case everywhere."[5] What is rather in question here is the thesis that it was principally the philosophes and their Enlightenment that first created that public space, which only later became politically oriented much on its own internal initiative. If, as they surely did, philosophes eventually became politically oriented, they did not do so in isolation from the public siege of absolutism taking place in the context of religious controversies that were private only in the sense that religion engaged the individual conscience.[6] Religion became a private matter largely as a result of those controversies; at midcentury, however, the regnant distinction still ran between the equally public temporal and spiritual domains.

To be sure, judicial Jansenism did not routinely employ the term public opinion, which waited until the physiocrats and the end of the century to become current coinage. Typically appealing to the "Public," the "judgment of the Public," or the "Tribunal of the Public," judicial Jansenism invoked the resultant "public outcry," or "cry of conscience," or the "witness of the faith." But this public's conscience was also a judgment and no stranger, therefore to the exercise

4. Keith M. Baker, *Inventing the French Revolution: Essays on French Political Culture in the Eighteenth Century* (Cambridge, 1990), p. 170.

5. "Mémoire fait vers 1760 par M. Bourgeois de Boisnes, alors premier président du parlement de Besançon, aujourd'hui secrétaire d'état, au sujet des parlemens, no. 7. Although Le Paige identifies Bourgeois de Boynes as the source of this memoir, Martin Mansergh has established Moreau's authorship in "The Revolution of 1771, or the Exile of the Parlement of Paris," (Ph.D. diss., Oxford, 1973), p. 55–56.

6. Habermas, *L'espace public,* p. 62.

of "reason" and the ways of "deliberation" and painstaking "persuasion." It also called for candor, simplicity, and right and denounced secrecy and the fait accompli as the habitual accomplices of despotism. Writing in 1757, the Jansenist magistrate Henri de Revol credited the *Unigenitus*-related controversies with having rent the "veil" concerning the "mysteries of the monarchy," thereby shedding "light" upon "these [constitutional] matters too little studied until now."[7] Although a clandestine journal itself, the *Nouvelles ecclésiastiques* kept pace with the English press in point of partisan political coverage, reporting in detail on sessions of the Parlement of Paris and even trying to penetrate the deliberation of the King's Council. That all of these protagonists were also simultaneously exploiting the distinction between the king's public and private wills shows how hopelessly entangled the old and new public / private paradigms in fact were, how imperceptibly the "new" politics grew out of the "old."

Also questionable here is the thesis that absolutism succumbed to a pervasive appeal to public opinion as such—succumbed, that is, apart from the diverse opinions the public actually professed. Appeals to public opinion by critics of absolutism and things "absolute" indeed abounded in the eighteenth century, but they did not occupy the discursive field alone. Often enough they encountered opposing appeals to public opinion by publicists who defended, if not divine-right absolutism, at least parts of the absolutist legacy, and that to the bitter end. How that public debate as well as appeals to public opinion conceptually disassembled absolutism is therefore the subject of this chapter.[8]

A Radical Gallicanism

Eighteenth-century French absolutism is inseparable from the Gallican Declaration of 1682, which had proclaimed the independence of both the French king from the church in temporal affairs and the French church from the papacy in spiritual affairs. By temporal power the Declaration explicitly designated that of absolute kings; by spiritual power it implicitly referred to an aristocracy of bishops. The declaration was mainly silent on the subject of relations between the two powers, except to reiterate Pope Gelasius's truism that, while each was to lend the other succor, they were to remain independent of each other in their respective domains.

The most influential restatement of the Gallican thesis for the 1750s and 1760s came not from a bishop, however, but from two Parisian Jansenist barris-

7. BPR: CLP, Ms. 541, no. 6, Revol to Le Paige, 24 Oct. 1757, dated by means of reference to no. 7.

8. For a similar critique of Habermas's thesis and the use to which it has been put, see Daniel Gordon, *Citizens without Sovereignty: Equality and Sociability in French Thought, 1670–1789* (Princeton, N.J., 1994), pp. 199–201.

ters: Gabriel-Nicolas Maultrot's and Abbé Claude Mey's two-volume *Justification of All the Sentences Delivered by the Secular Courts Against Schism,* which appeared in 1752.[9] The Huguenot diaspora's Holland-based *Gazette de Leyde* recommended the book as "seminal" in 1752, while the Parlement of Paris paid the *Apologie* the high compliment of popularizing its argument in the formidable remonstrances of 9 April 1753, which the *Gazette de Leyde* in turn serialized for readers unable to obtain them.[10] Relentless in its laicism, or its readiness to place the Gallican Church under the tutelage of the lay "prince," Maultrot's and Mey's treatise restated the Parisian barristers' celebrated consultations of 1727 and 1730. Behind these consultations loomed not the episcopal Gallicanism of 1682 but the earlier and more radical scholastic conciliarism of Almain, Gerson, Major, and even William of Ockham, to whose authority Maultrot's and Mey's *Apologie* sometimes openly appealed.[11]

As the *Apologie*'s full title suggested, the book was a defense of the secular courts' right to give orders and punish disobedience in such apparently spiritual matters as the church's public dispensation of the sacraments—a defense, in other words, of the parlements' action in the refusal-of-sacraments controversy. Because Maultrot and Mey acknowledged the classic distinction between the state's temporal and the church's spiritual authority, as well as the principle that the two "powers" ought not violate each other's authority, their strategy perforce consisted in further spiritualizing the church's authority to the point of divesting it of everything factual, exterior, public—of anything, in other words, that might have had a bearing on public tranquility and therefore of legitimate concern to the state. Where the sacraments of penance, the Eucharist, and extreme unction were concerned, the authors' strategy was to draw a sharp distinction between the private and interior dispositions required to partake of the sacraments, the so-called for intérieur, and the public access to these sacraments on the part of those who, like Jansenists, thought they had the required state of conscience. The conclusion was that the prince—that is, his courts—had the right and even the duty to maintain Catholic citizens in the tranquil possession of the sacraments absent formal conviction of some spiritual offense more serious than opposition to a bull that did not clearly distinguish heresy from orthodoxy.

This much was debatable enough, but it was ultimately crucial for Maultrot and Mey and their argument that they spiritualize not only the sacraments but also the entire internal governance of the Catholic Church. This they did with the conceptual help of an idealized image of "the primitive church" and its "happy centuries" when, "the spirit of charity . . . being the soul of its government, . . .

9. [Claude Mey and Gabriel-Nicolas Maultrot], *Apologie de tous les jugemens rendus par les tribunaux séculiers en France contre le schisme,* 2 vols. ("en France," 1752).

10. Joynes, "The *Gazette de Leyde,*" p. 155.

11. [Mey and Maultrot], *Apologie,* 1:482, 484–85.

the clergy with their bishop formed an ever standing tribunal to which sinners were cited and heard." By clergy Maultrot and Mey meant primarily the curés, upholding the long-standing Jansenist thesis that curés once governed the church with their bishops from the diocesan synod to the general council and that they should do so still. More recent was the authors' contention that "the people or at least the principal [members] of the faithful were present for [the sinner's] entire procedure" and that an excommunication was fulminated "only after . . . the most serious examination and exhausting all the means of gentleness and persuasion." The resulting excommunication was therefore always "the work of this small Council itself"—an ideal ecumenical council in miniature, as it were—"rather than of the person who presided over it." Maultrot and Mey moreover made it clear that in their opinion this primitive disciplinary procedure remained normative for the church, that all pastors including the pope could validly fulminate excommunications only with the "presumed consent of the church," which meant, in the last analysis, the whole church.[12]

A "ministry of charity and gentleness" as opposed to a "tyrannical despotism," the means of persuasion and consensual procedure as opposed to corporeal coercion—these were then the traits that honored the church during her happy centuries, as Maultrot and Mey always called them. What made these traits normative still was the Gallican principle derived from the medieval "doctors of Paris": that "although the [church's] keys have been *entrusted* to the Apostle Peter and to the other disciples, it is to the church that they were *given* in their persons because they were, so to speak, her deputies." The "authority of the keys," Maultrot and Mey further explained, "belong[ed] at once to the whole body and to its ministers, but in different senses: to the body as to the *property,* to the ministers as to the *usage* and *exercise.*" And like Le Gros earlier, the authors all but invited the accusation of ecclesial republicanism by boldly translating this principle into the analogy of a political republic. Just as in republics, they explained, "the judgment of the magistrate constitutes the judgment of the society, because the people consent to those charged to govern them, so is it the same with the church," where "ecumenical councils possess infallible authority because they sufficiently represent the universal church."[13]

Because even ecumenical councils pronounced infallibly only if they spoke for the universal church, they enjoyed no more right to lord it over the faith of the faithful than did a bishop in the case of excommunication. Although the authors did not spell it out, this much meant that simple priests were to accompany bishops to general councils. That principle of representation also meant that the lay faithful might legitimately make their public witness heard in reaction to an

12. Ibid., 1:507, 508–10, 513, 610, 633.
13. Ibid., 1:481–85.

unrepresentative council's decision, as had of course the barristers in reaction to the Council of Embrun. For by the authors' criteria no such decision, much less a papal bull, could become a rule of faith unless and until "it is no longer doubtful that it is consecrated by the acceptance of the universal church, when no clouds remain to obscure her submission, when *all attentive persons* are in a position to recognize that [the church] herself has spoken; that her witness is so public as not to be overlooked by anyone; and that the notoriety [of that witness] has attained such a degree of evidence that obstination alone is capable of hiding it and impeding its evidential force." Armed with such formidable criteria, Mey and Maultrot lovingly lingered over how long it had taken the decisions of some councils "now regarded as truly ecumenical" to win the church's universal consent. And not surprisingly so either, because any lay lament or "public outcry" *(cri publique)* against a recent decision or even an old one effectively belied the universal church's consent, failing which any disciplinary action—read: a refusal of sacraments—against recalcitrants constituted a "tyrannical vexation" and "visibly schismatic conduct."[14] The authors' criteria for valid consent—a devastatingly literal reading of Catholicism's *notae* or claims to unity, universality, and perpetuity—amounted to nothing less than total unanimity over time and thus functioned as a justification of minority dissent at any time.

Thus did the authors rejoin La Borde and Le Gros in defense of the "smaller number" as the likeliest bearers of Truth in the absence of unanimity and of the rights of the lay faithful as witnesses to that truth if not judges of it—two hallmarks of Jansenist ecclesiology throughout the century. But the legitimacy of the public outcry on behalf of truth was only the beginning of Mey's and Maultrot's laicism, because all the fear and force that their ecclesiology took away from the church it immediately reassigned to the lay prince—really his judges—by virtue of a kind of law of the conservation of constraint. Mey's and Maultrot's ideal church, it is true, was to be a gentle and charitable "assembly of the faithful," in which consensus would prevail by force of persuasion, consultation, and endless deliberation. But far from concluding in favor of a voluntary organization within but separate from the state—just about unimaginable to anyone in eighteenth-century France—the two Jansenist canonists nostalgically dreamed of an ideal Christian "empire" on the model of Theodosius's or Charlemagne's in which the prince—if not as lay Christian "outside bishop," then "even as pagan" political magistrate—would coerce his clergy to use the "ways of gentleness and persuasion." This state of affairs did not exclude the use of certain forms of state force against "heretics," so long as the church defined them by canonical procedures.[15]

14. Ibid., 1:41, 86.
15. Ibid., 2:20–25, 57–59, 67–97, 134–39, 176–78, 269–81, 327–46. The quotation about the rights of even "pagan" princes comes from p. 93.

Armed, then, with the prince's putative monopoly of force over everything external and contingent, combined with an Ockham's razorlike distinction between these and anything internal and spiritual, Mey and Maultrot encountered few if any matters so purely spiritual that they could not detect in them some elements of matter and fact, thereby rendering them fit for princely inspection. Not only, for example, were even ecumenical councils quite fallible in matters of fact, but whether they were ecumenical or not was itself a matter of fact which the prince was competent to judge. "Once the universal Church has spoken, the laity has no choice except that of submission," concluded Maultrot in a later pamphlet, "but the Prince, the Magistrate, even the simple Faithful," he added, "have the right to examine the exterior character of a judgment which is attributed to the Church in order to see if she has really spoken, if it is not just a small number of Bishops who have usurped her name."[16] Princes, moreover, had the right to examine whether "the judgment had been reached clearly, in such a manner as to abate the controversy." And should any of these criteria remain unobserved, the prince as protector of the canons was obliged to reject the judgment; or even if it met them all, as did the Council of Trent, the prince as political magistrate had the right to see whether under the name of doctrine anything had "slipped by which is contrary to the rights of the Prince, to the interests of his Crown, to the tranquility of his Realm, and to the liberties and maxims [read: the Gallican liberties] of whatever particular Church he is especially the protector."[17] And if such, finally, were the rights of princes with regard to decisions by ecumenical councils, how much more amply entitled would, say, Louis XV be in suspending civil obedience to the notoriously ambiguous and anti-Gallican bull *Unigenitus*. In doing so, that "prince" would not be infringing on his bishops' sacred right to proclaim whatever truth this bull contained, but merely forbidding them to make disciplinary use of the "exterior formula in which it is proposed."[18]

Although Mey's and Maultrot's *Apologie* was only one of many books and pamphlets to exemplify judicial Jansenism's tendency to construe Gallicanism as the nearly total subordination of church to prince, their treatise remained the bible of those tendencies until the French Revolution. In 1765, in reaction to the General Assembly's publication of its *Actes . . . concernants le religion*, which tried to restate the case for the church's independent spiritual authority, judicial Jansenist pamphleteers, including Maultrot himself, drew freely from the *Apologie* to justify the parlements' many victories over that spiritual authority since the book's publication in 1752. The Parlement of Paris's condemnation of Jesuit moral

---

16. [Gabriel-Nicolas Maultrot], *Les droits de la puissance temporelle, défendue contre la seconde partie des Actes de l'Assemblée du clergé de 1765 concernant la religion* (Amsterdam, 1777), pp. 26–27.

17. [Mey and Maultrot], *Apologie*, 1:348.

18. Ibid., 1:176.

theology in 1762, for example: was it not a clear infringement of the church's exclusive right to judge doctrine? Not so, Maultrot assured his readers, for "there are certain points of doctrine [namely moral ones] that have an intimate connection with the State."[19] The parlements' condemnation of the Jesuits' religious vows: did this not represent temporal interference in a matter of exclusive concern to God and the Jesuits? Far from it, replied Le Paige in his *Observations* on the Assembly's *Actes,* because whether the vow was validly contracted at all was a matter of fact that the prince could judge "by the light of reason" alone.[20] Parlementary orders to priests, finally, to administer the Eucharist and extreme unction to suspected Jansenists: was this not a temporal usurpation of the church's exclusive right to administer its most "august" sacraments? Not so, replied Maultrot, because the prince as political magistrate had the right "to maintain a citizen in the possession of the exterior advantages assured to all Christians, because the legal possession *[possessoire]* of even spiritual things is a purely profane matter."[21] With that breathtaking dictum judicial Jansenism went about as far in the direction of privatizing religion in the interests of public order as it was possible to go without actually using that vocabulary.[22]

If judicial Jansenism was so willing to materialize and factualize the spiritual in order to extend the state's control over the church, it was hardly likely to spiritualize something so matter-of-factual as ecclesiastical property in order to render it immune to taxation by the state. The period that witnessed the refusal-of-sacraments controversy hence also saw judicial Jansenists emerge as defenders of the monarchy's fitful attempts to tax clerical property, beginning with the controller general Machault d'Arnouville's attempt to impose the twentieth tax on the clergy in 1749. On the heels, for example, of Voltaire's globally anticlerical *La voix du sage et du peuple (The Voice of the Wise Man and the People),* in defense of Machault and the twentieth tax came the audibly Jansenist *Voice of the Priest,* which announced that, accustomed as they were to the episcopacy's "unjust excommunications," parish priests would willingly "suffer in even more palpable ways in the service of Your Majesty."[23] In the 1750s and 1760s that position enjoyed widespread sympathy, not only among Jansenist magistrates in the Parlement but among magistrates more generally, who viewed their case against the clergy, not as that of one privileged corps against another, but as that of the "entire state"

19. [Maultrot], *Les droits de la puissance temporelle,* p. 27.
20. [Louis-Adrien Le Paige], *Observations sur les Actes de l'Assemblée du clergé de 1765* (n.p., n.d.), pp. 71, 79–80.
21. [Maultrot], *Les droits de la puissance temporelle,* p. 82.
22. This is also the tendency of Jeffrey Merrick's argument in his *The Desacralization of the French Monarchy in the Eighteenth Century* (Baton Rouge, La., 1990), esp. pp. 78–104.
23. *La voix du prêtre* in *Recueil des voix, pour et contre les immunités du clergé* (London, 1750), p. 55.

against clerical "independence."[24] Jansenist espousal of state taxation outlasted Machault's short-lived attempt and took the form of an ever more comprehensive critique of the compatibility between the clergy's property and temporal position on the one hand and its "purely spiritual" functions on the other.

This along with other such tendencies reached a crescendo in reaction to the General Assembly's *Actes* of 1765, which reiterated the episcopacy's defense of its "immunities" to taxation.[25] Most surgical was the anonymous author of *The Right of the Sovereign over the Property of the Clergy and Monks*, who, even if he was not a Jansenist, reasoned with little more than the conceptual means available in judicial Jansenism.[26] Appearing in 1770, the pamphlet envisioned precisely the scenario in which the monarchy and the revolutionary National Assembly successively found themselves in 1789. The state owed three billion livres, and the payment of the interest on this debt, which consumed half of the annual revenues, did not leave enough to meet the state's ordinary expenses. Taxes could not be augmented because of the "dearness of all sorts of goods." What was then to be done? Considering and dismissing sundry alternatives in turn—cost-saving economies, additional loans, state bankruptcy—the author opted for the "surgical, decisive," and "simple" solution also adopted in 1789, namely the nationalization of all ecclesiastical property and its sale to private citizens, together with the transformation of ecclesiastics into paid "pensionaries of the state." Nowhere, not even in the literature produced by the prerevolutionary crisis of 1787–89, was the Revolution's solution to the state's fiscal problems more dramatically anticipated than here.

From the perspective of judicial Jansenism, the General Assembly's *Actes* of 1765 amounted to nothing less than "the revocation of the Declaration of 1682."[27] To be sure, the *Actes* concurred in principle with the divine-right theory of that

24. Quotations from unnumbered manuscript memoirs by the councillor Guillaume Lambert and the abbé Mey in BPR: CLP, Ms. 42 ("droit public"). For evidence of the Parlement's reluctance to side with the clergy in the controversy over the twentieth tax, note its refusal to condemn the barrister Daniel Bargeton's *Lettres: Ne repugnate vestro bono* (Paris, 1749), the chief pamphlet to appear in support of Machault's attempt tax the clergy, in the manuscript "Journal de Rolland d'Erceville," AN: AB XIX, Ms. 3336/2, fols. 9–10.

25. *Actes du l'Assemblée générale du clergé de France sur la religion, extraits du procès-verbal de ladite assemblée, tenue à Paris, par permission du roi, au couvent des Grands-Augustins, en mil sept cent soixante-cinq* (Paris, 1765), pp. 29–30.

26. [Cerfvol], *Du droit du souverain sur les biens fonds du clergé et des moines, et l'usage qu'il peut faire de ces biens pour le bonheur des citoyens* (Naples, 1770), pp. 124–46, but especially p. 138. For a fuller analysis of this pamphlet and its relation to judicial Jansenism, see Dale Van Kley, "Church, State, and the Ideological Origins of the French Revolution: The Debate over the General Assembly of the Gallican Clergy," *JMH* 51 (Dec. 1979):649–52.

27. *Nouvelles ecclésiastiques, ou mémoires pour servir à l'histoire de la constitution Unigenitus* (Utrecht, 1728–1803), 27 Mar. 1766, pp. 54–55.

declaration in teaching that kings were not accountable to any ecclesiastical
authority in temporal matters and that they received their authority from God
alone. But this high-principled smokescreen, designed to obscure the view of the
inattentive citizen, did not prevent the perspicacious Maultrot from noting that,
whereas the Declaration of 1682 had proclaimed the independence of the temporal
authority "as a truth conformed to the word of God," the *Actes* of 1765 had
presented it as "no more than the teaching of the Clergy of France."[28] Besides,
added Le Blanc de Castillon, who employed Mey and Maultrot as his canonical
consultants, the episcopal *Actes* of 1765 pointedly failed to imitate the Assembly of
1682 in explicitly condemning Cardinal Bellarmino's theory of the church's indirect
power, which allowed for papal intervention in a state's affairs whenever "sin"
was clearly involved. Tantamount to endorsing that doctrine, the "capital error of
the *Actes*," charged the avocat général of the Parlement of Aix, was "to have
excluded the . . . Prince's right of inspection over everything that is not entirely
profane, instead of restricting the innate power of the Church to what is purely
spiritual."[29] And if the pronouncements of the *Actes* on the subject of the first
Gallican article lacked candor, its commitment to the others was even more
casuistical. Its description of *Unigenitus* as an "irreformable judgment," its publication of a recent encyclical letter without any protest against this document's
presumption of papal infallibility—all this and more, maintained the avocat général, breathed an "ultramontanist spirit in blatant disharmony with the conciliarist
tradition of the Gallican Church.[30]

Some of these accusations ring true. The protracted exigencies of defending
Unigenitus and then the Jesuits had gradually cast the French episcopacy into an
ultramontanist posture that, restricted to La Fare, Tencin, and a few other firebrands in the 1730s, had become more general and accentuated by the 1760s. To
demote the Gallican liberties from the status of Catholic truth to national "opinion" was indeed to invite the opinion that that opinion might change. More clearly
than the *Actes* themselves, moreover, the episcopal defense of those *Actes* added up
to a discreet retreat in the face of a judicial Jansenist offensive that itself had altered
the spirit of the Declaration of 1682 to mean the nearly total subordination of
church to state, along with the laicization and republicanization of the church
itself. That meaning may have recalled various forms of Protestant erastianism, or
the most radical wing of the pre-Reformation conciliarist movement represented
by Robert Ockham and Marsilius of Padua. But no more than the General

28. [Maultrot], *Les droits de la puissance temporelle*, pp. 7–8. See also *Nouvelles ecclésiastiques, ou
mémoires pour servir à l'histoire de la constitution Unigenitus* (henceforth *NE*), 3d ed. (Utrecht, 1728–1803),
27 Mar. 1766, p. 54.

29. Jean-François-André Le Blanc de Castillon, *Réquisitoire du 30 octobre 1765* in BPR: CLP, Ms.
562, pp. 57–58.

30. Ibid., pp. 29–31, 97–98.

Assembly of 1765 did midcentury judicial Jansenism reflect the mainly episcopal Gallicanism of 1682.

What about royal Gallicanism, then, the subject of that declaration's first article? For it may seem as though judicial Jansenism's noisy defense of the temporal prince's power over all "exterior" aspects of the church's ministry should have involved it in defense of integral absolutism—in a defense, that is, of the monarchy's power over its lay subjects at least as absolute as that over its clerical ones. Declarations of fervent royalism aside, however, judicial Jansenism's "prince" tended to function as a code word for the Parlement of Paris. "Having established . . . that the Prince is not thought to have pronounced authentically as legislator unless his wishes have received the character of public law by the Parlement's registration," disarmingly explained an anonymous *Discourse on the Origins of Our Present Troubles* in a footnote, "it is superfluous to alert [the reader] that on each and every occasion that we henceforth mention the authentic decisions of the Prince, we always suppose them to be clothed in that essential form."[31] By Parlement, moreover, judicial Jansenism increasingly meant something like the nation. The paradox of judicial Jansenism's exaltation of the monarchy in relation to its clerical subjects, the better to undermine it with respect to its lay subjects, accurately reflects the diversity of its origins. From the royal courts it inherited the tendency to extend the state's authority over its feudal and ecclesiastical competitors, while from both the Catholic League and the Protestant *réforme* it retained the constitutionalist challenge to that authority, at least in absolutist form.

A Constitutional Monarchy

The book that dominated Jansenist and parlementary thinking about France's political constitution during the 1750s and 1760s was undoubtedly Louis-Adrien Le Paige's *Historical Letters on the Essential Functions of the Parlement, on the Rights of Peers, and on the Fundamental Laws of the Realm.*[32] Published in two volumes at the height of the refusal-of-sacraments controversy, the book quickly became, in the words of one historian, "the breviary of young magistrates all over France."[33] Like Mey's and Maultrot's *Apologie*, whose influence it rivaled, the book's principal theses appeared in all syllables in the Parlement of Paris's remonstrances, in this case in those directed against the Grand conseil dated 27 Novem-

31. *Discours sur l'origine des troubles présens de la France* (n.p., n.d.), p. 352 n. Clearly composed and published during the refusal-of-sacraments controversy, the anonymous book was written by Joseph Barré, according to Bernard Plongeron, *Théologie et politique au siècle des lumières* (Geneva, 1973), p. 71.

32. [Louis-Adrien Le Paige], *Lettres historiques sur les fonctions essentielles du parlement, sur le droit des pairs, et sur les loix fondamentales du royaume*, 2 vols. (Amsterdam, 1753–54).

33. Mansergh, "Revolution of 1771," p. 316.

ber 1755.[34] The book's foremost agenda was to justify the Parlement's disobe-dience to repeated royal orders that had led to its dispersion and exile in May 1753. The principal tack taken by Le Paige was the same one employed with ever greater frequency by the magistrates themselves in their confrontations with the king: to argue that the Parlement's duty to obey the king's real or permanent will as expressed in the monarchy's "fundamental laws" took precedence, in cases of conflict, over the king's "momentary will" as expressed in verbal orders or simple arrêts du Conseil. On this relatively conservative reading of Le Paige's *Lettres historiques,* the Parlement's role was to be a purely passive and judicial one, that of "repository and conservator of the State's constitutive laws." Far from taking the legislative initiative, the Parlement was rather to oppose all legislative innovations or, in Le Paige's words, "to oppose like an iron wall everything that might weaken the authority or [interrupt] the tradition of the [fundamental] laws." These funda-mental laws were ones so basic to the monarchy that they could not be altered without endangering the monarchical state itself: the Salic Law, for example, regulating the order of succession to the monarchy, or the "law" apparently discovered by Le Paige that reserved all criminal justice to the parlements so that the king alone might dispense grace in the form of pardons.[35] From Le Paige's perspective, the destruction of the parlements would entail that of the monarchy itself in the sense that the monarchy would thereby throw aside its self-imposed and salutary restraints and run the risk of degenerating into a despotism.

Even as they stood, these "conservative" contentions justified the increas-ingly radical resistance of the Parlement of Paris to the king's legislative wishes. But they also came embedded in a version of French constitutional history that rooted the Parlement of Paris's right of registration and remonstrance in a sup-posedly lineal descent from both the Merovingian royal court *(Cour royal)* and general assemblies *(parlemens généraux, placites généraux, cours plenières)* consist-ing of the entire Frankish nation, including even the women. To be sure, that part of its lineage going back to the Merovingian Cour royal by way of the medieval court of peers *(Cour des pairs)* identified the Parlement only with the king's justice, entitling it at best to speak to the nation on behalf of the king. But coequal descent from the side of the Frankish general assemblies entitled the Parlement to speak to the king as representative of the nation, inasmuch as these assemblies had once literally consisted of the whole Frankish nation and had possessed the constitu-tional right to consent to—or to veto—all of their kings' legislative initiatives. Whatever Le Paige's conscious intentions may have been—and even if recoverable they are hardly to the point—his textual logic invited the conclusion that the

---

34. Jules Flammermont, *Remontrances du parlement de Paris au XVIIIe siècle,* 3 vols. (Geneva, 1978), 2:26–27. See also 3:727–31.
35. [Le Paige], *Lettres historiques,* 1:12, 32–33.

eighteenth-century Parlement of Paris had inherited the quasi-legislative role once possessed by those assemblies and that, still representing those assemblies, the Parlement's constitutional rights of free registration and remonstrance were the eighteenth century's functional equivalents of the Frankish nation's erstwhile right to assent or to "murmur" its disapproval. How were readers of the *Lettres historiques* easily to avoid concluding that the Parlement exercised a species of national legislative cosovereignty in view of the text's reiterated premises that the Parlement was "just as old as the monarchy itself," that its authority was "the same as in Clovis's time," or that Frankish kings were not the only "founders of the monarchy?"[36]

Thus the seemingly absolutist formula, "for such is our good pleasure," with which royal declarations routinely concluded originally meant—and still should mean, according to Le Paige—that "such is the deliberation of the king and his plenary court or, in other words, such is the deliberation of the Parlement." Le Paige thereby also revealed his partial dependency on François Hotman, from whose *Francogallia* this exegesis was derived and whose constitutional and historical theses Le Paige updated for eighteenth-century purposes. These purposes meant that the Parlement of Paris had to replace the long defunct Estates General as the true successor of the Merovingian national assemblies, and so Le Paige accordingly went out of his way to snub the Estates General in a footnote in his *Lettres historiques.*[37] That also entailed taking a position against the comte Henri de Boulainvilliers and his similarly entitled *Historical Letters on the Parlements or Estates General,* which, first published in 1727, had equated the Frankish nation with the nobility and the parlements with the Estates General.[38] Yet Le Paige remained indebted to Boulainvilliers for more than the title of his book, borrowing the powerful pejorative *despotism* to describe the development of Bourbon absolutism.[39]

Le Paige's very parlementary version of French constitutional history also had predecessors. Etienne Pasquier, as has been noted, began substituting the Parlement of Paris for the Estates General in his histories as early as the late sixteenth century, and the constitutional literature of the Fronde completed that task, especially Louis Machon's *Véritables maximes du gouvernement de la France,* originally published in 1652 and republished by Jansenist barristers as *Judicium Francorum* during the political crisis of 1730–32. Le Paige's debt to the proparle-

---

36. Ibid., 1:11–12, 18–19, 89–92, 152–53.

37. Ibid., 1:86–87, 142 n.

38. Henri de Boulainvilliers, *Histoire de l'ancien gouvernement de France, avec les XIV lettres historiques sur les parlemens ou Etats-généraux, par feu M. le comte de Boulainvilliers,* 3 vols. in 2 (The Hague and Amsterdam, 1727), 2:50.

39. On Boulainvilliers's use of term "despotism," see his unpaginated introduction and especially ibid., 1:253–54, where he accused even Bossuet of having preached "despotism."

mentary literature of the Fronde is also evident in his pungent and immensely influential little *Letter on the Lit de Justice*, which, appearing in 1756, restated parts of the avocat général Omer Talon's speech before the Parlement of Paris shortly before the outbreak of the Fronde on 15 January 1648.[40]

Omer Talon had contended that the lit de justice assembly had not originally been an exercise in "sovereign authority, spreading terror everywhere, but rather like an assembly of deliberation and counsel."[41] As restated by Le Paige in his little *Lettre* and combined with his version of French constitutional history, that thesis completely subverted the meaning of the lit de justice assembly and made it into a mute testimony to something like national sovereignty. What had once upon a time been a "solemn seance" of king with his Parlement, a "veritable and serious deliberation" in which the nation's "wise Senators were free to enlighten the King," had by Le Paige's time become a "strange inversion of the ancient usage," had degenerated into a "mute scene" relative to the king, designed less to consult suffrages than to subjugate them. Nonetheless the contemporary ceremony's formality of having magistrates opine in inaudible tones stood as a mute witness or *témoignage* to antique constitutional "truth," to wit that their free suffrages were essential.[42] Like Le Paige's *Lettres historiques*, moreover, his *Lettre sur les lits de justice* proved immensely influential, going through four editions, including two in 1787, when it theoretically fortified the Parlement's refusal to accept the results of lit de justice assemblies on the eve of the Revolution.

Along with other judicial Jansenist publications in the 1750s, notably the Parlement's monumental remonstrances of 9 April 1753, Le Paige's *Lettre sur les lits de justice* also pioneered the pejorative use of the adjective *absolute*. In contrast to the time when the "the truth spoke and could make itself heard, . . . everything in today's lit de justice assembly," Le Paige lamented, "concludes with an act of *absolute* power." Equated with an "act of the king's will alone" or, worse yet, an order to "blindly follow the momentary whims of the prince," an "act of absolute power" also stood pejoratively opposed to "light," "knowledge," and a "veritable deliberation," as well as to the "freedom of suffrage" necessary to law.[43] As nothing was more semantically essential to absolutism than Bishop Bossuet's classic distinction between divine-like "absolute government" as opposed to degenerative "arbitrary government," Le Paige's clear tendency to conflate the two was anything but innocent. That tendency reached its apogee in the voluminous literature of pamphlets and books accompanying the trial of the Jesuits, which, under the pretense of judging the society's "despotic" constitution, in fact

---

40. Omer Talon, *Harangue faite au roi [le 15 janvier 1648] par monsieur Talon, son advocat général au parlement de Paris* (Paris, 1649).

41. Quoted in [Louis-Adrien Le Paige], *Lettre sur les lits de justice* (n.p., 1787 ed.), p. 14.

42. Ibid., pp. 7–10, 13–17.

43. Ibid., pp. 2, 4, 7, 11. Emphasis mine.

amounted to the condemnation of Bourbon absolutism. For it was then that the equation between absolute and despotic became banal, enabling Ripert de Monclar, the Jansenist procureur général of the Parlement of Aix, to observe in 1762 that the general of the Society of Jesus was no less despotic for being susceptible to deposition, because such was the only "counterweight" in "despotic Empires" to "*absolute* power."[44] Le Paige himself was hardly an innocent bystander in the term's further fall from grace, for he, along with the abbé Christophe Coudrette, in their seminal *Histoire général* of the society accused it of being at once an "absolute monarchy" and a "universal despotism."[45]

Directed against the Jesuits and designed to defend Jansenists, Le Paige's antiabsolutist constitutionalism nonetheless represents, as we have noted, a reworking of materials inherited from the Fronde, even from the wars of religion. Was his constitutionalism hence incidental to his Jansenism? Hardly, because Le Paige was able to give material a singularly Jansenist, even figuratist form. His *Lettres historiques* subtly cast the parlementary magistrates as a faithful constitutional remnant within a politically defected nation, steadfastly committed, like the Jansenist minority within the post-*Unigenitus* church, to witnessing to Truth amidst the apostasy of despotism in post-Frondish France. The truth to which the magistrates faithfully witnessed was mainly constitutional truth, attested to by French history rather than by divine revelation, yet hardly less hoary and invariable than Jansenism's parallel conception of patristic and especially Augustinian truth. And just as the Jansenist "small number" had sustained persecution throughout the century, so the magistrates' unenviable yet glorious lot was passively to sustain persecution by being intermittently exiled hither and yon, as they were in 1732 and again in 1753 and 1757.

However Jansenist in form and inspiration, Le Paige's constitutionalism unquestionably valorized the Parlement of Paris at the expense of the Estates General, raising the question of whether his highly influential "figuratist" reading of French institutional history marks a retreat from the conciliar audacities of, say, Nicolas Le Gros writing on the morrow of *Unigenitus*. Did not Le Gros's persuasive parallels between general councils and the Estates General amount to a clearer statement of the thesis of national sovereignty than Le Paige's more figuratist resuscitation of distant Merovingian national assemblies in the form of a company of venal office holders? Later on, after Chancellor Maupeou's temporary purge or suppression of the parlements in 1771, Le Paige's colleagues Mey and

44. Jean-Pierre-François Ripert de Monclar, *Comte rendu des constitutions des Jésuites par M. Jean-Pierre-François Ripert de Monclar, procureur général du roi au parlement de Provence* (n.p., 1763), pp. 83–84, 90. Emphasis mine.

45. [Christophe Coudrette and Louis-Adrien Le Paige], *Histoire générale de la naissance et des progrès de la compagnie de Jésus en France et analyse de ses constitutions et privilèges,* 4 vols. (Paris, 1761), 1:19; 2:225.

Maultrot would in fact apply their radical conciliarism to the French state and, like Le Gros, elaborate a kind of conciliar constitutionalism that theoretically rehabilitated the Estates General as the nation's representative organ. After the return of the parlements in 1774, Mey's and Maultrot's conciliar constitutionalism continued to gain ground at the expense of Le Paige's "figuratist" variety, even within the confines of the Palais de justice. But in the 1750s there was no more prospect of a meeting of the Estates General than there was of the restoration of the Merovingian dynasty, in which case it made good political sense to use the Merovingian myth of an original national contract to legitimate the opposition of an institution which was at least alive and doing rather well in Paris at that time.

Even by itself, however, the *Lettres historiques* invited a radical reconsideration of political representation in relation to the Parlement, as is evident in Le Paige's correspondence with Charles-François Henri de Revol, a councillor in the Parlement of Paris. In private colloquia with Le Paige and other erudite magistrates like Durey de Meinières in the 1740s, Revol denied any historical connection between the eighteenth-century parlements and ancient Frankish assemblies. Although he agreed that such assemblies had really existed under the Merovingian and Carolingian dynasties, and had once even possessed the right to consent to new laws and taxes, Revol also held that the Capetian kings had evaded the obligation to convoke them even before both monarchy and assemblies had succumbed to "feudal anarchy." If, since then, the monarchy had stumbled from feudalism's "somber and stormy night" into the dawn of a "happy despotism," it was with the help of royal judges bearing no connection to Frankish assemblies.[46] And if French kings were still duty-bound to convoke the Estates General, which was the only institution plausibly related to the earlier assemblies, theirs was a duty for which they were answerable to God alone, the nation lacking the constitutional wherewithal to make them fulfill it.[47]

Upon reading Le Paige's *Lettres historiques,* however, the scales fell from Revol's eyes. Convinced by Le Paige's historical demonstration that the original "parlemens généraux had insensibly melted into the court of our kings," and that this medieval court was in turn the ancestor of the Parlement of Paris, Revol concluded that the Parlement indeed legitimately spoke for the nation and its "veritable public law." Convinced as well by Le Paige's argument that the Estates General were not the true successors of the Frankish general assemblies, because these had laid down the law whereas the Estates General had supplicated on

46. BPR: CLP, Ms 42 ("droit public"), in particular the manuscript "Dissertation sur la question si les Roys sont quelquefois obligés d'assembler les Etats généraux," fols. 598–618.

47. BPR: CLP, Ms 560: "essay sur le droit public de notre nation sous la troisième race," unnumbered Ms; and "Essay sur le droit public de France ou Extraits de différents auteurs concernant toutes les matières du droit public sous les trois races de nos Roys. Touts ces extraits ont été lus dans les conférences tenus chez monsieur en 1741, 1742, 1743, 1744, 1745, 1746," also unnumbered.

bended knee, Revol concluded that the Parlement was more effective than the Estates had ever been, since, being the king's chief court as well, it remained "always and necessarily assembled as compared with the session of the Estates, whose existence depended on the king's whim."[48]

There remained one caveat for Revol, however, and that was the fact that the Parlement could simply not take the place of the Estates General where consent to taxes was concerned. The nation's delegation to consent to taxes—the one area where the Estates General had spoken with authority—had to be specific and direct, whereas the Parlement's mandate to defend fundamental laws was general and permissibly indirect. All the Parlement could do was to grant provisional authorization to raise taxes in cases of dire necessity and meanwhile to endear itself to the nation—especially, Revol stressed, to the Third Estate—by steadfastly defending the principle of the rights of all proprietors to consent to all governmental subsidies. And so he urged Le Paige to write another volume of his *Lettres historiques* that would defend the nation's right to tax itself.[49]

But Le Paige's *Lettres historiques* proved to be only a temporary intellectual stopover for Revol. Ever more appalled, as the refusal-of-sacraments controversy escalated, by both the extent of ministerial despotism and the audacity of the Parlement's riposte, Revol was arguing by 1757 that a revised edition of the Estates General was needed in order to cope with the constitutional crisis. Whereas the Parlement's only "procuration from the nation" was passively to defend the repository of fundamental law, he argued, a new "meeting of all free citizens" might more "faithfully" revive the powers of the ancient Frankish assemblies and "effect some veritable change in the constitution of the monarchy and in the legitimate power of the ruling house." Speaking for commoners, Revol made it clear that the national assembly he contemplated would be composed quite differently from the medieval Estates General, because "the Third Estate had [since] come to share the nobility's rights as Franks." At the same time, however, Revol remained wedded to the traditional notion of a mandate binding the deputies to the wishes of their constituents, stipulating as he did that his assembly would be one "where each town or canton would give its deputies a special procuration in which the innovation desired by the nation would be spelled out." Thus did Revol precociously reveal in 1757 the limits that judicial Jansenist constitutionalism would encounter in the ultimate crisis of 1787–89.[50]

But the nation's Estates General and its possible analogy to the ecumenical council had not been forgotten by other Jansenist constitutional theorists during

48. BPR: CLP, Ms 42, fols. 506 ff.
49. Ibid.
50. Ibid., Revol to Le Paige, 25 Oct. 1757, unnumbered; and CLP 541, Revol to Le Paige, 6 Oct. 1757.

the 1750s either. Writing in 1755 against the Gallican clergy's claim that church property was immune to taxation, the jansénisant abbé Etienne Mignot argued that the clergy enjoyed only the "administration" of property owned by the church, which he defined as "the whole society of the faithful," including, of course, all laypersons, just as the king was "the simple administrator of the state," which he carefully declined to define.[51] But by accepting Le Paige's version of the legislative cosovereignty of early Frankish assemblies, and then—taking leave of Le Paige—by regarding the Estates General and not the Parlement as immediate successors of these assemblies, Mignot made it clear that the Parlement consented to taxes only "as an abbreviated [Estates General], and as their representatives."[52] And writing a few years earlier, in a harbinger of things to come, Le Paige's colleagues Mey and Maultrot denied bishops the right to refuse the sacraments to whomever they pleased on the grounds of conciliarism's classic distinction between spiritual power in itself, deeded by Christ to the whole church, and the subordinate right to exercise that power, only delegated to the ministers of the church. But just in case the king refused to permit his parlements to force the constitutionary bishops to be canonical dispensers of the sacraments, these two Jansenist barristers reminded the king that as political magistrate he, too, enjoyed only the "exercise and not the property" of the crown's—or the nation's—rights. The conclusion they drew from these premises was that the king had no right *not* to exercise the crown's—or the nation's—rights against sacrament-refusing bishops.[53]

"The Language of Patriotism"

Yet no mere summary of its printed utterances about church and state during the 1750s and 1760s does justice to judicial Jansenism's power as a movement of opposition to royal absolutism and the ecclesiastical hierarchy. Much more than its hundreds of anonymous books and pamphlets or its array of precedents and syllogistic arguments, judicial Jansenism was above all a language. The Jesuit Dominique Colonia came to something like this conclusion when, casting about for a way to justify the inclusion of so many anonymous books in his *Jansenist Library, or an Alphabetical Catalogue of the Principal Jansenist Books*, he finally pointed to their "precious jargon." Closer to the spirit of that jargon, however, was the Jesuit Antoine-Joseph Cerutti's characterization of it as "the language of

51. [Etienne Mignot], *Traité des droits de l'état et du prince sur les biens possédés par le clergé*, 2 vols. (n.p., 1755), 1:109–110; 2:336–37.

52. Ibid., 1:183–85. See also 2:393–94.

53. [Maultrot and Mey], *Apologie*, 2:353, but in general 349–59.

patriotism mixed with that of rebellion."[54] However begrudgingly, Cerutti's
phrase captures eighteenth-century Jansenism's essence as a kind of loyal opposition whose genius was precisely to oppose absolutism and the episcopacy in terms
of traditions that neither could entirely disavow. That language also reflects
Jansenism's experience of persecution, and its consequently defensive preoccupation with the twin questions of legitimate authority and the limits of obedience.

Whether in the domains of church or state, then, judicial Jansenism typically
excoriated "despotism," "tyranny," indeed all kinds of "arbitrary power" and
"unlimited authority" manifesting themselves in "assaults" *(voies de fait)*, if not
by outright "acts of authority" *(coups d'autorité)*, and animated, finally, by the
omnipresent "spirit of domination" and "blind obedience." Against these marks
of unbridled concupiscence Jansenist language proclaimed authority conceived as
a trust or "ministry" hedged about by "legitimate limits." These most often
consisted in "sound maxims," "ever constant usages," or better still "immutable
laws" if not "holy" ones, preferably collected in some kind of "repository" *(dépôt)*
where the laws kept wholesome company with "verities." These laws and verities—or laws *as* verities—were not so much legislated as they were witnessed to by
assemblies, in the state by the Parlement's "assembly of chambers" and in the
church as "assembly of the faithful," and solemnized by means of a "serious
deliberation" reflecting the "participation of everyone" *(concours de tous)* or,
better yet, a "unanimous consent." The respect for the necessity of concord and
unanimity, the spirit of counsel and deliberation, the submission and witness
voluntarily rendered to eternal truth and immutable law—these had all more
abundantly flourished in the distant past, in an ecclesiastical context during the
patristic "comely days of the church" in a political one during the Merovingian
and early Carolingian "ancient splendors of the monarchy." But alas! The seed-
lings sprung from this distant harvest had been more recently choked out by the
thorns and thistles of doctrinal and constitutional "innovation," sown insidiously
by the hand of "despotism," in the face of whose "pomp" and "haughty airs"
meek "charity" and "timid truth" could at best stammer "prayers" and "humble
remonstrances."

Even the briefest analysis of this language soon uncovers the various layers
of judicial Jansenism's origins. Its characteristic reverence for all things ancient
and horror of all "novelty" is of course to some degree common to all varieties of
Christianity, which has tended to venerate the first five centuries of its history as

54. Dominique de Colonia, *Bibliothèque janséniste, ou catalogue alphabétique des principaux livres
jansénistes, ou suspects de jansénisme, qui ont paru depuis la naissance de cette hérésie*, 4 vols., 2d ed. (n.p.,
1731), 1:9–13; and Joseph-Antoine Cerutti, *Apologie de l'institut des jésuites*, 2d ed., 2 vols. in one (n.p.,
1763), 1:10.

normative. Like sixteenth-century Protestantism, however, Jansenism accentuated this tendency, reinforced in its case by sustained persecution and the closely
related judicial milieu's reverence for legal precedents. Jansenists typically regarded the Truth (usually capitalized) as definitively residing in a repository of
which the church should have been the faithful guardian, just as the Parlement
prided itself on being the repository of venerable and fundamental laws. It is
indeed hard to tell in this case whose language is being contaminated by whose,
the Jansenists' in thinking of the faith as deposited in a musty moth-eaten register,
or the Parlement's in thinking of law as something immutably true, delivered once
and for all unto the saints. Similarly, Jansenism's tendency to garland itself in
terms of "love," "charity," and "truth" is, to be sure, broadly Christian. Yet the
peculiar emphasis given these terms in Jansenism warrants their being regarded as
characteristic. Charity, along with concupiscence, was one of the principal delectations or affections into which Jansenists divided the world of human motivation,
and throughout the eighteenth century Jansenists christened themselves as the
"friends" or "defenders" par excellence of Truth.

   Reflecting judicial Jansenism's odyssey from theology to politics by way of
ecclesiology is the movement's progressively wider application of the oppositional terms "love" and "fear." These terms belonged first and foremost to
penitential theology: love designated true contrition, by definition love for God,
which Jansenists thought necessary for absolution, while mere fear of sin's punishments characterized inferior attrition, with which Jesuit casuistry contented
itself. By the advent of *Unigenitus* if not earlier, however, Jansenist ecclesiology
had appropriated "love" and its ways as the defining characteristics of the episcopal ministry. In contrast to the state's "exterior" and "coactive" space, where
inspiring fear and using force were appropriate means, the episcopal office,
Jansenists never tired of repeating, was a "ministry and not an empire," which
"governs with gentleness and . . . inspire[s] obedience with love." Yet while
continuing to reiterate this contrast in ecclesiastical contexts during the 1750s and
1760s, Jansenist constitutionalism recalled La Borde's and Le Gros's application
of conciliarism to the state, and ended by deciding that love ideally characterized
the king's "ministry" as well as the bishop's. Judicial Jansenist constitutionalists
thereafter increasingly relegated fear to the secular hell of "despotism," where it
kept infernal company with Montesquieu's better-known emphasis on fear as the
defining principle of despotism in his *Spirit of the Laws*. The judicial Jansenist
insistence on love, however, as the essential link between king and subjects
remained more contritional and subversive than the aristocratic "honor" that
Montesquieu thought characteristic of monarchical constitutions.

   Also typically Jansenist are such pejoratives as "spirit of domination" and
"blind obedience." The spirit of domination (as opposed to the spirit of charity) as

one of the distinguishable marks of the concupiscent beast has a pedigree going back beyond Saint Augustine's *De Civitate Dei*, where the *libido dominandi* or *cupiditas dominationis* is identified as characteristic of the "earthly city" *(civitas terrena)*, to the Vulgate New Testament, where Christ enjoins his disciples to be "ministers" or "servants," unlike the "rulers of the Gentiles," who "dominate" and "wield power."[55] In contrast, the equally pervasive pejorative blind obedience has a Jesuitical origin, appearing in the society's constitutions, where a "kind of blind obedience" *(caeca quadam obedientia)* is enjoined upon the professed.[56] Seizing upon this phrase, Jansenists saw in it the quintessence of Jesuitical servility, the very obeisance demanded of them in the case of the bull *Unigenitus*. From here it was a short step to seeing blind obedience as the inevitable accomplice of monarchical high-handedness, the necessary underside of the spirit of domination. Nothing is more common, aside from "despotism," than these two pejoratives in prerevolutionary political pamphleteering; yet they remained linguistic quasi-monopolies of judicial Jansenism until the 1760s or thereabouts.

The ultimate linguistic defense against acts of arbitrary authority was the Jansenist insistence on the necessity of "unanimity" or "unanimous consent" on the one hand, and to the inviolability of the individual's or small number's "conscience" on the other. However contradictory these two appeals might seem at first blush, they functioned complementarily in judicial Jansenist semantics, for the small number's conscience legitimated its cry of protest precisely in the absence of the required unanimity. The appeal to unanimity was of course Catholic enough, finding legitimation in Saint Cyprian's *De Unitate Ecclesiae*, Saint Augustine's writings against the Donatists, and the fifth-century Saint Vincent de Lerin's *Commotorium*.[57] What was distinctively Jansenist was the use of the criterion of unanimity to justify the protestations of a condemned minority as well as to hurl the accusation of "schism"—also one of the worst pejoratives in the Jansenist lexicon—against the persecuting majority. Although not without both

55. Saint Augustine, *De Civitate Dei contra Paganos* (Leipzig, 1825), in praefatio, p. 3, and especially liber V, caput XIX, p. 160; and secundum Mattheum (20:24–28), and secundum Marcum (10:42–45), in *Biblia Sacra juxta Vulgatam* (Stuttgart, 1983), pp. 1557, 1593.

56. *Constitutions des jésuites, avec les déclarations, trauduites sur l'édition de Prague*, 2 vols. (France, 1762), 2:294. The given French translation reads: "une espèce d'obéissance aveugle," 2:293.

57. Saint Cyprian, *De Lapsis* and *De Ecclesiae Catholicae Unitate*, ed. Maurice Benevot (Oxford, 1971), especially pp. 70–80; his *Lettres*, trans. Sister Rose Bernard Donna, C.S.J. (Washington, D.C., 1964), pp. 30, 194, 297; and Saint Augustine, *Scripti contra Donatistas*, pars 1, in *Corpus Scriptorum Ecclesiasticorum Latinarum*, vol. 54, ed. M. Petschenig (Leipzig, 1908). liber 2, caput iii:5, p. 179. For a couple of explicit appeals to Saint Cyprian, see Vivien de La Borde, *Du témoignage de la vérité* (n.p., 1714), pp. 83, 1167–68; and Nicolas Le Gros, *Du renversement des libertés de l'église gallicane*, 2 vols. (n.p., 1716), 1:171–72.

patristic and scholastic origins, the appeal to conscience against the institutional church, on the other hand, aligned Jansenists with persecuted Huguenots.[58]

Hard behind these most specifically Jansenist contingents in judicial Jansenism's semantic formations marched late-medieval Gallicanism's phalanx-like legacy, with its bristling array of interlocking ecclesiastical definitions and catchwords—the church as "assembly of the faithful" *(congregatio fidelium)*, which possessed the "property" *(proprietas, dominium)* of the Petrine keys and "delegated" their "usage" or "exercise" *(usus, utendum)* to the bishops as "ministers" and so on. Already exploited by both Huguenot publicists and League apologists, the late-medieval "school of Paris"—Jean Gerson, Jacques Almain, John Major—are the immediate sources of this conceptual apparatus and vocabulary, which in turn have roots in earlier canon law and the Vulgate New Testament. When, as we have seen, judicial Jansenism began to transfer this radical conciliar conception of ecclesiastical authority to the French state, it retained the telltale vocabulary, conferring on the "nation" the "property" of its ultimate legislative "authority" or "power" while delegating its "usage" or "exercise" to the king as "minister" or "administrator."

Bringing up the rear, as it were, and providing the whole with a kind of legal and logistical support, came the parlementary linguistic legacy, with its veneration for "ever constant usages," "invariable rules" and "sound maxims," as well as its horror of "acts of authority" *(coups d'autorité)*, illegalities or *voies de fait*, and all that smacked of the "arbitrary" and "despotical." Proparlementary propaganda may plausibly lay claim to the terms *despot* and *despotical* themselves. For after a brief appearance in the French fourteenth century in both scholastic Latin and the vernacular, the terms were driven from the field as unauthentic Latin by Renaissance humanism—both Protestant pamphleteering and the literature of the League contented themselves with *tyranny* and *tyrannical*—only to reappear in the vernacular in proparlementary pamphlets during the Fronde of the seventeenth century. The judicial milieu's midwifery also seems to have been instrumental in the birth of the more general term *despotisme* toward the end of the same century.[59] Yet the terms *despot, despotical,* and *despotism,* as well as the untranslatable expression *voie de fait,* well illustrate the difficulty in disentangling parlementary and Jansenist vocabularies—and therefore the point of the concept of "judicial Jansenism." One of Jansenism's first and most faithful social constituencies was the judicial

58. On the conscience, see Jacques Le Brun, "La conscience et la théologie moderne," in *La révocation de l'édit de Nantes et le protestantisme français en 1685,* ed. Roger Zuber and Laurent Theis (Paris, 1986), pp. 113–33.

59. On despotism, see R. Koebner, "Despot and Despotism: Vicisssitudes of a Political Term," *Journal of the Warburg and Courtauld Institutes* 14 (1951):275–482; and Melvin Richter, "Despotism," in *Dictionary of the History of Ideas: Studies of Selected Pivotal Ideas,* 4 vols., ed. Philip P. Wiener (New York, 1973), 2:2–18.

milieu, and it is hardly accidental that the son of a parlementary lawyer, "the great" Antoine Arnauld, should have employed the distinction between fact *(fait)* and principle or law *(droit)* to argue that Jansenists need not entirely accept a papal bull that said that five propositions were not only heretical or false but were in fact to be found word for word in Cornelius Jansen's *Augustinus.*

At the height of its influence during the refusal-of-sacraments controversy, judicial Jansenism deployed its characteristic language in the form of books, pamphlets, and published remonstrances against some of the Old Regime's most sacrosanct institutions, and with devastating effect. In the name of doctrinal Augustinianism, the ideology denounced the heretical Pelagianism and perverse morality of the Society of Jesus and called upon all good Catholics to uproot them. In the name of episcopal Gallicanism, it denounced the "foreign" and "Italian" influences of the Jesuits and the Jesuit-dominated papacy and called upon "every good Frenchman" to eradicate them. Yet in the name of parlementary and Richer-ist strains of Gallicanism, it denounced the "spirit of domination" and "system of independence" of this very Gallican episcopacy and called upon the "prince" to subjugate them. This abstract prince, moreover, was only apparently the monarch because, in the name of parlementary constitutionalism, judicial Jansenism did not hesitate simultaneously to denounce the "despotism" and *voies de fait* of this same monarchy, or at least its ministers, and called upon all loyal "patriots"—and this well before the advent of the patriot movement in 1771—to oppose them.

Opposing the "court of Rome" in the name of the Roman Holy See, "ministerial despotism" in the name of the monarchy conceived as a ministry, and the Gallican bishops in the name of pristine Gallicanism, judicial Jansenism was no less damaging in effecting maneuvers thus circular, and for giving battle at such close quarters to the institutions it opposed. Indeed, its self-defensive formation of persecuted innocence and orthodoxy in part lent credibility to the movement's oppositional message and gave it its hybrid religious-ideological punch. After the final breakdown of the Old Regime in 1789—and increasingly as one approached that point—intellectual strains quite peripheral to and distant from its spirit and institutions could become politically relevant. Until then, however, a movement that seemed to speak in the name of all that was venerable and sacrosanct in the Old Regime's repertory of institutions and traditions in fact undermined eighteenth-century absolutism the more effectively. That same stance of persecuted orthodoxy is also a sense in which the movement, although taking on an ever more secular hue, continued to bear an authentically Jansenistical cast. Originally accused of crypto-Calvinism, Jansenists responded that they alone were orthodox Catholics, equidistant from schismatic Calvinists and Molinistic Jesuits. Charged with subverting the ecclesiastical hierarchy, they maintained that they alone were good Gallicans and that their persecutors within the episcopacy were really ultramontanists. Sporadically accused of republicanism, they parried with the assertion that they alone were true monarchists and that their Jesuitical opponents were at once the assassins of kings and the apologists of despotism.

If in the beginning *Unigenitus* was the papal word that brought judicial Jansenism into existence, then the Jesuit was the unholy spirit that improvidently maintained it. For in the Jesuit, judicial Jansenism encountered its ideal antiego, symbolically magnifying everything it opposed. Purveyor of a theology that replaced God with man as the arbiter of salvation and a morality (probabilism) that enthroned vice in the place of virtue, the Jesuit was immorality incarnate and the unavowed accomplice of "encyclopedic" unbelief. Huckster of a devotional style that concupiscently riveted the penitent's attention on corporeality and encouraged a mechanical reliance on externals, the Jesuit was a promoter of both superstitious ignorance and persecutory fanaticism. Juror of special obedience to the papacy and the abettor of the political ambitions of the court of Rome, the Jesuit was the archenemy of the Gallican liberties and national freedoms everywhere. Swearer of blind obedience to his superior general, who acted without constitutional restraints, the Jesuit was at once the incarnation of servility and of despotism, the advocate of free will with no will of his own. Traditional confessor of Europe's Catholic princes and at home amid court intrigue, the Jesuit was at once an incorrigible "abettor of despotism" *(fauteur du despotisme)* and the perennial assassin of princes. And the Jesuit conspired by definition. In 1757 the Jansenist magistrate Revol was sure that the "black cluster of [Jesuit] royal confessors" was conspiring with the devout "ministerial cabal" to persuade Louis XV that the parlements were his enemies, echoing the conviction earlier voiced by the Parlement itself that certain elements at court had "formed a systematic and studied plan" to "destroy the entire magistracy in France."[60] That conviction did not prevent Revol or most other parlementaires from suspecting that the Jesuits had conspired to put Damiens up to his apparent attempt on Louis XV's life the same year.

This conspiratorial bent is one of many traits shared by judicial Jansenism with what Bernard Bailyn and Gordon Wood have called "radical Whiggism" or "commonwealthman" ideology in eighteenth-century England and colonial America, an outlook that gave the American Revolution its main ideological component.[61] For both movements the detestation of Jesuits and the capacity to

60. BPR: CLP, Ms. 541, no. 6, Revol to Le Paige, 6 Oct. 1757; and "Très humbles et très respecteuses remontrances, que présentent au roi notre très honoré et souverain seigneur, les gens tenant sa cour de parlement, 4 août 1756," CLP, Ms. 539, no. 152.

61. Bernard Bailyn, *The Ideological Origins of the French Revolution* (Cambridge, Mass., 1967); and Gordon Wood, *The Creation of the American Republic* (Chapel Hill, N.C., 1969). See also J. G. A. Pocock, *The Machiavellian Moment: Florentine Political Thought and the Atlantic Republican Tradition* (Princeton, N.J., 1975); and Caroline Robbins, *The Eighteenth-Century Commonwealthman: Studies in the Transmission, Development and Circumstance of English Liberal Thought from the Restoration of Charles II until the War with the Thirteen Colonies* (Cambridge, Mass., 1959).

detect conspiracies were symptomatic of a profound distrust of all forms of political power and a consequent tendency to hedge it about with as many restraints or "just limits" as possible. Both movements therefore excoriated "blind" or "passive" obedience in the name of "conscience" or "reasoned" obedience and defended various "liberties" like those of the Gallican Church or the Magna Carta against "domination." Both movements therefore also defended supposedly ancient constitutions against "despotic" usurpations whether in church or state, judicial Jansenism's constitutions having origins in the pre-Gregorian church and the forests of Franconia, and radical Whiggism's ultimately in pre-Norman or pristine Anglo-Saxon England. Both movements worried about the nefarious influence of the recipients of "ministerial" pensions in the surviving hulks of once more representative constitutional bodies, like the Parlement's lower judicial chambers or the Parliament's House of Commons, although, based as it was in continental France, judicial Jansenism did not enjoy the luxury of opposing standing armies, as did commonwealthman Whigs in insular England. And speaking of "luxury," both movements condemned it and associated it with decadence and despotism. Part of the parlementary parti janséniste's perennial opposition to royal finance and borrowing, for example, lies in its century-long moral opposition to all forms of commercial interest.

In part a set of comparable origins accounts for these similarities between judicial Jansenism and commonwealthman ideology, commonwealthman ideology in Puritanism, insular "antipopery," and the constitutionalism of the English Civil War; judicial Jansenism in "puritanical" Jansenism, Gallican anti-ultramontanism, and the parlementary constitutionalism of the Fronde. Both Puritanism and Jansenism in turn echoed the sixteenth-century Reformation—in Jansenism's case the Calvinist réforme—and the Catholic counterreformation both. The two movements therefore not surprisingly drew inspiration from many of the same sources: the late medieval conciliarists, the sixteenth-century Calvinist monarchomachs, and such seventeenth-century natural-law theorists as Hugo Grotius and Samuel Pufendorf. By the 1770s, moreover, the two oppositional traditions ceased to be merely parallel and began to interact more directly, colonial American commonwealthmen like John Witherspoon steeping themselves in the Jansenist Sorbonnist Charles Rollin's history of the Roman Republic and judicial Jansenists like Mey and Maultrot quoting extensively from the works of Algernon Sidney's *Treatise on Civil Government*, Lord Bolingbroke's *Craftsman*, and Thomas Gordon's essay on Tacitus.[62] In the 1770s both movements also became deeply implicated in organized "patriotic" protests, commonwealthman ideology in both the Stamp Act protest in the American colonies and John Wilkes's

---

62. Wood, *The Creation of the American Republic*, p. 53; and Patrice Higgonet, *Sister Republics: The Origins of French and American Republicanism* (Cambridge, Mass., 1988), p. 141.

movement against general warrants and in favor of parliamentary reform in England, judicial Jansenism in the "efforts of patriotism" against Chancellor Maupeou's "constitutional revolution" at the expense of the French parlements.

If, then, the commonwealthman tradition is commonly accounted a secular political ideology despite its partly Puritan origins, why should not what we have called judicial Jansenism be similarly considered despite its partly Jansenist origins and continuing association with bona fide "witnesses to the Truth," especially since by the 1760s the movement was attracting fellow travelers with little grounding or interest in Jansenism's theological tradition? The answer is that judicial Jansenism was indeed an ideological as well as a religious movement and that its history in the eighteenth century is in part that of a transition from religion to political ideology. Religions and political ideologies are obviously not mutually exclusive. However otherworldly or transcendent—perhaps even in proportion as they are otherworldly or transcendent—religions typically carry plenty of implications for the organization or reorganization of the here and now, and this was particularly so in Jansenism's case, what with its original and profound tendency to desacralize everything short of a hidden God. Nor are modern ideologies typically devoid of religious or transcendent elements, as the persistence of the sermonic jeremiad in colonial commonwealthman oratory eloquently demonstrates.[63]

Yet it was precisely an aspect of even "judicial" Jansenism's still transcendent character—that is, its reluctance to acknowledge let alone valorize anything between the bipolar realms of charity and concupiscence—that inhibited it from embracing political "virtue" and therefore limited its potential for political reconstruction. Political virtue—the capacity without grace for disinterested dedication to the political commonwealth—is what defines commonwealthman ideology and was of course essential to the political message of, say, Montesquieu, Mably, and Rousseau, even in less virtuous France. But except in the many cases of hybrid discourse, political virtue is conspicuous in judicial Jansenist discourse mainly by its absence. And although that absence hardly detracted from judicial Jansenism's immense powers of defense and deconstruction, it proved a serious liability when reconstruction was in order. That liability bore a distinctively Augustinian imprint, and it is in part for that reason that the term *ideology* seems unsatisfactory as a shorthand description of judicial Jansenism's case.

Devout Discourse in Defense of Throne and Altar

In contrast to judicial Jansenism's reticence on the subject, "virtue" figures prominently enough in the opposing discourse of the parti dévot. Appropriately so, too, because Molinistic theology allowed for the production of human virtue with only

---

63. Perry Miller, "From Covenant to the Revival" in his *Nature's Nation* (Cambridge, Mass., 1967), pp. 90–120.

minimal help from divine grace. Or perhaps the plural *virtues* is the better term, because the parti dévot's "virtue" readily collapsed into Christianity's traditional theological and moral virtues and did not add up to the citizenry's selfless dedication to the commonweal denoted by the same term in commonwealth ideology and in the political thought of Montesquieu and Rousseau. On the contrary, devout discourse's political virtue consisted precisely in the blind obe-dience—or "absolute submission," in that discourse's less pejorative parlance—excoriated by judicial Jansenism as well as in the commonwealthman tradition. For while judicial Jansenism's was above all a discourse on the limits of obedience if not on outright disobedience, devout discourse was above all about the extent of obedience to legitimate if not to illegitimate authority. This language of obedience maintained itself even in situations of de facto disobedience to existing authorities, a semantic act of no mean proportions.

In both church and state, therefore, devout discourse exalted "supreme power," "hierarchy," and "legitimate authority," and invested these with "dig-nity," "glory," "majesty," "superiority," an "exterior jurisdiction," above all "sovereignty" itself. In the place of judicial Jansenism's "prince" or "chief," devout discourse typically substituted a more majestic "sovereign" or "sovereign master"; where judicial Jansenism spoke of the Roman Holy See, distinguishing it from the Court of Rome, devout discourse referred unapologetically to the pope or, better yet, the "sovereign pontiff." Symptomatic of devout discourse's cozy proximity to political and ecclesiastical powers and principalities is the textual prominence of the adjective "absolute" and the adverb "absolutely." Both bishops and political sovereigns were routinely qualified as absolute. And while the dispensation of the sacraments, for example, depended "absolutely on the will of the bishops," the political sovereign was for his part "absolutely the master to refuse" whatever he wished, for instance to hear parlementary remonstrances.[64]

These absolute and sovereign powers enacted "decisions" and "acts" and imposed these with "discipline." In sharp contrast, again, to the pejorative view of them as illegal in judicial Jansenist discourse, the many "acts of authority" figured favorably in devout discourse, emanating as they proudly did from an ecclesiasti-cal "jurisdiction" or political "legislative apparatus" as visible and "exterior" as the Jansenist conscience was invisible and internal. These disciplinary acts and decisions descended upon a population of political "subjects" and ecclesial "flocks" *(ouailles, brebis, troupeaux)*, who, unlike contentious Jansenist "citizens" and lay "faithful," liked to "listen" respectfully to their "superiors" and always responded with "simplicity," "docility," or "obedience without reserve" and a

---

64. The phrase about the bishops comes from Le Corgne de Launay, *Les droits de l'épiscopat sur le second ordre, pour toutes les fonctions du ministère ecclésiastique* (n.p., 1760), p. 79; and the one about the political sovereign comes from Jean-Georges Lefranc de Pompignan, *Défense des Actes du clergé de France, publiée en l'assemblée de 1765, par M. l'évêque du Puy* (Louvain, 1769), p. 377.

"submission without limits." Or at least once upon a time things were thus, for all was not now well in the devout Garden of Eden either. Alas! A host of "opinionated heretics," "frondeurs," and "refractories" had recently arisen; a combination of castoff Calvinist "sectaries" and newfangled philosophical "unbelievers," they fomented "discord," "sedition," and "tumults," culminating in "revolt" and "resistance" bordering on "rebellion" and "revolution." The scourge of their century, these new "factions" directed their venom first against the ecclesiastical hierarchy, seeking to "violate" its purity, "contravene" its canons, and "divest" it of authority, but ultimately they aimed to undermine the political order as well.

This heretical activity took on conspiratorial proportions in the devout imagination, just as the Jesuit's did in the Jansenist imagination. The parti dévot's original version of a Jansenist plot was the Bourgfontaine conspiracy uncovered in 1654 by the Bordelais barrister Jean Filleau, who was also a scourge of prerevocation French Protestants. According to Filleau's account of the plot, Jansen and Saint-Cyran and five others had met in Bourgfontaine in 1621 in order to contrive the destruction of Catholicism and the establishment of Deism in France. This they planned to do by disguising the Calvinist heresies of divine predestination and irresistible grace as orthodox or Augustinian Catholicism and by exaggerating the requirements for partaking of the sacraments of penitence and the Eucharist. Catholicism's sacramental system would come to seem so inaccessible to the faithful as to disenchant them with its practices, while the doctrine of predestination and unmerited grace would convince them that Christ and the incarnation played no real role in their salvation, leaving the field to a triumphant Deism in France.[65]

Filleau's seventeenth-century version of the plot acquired new life at the height of the Enlightenment in the work of the Jesuit Henri-Michel Sauvage, who, convinced that the original plotters had all but achieved their religious goals, shifted the emphasis from dogma to ecclesiology. For the Jansenist conspirators' aim, he maintained, had also been to transform the Catholic Church's aristocratic monarchy into an "aristo-democratical" polity vesting its ultimate spiritual authority in the whole church while delegating its daily exercise to the bishops, the lay faithful's mandatories. Appropriately, lay lawyers and their peremptory judgments had taken the place of bishops and their mandamuses as the Jansenists' real magisterium.[66] From there it was a short step for others like Pierre-François Lafitau, Bishop of Sisteron, to expand the plot by making Jansenist ecclesiology an intermediate staging point for a final assault on absolute royal authority. Political heretics as much as doctrinal ones, Jansenists had adopted the conciliar

65. Jean Filleau, *Relation juridique de ce qui s'est passé à Poitiers touchant la nouvelle doctrine des jansénistes* (Poitiers, 1654).

66. Henri-Michel Sauvage, *La réalité du projet de Bourgfontaine, démontré par l'exécution,* 2 vols. (Paris, 1755), 2:142–43, 147–48, 191–92, 200–201.

maxim that political as well as ecclesiastical communities retained the ownership of their sovereignty, delegating its "usage" to accountable "chiefs." Entrenched in the parlements, "political" Jansenists had already manipulated these courts into proclaiming these political heresies in advance of yet more sinister designs on absolute monarchy.[67]

Given this devout defense of legitimate authority in both church and state, it is hardly surprising that the Bishop of Le Puy, Jean-Georges Lefranc de Pompignan, should have singled out the nouns "power" and "jurisdiction" and the adjectives "absolute" and "exterior" for explicit defense against the mainly Jansenist critics of the General Assembly's *Actes* of 1765. Weighing his words carefully, the bishop insisted that the church no less than the state rightfully called itself a power possessed of a jurisdiction capable of producing exterior effects and rendering absolute judgments. That this exchange may have been, in the bishop's own words, "only a dispute over words" only highlights its significance. And that he tied his defense of these words so closely to a defense of an absolute monarchy signifies what is palpable even at first glance—that devout language was essentially that of Bodin and Bossuet, that is, of late sixteenth-century and seventeenth-century absolutism.[68] For even when speaking of Religion (like Jansenist Truth, devout Religion was always capitalized), devout discourse always deployed much the same imperial terminology, revering its "august" sacraments and the "majesty" of its "exterior cult."

The term *majesty* was a Roman imperial title before being appropriated by French jurists to describe their king and his "sovereignty" in the sixteenth century. *August* was of course another imperial title taken by a medieval French king as well as by the devout dauphin, Louis-Auguste, in 1754, while the emphasis on religion's exterior features smacked of not only devout Catholicism's affective piety, but the spectacle of royal pomp and ceremony. It is hard to imagine a Jansenist having delivered such a sermon as did Henri Griffet in defense of the "exterior cult that we render . . . to the Sovereign Master," exulting in Catholic worship's "sensible apparatus" *(un appareil sensible)* and the "august pomp of [its] ceremonies," in contrast to "a simplicity contrary to the spirit of the church" and a "purely interior cult."[69]

More than in the case of judicial Jansenism, therefore, the parti dévot's language was that of an ideology. Aside from the mandatory references to generic Religion, devout discourse was not noticeably religious. Gone, by the 1750s, were

---

67. [Pierre-François Lafitau], *Entretiens d'Anselme et d'Isidore sur les affaires du temps* ("en France," 1756).

68. Lefranc de Pompignan, *Défense des Actes du clergé de France*, pp. 153–55.

69. Henri Griffet, "Sur le culte extérieur," in *Sermons pour l'Avent, le carême, et les principaux fêtes de l'année, prêchés par M. père H. Griffet, prédicateur ordinaire du roi*, 4 vols. (Liège, 1773), 3:166–67, 169, 170–72.

Languet de Gergy's heroic attempts to justify the theology underpinning the bull *Unigenitus;* Christophe de Beaumont, Languet's successor in a sense, contented himself with the bald assertion that the truth of the bull lay in the logical "contra-dictories" of the propositions it condemned.[70] The "ideology" in question was that of the absolutist alliance of monarchy and episcopacy. More than half a century before the French Revolution, devout spokesmen were already proclaim-ing the necessary defensive alliance of throne and altar. "Let [Jansenists and parlementaires] leave altar and throne as they have always been," cried Pierre Lafitau, Bishop of Sisteron, in a typical passage. The bishops, he specified, should be "masters" to command in the church and in position to be obeyed *(en possession d'être obéis)*, while the king should be the "sole absolute and independent master to command in the State."[71]

This defense of absolutist throne and episcopal altar was not very stellar. With the exception, perhaps, of the abbé Nicolas-Sylvestre Bergier's distinguished tracts against "incredulity," the eighteenth-century French parti dévot proclaimed nothing in the way of Catholic apologetical literature as compelling as Bossuet's *Exposition de la religion chrétienne (Summary of the Christian Religion)* in the seventeenth century or Hughes-Félicité de Lamennais's *Essai sur l'indifférence en matière de religion (Essay Concerning Religious Indifference)* in the nineteenth century. Because the edicts of Fontainebleau and of 1695, as well as the Gallican Declaration of 1682 and the bull *Unigenitus*—the legislative legacy, in short, of Louis Quatorzian absolutism—ran mainly in its favor, the eighteenth-century French episcopacy had only to defend this legacy against all "frondish" and "sectarian" comers in order to maintain its favored position at the right hand of divine-right monarchy. But the defense of laws and legalities is hardly the stuff of inspired apologetics or classics in political thought.

It is also very misleading. For the bland uniformity—or "unity," as its spokespersons would surely have had it—of the devout idiom nonetheless veils a growing alienation from the monarchy, as we have already noted, in response to the breakdown of royal religious policy in the 1750s and 1760s. In the very long run, of course, this estrangement between monarchy and episcopacy, along with the resultant rise of episcopal ultramontanism, weighed heavily on the fate of the Old Regime, both on the eve of the Revolution and during its attempted Restora-tion on the morrow.

The parti dévot's defense of its sacrosanct jurisdiction entailed in the first place a defense of the Edict of 1695, which had reinforced episcopal authority over parish priests. That much meant a refutation of the Richerism or curé-centered

---

70. Christophe de Beaumont du Repaire, *Mandement et instruction pastorale de Monseigneur l'arché-vêque de Paris, touchant l'autorité de l'église* (Paris, 1756), p. 53.

71. [Lafitau], *Entretiens d'Anselme et d'Isidore,* pp. 13–14, 195–96.

parochialism still sponsored by the Jansenist press and personified by the likes of Maultrot or Travers. So while for Mey and Maultrot the Edict of 1695 did not even merit the name of a law, having failed among other things to win the "applause" of the entire nation, for the devout Sorbonne doctor Le Corgne de Launay, this "celebrated" edict was "one of the most beautiful monuments in the reign of Louis XIV, in which his wisdom had played no less a part than had his piety."[72] Le Corgne's *Rights of the Episcopacy over the Second Order,* published in 1760, proceeded to enumerate these rights. Having alone received their "spiritual power" from Christ directly, and not merely to administer but to "possess" it, the apostles and their successors alone "possessed" the "power" to "delegate" the "power" to preach, confess, absolve penitents, and to appoint assistant vicaires.[73] A bishop also possessed the right *not* to follow the advice of his curés or cathedral clergy, lest these latter become the real "sovereign arbiters of the whole ecclesiastical government" and forget "their obedience toward the episcopacy."[74] The intended effect of Le Corgne's ecclesiology was to transform the whole clerical second order into mere delegates of the bishops, with no independent spiritual authority of their own.

In order to divest the second order of all these "powers" to the exclusive benefit of the bishops, Le Corgne de Launay separated them from the sacrament of ordination, and therefore demoted ordination to a mere susceptibility of receiving these powers by way of episcopal appointment. Where Richerist ordination, then, conferred full spiritual powers that episcopal approbation assigned and restricted only to a given territory, Le Corgne de Launay's ordination conferred at best a potential for receiving sacerdotal powers that episcopal approbation actualized and even extended. And as did Languet before him, Le Corgne justified this demotion of curial status by recalling that Christ had addressed his injunction to preach to his twelve apostles alone, exclusive of the seventy-two disciples also commissioned by Christ, whom Jansenists regarded as the biblical prototypes of parish priests. Christ's commission to the seventy-two, argued De Launay, was unique to that time and place and effected no transmission of spiritual authority to any of their successors. To these and other appeals to the Scriptures and tradition, Le Corgne, unlike Languet, surprisingly added some appeals to philosophical "reason" and "experience." Just as Montesquieu, at least according to Le Corgne, had argued that a numerous nobility needed a Senate to regulate its affairs, so Le Corgne himself maintained that the clerical order, a kind of "aristocracy," needed an episcopal Senate in order to avoid "Presbyterian [i.e., Jansenist] fanaticism"

72. Le Corgne de Launay, *Les droits de l'épiscopat sur le second ordre,* p. 51.

73. Ibid., on power to preach, pp. 35–36, 40–45; on power to confess and absolve, pp. 69–71, 76; on sacraments in general, p. 65; on right to appoint vicaires, p. 150; on possession of spiritual power, p. 154.

74. Ibid., pp. 84–85.

and "anarchy." The example of England's seventeenth-century Puritan Revolution came to Le Corgne's aid at this point, conveniently proving as well that "sectarian" attacks on the episcopacy were tantamount to attacks on the outworks of monarchy.[75]

But Le Corgne might just as well have saved his anathemas. Fleury and his episcopal appointees had done their work thoroughly, having all but purged the beneficed lower clergy of Jansenists. Aside from pockets of resistance here and there and despite unabated Jansenist rhetoric on the subject in the *Nouvelles ecclésiastiques* and pamphlets, Richerist parochialism as such no longer posed much of a threat to the episcopacy in the 1760s. As his nervous reference to Presbyterianism and the English Civil War suggests, Le Corgne was probably all too aware that the episcopacy's chief enemy in 1760 was the Paris Parlement seemingly intent upon playing the role of the English Parliament, and that disaffected Jansenist curés were likely to be troublesome only to the extent that the parlements chose to defend them. That is to say that the chief threat to the episcopacy was Jansenist laicism, as represented by the Parisian judicial community armed with its arrêts, consultations, and remonstrances.

The episcopal defense's starting point was again the Edict of 1695, especially those provisions (articles 30 and 35) that seemed to give the Gallican Church exclusive jurisdiction over litigation concerning doctrine, the sacraments, ecclesiastical discipline, religious vows, and "other purely spiritual matters." The only intervention by the secular courts in these "purely spiritual matters" allowed by the Edict of 1695, argued Christophe de Beaumont in his militant mandamus of 1756, was by way of the civil appel comme d'abus, which might at most fault the form of an ecclesiastical court's procedure, not the judgment itself.[76] The proper role envisioned by the edict for the secular courts was moreover to aid and abet the work of the church and her ministers, added the cardinal de Soubise, and not to obstruct them, as the parlements were doing.[77]

Jansenist jurisprudence easily outflanked the parti dévot's stationary legalistic defense, as has been noted, by using criminal procedure and arguing that the public and external refusal of sacraments was *not* a purely spiritual matter. A genuinely religious response to this jurisprudence by devout apologists would have surely taken its criteria of externality and publicity head on and argued frankly for the necessarily external and public character of Catholic Christianity.

75. Ibid.: on English example, pp. 3–5; on apostles as sole recipients of Christ's injunction to preach, 9–11; on sacerdotal power, 69–71. Other arguments from Scripture and tradition are to be found on pp. 23–25, 35–36.

76. Christophe de Beaumont, *Mandement et instruction pastorale, . . . touchant l'autorité de l'église*, p. 42.

77. AN: 177mi (Chartrier de Tocqueville), 75, Ms. 12, mémoire du cardinal de Soubise, fols. 20–21.

Such a defense would have moreover gone well with devout Catholicism's highly affective and palpable religious sensibility; it would also have sought out and challenged Jansenism's religious introspection at its interior center.

Among devout apologists, however, only the Bishop of Puy, Lefranc de Pompignan, resolutely picked up this implicitly religious gauntlet. The "invisible and purely interior faith" that judicial Jansenism placed beyond the reach of the "prince" was "without consequence," Pompignan held. Catholicism's cult, ceremonies, sacraments, and preaching were on the contrary all very public and exterior, he had already observed as the General Assembly's spokesman to the king in 1755, and he later rhetorically asked, "if all of that fell under the purview of the secular authority, on the grounds that all of it was exterior and public, . . . what must one conclude?" Clearly that the state would rightfully "decide whether such and such a book in dispute among Christians was canonical or not, whether the word of God was entirely contained in the Holy Scriptures or whether . . . part of it should be acknowledged as having been transmitted by word of mouth from the Apostles to ourselves" and whether this and that and so on until, the state having decided on all of these "exteriors," nothing remained of Catholicism except a religion "entirely human in its essence." What was in the last analysis at issue between himself and his judicial Jansenist opponents, maintained the bishop, was nothing less than the "divinity" of the Christian religion.[78] The irony, of course, is that in thus publicizing the spiritual while denying that the public refusal of sacraments to Jansenists and others did any serious damage to them as "citizens," the parti dévot tended to separate citizenship from religion and thereby privatize the latter as much as judicial Jansenism's interiorization of religion did. That tendency was to reach its culmination during the Revolution when the neodevout or "refractory" clergy that opposed the Civil Constitution of the Clergy counseled lay parishioners to have as little to do with the constitutional clergy as possible, even if it meant registering their marriages and births with the lay state instead.[79]

Be that as it may, that properly religious response was a minor motif, even in the works of Lefranc de Pompignan. The more dominant theme was a political and ecclesiological response that, faced with the accusation that the French episcopacy had become traitorously anti-Gallican, tried to underscore the episcopal character of true or "orthodox" Gallicanism and defended this orthodoxy against

78. Lefranc de Pompignan, *Défense des Actes du clergé de France*, pp. 337–38; and "Remontrances au roy concernant les refus de sacrements," in *Collection des procès-verbaux des assemblées générales du clergé de France*, vol. 8, pt. 1, no. 5, p. 182.

79. Yann Fauchois, "Les évêques émigrés et le royalisme pendant la Révolution," in *Les résistances à la Révolution: Actes du colloque de Rennes, 17–21 septembre 1985*, ed. François Lebrun and Roger Dupuy (Paris, 1987), pp. 386–95; and "Révolution française, religion et logique de l'état," in *Archives de sciences sociales des religions* 66 (July–Sept. 1988):9–24.

the "heretical" lay and parlementary Gallicanism that had become part of judicial Jansenism.[80] Proudly extolling, for example, the "precious liberties" that so happily distinguished the Church of France from other Catholic Churches," Le Corgne de Launay made it clear, as has been seen, that these liberties, in his opinion, consisted in the distribution of sacerdotal power among an independent aristocracy of bishops, but not among a dependent presbytery of priests.[81] For Lefranc de Pompignan, too, the Gallican tradition meant that the government of the church was a "monarchy essentially tempered by an [episcopal] aristocracy." But more explicitly than Le Corgne, Pompignan defended this episcopal aristocracy against the lay state.[82] The famous Gallican Declaration of 1682, he maintained, had not meant, in defending temporal power against the papacy's pretensions of indirect temporal power, "to confuse the true liberties of the Gallican Church with a shameful slavery which, against the institution of Jesus Christ, would enfeoff the ecclesiastical ministry to the secular Power."[83] The "emperor is in the church" just as truly as the "church is in the empire," thundered Christophe de Beaumont, quoting Saint Ambrose against Saint Optatus of Mileva, and that meant, according to the metropolitan archbishop, that "in spiritual matters the Laws of the Church oblige the Emperor and he can never put himself above them."[84]

But these gestures of independence sat uneasily with the posture of bended knee; admonitions were barely audible when articulated in the parti dévot's habitual language of submission and obligation. Better therefore to distinguish as sharply as possible between the king and his parlements—to divide, if not to conquer, at least to defend—and to stress, as did Lafitau, that "it is the king and not the parlements that we ought to obey."[85] And better still to take the rhetorical offensive, to throw the parlements and their Jansenist apologists on the defensive by calling attention to the ecclesial laicism and political republicanism underlying their professions of Gallican and royalist faith. That rhetorical tactic was the more effective in that it was not simply "rhetorical," and had only to accent certain elements that, though muted, were audible enough in the rhetoric of judicial Jansenism.

Thus, for Abbé Bertrand Capmartin de Chaupy, writing on behalf of the royal cause in 1754, the original villain was Edmond Richer, who, first among Frenchmen, had laid down the anti-French principle that whatever "power gov-

80. Fauchois, "Les évêques émigrés et le royalisme pendant la Révolution," pp. 386–87.

81. Le Corgne de Launay, Les droits de l'épiscopat sur le second ordre, pp. 336–37.

82. Lefranc de Pompignan, Défense des Actes du clergé de France, pp. 202, 233.

83. Ibid., p. 348.

84. Christophe de Beaumont, Mandement et instruction pastorale . . . touchant l'autorité de l'église, p. 20.

85. [Lafitau], Entretiens d'Anselme et d'Isidore, pp. 109–10.

erned Society belonged to that society which retained its property while relinquishing only the exercise." Without either spiritual or temporal authorities on
their side, "the Jansenists," Chaupy held, "had found Richer's doctrine too favorable to their interests not to follow it"; Montesquieu, the *Encyclopedia* and the
anonymous author of the *Lettres historiques* then applied Richer's principle to the
French state; and finally "the Parlement [of Paris] let itself be carried away by the
torrent."[86] In two anonymous pamphlets, Chaupy artfully dissected the language
of Le Paige's *Lettres historiques* and several parlementary remonstrances, showing
how, outdoing the *Judicium Francorum*, they confounded "society" and "sovereignty," the better to concentrate effective power in the Parlement; and how,
following the memoir of 1730, they used the word "chief" in the place of "king,"
the better to demote him to the level of parlementary first president.[87] For Lafitau,
writing at the same time, Edmond Richer had only repeated what Calvin, Luther,
Almain, and Major had taught before, namely that "all jurisdiction over the
community belongs to that community in preference to those who are its chiefs."
Although religiously a mere "castoff from the sect of Calvin," Jansenism had
drawn its political principles from all of these sources and, beginning with the
heresy of "opposition itself to the Bull *[Unigenitus]*," had developed into a "sect
more opposed to royal authority" than any other before it, "aspiring everywhere
to a republican liberty." Like Capmartin de Chaupy, Lafitau held Jansenists
responsible for corrupting the parlements, which, following Richer, had recently
proclaimed "our kings . . . dependent on their subjects," transferred "supreme
authority to . . . the new nation," and anointed themselves as its mouthpiece."
Like Chaupy, too, he invoked the spectre of the executed Charles I of England,
victim of Parliament and sectarian Puritans, to dramatize judicial Jansenism's
threat to the throne.[88]

The case of the seventeenth-century English Revolution also suggested that
monarchy and episcopacy stood or fell together. Had not the Presbyterian revolt
against the "yoke of the episcopacy" been followed by an "unprecedented attack
on the Crown and the life of their King?" asked Le Corgne de Launay in defense
of the episcopacy?[89] In unison, devout apologists intoned this theme. "Let the
King only pierce the mystery of iniquity," and he "would clearly see that under the
pretense of giving the King all power over the altar, the sworn [Jansenist and

---

86. [Bertrand Capmartin de Chaupy], *Observations sur le refus que fait le Châtelet de reconnaître la
Chambre royale* (France, 1754), pp. 196–98.

87. Ibid., on "sovereignty" and "society," p. 199; on "chief," pp. 204, 206, 238–39; and in general,
pp. 196–241. See also his *Réflexions d'un avocat sur les remontrances du parlement, du 27 novembre, 1755, au
sujet du Grand conseil. A M. le président de Xxx* (London, 1756), pt. 1, pp. 14, 48–49, 52–53, 57–60, 64–66,
78–79, 80–83.

88. [Lafitau], *Entretiens d'Anselme et d'Isidore*, pp. 110–12.

89. Le Corgne de Launay, *Les droits de l'épiscopat sur le second ordre*, p. 5.

parlementaire] enemies of his glory aim at nothing less than the immolation of his own [secular] authority"—thus Lafitau, in support of the thesis that "heresy will never put up with a master."[90] "Episcopal authority is the strongest rampart of royal authority . . . [for] it is by means of the cooperation of these always united powers, lending each other mutual support, that the French monarchy has arrived at the point of perfection that has been the glory of the past two reigns"—thus the General Assembly of the Gallican Clergy, remonstrating to the king in defense of the Jesuits in 1762.[91] If the "property of the power of the [sacerdotal] keys" indeed belonged to the whole "Christian society," and the pastors enjoyed "only its usage"—thus Lefranc de Pompignan, reasoning from this well-known conciliarist principle—then "this supposed law should apply . . . to every kind of administration, and bishops in their sees would be no more than . . . mandatories of the people, if only because even the most absolute monarchs would . . . be little more than that on their thrones."[92]

The tactic of associating monarchy with episcopacy in a common defense against republicanism remained incomplete without a spirited defense of divine-right absolutism, however. Nor were midcentury devout apologists unworthy of this challenge, going as far if not further than anything that had ever been said on behalf of absolute monarchy in the seventeenth century. Without forswearing the traditional constraints of divine, natural, or "fundamental" law, they saw to it that these constraints remained metaphysical rather than constitutional ones—their king literally accounted to God alone—at least so far as the king's relations to his lay subjects were concerned.

Holding, with the jurist Antoine Loisel, that French kings owed their scepter to God and "their sword," Capmartin de Chaupy argued that the logic of Anselm's famous ontological argument for God's existence held for the French monarchy as well. That is, just as it sufficed to conceive of some desirable "perfection" in order to attribute it with confidence to God, so it sufficed to think of some "quality" whose possession would make the monarchy "purer" in order to conclude that the French monarchy in fact possessed it. Holding as well, this time with Justinian's Code, that the French king, like the Roman emperor, was a "living law" *(lex animata)*, Chaupy concluded that the "will of the king is the supreme law of the Realm"—except of course for "fundamental laws," a denomination he limited to precisely those laws that defined the monarchy as absolute and perpetual.[93] Whereas in judicial Jansenist parlance the king was at best the

90. Ibid., p. 191.

91. "Remontrances," in *Collection des procès-verbaux des assemblées du clergé de France*, vol. 8, pt. 2, no. 111 in "pièces justicatives," pp. 362–63.

92. Lefranc de Pompignan, *Défense des Actes du clergé de France*, pp. 222–23.

93. [Capmartin de Chaupy], *Observations sur le refus que fait le Châtelet de reconnaître la Chambre royale*, pp. 6–8.

"administrator" of his realm, for Chaupy the king was literally the "master" and "possessor" of his sovereignty. Putting into so many words the notorious definition of the state falsely attributed to Louis XIV, Chaupy maintained that in such "pure monarchies" as the French case, "the king is the state," that therefore "the will of the king is the will of the state."[94] For the Bishop of Sisteron, too, "the property of government," not just its administration, "resides in the king alone" because "his authority is independent of any other except God, who immediately confided it to him." The king was therefore not a "chief" but the "sole master, absolute and independent to command in the State."[95]

Both Chaupy and Lafitau similarly rang the tocsin of royal violence against the pretensions of the magistracy, whose only legitimate function, they maintained—quoting Louis XIII in 1635—was to dispense justice as between Master Peter and Master Paul. These pretensions were not only constitutional but social: their self-anointed title of "court of peers" did not prevent Chaupy from seeing them for the common "robins" and "intruders" they once were; and their self-imposed responsibilities as "assessors of the throne" did not dim Lafitau's memory that they had still harangued the king on bended knee as delegates of the Third Estate in 1614. Chaupy then compared the Parlement's "vain words" with the king's potentially "terrible blows," which could "dumbfound, transform, or disperse the parlements entirely," while Lafitau foresaw the day when, however it might hurt his goodness, His Majesty would be forced to "sever the head of this monster." There followed a list of suitably surgical suggestions for judicial and constitutional reform that remarkably anticipated the substance of Chancellor Maupeou's coup fifteen years later.[96]

The parti dévot's exaltation of absolute monarchy continued unabated in the debate accompanying the trial of the Jesuits. Provoking as it did the accusation that the Jesuits' constitutions were despotic and therefore incompatible with the constitution of France, this debate inevitably raised questions about the nature of that constitution, whether it provided for an absolute monarchy or one limited by the parlements on behalf of the nation. This opportunity to link the cause of the Jesuits to that of the monarchy was too good to miss. Speaking as an expert on his society, Claude Frey de Neuville, for example, thought the French king's authority more unlimited than even the much maligned Jesuit general's because, unlike his, the king's admitted of "neither inspection nor limitation." That authority was "entirely born, lives only in and through him, and only dies—or rather does not

94. [Capmartin de Chaupy], *Réflexions d'un avocat sur les remontrances du parlement*, pt. 1, pp. 53–55.

95. [Lafitau], *Entretiens d'Anselm et d'Isidore*, pp. 13–14, 195–96.

96. [Capmartin de Chaupy], *Réflexions d'un avocat sur les remontrances du parlement*, pt. 1, pp. 145–48; [Lafitau], *Entretiens d'Anselme et d'Isidore*, pp. 108–9, 191–95.

die at all—with him."[97] If with this parenthetical aside Neuville stopped short of entirely blurring the distinction between the king's two bodies, another Jesuit was less cautious when, in a justificatory memoir, he equated the king's will with the "sovereign depository and authority of the laws"—terms that he must have known were antithetical in parlementary parlance and that indeed conflated the two bodies.[98] Hardly less absolute than the others, Lefranc de Pompignan's monarch likewise received his sovereignty directly from God, responded "to God alone," owed "no account to his people," and "reigned alone in his states," except for help from his magistrates, who were "first subjects and nothing more."[99] Yet not all the talk about the absolute power and sovereignty of the king and about submission to him could entirely obscure the consideration that, in the minds of these devout apologists, the Gallican Church, too, possessed a sovereign and independent if spiritual domain, and that the monarchy's writ stopped where the church's began. To the extent possible, they couched this incipient no to the French Caesar in their accustomed language of absolute power, obligation, and obedience. Consider, for example, the following typical passage from Lefranc's *Défense:*

> There is nothing wiser nor more prudent—no, there is not so much as anything prudent and wise in religion, except to obey the Church without examining apart from her. Jesus Christ is the guarantor of what she teaches. With such a guarantee one need not fear seduction. The pressing obligation to submit is inseparable from the absolute certainty of not being mistaken. In that respect princes have no privilege that distinguishes them from other men. They would be the most unfortunate of men if they had. Their happiness consists in being children of the Christian Church, and being obligated in that capacity to listen to her voice with the same submission as the very least of their subjects.[100]

The same point could be put more actively without leaving the language of command and obedience, as did Christophe de Beaumont when he reminded his parishioners that within the church it was for priests "to command" and for kings "to obey," and as did the General Assembly's *Actes* of 1765, which recalled that, as one of the two "powers" instituted by God, the church "governed" as well as the state.[101]

Where this language faltered, where it threatened to break down altogether,

97. [Claude Frey or Pierre-Claude de Neuville], *Observations sur l'institut de la société des Jésuites* (Avignon, 1761), p. 45.

98. *Réponse à quelques objections publiées contre l'institut des Jésuites,* in BN: CJF, Ms. 1612, fol. 186.

99. Lefranc de Pompignan, *Défense des Actes du clergé de France,* pp. 215, 217, 232–33.

100. Ibid., p. 324.

101. Christophe de Beaumont, *Mandement et instruction pastorale . . . touchant l'autorité de l'église,* pp. 20–21.

was precisely at the point of conflict between the two powers at which submission to the hierarchical church clearly entailed disobedience to the state. And for devout spokesmen habituated to a plenum of power and obedience, it was precisely such a frightening gap between the two powers that opened up with the reorientation of royal sacramental policy between 1754 and 1757, only to grow wider with the government's acquiescence in the suppression of the Jesuits and growing nonenforcement of the suppression of Protestants.

What to do? How to acknowledge the need for disobedience without uttering these accursed syllables? In a tack taken by many of his colleagues, Lafitau held that the royal Declaration of 2 September 1754, which imposed silence on the subject of *Unigenitus*, simply did not apply to bishops, duty-bound as they were to proclaim all truth, especially since previous declarations of the sort had nominally excepted the bishops. But just in case the Declaration of 1754 differed from its predecessors in this respect—he well knew it did—he added for good measure that "however sovereign and independent royal authority might be in relation to everyone except God, it could never have authorized the inclusion of bishops in the silence it has imposed," because "silence," as he explained it, "is itself a true language for the church, by means of which she teaches even when she hushes, . . . and opposes when she does not protest." Sooner that they be flagellated in synagogues like Christ's disciples, Lafitau concluded, than that they "apostatize by holding their peace."[102] Others were blunter. Caritat de Condorcet, Bishop of Auxerre, for example, publicly admonished the king that in relation to the church he was a mere "protector" and no longer a master, while Le Corgne de Launay, if he was indeed the author of the General Assembly's *Actes*, warned the king that it was "better to obey God than man."[103]

Perhaps the parti dévot's most politically subversive utterance during the latter 1750s and 1760s was its chronic mispunctuation of Saint Paul's well-known injunction to obedience in Romans 13:1–2: "Let every soul be subject to the higher powers, for there is no power but of God: the powers that be are ordained of God" (or in the Vulgate's Latin: *Omnia anima potestatibus sublimioribus subdita sit. Non enim potestas nisi a Deo; quae autem sunt, a Deo ordinatae sunt.*) Now where most editions of the Vulgate generally placed the comma between the *sunt* and *a Deo*, conveying the meaning that all powers and principalities without exception were ordained by God, both Christophe de Beaumont's incendiary mandamus of 19 September 1756 and the General Assembly's manifesto of 1765 placed it between

102. [Lafitau], *Entretiens d'Anselme et d'Isidore*, pp. 177–78.

103. Caritat de Condorcet, Bishop of Auxerre, *Mandement de Monseigneur l'évêque d'Auxerre, publié le dimanche 7 novembre dans son église cathédrale* (Auxerre, 1756), p. 4, in BN: Mss. Fr. 22093 (98); *Actes de l'Assemblée générale du clergé de France sur la religion*, p. 43.

Deo and *ordinatae*, suggesting that only "ordained" or legitimate powers enjoyed God's imprimatur, and that it was permitted to resist ones that did not.[104] To judicial Jansenists posing as the monarchy's best defenders, these mistranslations and mispunctuations were all too calculated—proof positive, if any were needed, of the parti dévot's subversive inheritance from the Catholic League. And although these suspicions wildly overshot the mark, they were hardly allayed by Lefranc de Pompignan's defense of the dubious punctuation of Romans 13:1–2, to the effect that the Latin indeed allowed for a distinction between "legitimately instituted power" and "irregular" or "vicious" power, and that the real distinction was "the power of a magistrate who governed a civil society" and that of Saint Augustine's "brigand or pirate who infected the roads or seas."[105] Although these caveats did not affect the episcopacy's loyalty in the longer run, they did so in the shorter run, being a factor in the bishops' abandonment of the monarchy in its penultimate hour of need, in 1788.

Now if defending themselves against judicial Jansenism's subversive appropriation of the Gallican label prompted second thoughts about obedience to divine-right monarchy in the minds of some devout apologists, that defensive stance put even greater strains on their loyalty to the more traditional, or conciliar, tenets of the Gallican legacy. Confronted, in other words, by a Gallicanism construed to mean the democratization and laicization of a church wholly under the thumb of the state, the Gallican episcopacy was bound to suffer a kind of identity crisis and to become, in short, less Gallican. As usual, it was Lefranc de Pompignan who best articulated his colleagues' dilemma. Insisting, as has been noted, on the Gallican Church's independence from the state and describing its government as a papal "monarchy tempered by an [episcopal] aristocracy," he admitted that if choose he must between being the pope's vicar and the people's mandatory, accountable to lay judges, to say nothing of Jansenist "women," he would undoubtedly embrace the first. For most practical purposes, at least, the ultramontanist theologians maintained the church as a "mixture of aristocracy with monarchy" instead of reducing it to the "shameful slavery of the state" or the "tumults and discords" of "popular tribunals."[106]

A compromising admission, this, confirming judicial Jansenism's worst suspicions. These soon found additional evidence to fasten upon. In response, for example, to the accusation that the General Assembly of 1765 had avoided the

---

104. Ibid., p. 15, which translated the passage as though this were the punctuation in Latin: "Deux puissances sont établies pour gouverner les hommes: l'autorité sacrée des Pontifes et celle des Rois; l'une et l'autre viennent de Dieu, de qui émane tout pouvoir bien ordonné sur la terre." On Christophe de Beaumont's punctuation of the same passage, see [Jean-Pierre Grosley], *Lettre d'un solitaire sur le mandement de M. l'archévêque de Paris, du 1 mars 1757* (n.p., 1757), pp. 9–10.

105. Lefranc de Pompignan, *Défense des Actes du clergé de France*, pp. 474–75.

106. Ibid., pp. 203, 205.

expressions consecrated by that of 1682, Lefranc de Pompignan pleaded guilty to the opinion that "whatever the respect" that subsequent assemblies of the clergy had paid to the one held in 1682, they had "never considered its authority as equal to that of the universal church or an ecumenical council."[107] Such was also the judgment of the archbishops of Narbonne, Lyon, and Toulouse and the Bishop of Orléans, who, appointed by Louis XV to examine the high view of the Gallican Declaration held by François de Fitz-James, the jansénisant Bishop of Soissons, rather inclined to view it as a venerable but debatable "opinion" or "sentiment" that did not fall under the heading of faith or dogma.[108] All, however, were outdone by Henri-Jacques de Montesquiou, Bishop of Sarlat, who informed his diocesan clergy in a published pastoral instruction that God's word was "not the foundation of our [Gallican] liberties, for the word being unchangeable and uniform, all the churches that do not possess such liberties would then be governed against the word of God."[109] About the same time, the Bishop of Langres, Montmorin de Saint-Herem, gave it out as his opinion that the Declaration of 1682 was more than just an opinion. But in the same breath he told his diocesan clergy that the "particular certitude" attributable to the article concerning the independence of the temporal power was "much superior to that of the other articles, leaving his clergy to wonder exactly what he thought of these.[110]

This strategic retreat from the Declaration of 1682 was not without repercussions on the rhetorical tactic of associating throne with altar. For it threatened to transform the hitherto touted alliance between absolute throne and episcopal altar into an alliance between absolute throne and papal altar. As early as 1753 the marquis d'Argenson complained of an "insane and fanatical" mandamus by the Bishop of Montauban, which attributed France's good fortune to "papism" and England's many misfortunes to "heresy." England's revolutions of the previous century and consequent exile of her legitimate kings were presented as the direct consequence not of Puritans or Presbyterians but of the earlier secession from the papal fold.[111] D'Argenson was probably not imagining things, because the Bishop of Sisteron, said much the same thing just a few years later. Although the altar he defended was in part an episcopal one—"the bishops should be sole masters with their [papal] chief to command in the church"—he also disarmingly noted that his

107. Ibid., p. 472.

108. *Mémoire au sujet de l'instruction pastorale*, in François de Fitz-James, *Oeuvres posthumes de Monseigneur le duc de Fitz-James évesque de Soissons*, 2 vols. (Avignon, 1769), 2:197–200, 212–13, 224–25. Fitz-James offending pastoral instruction of 1762 is to be found in ibid., 1:18–20.

109. Henri-Jacques de Montesquiou, *Instruction pastorale de Monseigneur l'évêque de Sarlat au clergé séculier et régulier et à tous les fidèles de son diocèse. 28 novembre 1764* (n.p., n.d.), pp. 11, 16.

110. Montmorin de Saint-Herem, *Lettre pastorale de Monseigneur l'évêque de Langres au clergé de son diocèse. 1 août 1763* (n.p., n.d.), p. 9.

111. René-Louis de Voyer, marquis d'Argenson, *Journal et mémoires du marquis d'Argenson*, ed. E.-J.-B. Rathery, 9 vols. (Paris, 1911), 8:148.

judicial Jansenist opponents readily abided "neither king nor pope at their head."[112]

The suppression of the Jesuits and criticism of the General Assembly's *Actes* finally hardened these reactions into the form of a litany. The *Reflections of a Papist and Royalist Frenchman,* the title of another pro-Jesuit pamphlet published in 1764, by itself speaks volumes, as does a *Letter from a Cosmopolite* anonymously published the same year, which announced the formation of a conspiracy against throne and altar.[113] The reason that the Jesuits succumbed in France, explained the anonymous author of a pro-Jesuit pamphlet published in 1761, was that "in France the Jesuits were too Roman and in Rome they were too French." That is, he enlarged, that the Jesuits were "at once Papist and Royalist, and those who condemned them mean to put up with neither Pope nor King."[114] Yet another pious pamphleteer raised a "cry of indignation" in reaction to Le Blanc de Castillon's *Réquisitoire,* and, in his "double title" of "Catholic" and "Frenchman," called for "vengeance" and "a reparation" on behalf of both a Bourbon "Crowned Head" and a papal "Holy See," seat of the "First of Pastors."[115] Well before it described a political reality of the counterrevolution and the Bourbon Restoration, an absolute Bourbon "throne" and a papal "altar" began huddling together, if not in fact, at least in the rhetoric of the mid-eighteenth-century parti dévot in France.

Religion and "Reason" in Eighteenth-Century France

These devout defenders of throne and altar directed their shafts not only against Jansenist "sectaries" and parlementary Gallicans, but also against philosophes, or those whom Lefranc de Pompignan called "the so-called bold thinkers *(esprits forts)* of our day."[116] Yet in rhetorically linking Jansenist magistrates with incredulous philosophes, devout apologists were only imitating the tactics of Jansenists, who from the late 1740s regularly denounced the collusion between philosophes and Jesuits. By minimizing the gravity of original sin, the depths of the fall, and human nature's consequent dependency on divine grace, the Molinistic or neo-Pelagian theology—so ran the Jansenist argument—prepared the way for the franker philosophic rehabilitation of human nature and moral validation of ego-

112. [Lafitau], *Entretiens d'Anselme et d'Isidore,* pp. 110–11, 195–97.

113. *Réflexions impartiales d'un François papiste et roialiste sur le réquisitoire du maître Omer Joly de Fleury et l'arrêt du parlement de Paris du 1 juin 1764* ("à Alais: chez Narcisse Buisson imprimeur à l'enseigne du probabalisme, ce 12 juin 1764"); and *Lettre d'un cosmopolite sur le réquisitoire de M. Joly de Fleury, et sur l'arrêt du parlement de Paris du 2 janvier 1764* (Paris, 1765). See also *NE* 28 Aug. 1765, p. 142, on the subject of this *Lettre.*

114. *Compte rendu au public des comptes rendus aux divers parlements et autres cours supérieures,* 2 vols. (Paris, 1765), 1:vii–viii.

115. *Cri d'un François catholique après la lecture du réquisitoire de M. Le Blanc de Castillon, sur les Actes du clergé* (Soleure, 1766), pp. 12, 22.

116. Lefranc de Pompignan, *Défense des Actes du clergé de France,* p. 207.

centric self-interest. How comes it, asked the *Nouvelles ecclésiastiques* in its review of Claude-Adrien Helvétius's *De l'esprit (On the Mind)* in 1759, "that the Buffons, the Montesquieus, the De Prades, the Encyclopedists, [and the author of] *De l'esprit* should have dared at this moment to unfurl the standard of impiety?" His answer was that these "unbelievers . . . had had precursors": namely the Jesuits, what with their "Pelagian doctrine and the corrupt ethic that flows from it, and which for the past two centuries has inundated the entire earth like a deluge."[117]

The prevalence of these mutual denunciations of complicity with "philosophism" or "encyclopedism" during the 1750s and 1760s reflects the emergence of the Enlightenment—or the "lights," as contemporaries called the movement—as a self-conscious movement and contestant for attention in the public sphere. For the same two decades that weathered the refusal-of-sacraments controversy and the suppression of the Jesuits also witnessed the publication of Montesquieu's *Spirit of the Laws,* Buffon's *Natural History,* Voltaire's *Philosophical Dictionary,* Rousseau's *Emile* and *Social Contract,* and volume after volume of Diderot's and d'Alembert's *Encyclopedia*—the defining works, in a word, of the French Enlightenment.

In these and other works, as is well known, self-styled philosophes or men of letters *(gens de lettres)* set out to replace concern for confessional orthodoxy with at most a tolerant natural religion, loyalty to Christendom with dedication to civilization, the works of Catholic charity with the practice of beneficence or *bienfaisance,* the quest for a transcendent *summum bonum* with a terrestrial happiness *(bonheur),* and hope in divine providence with the prospect of secular progress. As necessary conditions to these goals, the philosophes rejected the doctrine of original sin in favor of a malleable if not infinitely perfectible human nature and rejected faith or even unaided reason in favor of a reason in harness to experience and the observation of nature. This agenda clearly set this nascent "party of humanity" off from either Jansenist or pious parties; and enlightened manifestos stood out by virtue of the pox they pronounced on both religious houses. Indeed, one of the most salient features of the eighteenth-century French intellectual landscape was this sharp triangular set-to between Jansenist, devout, and philosophe. This situation differed markedly from elsewhere in Catholic Europe, where a more muted Enlightenment made common cause with what was called Jansenism, as well as from Protestant Europe, where lights often shaded imperceptibly into religious dissent.[118]

---

117. *NE* 23 Jan. 1759, pp. 17–18.

118. See, for example, Emile Appolis, *Le "Tiers parti" catholique au dix-huitième siècle* (Paris, 1960); Samuel J. Miller, "Enlightened Catholicism" in his *Portugal and Rome, c. 1748–1830: An Aspect of the Catholic Enlightenment* (Rome, 1978); Bernard Plongeron, "Recherches sur 'l'Aufklärung' catholique en Europe occidental, 1770–1830," *RHMC* 16 (1969):555–605; and Dale Van Kley, "Piety and Politics in the Century of Lights," in *The Cambridge History of Eighteenth-Century Political Thought* (Cambridge, forthcoming).

Such characterizations of the French Enlightenment during the 1960s and 1970s as Peter Gay's tended to emphasize the movement's empiricism, environmentalism, and realism.[119] The evidence that this historiography plausibly pointed to is that most of the philosophes were self-conscious converts to John Locke's empiricism, eventually transforming the English philosopher's thesis of the experiential origin of ideas into the dogma that all thought is at bottom sensation. Just about all French philosophes also disavowed the deductive rationalism of their continental Cartesian forebears, replacing their proud and overambitious "systematizing mind-set" (esprit de systéme) with a modest and undogmatic "systematic spirit" (esprit systématique). But to have preached Lockean empiricism is one thing; to have consistently practiced it is another. More recent studies of the French Enlightenment have uncovered the continuing influence of normative notions of nature, natural law, and natural rights—notions derivative from "right reason" but hardly from empirical observation—as well as of elements of Cartesian rationalism.[120] It is arguably the combination of Lockean empiricism with Cartesian rationalism that gave the French Enlightenment its peculiar punch. It is hard, for example, to imagine how Locke's doctrine of the mind's dependency on sense perception for ideas could have led Diderot to materialism and atheism had not the Cartesian legacy's radical separation of body from soul obliged him to eliminate "soul" from his epistemology as soon as any sensate origin of thought was conceded.

The same holds for the French Enlightenment's political thought. By itself, empiricism's insistence on the experiential origin of thought tended to justify all beliefs, customs, and institutions as natural and inevitable responses to their different cultural and geographical environments, as indeed it nearly did in the case of Montesquieu's Spirit of the Laws. At the end of the century—and in reaction to the French Revolution—enlightened empiricism fortified that strain in an emergent conservatism that valorized the inertia of tradition and custom over rational deliberation with a view toward change. When and to the degree that philosophes found their own political voice in the political conflicts of the day, they held a close empirical examination of state and society in tension with a normative and rationalist critique of them.

But with some obvious exceptions, that is what the philosophes did not do in the 1750s and 1760s. For it was hard for people who put no stock in the sacraments to take sides in such controversies as the refusal of sacraments to Jansenists. If, then, the French Enlightenment is understood as the thought of the philosophes, and if politicization be thought of as active engagement in the political conflicts of

119. Peter Gay, The Enlightenment: An Interpretation, 2 vols. (New York, 1967–69).
120. For example, Keith M. Baker, Condorcet: From Natural Philosophy to Social Mathematics (Chicago, 1975).

the day, then politicization came late to that Enlightenment. If, however, the Enlightenment is understood more broadly as a set of secular appeals, whether to reason, nature, or sensate experience, that replaced older ones such as to revelation, tradition, or historical precedents, then that Enlightenment indeed played a role in the confessional conflicts of these decades in the form of "enlightened" appeals by some of the antagonists in these conflicts, whether otherwise enlightened or not. Although these appeals did not govern the direction of either the judicial Jansenist or devout positions, they took each line of argument further than traditional ones might have done. Discernible also is a tendency for the natural-law legacy and rationalism to side with judicial Jansenism, and for empiricism to come to the aid of the clergy and the parti dévot.

A good example of reason and the natural-law tradition in the service of judicial Jansenist agenda is the barrister François Richer's *On the Authority of the Clergy, and of the Power of the Political Magistrate in the Exercise of the Function of the Ecclesiastical Ministry*. This two-volume treatise, published on the occasion of the controversy over the General Assembly's *Actes* of 1765, was read widely enough to have later circulated under Jansenist auspices in Maria Theresa's Austria.[121] Like the Rousseau of the *Social Contract*, Richer began with the question of why, given natural liberty, people had everywhere accepted the restraints of society. Richer found the answer less in technological prowess than in the long period of helplessness preceding maturity, rendering stable and authoritarian families indispensable. But after these families had broken up due to the death of patriarchal chiefs, the "passions and the inherent vices of humanity" created a state of perpetual war, whence the need to appoint a "conventional chief" in place of the "natural chief," heralding the advent of the state. In the resulting social contract, the chief or "sovereign" agreed to promulgate "the most suitable rules" for the general welfare, in return for which the "nation" promised "the most prompt and blind obedience." The Hobbesian rigor of the contract's terms was nonetheless softened by their apparent compatibility with the chief's quality as a "representative," even "mandatory" of the nation.[122]

The author credited these constitutional insights to the help of "reason" attuned to the teachings of "nature," although he also thought them confirmed by biblical authority. These sources again collaborated to produce another principle, that the "conservation and the agreements of terrestrial life" had been the "unique motive" behind the formation of civil societies." Religion had had no hand in it.

---

121. [François Richer], *De l'autorité de clergé, et du pouvoir du magistrat politique sur l'exercise des fonctions du ministère ecclésiastique*, 2 vols. (Amsterdam, 1766). On the authorship of the book, see Edmond Préclin, *Les jansénistes du dix-huitième siècle et la Constitution civile du clergé: Le développement du richérisme, sa propagation dans le bas clergé* (Paris, 1929), p. 416. On the circulation of the book in Austria, ibid., p. 432.

122. [Richer], *De l'autorité du clergé*, 1:1—27.

Before divine revelation, "the cult inspired by enlightened nature and guided by reason" was not dependent upon society for its celebration, for "each man" in this Rousseauian state of nature had fulfilled all he owed to his creator "within the most profound solitude and without any sort of communication with his fellows." The effect of this account of the origin of the state was to give priority to the interests of civil society over those of religion, at least so far as temporal arrangements were concerned. Nor had the advent of Christianity much altered this primitive state of affairs. For Christianity had established an altogether different sort of society—the Church—consisting of a "corps of travelers on earth" en route to their "other country" or "the bosom of God himself." In contrast to the State, which employed physical force to rule corporeal bodies, the Church employed the gentler arms of grace and reason to persuade "our souls, or pure spirits" to accept its authority. Such spiritual authority as the Church rightfully possessed was moreover the property of the whole Church, or the assembly of all the faithful; the ecclesiastical hierarchy only administered the power of the keys. Though it was true that priests received their ministry directly from Christ, it was "no less true," Richer insisted, that they exercised it "only in the name of the Church" and could undertake nothing "without its presumed consent."[123]

Much of this seems vaguely familiar. It is as if Richer had imperceptibly strayed from the stark, austere plain of simple contracts and states of nature into a thickening forest of scriptural and early Church precedents. Before he could proceed any further, however, another contract intervened, this one between the Church and the prince become Christian. For when the band of travelers which was the Church had first asked the prince for the "liberty of passage" through his lands, the prince's duty to maintain "good order" had obliged him to undertake a detailed examination of "all the views and intentions of these foreigners," including their doctrine, morals, liturgy, and government. None of this meant, to believe the author, that the prince had actually judged dogma; he had only ascertained that the "good order of the State" was in no way compromised. If as a result of this examination the travelers had obtained a safe conduct, they for their part had agreed to abide strictly by the Scriptures and the tradition of the early Church, while the Sovereign for his part had sworn "to maintain them in the free exercise of the dogmas, moral code and discipline."[124]

Far from bringing him back to philosophical states of nature and natural religion, however, this second contract only hastened this pilgrim's progress toward the promised land of judicial Jansenist conclusions. For this contract, not as two-sided as it might appear, had already put the "Sovereign" as "political magistrate" in control of everything affecting "good order," therefore everything

123. Ibid.: on origin of cult, 1:1–27, on status of church in state, 1:27–32, 39–40; and on authority within church, 1:75–77, 107.

124. Ibid., 1:125–29.

external about the Church. The prince's promise to protect the Church's doctrine and discipline—read: his rights as "outside bishop" and "protector of the canons"—further entitled him to protest these rules against the ministers themselves. Hence, for example, the prince's obligation to oppose any novel doctrine—the bull *Unigenitus?*—that an ecclesiastical cabal might attempt to foist upon the Church. Hence, too, his obligation to examine all the exterior circumstances of a Church council to ascertain its ecumenicity, as well as his right to impose silence on religious disputes, invalidate unjust excommunications, prevent public refusals of sacraments—all this and more, without ever infringing upon the spiritual. Most of this could have come from Le Paige or Maultrot.[125]

Not all of it, however. For the treatise's enlightened social contracts and states of nature do not simply serve as neutral containers of Jansenist and Gallican contents. Rather, they display a chrysallis-like effect, in some cases making more explicit what was implicit before; in others, changing the contents radically. More explicit are the author's transformation of the Catholic priest into moral henchman for the State—"the organ of those charged with announcing the divine word ought always to be at the orders of the government"—as well as his starker statement of judicial Jansenism's criteria for the infallibility of Church councils—"only when human passions are silent" does "the necessary liberty to receive the Holy Spirit" obtain. Examples of radical change are his advocacy of the marriage of priests—the "good order" of the State includes the propagation of the human species—and his willingness to legalize divorce, which he justified by distinguishing between the civil contract, or "matter," and the inessential sacrament or its "benediction." These modest proposals, along with the contention that ecclesiastical property was a contradiction in terms, point clearly to the legislation of the Revolution.[126]

Judicial Jansenists were not alone, of course, in having recourse to reason and natural law to argue their case. That their devout opponents could do at least as much on behalf of throne and altar is apparent in the case of the redoubtable Lefranc de Pompignan, who, in his defense of the General Assembly of 1765, singled out Richer's more "philosophical" treatise for malign attention. Tactically postulating society's emergence from a state of nature, the future bishop of Vienne first argued the "enlightened" utility of religion by contesting the principle that mundane considerations alone could have effected such a transition. Religion, he argued, entered into the very "constitution of every body politic, and it would

125. Ibid., 1:393–96, 414–21; 2:8–9, 38–43, 95–99. For an idea of how far he strays from the Enlightenment, consider the following utterance: "or il suffit en matière de religion, qu'une doctrine soit nouvelle et inconnue aux premiers tems, pour être fausse" (ibid., 1:133).

126. Ibid.: on nature of priest and authority of general councils, 1:211–14, 238, 247–48, 418; on marriage of priests and divorce, 1:146–59, 190–93; and on ecclesiastical property, 1:151–53, 163–65, 174–75, 189–92.

have been impossible to associate men under a civil government if Religion, anterior to these human establishments, had not been the foundation and the tie."[127] Having sufficiently loosened Richer's social contract to incorporate religion at its core, the bishop of Le Puy next bore down on the principle that "by natural law and imprescriptible right" every society possessed the "power of government" and only delegated the usage to its chiefs—the principle of national sovereignty, in other words, stated in judicial Jansenist terms. Accepting, again, the notion of a passage from a state of nature to one of civil government accompanied by a contract, Pompignan's second step was to contest the principle that it was sovereignty itself—the power of life and death over other humans—which the community could have ever delegated to any government by virtue of natural law. Given the "natural equality" of the "primitive state," the bishop cogently argued that nature gave to no person or group any right over human life. Sheer numbers or express conventions did not legitimate a power that no one rightfully possessed over either one's own life or anyone else's, even if exercised in the act of self defense. Rendered powerless by this very equality to mitigate the fall's disorderly effects, men had received from the hand of their creator the gift of sovereignty necessary to create governments. "It is He who has come to their aid. His absolute power had enabled their impotence." With a stridency and accent that looked forward to the abbé Barruel and counterrevolutionary thought in general, the bishop of Le Puy concluded that the "Supreme Arbiter of their life" was "also the unique and necessary principle of all sovereign authority."[128]

While Lefranc de Pompignan wielded reason and natural law in defense of divine-right monarchy, the anonymous author of *The Respective Rights of Church and State* showed how empiricism could be used in defense of privilege and Catholic tradition.[129] But not before a feint in the opposite direction, for his argument, much like Richer's, began with a contractual transition from nature to the state that subordinated religious to civil laws, and then proceeded to a subsequent contract that subordinated Christianity to the state's approval and inspection. But at precisely this juncture his path diverged sharply from Richer's. This was due perhaps in part to his accent on "sentiment" as opposed to reason, but mainly to his Montesquieuian, empirical, yet unimpeachably "enlightened" emphasis on the "strange circumstantial vicissitudes" and "conjunctural whimsicalities" encountered by different peoples. The main effect of these, in his view, had been to refract the application of natural law into the bewildering variety of particular laws that we observe. Though natural law had inspired the formation of all constitutions, each "legislator" had had to adjust it according to the nation's physical and climatic circumstances, "factitious inclinations," and even errors, but

127. Lefranc de Pompignan, *Défense des Actes du clergé de France*, pp. 132–34.
128. Ibid., pp. 206–10, 233.
129. *Les droits respectifs de l'état et de l'église rappellés à leurs principes* (Avignon, 1766).

infallibly with a view toward the "best possible condition." Even the most apparently bizarre laws were therefore "nonetheless respectable" because the "idea of the best possible" had dictated their formation; to understand them a detailed empirical examination of the circumstances that produced them was necessary. The science of politics was therefore not reducible to a "system of geometrical order" but was rather a "calculus of proximities and simple approximations."[130]

The author's more empirical cast of mind thus led him to a proto-Burkean veneration for the delicately complex and infinitely variegated texture of all positive law, seen as the embodiment of the wisdom of the past. Consistent with himself, he did not exclude the clergy's privileged constitutional position from his all-embracing ken. The existence of a separate and even coercive ecclesiastical jurisdiction, the clergy's "titles of honor" and "exterior prerogatives," the Church's extensive property holdings—all these represented "universal reason's" infallible application of "natural law" to achieve the "best possible," which included the respect due to the ministers of a religion serving as spiritual foundation to the State. For "if in order to assure the repose of society it was necessary to fortify the observation of human laws by means of a principle of religion and a motive of conscience," was it not "equally advantageous," he asked, "to imprint on the people's soul a particular sentiment of respect for the censors of their conscience and the ministers of their religion?"[131]

By the 1760s, then, if not earlier, enlightened concepts began to find their way into the Unigenitus-related debates and to radicalize the opposing positions to some degree. The other side of the coin is that these controversies also began to attract the attention of some philosophes and to politicize them to some degree. The point is not exactly that the French philosophes were more Catholic than they knew—that they were, of course, is Carl Becker's argument in his classic The Heavenly City of the Eighteenth-Century Philosophers—but rather that proximity to the "old" politics of religious controversy helped politicize an Enlightenment that had kept its political message mainly implicit until then. For not all philosophes viewed the Unigenitus-related controversies from heights so Olympian as Voltaire's before 1770, or in a manner quite so megalomaniacal as that of Rousseau, who thought that he had spared France a revolution in 1753 because he had distracted the nation's attention from the refusal of sacraments to that of the comparative virtues of Italian and French music.[132]

Take, for example, the case of René-Louis de Voyer, marquis d'Argenson,

130. Ibid.: on contract, pp. 1–19; on empirical accommodations, pp. 19–24.

131. Ibid., pp. 64–66, 71–73, 102–4. I accept the corollary that Edmund Burke himself is to be regarded as a legitimate child of Enlightenment thought. On this, see Frederick Drayer, "The Genesis of Burke's Reflections," JMH 50 (Sept. 1978):462–79.

132. Jean-Jacques Rousseau, Les confessions, ed. Jacques Voisines, Classiques Garnier series (Paris, 1964), pp. 455–56.

who served Louis XV as an intendant and minister of foreign affairs before finishing life as a disgruntled memoirist in the late 1740s and 1750s. Although his biography belongs to the first half of the century, d'Argenson may lay claim to the title of at least a minor philosophe in his various capacities as a member and the memoirist of the philosophical Entresol Club, a protégé of the abbé de Saint-Pierre, a lifelong friend and correspondent of Voltaire, and the author of some highly "philosophical" *Considérations* on the French government.[133] Optimistic about humanity, he tended to divinize the "dictates of nature," regarded "self love" as the mainspring of moral action, and urged a program of local self-government and economic laissez faire long before physiocracy attached its label to a similar combination of proposals later in the century.[134] At the same time his enlightenment"was not unalloyed with religious elements, bearing as he did the name of a family with impeccably devout credentials. His grandfather had been a charter member and memoirist of the Company of the Holy Sacrament and his father the Paris lieutenant of police who had overseen the destruction of Port-Royal, while his younger brother, the comte d'Argenson, championed the cause of the episcopacy against the Jansenists and parlements as a secretary of state and unofficial head of the parti dévot at Versailles.

Whether as proto-philosophe or secularized dévot, d'Argenson began his career as a sincere if reforming royalist. For in the 1730s, when he probably wrote his *Considérations,* the monarchy was the only conceivable agent for the socially egalitarian and democratic reforms he contemplated. What he expected of royal authority was to continue to "inundate" France until, having "overturned every remaining obstacle," nothing would remain for it to do except to identify its "interest" entirely with that of its equalized subjects and, enlightened by their "counsels of reason," govern with their maximum bonheur in view.[135] That the attainment of these aims required absolutist means, d'Argenson made clear by specifying that "the right of the Commons and Parliament in England, [as well as] that of the national and provincial estates or [parlementary] remonstrances in our country, are not so much remedies as evils, seeing that they divide public power which ought to be one and single-minded."[136]

While administrative democracy would assure it of reason and economic freedoms would orient it toward happiness, the authority of this monarchy

133. René-Louis de Voyer, marquis d'Argenson, *Considérations sur le gouvernement ancien et présent de la France* (Amsterdam, 1765). D'Argenson is treated as a philosophe by Peter Gay in *Voltaire's Politics: The Poet as Realist* (New York, 1965), pp. 103–8.

134. On the thought of the marquis d'Argenson and his relation to Saint-Pierre and the Entresol, see Nannerl O. Keohane, *Philosophy and the State in France: The Renaissance to the Enlightenment* (Princeton, N.J., 1980), pp. 362–91.

135. D'Argenson, *Considérations*, pp. 104–5, 156–57.

136. Ibid., pp. 19–20.

"would . . . thereby be balanced but not shared."[137] The local democracies that d'Argenson envisioned would have been advisory, not legislative; the freedoms he urged would have been civil, not political. Neither would he have challenged the Bodinian indivisibility of monarchical authority that, for all d'Argenson's abhorrence for Turkish "despotism," would have remained as all-powerful as his mentor Saint-Pierre's *despoticité* or the later physiocrats' "legal despotism."[138]

What a contrast, then, between this advocate of enlightened absolutism in the 1730s and the proparlementary memoirist of the 1750s. Already in 1749 he sounded like a radical English commonwealthman, regretting that by means of a "few court favors" the royal ministry was successfully "corrupting and winning over the Parlement of Paris and some of the provincial ones, just as the kings of England did to their national Parliament."[139] In the following years d'Argenson's sympathy with the Paris Parlement seemed to increase in proportion as it proved its independence from the monarchy and willingness to resist the royal will. By 1754 he thought that "only the Parlement could save the State" in the event of a fiscal disaster because people "had to enjoy our confidence, and we know how useful a *national senate* is to the realm."[140] That d'Argenson had indeed come to think of the Parlement as in some sense representing the nation and entitled to a legislative share in the exercise of sovereignty he made clear a year and a half later when, reacting to the Le Paigian thesis that the parlements made up so many "classes" of a single national parlement, he commented that "this points directly to an assembly of the Estates General of the realm or—what would have an even greater effect—to the union of all the parlements joined to the princes and peers. Whence," he further speculated, "the makings of a national government, presenting moreover this additional advantage: that the clergy plays no part in it."[141]

"That villainous sacerdoce"—it is surely d'Argenson's disgust with the clergy, particularly its performance in the refusal-of-sacraments controversy, that best accounts for his disillusionment with the monarchy and growing sympathy for the parlements in the 1750s. Other candidates as catalysts in d'Argenson's political reactions are not wanting: in his own words, the "little people weighed down [by royal taxation] and wasted by misery; the financiers, "triumphant over

137. D'Argenson, *Considérations*. pp. 104–5.

138. Ibid., pp. 25–26. For the abbé de Saint-Pierre's espousal of *despoticité* and its relation to the thought of Boulainvilliers and d'Argenson, I am indebted to an unpublished paper by Harold Ellis entitled "Montesquieu and his Predecessors" delivered in a session on "The Uses of History in Eighteenth-Century France" at the annual meeting of the American Historical Association in Chicago, December 1986.

139. D'Argenson, *Journal et mémoires* (April 1749), 5:143–44. This account of the course of d'Argenson's political thought is obviously at variance to that of Peter Gay, according to whom he remained hostile to the parlements. See his *The Enlightenment: An Interpretation*, 2:503.

140. Ibid. (9 October 1755), 9:104–5.

141. Ibid. (4 July 1756), 9:294.

everything, and busily reviving the reign of the Jews"; and, last but not least, a "philosophical wind from England", which, he thought, increased the attraction for a "free and antimonarchical government." Yet none of these considerations compete successfully, in his *Journal*, with the attention given to the refusal-of-sacraments controversy and other *Unigenitus*-related issues. It was the "villainous sacerdoce," he thought, and not the Parlement, that had really undermined royal authority. "Who in effect," he asked, "attacks it and disobeys it, if not the bishops? And who supports it for the sake of [religious] peace and [ecclesiastical] good order, if not the Parlement?" Instead of his hoped-for enlightened monarchy leveling corporate barriers in order to introduce democracy and the rule of reason, it was, he now realized, "the Jesuits who, beginning with the constitution *[Unigenitus]*, had turned all the corps . . . into carcasses and now awaited the turn of the Parlement of Paris, after which, with only the corporation of flatterers still standing, all good would have entirely vacated the throne and evil alone would get a hearing."[142]

Paralleling d'Argenson's move away from enlightened absolutism toward the contentious Parlement was a move away from the bull *Unigenitus* toward Jansenism, as though his devout lineage and enlightened reformism stood or fell together. It is true that d'Argenson had always disapproved of the politics of persecution, including Cardinal Fleury's with respect to Jansenists, because its main effect was to produce more Jansenists. But while in 1739 he deemed *Unigenitus* to be "very orthodox and worthy of success, so far as doctrine and church discipline are concerned," in 1755 he thought that the bull proposed "a cantankerous God, the author of all the greedy vices of our infamous priests." And while in 1739 d'Argenson deemed Jansenism to be a troublesome heresy and thought that laypersons and "even clerics of the second order . . . ought to submit blindly to their [episcopal] pastors" on the subject of *Unigenitus*, by 1757 he applauded the lay judges' appeal against the bull, congratulating the Parlement for having thereby "saved religion" and deploring the "despotism of the bishops" for having behaved "cavalierly toward their curés." Behind the quarrel between Molinists and Jansenists d'Argenson discerned the intrigue of "sacerdotals" against "nationals," these latter being the harbingers of a "great Revolution in religion as in the government."[143]

In contrast to the marquis d'Argenson, who was at most a protophilosophe, Denis Diderot was one of the major figures of the High Enlightenment, best

142. Ibid.: on taxes, financiers, and England, 3 Sept. 1751, 6:464; *Unigenitus* and refusal of sacraments, 9 Oct., 1755, 9:104–5; on "villainous sacerdoce," 27 Mar. 1755; and on Jesuits and leveling, 14 Aug. 1751.

143. Ibid.: on contrasting views of *Unigenitus*, Feb., 1739, 2:90–92, and 27 Mar. 1755, 8:463; on contrasting views of Jansenism, Feb., 1739, 2:90–92, and 20 Jan. 1755, 8:415; and on "nationals" versus "sacerdotals," 23 June 1754, 8:313.

known in his own day as the principal editor of the *Encyclopedia*. And while *Unigenitus* figured prominently in d'Argenson's political education, Diderot referred to the bull very little and then only in terms of the most sovereign contempt. Yet unlike d'Argenson, who found his way to enlightenment from a devout family upbringing, Diderot came to it from from a vaguely Jansenist direction.

Diderot's father, a pious cutler established in Langres, destined this bookish son for an ecclesiastical career and had him tonsured at the tender age of twelve with this end in view. But when an aged uncle's benefice failed to fall to the family upon the death of its incumbent, Diderot apparently decided to join the Jesuits, from whom he had received his education in Langres, until a still unexplained falling out with the society caused him to pursue his education in Paris around 1729. Although Diderot may have briefly attended the Jesuits' celebrated College of Louis-Le-Grand upon arrival in the capital, it is now all but settled that he pursued his master of arts degree in philosophy at the University of Paris's College of Harcourt, whose Jansenist ambiance still awaited Cardinal Fleury's policy of educational purge.[144] What was not known until recently is that after obtaining the master of arts degree in 1732, Diderot undertook three full years of theological study at the Sorbonne or the College of Navarre—probably the Sorbonne—to the point of taking an advanced degree, or *quinquennium*, in 1735. The Sorbonne that Diderot would have attended had not yet formally rescinded its 1717 appeal of *Unigenitus* to a general council or had its faculty entirely purged of appellants, neither of which occurred until 1739. After taking the quinquennium Diderot abandoned theology and did not do the minimum necessary to obtain a benefice, whether because he preferred to study mathematics on his own, as he later claimed, or because he fell in love, as he also claimed, or because he balked at signing the Formulary of Alexander VII, which he is unlikely to have later admitted.[145]

These biographical facts bear at least implicitly on Diderot's first explicit political utterance, the article entitled "Political authority," which appeared in the first volume of his *Encyclopedia* in 1751 and with which this chapter began. This notorious article justified all political authority by reason of natural law, the consent of the governed, and the existence of an explicit or tacit contract stipulating the conditions and limits of rule. To justify these premises Diderot argued that the grant of unlimited authority to any human agency was a usurpation rather than a vindication of divine sovereignty, that Saint Paul himself had recommended only a "reasonable obedience," and that it was in the light of that

144. Arthur Wilson, *Diderot: The Testing Years* (New York, 1957), pp. 9–36.

145. Blake T. Hanna, "Diderot théologien," *Revue d'histoire littéraire de la France* 78 (1978):19–35. See also Huguette Cohen, "Jansenism in Diderot's *La Religieuse*," in *Studies in Eighteenth-Century Culture* 2, ed. Harry Payne (Madison, Wisc., 1982), pp. 75–91.

obedience that readers should interpret Paul's preachments in favor of the "powers" in Romans 13:1–2, which meant that only "just and regulated" powers came from God. Far from deriving any explicit justification for resistance from these contractual premises, however, Diderot stressed the obligation of subjects to remain obedient to the Bourbon dynasty, restricting them to prayers alone in response to royal injustice.[146]

But the guardians of the existing ecclesial and political principalities and powers were not thrown off Diderot's track by this seeming non sequitur. And so the Jesuits' *Journal de Trévoux* denounced the article for undermining the divine basis of political authority, for mistranslating and misinterpreting Saint Paul, and for relying heavily on a "heretical" English *Treatise on the Power of the Kings of Great Britain*. This article was no small factor in the Royal Council's decision to condemn the *Encyclopedia* as "tending to destroy royal authority" and to withdraw the royal privilege for its publication in 1752.[147]

Modern scholarship has tracked down the obvious clues concerning this article's intellectual debts—the English treatise, which Diderot and d'Alembert both adamantly denied having read, and a certain *Treatise on the Rights of the Queen over the Divers States of the Spanish Monarchy*, published under the auspices of Louis XIV in 1667 and alleged as one of their sources by the two editors when the *Encyclopedia* resumed publication in 1753.[148] To these may be added the works of such seventeenth-century Protestant natural-law theoreticians as John Locke, Hugo Grotius, and Samuel Pufendorf; for in both Grotius's *De jure Belli et Paci* and Pufendorf's *Du droit des gens* Diderot could have encountered arguments using contract theory to justify unconditional obedience similar to the one he elaborated in his much maligned article on political authority.[149]

Be all that as it may—and this is not to gainsay any of it—what strikes the ear attuned to the themes and changes of ecclesiastical controversy are precisely the Gallican and Jansenist ones. Whether sincerely meant or not, Diderot's ingenious appeal in the article's fourth paragraph to God's absolute power in order to establish the limited character of all human authority draws out the most radical

---

146. Denis Diderot, *Oeuvres politiques*, ed. Paul Vernière, Classiques Garniers series (Paris, 1963), pp. 9–20.

147. Wilson, *Diderot: the Testing Years*, pp. 130–60; *Mémoires de Trévoux* (Mar. 1752), pp. 457–60.

148. If Diderot and d'Alembert had read the English treatise, they would have probably read the translation entitled *Traité du pouvoir des rois de la Grande Bretagne* (Amsterdam, 1714). The treatise that they invoked as one of their sources, the *Traité des droits de la reine sur différents états de la monarchie d'Espagne* (Paris, 1667), was safe to appeal to, not only because it had been published under the auspices of Louis XIV on behalf of his claims to parts of the Spanish Netherlands but also because the Parlement of Paris had recently cited it in its nearly contemporaneous "great" *Remontrances du parlement au roi du 9 avril 1753* (n.p., 1753), pp. 3–4.

149. Jacques Proust, *Diderot et l'Encyclopédie* (Paris, 1917), pp. 341–403; and John Lough, "The *Encyclopédie* and the Remonstrances of the Paris Parlement," *Modern Language Review* 51 (1961):393–95.

implications from the Augustinian insistence on divine transcendence. If no Jansenist had ever quite put the matter that way, someone surely should have, although Diderot's article clearly echoes some passages from Pierre Nicole's essay *De la grandeur* ("On Greatness") in his widely read *Moral Essays*, as well as Pascal's *Trois discours sur la condition des grands (Three Discourses on the Condition of Great Personages)*, which Nicole had republished as a sequel to his own essay.[150] Moreover, to appeal, as Diderot next did, to Saint Paul's recommendation of reasonable obedience (*rationale obsequium vestrum*, Romans 12:1) in order to justify a limited obedience to the ecclesiastical and political powers—to qualify, as it were, Paul's advice in Romans 13:1–2 with that in Romans 12:1—was altogether banal in Jansenist polemical literature in the wake of *Unigenitus*—so banal that Languet de Gergy took the bother to refute this exegesis of Romans 12:1 in one of his pastoral instructions in 1719.[151]

In contrast, Diderot's reinterpretation of Romans 13:1–2 as meaning that only "just and limited" powers enjoyed God's blessings was not typical of Jansenist literature, which until 1770 tended to accuse the Jesuits and the parti dévot of this subversive rendering. But—more consistently Gallican than the Jansenists— Diderot's exegesis was indeed quite true to the classic Gallican treatises of the late Middle Ages, notably Jacques Almain's and John Major's. Jansenists themselves would revert to that rendering after 1770. It was perhaps directly from those sources, too, that Diderot derived the classic Gallican distinction between the "property" of public authority, vested inalienably in the "body of the nation," and the "exercise" or "administration" of that property, which the nation might contractually delegate to a prince. But Nicolas Le Gros had already exchanged these originally Latin distinctions for French currency in his *Du reversement des libertés de l'église gallicane* in 1717; as Diderot wrote, Mey and Maultrot were preparing to use them to good effect in their collaborative *Apologie de tous les jugements* published in 1753. Even more closely associated with the Jansenist cause in the eighteenth century was another of Diderot's distinctions, that between a "chief," who "governs according to the laws of justice," and an "absolute master," who governs "according to his caprice." For it was the Jansenist barristers' famous consultation of 1730 that, along with the Royal Council's condemnation, had criminalized the word *chief* for the remainder of the century.

The point of this brief textual digression is not to suggest that Diderot was a

150. Pierre Nicole, "De la grandeur," in *Essais de morale, contenus en divers traités sur plusieurs devoirs importants*, 3 vols. (Paris, 1715), 2:120–21 in pt. 1; 141, 146 in pt. 2. Pascal's three *Discours* are reprinted at the end of pt. 2, pp. 179–89; the second *Discours* is especially suggestive.

151. On the ubiquity of this appeal see Bernard Plongeron, "Recherches sur l'aufklärung catholique en Europe occidentale, 1770–1830," pp. 578–79; and for Languet de Gergy's refutation of it, see *[Deuxième] instruction pastorale, contenant un deuxième avertissement à ceux qui dans son diocèse se sont déclarés appellans de la constitution Unigenitus* (n.p., 1719), pp. 78–79.

Jansenist in 1750 or even in 1732 but only that he had obviously not studied theology and ecclesiology in the still Gallican and jansénisant Sorbonne in the 1730s for nothing. It is also to suggest that, for all the disdain he subsequently affected for the enlightened century's residual religious disputes, the great set-to over *Unigenitus* may have been a crucial catalyst in Diderot's own politicization, as it also was in the case of some of his fellow philosophes. As it happened, the year that witnessed the first volume of Diderot's *Encyclopedia* and his article on political authority, 1751, was also the first year that the police inspector Joseph d'Hémery, who specialized in the surveillance of authors, printers, and book-sellers, kept a journal about the books and pamphlets that came to his attention. Of those whose orientation is evident from their titles, their authors, or from d'Hémery's own comments, thirty-seven were more or less "philosophical" and forty-eight published "by the care of the Jansenists," as the police inspector routinely put it. Although for the most part philosophical productions and Jansenist books missed each other, addressing different subjects, they occasionally competed on common ground, as in the case of the controversy over the government's attempt to tax the clergy.[152] The overall proportions and minimal intersection between the two kinds of works in d'Hémery's journal probably remained the same for the next two decades, with the trial of the Jesuits taking the place of clerical taxation as an area of common concern. But that area expanded dramatically in 1771, when a new chancellor provoked a crisis in the monarchy's relation with the parlements over an issue only indirectly related to religion.

152. Joseph d'Hémery, "Journal de la librairie," 12 Nov. 1750–31 Dec. 1751, in BN: Mss. Fr., Ms. 22156, A–D 96.

CHAPTER 5

From Religious to Ideological "Parties"

HARDLY HAD THEY RETURNED FROM THEIR ANNUAL AUTUM-
nal recess in December 1770 than the magistrates of the Parlement of Paris
received from their chancellor a royal edict that, had they registered it, would have
been tantamount to a disavowal of all the constitutional gains they had made at the
expense of royal absolutism during the preceding twenty years. Defending the
king's undivided and divinely ordained sovereignty against his disobedient magistrates' esprit de système, this so-called Edict of December explicitly condemned
the theses that the Parlement of Paris, together with France's thirteen provincial
parlements, constituted the various "classes" of a single national parlement, that
these parlements legitimately represented the French nation vis-à-vis the king, or
again that this representative capacity entitled them to refuse their consent to royal
declarations and edicts—including of course the Edict of December. The same
edict also outlawed the practice of the judicial strike—that is, the suspension of the
administration of routine justice—by means of which the Parisian magistrates had
been able to make good their now proscribed constitutional claims.[1]

The presumed author of this provocative edict was the new chief of justice or
chancellor René-Nicolas-Charles-Augustin de Maupeou, himself a former councillor and president in the Parlement of Paris. And if by means of this edict
Maupeou or Louis XV had hoped to goad the Parlement into a punishable act of
disobedience, he probably succeeded beyond his own expectations. Faced with the

---

1. François-Andre Isambert et al., eds., *Recueil des anciennes lois françaises depuis l'an 420 jusqu'à
la Révolution de 1789* (Paris, 1821–33), 22:501–7.

unattractive alternatives of signing their own constitutional death warrant or inviting it by defying the edict's express provisions, the Parlement chose the latter course, refusing either to register the edict or to administer routine justice after the king forcibly registered the contested edict in a royal lit de justice assembly on 7 December. The magistrates' unanimous resistance first obliged Maupeou to exile each and every one of them—the more moderate ones to their country estates and notorious "troublemakers" to sundry remote and inhospitable locations—and then to replace the Parlement's entire judicial personnel with hastily impressed recruits. The continued defiance of other Parisian courts, notably the *Cour des aides,* as well as the provincial parlements, further challenged the chancellor's improvisational prowess, forcing him either to abolish or to purge these courts as each in turn refused to register the new edicts legalizing the previous improvisations. In this way one expedient led to another, all of them adding up to the reconstitution of France's entire judicial system and the replacement of much of its personnel.[2]

"The revolution perpetrated on the constitution of the French monarchy by M. de Maupeou," as the Parisian "publicist" Pidansat de Mairobert's *Journal historique* called it, did not ultimately escape the fate traditionally assigned to revolutions, coming as it did full circle with the restoration of the old parlements by the new King Louis XVI in 1774. Nor did the reformist aspects of Maupeou's coup, like ending the sale of offices in the parlements, amount to very much more than justificatory afterthoughts, the original thoughts having had to do with obscure maneuvering among court factions including Maupeou's own.[3] Despite the plaudits of Voltaire, the reforms themselves remained unconvincing, resulting in neither cheaper nor better justice nor in any sustained attack on the luxuriant undergrowth of purchasable offices and the privileges they conferred. The coup's most lasting institutional legacy was to have broken the internal discipline of the Parisian Barristers' Order, which capitulated to Maupeou in 1771 and escaped once and for all from Jansenist control after its restoration in 1774.[4] If the coup also righted the imbalance among the realm's chief corps that resulted from the parlementary victory over the church in 1757, the new balance was one of collective fragility. By exposing the vulnerability of the parlements to determined royal action, the coup weakened the whole fabric of the corps, making a defensive alliance among them more likely and a demagogic appeal to public opinion more tempting.

2. The standard narrative accounts of Chancellor Maupeou's judicial and constitutional reforms remain Jules Flammermont, *Le chancelier Maupeou et les parlements,* 2d ed. (Paris, 1885); and Jean Egret, *Louis XV et l'opposition parlementaire* (Paris, 1970), pp. 133–228.

3. See, in particular, William Doyle, "The Parlements of France and the Breakdown of the Old Regime," *FHS* 6 (Fall 1970):515–58; and Martin Mansergh, "The Revolution of 1771, or the Exile of the Parlement of Paris" (Ph.D. diss., Oxford, 1973).

4. David A. Bell, *Lawyers and Citizens: The Making of a Political Elite in Old Regime France* (Oxford, 1994), pp. 129–63.

But Maupeou's constitutional coup compensated for the poverty of its institutional reforms by effecting more lasting changes in the more pliable domain of political culture. Parallel to the contemporaneous coalition in support of John Wilkes and parliamentary reform in England, as well as to the "patriots" who protested against the Stamp Act in the American colonies, a "party of patriotism" rapidly took shape in support of the suppressed parlements in France. By "patriot party" Mairobert pointed not to a modern political organization but to an informal coalition of groups and individuals associated in defense of the parlements and against Maupeou. This loose coalition temporarily harnessed the corporate discipline of the Parisian Order of Barristers and orchestrated the publication and distribution of more than five hundred books and pamphlets or *maupeouana,* which, though much less numerous than the Fronde's thousands of mazarinades, are visibly closer to the Revolution in their explicit appeal to the "nation" and its putative "public opinion" against Maupeou's "despotism."[5] In response, Maupeou and some of his fellow maligned ministers mobilized not only the censorial efforts of the Paris police but also a sort of party or political coalition of their own. On behalf of his "reforms" Maupeou was able to count on the support of some of his enemies' enemies, among them clergymen and some rank-conscious nobles long fed up with the "bourgeois" parlementaires' pretensions; yet he also enlisted the services of some talented publicists like the journalist-barrister Henri-Simon Linguet. Although unsanctioned by contemporary usage, the term *ministerial party* will be used here to designate this pro-Maupeou coalition, which, with obvious ministerial help, published a hundred or so pamphlets in defense of "reform" and the absolute monarchy that had promulgated it. To defend royal ministers, however, was perforce to defend the monarchy that employed them, and in thus pleading the monarchy's case in pamphlet form and implicitly accepting public opinion as judge, this ministerial party's propaganda may well have undermined divine-right monarchy more effectively than it defended it.[6]

As it happens, the three Maupeou partisans who play the most ignominious roles in one of the patriot party's most successful pamphlets—Jacques de Flesselles, Foullon de Doué and Berthier de Sauvigny, who figure in the anonymous *Personal and Confidential Correspondence*—were among the very first victims

5. The best and most recent work on the "patriots" and "patriot constitutionalism" is now Durand Echeverria's *The Maupeou Revolution: A Study in the History of Libertarianism* (Baton Rouge, La., 1985), pp. 37–122. But this book has already been supplanted in some important respects, especially on the subjects of public opinion and the publication of patriot propaganda, by Shanti Marie Singham's "'A Conspiracy of Twenty Million Frenchmen': Public Opinion, Patriotism, and the Assault on Absolutism During the Maupeou Years" (Ph.D. diss., Princeton University, 1991).

6. Echeverria, *The Maupeou Revolution,* pp. 125–77. Because both Simon-Henri Linguet and Voltaire pamphleteered on behalf of Maupeou and his revolution, Echeverria's decision to treat them separately from "the royalists" seems unjustified. Still useful on this subject is David Hudson's "In Defense of Reform: French Government Propaganda during the Maupeou Crisis," *FHS* 8 (1973):51–76.

of the triumphant stormers of the Bastille in 1789, who forced Flesselles in particular to confess his past sins in the "service of despotism" before severing his head and parading it on a pike.[7] But such anecdotal and melodramatic evidence is not really needed to underscore the long-term significance of the changes in political culture wrought by the Maupeou episode. For it was the faithful remnants of the patriot party who, still under that banner, led the prerevolutionary charge in 1787–88 against the "despotism" of the royal ministers Alexandre de Calonne and Loménie de Brienne, who in turn followed Maupeou's example in subsidizing pamphlets that renewed the charge of "aristocracy" against the parlements and their partisans.

By the same token, the patriot-ministerial confrontation of the Maupeou era represents an evident secularization of the political debate in France in comparison with that of the preceding decades. In the 1770s, open debate about the putative existence and nature of France's "constitution" displaced discussions about the "constitution" *Unigenitus* and that of the Society of Jesus at the center of the new French "public sphere." Symptomatically, perhaps, French philosophes abandoned the aloof disdain characteristic of their attitude toward the Jansenist and *Unigenitus*-related controversies and now entered the new public space on both sides of the controversy. On the patriot side, for example, Denis Diderot wrote hauntingly of confronting the "hideous head of despotism," which Maupeou's unceremonious rending of the spider's web of constitutionality had exposed to plain view. Although they hardly made Diderot into a partisan of the parlements, the events of the Maupeou era prompted him to radicalize his conception of the constitutional contract between king and subjects, abandoning a mutually binding or synallagmatic contract for one that the people alone might renounce on the grounds of despotic royal behavior.[8] And from his estate at Ferney, on the ministerial side of the debate, Voltaire committed himself to the defense of Maupeou's "enlightened" reforms and something like absolute monarchy in the most unguarded terms and at the momentary cost of his popularity and reputation for integrity. Preferring, he repeatedly explained, "to live under the paw of a lion than to be continually exposed to the teeth of a thousand rats like myself," he objected in principle to the parlements' attempt to "raise a hundred democratic thrones on the ruins of a throne that has endured for nearly fourteen centuries."[9]

7. [Jacques-Mathieu Augéard], *Correspondance secrète et familière de M. de Maupeou, avec M. de Sorhouet, conseiller au nouveau parlement,* in *Les efforts de la liberté et du patriotisme contre le despotisme du Sr. de Maupeou, chancelier de France,* 6 vols. (London, 1775), 2:32, 62–63, 95–96; and Prosper-Siméon Hardy, "Mes loisirs, ou journal d'événements tels qu'ils parviennent à ma connoissance," in BN: Mss. Fr., 8 vols., Ms. 6687 (14 July 1789), p. 389.

8. Denis Diderot, *Observations sur le Nakaẓ* in *Oeuvres politiques,* ed. Paul Vernière, Classiques Garnier (Paris, 1963), p. 358.

9. Quoted in Echeverria, *The Maupeou Revolution,* pp. 155–56. On Voltaire's penchant for royally sponsored reform over representative government, at least in the French context, see in general

Such evidence points up the knotty problem of the relationship between the French Enlightenment and the political thought and rhetoric of the late eighteenth century, and of these in turn to the French Revolution. Were the participants in the debate over Maupeou's reforms mainly philosophes and their disciples, their entry into the public sphere representing the first massive application of hitherto abstract enlightened principles to the French polity? As early as 1777 the former patriot publicist Pidansat de Mairobert said so, identifying the antidespotic patriot movement as the final and most explicitly political stage of a "philosophical movement" that had begun with the anti-"fanatical" encyclopedists and had continued with the antimercantilist physiocrats.[10] Yet in the heat of battle just five years earlier the same Pidansat de Mairobert had observed that it was Jansenism that had "transformed itself into the party of patriotism," having redeployed its forces from papal despotism and against the political counterpart.[11]

Which of these two Mairoberts should we believe? What this chapter will argue is that, although still close to the event, Mairobert's attempt at historical reconstruction in 1777 is less reliable than his ground-level observations in 1772; and that, although it commanded numbers of "enlightened" allies, the patriot movement of the early 1770s was a transformation of what had been known as the parti janséniste in the 1750s and 1760s. That ancestry makes it less surprising that when Maupeou sought allies against these rechristened patriots, he should have found some of them among Jansenism's traditional enemies, namely ex-Jesuits (as Mairobert recalled, their society had been disbanded in France in 1762) and their partisans among the bishops and courtiers—in other words, the parti dévot. This chapter will therefore also argue that the pro-papal parti dévot stands at the origin of the late-eighteenth-century ministerial party and its rhetorical tactics. Even if correct, however, this account of the religious origins of France's prerevolutionary political alignments does not exclude the possibility that the more "enlightened" Mairobert might have noted something true about the Enlightenment in 1777. For the proximity of the Enlightenment undoubtedly contributed to the transformation of these hitherto religiopolitical parties into ideological-political ones. And however distortingly, Mairobert's version of the Enlightenment's three successive stages testifies to the politicization of the philosophical movement itself in the course of its contact with Jansenist patriotism and the parti dévot in prerevolutionary France.

---

ibid., pp. 147–68; and Peter Gay, *Voltaire's Politics* (Princeton, N.J., 1959). Voltaire's pamphlets in defense of Maupeou are in his *OC*, ed. Louis Moland, 52 vols. (Paris, 1877–85), 28:386–424.

10. Mathieu-François Pidansat de Mairobert, "Avertissement des éditieurs" in Louis Petit de Bachaumont, *Mémoires secrets pour servir à l'histoire de la république des lettres en France, depuis MDCCLXII jusqu'à nos jours*, 36 vols. (London, 1784–88), 1:3–4.

11. Mathieu-François Pidansat de Mairobert, *Journal historique de la révolution operée dans la constitution de la monarchie françoise, par M. de Maupeou, chancelier de France*, 7 vols. (London, 1774–76), 20 Jan. 1771, 2:351.

The "Patriotic" Pamphlets

When such late eighteenth-century observers as Mairobert used the term Jansenism, they no longer designated an austere group of theological and moral
disciples of Saint Augustine but rather what we have here characterized as judicial
Jansenism: an already politicized combination of elements of Gallicanism, parlementary constitutionalism, and Jansenism more narrowly defined. Its anti-Jesuitical and antipapal protonationalism and its defense of a putatively ancient
constitution against "despotism," in continued association with a "puritanical"
religious "conscience" against all forms of "domination," as we have seen, made
this Jansenism in many respects the Gallic counterpart to the "real Whiggism" or
commonwealthman ideology then current in England and the American colonies.
In looking for a Jansenist presence in the pamphlet literature of the patriot
movement, therefore, it is imperative to bring to bear the wider meanings that this
term had acquired, especially those having to do with the varieties of parlementary constitutionalism on which Jansenists had left their inimitable imprint.

By far the most prevalent form of parlementary or magisterial constitutionalism in the patriot pamphlet literature of the period 1771–75 rooted the
Parlement of Paris's rights of remonstrance and registration in its supposedly
lineal descent from the medieval Court of Peers and ultimately from the much
earlier Merovingian Royal Court *(Cour royal)* and General Assemblies *(parlemens
généraux)* of all Frankish warriors. Because in this reconstruction of French
institutional history these primitive assemblies had consisted of the entire Frankish nation, which, when assembled, possessed the right to accept or annul all of the
Merovingian kings' legislative initiatives, it followed that the Parlement of Paris as
its legitimate institutional descendant was also "in its own manner possessed of a
role in legislation," and therefore also entitled to the quality of "representative of
the Nation, for stipulating its interests." Yet, continued the anonymous *Letter from
Monsieur Xxx, a Councillor in the Parlement, to Monsieur the Count of Xxx*, this
capacity as representative of the nation did not prevent the Parlement from also
being the successor of both the Merovingian royal court and the medieval court of
peers and, as the offspring of those royal institutions, from being the king's only
legitimate "mouthpiece vis-a-vis the Nation."[12] From these historical and constitutional premises pamphleteers like the anonymous author of a *Letter
from a Bourgeois of Paris* also frequently drew the corollary that the lit de justice
assembly had once been a genuine consultation between the king and his trusted
magisterial councillors and had only recently degenerated into a display of arbitrary force—that "this solemn assembly," in that pamphlet's words, "once intended to enlighten the king and show him the truth, had become instead a dumb

---

12. *Lettre de Monsieur Xxx, conseiller au parlement, à M. le comte de Xxx* (n.p., 1771), pp. 11–12.

scene just as distressing for its members as it is useless for the instruction of the king."[13]

However ancient these pamphlets thought the origins of the Parlement of Paris to be, the thesis of those ancient origins was quite recent, at least in that precise form, having found expression less than twenty years earlier in the two-volume *Lettres historiques sur les fonctions essentielles du parlement*. And however recent the deformation of the lit de justice assembly—it was that assembly, we now know, and not its deformation that was recent—the thesis of that degeneration was more recent still, having appeared in a book entitled *Discours sur les origines des troubles présens en France (Discourse on the Origin of the Present Troubles in France)* and in a pamphlet entitled *Lettre sur les lits de justice*, both published in 1756. The author of the two *Lettres* was of course Louis-Adrien Le Paige, among other things the personal librarian and legal consultant to the king's cousin the Prince de Conti, who, as secular head of the Order of Malta, also employed Le Paige as his judicial bailiff over the order's privileged Parisian domain called the Temple. Already a frondeur on the Protestant and Jansenist side in the latter 1750s, Conti had thrown himself heart and soul into the patriot protest against Maupeou's coup, sponsoring a quasi-official *Princes' Protest* against the Edict of December—and retrospectively making a strong case for the influence of Le Paige on the contents of this and other documents in the patriots' protest literature.[14] And Le Paige was also a Jansenist in just about every sense of that term.

In his *Lettres historiques*, as we have seen, Le Paige had given his reworking of sixteenth-century and Frondish constitutionalism a markedly Jansenist cast. And as it happens, a similarly Jansenist tone pervades much of the anonymous patriot pamphlet literature of 1771–75. The apparently disobedient magistrates had only done their "solemn duty to refuse until death" to act in complicity with Maupeou's constitutionally heretical edict against the "dogma of our national constitution," maintained, for example, the *Petition to the King by the Estates General of France*. Far from having seditiously challenged the king's rightful authority, added the *Lettre de M. Xxx, conseiller au parlement*, they had only uttered a "cry of conscience" and defended the "always subsistent [fundamental] laws" by "passively" refusing to "lend their ministry" to Maupeou's projected transformation of France into a despotism. The *Lettre d'un bourgeois de Paris*

13. *Lettre d'un bourgeois de Paris à un provincial, à l'occasion de l'édit de décembre 1770* (n.p., n.d.), p. 8, in BPR: CLP, Ms. 800, no. 14. See also *Lettres d'un homme à un autre homme* (n.p., n.d.); and *Le parlement justifié par l'impératrice de Russie, ou lettre à M. Xxx dans laquelle on répond aux différents écrits que M. le Ch[ancelier] fait distribuer dans Paris* (n.p., n.d.), pp. 106–7, 109.

14. *Protestation des princes du sang contre l'édit de décembre 1770, les lettres patentes du 23 février 1771, et contre tout ce qui s'en est ensuivi ou pourroit s'ensuivre; signifiées et déposées au greffe du parlement, et lues en présence de MM. du Conseil siégeant au palais, le 12 avril 1771* (n.p., n.d.), of which Le Paige's handwritten copy is in BPR: CLP, Ms. 569, no. 147.

maintained that Maupeou's "despotism" had replaced the "love" hitherto characteristic of relations between the French monarchy and its subjects with a reign of
"fear," in the teeth of which the magistrates had dutifully persisted in "presenting
the truth to the king."[15]

But coexisting uneasily with this Le Paige-like magisterial constitutionalism
in the pamphlet literature of the patriot movement is another strain that, however
respectful of the parlements and grateful for their stand against Maupeou, clearly
questioned their claim of being direct descendants of the Frankish national assemblies and the representatives of the French nation. Instead, this strain touted the
candidacy of the defunct Estates General. These two somewhat competitive
constitutionalisms were not mutually exclusive. Witness the anonymous *Requête
des Etats-généraux de France au roi,* which, locus classicus though it was of Le
Paigian figurist constitutionalism, put the nation's putative grievances into the
mouth of the Estates General and not the parlements; or the equally proparlementary *Conversation Between a Barrister and Monsieur the Chancellor,* which conceded
that, where consenting to taxes was concerned, the Parlement had at best acted in
virtue of a mandate provisionally granted by the Estates General of Blois in
1577.[16] Also very respectful of the parlements, the widely read *The Inauguration of
Pharamond* went further, calling for the restoration of a supposedly original
National Diet for the purpose of constitutional legislation and explicitly arguing
that "even the Parlements . . . are never more competent to deliberate concerning
a new law than they are concerning the establishment or prorogation of a tax, for
the reason that no tax can be established or continued except in virtue of a law
whose rationale is the public utility recognized as such by the nation."[17]

One of the defining features of the patriot party's more radical fringe is
arguably the peremptoriness of this antiparlementary bias. The much commented
upon *Letters from One Man to Another,* for example, laid it down in no uncertain
terms that "the parlements do not compensate for the loss of the Estates General
which they certainly do not represent: in no way where taxes are at issue can the
Estates General be supplanted by the parlements, which have acquired I know not
how the right of registration." The immensely successful and satirical *Correspondance secrète et familière* would boldly call this supposed right a "felony" and a
"usurpation."[18] Pidansat de Mairobert's radical *Journal historique* also frequently

---

15. *Requête des Etats-généraux de France au roi,* pp. 18–19; *Lettre de Monsieur Xxx, conseiller au
parlement,* pp. 28–29; *Lettre d'un bourgeois de Paris,* pp. 20–21.

16. *Conversation entre un avocat et M. le chancelier* (n.p., 1771), pp. 31–32. This pamphlet is simply a
different edition of the one entitled *Plan d'une conversation entre an avocat et M. le chancelier,* in BPR: CLP,
Ms. 805, no. 2.

17. *Inauguration de Pharamond, ou exposition des loix fondamentales de la monarchie françoise; avec
les preuves de leur exécution, perpétuées sous les trois races de nos rois,* in *Les efforts,* 4:188–89.

18. *Lettres d'un homme à un autre homme,* pp. 202–3; and *Correspondance secrète et familière,* in *Les
efforts,* 2:45, 99.

faulted the patriot pamphlets that came to his attention for being "very *parlementaire*" and blamed the parlements themselves for the "weakness of repeating [in their remonstrances] that the king holds his crown from God alone," a "proposition," according to Mairobert, "which should never have been advanced in a century as enlightened and philosophical as our own."[19]

A century distinguished by its enlightenment and philosophy? Has Pidansat de Mairobert's *Journal historique* taken us across a line separating not only moderate from radical patriotism but vaguely "Jansenistical" from "enlightened" patriotism as well? What reinforces this impression is that Mairobert faulted other anonymous patriot publications for being both too Jansenist and too parlementaire, and he derived special encouragement from such "enlightened" adhesions to the patriot cause as those of the philosophes Claude-Adrien Helvétius and the Baron d'Holbach.[20] The same *Lettres d'un homme à un autre homme* that so peremptorily challenged the Parlement's right to register taxes emits a similar if more subdued philosophical glow. Written, according to Mairobert, in the "lively style of a man about town" *(homme du monde)*, a veritable "Fontenelle of politics," this pamphlet characteristically celebrated the "few lights" bestowed on France by Louis IX and the thirteenth century, lights that began to "dissipate the darkness of barbarism" and medieval "trouble and ignorance."[21] The comte de Lauraguais' *Tableau of the French Constitution*, although still significantly dependent upon a Le Paige-like version of France's institutional past, obviously chafed at this dependence and sought to rehabilitate the Estates General.[22] Fifteen years later the same Lauraguais would develop a constitutionalism that, however historical and "gothic" by revolutionary standards, espoused a very different notion of national representation, which drew liberally from the political thought of Jean-Jacques Rousseau.[23]

Yet the "influence of the Enlightenment" in a given patriot pamphlet is by no means measurable in terms of its announced preference for the Estates General over the parlements. Take, for example, the two-volume *Maxims of French Public Law,* that massive summa of patriot constitutionalism, which despite Mairobert's

19. Mairobert, *Journal historique:* on being too parlementaire (25 July 1772), 1:217; on proposition of holding crown from God alone (13 Feb. 1772), 2:309; and on enlightened and philosophical century (17 June 1771), 1:364–65.

20. On being too Jansenist, ibid. (13 December 1772), 3:390–92; on philosophical adhesions, see Echeverria, *The Maupeou Revolution,* pp. 56–57.

21. Mairobert, *Journal historique* (6 Aug. 1771), 2:69–70; and *Lettres d'un homme à un autre homme,* pp. 171–72, 180–81.

22. Louis-Léon-Félicité, duc de Brancas, comte de Lauraguais, *Tableau de la constitution françoise, ou autorité des rois de France, dans les différens âges de la monarchie* (n.p., 1771), pp. 60, 70–78.

23. Lauraguais, *Receuil de pièces historiques sur la convocation des Etats-généraux et sur l'élection de leurs députés* (Paris, 1788), pp. 101–12; and *Dissertation sur les assemblées nationales, sous les trois races des rois de France* (Paris, 1788), pp. 11–14, 98.

objection that it revealed "too marked an interest in the Company [the Parlement]," contained one of the patriot movement's most radical statements of the Estates General's constitutional powers and of the need for its immediate convocation. To be sure, these *Maximes* came out in defense of the parlements in the context of Chancellor Maupeou's constitutional coup and went to considerable lengths to establish the Parlement's immemorial right to register royal edicts and declarations, without, however, following Le Paige into the recesses of Merovingian Gaul. At the same time the treatise precociously demonstrated how a kind of parlementary constitutionalism could take theoretical leave of the parlements, and how very precipitous could be the descent from an admission of the nation's fiscal sovereignty to an acknowledgment of its global legislative sovereignty. The treatise's assertion of the nation's right to consent to all subsidies was indeed among the first salient features amidst its mountainous prolixity, as its insistence upon the Parlement's right of registration was among its last. Below these two conspicuous landmarks, however—and as it were supporting them—lay a seemingly trackless rubble of erudition, which included the dictum of classical natural law *suprema lex salus populi esto* ("The supreme law is the people's welfare") and the maxim that nations as political communities always retained the proprietorship of their sovereignty and only delegated its exercise to kings as their mandatories.

Once in motion, these two premises dislodged conclusions that fell thick and fast. No king could prescribe against the nation any more than a mandatory could prescribe against his mandate, but a nation could prescribe against its king in whatever way it chose. The nation, when assembled, could change the form of its government, from a hereditary monarchy to an aristocracy or a democracy. If the king should refuse to assemble the nation, its Estates General could assemble themselves at the behest of a single province, just as a single church could assemble a general council in the face of papal ill will. By the time the two volumes of *Maximes* had fully settled, the whole structure of Bourbon absolutism—divine right, automatic hereditary succession, lettres de cachet, Antoine Loisel's "si veult le roi si veult la loy" ("the king's will is the law's will"), the phrase "car tel est notre bon plaisir"—found itself buried beneath a rock slide of erudition from which no excavation seemed possible.

To be sure, the natural-law tradition figures importantly among the *Maximes'* intellectual sources, particularly for the axioms that rulers were supposed to govern in the interest of their people, and that the people's consent in the form of some kind of contract lay at the origin of all legitimate political communities. Although by the 1770s the natural-law tradition was common to both Jansenism and the Enlightenment, the form of it most conspicuous in the pages of the *Maximes* was that bequeathed by the seventeenth-century Protestant theoreticians Hugo Grotius and Samuel Pufendorf. But both of these theorists had drawn rather absolutist conclusions from natural-law premises, the most flagrant of them being that the people's initial choice of their form of government or particular dynasty was irrevocable and that resistance to it was illegitimate; these sources were therefore eventually inconvenient for the *Maximes'* ultimate political purposes. At that point Anglo-Saxon commonwealthman ideology's more radical rendering of the natural-law tradition came to the *Maximes'* rescue, most especially Algernon Sidney's *On Civil Government,* which did indeed allow for the right of popular resistance and for the possibility of a willful "dissolution of the government." The *Maximes* even had recourse to John Locke's *Two Treatises on Civil Government.* Page upon translated page of the *Second Treatise* appears in the *Maximes,* including the notorious passage specifying that "the people will judge" in cases between themselves and their government.[24]

Yet the *Maximes'* ultimate and most characteristic recourse was to the authority of the late-medieval "school of Paris"—Jean Gerson, Jacques Almain, John Major—and to its crucial distinction between the *property* and *source* of political power on the one hand, always retained by the whole community, and the *exercise* or *use* of that power on the other hand, revocably delegated to kings or rulers. Symptomatic of that Gallican influence in pages of the *Maximes* is the argument for national sovereignty by analogy to the whole Catholic community and the ecumenical council's superiority over the papacy—hardly a typical argument for an anti-Catholic Enlightenment.[25] On the contrary, it is altogether Gallican and therefore also Jansenist to the extent that Jansenists had made conciliar Gallicanism one of the hallmarks of their ecclesiology. Nicolas Le Gros and Vivien de La Borde had of course already used the conciliar analogy to effect the transfer of sovereignty from monarchy to nation and its Estates General in the wake of *Unigenitus;* and although Le Paige's version of parlementary constitutionalism had eclipsed the conciliar analogy during the 1750s and 1760s, it was not far below the surface of Mey and Maultrot's *Apologie de tous les jugemens,* published in 1752.[26] During the patriot protest itself the conciliarist argument stood out conspicuously in the anonymous and incendiary *Manifesto to the Normans* in 1772, as well as in Guillaume Saige's *The Citizen's Catechism* in 1775.[27]

Of course the Le Paige-like version of patriot constitutionalism also identi-

24. [Gabriel-Nicolas Maultrot, Claude Mey et al.]., *Maximes du droit public françois, tirées des capitulaires, des ordonnances du royaume, et les autres monumens de l'histoire de France,* 2 vols., 2d ed. (Amsterdam, 1775), 1:309–10, 317, 374; 2:84–89.

25. Ibid., especially the "Dissertation sur le droit de convoquer les Etats-généraux," appended to the end of the first volume and paginated separately, pp. 17–18, but also 1:167–69, and 2:154–60.

26. [Gabriel-Nicolas Maultrot and Claude Mey], *Apologie de tous les jugements rendus par les tribunaux séculiers en France contre le schisme,* 2 vols. (France, 1752), esp. 1:481–85; but also Nicolas Le Gros, *Du renversement des libertés de l'église gallicane,* 2 vols. (n.p., 1716), esp. 1:336–37, 343–45.

27. *Manifeste aux Normands* (n.p., n.d.), in *Les efforts,* 6:8, 12–13; and [Guillaume Saige], *Catéchisme du citoyen, ou éléments du droit public françois, par demandes et réponses; suivi de fragments politiques; par le même auteur* ("en France," 1788, although originally published in 1775), pp. 24–25, 74–76, 96–97, 115.

fied the nation as the source of sovereignty, differing from the *Maximes* in entrusting the exercise of sovereignty to king and Parlement rather than to king, Estates General, and Parlement, with the latter in the role of some species of supreme court. While both of these jansénisant genres of patriot constitutionalism, then, embraced the thesis of national legislative sovereignty, they variously moderated its exercise by entrusting it to constitutional combinations of king, Estates General, and Parlement and by requiring something like unanimity among them. The spirit of these combinations was hence also profoundly defensive, as was the character of Jansenism itself, the intention being to divide the exercise of sovereignty among corporate groups and institutions in such a way as to mitigate the exercise of power and the attendant threat of "despotism." At this point in the century the threat of despotism was the exercise of royal or ministerial power, and the counterpoise to it the nation's corporate groups and institutions. Yet it is easy to see that, in the absence of either absolute monarchy or corporate groups and institutions, the profound tendency of patriot constitutionalism would be to divide sovereignty to the extent of investing it in the individual *âmes* and consciences of all social constituents and erecting their required consensus or unanimity as the ultimate barrier against the "despotism" of even representative bodies. In the absence of a "reliable" episcopacy, Jansenist ecclesiastical thought had already undergone such an evolution; in reaction to Le Paige's corporate constitutionalism, Henri de Revol had precociously undergone a secular version of such an evolution in the 1750s. A similarly secular counterpart to something originally ecclesiastical, finally, is also apparent in patriot constitutionalism's profound respect for the French past—a counterpart, in effect, to Jansenism's profound respect for the patristic past—tending to see in history a repository of constitutional truth and so many mute testimonies against despotism and usurpation.

Such a textual "presence" beneath patriot constitutionalisms is no doubt real enough to the already converted, but it may well strike the religiously unattuned as insubstantial. But perhaps those Jansenist elements are more apparent in the case of patriot literature's many expressions of anti-Jesuitism. After all, the dissolution of the Society of Jesus in France had by no means satiated the Jansenists' animus against their century-old theological enemies and persecutors, while the corpus of polemical patriot literature is nothing if not awash in insults to Jesuits. Yet even this sort of evidence is difficult to interpret because anti-Jesuitical rhetoric had taken on the same ecclesial and political overtones as had Jansenism as a whole, and had therefore become available to diverse "patriots" like Mairobert on the lookout for convenient symbols of despotism and ultramontanism. It was natural enough that ex-Jesuits should have been suspected as implicated in Maupeou's coup against the parlements and excoriated accordingly, given the parlements' role in the formal dissolution of their company just a few years earlier.

Expressions of anti-Jesuitism, then, cannot be taken as evidence of Jansenism strictly defined except when they continue to bear some confessional content, as they do in the anonymous *The Parlement Vindicated by the Queen-Empress of Hungary, and by the King of Prussia,* or—even more conclusively—when they reach pathological proportions, as in the case of two anonymous pamphlets entitled *The Point of View* and *The Fulfillment of Prophecies.*[28] The same two pamphlets also implicate the short-lived *Supplement to the Gazette of France,* which ran through thirteen numbers between late 1771 and 1773. Indeed, having respectfully reviewed *Le point de vue,* the *Supplément* positively anticipated the publication of *L'accomplissement des prophéties* by suggesting that the Jesuits had not only plotted Maupeou's coup but had successfully prophesied it as well.[29]

If in spite of these few firm conclusions anti-Jesuitism remains imperfect as evidence of Jansenism, it would seem otherwise for specifically theological references, including ones to *Unigenitus.* On only one occasion, however, did Jansenism come out into the open to confront Maupeou's Edict of December in its unique armor of faith. Divulging his "figurist" *Reflections on Present Events,* the anonymous author explained France's fall into despotism as a long-suffering Jehovah's delayed punishment for the eighteenth century's "flood of corruption, injustice, irreligion, and impiety which have inundated all estates and professions." Standard sermonic fare, this, and just as probably Jesuitical? Perhaps. But look again, because France's paradigmatic sin, in this pamphleteer's estimation, turns out to have been especially subtle, "of a sort to wound the heart of God more directly, and therefore also to merit a severer vengeance than even the grossest of crimes." That subtle sin was none other than an "insulting disdain for the truth" in the form of the theological Molinism of the bull *Unigenitus,* which replaced love or contrition with fear or attrition as the principle governing relations between God and men. Molinism had now given birth to the fearful and despotic Edict of December henceforth governing relations between king and subjects. What justice, reflected these *Réflexions.* "In a word, State Molinism is now trying to follow in the footsteps of Religious Molinism. Our punishment has been exactly tailored to our sin." There followed a long list of "parallels": "the bull *Unigenitus* and the Edict of December 1770"; "Molinism introduced by the Jesuits" and "despotic

---

28. *Le parlement justifié par l'impératrice reine de Hongrie, et par le roi de Prusse; ou seconde lettre, dans laquelle on continue de répondre aux écrits de M. le chancelier* (n.p., n.d.), in *Les efforts,* 4:209–10; *Le point de vue, ou lettres de M. le prés . . . à M. le duc de N.* (n.p., 1772), p. 6, in BPR: CLP, Ms. 811, no. 5; and *L'accomplissement des prophéties. Pour servir de suite à l'ouvrage intitulé Le point de vue. Ecrit intéressant pour la maison de Bourbon* (n.p., 1772), in BPR, CLP, Ms. 811, no. 6.

29. *Supplément à la Gazette de France* (n.p., n.d.), 1 May 1772, on subject of *Le point de vue,* and 1 June 1773, on *L'accomplissement des prophéties,* in *Les efforts,* 5:134, 232. For further evidence of the *Supplément*'s Jansenist editorship, see Mairobert, *Journal historique* (24 Apr. 1772), 3:83; and (13 Dec. 1772), 3:391–92.

authority introduced by Maupeou"; "the Jesuits accusing the opponents of the bull of doctrinal innovation" just as "the Chancellor . . . is now accusing the parlements of constitutional innovations"; and so on.[30]

The Authorship of Anonymous Pamphlets

Buried in the middle of one of the bulkier *recueils,* or bound collections, consisting of contemporary publications and personal notes and letters of the Jansenist lawyer Le Paige, is a one-page manuscript entitled "outline for a *State Molinism,* a small writing in manuscript." Written in Le Paige's neat but minuscule hand, the manuscript contains the parallelisms that conclude the published *Réflexions sur les affaires présentes.* This rather conclusive evidence for Le Paige's authorship of this pamphlet is further buttressed by his handwritten additions and corrections in his personal copy, including the date of its publication, 14 May 1771.[31] Le Paige's authorship of the pamphlet should come as no surprise, combining as it does his twin fortes as theologian and political éminence grise. An exercise in political commentary in the Jansenist or figurist mode, it attempted to spell out the political implications of the prophecies of general defection or apostasy which he and his coreligionists thought they discerned in the Old and New Testaments and whose fulfillments they were witnessing in post-*Unigenitus* France.

Is it possible to go beyond this single identification and connect Le Paige to other anonymous patriot pamphlets? It would surely seem so. For another of these bulky recueils contains a long letter dated 20 March 1772 from Le Paige to the exiled magistrate Jean-François Alexandre de Murard in which the Jansenist barrister eloquently defends the parlementary principle of unforced registration, calls for the monarchy's reconversion to the penance of "good laws" and the constitution, and suggests such reforms as the restoration of French royal taxes on the foundation of national consent, the virtual elimination of the use of lettres de cachet, the abolition of the "tyranny" of the intendants and provincial governors, and finally the purging of morals and the nation's excessive taste for "luxury," along with the "restoration of the national spirit, honor, disinterest, and the love of truth and candor." All of this was to be effected, if not by the Estates General, at least by an assembly of notables in which those distinguished by "merit" would play their deserved role.[32]

Le Paige did not usually retain copies of his own letters, so why did he make a copy of this one? Was it perhaps to serve as an outline for a pamphlet entitled *Requête des Etats-généraux de France au roi,* which appeared some three or so

30. *Réflexions sur les affaires présentes* (n.p., n.d.), pp. 1–7, in BPR: CLP, Ms. 811, no. 8.
31. BPR: CLP, Ms. 569, no. 173, "plan du molinisme d'état, petit écrit en manuscrit"; and CLP, Ms. 811, no. 8, "14 mai 1771."
32. BPR: CLP, Ms. 571, no. 26, "20 mars 1772 à m. le p. de Murard."

months later and bears an uncanny resemblance to Le Paige's epistolary agenda, including the call for a sort of permanent assembly of notables–what the pamphlet called an Order of the Fatherland *(Ordre de la patrie)*–to advise the king in all of the areas of suggested reform?[33] Unlike the letter, the pamphlet only hinted at the necessity of convoking the Estates General to consent to royal taxes, but it compensated for this measure of moderation with the audacity, in the words of Mairobert, of a "vigorous and terrible" portrait of the Sun King Louis XIV and the advice to his successor to "leave your palaces inhabited by high society and pleasure once in awhile and get acquainted with the vast reaches of your State."[34] Le Paige's handwritten corrections in his own published copy of the pamphlet further implicate him in its composition, an authorship already strongly suggested by the pamphlet's very theological anti-Jesuitism and version of French institutional history.

It would be tedious indeed to review here every scrap of evidence linking Le Paige to particular patriot pamphlets. Suffice it to say that that evidence–handwritten corrections in his personal published copies, similarity between these pamphlets and yet other manuscripts, the presence in some of these pamphlets of telltale language–points rather surely to Le Paige as author of at least twenty pamphlets, including several mentioned earlier, such as the many *Lettres*, one from a *François aux victimes d'Ebrouin (Letter by a Frenchman to the Victims of Ebrouin*, another from an *ancien magistrat à un duc et pair*, two more from a *bourgeois de Paris à un provincial*, and yet another from a *M. Xxx, conseiller au parlement, à M. le comte de Xxx*, as well as the figurist and anti-Jesuitical *Le point de vue* and *L'accomplissement des prophéties*. This number is, moreover, a conservative one. In sum, Le Paige's "influence" on the literature of the patriot movement turns out to be influence indeed, exercised directly by himself on much of its content and form.

If this torrid output seems beyond the energy and resources of even a very industrious barrister, it is well to remember that, along with many of his colleagues in the Parisian Order of Barristers, Le Paige had gone "on strike" even as a legal consultant in protest against Maupeou's edicts and his "scab" parlements and hence had nothing better to do with his time. Moreover, he enjoyed the protection of the Prince de Conti and the enclosure of the Temple, which, as a juridically immune enclave, was off-limits to both Maupeou's parlement and to the Paris lieutenant of police. All the same, Le Paige's pamphleteering activities and the Temple's secret printing presses eventually provoked enough suspicion so that, in early September 1772, the Maupeou parlement ordered Le Paige's arrest after he

33. *Requête des Etats-généraux de France au roi*, pp. 80–87.

34. *Journal historique* (25 July 1772), 3:216, but see also ibid., 17 May 1772), p. 121, on the subject of the pamphlet's appearance. The quotation about Louis XV's palaces, etc., comes from *Requête des Etats-généraux de France au roi*, pp. 46–47. For the "terrible portrait" of Louis XIV, see ibid., pp. 34–36.

failed to appear for interrogation. Le Paige himself fled for parts unknown, while Conti ostentatiously arranged for a formal inspection of the Temple.[35] Le Paige did not return to the Temple until January 1774, and the dramatic trailing off of patriot publications in late 1772 and 1773 may be attributable in part to his absence.[36]

Sixteen years later, as prerevolutionary pamphlets grew ever more revolutionary, the nearly blind octogenarian Le Paige grumbled in the margins of one of those pamphlets that "we [should] be doing what was done in 1771, and have everything [to be published] reviewed by the same pair of eyes," presumably his own.[37] That those eyes had been his is indicated by a stray letter from the young Jansenist barrister—and future revolutionary—Armand-Gaston Camus, asking Le Paige in 1771 "to please look over" a manuscript pamphlet against Maupeou "and to use it as he deems apropos."[38] And that Le Paige's supervision of patriot pamphleteering may sometimes have included collaboration is strongly suggested by the story of the composition of the *Inauguration de Pharamond,* a pamphlet universally respected in patriot circles and regarded by the *Supplément de la Gazette de France* as "the most learned and profound of all those [works] which have yet appeared on the subject."[39] Although the Bachaumont memoirs attributed the pamphlet to one Martin de Morizot, the Parisian police suspected a Jansenist Barnabite monk named Isidore Mirasson, who, arrested on 6 August 1771, conveniently accused someone "unknown to him" called Vialdome, whom he had encountered working on the manuscript of the *Inauguration* while living in poverty in the Temple.[40] Mirasson himself admitted to having allowed Vialdome the use of the Barnabites' library, as well as to having "made some corrections on" sections of the book as Vialdome transcribed them.[41] But it is hard to believe that while working on such a manuscript in the Temple he had not received a little editorial assistance from Le Paige, whose own copy of the book contains a few handwritten additions and corrections. In a letter written to his brother while in

35. On Le Paige's flight from Paris, see Mairobert, *Journal historique* (8, 12, 14 Sept. 1772), 3:271–72, 276, 278; and Le Paige's own letters from his place of hiding to his brother and Conti in BPR: CLP, Ms. 571, nos. 48–63.

36. On Le Paige's return to the Temple, see Hardy, "Mes Loisirs," Ms. 6681 (20 Jan. 1774), p. 280.

37. BPR: CLP, Ms. 928, no. 6, on reading the second part of Pierre-Jean Agier's *Le jurisconsulte nationale.*

38. BPR: CLP, Ms. 560, no. 160: "M. Camus prie Monsieur Le Paige de vouloir bien voir cet écrit, et en faire l'usage qu'il jugera à propos." The manuscript in question is entitled "Observations sommaires sur les opérations du 13 avril 1771." Although no pamphlet by that title appeared in 1771, Camus's manuscript may well have seen the light of day under another title.

39. *Supplément à la Gazette de France* (6 Mar. 1772), in *Les efforts,* 5:114. See also Mairobert, *Journal historique* (7 Mar. 1772), pp. 5–13.

40. Bachaumont, *Mémoires secrets,* 24:181.

41. BA: AB, Ms. 12401, nos. 139–50, interrogations of Dom Isidoire Mirasson by Miché de Rochebrune on 27, 28, and 29 Aug. 1772.

hiding a few months later, Le Paige acknowledged that he was suspected for his complicity in the work, and did not exactly deny it.[42]

Le Paige could not have been the principal author of the *Inauguration*, however, because its constitutionalism was much less favorable to the parlements than was his. The constitutionalism of the *Inauguration* therefore had more in common with that of the monumental *Maxims of French Public Law*, which, however respectful of the parlements, still clearly subordinated them to the nation as better represented in the Estates General. Like the *Inauguration*'s national diet, the *Maximes*' Estates General possessed full legislative sovereignty, explicitly including the right to change the French monarchy into an aristocracy or democracy if it chose.[43]

But the *Maximes*, as we have already noted, do not really take leave of Jansenist turf. Wrongly attributed by Mairobert to the parlementary magistrate Michau de Montblin, who in fact did not survive his exile during the Maupeou revolution, the treatise was in fact the product of a collaborative effort by parlementary barristers who, like Le Paige, were chafing at the bit of their self-imposed regime of legal inactivity. Although the total number of contributors to this enterprise is uncertain, the most important were our old acquaintances, the abbé Claude Mey and Gabriel-Nicolas Maultrot, the latter apparently the author of a pungent little *Dissertation on the Right to Convene the Estates General* that was appended to the *Maximes*' second edition. The similarity noted earlier, then, between the Gallican and specifically conciliar argumentation of the *Maximes* and that of the *Apologie de tous les jugemens* published in 1752 is hardly coincidental, for Mey and Maultrot were in part the authors of both treatises.[44]

Rounding out this list of the *Maximes*' known contributors are the lawyers Aubri, son of the author of the famous consultation against the Council of Embrun in 1727 and noted by the Bachaumont memoirs at the time of his death as a "lawyer renowned above all in the Jansenist party"; and André Blonde, another canonist and known chiefly in the 1770s for his Jansenistic refutation of the abbé Bergier's somewhat Molinistic apologetical writings against Rousseauian deism and Holbachian atheism.[45] Blonde was also the author of two other widely noted

---

42. Le Paige's corrections and additions are in his personal copy of the *Inauguration* in BPR: CLP, Ms. 815, no. 5, pp. 16, 65, 135. These additions and corrections did not appear in any published edition. For his epistolary remarks about his suspected complicity in the writing and publication of the pamphlet, see BPR: CLP, Ms. 571, fol. 50, Le Paige to his brother, 14 Sept. 1772.

43. *Maximes du droit public françois*, 1:155, 237–38, 267–69.

44. On attribution by Mairobert, see *Journal historique* (23 Aug. 1772), 3:252. On authorship of *Maximes*, see L.-G. Michaud, ed. *Biographie universelle ancienne et moderne*, 83 vols. (Paris, 1811–55): on Maultrot (and Blonde), 27:311–14; on Mey, 28:162–63.

45. On Aubri, see Bachaumont, *Mémoires secrets*, 34:10; for André Blonde in general, see Michaud, *Biographie universelle*, 4:448–49; and as anti-Molinist, see his *Lettre à M. Bergier, docteur en théologie et principal du collège de Besançon, sur son ouvrage intitulé: Le déisme réfuté par lui-même* (n.p., n.d.).

anti-Maupeou pamphlets, namely the *Le parlement justifié par l'impératrice de Russie* and *Le parlement justifié par l'impératrice reine de Hongrie et par le roi de Prusse.*[46] The Jansenist tone of this latter pamphlet's anti-Jesuitism is therefore hardly accidental. Anathase-Alexandre Clément de Boissy, a councillor in the Paris *Chambre des comptes*, is usually credited with the authorship of the highly successful *Mayor of the Palace*, suffused though that pamphlet is with Le Paigian parlementary constitutionalism. "People grab it on all sides, and I have had it said to my face that it is a chef-d'oeuvre," despairingly confided the fictional Sorhouet to Maupeou in the satirical *Correspondance secrète et familière.*[47] But whether Boissy or Le Paige wrote it makes no difference for this tally of Jansenist pamphleteers: Clément de Boissy was a member of an integrally Jansenist family that included Clément de Barville, solicitor general of the Paris *Cour des aides;* Clément de Feillet, councillor in the Parlement of Paris; and the abbé Augustin-Charles-Jean Clément de Bizon, treasurer of the cathedral church of Auxerre and future constitutional bishop of Versailles. Finally, the Parisian police's search of the premises of one Zacarie-Mathieu de Ponchon, chevalier de Montfort, turned up evidence of his authorship of a small pamphlet entitled *Franches et loyales représentations de la noblesse (Frank and Loyal Remonstrances by the Nobility)*. If not himself a Jansenist, he was in the police informer's estimation "connected to many Jansenists"– principally the Le Nain and d'Asfeld families–and had loudly blamed Maupeou's coup on the Jesuits in some of his impromptu café commentaries.[48]

It is surely time to take inventory and see what all these pamphlets and books amount to in relation to the patriots' polemical production as a whole. Of about eighty pamphlets carefully perused in the course of this study, nearly half, or thirty-eight of that number, can safely be labeled as Jansenist by reason of textual or authorial considerations. These raw figures call for several refinements. First, the total of eighty refers to the unofficial and anonymous publications that bear the personal stamp of one or several authors and, with the exception of Lamoignon de Malesherbes' highly characteristic remonstrances written as president of the Paris Cour des aides and the playwright Caron de Beaumarchais' equally eccentric judicial memoirs against the Maupeou parlement in 1773, does not include the much more numerous official pronouncements–remonstrances, judgments, entreaties, etc.–of the various parlements and other judicial bodies, pro-

---

46. Augéard, *Memoirs secrets*, p. 44.

47. *Correspondance secrète et familière* in *Les efforts*, 2:101. For Clément de Boissy as author of *Le maire du palais* as well as of the pamphlet *Vues pacifiques sur l'état actuel du parlement* (n.p., n.d.), see Antoine-Alexandre Barbier, *Dictionnaire des ouvrages anonymes*, 4 vols. (Paris, 1873–1889), 2:320; and Michaud, *Biographie universelle*, 8:408–9. For evidence of Clément de Boissy's Jansenism, see his publications under the pseudonym of "Fontenay" on the eve of the Revolution, such as *De la grace de Dieu et de la prédestination* (n.p., 1787), *Abrégé de l'ancien et du nouveau testament* (Paris, 1788), and others.

48. BA: AB, Ms. 12392, nos. 202–3, dossier dated 7 Feb. 1771; no. 205, search by Commissioner Hubert Mutel, 25 Mar. 1771; and nos. 208–13, interrogation by Mutel, 30 Mar. 1771.

nouncements that usually assumed the form of pamphlets. Second, this figure includes only whole works, and does not count either multiple editions of a single work or the several parts of works that appeared in installments, such as the famous *Correspondance secrète et familière* and the *Lettres d'un homme à un autre homme*, or the successive numbers of a periodical such as the thirteen odd numbers of the *Supplément à la Gazette de France*. The eighty are hence a significant percentage of the patriots' total literary production from 1770 to 1775; Durand Echeverria's exhaustive bibliography includes less than a hundred and twenty such "individual" publications, including the many quasi-official "records" or "accounts of what has happened" in this or that parlement.[49] Finally, thirty-eight is a conservative figure, and does not exclude the possibility that other less clearly identifiable pamphlets may have been written by Jansenists as well.

Not only is the figure thirty-eight numerically significant, but it includes most of the major pamphlets of the protest—the ones that apparently made the biggest impression and gave rise to the most comment. The most glaring exceptions to this rule are Lamoignon de Malesherbes' memorable remonstrances as president of the Cour des aides; the spectacularly successful *Correspondance secrète et familière*, which the Parisian barrister Jacques-Mathieu Augeard owned up to having written in his subsequently published memoirs; and the *Lettres d'un homme à un autre homme* written by Guy-Jean-Baptiste Target, yet another Parisian barrister who went on to play an important role in the early phases of the Revolution.[50] Constituting as it were a separate wing or flank of the patriot front, Augéard, Malesherbes, and Target had found their own paths to the thesis of national sovereignty, and it may readily be granted that these paths were illuminated in part by the French Enlightenment. Indeed, Target, whose *Lettres* strike an audibly enlightened tone, was at that moment moving out of the parlementary and Jansenist circles that had first formed him and into the philosophical salon of Madame Geoffrin, while Malesherbes could lay claim to being at least a lesser luminary in the century's firmament of lights.[51]

49. Echeverria, *The Maupeou Revolution*, pp. 305–14.

50. Augeard, *Mémoires secrets de J.-M. Augéard, secrétaire des commandements de la reine Marie-Antoinette, 1760–1800* (Paris, 1866), pp. 44–45, 65. Augéard also took credit for the *Oeufs rouges. Première partie. Sorhouet mourant à M. de Maupeou, chancelier de France* (n.p., 1772); and *Mandement de Monseigneur l'archévêque de Paris, qui proscrit l'usage des oeufs rouges, à commencer du vendredi dans l'octave de l'ascension jusqu'à la résurrection des morts exclusivement* (Paris, 1772). In an anonymous pamphlet written on the eve of the Revolution, however, Augeard hinted that President Chrétien-François de Lamoignon may also have contributed to the composition of the *Correspondance secrète*. See [Augéard], *Les mânes de Madame la présidente Le Mairat à M. de Lamoignon, quatrième président au parlement, et garde des sceaux* (n.p., 1788), pp. 3–4.

51. On Target's early career, see Dale Van Kley, *The Jansenists and the Expulsion of the Jesuits, 1757–1765* (New Haven, 1975), pp. 100–101; and Charles O'Brien, "New Light on the Mouton-Natoire Case (1768): Freedom of Conscience and the Role of the Jansenists," *JCS* 27 (1985):65–82.

That said, it would be misleading to draw too sharp a line between the enlightened and Jansenistic flanks of the patriot movement. On the one side, Lamoignon de Malesherbes had learned his constitutionalism at the feet of Abbé Pucelle, the great Jansenist magistrate of the century's first decades, while both Augeard's and Target's constitutionalism remained very historical and heavily indebted to that of Le Paige.[52] Even the self-consciously enlightened Pidansat de Mairobert could rail against the Jesuits in accents barely distinguishable from those of Jansenists.[53] And on the other side, the forensic necessity of appealing to the broadest possible constituency forced Jansenists further to secularize their sectarian constitutionalism: to reconceptualize, for example, the magistrates' venal offices in terms of the natural right of property, and their representative role in the language of natural law. This was especially true of Mey's and Maultrot's *Maximes du droit public françois*, which drew heavily, as has been noted, from such seventeenth-century natural-law theoreticians as Pufendorf and Grotius, as well as such Anglo-Saxon commonwealthman ideologists as Sidney and Locke. In one of his pamphlets, the Jansenist André Blonde even quoted from that boldest of the century's atheistic statements, Baron d'Holbach's *Nature's System*.[54]

Pidansat de Mairobert then had it about right: in rebaptizing itself as the patriot party, the Jansenist party became at once more and less than it had been. It remains the case, however, that until less than twenty years before the Revolution the century's most frontal protest against Bourbon absolutism was organized largely if not exclusively by Jansenists.

The Printing and Distribution of Patriot Pamphlets

These "antichancellor writings," as the Parisian bookseller Siméon-Prosper Hardy called them, were the objects of eighteenth-century France's most massive censorial crackdown. By the time it was over, all branches of the printing industry had been affected, including the content of French-language newspapers printed outside of France.[55] The initial phase of this governmental effort was extrajudicial, its principal agent being the police inspector—and "literary specialist"— Joseph d'Hémery, made familiar by the work of Robert Darnton. With the help of commissioners Hubert Mutel and Miché de Rochebrune, d'Hémery acted under

52. On Malesherbes' constitutionalism, see Pierre Grosclaude, *Malesherbes, témoin et intérprète de son temps* (Paris, 1961), pp. 55–60.

53. Mairobert, *Journal historique*, 1:75, 93, 113, 127, 248, 250, 265, 287.

54. [André Blonde], *Le parlement justifié par l'impératrice de Russie*, pp. 119–20.

55. Robert Darnton, "Reading, Writing, and Publishing," in *The Literary Underground of the Old Regime* (Cambridge, Mass., 1982), pp. 167–208; and Jeremy Popkin, "The Gazette de Leyde under Louis XVI," in *Press and Politics in Pre-Revolutionary France*, ed. Jack R. Censer and Jeremy Popkin (Berkeley, Calif., 1987), pp. 88–89.

the authority of the Parisian lieutenant of police Gabriel de Sartine.[56] But in March 1772 the Maupeou parlement also got into the act with its own noisy judicial investigation under the direction of the court reporter Valentin Goezman, who later suffered a spectacular literary drubbing at the hands of the playwright Caron de Beaumarchais.

As the title of d'Hémery's report makes clear, the targets of this censorial effort were at once the "authors, printers, booksellers, and peddlers of scurrilous pamphlets *(libelles)* since the Edict of December 1770." Unless the flights of Blonde and Le Paige can be counted as successes—they were of sorts—and apart from the case of Dom Isidore Mirasson, the only writers that this vast repressive effort turned up were the chevalier de Montfort, author, as we have noted, of the *Franches et loyales représentations de la noblesse,* and one Claude-Antoine Boulemier, the author of a small ode against the chancellor.[57] The investigation was hardly more successful where printers were concerned.[58] The brunt of the crackdown therefore fell on the booksellers, street peddlers, and the much more numerous individuals guilty of selling, copying, distributing, or procuring some "antichancellor writings"—occasionally only of uttering some "antichancellor" remarks.

The resultant collection of "embastilled" unfortunates makes it possible to measure the presence of Jansenism at the lower levels of the patriot movement's constituency and distributional infrastructure. Owing to the fragmentary state of both the Bastille's archives and the trial records of the Maupeou parlement, the collection of names is incomplete. Yet a list of eighty-five individuals subjected to intense surveillance, attempted arrest, arrest and imprisonment, or sometimes trial probably represents close to three-fourths of the total, and hence provides an adequate sampling. Of this number, twenty-eight and possibly thirty, or about one-third of the total, were Jansenists or jansénisants in rigorous senses of these terms. The figure is again a conservative one because it cannot include Jansenists whose identity is unapparent on the basis of the often sketchy information available.

What constitutes evidence for Jansenism? Although in some cases the evidence may ring efficaciously only in the ears of the initiates—the use of the phrase "friends of the Truth" in an interrogation, for example—in others it would seem sufficient for all. Consider the case of four unmarried women arrested on 5 September 1771. Forced by suspicious commissioners to dismount from their carriage at the Paris "hell's gate" upon returning from an outing in Arcueil, these

56. Robert Darnton, "A Policeman Sorts His Files: The Anatomy of the Republic of Letters," in *The Great Cat Massacre and Other Episodes in French Cultural History* (New York, 1984), pp. 145–89.

57. BA: AB, Ms. 12387, no. 173.

58. BN: Mss. Fr., Ms. 22101, A-D 41, fols. 70–71, 100–105; BA: AB, Ms. 12392, nos. 73, 78–81, 93, 111, 140–41, 179.

women displayed a suspicious waddle in their movements that turned out, upon inspection, to be caused by part of an edition of an anti-Maupeou pamphlet attached to the undersides of their petticoats. The obligatory arrests were almost as embarrassing to the police as to the women and their families, because the four in question were hardly nobodies: Françoise-Julie Danjean, daughter of a well-known Parisian architect; Démoiselle Gerbier de La Massilaye, sister of the famous parlementary barrister by the same name; Démoiselle Heuvrard, the trusted chambermaid of the *maître des requêtes* Guillaume Lambert; and Anne-Madeleine Morin, the first cousin of the bookseller Butard, long established "at the ensign of Truth" on the rue Saint-Jacques—all of them notoriously Jansenist as well as prominent Parisian families. They are "the most outrageous Jansenists," was all a police spy could find to report to Sartine concerning Gerbier mother and daughter after the police had allowed the latter to return home.[59]

But the police learned little from the less fortunate Danjean and Morin, who endured a four-month stay in the Bastille, not in this case because the prisoners knew nothing but because in the purest tradition of Port-Royal they insisted upon keeping their biblical yeas to a tight-lipped minimum. Typical of their indomitable nays under interrogation are those of Julie Danjean, who, when asked by Commissioner Mutel whether she knew the author—in fact Le Paige—of the pamphlet that they had been carrying *(Réflexions générales sur le système projetté par le maire du palais, pour changer la constitution de l'état [General Relections on the Mayor of the Palace's Systematic Design of Changing the French Constitution])* responded that "she had nothing to respond" because "neither the law of God nor that of honor obliged her to inform on her brothers."[60]

But the Jansenist presence at the lower reaches of the patriot movement looms even larger when subjected to a more qualitative analysis equidistant from these statistical or anecdotal extremes. Many—even most—of those arrested, investigated, or harassed by the police or the Maupeou parlement were in fact related to one another as strands of small distribution webs which, in five of six cases, led to a Jansenist center.

At or near the center of the one involving the four Jansenist spinsters, for example, was a certain Vion, alias Jean-Pierre Dumont, a sometime Dominican monk who, having been obliged to leave his order in 1741 after running afoul of the Archbishop of Embrun "over matters relating to the constitution *[Unigenitus]*," had since lived in Paris above Butard's Jansenist bookstore and in contact with the "the most important Jansenists and especially with the Gerbiers,

59. The quotation is from a report by a police spy, or *mouche*, dated 8 Feb. 1772, in BA: AB, Ms. 12392, nos. 377–78; for basic information on this case, see Ms. 12403, no. 221; BN: Mss. Fr., Ms. 22101, A-D 41, fol. 158, report of 18 Feb. 1771; and Mairobert, *Journal historique* (15 Sept. 1771), 2:140–41.

60. BA: AB, Ms. 12392, no. 313, interrogation of Julie Danjean in Bastille by Hubert Mutel on 21 Sept. 1771.

the Butards, the Danjeans, etc., etc."[61] The police finally did get Anne-Madeleine Morin to confess by means of indisputable evidence that it was this Dumont, or Vion, who had engaged her to write to a certain Abbé Le Chanteux at Arcueil, asking him to accept and store cases of pamphlets that she and her sister "pilgrims" then picked up, not only on 5 September but also on previous and more successful occasions. But that is about as much as the police ever learned. The abbé Le Chanteux convinced the police that he had been an unwitting accomplice of Morin and Dumont, while Dumont or Vion, spectacularly arrested by d'Hémery on 19 September, stubbornly refused to divulge the identity of the pamphlet's printer or distributor in Arcueil. As for the Parisian connection, Morin revealed that she and her companions had deposited their previous stock at the hôtel of the chamber-maid's master Guillaume Lambert, a sometime member of the Parlement's magisterial *parti janséniste*, whose Jansenist zeal had not been dampened by his recent promotion to the royal council. The police did not apparently think it appropriate to importune Lambert himself.[62]

D'Hémery and Mutel stumbled onto another such distributional network on 10 June 1772, when, tipped off by a police spy or a neighbor, they arrested an out-of-work tailor named Prestrelle and his family, whom they caught in the act of recopying patriot pamphlets and found in their possession a sizable collection. Recently immigrated from Noyon, the indigent Prestrelle family was selling their copies to one François-Amadée Kaufmann, an interpreter and secret agent of the French diplomatic service, who on orders from his superiors was busily ingratiating himself with the Saxon and Prussian ambassadors by procuring the pamphlets they desired. Unable to go further in the direction of demand, the police then tracked down the Prestrelle's source of supply, which led them to a minor employee of the indirect tax farmers, or General Farm, a man named De La Roche, whom the police arrested the following day. Also caught *en flagrant délit*, De La Roche for his part pointed to a fellow employee of the General Farm, who in turn had been getting the pamphlets from his brother, an out-of-work procurator at the Paris Châtelet, who in d'Hémery's words was a "young man entirely devoted to the Jansenist party" and bent upon "imitating one of his uncles named the abbé de François, a former inmate of the Bastille and prominent Jansenist canon in Troyes."[63]

61. BN: Mss. Fr., Ms. 22101, A-D 41, fol. 160, report dated 19 Sept. 1989. On Dumont's or Vion's arrest and previous difficulties apropos of *Unigenitus*, see Hardy, "Mes loisirs," Ms. 6680 (19 Sept. 1771), p. 279.

62. BN: Mss. Fr., Ms. 22021, A-B 41, fols. 159–60. See also BA: AB, Ms. 12392, no. 301, d'Hémery to Sartine, 19 Sept. 1772; nos. 318–19, interrogation of Morin by Mutel at Bastille on 23 Sept. 1771; and nos. 321–22, interrogation of Dumont or Vion by Mutel on 24 Sept. 1771.

63. BA: AB, Ms. 12403, nos. 48–50, d'Hémery to Sartine, 10 June 1772; Kauffmann's declaration (no. 154) is dated 10 July 1772. On Prestrelle and De La Roche, see BN: Mss. Fr., Ms. 22101, A-D 41, fols.

This Jansenist brother, named François de Quiney, concocted a cock-and-bull story about his own source of supply until the Jansenist colporteur La Gueyrie, who had been arrested earlier that June, indicated the widow Mecquignon and sons, booksellers established on the rue de la Juiverie, as his own principal source. At that point François de Quiney confessed that he too had gotten his pamphlets from Mecquignon, but from Mecquignon herself the police learned nothing except that she sometimes went with her servant Jeanneton to the enclosure of the Temple "to consult Monsieur Le Paige."[64] Invoking her "honor and conscience" and the "commandment of charity," and refusing repeatedly to take the oath because her first one was "irrevocable," this Jansenist widow remained steadfastly silent throughout her stay in the Bastille and her trial by the Maupeou parlement, which sentenced her to a nine-year exile from the environs of Paris. Fortunately for her, the dauphine Marie-Antoinette took a benevolent interest in the widow's plight, obtained the king's pardon, and invited her whole family to dinner at Versailles—all this over the protests of the Archbishop of Paris, who objected that "that widow is Jansenist, receives no one but Jansenists, and sells no books except Jansenist ones."[65]

The conspicuous role of Jansenists at all levels of the patriot movement strongly suggests that that movement sought out and spread by means of the same clandestine channels of communication originally set up for the dissemination of Jansenist ephemeral literature, in particular the weekly *Nouvelles ecclésiastiques*. The fact that, when arrested, the Jansenist colporteur La Gueyrie was carrying fifty numbers of the *Nouvelles ecclésiastiques*, as well as such anti-Maupeou pamphlets as the satirical *Mandement de l'archévêque de Paris qui proscrit l'usage des oeufs rouges (Mandemus by the Archbishop of Paris Proscribing the Use of Red Eggs)*, lends additional credence to this possibility. La Gueyrie's interrogation and his confiscated account book amply confirm Pidansat de Mairobert's assertion that

178–79, report of 10–11 June 1772; and AN: X2b, Ms. 1400, interrogation of Prestrelle family by Mutel on 10, 16 June 1771, and by Goezman on 27 Feb. 1773; perquisition and interrogation of De La Roche by Mutel and d'Hémery on 11 June 1771; and perquistion and interrogation of Quiney brothers on 10–11 June 1771.

64. Quotation from Mecquignon's interrogation and confrontation with La Gueyrie by Jean Serreau on 19–22 June 1771 in AN: X2b, Ms. 1400. See also confrontation of François de Quiney with Mecquignon at Bastille on 23 June 1771.

65. The quotation from Mecquignon is from her requête to Maupeou's parlement of Paris in BA: AB, Ms. 12403, no. 421. Mecquignon's sentence is in *Arrest de la cour de parlement, qui condamne différens particuliers au bannissement et au blâme, etc. pour avoir colporté et vendu différens libelles contre l'autorité du roi et l'honneur des magistrats. Du 29 janvier 1774* (Paris, 1774), p. 23, in NL, case wing folio oZ 144, .A1, vol. 8, no. 77. On Mecquignon's pardon and Archbishop of Paris see Siméon-Prosper Hardy, "Mes loisirs, ou journal d'événements tels qu'ils parviennent à ma connoissance," 8 vols. in BN: Mss. Fr., Ms. 6682 (29 Jan.; 11, 23 Feb.; and 9 Mar. 1774), pp. 280, 287, 297, 305, respectively. The Archbishop's attitude toward this family as reported by Hardy is confirmed by a letter from that prelate dated 17 June 1772 in BA: AB, Ms. 12403, no. 98.

he was a regular distributor of the *Nouvelles,* both in Paris and in the provinces. Hardly different is the case of Le Sage: according to Mairobert a "big Jansenist and a big distributor of Ecclesiastical Gazettes." Denounced as a peddler of anti-Maupeou pamphlets and arrested on 27 October 1772, Le Sage was found in possession of another fifty numbers of the *Nouvelles* and letters from the provinces requesting more.[66]

Le Sage's footsteps led in some very strange directions, however, among them the patriot movement's only incontestably "philosophical" or "encyclopedic" distributional nexus uncovered by the police. Le Sage, as it happened, worked as a shopboy *(garçon)* for a certain bookseller named Etienne Devaux, who had served time in the Bastille for selling antireligious and pornographic books and who, far from mending his ways after his release, added anti-Maupeou pamphlets to his prohibited stock until death closed down his business in 1772. What his death and the necessary inventory of his effects eventually revealed was that Devaux had plied his prohibited commerce in close cooperation with a policeman *(exempte de police)* named Joseph Archier, who was able to provide the ailing Devaux with the indispensable legal protection as well as to procure the philosophical and pornographic books from somewhere outside Paris. And indeed the perquisition of Devaux's stock turned up mainly pornographic and philosophical books ranging from *Celebrated Girls of the Eighteenth Century* to Voltaire's *Precis of the Century of Louis XV.*[67]

For anti-Maupeou pamphlets, however, Archier had recourse to Le Sage, who of course enjoyed access to the Jansenist distributional underground. But Archier had also exploited others, including a defrocked Benedictine monk named Guillaume Imbert. Denounced by Archier and arrested in turn, this former monk confessed to having indeed sent a couple of hawkers of anti-Maupeou pamphletary wares in Archier's direction because Archier had told him that he needed the pamphlets for an important parlementary magistrate, who turned out to be none other than the pious Jansenist Rolland de Challerange. But the unfortunate Imbert himself was found in possession of all manner of antireligious philosophical books, which, he apologetically explained, he had borrowed or bought from Archier for the express purpose of writing a "systematic refutation." A self-proclaimed acquaintance of the philosophes d'Alembert and Madame Geoffrin,

66. La Gueyrie's account book as a colporteur along with the numbers of the *Nouvelles ecclésiastiques* confiscated from both him and the colporteur Le Sage are in AN: X2b, Ms. 1400. The quotation about La Gueyrie as Jansenist is from a letter by Serreau to Sartine dated 3 June 1772 in BA: AB, Ms. 12403, no. 39. See also Mairobert, *Journal historique* (27 Oct. 1772), 2:319; and Hardy, "Mes loisirs," BN: Ms. Fr. 6681 (20 Oct. 1772), p. 107.

67. This list of seized books, along with the interrogations of two other shopboys of Devaux's named Veille and Lamare by Goezman on 22–23 Feb. 1773, are in AN: X2b, Ms. 1400. See also Hardy, "Mes loisirs," BN: Ms. Fr. 6681 (26 Oct. 1772), p. 107.

Imbert boasted a collection of books and pamphlets in which Diderot's *Pensées sur la nature (Thoughts on Nature)*, d'Holbach's *Système de la nature*, and Voltaire's *Sermon des cinquante (Sermon by the Fifty)* sat uneasily next to Le Paige's *Lettre sur les lits de justice*, La Chalotais' judicial *Compte rendu* against the Jesuits, and some numbers of the Jansenist *Supplément à la Gazette de France*.[68]

Nothing better illustrates the ideological promiscuity of the patriot movement, at least at its fringes, than this juxtaposition of encyclopedic and Jansenist literary undergrounds, persons, and books in the Devaux-Archier case, unless it is the case of François de Quiney, the "entirely Jansenist young man" whom d'Hémery arrested earlier for buying anti-Maupeou pamphlets from the widow Mecquignon and then giving them to his brother for distribution elsewhere. "I suppose I had better be prepared for the worst, since brother has already been pitted against brother, a mother against her children, . . . relatives against relatives, and friends against friends," de Quiney wrote resignedly to the lieutenant of police Sartine after extrajudicial "confrontations" had been conducted with his mother, brother, and Mecquignon, and he had himself spent three months in the Bastille. "And thus," he continued more bitterly, "have I witnessed the overthrow, if not of divine laws, at least the laws of nature which even the most barbarous nations respect—and that by means of this very imposing display of justice that ought to be used to uphold these same laws. Ah," he concluded, "how Monsieur Rousseau is right to say that we have only the appearance of humanity. And thus, Monsieur, I am content so long as I enjoy the good fortune of not thinking." Misery loves company. For thus did persecution convert—or deconvert—a disciple of Saint Augustine into a disciple of that self-anointed spokesman for the persecuted of even an "enlightened" century: namely, Jean-Jacques Rousseau.[69]

"Acts of Schism"

Evidence of Jansenist participation in the patriot movement calls for some explanation. Why would Jansenists have run the risk of compromising their religious identity by throwing themselves body and soul into a movement so apparently devoid of religious meaning as a political protest against Maupeou's constitutional coup? Was it just in repayment for past services rendered by the parlements to the Jansenist cause, notably judicial protection from public refusals of sacraments in

68. The interrogations of Imbert by Rochebrune in Bastille on 10 December 1772 are in BA: AB, Ms. 12400, nos. 94–97; and by Goezman in Conciergerie on 20 Feb. and following days, 1773, in AN: X2b, Ms. 1400. For the inventory of Imbert's papers and books, and the letter from Rolland de Challerange to Archier, dated 29 July 1771 at Etampes, see ibid.

69. D'Hémery's description of François de Quiney is in BN: Mss. Fr., Ms. 22101, A-D 41, fols. 178–79, report of 10–11 June 1772. The prisoner's letter to Sartine, dated Sept. 1772, is in BA: AB, Ms. 12403, no. 286.

the 1750s and the dissolution of the Jesuits in the 1760s? Or did the Maupeou coup itself have a religious agenda that has hitherto eluded the attention of the event's many historians?

The event's possible religious dimension is indeed likely to be elusive. Consider, for example, the possibility that Maupeou's antiparlementary revolution meant that the Archbishop of Paris and other like-minded prelates found themselves able to resume their policy of depriving suspected Jansenists of the sacraments of the viaticum and extreme unction. But if they did so, how are we to know in the absence of any judicial affaires on behalf of Jansenists, which would be unlikely in Maupeou's courts? To be sure, the Jansenists' vigilant *Nouvelles ecclésiastiques* might have been trusted to bring every last such incident to the attention of its outraged readers, as it had certainly done during the 1750s and 1760s. But in 1770 this hitherto feisty journal began to retreat from the politically controversial and to restrict its coverage to "ecclesiastical news" more narrowly defined. The reason, hinted the anonymous *Supplément à la Gazette de France,* was that "after thirty years or more of fuss and bother, thirty million [livres] and thirty thousand spies," the police had finally penetrated the anonymity of the Jansenist weekly.[70] In short, the periodical was pretty definitely on probation, which may be why it had little to say about Maupeou's revolution. Nor did the *Supplément* itself pick up the slack in the reporting of mixed political-ecclesiastical events.

Fortunately another source comes to the rescue, namely the manuscript diary of the Parisian bookseller Siméon-Prosper Hardy. Hardy has hardly suffered from neglect at the hands of historians; along with Arthur Young's *Travels,* his diary is among the most cited sources on France on the eve of the Revolution, particularly on the subject of pamphlets and popular disturbances. But what seems largely to have escaped historiographical attention is Hardy's Jansenism—a Jansenism brazen enough to have accepted as authentic all the miracles attributed to the Deacon Pâris and persistent enough to have seized every occasion to extol the memory of Port-Royal. What makes Hardy's Jansenist testimony especially interesting is that it is that of a pious yet highly anticlerical Parisian bourgeois, strategically located in the largely Jansenist quarter of Saint-Jacques, next to another Jansenist bookseller, Jacques Butard, "at the ensign of the Truth."

So it is Hardy, for example, who indignantly informs us that most of the clerical councillors for Maupeou's new Parlement of Paris had been recruited by none other than the anti-Jansenist Archbishop of Paris, Christophe de Beaumont, who raided his cathedral clergy for that purpose.[71] But what particularly outraged

---

70. *Supplément à la Gazette de France* (16 Aug. 1772), in *Les efforts,* p. 152.

71. Hardy, "Mes loisirs," BN: Ms. Fr. 6680 (24 Apr. 1771), p. 253; and Ms. 6681 (20 Feb. 1772), p. 24. This testimony is confirmed by Mathieu-François Pidansat de Mairobert in "Lettre V sur le clergé," *L'espion anglois, ou correspondance secrète entre Milord All'eye et Milord All'ear,* 10 vols. (London, 1784)

Hardy, aside from the persecution of his beloved parlements, was that the Maupeou coup gave ecclesiastics the green light to resume the sacramental harassment of appellants of *Unigenitus* and other suspected Jansenists, persecution that the old parlements had stopped. Although obviously acting with the approval of the archbishop, the ecclesiastics in question were second-order curés, the products of the episcopal purge of the Parisian priesthood; and this pious bourgeois bookseller's opinion of them shows why, despite some initial enthusiasm for the Revolution, they would be unable to repeat in 1789 anything like the popular role they had played in the Paris of the Catholic League or even of the religious Fronde.

The first recorded victim of this renewed anti-Jansenist offensive was a sort of lay saint, one Claude Boucherette Du Roule, who, son of a well-known Parisian barrister, "had been living for a long while as a simple individual in the profoundest retreat while devoting himself to penitence and other good works" in the once pretty Jansenist and soon-to-be revolutionary Saint-Antoine quarter of Paris. Finding himself at extremities in April 1772, he requested viaticum and extreme unction, only to be refused by the entire resident clergy of the Sainte-Marguerite parish. They had apparently acted on the instructions of the Archbishop of Paris, who insisted that Du Roule name his confessor. In the absence of the exiled Parlement of Paris, the ultimate "public scandal" of death without the sacraments was avoided only by the quick action of the lieutenant of police, Gabriel de Sartine. Sartine had Du Roule transferred to the rue de la Mortellerie, where he was ministered to by the more irenic curé of Saint-Gervais.[72]

Du Roule's case was followed in the next two years by several others in Paris or the Paris region, all of them duly noted by the indignant Hardy.[73] In the course of the same years, the remaining Jansenist refugees among the monastic communities in the Paris region unhappily found themselves the objects of the archbishop's rekindled zeal: the monastic personnel of the Hôtel Dieu, the chief Parisian hospital and poor house, got a new set of administrators to the archbishop's liking; so, too, the Saint-Magloire convent in the rue Saint-Denis and a Carmelite monastery in Charenton.[74] Finally, on 7 March 1774, even the recently restrained *Nouvelles ecclésiastiques* broke its long silence, running the risk of a belated and understated issue devoted to these renewed "acts of schism."[75] The

---

1:186. The clerical councillors were the abbés Lucker, Le Sage, Desplasses, and the archbishop's nephew de Beaumont.

72. Hardy, "Mes loisirs," BN: Ms. Fr. 6681 (14 May 1772), p. 59.

73. Ibid., 3 Oct. 1772, p. 106; 27 Feb. 1773, p. 162; 7, 16 Apr. 1773, pp. 180, 182; 30 July and 12 Aug. 1773, pp. 213, 217; 15, 27 Feb. 1773, pp. 291–92.

74. On hospitals and monasteries, ibid., Ms. Fr. 6680 (21 Aug., 25 Dec. 1771), pp. 273, 299; and Ms. Fr. 6681 (10, 12 May 1772), pp. 25–26, 58; (11–12 May 1773), pp. 187–89.

75. *Nouvelles ecclésiastiques, ou mémoires pour servir à l'histoire de la constitution Unigenitus* (henceforth *NE*), 3d ed. (Utrecht, 1728–1803), 7 Mar. 1774, pp. 37–38; and Hardy, "Mes loisirs," BN: Ms. Fr. 6681 (10 Mar. 1771), p. 310.

Nouvelles correctly attributed them, not to royal religious policy as such, which remained pretty much unchanged during the Maupeou episode, but to Christophe de Beaumont, who profited in piecemeal fashion from the dispersal or purging of the old parlements "to commit," as the Jansenist journal put it, "these new acts of schism after which his heart has pined for so many years."[76]

Perhaps the pettiest "act of schism" to come to Hardy's outraged attention involved an unfortunate schoolmistress who absentmindedly left her book of liturgical offices on her chair in the parish church of Saint-Sulpice after attending mass there one Sunday morning in 1774. Turned in to the church sacristan, the book fell into the hands of one of the church's vicaires, who, finding in its pages a portrait of the deceased Jansenist "saint," the deacon Pâris, brought this incriminating evidence to the attention of the curé, who sent it to the *grand chantre* of the cathedral church. This prelate in turned informed the archbishop Christophe de Beaumont, who finally delegated the task of investigating "such an important fact" to one of his grands vicaires, the abbé de L'Ecluse or Delescluse. The terrified schoolmistress confessed to seeing nothing amiss in using the "venerable deacon's" portrait as a bookmark, and her catechism pupils, who were each interrogated separately, had apparently learned nothing from their teacher to the detriment of the bull *Unigenitus*. Nonetheless de L'Ecluse dismissed the schoolmistress, allowing her only enough time to collect some of her tuition—and "to which he added the injustice of refusing to return her book of offices." "Thus," commented Hardy indignantly, "have these turbulent and fanatical ecclesiastics profited . . . from present circumstances to exercise with tranquility their false and indiscreet zeal, in tormenting simple laypeople with ridiculous gestures which are an affront to common sense."[77]

Who, it might be asked, was Jacques de L'Ecluse? He had long been one of the archbishop's grands vicaires, but he had also once been the curé of the parish church of Saint-Nicolas-des-Champs—until 1759, when the old Parlement of Paris had banished him from the realm for life for having refused the viaticum and extreme unction to one of his appellant parishioners.[78] So his renewed presence in Paris in the 1770s calls for explanation, and is part of a wider pattern also assiduously noted by Hardy. Availing himself of a royal declaration of amnesty promulgated on 15 June 1771 for precisely such exiled priests (and docilely registered by the Maupeou parlement four days later), Christophe de Beaumont systematically brought such exiled priests as well as ex-Jesuits back to the archdiocese of Paris and found supplementary benefices for them wherever he could,

76. *NE* 7 Mar. 1774, pp. 37.

77. Hardy, "Mes loisirs," BN: Ms Fr 6681 (22 Feb. 1774), pp. 296–97.

78. BN: CJF, Ms. 1569, fols. 306–14; and *Arrest de la cour de parlement. Extrait des registres du parlement. Du 17 janvier 1759* (Paris, 1759).

in de l'Ecluse's case as superior to the Ursuline convent in Saint-Cloud.[79] These priests in turn often perpetrated the new "acts of schism." Another such case is that of the abbé—and ex-Jesuit—Madier who, driven by the Parlement from the parish of Saint-Séverin in 1756, found himself reimposed by the archbishop on the same parish as its curé in 1771 and named confessor to the king's sisters, with an annual pension of ten thousand livres. As curé of Saint-Séverin the unrepentant Madier then denied the last sacraments to two octogenarian appellants in 1773.[80]

Madier was not the only ex-Jesuit to benefit from the archbishop's largesse. Witness one Reverend Père Garnier, in 1772 reincarnated as the abbé Garnier and newly installed as chaplain of the convent of the Holy Sacrament; or another ex-Jesuit promoted as curé over the head of the long-resident vicaire of the village church of Ivry in 1774.[81] The curé in question had apparently obtained this position on the recommendation of the king's sister, Madame Louise de France, who had undergone a highly publicized "devout" or Jesuit-oriented religious conversion in September 1771 and then taken up residence as a novice in the Carmelite convent of Saint-Denis. Saint-Denis thereafter functioned as the spiritual Jerusalem of the ministerial and episcopal parti dévot, attracting weekly visits from the Archbishop of Paris, accompanied by Louise's confessor, Madier, as well as an occasional visit by Maupeou himself, who deemed it politically prudent, according to Mairobert's *Journal historique*, occasionally "to play the dévot."[82]

From Saint-Denis emanated the project not only of persuading other French bishops to employ ex-Jesuits in their dioceses but of reestablishing the society itself on a legal footing in France. This latter initiative survived even the papal dissolution of the society in the brief *Dominus ac redemptor*, fulminated by Clement XIV in 1773 under pressure from the Bourbon courts of Naples and Madrid, after which it assumed the form of a proposal to regroup the disbanded Jesuits as a congregation of secular priests. Hostile reaction to *Dominus ac redemptor* briefly cast the ultramontanist parti dévot into the role of an opposition more papal than the pope—indeed threatened, as Hardy ironically noted, "to produce a new genre of appellants very different from those whom the Jesuits have persecuted for so long." This opposition struck the secretary of foreign affairs, the duc d'Aiguillon, as sufficiently "violent" and "fanatical" as to give him pause, prompting him to

79. *Déclaration du roi, portant rappel des prêtres décrétés ou bannis. Donné à Marly le 15 juin 1771. Registré au parlement le 19 juin 1771,* in BPR: CLP, Ms. 570, no. 262. See also Mairobert, *Journal historique* (27 June 1771), 1:373. On De L'Ecluse's appointment, see Hardy, "Mes loisirs," BN: Ms. Fr. 6681 (6 Sept. 1772), p. 94.

80. On Madier or Madrier see Hardy, "Mes loisirs," BN: Ms. Fr. 6680 (3 Oct. 1771), p. 281; on his refusal of sacraments to octogenarian priests, ibid., Ms. Fr. 6681 (7, 16 Apr. 1773), pp. 180–82; and (15, 27 Feb. 1773), pp. 291–92. On Madier's original exile by the Parlement, see BN: CJF, Ms. 1487, fol. 288.

81. Hardy, "Mes loisirs," BN: Ms. Fr. 6681 (8 May 1772), p. 57.

82. Ibid., Ms. Fr. 6680 (9 July and 29 Dec. 1771), pp. 262, 299; and Ms. Fr. 6681 (13 Sept. and 20 Oct. 1773), pp. 227–28, 236; and Mairobert, *Journal historique* (6, 10 Feb. 1772), 2:369, 373–74.

solicit from Clément XIV an additional brief reaffirming the authority of *Dominus ac redemptor.*[83]

If the Maupeou coup did not finally produce the triumphal restoration of the Company of Jesus in France, it witnessed many mini-triumphs of Jesuit-sponsored devotions, at least in Paris. On 10 January 1772 it was the celebration in the church of Saint-Roch of a first annual mass patronized by the Archbishop of Paris and christened "the triumph of the faith." The faith in question, according to Hardy, was that of the "turbulent ecclesiastics and disturbers of the public peace," because the triumph referred to the "destruction of the parlements." "Everyone murmured against this novelty," he further reported, "especially at a time when the faith, far from growing stronger and achieving any triumphs, . . . has on the contrary been weakening day by day." On 1 May 1772 it was the veneration of a relic of the newly canonized (1767) but Molinist Saint Jeanne-Françoise-Fremyot de Chantal—co-founder with François de Sales of the order of the Visitation of Holy Mary—in the church of Saint-Médard at the instigation of its curé, Hardy de Levaré, another of the many exiled priests who had recently returned to Paris. The date of 1 May had not been randomly chosen, for it was calculated to compete with the anniversary of the death of the uncanonized Jansenist deacon Pâris, whose tomb was still located in the graveyard of that church and whose devotees were still wont to congregate in some numbers on that day, "as though," commented Hardy, "the voice of the people, recognized by all ages as the voice of God himself, had not sufficiently canonized the virtues and miracles of this holy personage, whose glory and merit certain people have made it their business to obscure."[84]

If the political implications of these devotions were not obvious enough, Hardy had repeatedly to hear them spelled out in all syllables on the occasion of the many processions that he was obliged to attend as adjunct syndic of the Parisian booksellers guild. On one such occasion, on 7 October 1771, the procession headed ominously toward the Carmelite convent in the faubourg Saint-Jacques, where the chagrined bookseller listened to one Abbé Rétard extol Madame Louise's recent profession of monastic vows and explain how, although France had reason enough to fear the wrath of God until then, everything had forthwith changed for the better—"by which he undoubtedly referred," Hardy was sure, "to the recently destroyed parlements and the ecclesiastics thereby put into possession of the right to disturb the public peace by their harassments so opposed to the spirit of the Gospel and the good of religion." In another procession which wound up at the College Mazarin, Hardy endured the underprincipal's

83. Ibid., Ms. Fr. 6681 (8 Sept. 1773), p. 226; and Lucien Laugier, *Un ministre réformateur sous Louis XV: le triumvirat, 1770–1774* (Paris, 1975), pp. 485–86.

84. Hardy, "Mes loisirs," BN: Ms. Fr. 6681, 10 Jan. 1772, p. 141, on Saint-Roch; 1 May 1772, p. 55 on Saint-Médard; 28 June 1772, p. 76 on Saint-André-des-Arts.

pointed eulogy of Mazarin, the seventeenth-century cardinal-minister for whom the college was named, joined to the observation that the effect of calumny was always short-lived—a phrase obviously intended, Hardy was sure, "at once to canonize and exculpate the great personage [Maupeou] who at the present moment is no less odious to the nation than was his celebrated eminence [Mazarin] in his own time and who, according to his zealous partisans, is [like the cardinal] a victim of the blackest calumny."[85] What Hardy might have added but probably did not know was that in the early 1650s Mazarin was particularly odious to a largely Jansenist Parisian priesthood, whereas in the early 1770s Maupoeu numbered Parisian priests among his most zealous partisans.

The Sorbonne's clarion sounding of Maupeou's virtues signaled another open season on excessively Augustinian doctors within its precincts—and the difference between the Jansenist Sorbonne of the seventeenth and early eighteenth centuries and the absolutist and Molinist one of the 1770s. One Jacques-Albert Hazon, a regent-doctor of the faculty of medicine, found himself forbidden to preside over any public functions for ten years for having found a kind word for such skeletons in the Sorbonne's closet as Antoine Arnauld, Laurent Boursier, and Nicolas Petipied in a "Historical Eulogy of the University of Paris," delivered on 11 October 1770. Hazon, who was already seventy, was not likely to outlive this interdiction. And another lettre de cachet felled Doctor Xaupi, the theological faculty's eighty-eight-year-old dean, prohibiting him from exercising his functions or even attending the faculty's monthly assemblies until he could prove that a benefice he possessed in the cathedral church of Perpignan did not require his residence there. But his real fault was to have signed a legal consultation written by the inevitable Jansenist duo, the abbé Claude Mey and Gabriel-Nicholas Maultrot, on behalf of some second-order curés against the cathedral chapter in the neighboring diocese of Cahors.[86]

But the case that best illuminates the religious underside of Maupeou's constitutional revolution is another miscarriage of academic justice, this one involving the College of Auxerre, where numbers of Jansenist professors had evidently congregated under the long and protective episcopacy of Charles de Caylus. Things had drastically changed under Caylus's militantly anti-Jansenist successors Caritat de Condorcet and Champion de Cicé, who spent much of their pastoral energy purging their largely Jansenist cathedral and parish clergies. The college did not escape this episcopal purge. In 1773 Champion de Cicé somehow obtained a sentence from the local bailiwick court condemning two professors to

85. Ibid., Ms. Fr. 6680, 7 Oct. 1771, p. 281 on Carmelite convent sermon; 12 Dec. 1771, pp. 296–97, on Collège Mazarin sermon.

86. Ibid., Ms. Fr. 6680, 2 Sept. 1771, p. 275, for Hazon affair; and Ms. Fr. 6681, 1 Dec. 1772, 14 Mar. 1773, pp. 119, 169–70, for Xaupi affair. On Hazon affair, see also the printed *Arrest du Conseil du roi. Du 18 aoust 1771. Extrait des registres du Conseil du roi* (Paris, 1771) in BN: Mss. Fr., Ms. 22101, A-D 41, fol. 151.

perpetual galley labor and confiscation of property, two more professors to perpetual banishment from Auxerre as well as confiscation of property, and three others to somewhat lesser penalties. Among their stated crimes were not only "having raised the youth in a spirit of contentiousness and disobedience toward the Laws of the Realm concerning matters debated in the Church"—against *Unigenitus*, in other words—but also for having "explained and commented on seditious, injurious, and calumnious *libelles* against the Government and the honor of its Ministers and Magistrates"—that is, for having directed the students' attention to pamphlets against Maupeou and his replacement parlements. It was the chief of these parlements, that of Paris, which on 25 February 1774 appropriately upheld this sentence by the *bailliage Cicé*, as it was derisively christened.[87]

The Ministry's Pamphlets and the Parti Dévot

That Maupeou's constitutional coup possessed a devout religious dimension is just as certain, then, as that the patriot protest possessed a Jansenist one. That dimension is most apparent in new "acts of schism" recorded by Hardy, as well as in the reappearance of some of the parti dévot's chief constituents, namely the ex-Jesuits and curés previously exiled by the Parlement of Paris. At the same time devout religiosity asserted itself more positively by means of certain devotions, like that of the Sacred Heart of Jesus. The Parisian archiepiscopal palace and the Carmelite convent at Saint-Denis functioned as the party's spiritual outposts—the party's Antioch and Jerusalem, as it were—the former as long as the aging Christophe de Beaumont remained there, the latter since Louise de France had taken up residence as a Carmelite novice. But Versailles remained the party's spiritual Rome, with or without Jesuit confessors and preachers, what with such illustrious lay sponsors as the king's other sisters, Mesdames de France; the minister of state Henri-Léonard Bertin; and the seemingly indestructible governor of the royal children, the duc de La Vauguyon, who nonetheless died in 1771 "regretted by no one," to believe Hardy, "except for the Archbishop of Paris and the Jesuits."[88]

But how if at all did the parti dévot's political and religious sensibility make itself felt in the hundred or so pamphlets subsidized by Maupeou in an effort to plead the monarchy's case in the public forum? Unfortunately, no devout counterpart to Le Paige is at hand to help crack the anonymity of these pamphlets, nor did Le Paige himself know very many of their authors. And because the Maupeou

---

87. Hardy, "Mes loisirs," Ms. Fr. 6681 (7, 11, 24, and 29 Nov.), pp. 243, 244–45, 250, 253, respectively; and ibid., 26 Jan., 25 Feb. 1774, pp. 278–79, 298. See also the printed *Arrest de la cour de parlement . . . du 25 février 1774* (Paris, 1774), in NL, case wing folio oZ 144, .A1, vol. 8, no. 82.

88. Hardy, "Mes loisirs," BN: Ms. Fr. 6681 (4 Feb. 1771), p. 65.

ministry allowed these pamphlets to circulate freely, the Parisian police made no attempt to identify their authors, either. Only a few of these pamphlets can therefore be connected to card-carrying members of the clerical parti dévot—among Catholic clergymen, a certain abbé Joseph-François Marie (or Mary), one of the chancellor's clerical councillors in his makeshift parlement of Paris and the author, according to Le Paige, of several pro-Maupeou pamphlets; and the barrister and abbé Pierre Bouquet, a "kind of erudite" on good terms with the duc de La Vauguyon and the archdevout La Motte, Bishop of Orléans, and the author of some *Lettres provinciales* highly critical of patriot constitutionalism.[89]

Among laymen, the cases of the barrister Jacob-Nicolas Moreau and Simon-Henri Linguet are more ambiguous. Sons of persecuted Jansenist professors of philosophy, both revolted against their upbringing. Moreau first distanced himself from the Parlement of Paris's pro-Jansenist stand in the controversy over the refusal of sacraments in the 1750s and thereafter defended the monarchy against the parlements until neither monarchy nor parlements remained standing. Linguet first raised his voice in public defense of the Jesuits in the pamphlet debate accompanying their trial in the 1760s, and later assumed the mantle of an apostle of despotism until that term fell once and for all from favor in 1789. Although Moreau acknowledged only his monumental *Leçons de morale, de politique, et de droit public (Lessons in Ethics, Politics, and Public Law)* during this period and claimed to have put youthful pamphleteering behind him, it is hard to believe that this sinecured "royal historiographer" did not write one or two pamphlets; Linguet was most certainly the author of three or four.[90] If nothing else, the two careers illustrate the close connection in eighteenth-century France between the defense of the Jesuits and integral absolutism on the one hand, and between Jansenism and parlementary constitutionalism on the other.

A thematic dredging of the same pamphlets yields little more in the way of a blatantly devout Catholic presence, unless the many accusations of Jansenism may

89. On Abbé Marie or Mary, see Michaud, *Biographie universelle*, 26:648–49; and on Pierre Bouquet, Jacob-Nicolas Moreau, *Mes souvenirs*, ed. Camille Hermelin, 2 vols. (Paris, 1898), 1:176–77. Le Paige attributed the following pamphlets to Marie: *Considérations sur l'édit de décembre 1770* (BPR: CLP, Ms. 804, no. 7); and *Observations sur l'écrit intitulé: Protestations des princes* (CLP, Ms, 569, no. 190).

90. On Linguet see Darlene Gay Levy, *The Ideas and Careers of Simon-Nicolas-Henri Linguet: A Study in Eighteenth-Century French Politics* (Urbana, Ill., 1980), esp. pp. 8–16; and *NE* 15 Dec. 1731, p. 241, where Linguet's Jansenist father figures as a victim of Cardinal Fleury's persecution. On Moreau see his *Mes souvenirs*, esp. 1:1–12, 286–330; and Dieter Gembicki, *Histoire et politique à la fin de l'ancien régime: Jacob-Nicolas Moreau, 1717–1803* (Paris, n.d.). Le Paige attributed the following pamphlets to Linguet: *Réflexions d'un citoyen sur l'édit de décembre* (BPR: CLP, Ms. 804, no. 8); *Nouvelles réflexions d'un citoyen sur l'édit de décembre* (ibid., no. 9); *Remontrances d'un citoyen aux parlemens de France* (ibid., no. 11); and less certainly the *Réponse d'un citoyen qui a publié ses réflexions* (ibid., no. 10). In addition, it is all but certain that he is the author of the anonymous *La tête leur tourne* (n.p., n.d.), also in BPR: CLP, Ms. 810, no. 8; and of some *Recherches sur les Etats-généraux* (n.p., n.d.), both of which were republished in 1788.

count as such. The abbé in the anonymous *Entretien d'un ancien magistrat et d'un abbé (Conversation Between a Retired Magistrate and an Abbé)*, for example, accused his magisterial conversant of having invoked the authority of the Estates General "with no better faith than the Sectaries [Jansenists] have called for an Ecumenical Council," clearly implying the close proximity of the two sets of appellants. By itself, however, anti-Jansenism is no better evidence for a devout religious presence than anti-Jesuitism is of a Jansenist one. What makes charges of Jansenism into plausible indications of devout religiosity is that they often come paired with accusations of philosophical or encyclopedic unbelief. The pejorative coupling of Jansenism with philosophism became part of the parti dévot's rhetorical stock-in-trade during the eighteenth century—the anti-Jansenist Moreau, for example, was also the author of the well-known antiphilosophical *Histoire des cacouacs (History of the Cacouacs)*—just as the linking of Jesuitism with philosophism was routine rhetorical fare for the parti janséniste. More to the point, the anonymous *Final Word in the Affair* blamed patriot opposition's "republican spirit" and rhetorical antidespotism on a "self-styled Philosophy" that had been joined by a "Sect." This sect the pamphlet later described as "the most dangerous perhaps that might ever have existed in a State" because, "enemy of Kings as well as of Pontiffs, . . . "it is the enemy of every kind of authority."[91]

Although evidence of a devout presence, anti-Jansenism is only one of the salient features of Maupeou's pamphlet defense. Another was the incendiary charge that the old parlementary magistrates had constituted a "monstrous hereditary aristocracy," a throwback to medieval feudal aristocracy, whose selfish and particularistic "corporate spirit" *(esprit de corps)* and "particular interest" *(intérêt particulier)* expressed themselves in the "gothic" style of its parlementary constitutionalism. This charge drew inspiration from a royalist version of French history most immediately indebted to the works of such early eighteenth-century publicists as the marquis d'Argenson and the abbé de Saint-Pierre, which had featured the king as civil liberator of the people from the yoke of feudal oppression and the barbarous Middle Ages.[92] When, for example, Linguet maintained that "the absolute independence of the Master is the rampart of the liberties of the subjects, and the surest guarantee of their welfare," he was only repeating d'Argenson's contention that "feudal right" had been a "usurpation of royal authority," while the resurrection of royal power at the end of the Middle Ages had entailed the

---

91. *La fin mot de l'affaire* (n.p., n.d.), pp. 16–18.

92. The "monstrous hereditary aristocracy" comes from [Linguet], *Réflexions d'un citoyen sur l'édit de décembre*, pp. 16–17, while the complaints about a "gothic style" and the magistracy's "particular interest" come, respectively, from the *Réflexions d'un vieux patriote sur les affaires présentes* (n.p., n.d.), pp. 21–23; and Voltaire's *Sentiments des six conseils établis par le roi et de tous les bons citoyens*, in *OE*, 28:399. On d'Argenson and Saint-Pierre, see Nannerl O. Keohane, *Philosophy and the State in France: The Renaissance to the Enlightenment* (Princeton, N.J., 1980), pp. 361–91.

decline of the nobility and the rise of social democracy, which he thought "as much the friend of monarchy, as Aristocracy is its enemy."[93]

Is the charge of "aristocracy" a typically devout one? Although the Jesuits' *Journal de Trévoux* occasionally indulged in biting reprimands of noble arrogance and uselessness, antiaristocratic sentiment was hardly the mainstay of the late eighteenth-century parti dévot, while any search for anterior evidence would have to insist on the devout lineage of the d'Argenson family or go all the way back to the antiaristocratic sentiment of some of the literature of the Catholic League in the 1590s.[94] Such mid-eighteenth-century devout defenders of the monarchy as the abbé Capmartin de Chaupy or Lafiteau, Bishop of Sisteron, had on the contrary reproached the magistrates for being uppity bourgeois, fraudulently claiming succession to the true Court of Peers and social equality with the realm's nobility.[95] Nor, however, despite the protophilosophic precedents of d'Argenson and the abbé de Saint-Pierre, was the charge a specifically enlightened one. Voltaire, surely the Enlightenment incarnate, did not rebuke the parlementaires as feudal or aristocratic in the pamphlets he wrote; on the contrary, he echoed recent devout rhetoric in maintaining that the magistrates were men whose "grandfathers were our farmers, postmen, or who wore the livery."[96]

Rather than either devout or enlightened sources, royalist historiography of the late sixteenth and seventeenth centuries is perhaps the likeliest origin of the antiaristocratic rhetoric of the pro-Maupeou pamphlets, for "feudal anarchy" and "aristocratic usurpation" were already commonplace complaints regarding the Middle Ages in such seventeenth-century royalist histories of France as those by the père Gabriel Daniel and Eudes de Mézeray.[97] Whatever its origin, the rhetoric as employed in Maupeou's behalf differed from earlier examples in extending the potent charge of aristocracy and feudalism from, say, the dukes and peers of the realm to the parlementary magistracy. Although it failed to affect public opinion's general support of the exiled magistracy in the early 1770s, it proved far more explosive in 1788.

If ministerial propaganda's antiaristocratic rhetoric did not, then, clearly derive from devout precedents, another component of its royalist reading of the

---

93. [Linguet], *La tête leur tourne*, pp. 17–18; and d'Argenson, *Considérations sur le gouvernement ancien et présent de la France* (Amsterdam, 1765), pp. 103, 124.

94. On the *Journal de Trévoux*'s antinoble bias see Jack R. Censer, *The French Press in the Age of the Enlightenment* (London, 1994), p. 114.

95. [Pierre-François Lafitau], *Entretiens d'Anselme et d'Isidore sur les affaires du temps* (France, 1756), pp. 108–9; and [Bertrand Capmartin de Chaupy], *Observations sur le refus que fait le Châtelet de reconnaître la Chambre royale* (France, 1754), pp. 73–74.

96. Voltaire, *Très humbles et très respectueuses remontrances du grenier à sel* (1771) in *OC*, 28:403.

97. Harold Ellis, *Boulainvilliers and the French Monarchy: Aristocratic Politics in Early Eighteenth-Century France* (Ithaca, N.Y., 1988), pp. 31–39. See also J. Q. C. Mackrell, *The Attack on "Feudalism" in Eighteenth-Century France* (London, 1988), pp. 17–47.

French past, namely its exalted view of monarchical sovereignty, most surely did. Indeed, some of the formulations of monarchical sovereignty in that literature were as unguarded as anything that had been said at the height of the Bourbon dynasty's prestige under Henry IV or Louis XIV, and seemed designed to substantiate the patriot opposition's worst "despotic" nightmares. In ministerial pamphlets, a depaternalized monarchical "master" *(maître)*, who lorded it over mere valets and servants, belligerently confronted the benign "chief" *(chef)* of patriot pamphlets, who was a sort of constitutional *primus inter pares*. Similarly, ministerial propagandists vested the "property" *(propriété)* of the state in this master, defying the patriot tendency to vest it in the nation and to confide only its administration to its chief.[98]

For a certain number of Maupeou's pamphleteers, including Linguet in *La tête leur tourne (Their Heads Are Spinning)*, the power of their royal master effectively "raised him above the laws, so that he might change [the laws], abrogate them, reestablish them, make new ones—a power, in fine, which only he himself can limit, and whose cause may not be obstructed by any [other] will whether particular or general. Such is the French constitution." Principles such as these both justified and found justification in the supposedly ancient summary of the French constitution in the lapidary phrase, *Si veut le Roi, si veut la Loi* ("As the king wills, so wills the law"), as reported by the sixteenth-century jurist Antoine Loisel.[99]

This almost anticonstitutional view of the French monarchy may be regarded as a devout legacy, not only because it is indebted to a counterreformational exaltation of the monarchy going back to the late sixteenth and early seventeenth centuries but because it stands in direct succession to an almost identical view of the monarchy as articulated by such midcentury episcopal and Jesuitical apologists as Balbani, Capmartin de Chaupi, Lafitau, and Lefranc de Pompignan. Like them, Maupeou's publicists continued to speak the language of "sovereignty," "authority," and "power," describing these as "legitimate," "supreme," and of course "absolute" in relation to "subjects" whose "obligation" was to "obey" and "submit." The submission enjoined upon subjects by pro-Maupeou pamphleteers was perhaps a little less harsh than in the 1750s, absolute or "limitless" submission sometimes giving way to a "sweet and peaceful" variety, and the

---

98. These references are, in order, from [Charles, marquis de Villette], *Le soufflet du maître perruquier à sa femme*, p. 14; *Les bons citoyens, ou lettres des sénat-graphs, écrits par des gens respectables* (Rouen, 1771), pp. 5–6, in BPR: CLP, Ms. 810, no. 26; *Réponse à la lettre d'un magistrat à un duc et pair, sur le discours de M. le chancelier au lit de justice, du 7 décembre 1770* (n.p., n.d.), p. 10, in BPR: CLP, Ms. 804, no. 6.

99. [Linguet], *La tête leur tourne*, pp. 14–15. Loisel's formula is invoked in [Marie], *Considérations sur l'édit de décembre 1770*, p. 58; and *Examen analytique et raisonné d'un écrit qui à pour titre: Protestation des princes du sang* (n.p., n.d.), in BPR: CLP, Ms. 814, no. 18. Mey turns the formula on its head in *Maximes du droit public françois*, 2:115.

subject itself occasionally rising to the rank of citizen.[100] Yet the parlements as well as all other corps remained, in the words of Linguet, "absolutely dependent on the will of our kings," or, as the marquis de Villette put it, bound to "submission to the velleities *(volontés)* of the monarch," who for his part continued in the roles of "sovereign" and "master" in the business of peremptorily giving "orders" and "commands."[101]

But the early 1770s were not after all the 1750s; in at least a diffuse way, another two decades of secular lights had made for some important differences in even the devout defense of the monarchy. The midcentury clerical apologists—they were not quite publicists—had articulated their view against the Jansenist parlements and in defense of the bull *Unigenitus*, which had become a symbol of royal authority, as well as on the model of their very anti-Gallican conception of the papacy's authority over the church.[102] Yet while they had exalted the king's power over his lay subjects, the better to restrain him by divine law in relation to the spiritual power of the church, their more journalistic and ministerial successors of the Maupeou era contented themselves with only the fewest and most perfunctory references to things divine—even to divine right—and argued the monarchy's case on the grounds of either natural law or, more often, historically demonstrated utility.[103] In a sampling of forty pamphlets, only one, Linguet's *La tête leur tourne*, specifically invoked God as the ultimate source of the king's "independent" and "absolute power"; only one other described his authority as "sacred."[104] Royalty's baroque accoutrements, like "glory," "majesty," "splendor," and "dignity," similarly receded in comparison to their status with the midcentury panegyrics, garnering only a mention apiece in the same sampling.

What the king lost in divinity and majesty, however, he gained in human will, for he remained the locus of as much "will" and as many "velleities" in the early 1770s as in the preceding two decades. To be sure, that royal willfulness is obviously also part and parcel of the devout legacy, given that tradition's long-standing defense of the free human will against Jansenist grace. But the combination of the secularization—and humanization—of the devout tradition's representa-

---

100. [Linguet], *Remontrances d'un citoyen aux parlemens*, p. 14.

101. Ibid., p. 29; and [Villette], *Le soufflet du maître perruquier*, p. 27.

102. Dale K. Van Kley, *The Damiens Affair and the Unraveling of the Old Regime, 1750–1770* (Princeton, N.J., 1984), pp. 194–98, 211–19; and *The Jansenists and the Expulsion of the Jesuits from France*, pp. 137–62.

103. Echeverria, *The Maupeou Revolution*, pp. 125–77. See, for example, *La tête leur tourne*, p. 14; or *Réflexions d'un maître perruquier sur les affaires de l'état*, pp. 14–16. Patriot constitutionalism also contributed to the obliteration of Bossuet's distinction by equating *absolute* with *arbitrary* or *despotic*, as [Linguet's] *Nouvelles réflexions d'un citoyen sur l'édit de décembre 1770* perceptively observed at the time, p. 29.

104. [Linguet], *La tête leur tourne*, p. 14; and [Marie], *Observations sur l'écrit intitulé: Protestations des princes*, pp. 41, 45.

tion of the monarchy with the same tradition's retention of will as one of the king's foremost attributes was a devastating one. For it produced a conception of royal power as an exercise in will so unrestrained as to all but obliterate Bishop Bossuet's hallowed distinction between arbitrary and absolute power. In thus distilling the essence of monarchy into will, however, this rhetorical tactic ran the obvious risk of making the monarchy more vulnerable to patriot opposition if and when, as eventually happened, that discursive tradition came to express itself in comparably willful terms.

More frontally than in the 1750s and 1760s—and in a manner to make even Bossuet stir uneasily in his grave—the Maupeou period's defenders of the monarchy also questioned the very existence of constitutional or fundamental law. "These *fundamental laws,* about which so much noise is made . . . and which are nowhere to be found, are they any better known and spelled out" for all that, asked an irate Linguet, obviously out of patience with the parlements' "faithful archives, where its corporate spirit blends so happily with the spirit of the law?"[105] Reminding the parlementaires that there were kings such as Frederick the Great who would teach them to "find out about affairs of state from the Gazettes," the anonymous *Henry the Great's Response to the Parlements' Remonstrances* warned them also that they "could appeal all they wanted to their fundamental laws (of which God alone knows the originals). He [the king] will simply make some new ones to suit his convenience, to which they will be obliged to submit."[106] The anonymous author of a *Letter from M. D. L. V., a Barrister in the Parlement* went further, denying not only the historical existence of fundamental laws but their very possibility, "diametrically opposed as these were to good sense as well as to right reason." No more than his predecessors could Louis XV legally bind his successors, who would be free to legislate "apropos of the welfare of our descendants."[107]

Combining devout moralism with some Montesquieuian relativism, the abbé J.-F. Marie's skeptical and royalist assault on fundamental law went so far as to come full circle and paradoxically resubject the monarchy to a kind of national will. In imprudently parroting parlementaire palaver, Marie charged, the princes' *Protestation* had confounded "the civil order with the moral order, or rather assimilated the mobile and variable laws of the former with the constant laws of the latter. In morality," he explained, "all is immutably true, while in politics what is true for one time can become error in another," with the result that "the antiquity of laws gives them no title to irrevocability." Abbé Marie's audacious

105. [Linguet], *Remontrances d'un citoyen aux parlemens de France,* pp. 20, 42–43.

106. *Réponse de H[enri] le Grand aux remontrances des parlemens* (n.p., n.d.), pp. 4–5.

107. [Linguet], *Remontrances d'un citoyen aux parlemens de France,* pp. 20, 42–43; *Réponse de H[enri] le Grand aux remontrances des parlemens* (n.p., n.d.), pp. 4–5; and *Lettre de M. D. L. V. avocat au parlement,* p. 34.

line of reasoning produced the startling conclusion that not even absolute monarchies had any "absolute consistency, because the same laws do not always
produce the same effects, because alterations in the principles and character of a
nation necessarily entail new needs and precautions. If authority does not adjust to
popular changes, the diverse pieces of that immobile monarchy will lose flexibility
and eventually fall apart."[108] The royal will was similarly indistinguishable from a
changing "national spirit" for the author of a *Letter from a Parisian Barrister to the
Magistrates of the Parlement of Rouen*—a national spirit "to which laws and ordinances cannot give orders and to which political institutions must themselves give
way."[109]

As on the patriot side, a radical, potentially subversive strand of ministerial
pamphleteering therefore stands out in contrast to a moderate one. And what
distinguishes this radical strand is in part its skepticism about the relevance or
even accessibility of the past. While a moderate defender of the monarchy like
Moreau attempted to fashion a royalist version of French history in order better to
compete with the parlementary and patriot versions, the likes of Linguet and
Marie turned their backs on history entirely and, renewing contact with a line of
royal apologetics represented most recently by the abbé de Saint-Pierre during the
Regency, argued the case of the royal will in utilitarian terms alone.[110] Even
sharper, then, was the contrast with patriot pamphleteering. For where patriot
pamphleteering—especially the more Jansenist versions of it—all but eliminated
the flesh and blood monarch in favor of immutable fundamental laws as they
supposedly existed by national consent during the monarchy's earliest centuries,
this more radical wing of the ministerial front strove to free the monarchical will
from the constraints of the past however construed. But these radical and moderate wings of the ministerial front were no more manned by enlightened and
devout recruits, respectively, than were the patriot party's radical and moderate
flanks composed of enlightened and Jansenist ones, in that order. For just as some
of the most radical patriot constitutionalism had roots in Jansenist conciliarism
and its vision of a pristine patristic revelation—for Jansenists the touchstone of all
ulterior theologizing—so some of this radical ministerial anticonstitutionalism
arguably had roots or at least a counterpart in a devout apologetical tactic developed during the eighteenth century's earlier decades.

108. [Marie], *Observations sur un écrit intitulé: Protestations des princes,* pp. 12–13.
    109. *Lettre d'un avocat de Paris aux magistrats du parlement de Rouen, au sujet de l'arrêt de cette cour,
du 15 avril 1771,* p. 5. See also [Marie], *Considérations sur l'édit de décembre 1770,* pp. 62–65.
    110. On Moreau's effort to build an archival arsenal in defense of the monarchy see Kieth M. Baker,
"Controlling French History: The Ideological Arsenal of Jacob-Nicolas Moreau," in *Inventing the French
Revolution: Essays on French Political Culture in the Eighteenth Century* (Cambridge, 1990), pp. 59–85. On
the abbé de Saint-Pierre's utilitarian absolutism see Thomas E. Kaiser, "The Abbé de Saint-Pierre, Public
Opinion, and the Reconstitution of the French Monarchy," *JMH* 55 (Dec. 1983):618–43.

That apologetical effort, undertaken by the Jesuits Jean Hardouin and his disciple Isaac Berruyer, had audaciously challenged the authenticity or at least the accessibility of much of the historical and documentary evidence of Christian revelation, like the writings of the church fathers and the pronouncements of church councils. Thereby freed from the constraints of both ecclesiastical and dogmatic history—so ran the strategy of this apologetic—the papal magisterium would be free to define what the church had presumably always believed as it infallibly saw fit. In the works of Jean Hardouin, who wrote during the earlier decades of the century, this apologetic took the crude form of challenging the authenticity of all the church's documentary evidence except for the Vulgate before the fourteenth century, at which time some atheistical monks forged all of the patristic and conciliar evidence in an attempt to undermine papal authority.

Hardouin's disciple Isaac Berruyer took a subtler tack, holding that the meanings of terms and the systems of reference of such ancient documents were so time-bound as to render their meaning all but impenetrable to the eighteenth-century understanding. Berruyer therefore hoped to improve on "dry and sterile" precis and vernacular translations and felt free to make the ancient protagonists of the Hebrew Scriptures "speak as they would speak today if they were among us" and to present a "living and animated tableau of the adorable perfections of the great Master who we have the honor to serve."[111] This he did with scandalous effect in his multivolume and novelistic *History of the People of God*. But the intended effect, as in Hardouin's work, was to emancipate the papacy from documentary evidence of just about any kind, allowing it to define or redefine the Catholic dogmatic tradition in the sense of the bull *Unigenitus*. Hardouin and Berruyer were hence predictably outspoken Molinists and anti-Jansenists, defending not only the authority of the papal present against the patristic past but an essentially benign view of fallen humanity against the Jansenist insistence upon the fall's tragic consequences. Because, thought Berruyer, fallen humanity might conquer sin with the help of sufficient grace, that "grace . . . would give far more perfect worshipers to God than his original justice would ever have done in the absence of the passions . . . and in the serenity of . . . pristine innocence."[112] Intoned as one word in the pages of the *Nouvelles ecclésiastiques*, Hardouin-Berruyer and Company figured as the Jansenist weekly's chief bêtes noires during the century's central decades.[113]

111. Isaac-Joseph Berruyer, *Histoire du peuple de Dieu, depuis son origine jusqu'à la naissance du messie*, 10 vols. (Paris, 1753), 1:xxviii, xxxv, lxxviii.

112. Ibid., p. xiii.

113. This account of Hardouin's and Berryer's apologetical efforts on behalf of tradition is dependent upon Robert R. Palmer's classic *Catholics and Unbelievers in Eighteenth-Century France* (Princeton, N.J., 1947), pp. 65–76. *NE* devoted a special issue to Berruyer—and to the Bishop of Soisson's "pastoral" refutation of Berruyer's *Histoire du peuple de Dieu*—on 19 March 1760, pp. 49–64, but other numbers of the clandestine journal are peppered with pejorative references to the Hardouin-Berruyer duo.

The distance between the epistemological liberation of the papacy from its patristic and especially Augustinian past and the liberation of the monarchy from its Frankish and putatively constitutional past is not a great one, especially in view of the role that eighteenth-century Jesuits had played in the defense of the French monarchy. The most visible bridge between the two is perhaps the avocat-abbé Pierre Bouquet's *Provincial Letters,* a stout book published in late 1772.[114] Although "very royalist" and a self-anointed defender of the monarchy, Bouquet apparently wrote at the behest of the ministry's devout stalwart Henri-Léonard Bertin rather than the sometime parlementaire Maupeou.[115] This difference in ministerial sponsorship symbolizes if it does not explain Bouquet's Berruyer-style epistemological assault upon the documentary bases of Le Paige's historical constitutionalism, underscoring as it did the relative paucity and dubious authenticity of these documents, as well as the formidable semantic barriers to their proper interpretation. Bouquet did not go so far as to deny the possibility of any reliable knowledge about the French constitutional past. But he came pretty close, going so far as to raise doubts about the Salic Law, which regulated the succession to the French throne—the one "fundamental" law that just about all defenders of the monarchy accepted.[116] In any case he went too far for Maupeou, who had the book condemned by a decree in council for "containing dubious assertions and inexact notions about the history of the monarchy"—and thereby procuring for the book a brief succès de scandale. With friends like that, the French monarchy hardly needed any "patriot" enemies.[117]

A Monarchy in Search of an Identity

In fact, the monarchy's devout friends had reason to be disappointed by the result of the Maupeou coup, which, despite the reprieve it gave to bishops in their war with the parlements, had not culminated in the restoration of the Jesuits, much less in a general reorientation of royal religious policy. And so the last years of Louis XV's reign were witness to a frenetic attempt by bishops to convert the monarch if not the monarchy, in the evident hope that the one would lead to the other. "Let

114. Pierre Bouquet, *Lettres provinciales ou examen impartial de l'origine, de la constitution, et des révolutions de la monarchie française* (La Haye: "chez Le Neutre, a l'enseigne de la Bonne Foi," 1772). The title is almost certainly a satirical reference to Pascal's *Lettres provinciales,* as the supposed publisher and his ensign is a satirical reference to Butard's Jansenist printshop-bookstore "at the ensign of the Truth" on the rue Saint-Jacques. In his copy of the book, (BPR: CLP, Ms. 812, no. 2) Le Paige noted that Bouquet was an "élève tonsuré," by which he probably meant that Bouquet was a tonsured graduate of a Jesuit college.

115. Mairobert, *Journal historique* (10, 12 Dec. 1772), 3:384–85, 390.

116. On this book I am dependent on an untitled and unpublished paper presented by D. Carroll Joynes at the meeting of the American Historical Association in Chicago, Dec. 1986.

117. *Arrêt du Conseil d'état du roi, qui supprime un imprimé qui a pour titre, Lettres provinciales. Du 28 novembre 1772.* (Paris, 1772), in BN: Mss. Fr., Ms. 22100, A-D 41, no. 184.

Louis be reborn with Jesus Christ," implored Jean-Baptiste de Beauvais, Bishop of Senez, in an Easter sermon delivered in the presence of the old king himself only a year or so before his death. "[L]et him be reborn today, and . . . the nation entire will be reborn with her master."[118] The devout strategy, as this sermon reveals, was to begin with the personal conversion of him who linked the realm to God, whereupon the reopened conduits would send divine grace coursing through the body politic to the detriment of both Jansenist heresy and philosophical unbelief.[119]

That conversion was not to be—or at least not until a fatal bout with smallpox extracted a deathbed confession from him in May 1774. Until the end the king retained Du Barry as titled mistress, providing grist for more antiroyal *mauvais discours* quite apart from the fallout from Maupeou's constitutional coup. Although some of these echoed the religious content of previous decades, they typically concentrated their fire on the monarchy's collapse into immorality, imbecility, and despotism. Still pitying Louis XV for the negligence of Fleury's tutorship and for being the dupe of the "Jesuitical system," the anonymous *Remonstrances of the Basoche* reproached the king for a political coup that was "the first act of despotism," but also for a love life that "began with the nobility," descended to the bourgeoisie, and "finished with the dregs of the people."[120] Others dismissed the king as an imbecile or for being "without a head," while one Dominique Huguet found himself in the Bastille for having reportedly said that the king "did well to go to Compiègne, Fontainebleau, Marly, and Versailles, but would do even better to go to Saint-Denis."[121]

To the royal burial site at Saint-Denis the king finally went on 11 May 1774. Preaching the dead king's funeral oration there a few months later, not even the Bishop of Senez "could . . . dissimulate how much the demonstration of their love seemed to fall upon hard times and grow colder among Frenchmen."[122] In fact,

---

118. Jean-Baptiste-Charles-Marie de Beauvais, Bishop of Senez, "Sermon sur l'immortalité de l'âme," in *Sermons de Messire Jean-Baptiste-Charles-Marie de Beauvais, évêque de Senez*, 4 vols. (Paris, 1787), 1:186–87.

119. On the episcopal strategy to rechristianize France, see Hermann Weber, "Das Sacre Ludwigs XVI vom Juni 1775 und die Krise des Anciens Régime," in *Vom Ancien Régime zur Französischen Revolution: Forschungen und Perspektiven*, ed. Ernst Hinrichs, Eberhard Schmitt, and Rudolf Vierhaus (Göttingen, 1978), pp. 539–69.

120. *Remontrances de la basoche* in BA, AB, Ms. 12389, fols. 174–83.

121. On king as fool *(benêt)*, interrogation of Claude de Veugny on 8 Mar. 1771 in BA, AB, Ms. 12393, no. 290; on king as having no head, see interrogation of the abbé Jharse or d'Iharse on 21 Apr. 1771, Ms. 12390, no. 60; and on king at Saint-Denis, see interrogation of Dominique Huguet on 8 Feb. 1771, Ms. 12390, no. 33. See also Shanti Marie Singham, "A Conspiracy of Twenty Million Frenchmen," pp. 163–215.

122. Beauvais, "Oraison funèbre de Louis XV le Bien-Aimé, prononcé dans l'église de l'abbaye de Saint-Denis, le 27 juillet 1774," in *Sermons*, 4:243.

the king's demise provoked discourse as scurrilous and pointedly sacrilegious as any that had appeared during his lifetime. "Here, by the grace of God, lies Louis XV," was one of the many epitaphs that circulated after the king's death, maliciously playing on the Bourbon monarchy's claim to rule by the grace of God alone. "He died, didn't he?" reportedly replied the abbot of Sainte-Geneviève when asked why Paris's patron saint had not answered Parisians' prayers on the occasion of the late king's illness.[123] The unregretted Louis "the Beloved" continued to bedevil the reputation of the monarchy even from his grave, as such systematic and scandal-mongering exposés of his reign as *Anecdotes sur Madame la comtesse Du Barry (Anecdotes about Madame the Countess Du Barry)* and the *Vie privée de Louis XV (The Private Life of Louis XV)* appeared after his death. As a title like *Vie privée* indicates, these exposés continued to widen the distance between the king's two bodies, portraying the private one as debauched and the public one as despotic. Indeed, the aftermath of the Maupeou episode signaled the transition from an antiroyal mauvais discours with significant traces of religious content to ones that were simply and secularly mauvais—the transition, that is, to the thoroughly discredited and desacralized monarchy of the clandestine literature so engagingly studied by Robert Darnton.[124]

Devout hopes hence centered on the deceased king's grandson and successor as Louis XVI, a man of exemplary piety and unimpeachable morals. The man of that hopeful hour was again the Bishop of Senez, who now dared hope that "honor, faith, and virtue [are] not yet entirely extinguished from the hearts of the French," and that the new king's "zeal" and good intentions might justify the title of the "restorer of morals" with which the bishop proposed to christen him.[125] At the royal court, this restoration of manners and morals took such obvious form as exiling compromising leftovers of the previous reign like Madame du Barry and the comte de Saint-Florentin and by appointing devout ministers like Louis-Nicolas, comte de Muy, the new secretary of war. But the most signal triumph of the parti dévot was the consecration and coronation ceremony at Reims, which Louis insisted upon retaining in its integrity. The few liberties taken with tradition rather reinforced the role of the clergy and highlighted the principle that the king "held his power from God, that he held it from God alone, and that he was accountable for it only to God." Where the ceremonial text, for example, called for the bishops of Beauvais and Laon to turn toward the people and rhetorically ask them if they would take the candidate as their king, these bishops remained

123. Cited in Jeffrey Merrick, "The Politics of the Pulpit: Ecclesiastical Discourse on the Death of Louis XV," in *History of European Ideas* 7 (1986):149.

124. Robert Darnton, "Reading, Writing, Publishing," in *The Literary Underground of the Old Regime* (Cambridge, Mass., 1982), 199–208; and *The Forbidden Best-Sellers of Pre-Revolutionary France* (New York, 1995), pp. 137–66, 197–246, 337–89.

125. Beauvais, "Oraison funèbre de Louis XV le Bien-Aimé," in *Sermons*, 4:217, 265–66.

unmoved while facing the king, altogether suppressing this vestigial gesture toward the principle of popular consent. Louis XVI himself was observed to have followed the ceremony with a religious earnestness, in sharp contrast to his brothers, who did not. Nor, once crowned, did Louis XVI neglect to touch hundreds of victims of scrofula, and that for the first time since 1738, when his predecessor had abandoned the practice. But he performed that ritual only after he had confessed and taken communion in the abbatial church of Saint-Remy, as though the Bourbon monarchy's miraculous powers depended on the church and its sacraments.[126]

Although this consecration and coronation ceremony struck articulate observers like Pidansat de Mairobert as spectacle or theatre—or at least something less than religious revival—the devout and episcopal strategy of resacralizing the kingdom from the head on down seemed to bear fruit on the occasion of the papal jubilee of 1776, which, unlike the one fifty years earlier, proceeded unhindered by Jansenist curés and their parsimonious ideas about divine grace. "At the very moment when impiety is redoubling its applause at its own successes, and in the midst of this capital, the center and foyer of the epidemic, have we not just seen the old fervor rekindle itself with an éclat that has taken even us by surprise?" rejoiced the Bishop of Senez preaching the comte de Muy's funeral oration in April 1776.[127] Even Pidansat de Mairobert wryly confessed to being tempted to become a penitent too, lest he "miss such a fine occasion," Catholic piety having become "a style, a craze, competitive with high hairdos and big earrings."[128]

No such national resacralization under royal leadership was to occur, however, despite an upturn in vocations in some religious orders. By 1775 religious controversy had done far too much damage to royal religion—even to religion itself—for any king's personal piety to prevail against all the competitive forces and factors both new and old. That personal piety did not even prevent Louis XVI from becoming the object of seditious discourse in his turn, his putative impotence taking the place of his predecessor's prurience, and a cuckolding by a cardinal taking the place of the reputed debauchery of the *Parc aux cerfs*.[129] From the perspective of an older Old Regime, then, the period from the death of Louis XV to the onset of the Revolution was a confusing one, a witness to the monarchy's tentative quest for a new identity as well as the fissuring of older patterns of opposition, as both absolutism and opponents of absolutism tried to come to

126. This account of the sacre is heavily dependent on Weber's "Das Sacre Ludwigs XVI"; the various quotations are taken from Mairobert, *Espion anglois*, 1:344–48.

127. Beauvais, "Oraison funèbre de M. Louis-Nicolas-Victor de Félix, comte du Muy, maréchal de France, chevalier des ordres du roi, ministre et secrétaire d'état au département de la guerre, prononcé dans l'église de l'Hôtel des Invalides, le 24 avril 1776," in *Sermons*, 4:348.

128. Mairobert, "Le jubilée," *Espion anglois*, 3:101–2.

129. Darnton, *The Literary Underground of the Old Regime*, pp. 199–208.

terms with the Enlightenment as a political force. That the monarchy's experimentation with a new persona ultimately reached a dead end in 1793 does not
detract from the fascination of the effort.

No attempt to resacralize the post–Louis Quatorzian monarchy could do so
without the close association with the episcopacy. Yet even before his coronation
Louis XVI seriously compromised that alliance by deciding to undo Maupeou's
"reforms" and to recall the old parlements to the applause of Jansenist and
patriotic opinion. Buoyed by that victory, the forces of patriotism had no reason to
leave the field of commentary on the royal sacre uncontested, and so answered the
bishops in a number of books and pamphlets published in 1775, including an
augmented second edition of Mey's and Maultrot's massive *Maximes du droit
public françois*. This edition included a detailed demonstration of how the abettors
of despotism had gradually edited out all textual evidence of the French monarchy's elective origin from the coronation script. The anonymous *Le sacre royal*,
meanwhile, insisted on the historical reality of a contractual "social pact," giving
legislative power to the nation.[130] Claude Martin de Marivaux's *L'ami des loix
(The Friend of the Laws)* and Guillaume-Joseph Saige's *Catéchisme du citoyen (The
Citizens's Catechism)*, both published in 1775, were somewhat less weighed down
with historical erudition, allowing the thesis of national sovereignty to stand out
in greater relief.[131]

Saving facts until later, Saige's *Catéchisme du citoyen* began with a clarion
enunciation of Rousseauian principles. "Sovereign power," he argued, "resides in
the general will alone"; the general will was the "necessary tendency . . . toward
the happiness of all"; that tendency had its basis in each individual's "love of self"
(amour de soi). With the aid of such preliminary premises it was easy for Saige to
conclude that "the sovereign authority cannot legitimately reside except in the
body of the people."[132] But once caught in the web of historical fact, Saige's
"patriotic" version of France's historical "constitution" began to resemble a
parlementary if not a Jansenist one. Like Mey and Maultrot or Revol before them,
Saige thought the nation's legislative will best articulated by the Estates General,
suitably tied to its constituents by a binding mandate; like Le Paige, however, he

130. *Le sacre royal ou les droits de la nation reconnus et confirmés par cette cérémonie*, 2 vols. (Amsterdam, 1776). On this treatise, see Marina Valensise, "Le sacre du roi: Stratégie symbolique et doctrine
politique de la monarchie française," *Annales* (May–June, 1986):560–71.

131. On the subject of Guillaume-Joseph Saige, as well as on political thought generally at this
juncture, see Keith M. Baker, "French Political Thought at the Accession of Louis XV," and "A Classical
Republican in Eighteenth-Century Bordeaux: Guillaume-Joseph Saige," in *Inventing the French Revolution*, 109–52.

132. [Guillaume-Joseph Saige], *Catéchisme du citoyen, ou éléments du droit public françois par demandes et réponses* (Geneva, 1775), pp. 9–10.

reserved an honored place for the various "classes" of a French Parlement that, with its center in Paris, dated from the beginnings of the French monarchy and still defended French constitutional "liberty." Saige's "constitution of the church" also located the "plenitude of power" not in the papacy but in the whole body of the faithful, represented by the general council, in which he found ample place for parish priests, successors of the "seventy disciples of Jesus Christ, and the elders of the primitive church."[133] Such was Saige's veneration of this constitution of the French church and state that, although regarding it as willed and still upheld by national sovereignty, he also gave it quasi-Jansenist legitimation as the testimony of "the tradition and the political belief of the first centuries of our monarchy."[134]

That Saige's *Catéchisme* should also have witnessed a certain if limited coalescence between Rousseauism and Jansenist constitutionalism in post-Maupeou patriotic thought calls for brief commentary. For few religious or quasi-religious phenomena could have started from points further removed from each other than Jansenism and Rousseauism: on the Jansenist side, the conviction of the radical corruption and servitude of human nature unless saved by divine grace; on the Rousseauian side the equally fervent conviction of the radical innocence and moral freedom of human nature in spite of and beneath the ongoing corruption of social and institutional circumstances. While Rousseau's belief in the possibility of moral virtue without grace owed more to devout Catholicism than to Jansenism, his conviction of personal justification was more akin to Calvinist justification by faith than to either variety of French Catholicism. And although Rousseau, along with the philosophes, rejected all forms of special revelation and supernatural intervention, he noisily broke with other philosophes over their celebration of civilization and disparagement of religion, making Rousseauism at least a quasi-religious phenomenon.[135] How Rousseauism's simultaneously vaporous and personal religiosity might have been expected to condense in the public political forum is not made much clearer by Rousseau's explicitly political pronouncements, which, although they did not directly engage contemporary political debate, lent themselves to exploitation by all parties to that debate. Rousseau's valorization of the exercise of will in politics, his many strictures against aristocracy and particular interests, his espousal of the possibility of a unitary and indivisible general interest—these, for example, had more potential in the service

133. Ibid., pp. 33–34, 41–42, 46–47, 60, 74–77, 96–97, 120.
134. Ibid., pp. 24–25.
135. My conception of Rousseauism as a quasi-religious phenomenon owes most to Carol Blum's *Rousseau and the Republic of Virtue: The Language of Politics in the French Revolution* (Ithaca, N.Y., 1986); and Jean Starobinski's classic *Jean-Jacques Rousseau: Transparency and Obstruction*, trans. Arthur Goldhammer (Chicago, 1988). See also Philippe Lefebvre, *Les pouvoirs de la parole: L'église et Rousseau, 1762–1848* (Paris, 1992).

of the monarchical or ministerial cause than in the patriot one. And impressed they were by that cause in the confrontation of 1789.[136]

That much said, other aspects of Rousseauism were more adjacent to judicial Jansenism, making it possible for "patriotism" to bring them together for a political season or two, both before 1789 and even beyond. For one thing, Rousseau's growing appreciation of the pervasive influence of social corruption tended so to efface humanity's radical innocence as to put it into a category with vestiges of the image of God, and Rousseau's growing paranoia as life went on so tended to thin the ranks of his putative virtuous as to render them hardly more numerous than the Jansenist elect. Hence, in part, the proximity of Jansenist and Rousseauist appeals to the "upright heart" *(coeur droit)* against the passions and pervasive amour propre; sincerity and simplicity against calculation and prevarication; the individual conscience and integrity against raw numbers and sheer force. The resultant contamination by a Rousseauian virtue and more active political will is one of the factors that made judicial Jansenism more exportable as radical patriotism, while judicial Jansenism gave Rousseauism a more corporate constituency, thereby taming its ideological impact at least in the shorter run. For Rousseau's clear doctrine of popular sovereignty as enunciated in the *Social Contract* was also close enough to judicial Jansenism's more historically oriented and corporate national sovereignty to have produced the mutual contamination of constitutional outlooks evident in Saige's *Catéchisme.* When combined, moreover, with a minority mentality, Rousseauian and judicial Jansenist constitutionalism engendered a similar suspicion of representative bodies and legislative majorities in defense of the real "people" or veritable "faithful"; a similar validation of an electorate's spontaneous "hue and cry" in the absence of binding mandates; and a similar vindication of individual consciences and supposedly silent majorities in the name of the general will.

Not all of these similarities are coincidental. After his conversion from Genevan Calvinism to Catholicism, Rousseau himself confessedly lived through a Jansenist phase when he read through the Port-Royalist corpus.[137] Arnauld and Pascal coined and developed the concept of the general will, which Rousseau along with others appropriated and secularized. And the validation of the "general interest" in opposition to the "particular interest" was banal enough in Jansenist literature well before the publication of Rousseau's first prize-winning

---

136. Rousseau's indebtedness to absolutist political thought is underscored by Nannerl O. Keohane in *Philosophy and the State in France,* pp. 442–43. For an argument stressing the adaptability of Rousseau's political thought to different and even opposed causes, see Joan McDonald, *Rousseau and the French Revolution* (London, 1965).

137. Jean-Jacques Rousseau, *Les confessions,* ed. Jacques Voisine, Classiques Garnier (Paris, 1964), pp. 267, 273, 280–81.

discourse.[138] Without underestimating the deep gulf generally separating Jansenism and Rousseauism, then, it is worth observing these points of contact between them, and to note, with Roger Barny, that it was the overlapping Jansenist and patriotic milieux that produced the first appreciative contingent of the *Social Contract*'s readers.[139]

If the monarchy did not derive any immediate benefit from Rousseauism's debut on the political scene, then neither did the Parlement. For the restored Parlement of Paris singled out Saige's and Marivaux's Rousseauian pamphlets for condemnation shortly after the royal sacre on 30 June 1775, thereby alienating a segment of advanced patriotic opinion. "Such is the absurdity of that Company, chronically contradicting and inculpating itself . . . and pronouncing its own condemnation," complained Pidansat de Mairobert.[140] That absurdity was not without political method, however, one dictated by the need for institutional allies in the light of the Parlement's vulnerability as revealed by the Maupeou coup. In distancing itself from the radical fringe of patriotic opinion, the Parlement courted the alliance of none other than the episcopacy. And so in a "capucinal harangue" delivered on 7 September 1775 that Mairobert found "revolting," the Parlement's avocat général Antoine Séguier called off the sovereign court's long war against the clergy, "announcing that the moment had come for the reunion of that order with the magistracy, and that a precious harmony ought henceforth to reign among them, and bring back the reign of religion."[141] The same parlementary raison d'état presided over the condemnation of Boncerf's *Inconveniences of Feudal Rights* at about the same time, a logic in this case designed to court the support of the princes and peers and in particular of the prince de Conti, who brought the book to the Parlement's attention.[142] One result of these exercises in political fence-mending is that, whereas before 1771 the parlements had sometimes lent discreet support to attacks on the clergy's immunity to secular taxation, after 1775 they tended to close ranks with the upper clergy among other Montesquieuian corps in a common defense of "property." The thesis that an "aristocratic reaction" or regrouping took place during the last fifteen or twenty years before the

138. Patrick Riley, *The General Will Before Rousseau* (Princeton, N.J., 1986); and Keohane, *Philosophy and the State in France*, pp. 273–82, 433–49.

139. Roger Barny, *Prélude idéologique à la Révolution française: Le Rousseauisme avant 1789* (Paris, 1985), pp. 90–120.

140. Mairobert, "Lettre II, sur le sacre de Louis XVI, et sur les monumens et écrits qui ont paru à cette occasion," *L'espion anglois*, 1:351–52.

141. Ibid., "Letter XVII, sur l'assemblée du clergé, et sur ce qui s'est passé depuis son ouverture, au commencement de juillet, jusques à sa clôture en décembre," 2:237.

142. François Boncerf, *Les inconvénients des droits féodaux* (London, 1776); and *Arrêt de la cour de parlement, qui condamne une brochure intitulée: Les inconvénients des droits féodaux, à être lacérée et brûlée au pied du grand escalier du palais, par l'exécuteur de la haute justice.* (Paris, 1776).

Revolution may have fallen upon revisionist times as social history, but it is far from implausible as political history.

That the monarchy would not be a party to this parlementary-episcopal rapprochement was due not only to its chronic need for additional revenues but also to the appointment of Anne-Robert Turgot as controller general of finance in 1775–76. For while devout bishops suspected Turgot as an irreligious philosophe who challenged their interpretation of the royal sacre and advocated the civil toleration of Protestants, magistrates and bishops alike opposed him as a physiocrat or enlightened *économiste*, as French advocates of the "natural laws" of the market place and the policy of laissez faire were then known. As expounded by François Quesnay and the "friend of humanity" Victor Riqueti, the marquis de Mirabeau, physiocratic economic theory favored such "natural" or unfeudal forms of property as brought labor, capital, and above all land into a closer working relationship, which, empowered by the free play of the profit motive, would increase production, assure the state of an enhanced revenue, and provide the propertyless with cheaper commodities.[143] Although Turgot did not share the movement's dogmatic preference for agriculture and the soil as the only source of additional wealth, he entirely shared its general bias against such "unnatural" and unproductive forms of property as venal offices, redundant benefices, and seigneurial or feudal rights. That bias lurked behind Turgot's six famous edicts further freeing the grain trade and abolishing the guilds and some venal offices. The bias was still more evident in pamphlets that circulated in support of Turgot's total program, such as Boncerf's *Disadvantages of Feudal Rights*. The Parlement's opposition to these edicts, voiced in two rounds of remonstrances and Antoine Séguier's harangue of 12 March, was not the most decisive factor in Turgot's later fall from power.[144] Yet that opposition put it perilously on record in defense of every form of privileged property and further compromised it in patriot opinion. The thesis that a formally privileged nobility was essential to a monarchical constitution also made its way into parlementary pronouncements at this point.[145] Although it helped solidify the Parlement's new working alliance with the princes and peers in 1776 and enjoyed unimpeachably enlightened legitimation in Montesquieu's political science, that thesis would prove to be a political liability in 1788.

Although physiocratic opinion was far from the same as encyclopedic opinion as such—the movement encountered no little enlightened opposition—the net

143. On the marquis de Mirabeau, François Quesnay, and physiocracy, see Elizabeth Fox-Genovese, *The Origins of Physiocracy* (Ithaca, N.Y., 1976); and *Les Mirabeau et leur temps, Acts du colloque d'Aix-en-Provence* (Paris, 1968), pp. 1–87.

144. Edgar Faure, *La disgrâce de Turgot*, Trente journées qui ont fait la France series (Paris, 1961), pp. 480–522.

145. "Remontrances du 2–4 mars 1776" and "Remontrances du 8–19 mai 1776," in Jules Flammermont, *Remontrances du parlement de Paris au dix-huitième siècle*, 3 vols. (Geneva, 1978), 3:287–88, 291, 378.

effect of Turgot's brief tenure as controller general was to bring philosophical opinion in general around to the side of the monarchy and ministerial policy, despite Turgot's fall from power in May 1776.[146] Whereas Voltaire's defense of the ministry was the exception during the Maupeou episode, it was to become more normal than not after 1775. Physiocracy's political program was moreover admirably tailored to the defense of the monarchy's undivided and unitary power. In line with its penchant for simplicity and economy, physiocracy abhorred Montesquieuian intermediate powers and Anglo-Saxon checks and balances, and hence the sort of constitutional barriers to the monarchy's will represented by the parlements and even the Estates General. And in proclaiming the king to be the co-proprietor of all the net revenue of the realm, physiocracy hoped not only to solve the monarchy's fiscal problems but to give it a stake in the realm's material welfare, which, combined with a free press and an informed public opinion, was supposed to form a more effective barrier to arbitrary government than any privileged corps. Against these corps, physiocrats tended to look to the monarchy and its ministers—to legal despotism, as the phrase went—for the force needed to break the self-interested resistance of privilege and prepare the way for the rule of natural law.[147]

In spite of the obvious enmity between enlightened physiocracy and devout Catholicism, physiocracy was not an altogether implausible substitute as the regnant ideology for a monarchy in need of an updated identity. The replacement of the one by the other might not have been as abrupt as it at first appears because, as is appropriate to this ideologically promiscuous period, physiocracy was not entirely discontinuous with some moments in the history of devout Catholicism. Physiocracy's economic agenda was in a sense a secular legatee of Fénelon's and Beauvilliers's Christian agrarianism and hence of the late seventeenth-century parti dévot. Both looked to agriculture and the soil for virtue and wealth, both believed in the beneficent effects of free trade and commerce, both preferred peace to the pursuits of glory and conquest, and both hoped, each at its particular juncture, that a new king might take the advice of the right mentor and model himself after the selfless Télémaque. Although innocent of Fénelon's mystical quest for pure love and the annihilation of amour propre, physiocrats shared the Bishop of Cambrai's preoccupation with virtue and, in comparison with other philosophes, professed due respect for the deity, distancing themselves from both d'Holbachian atheism and Voltairian fixation on the infamous thing.

Nor, for that matter, were connections to the eighteenth-century parti dévot

146. See, for example, Mairobert's favorable account of the forced registration of Turgot's edicts in the lit de justice assembly of 12 Mar. 1776 in "Lettre XXVIII, lit de justice du 12 mars 1776: Evénements qui l'ont précédé et suivi," *L'espion anglois*, 3:94.

147. On the political thought of physiocracy see Léon Cheinisse, *Les physiocrates* (Paris, 1914); and Eugène Daire, ed. *Physiocrats*, 2 vols. (Paris, 1846).

lacking. Physiocrats, too, combined a generous conception of human capacities with a sufficient if secular grace for all, at least in pedagogical grace. Would but the king adopt his proposed political catechism and have it taught to all school-children, Turgot assured Louis XV in 1776, and "ten years from now your nation would be unrecognizable . . . and infinitely superior to all other peoples past and present."[148] As a self-conscious movement, animated with missionary zeal and armed with propagandistic media like the abbé Nicolas Baudeau's *New Ephemerids for the Citizen,* physiocracy bore a religious aspect, prompting even sympathetic observers to refer to its founders as proselytes, to its theory as doctrine, and to the whole movement as a sect.[149] These points of contact with devout Catholicism extended even to biography. Two of the controller general's collaborators, André Morellet and Loménie de Brienne, had also been fellows in the Molinistic Sorbonne in the late 1740s.[150] Another, the marquis de Condorcet, had a zealously devout uncle, the scourge of Jansenists as Bishop of Auxerre. Turgot himself had intervened in the refusal-of-sacraments controversy with a pamphlet called *Le conciliateur (The Conciliator),* which had conciliated more Molinistically than otherwise. However remote they may seem to us today, these connections and relations were not lost on contemporaries like the young councillor Jacques Duval d'Eprémesnil, who, as the conflict between the Parlement and Turgot came to a head in 1776, accused the économistes of being secularized successors of the Jesuits.[151]

As it happened, Jesuits, or rather ex-Jesuits, again occupied the attention of the Parlement of Paris at about the same time. For in the spring of 1777 the Parlement's parti janséniste—in this case, Louis-Alexandre Angran, Pierre-Daniel Bourrée de Corberon, and the inevitable Robert de Saint-Vincent—succeeded in provoking several sessions on the subject and in persuading the Parlement to investigate ex-Jesuits rumored to be regrouping in Lyon and trying to establish a new institutional base within the chaplaincy of the Ecole militaire.[152] But neither rhetorical assimilation of Jesuits to physiocrats nor the scapegoating of ex-Jesuits themselves could altogether obscure a growing distance between the Parlement of

148. Anne-Robert Turgot, "Memorandum on local government," *The Old Regime and the French Revolution,* ed. and trans. Keith M. Baker (Chicago, 1987), p. 102.

149. Mairobert, "Lettre première, sur les économistes, sur M. Turgot, sur la nouvelle législation concernant le commerce des grains, et sur les émeutes," *L'espion anglois,* 1:275–319.

150. André Morellet, *Mémoires inédits de l'abbé Morellet, de l'académie française, sur le dix-huitième siècle et sur la Révolution,* 2d ed., 2 vols. (Paris, 1822), 1:1–22.

151. Faure, *La disgrâce de Turgot,* p. 438. For another example of Jansenist reaction to physiocracy, see André Blonde, *Lettre d'un profane à monsieur l'abbé Beaudeau, très-vénérable de la scientifique et sublime Loge de la Franche-Economie* (n.p., 1775).

152. Mairobert, "Lettre XI: Dénonciations au parlement contre les ex-jésuites," *L'espion anglois,* 5:273–303.

Paris and Jansenism's ecclesiastical agenda that the new parlementary-episcopal rapprochement carried in its train. For if the parlements and the episcopacy were to stand together in defense of "property" high and low, the parlements had perforce to spare episcopal susceptibilities in such causes as the rights of parish priests, not to mention civil toleration of Protestants, both of them dear to Jansenists.

Thus it happened, for example, that the Parlement of Paris indifferently folded its arms while Turgot and his philosophical colleague Lamoignon de Malesherbes tried in vain to talk the General Assembly of the Clergy of 1775 into relinquishing the principle of clerical immunity to royal taxation, a reform to which Jansenists were generally sympathetic. And it was the Protestant minister Jacques Necker, not the episcopacy or the Parlement, who sponsored the modest increase in the *portion congrue* for poor parish priests in 1780. And so it happened, too, that the Parlement of Paris lent no help to Malesherbes's attempt to persuade the General Assembly of 1775 to recognize the legality of Protestant marriages in "the desert" and turned a deaf ear to the pro-Protestant entreaties of Jansenist magistrates like Robert de Saint-Vincent and Anne-Charles-René de Bretignières just a few years later, in 1778. It would take all of the tireless Robert de Saint-Vincent's persistence to prod the Parlement into an examination of the Archbishop of Paris's new ritual in 1786.[153]

The effect of the parlementary-episcopal rapprochement on property was to split the Jansenist or patriot agenda in the decade before the Revolution as well as to make parish priests available as potential allies of the monarchy. Without ever entirely abandoning the cause of the parlements, Jansenists most interested in ecclesiastical reform found themselves obliged to look as much to the monarchy as to the parlements for redress. Although Le Paige's primarily figurist constitutionalism kept him and others loyal to the Parlement of Paris until and even beyond the götterdämmerung of 1789, Mey's and Maultrot's conciliar constitutionalism, modeled after their ideal of the primitive church, kept them more active on behalf of Richerist causes and enabled them more easily to transfer their allegiance from parlements to Estates General in 1789. In the campaign for civil toleration of Protestants, similarly, the Jansenist theologian Louis Guidi wrote his pro-Protestant pamphlets in 1775 on behalf of Malsherbes and Turgot, not the Parlement of Paris.[154] So discontinuous did Jansenism's political and ecclesiastical

153. On the Jansenist campaign for toleration of Protestants within the Parlement of Paris see Charles O'Brien, "The Jansenist Campaign for Toleration of Protestants in Late Eighteenth-Century France: Sacred or Secular?" *JHI* 46 (1985):523–38. On Robert de Saint-Vincent's case against the archbishop's ritual, see his *Dénonciation du nouveau Rituel de Paris, aux chambres assemblées, par M. XXX, du mardi 19 novembre 1786* (N.p., n.d.).

154. Geoffrey Adams, *The Huguenots and French Public Opinion, 1685–1789* (Waterloo, Ontario, 1991), pp. 238–42; and Mairobert, "Lettre XVII, sur l'assemblée du clergé," *L'espion anglois,* 2:222–32.

agendas become after 1775 that it will be necessary to take them up separately in the remaining chapter.

The years following the failure of Maupeou's coup, then, significantly blurred without completely altering the political patterns as they had emerged from that coup. On the one hand, the monarchy in the person of a pious and morally exemplary new king found itself estranged from its traditional episcopal support while enjoying some unexpected goodwill from philosophical opinion and the second order of the clergy. A reform-minded monarchy in alliance with physiocratic philosophes and Richerist priests against the noble and mitred privileged—such a configuration was not outside the realm of political possibility, assuming, of course, that the king himself would have the courage of these new convictions and would not, like Lot's wife, nostalgically look back toward the conflagration of privilege in 1789. On the other hand, the Parlement of Paris firmed up a growing alliance with the princes and peers and engineered a domestic "diplomatic revolution" by means of its staged rapprochement with the bishops. In doing so, however, it alienated radical patriotic opinion and a part of what remained of its Jansenist constituency. That the Parlement in alliance with princes and some bishops might bring the monarchy to its knees was clear enough, if only from the memory of the Fronde. What was less clear was whether such allies could take the place of patriotic Parisian opinion in the uncharted confusion that followed.

CHAPTER 6

From Ideology to Revolution
and Counterrevolution

AMONG THE VARIOUS CANDIDATES FOR THE DISTINCTION of being the last day of the Old Regime in France, the claim of 23 June 1789 is as strong as any. On that day Louis XVI arrived at the Salle des menus plaisirs accompanied by much of the court to address a plenary session of the Estates General of his realm—the first such meeting in 175 years—and presented two declarations, as though for registration by the assembly. The very first article of the first declaration maintained the distinction between the clergy, the nobility, and the Third Estate as essential to the realm's constitution, and therefore annulled the decision of the Third Estate, or Commons, taken three days earlier, whereby it had declared itself to be France's National Assembly," duly authorized by the nation to legislate in its interests with or without the other two orders. Another crucial provision of the same declaration laid it down that the "antique and constitutional rights of the three orders," as well as the form of future meetings of the Estates General, would be off limits to deliberation by the three orders meeting in common, implying that any change in such constitutional matters would require the consent of each of the three orders deliberating separately, to say nothing of the king. Having finally reminded the deputies that all of their decisions would indeed require his "special approbation," the king and his whole court left the assembly, followed by the nobility and most of the clergy, leaving behind his master of ceremonies, the marquis de Dreux-Brezé, to tell the delegates of the Third Estate that they were to leave as well.[1]

1. M. J. Madival and M. E. Laurent, eds., *Archives parlementaires de 1787 à 1860, première partie (1787–1799)*, 94 vols. to date (Paris, 1867–), 23 June 1789, pp. 142–46.

Accounts of exactly what happened next vary somewhat in detail. But by most accounts the first person after Brezé to open his mouth was Honoré Riquetti, comte de Mirabeau, wayward son of the founder of physiocracy and renegade noble representing the Third Estate at Aix-en-Provence. Like those provincial nobles who put themselves at the head of commoner revolts during the Fronde, Mirabeau put himself at the head of the Commons's delegation and told Brezé that if he really wished them to leave he would have to call on military force, because they "would not quit their seats except by the power of bayonets."[2] By most accounts, too, the next delegate to speak was Armand-Gaston Camus, a Jansenist barrister in the Parlement of Paris and, as noted earlier, a veteran of Chancellor Maupeou's constitutional coup of 1771–74. As a close witness of many a royal-parlementary confrontation, including the recent ones of the prerevolution, Camus knew a disguised lit de justice assembly when he saw one and so proposed the strongest possible response: not to protest or to remonstrate but "to persist without reservation in our preceding arrêtés" or legislative decisions.[3] The third person to speak was apparently Antoine Barnave, a Protestant barrister in the Parlement of Grenoble in Dauphiné, who reminded the deputies that these arrêtés included the one that had declared them a National Assembly, whereupon, after additional speeches, including one by the abbé Emmanuel-Joseph Sieyès and another by Mirabeau, the assembly voted unanimously in favor of Camus's motion. Louis capitulated to the Third Estate's defiance several days later, ordering the other two orders to join the National Assembly on the twenty-seventh, a capitulation that the Parisian municipal revolution and fall of the Bastille of 12–14 July memorably confirmed. And thus, in a sense, did the Fronde, the long Jansenist resistance, and the Protestant réforme have the last word about absolutism after all.

That last word, it is true, was a delayed one—an echo, as it were, because religion and religious issues had hardly been the order of the day during the last fifteen years of the Old Regime. Among the orators in that historic last session of the Estates General and first of the National Assembly, Sieyès hardly spoke in the accents of an abbé and Barnave said nothing that identified him as a Protestant, which he remained in a mainly ancestral sense. And although Camus's Jansenism was still alive and well enough to sound altogether like itself, even he articulated

---

2. Ibid., p. 146; Honoré-Gabriel Riquetti, comte de Mirabeau, "Treizième lettre," *Courrier de Provence, pour servir de suite aux lettres du comte de Mirabeau à ses commettans,* 2 vols. (Paris, 1789), 23–25 June 1789, 1:9–10. However, Le Hodey de Sault Chevreil in his *Journal des Etats-généraux,* 35 vols. (Paris, 1789–90), 25 June 1789, 1:204–6, has the cry of defiance arising spontaneously from the whole assembly, while Bertrand Barère in his *Le point du jour,* 27 vols. (Paris, 1789–91), 25 June 1789, 1:42–44, makes Camus the first speaker.

3. Le Hodey's *Journal des Etats-généraux* (23 June 1789), 1:204–5, has Pisand de Galand and Barnave speaking before Camus, but all sources agree that it was Camus who made the motion that the assembly "persist" its preceding arrêtés.

what had become more like an inheritance than a heresy. That much may not have distinguished patriot Jansenism—or Jansenist patriotism—from enlightened encyclopedism, which by the 1780s was likewise past its prime as a self-conscious and coherent movement. But patriot Jansenism was also a divided legacy on the eve of the Revolution, as we have seen, pitting proponents of the constitutional reform of absolutism against proponents of ecclesiastical reform in alliance with absolutism. Even that divided legacy was far from having the discursive field to itself, juxtaposed as it was with what remained of the politics of devout Catholicism—the other chief religious legacy—not to mention encyclopedic, Rousseauian, and physiocratic thought.

Yet even fragmented inheritances can give direction and set limits to political action of the inheritors, conditioning if not determining it in ways apart from the conscious intention of the actors. It remains to be seen whether and how the Old Regime's various religious legacies did so in the separate domains of constitution making and ecclesiastical reform.

Patriot Pamphleteering in the Prerevolution

A restored but weakened Parlement of Paris remained the Old Regime's primary arena of constitutional contestation after 1774, even though no single issue galvanized opinion and clarified ideological divisions as had the *Unigenitus*-related controversies of the 1750s and 1760s or Chancellor Maupeou's constitutional coup in the early 1770s. In the absence of such "public" issues the center stage gave way to a series of salacious "private" courtroom cases, which, though apparently unrelated to the religious concerns of a previous generation, dramatized some of the constitutional and social issues to which those concerns had given rise and, by restating them in intensely personal and moral terms, literally brought them home to ordinary Frenchmen in a way that earlier cases had not.[4] For each of them seemed to issue an indictment of despotism, aristocracy, or sometimes both in a way that anticipates the conflation of the two pejoratives that was to occur in the Revolution. Coming at the beginning of this period, for example—in fact, while the Maupeou parlement still existed—the case of the commoner Véron-Dujonquay family against the comte de Morangiès dramatically translated the ministerial case against the patriot aristocracy into concrete social imagery, although, as Sarah Maza points out, the Véron family's lawyer, Jacques-Vincent Delacroix, also skillfully cast Morangiès as the perfect despot. And coming at the end of the period—indeed, as the prerevolution was turning into the French Revolution—the case of the banker Guillaume Kornmann against his adulterous wife ended in an

4. Sarah Maza, *Private Lives and Public Affairs: The Causes Célèbres of Prerevolutionary France* (Berkeley, Calif., 1993).

explicit indictment of despotism and even the controller general Alexandre de Calonne, although it also condemned the sexual mores of court society and hence aristocracy as well.

If Louis XVI himself remained relatively unscathed by these indictments, it was not only because he seemed benign and personable in contrast to his grandfather but because little remained except his person either to like or dislike. For by the 1780s a century of desacralizing religious conflict had done its worst, stripping the king of his public patriarchal qualities and leaving him, as Lynn Hunt has shown, with at best the role of benevolent father to play.[5] Illustrative of this process of domestication is the depiction of the king in what would seem to have been sacral absolutism's last redoubt: the salons of the Royal Academy of Painting as described by the Bachaumont *Mémoires*.[6] While in 1761 Michel Vanloo still portrayed the king with all of the attributes of royalty, in 1785 an obscure painter named Dubucourt pictured Louis XVI ordinarily clad and incognito, "unaffectedly hiding all the decorations that might give him away," the better to give alms to a poor peasant boy whose grateful parents have just recognized their royal benefactor nonetheless. Evident in all the pamphlets of the prerevolution, the role of affectionate and benevolent "father of his people" would help Louis XVI survive the events of the collapse of absolutism and the onset of the Revolution, but would finally prove incompatible with what remained of his quality as "eldest son of the church."

A little out of its element in this new personal and private world, the Parlement of Paris's parti janséniste meanwhile continued to dominate a diminished domain of public affairs to an extent out of proportion to its dwindling numbers. For even in the 1780s a Parlement quite docile in fiscal matters remained persistent in areas where Jansenism was indirectly concerned. The Parlement's opposition, for example, to the ministry's "despotic" tampering with the sacrosanct constitutions of the Benedictine congregation of Saint-Maur, a long-time Jansenist preserve, elicited three successive remonstrances, all of them written by the Jansenist canonist Henri Jabineau.[7] And the Parlement's charge that "charity had given way to despotism" in the new administration of the reorganized and

5. Lynn Hunt, *The Family Romance of the French Revolution* (Berkeley, Calif., 1992), pp. 49–52; and Jeffrey Merrick, "Fathers and Kings: Patriarchalism and Absolutism in Eighteenth-Century French Politics," *Studies on Voltaire and the Eighteenth Century* 308 (1993):281–303.

6. Louis Petit de Bachaumont, *Mémoires secrets pour servir à l'histoire de la république des lettres en France, depuis MDCCLXII jusqu'à nos jours*, 36 vols. (London, 1784–88), 30:190–93. I thank Berdanette Fort for permission to cite this evidence as brought to my attention in her unpublished paper, "The *Salons* in the *Mémoires secrets*: Art History in the Making."

7. Jules Flammermont, *Remontrances du parlement de Paris au dix-huitième siècle*, 3 vols. (Geneva, 1978), 3:501–14, 531–42, 603–17, and dated 4 Sept. 1783, 10–15 Feb. 1784, and 13 Feb. 1785. On Jabineau's authorship, see Lefebvre de Beauvray, "Mémoires pour servir à l'histoire du XVIIIe siècle," 2 vols. in 1 in BN: Mss. Fr., Ms. 10364, 2:73.

relocated Quinze-Vingts hospital for the blind—another long-standing Jansenist preserve—played variations on a theme originally set in oppostion to the Archbishop of Paris's attempted reform of the Hôpital général during the 1750s.[8] The composer of these remonstrances was Duval d'Eprémesnil, whose Jansenistical Catholic piety apparently found some "analogy between the convulsions of the appellant deacon [Pâris] and those effected by Doctor Mesmer" and his modish animal magnetism.[9]

What at once clarified both the period's ideologically diffuse quality and ended the Parlement's timidity in fiscal matters was the rapid succession of events now known as the French prerevolution.[10] Informed in 1786 by his controller-general Calonne that the government's debt and annual deficit were no longer amenable to ordinary fiscal remedies, Louis XVI, on Calonne's advice, convoked a handpicked Assembly of Notables, the first such since 1626. While waiting for that assembly to meet, Calonne and his staff elaborated a series of far-reaching reform proposals of vaguely physiocratic inspiration, the most important of them being the replacement of existing direct taxes with a "territorial subvention" levied in kind on all land regardless of the social status of its owners, along with the creation of advisory provincial assemblies similarly composed of landowners without respect to rank or order. Calonne also proposed to abolish internal tolls and tariffs as well as other impediments to the free circulation of merchandise and commodities, especially grain. The purpose of laying these proposals before an Assembly of Notables was in part to disarm in advance the Parlement of Paris, which would eventually have to register these measures.

From the outset, events conspired against Calonne's attempt to manipulate public opinion. By the time the assembly met, Calonne himself and two other ministers had fallen sick, wasting precious time and allowing Parisian pamphleteers to convince the idle notables that something foul was afoot. Worse yet, these pamphleteers included Calonne's popular predecessor Jacques Necker, who, although in a state of disgrace vis-à-vis the king since his fall from the ministry in

---

8. Flammermont, *Remonstrances*, 3:484–501, 558–86, 617–26, 661–63, dated 27–29 May 1783, 21–23 May 1784, 6 Mar. 1785, and 25 Aug. 1786. The quotations are from the remonstrances of 21–23 May, p. 583.

9. On Duval d'Eprémesnil's Jansenism see Armand-François, comte d'Allonville, *Mémoires secrets de 1770–1830, par M. le comte d'Allonville*, 6 vols. in 3 (Brussels, 1838–45), 1:235. The quotation about Jansenist and Mesmerist convulsions comes from *Correspondance secrète, politique, et littéraire*, 18 vols. (London, 1787–90), 17:210. On Mesmerism and Cogliostro, see Robert Darnton, *Mesmerism and the End of the Enlightenment in France* (New York, 1970).

10. The expression is Jean Egret's, whose *La Pré-Révolution française, 1787–1789* (Paris, 1962) remains indispensable for the period. Much has been added, however, by William Doyle's *The Origins of the French Revolution* (Oxford, 1980), Bailey Stone's *The French Parlements and the Crisis of the Old Regime* (Chapel Hill, N.C., 1986), and Vivian Gruder's many articles, among them "The Society of Orders at its Demise: The Vision of an Elite at the End of the Old Regime," *FH* 1 (Oct. 1987):210–37.

1781, remained alive and well enough in Paris to undermine Calonne's credibility on the subject of the deficit. It was therefore with great difficulty that Calonne fended off the demand to see the monarchy's accounts and convinced the notables of the reality of the deficit, whereupon they attributed it uniquely to his mis-management. They also opposed the elimination of social distinctions in his proposed provincial assemblies. And although they accepted the principle of fiscal equality implied by the proposed territorial subvention, the notables objected to the tax as such, some of them alleging their own constitutional incompetence and the need for parlementary registration, even for consent by the long defunct Estates General. Nagged by the notables and pilloried in the pamphlets, Calonne fell from power in April and headed for England shortly thereafter, the first of the Revolution's émigrés.

Calonne's most notable critic before becoming his successor, the new first minister Loménie de Brienne, Archbishop of Toulouse, then revamped his pro-posals and began sending them to the Parlement of Paris after dismissing the still uncooperative Assembly of Notables. Some of these proposals—for provincial assemblies, for example—survived the gauntlet of parlementary registration more or less unscathed. But it was otherwise with the edicts establishing Calonne's revised land tax and a new stamp tax, on which the Parlement fixed its fire. Like the notables, the parlementaires accepted—or at least did not object to—the princi-ple of fiscal equality, but, also like the notables, they pleaded their own incompe-tence to approve the new taxes and appealed to the authority of the nation in the Estates General. Caught off guard, Brienne and his ministerial cohort, Chancellor Lamoignon, retaliated with the tried although not very true expedients of a lit de justice assembly on 6 August 1787 and the exile of the still recalcitrant magistrates to a provincial city, Troyes, shortly after.

The exiled Parlement was brought back to Paris in September by an agree-ment whereby the ministry dropped its demands for fiscal edicts in return for the new loans and the prolongation of existing twentieth taxes until the Estates General could meet. But this compromise, too, unraveled when on 19 November a supposedly advisory *séance royale* or "royal session" in the king's presence degen-erated into another lit de justice assembly and forced registration of five successive years of government loans, and the Parlement again remonstrated against this assembly. The ministry then arrested two of the most outspoken magistrates and exiled the duc d'Orléans—the princes and peers had been meeting as part of the Parlement—whereupon the Parlement publicly remonstrated against the mon-archy's practice of extrajudicial arrests and the use of lettres de cachet. When, a few weeks later, a young magistrate named Goislard de Montsabert publicly accused the ministry of arbitrarily revising the existing twentieth tax rolls, Brienne and Lamoignon abandoned efforts at compromise and began planning an anti-parlementary coup not unlike the one attempted by Chancellor Maupeou eighteen years earlier. Getting wind of this coming coup, the magistrates swore a kind of proto-"tennis-court" oath on 3 May 1788, promising each other not to accept positions in any substitute parlement, and also laid down a fledgling declaration of fundamental rights, the Revolution's first.

These events signaled the crisis point of the Old Regime's last parlementary-ministerial set-to. The government made another attempt to arrest parlementary ringleaders, who, forewarned, took refuge in the Parlement's assembled chambers, provoking a siege of the Palais de justice by royal troops. This marathon "session of thirty hours" ended only after the two magistrates, namely Montsabert and d'Eprémesnil, identified themselves and submitted to arrest. In yet another lit de justice assembly on 8 May, the ministry unveiled its own constitutional solution: a national *Cour plénière* (plenary court), amalgamating representatives of provincial parlements with a curtailed Parlement of Paris, which would henceforth register whatever royal edicts and declarations the monarchy sent it. Although Brienne and Lamoignon did not, like Maupeou, profess to end venality of office, they abolished both torture in criminal procedure and the remaining seigneurial courts, thereby adding feudal and seigneurial rights to the widening public discussion of reform. The ministry then sent the Parlement of Paris on vacation sine die, and after it the provincial parlements, as each of these protested in turn against the "military" registration of the May edicts.

Viewed from the perspective of the century's earlier and often religion-related confrontations, this sequence of events bore a still familiar aspect. The Parlement of Paris, it is true, had never before appealed to the Estates General; yet the thinking that led to this appeal had been going on there ever since the sacramental controversy in the 1750s—indeed, in an indirect form ever since the appeal of the bull *Unigenitus*. It is also true that the monarchy had never before faced the organized opposition of the princes and peers, whom Louis XVI, in sharp contrast to his grandfather, had permitted to meet with the Parlement of Paris throughout his reign. Yet the junction of the parlementary magistrates with the princes and peers as France's Court of Peers and national representative body fulfilled one of Le Paige's pet projects, spelled out in the pages of his *Lettres historiques*. And however diminished in numbers and influence in comparison to the 1750s or 1730s, identifiably Jansenist magistrates like Fréteau de Saint-Just, Goislard de Montsabert, and Robert de Saint-Vincent remained so conspicuous within the leadership of the parlementary opposition that the marquis de Bouillé, writing during the Restoration, still blamed the demise of the Old Regime on the Parlement's parti janséniste.[11] In Brienne, these long Jansenist memories per-

---

11. François-Claude Amour, marquis de Bouillé, *Mémoires du marquis de Bouillé*, eds. Berville and Barrière, 2d ed. (Paris, 1822), pp. 64–65. For evidence of Goislard de Montsabert as Jansenist, see Henri Jabineau's *Lettre d'un magistrat au parlement de Paris sur l'édit concernant les non-catholiques* (n.p., 1787).

ceived the theology student in the Molinist Sorbonne of the 1740s, while in Calonne they could not forget d'Aiguillon's hatchet man in Brittany on the wrong side of the events that had culminated in Maupeou's coup.

These continuities are even more salient in the immense pamphlet production provoked by the prerevolutionary political crisis, especially on the patriotic side. Pamphleteers sympathetic to the Parlement of Paris and its appeal to the Estates General joined battle with "ministerial despotism" under the same banner of patriotism first unfurled as a "party" standard against Maupeou and the ministry in 1771. Numbers of patriotic pamphlets that appeared in 1787–88 in fact represented reprints of pamphlets that had first appeared in 1771 or even earlier. Among them were not only Saige's *Catéchisme du citoyen* but even Le Paige's *Lettre sur les lits de justice,* which, originally published in 1756, went through several new editions, including one with an updated introduction and a new title, *A Citizen's Reflections on Lit de Justice Assemblies.*[12] A pamphlet that struck Calonne as singularly seditious, an anonymous *Dissertation on the Right to Convoke the Estates General* that argued that the Estates General might convoke themselves, was a detached appendix to the first volume of the second edition of Mey and Maultrot's *Maximes du droit public françois,* which appeared in 1775.[13] But by no means did all of this Jansenist and patriotic persistence take the form of reprints. That even Le Paige's brand of figuratist or narrowly parlementary constitutionalism was still a going concern in the prerevolution is evident, not only in the remonstrances of the Parlement of Paris themselves, but in a series of pamphlets reporting a supposed *Conference Between a Minister of State and a Councillor in the Parlement.*[14] Animated by the same outlook, these pamphlets belong in spirit to the earlier half of the parlementary phase of the political crisis, stretching from the summer of 1787 to the lit de justice assembly of May 1788, although the last in this

12. [Louis-Adrien Le Paige], *Réflexions d'un citoyen sur les lits de justice* (n.p., 1787), with a new introduction updated by means of a few references to Maupeou's constitutional revolution of 1771. For a list of such reprints, see the catalogue of the pamphlets republished in section 5 of Pergamon Press's microfiche *The French Revolution Research Collection* (Oxford, 1990), a section edited by Jeremy Popkin and Dale Van Kley.

13. [Maultrot], *Dissertation sur le droit de convoquer les Etats-généraux, tirée des capitulaires, des ordonnances du royaume, et les autres monuments de l'histoire de France* (n.p., 1787). See also Bachaumont, *Mémoires secrets,* 36:34–35; and Charles-Alexandre de Calonne, *Lettre adressée au roi, par M. de Calonne, le 9 février 1787* (London, 1789), pp. 13–14.

14. *Conférence entre un ministre d'état et un conseiller au parlement* (n.p., n.d.); *Suite de la conférence du ministre avec le conseiller* (n.p., 1787); *Deuxième suite de la conférence du ministre avec le conseiller* (n.p., 1787); and finally *La nouvelle conférence entre un ministre d'état et un conseiller au parlement* (n.p., n.d.). See also Bachaumont, *Mémoires secrets* (9 Aug. 1787), 35:385–89, and (10 Dec. 1787), 36:232–33; and Siméon-Prosper Hardy, "Mes loisirs, ou journal d'événements tels qu'ils parviennent à ma connoissance," 8 vols., in BN: Mss. Fr., Ms. 6686 (28 Nov. 1787), p. 289; and Ms. 6687 (3 Oct. 1788), p. 104. Judging from the handwritten corrections in his copy of the first two pamphlets (BPR, CLP, Ms. 915, no. 6), Le Paige himself may have had a hand in their composition.

series appeared after Brienne's May edicts and antiparlementary coup and reacted to these events.

This pamphlet laid it down in audibly Le Paigian accents that the Parlement had been "born with the monarchy," existed "essentially and necessarily with it," and formed "an integral part of the constitution." Lest it be argued that the Parlement was just an appendage to the monarchy, the pamphlet traced the Parlement's ancestry to Frankish national assemblies, maintaining on Hotman's authority that these assemblies had "disposed of the Crown, regulated the royal succession, judged the great vassals, and collaborated with the Sovereign in the formation of the Laws." And lest the implication of legislative cosovereignty go undetected, the pamphleteer spelled it out that the eighteenth-century Parlement, successor of those assemblies, acted as it did by virtue of the "constitutional principle" that the king's will alone could "not make the Law," and that the "agreement of the nation" was necessary.[15] The pamphlet's conception of the law as capitalized Truth, in defense of which the Parlement as its "repository" should be prepared to suffer "persecution"—this language places the pamphlet in figuratist constitutional discourse.

But how, it might be asked, could anyone have thought Le Paigian or figuratist constitutionalism any longer apropos after the Parlement of Paris itself had confessed its constitutional incompetence to register the ministry's fiscal expedients and had appealed to the authority of the nation assembled in the Estates General? The Estates General's authority was acknowledged in the pamphlet itself, which declared at one point that the Parlement's magistrates were not representatives of the nation and did not wish to be so regarded, and that if the Estates General of Blois in 1576 had implicitly delegated to the Parlement the nation's right to consent to taxation, the terms of that delegation restricted that right to a merely provisional consent in cases of urgent necessity. The key to this apparent inconsistency lies in the pamphlet's assumption that the taxation of private property was a unique case, requiring the express consent of the proprietors in each new instance, whereas in other legislative matters the Parlement legitimately if indirectly represented the nation because in so doing it defended constitutional laws that enshrined the nation's historically expressed intent. France, in this view, already had a constitution; the Parlement of Paris was at once a part of it and defended it in its capacity as a supreme court.

That view, as we have seen, was Le Paige's ever since he had come to believe under the pressure of the events in the 1750s that the nation alone might legitimately tax itself. What is new in 1787 is that that view had also become the Parlement's under pressure from events of that year, although it had defended the

---

15. *La nouvelle conférence*, pp. 21, 25–27, 31–32. The pamphlet's reference to Hotman "dans son ouvrage sur la Gaule Française" is on p. 5.

Estates General's authority in fiscal matters in remonstrances in 1778.[16] But that view, as we have also seen, had long existed in tension with a competitive Jansenist constitutionalism, which, on the analogy of the general council, gave considerably more leeway to the activity of the Estates General. And while Le Paige's figuratist constitutionalism remained seasonal enough so long as the controversy mainly concerned new taxes, it was no longer adequate to the broadening of the constitutional agenda after the events of early May 1788. By arresting more magistrates, sending the parlements on vacation, and trying to replace the Parlement of Paris with a Cour plénière, the royal ministry itself enlarged this constitutional agenda, bringing conciliar constitutionalism into play in the pamphlets that followed.

Perhaps the best illustration of the politically radicalizing transition from figuratist to conciliar constitutionalism in the crucible of Brienne's constitutional coup is *The National Jurisconsult,* another of the pamphlets denounced as especially seditious by Calonne as an emigré in England.[17] Published in three installments between September 1787 and October 1788, its acknowledged author was Pierre-Jean Agier, one of the Paris Bar's few young Jansenists and a future alternate deputy to the Estates General.[18] The first part of the *Jurisconsulte,* favorably noted by Hardy in 1788, predictably took its greatest pains to establish the nation's natural right to consent to taxation. Although Agier did not neglect the "testimony" of history, he clearly preferred the *Maximes du droit*'s more peremptory argument that royal violations of this right were of no legal consequence because the king could not prescribe against the rights of the nation.[19] And even in this installment Agier distanced himself a little from the parlements, for while nodding respectfully toward the Estates General of Blois's supposed commission to the Parlement of Paris in 1576 to speak on their behalf in matters of taxation, Agier thought it strange that anyone had ever thought that constitutional "bodies that depend so much on the king and not at all on the nation . . . could ever represent the Estates." His constitutionalism nonetheless remained parlementary to the extent that it would have provided a very honorable place for the parlements in that constitution; Agier's main target was also "ministerial despotism" and not "feudal aristocracy."[20]

The pamphlet's second installment, although dated 28 May 1788, devoted

---

16. Flammermont, *Remontrances,* 3:404, dated 23–26 January.

17. Pierre-Jean Agier, *Le jurisconsulte national, ou principes sur les droits les plus élémentaires de la nation,* 3 vols. (n.p., 1788). Although the various parts were published as separate installments, all three installments were published as one pamphlet in 1788; it is this edition that is cited here. See also Calonne, *Lettre adressée au roi,* pp. 13–14.

18. Gustave Fallot, "Pierre-Jean Agier," in L.-G. Michaud, ed. *Biographie universelle ancienne et moderne,* 83 vols. (Paris, 1811–55), 56:90–94.

19. Agier, *Le jurisconsulte national,* 29–30, 77–78, 80–81.

20. Ibid., pp. 60–62, 72–73.

the bulk of its theoretical energy to extending the nation's right of consent to loans as well as to taxes, suggesting that most of it was written in reaction to the loans forcibly registered in the Brienne ministry's royal session of 19 November 1787.[21] The last pages of this installment reacted to Brienne's constitutional coup of 8 May and maintained that only the whole nation assembled in Estates General might legitimately replace the parlements with the proposed Cour plénière. Or, rather, the nation assembled in the Estates General *was* this plenary court, competent to verify not only loans, the territorial subvention, and other fiscal measures, but even laws of a constitutional or "fundamental" sort. Thereby did Agier's *Jurisconsulte* make the crucial transition from a narrowly fiscal agenda to a wider constitutional one.[22]

Reacting in turn to the *Jurisconsulte*'s second installment, Le Paige scribbled crabbedly in its margin that the Estates General was "so little the true plenary court that it possessed no [judicial] jurisdiction and was so little invested with the power of registration that it had had to ask the Parlement to register the Ordinance of Orléans." Agier just did not know his history, grumbled Le Paige, which would have taught him that the Parlement of Paris alone had succeeded to the Merovingian and Carolingian estates as the true Court of Peers. So if Le Paige had been heretofore only confusedly aware of the differences between his own brand of parlementary constitutionalism and the conciliar variety espoused by his close colleagues Mey and Maultrot, he was becoming clearer about it now. It was in reaction to Agier's pamphlet that Le Paige regretted that the "same pair of eyes" could not review everything in advance as in 1771.[23]

Those eyes could no longer be his, alas, and not only because he was half blind. And so Agier and others continued undeterred. Drawing out another corollary from the conciliar constitutionalist maxim that the nation might very well prescribe against the king—in plainer words, that it might change the form of the government—the *Jurisconsulte national*'s third installment went so far as to suggest that in the best of all political worlds France would be a republic. "I certainly desire with all my heart that we could adopt that form of government because I am persuaded that it is the only one in which men living in society can realize the degree of perfection of which their present condition is susceptible."[24] Failing that—because all of French history and manners militated against it—the French nation should at least reclaim her exclusive "legislative power," which she should never have allowed kings to usurp or to have delegated to the Parlement.

---

21. The second installement's separate title is *Le jurisconsulte national, seconde partie, ou nécessité du consentement de la nation pour autoriser les emprunts.* The events of May 1788 are visibly referred to in ibid., 2:8–12.

22. Ibid., 2:32–36.

23. BPR: CLP, Ms. 928, no. 6.

24. Agier, *Le jurisconsulte national,* 3:119–20, 155–56.

As for the king, he could no longer in truth "help himself to our pockets and tax us at his pleasure, . . . make us receive and execute his laws at the point of the bayonet," or "enjoy the extreme pleasure of being able to issue lettres de cachet—which is to say that he would have to behave like a king and not a despot." And as for the Parlement, its "principal glory" was to have conserved the nation's rights during the "violent interruption of the national assemblies," but the time to step aside and return to its purely judicial functions had clearly arrived.[25]

Agier's *Jurisconsulte national* at once recapitulated the radicalization of Jansenist constitutionalism in the eighteenth century and stretched that tradition's capacity to its farthest limits, unless that honor be reserved for Maultrot's three-volume *Origins and Just Limits of the Temporal Power,* published belatedly in 1789.[26] For it was left to this blind veteran of every *Unigenitus*-related battle since midcentury to invoke divine grace against the theological pillars of divine-right monarchy itself and, like a Gallic Samson, pull them down from within. Christianity featured miracles and mysteries enough, he opined, without postulating some species of direct infusion of divine grace onto kings to account for governments that the governed had instituted themselves, God "having abandoned the earth to men." There was no "sacrament established for the creation of kings," Maultrot maintained, because sacraments affected souls alone and the royal sacre was only the solemnization of a "social contract" that made kings the mandatories of the people.[27] The classic Gallican distinctions between physical coaction and grace, between mandatory and mandator, between administration and ownership, between the immortal crown and its mortal bearer—all these Maultrot worked and reworked to produce the "maxim" that "legislation belongs to the Nation alone . . . and the king has only the executive power."[28] In support of these propositions, Maultrot finally parted political paths with such eminent Jansenist predecessors as Arnauld and Nicole in favor of such Protestant publicists in the monarchomach mode as Jacques Abbadie, George Buchannan, Lohn Locke, and Emmerich Vattel—even Jean-Jacques Rousseau—who thus joined Jean Gerson and John Major in this canonist's canon. Indeed, Maultrot here went so far as to opt for the punctutation of Romans 13:1 in the Vulgate's Latin that seemed to make the verse mean that only "well-ordered" powers enjoyed God's approval and deserved obedience, a punctuation he and other Jansenists had held against the parti

25. Ibid., pp. 121, 155–56, 159–65. See also pp. 103–4, 107–89.

26. Gabriel-Nicolas Maultrot, *Origines et justes bornes de la puissance temporelle suivant les livres saints et la tradition sainte,* 3 vols. (Paris, 1789). For a penetrating treatment of this little-studied treatise, see Yann Fauchois, "Jansénisme et politique au XVIIIe siècle: Légitimation de l'Etat et délégitimation de la monarchie chez J.-N. Maultrot," *RHMC* 34 (1987):473–91.

27. Maultrot, *Origines et justes bornes,* 1:19–20.

28. Ibid. On grace and force see 1:19–20; on ownership and exercise or administration, 1:465 and 2:153; on mandator and mandatory, 2:23–24, 166–67; on crown and mortal bearer, 2:180–81; on coronation, 2:113–14, 141–42; and for quoted maxim, 2:84.

dévot until then.[29] And so did Maultrot end by appropriating the whole monarchomach tradition, along with some subversion from the dévot one.

Although the examples of Agier, Maultrot, and the anonymous author of the *Conférence* show that Jansenists were still antagonists in the political confrontation of the prerevolution, they should not convey the impression that Jansenist political discourse was limited to Jansenists. On the contrary, it was pervasive on the patriotic or proparlementary side—as diffuse, indeed, as "patriotism" itself had become in the wake of Maupeou's constitutional coup. Eloquently exemplifying that diffusion is the most popular patriotic pamphlet of the entire parlementary phase of the prerevolutionary crisis, the comte Emmanuel d'Antraigues's *Memoir on the Estates General,* which appeared in late 1788 and went through fourteen editions.[30]

Written by no Jansenist, d'Antraigues's *Mémoire* nonetheless espoused a radically conciliar view of Catholic Church governance and incidentally professed a view of divine grace as restrictive as any condemned by the bull *Unigenitus.* Hardly Protestant either, despite a distant Protestant ancestry, d'Antraigues nonetheless cited Hotman's *Francogallia* on the subject of France's original "constitution," and allowed that the religious wars of the sixteenth century and the "Protestant religion" in particular had "conserved liberty and energy in France during the reign of princes most minded to destroy them."[31] Neither a philosophic nor an antiphilosophic utterance, the *Mémoire* nonetheless echoed Rousseau's appeal to the "general will" and the right-headed "heart of a free man," maintaining that "man is born free," although obviously now in chains.[32] What held all of this together was precisely patriotic discourse itself, which, however indebted to Jansenist and Protestant sources, had by this time acquired a life of its own. Whence the *Mémoire*'s reverence for French history as a mute witness to antique constitutional truth, its assignment of legislative sovereignty to the Estates General and the role of persecuted defender of the constitution to the parlements, and its denunciation of "absolute power" and "ministerial despotism," as well as of "blind obedience" and the "desire to dominate."[33]

29. Ibid. On Jansenist predecessors see 1:91–92, 2:78–79, 83, 481–82. On Abbadie see 3:263–64, on Gordon, 3:317, on Locke, 2:172–73, on Rousseau, 3:64–65, on Vattel, 3:305–6, and on Almain and Gerson see 1:10–13, 305–17. On punctuation of Romans 13:1, see 1:183–84.

30. Emmanuel-Louis-Henri de Launay, comte d'Antraigues, *Mémoire sur les Etats-généraux, leurs droits et la manière de les convoquer* (n.p., 1788). On its author and the number of editions, see Guy-Chaussinand Nogaret, *La noblesse au XVIIIe siècle: De la féodalité aux lumières* (Paris, 1976), 34–36.

31. D'Antraigues, *Mémoire sur les Etats-généraux:* on Catholic Church governance see pp. 79, 143–44; on Jansenist-like view of grace, p. 106; on Hotman, pp. 10–11; on the formula "car tel est notre bon plaisir," pp. 161–62; on Protestants and wars of religion, p. 171.

32. Ibid.: for Rousseuian lines see pp. 7–8, 17–18; for some examples of his use of the expression "volonté générale" see pp. 25–29, 127, 234.

33. Ibid.: on value of history see pp. 7, 43–46, and on history as witness, pp. 167–69; on Estates

Whence, too, its espousal of such specific theses as that kings neither were divine nor reigned by virtue of special divine grace, that coronation oaths proved that the French kingship had once been elective, that the Estates General might convene themselves without royal authority, that the absolutist lit de justice ceremony had once been a national deliberative assembly, and so forth.[34]

Very much alive, then, on the eve of the Revolution, patriotic discourse was to contribute much to revolutionary ideology, most notably its rhetoric of antiabsolutism and antidespotism and its thesis of national legislative sovereignty. By the same token these and other patriotic pamphlets reveal the limitations of that discourse, limitations that stood in the way of its becoming revolutionary ideology as such. Chief among these were its reverence for history and for French history in particular—"that faithful witness to truth," as Maultrot called it—and its clear commitment to a corporate conception of the nation.[35] Implicit in the concept of the nation as corps was the notion that it consisted in corporate parts and parcels. More ambiguous from the point of view of emerging revolutionary ideology is the closely related notion of unanimity as a necessary precondition for constitutional law. Originating in part in Jansenist ecclesiology, that insistence on unanimity as applied to a corporate conception of the nation was to lead the Parlement of Paris to its fateful ruling of 25 September 1788 in favor of the "forms of 1614" for the Estates General, which were immediately construed to mean what Louis XVI later said they meant on 23 June 1789: that is, that any fundamental law required the unanimous consent of the clergy, nobility, and the Third Estate as separate and constitutional corps. In corporate form, then, that insistence was to lead not toward revolution but to counterrevolution. Yet the same hankering after unanimity was to survive the debacle of 25 September 1788 and, as applied to the individualized nation and to legislative assemblies, was to nag at revolutionary legitimacy not only from the right but also from the left. As such it is part of the French Revolution's conceptual inability to deal with division and disagreement.

The Ministerial Rejoinder

No more than in 1771 did patriotic pamphleteering go unanswered. Indeed, so continuous was the debate beginning in 1787 with the one that left off in 1774 that some of these answers took the form of reprints of pamphlets originally published

---

General, pp. 20–21, 47–56; on parlements and persecution, pp. 14–15, 117–18, 222–23; on absolute power, pp. 26–27, 35–36, 74; on ministerial despotism, pp. 40, 210–12; on desire to dominate, pp. 34–35; on passive obedience, pp. 62–63, 171.

34. Ibid.: on grace and divine right see pp. 61, 106, 160–61; on right to convoke Estates General, pp. 189–90; on lit de justice assembly, pp. 120–21. The *Mémoire* cites the *Maximes du droit public françois* on two occasions, pp. 163, 200.

35. Maultrot, *Origine et justes bornes,* 3:28.

in defense of Maupeou's reforms. This holds for an anonymous *Le songe d'un jeune Parisien*, republished as *Le songe d'un bon citoyen français (A Good French Citizen's Dream)* in 1788, and numbers of pamphlets by Linguet: his *Remontrances d'un citoyen aux parlemens de France*, republished as *Avis aux bons Français (Advice to Good Frenchmen)* in 1788, and his *Recherches sur les Etats-généraux*, which reappeared as *Quelle est l'origine des Etats-généraux? (What is the Origin of the Estates General?)* in the same year. Most probably written by Linguet, *La tête leur tourne* also reappeared in 1788 under the same title, minus its introductory references to Jansenists, which too obviously dated it a decade or two earlier.

Not that the monarchy or the ministry lacked for live defenders in 1787–88. Conspicuous by their absence, however, were bishops and ex-Jesuits, the monarchy's mainstays until the mid-1770s. One of the few clerical defenses of the monarchy to appear in the intervening years was Jean Pey's *On the Authority of the Two Powers* in 1781, which, like the writings of Languet de Gergy, defended both the absolute authority of the king and the sovereign power of the episcopacy against both Rousseau's conception of the social contract and Mey and Maultrot's radically Gallican ecclesiology.[36] During the prerevolutionary crisis itself the still loyal Lefranc de Pompignan was the only bishop to preach submission to the monarchy in a pastoral instruction, which provoked the predictable Jansenist rejoinders to his counsels of blind obedience.[37] Although not exactly enjoining disobedience, the General Assembly of the Gallican Clergy, meeting in 1788, actually remonstrated against the Brienne ministry's edicts of May 1788, even though Brienne himself was an archbishop.[38] The Gallican divines' curious inactivity on behalf of divine-right monarchy, which had its origin in their temporary alienation from the monarchy and rapprochement with the parlements during the ministry of Turgot, was now reinforced by Calonne's attempt to impose the territorial subvention on the church's landed property in 1787 and Brienne's and Lamoignon's sponsorship of an edict in favor of toleration of Protestants in 1787.

In the absence of bishops, the defense of the monarchy and ministry thus fell to barristers at odds with their order, like Gerbier, or to former Maupeou ministry commis, like Charles Le Brun. One remaining connection between the parti dévot and the ministerial barristers was the conspicuous presence in their ranks of such

36. Jean Pey, *De l'autorité des deux puissances*, 3 vols. (Strasbourg, 1781), 1:xlix, 30–31. On Rousseau, 1:204–12; 3:246–49; and on Mey and Maultrot, 1:234–39; 2:65, 71–86, 385; and 3:82–136.

37. Jean-Georges Lefranc de Pompignan, *Lettre pastorale de Monseigneur l'archévêque de Vienne, aux curés de son diocèse* (Vienne, 1788), esp. pp. 6–8. Two visibly Jansenist ripostes are Michel Blanchard, *Lettre de Michel Blanchard, magistrat du village de Morvieux en Dauphiné, à Monseigneur Georges Le Franc de Pompignan, en réponse à une instruction pastorale sur l'obéissance due aux puissances* (Paris, 1788), pp. 3–4, 6–7; and *Lettre à Monseigneur l'archévêque de Vienne, par un curé de son diocèse* (n.p., n.d.), pp. 12, 17.

38. Jean Egret, "La dernière assemblée du clergé de France (5 mai–5 août 1788)," *Revue historique* 219 (1958):1–15.

rebellious sons of Jansenist fathers as Linguet and Moreau, who picked up the gauntlet in 1788 where it had been left in 1772. Just as obviously on the monarchy's side as in 1771 were such Voltairians as the former barrister Jean Blondel, joined in 1788 by such philosophic former members of Turgot's physiocratic équipe as André Morellet and the marquis de Condorcet.[39] As in 1771 as well, the royal cause found itself in the dubious hands of anonymous hacks in the hire of royal ministers, particularly Brienne and Lamoignon but also Calonne and Necker, who imitated Maupeou in seeing to their own pamphlet defense. The smoke of complaints like Hardy's about the "multitude of miserable brochures which the ministers . . . are spreading around profusely" so filled the air by 1788 that there is bound to have been some real fire somewhere.[40]

Until the appearance of counterrevolutionary ideology, the parti dévot's political legacy perpetuated itself mainly in the form of a brittle, almost desiccated defense of the monarchy's indivisible Bodinian unity and sovereign will, combined with a dangerously demagogic attack on the privileges of the aristocracy. And with the bishops temporarily on the patriot side, the charge of aristocracy now embraced the upper clergy as well as the magistracy and nobility. To the extent that the ministerial pamphlet was historical, that history, as in the pro-Maupeou pamphlet, was a royal history that celebrated the rise of the monarchy's power along with the social liberation of the Third Estate at the expense of the twin hydras of "aristocratic domination" and "feudal anarchy." And far from attesting to any fixed constitution limiting the exercise of royal power, French history in the ministerial version of events showed the empirical necessity of absolute royal power, celebrating the prowess of the same Louis XI's and Richelieus denounced as despots in patriotic pamphlets and sometimes demonstrating, as had Abbé Marie in 1771, that "we do not have, strictly speaking, a constitution," nor even any "constitutional laws," but only a "paternal government" resulting from ancient conquest.[41]

No sooner had the parlementary phase of the conflict begun and the Parlement of Paris appealed to the Estates General than Jean Blondel's anonymously published *Barrister's Observations* set the ministerial tone. The pamphlet combined an assertion of the monarchy's sovereign will that would have shocked Bossuet (the king could "alienate whole provinces without accounting to anyone") with a demagogic appeal to the Third Estate and a precocious challenge to the traditional form of the Estates General ("if the Estates General were formed following the old usage, a considerable portion of the king's most enlightened subjects would be

39. For evidence of Blondel's Voltairianism, see his *Les hommes tels qu'ils sont et doivent être, ouvrage de sentiment* (Hamburg, 1758). Celebrating civilization and professing a belief in human perfectibility, this philosophical essay tried to construct a case for virtue on the basis of "amour propre alone."

40. Hardy, "Mes loisirs," BN: Ms. Fr. 6687 (18 July 1788), p. 21.

41. *Lettre d'un conseiller au parlement de Normandie* (London, [ce 26 août 1787]), pp. 16–17, 48–49.

excluded").[42] The pamphlet was "an impudent writing, a veritable libel," according to Hardy, "which could only have come from a mercenary pen."[43] As if to confirm Hardy's suspicions, the Brienne-Lamoignon ministry forced the *Gazette de Leyde* to print the entire pamphlet on pain of having its postal privileges revoked.[44]

But the prerevolutionary ministerial pamphlet's greatest season in the sun was in the summer and early fall of 1788. And although no one ministerial pamphlet enjoyed quite the same success as did d'Antraigues's *Mémoire sur les Etats-généraux*, Linguet dominated ministerial discourse by virtue of the sheer volume of his production: at least thirteen or fourteen pamphlets, not to mention his periodical *Annales politiques*, which continued to appear during the entire period.[45] Lest anyone think he had nothing to say after Maupeou's coup, he offered a comparison between that episode and Brienne's and Lamoignon's judicial reforms.[46] He was also the author of *France More English Than England*, *Ointment for the Burn*, and the incendiary *Advice to Parisians*.

No ex-Jesuit, to be sure, Linguet still thought it apropos in 1788 to refute the *Judicium Francorum*, as well as to ridicule the notion of unanimity "à la janséniste," holding it responsible for informing part of the patriot opposition.[47] Hardly a dévot adherent to the episcopal cause, Linguet was nonetheless readier than most bishops in 1788 to regard royal power as sacred—indeed, as "an emanation and image of divine power"—to enjoin obedience to absolute authority, and even to quote at that late date the "celebrated" Languet de Gergy against the Parlement of Paris.[48] Although not really a latter-day Leaguer, either, Linguet

42. [Jean Blondel?], *Observations d'un avocat sur l'arrêté du parlement de Paris, 13 août 1787* (n.p., 1787), pp. 12–13.

43. Hardy, "Mes loisirs," BN: Ms. Fr. 6686 (17 Aug. 1787), p. 180. Although Hardy here named Jacob-Nicolas Moreau, Linguet, Morellet, and Blondel as possible authors, the barrister Lefebvre de Beauvray was more probably right in attributing it to Blondel. See his "Mémoires pour servir à l'histoire de la fin du dix-huitième siècle," BN: Ms. Fr. 10364, 2:304, 325–26.

44. Jeremy Popkin, "The *Gazette de Leyde* and French Politics Under Louis XVI," in *Press and Politics in Pre-Revolutionary France*, ed. Jack Censer and Jeremy Popkin (Berkeley, Calif., 1987), p. 109.

45. Simon-Henri Linguet, *Annales politiques, civiles et littéraires du dix-huitième siècle*. On Linguet see Darlene Gay Levy, *The Ideas and Careers of Simon-Henri Linguet* (Urbana, Ill., 1980).

46. [Simon-Henri Linguet], *Réflexions sur la résistance opposée à l'exécution des ordonnances promulgués le 8 mai; suivies de la différence entre la révolution passagère de 1771, et la réforme de 1788, dans l'ordre judiciaire en France* (Brussels, 1788).

47. [Linguet], on *Judicium Francorum* see *Onguent pour la brûlure, ou observations sur un réquisitoire imprimé en tête de l'arrêt du parlement de Paris, du 27 septembre 1788, rendu contre les Annales de M. Linguet* (London, 1788), p. 28; on unanimity "à la janséniste," *La France plus qu'angloise, ou comparaison entre la procédure entamée à Paris le 25 septembre 1788 contre les ministres du roi de France, et le procès intenté à Londres en 1640, au comte de Stafford, principale ministre de Charles premier, roi d'Angleterre.* (Brussels, 1788), pp. 124–25.

48. On "sacred" authority, see [Linguet], *La France plus qu'angloise*, p. 16; on monarchy as "emanation and image of divine power," *Quelle est l'origine des Etats-généraux* (n.p., 1788), p. 4; on Languet de Gergy, *Onguent pour la brûlure*, p. 28.

conveyed a sense of impending apocalypse reminiscent of the literature of the League, calling on Parisians in 1788 to form a kind of sacred union, or at least a "wall" around their king against an "egotistical" if not heretical "aristocracy of magistrates."[49] And although vociferously opposed to philosophes and to physiocrats, Linguet had frequent and strategic recourse to the language of "utility" and "happiness" *(bonheur)* in defense of monarchy, and to the language of social equality against the aristocracy.

In Linguet's language, these devout echoes were part of a ministerial or monarchical discourse that also recalled d'Argenson's defense of untrammeled royal power in alliance with social democracy in the 1730s. It harked back as well to royalist historians' polemics against aristocracy and feudalism in the seventeenth century, Bodin's definition of monarchy as indivisible in the sixteenth century—perhaps even appeals to "reasons of necessity" and "reasons of public utility" by apologists of monarchical high-handedness in the late Middle Ages.[50] "As to the ministers," he avowed, "it is true—very true—that it is their cause I defend; yet it is also my own principles I maintain, having never varied from . . . my debut in literature to the . . . [latest] issue of my *Annales*."[51] And as applied to the monarchy, those same principles, he explained, consisted in dedication to *"true public welfare"* and the "true *advantages* of the *people*," and an "involuntary aversion for the *aristocracy*," including the English constitution; "not knowing," he added, "a more reasonable and even just government *in speculation* than *democracy*," but "seeing no solid, tranquil, or happy government *in practice* except for *monarchy*."[52]

More than any other ministerial pamphleteer, Linguet stretched this language to the revolutionary breaking point. He was among the first to denounce the "despotism of these supposed [parlementaire] enemies of ministerial despotism," thereby preparing the revolutionary conflation of despotism with aristocracy. He was also among the first to lump the "clergy, the nobility, and the magistracy" together as a single, self-interested aristocracy, making him one of the inventors of the thesis of a prerevolutionary aristocratic reaction.[53] "Well then,"

49. [Linguet], *Avis aux Parisiens. Appel de toutes conventions d'Etats-généraux où les députés du troisième ordre ne seroient pas supérieurs aux deux autres* (n.p., n.d.), pp. 2, 5. On Linguet's apocalyptic language and sense of time, see Jeremy Popkin, "The Prerevolutionary Origins of Political Journalism," in *The Political Culture of the Old Regime*, ed. Keith M. Baker, vol. 1 of *The French Revolution and the Creation of Modern Political Culture* (Oxford, 1988), pp. 218–19.

50. On these medieval justifications see Gaines Post, *"Ratio Publicae Utilitatis, Ratio Statis*, and 'Reason of State,'"* in *Studies in Medieval Legal Thought: Public Law and the State, 1100–1302* (Princeton, N.J., 1964), pp. 241–309.

51. [Linguet], *Réflexions sur la résistance opposée à l'exécution des ordonnances promulgués le 8 mai*, pp. 90–91.

52. [Linguet], *La France plus qu'anglaise*, p. 111.

53. Ibid., p. 8; [Linguet], *Avis aux provinces*, p. 2.

he also prophetically advised Frenchmen, "if you are determined at all costs to topple the throne, at least raise the entire nation on its debris."[54] That advice was proffered not in 1789 or 1790 but originally in 1771, reprinted in 1788. Yet not even these incendiary utterances entirely obscure an integral absolutism that Linguet was later to pay for with his head, and one that prevented ministerial language from becoming revolutionary discourse tout court. In order for anything like that to happen—in order, in other words, for it to contribute its antiaristocratic bias to revolutionary ideology—ministerial discourse would eventually have to shed that absolutism, together with the royalist version of French history that encrusted it, just as patriotic antidespotism would have to shed its commitment in a corporate nation along with its accompanying patriotic version of French history.

Or rather, to be more precise, ministerial discourse would have to shed its royal absolutism. As for absolutism as such, its legacy was to be just as ambiguous as the notion of unanimity was to be on the patriotic side. For if on the one hand counterrevolutionary ideology was to continue to associate absolutism with both royal and papal power, nothing would prevent some revolutionaries, on the other hand, from transferring the attributes of absoluteness and unity from the monarchy to the nation—or an assembly claiming to represent the nation.

The Sieyèsian Synthesis

Until late in 1788 this patriotic-ministerial standoff continued to dominate discourse, much as it had in 1771. That it had been the Parlement of Paris that had called for the Estates General, that there was a real prospect that the old assembly might meet after a hiatus of 175 years—these facts were of course new or relatively new. Yet the pamphlet and book debate continued to ring changes on familiar themes that recalled aspects of the Jansenist-devout controversy of the earlier eighteenth century, the mazarinade-royalist debate of the Fronde, the bons français-dévot confrontation of the early seventeenth century—even the monarchomach-League clash of the sixteenth century—as Major, Hotman, Pasquier, Talon and Boulainvilliers squared off against Bodin, Loisel, Bossuet, and Du Bos, and as though history had stood still. To be sure, Mably, Montesquieu, Rousseau, and Voltaire made frequent appearances in the citations as well, but as supporting or assimilated to either the patriot or ministerial cause, pitting for example a "general will" understood as the coincidence of corporate wills against a "general will" identified with the unitary will of the king. Veteran of every parlementary-ministerial confrontation of the eighteenth century since the 1730s, Le Paige experienced no difficulty organizing his collection of prerevolutionary pamphlets until late 1788, after which his organization symptomatically broke down.

54. [Linguet], *La tête leur tourne*, p. 12.

The few surviving philosophes like Condorcet, André Morellet, and their self-conscious disciples tended toward the ministerial side of the debate.[55] Typical of the situation as late as 1788 is the contrast between the book seller Hardy and the barrister Lefebvre de Beauvray. A partisan of the philosophes, Lefebvre de Beauvray continued to defend the "purity" of the king's intentions and to deplore the Parlement of Paris's "displaced" and "indiscreet" call for the Estates General, which he thought had prompted such pamphleteers as the anonymous author of *A Supplement to the Parlement's Remonstrances* "to denature the French Government, to confound it with that of England."[56] Lefebvre also persisted in associating what he called a "parlementary and republican cabal" with "certain sectaries who go by the names of Jansenists, Quesnelists, and convulsionaries," and missed no occasion to insult individual Jansenists, in particular Robert de Saint-Vincent, whose efforts in favor of toleration for Protestants in 1787 only deepened his suspicions of Jansenist intentions toward philosophes.[57] At the same time and in the sharpest contrast, the book seller Hardy singled out that "patriotic magistrate" Robert de Saint-Vincent for special praise, even on the occasion of his efforts on behalf of Protestants, seized every occasion to extol "those who are still today called Jansenists on account of their loyalty to the morality of the pious and learned solitaries of Port-Royal," and excoriated both ex-Jesuits and philosophes, whom he called "modern unbelievers."[58] As in 1771, he fervently supported the Parlement of Paris's "patriotic" battle against "arbitrary authority" and "oriental despotism," not only in spite of but because of its call for the Estates General. And he greeted the same pamphlet that so disturbed Lefebvre de Beauvray with the estimate that it displayed "nothing but solid and consequent reasoning, as able to hold the interest of publicists as it is of riveting the attention of good citizens and true patriots."[59]

That pamphlet, a discernibly Jansenist one, was one of the very few to unite the otherwise opposed theses of national sovereignty and an antiaristocratic

55. Condorcet's "ministerial" sympathies are evident in his espousal of provincial assemblies and continuing opposition to the meeting of the Estates General as late as in his *Sentiments d'un républicain, sur les assemblées provinciales et les Etats-généraux* (Philadelphia, 1788), 18–19.

56. Lefebvre de Beauvray, "Mémoires pour servir à l'histoire de la fin du XVIIIe siècle" in BN: Ms. Fr. 10364, 1:303–4. The pamphlet referred to is *Supplément aux remontrances du parlement, en réponse à la lettre d'un ami, du 24 août 1787* (n.p, n.d.).

57. On "republican cabal" see Lefebvre de Beauvray, "Mémoires pour servir à l'histoire," 1:118; on Jansenists, 2:62; on Robert de Saint-Vincent, 2:167–68. See also his comment about the Jansenist barrister Louis-Simon Martineau and his "ardent and republican genius," 1:243.

58. Hardy, "Mes Loisirs" in BN: on Robert de Saint-Vincent, see Ms. Fr. 6686 (26 Feb. 1787), p. 3; on Jansenists (19 Jan. 1788), p. 352; on "modern unbelievers" (22 Mar. 1788), p. 394; on ex-Jesuits (16 Jan. 1788), p. 349.

59. On "arbitrary authority" see ibid., Ms. Fr. 6687 (14 July 1788), p. 18; on "oriental despotism" (18 July 1788), p. 21; on *Supplément aux remontrances du parlement de Paris*, Ms. Fr. 6686 (11 Oct. 1787), p. 260.

conception of the nation before the autumn of 1788. What made that exception into a force at that time—what more massively began to force the hitherto opposing patriotic and ministerial languages together into a "national party," as another pamphlet called it—were the unprecedented events of late August and early September 1788 that dragged the whole debate into an institutional and ideological terra incognita, where no usable French past pointed the way.[60] The events in question had to do with the monarchy's imminent bankruptcy, the fall of Brienne and Lamoignon from power, the return of the parlements, and the royal convocation of the Estates General.

By securing the convocation of the Estates General, the Parlement of Paris's offensive, together with the monarchy's fiscal impasse, challenged the premises of Bourbon absolutism since the wars of religion, exposing pamphleteers like Linguet who had been defending it in such unmeasured terms. Although the monarchy itself maintained the absolutist fiction, it became ever more difficult to suppose that the king would consult with his assembled nation only to act according to his good pleasure. Yet by registering the royal declaration of convocation on 25 September "according to the forms of 1614," the Parlement of Paris exposed itself to a highly "aristocratic" misunderstanding, embarrassing patriotic publicists who had been defending advanced parlementary constitutionalism until then. Whatever the Parlement may have meant by the "forms of 1614," it was easy for such ministerial pamphleteers as Linguet to read the ruling as meaning numerically equal delegations by the three estates voting separately, and therefore as a telltale manifestation of aristocratic self-interest.[61] That interest grew more palpable in early December in the wake of a second meeting of the Assembly of Notables. Called by the new finance minister Jacques Necker to advise him on the forms of convocation and composition of the Estates General, the majority in this assembly not only interpreted the "forms of 1614" to mean what antiparlementary pamphleteers had maliciously speculated it meant, but—going well beyond the Parlement's own defense of its ruling—also laid it down that not even the assembled nation could change these forms.[62]

It was at this stage of the debate that a segment of noble opinion renewed the Parlement of Paris's claim in its remonstrances against Turgot's edicts in 1776 that

60. That the *Supplément aux remontrances du parlement* was in part Jansenist in inspiration can be deduced from its favorable reference to Arnauld and Nicole as opposed to Luther and Calvin, combined with its excoriation of the papacy's "tyrannical domination" on pp. 6–10, 11–13, 15. For the expression "national party" see the anonymous *Le roi et ses ministres, dialogues* (n.p., n.d.), which announced the emergence such a party in the interstices of the patriotic and royal ones, pp. 3–4.

61. For an attempt to reconstruct parlementary intentions behind the arrêt of 25 Sept. 1788, see Dale Van Kley, "The Estates General as Ecumenical Council: The Constitutionalism of Corporate Consensus and the *Parlement*'s Ruling of September 25, 1788," *JMH* 62 (Mar. 1989):1–52.

62. Assemblée des notables, *Motifs des douze notables, au bureau de Monsieur; pour adopter, contre l'avis des treize, l'avis qui a prévalu dans les cinq autres bureaux* (n.p., n.d.), pp. 4, 6–7.

the distinction between the orders was part of France's historic "constitution." Reinforcing the association between historical constitutionalism and the cause of aristocracy was the intervention in the debate by the high court nobility in the form of the *Mémoire des princes (The Princes' Memoir)*, which, signed by the king's younger brother Artois and several princes of the blood, impolitically tied the throne to the defense of this aristocratic constitution. Although this alliance of the princes and peers with the Parlement had realized Le Paige's dreams and had seemed to reinforce the Court of Peers' position vis-à-vis the monarchy after 1774, it became a liability amid a rapidly shifting public opinion in 1788. Feeling that ground shift beneath them, such erstwhile defenders of parlementary constitutionalism as the celebrated—and formerly jansénisant—barrister Jean-Baptiste Target had soon to acknowledge the existence of not one but "two dangerous enemies [that] menace the happiness and the liberty of Nations: ministerial Despotism and the Aristocracy of the highest classes," and like other pamphleteers began to call for the doubling of the Third Estate's delegation and the vote by head.[63]

The condemnation of both despotism and aristocracy entailed among other things the condemnation of both patriotic and ministerial versions of French history. If French history bore witness neither to a lost constitutional freedom in need of restoration nor to the civil benefits of a strong monarchy, it was good for nothing, at best a record, in the abbé Sieyès's words, of the long "night of [aristocratic] barbarity and ferocity" pierced only by a few rays of "pure despotism."[64] And indeed, this global condemnation of all of history—or at least all of French history—runs like a red thread through many of the "national" pamphlets that, sponsored by such political clubs as the famous Committee of Thirty, began to appear in the autumn of 1788, making secular bedfellows not only of former patriotic and ministerial antagonists but even of the most unlikely confessional candidates. "It is the salvation of France and not of the archives that we must heed," advised, for example, ex-Jesuit Joseph-Antoine Cerutti, perhaps remembering the dispersal of the Society of Jesus's French archives in 1762. "History is not our code," repeated the Protestant pastor Rabaut de Saint-Etienne in yet more peremptory fashion, perhaps recalling that, for French Protestants, history had hardly been a code. Even d'Antraigues, whose *Mémoire* circulated under vaguely "national" auspices, felt obliged to warn that the study of history "would be catastrophic to him who believed that . . . we have no other titles to our national

63. Jean-Batiste Target, *Suite de l'écrit intitulé: Les Etats-généraux convoqués par Louis XVI* (n.p., n.d.), pp. 36–37. See also his *Les Etats-généraux convoqués par Louis XVI* (n.p., n.d.), pp. 48–49, 53, 63, on enlarging the delegation of the Third Estate; and his *IIe suite* (n.p., n.d.), p. 14, for his continuing defense of the purity of the Parlement's intentions on 25 Sept. 1788.

64. Abbé Emmanuel-Joseph Sieyès, *Qu'est-ce que le Tiers-état*, ed. Edme Champion (Paris, 1982), pp. 36, 54.

liberty than those that, during eight centuries, have been covered with the dust of the archives."[65]

In the wake of this condemnation of both patriotic and ministerial versions of French history came a call for something like national regeneration.[66] Designating the rebirth brought about by conversion, whereby the Pauline "old man" became a new one, this technically theological term made its prerevolutionary debut in pamphlets in a less historical and hence more ministerial mode, as in Le Tellier's call to Frenchmen to help the king "consummate the great work of the regeneration of his realm, and to bring the magistracy back to its duty."[67] But the term soon became a feature of the "national" pamphlet, where it functioned in a politicized and secularized way, as though France herself was about to slough off the old regime—a term that also made its appearance in 1788—and take on the new. That the use of the term drew on religious energy is suggested by its prominence in pamphlets that parodied or borrowed heavily from Christian liturgical and confessional forms, as in Cordier's *Third Estate's Credo*, which called for the "regeneration of the State."[68]

Proparlementary patriotism did not remain aloof from this sacralization of secular politics either, as attested to by its many political "catechisms" and "professions of faith." Its most characteristic contribution was perhaps the transfer of royal majesty in the train of sovereignty to the nation. Long implicit in judicial Jansenist constitutionalism, this transfer became explicit with the invention of the crime of lèse-nation as a replacement of lèse-majesté, as when Augéard accused the keeper of the seals Lamoignon in 1788 of apostatizing his "patriotism" of 1771 by abetting Brienne's "despotism" against the parlements. "Is the crime of lèsenation any less heinous than that of lèse-majesté?" asked Augéard.[69] A little later, Maultrot similarly maintained that majesty, like sovereignty, belonged to the entire nation, with the consequence that the king himself might commit the crime of lèse-majesté—which, Maultrot thought, might better be thought of as lèse-Etat.[70] Like the term *regeneration*, the expression *lèse-nation* soon became common

---

65. Joseph-Antoine Cérutti, *Mémoire pour le peuple français* (n.p., 1788), p. 37; Jean-Paul Rabaut de Saint-Etienne, *Considérations sur les intérêts du Tiers-état, adressées au peuple des provinces, par un propriétaire foncier* (Paris, 1788), p. 13; and d'Antraigues, *Mémoire*, pp. 17–18.

66. On the use of this term in the French Revolution see also François Furet and Mona Ozouf, eds. *A Critical Dictionary of the French Revolution*, trans. Arthur Goldhammer (Cambridge, Mass., 1989), pp. 781–91.

67. Le Tellier, *Jugement du champ de Mars, rendu le peuple assemblé, les laboureurs y séant, du 26 décembre 1788* (n.p., [1788]), p. 24.

68. [Cordier], *Crédo du Tiers-état* (n.p., 1789), p. 1, 13.

69. [Jacques-Mathieu Augéard], *Les mânes de Madame la présidente Le Mairat à M. de Lamoignon, quatrième président du parlement et garde des sceaux* (n.p., 1788), p. 16.

70. Maultrot, *Origines et justes bornes*, 2:352–53.

parlance and arguably actualized itself when, in the wake of the royal session of 23 June, Mirabeau moved that the nation's representatives invest themselves with heretofore royal inviolability.

Accompanying these developments was a synthesis of the hitherto exclusively patriotic thesis of national sovereignty with the ministerial antithesis of the nation as composed of equally entitled commoners. The casualties of this synthesis were obviously the thesis of royal sovereignty and a corporate conception of the nation. At the center of this synthesis stood the abbé Emmanuel-Joseph Sieyès—a mundane abbé, but an abbé nonetheless—and his *What is the Third Estate?* Like the membership of the "national party" as a whole, Sieyès came to this point of synthesis dialectically. The first prerevolutionary pamphlet he wrote contained a strong statement of the thesis of national sovereignty, yet envisioned a united three orders seizing sovereign power in the name of the nation from royal ministers. His second pamphlet, written under the impact of the Parlement of Paris's ruling of 25 September 1788, excoriated the principle of privilege, even honorific privilege, and all but excommunicated the nobility from the nation, yet breathed nary a word about national sovereignty. *What is the Third Estate?* finally put these two theses together with a combination of Cartesian clarity and Rousseauian passion, vesting the nation with almost limitless power vis-à-vis all positive law, defining the nation in opposition to all privileged groups, and prophetically urging the Third Estate to seize the occasion of the meeting of the Estates General to declare itself the nation at the expense of both royal ministers and the privileged orders.[71]

What seems clear enough at the center of this national synthesis, however, was much more ragged around the edges. Recruiting from formerly patriotic and ministerial constituencies alike, it was bound to contain the tendencies of both, more or less pronounced in individual cases. Nothing in ex-Jesuit Cérutti's prerevolutionary pamphlets, for example, makes much sense except on the assumption that the upcoming Estates General was to lay down the law, to legislate with the king if not against him. Yet Cérutti was not very explicit about national sovereignty, while the rhetorical weight of his *Memoir for the French People* fell on the parlementary "conspirators" posing as the nation's legislators but secretly working to restore a feudal aristocracy.[72] Calling the king the "perpetual and hereditary dictator of the republic," Cérutti, like Linguet, advised the Third Estate to "huddle around the Throne," reminding them that they were "tied to the Throne by all their interests, as they were united to the Altars by all their dearest

71. Sieyès's first two pamphlets are *Vues sur les moyens d'exécution dont les représentants de la France pourront disposer en 1789* (n.p., 1789); and *Essai sur les privilèges* (Paris, 1788). My account of the progression of these pamphlets is dependent on Murray Forsyth, *Reason and Revolution: The Political Thought of the Abbé Sieyès* (New York, 1987), pp. 16–17.

72. [Cérutti], *Mémoire pour le peuple françois*, pp. 1–2, 15–16, 62.

convictions."[73] Radicalized by the noble-commoner set-to in his province, the Breton Jansenist barrister Jean-Denis Lanjuinais also denounced nobles as "living parasites" and inveighed against their appeal to oppressive precedents like the forms of 1614.[74] Yet none of this antinoble rhetoric entirely obscured his starting point in an antidespotic or patriotic constitutionalism that took its cues from Saige's *Catéchisme du citoyen*. Calling for the "reestablishment of our ancient constitution," Lanjuinais thought that it consisted in the "concourse of king, *grands*, and the people acting through their representatives, from which there would emerge a general and constant will that subjected all in the Empire to the Law alone."[75]

Not only, then, did the national synthesis contain both patriotic and ministerial tendencies, but patriotic and ministerial pamphlets more than held their own against their national rivals well into 1789—indeed, until the meeting of the Estates General itself. Whether because it was subsidized by ministers—in this case Necker—or by reason of residual rhetorical inertia, the ministerial pamphlet persisted in preaching a union of king and people against aristocracy. As 1788 turned into 1789 and elections to the Estates General proceeded, the ministerial reform agenda grew ever wider and more radical, as individual pamphlets called on the king and the Estates General to overhaul France's civil and criminal laws, to destroy the parlements, to abrogate feudal rights, to abolish hereditary nobility, to eliminate "useless" ecclesiastical benefices, to confiscate or at least to tax the church's property—even "to reform everything on land and on sea," in the words of the prayer with which a royalist pamphlet proposed that the Third Estate begin the meeting of the Estates General.[76] All these reform programs tended to assume the good pleasure of a strong king seconded by the Third Estate and directed against the "privileged" orders. The persistence of antiaristocratic ministerial discourse ensured in turn the continuation of a modified antidespotic patriotic discourse, which, whether articulated by magistrates or barristers or not, now tended to concede a doubled delegation and sometimes even the vote by head to the Third Estate, the better to call its distracted attention to the ministry's tactic of dividing and conquering. "Frenchmen, watch out for yourselves!" was the warn-

73. Ibid., pp. 61–62, 52–53.

74. On precedents see [Jean-Denis Lanjuinais], *Réflexions patriotiques sur l'arrêté de quelques nobles de Bretagne, daté du 25 octobre 1788* (n.p., 1788), pp. 16–17; on nobles and strategy for Third-Estate deputies, see his *Le préservatif contre l'avis à mes compatriotes, avec des observations sur l'affaire présente* (n.p., n.d.), pp. 15–16, 25.

75. [Lanjuinas], *Le préservatif*, pp. 18–19.

76. *Grand' messe votive, qui doit être célébré par l'aumônier du Tiers, à l'ouverture des Etats-généraux* (n.p., 1789), p. 5. For other examples, see Jeremy Popkin and Dale Van Kley, "The Pre-Revolutionary Debate," in catalogue for section 5 of Pergamon Press's *The French Revolution Research Collection* (Oxford, 1990), p. 12 and n. 79.

ing of a pamphlet by that title, "lest [the ministry] make a fulcrum of the Third Estate and use the nation to subjugate the nation."[77]

What is perhaps surprising so late in the Old Regime's day is the continuation of integral restatements of the constitutional program of the *Maximes du droit public françois*, sometimes to the point of plagiarism, until and even beyond the meeting of the Estates General. To be sure, late events left their mark on these pamphlets, taking such forms as the recognition of the principle of social equality in taxation, the need to eliminate all but honorific privileges, the necessity of reforming judicial procedure, and the desirability of the vote by head in the Estates General or whatever national assembly eventually took its place. This much granted, these pamphlets excluded any social agenda by focusing on a tried and true antidespotic patriotic political agenda that included the redefinition of the king as a paternal but desacralized "chief," the right of the Estates General to convoke itself without his consent, the nation's right to consent to all laws, including the imposition of taxes, the abolition of such strictures on personal freedom as lettres de cachet, governmental tampering with mail, and royal censorship, except perhaps of writings harmful to religion and morals, and a continued role for the parlements in the constitution. An anonymous *Observations on the Estates General* even cast the Parlement of Paris in the role of a registering body vis-à-vis the Estates General; others like the *Discourse for the Nation* featured some form of unanimity as the chief check to a national assembly's legislative whims.[78]

Writing under the Restoration, Madame de Staël remembered that the *Maximes* "agreed entirely with [the principles] proclaimed by the Constituent Assembly on the necessity of a balance of powers, on the consent of the nation to subsidies, on its participation in legislative acts, and on ministerial responsibility," posing the perennial question of why there had to be a revolution, or why it had to be as violent as it was.[79] The answer is in part that the elements of the *Maximes*'s Protestant, Jansenist, and patriot constitutionalism are far from the only ones to enter into the Revolution, or even into the Constituent Assembly's constitution. To some of those other elements we now turn.

The Constitutional Revolution

Much of the prerevolutionary propaganda written on behalf of the Third Estate suggests that if from the beginning of the meeting of the Estates General the

---

77. *Français, prenez y garde à vous!* (n.p., 1788), p. 7.

78. *Observations sur les Etats-généraux, et sur les réformes à faire dans l'administration* (n.p., n.d.); and *Discours à la nation, sur les principaux objets dont elle doit s'occuper dans sa prochaine assemblée, pour la régénération de l'état, par un Français* (n.p., 1789), pp. 25–26. For other examples of these kinds of pamphlets see Popkin and Van Kley, "The Pre-Revolutionary Debate," p. 12, n. 78.

79. Madame Germaine de Staël-Holstein, *Considérations sur la Révolution française* in *OC*, 15 vols. (Paris, 1820), 12:153.

monarchy had resolutely taken the Third Estate's side on the procedural issue of the vote by head or by order, it might have staved off this constitutional agenda as well as salvaged its fiscal situation by means of a little additional support for the Third on social issues. By doubling the Third Estate's deputies on 27 December 1788 and by its quite democratic electoral regulations of 24 January 1789, the monarchy had encouraged the Third's expectations that it would take its side on the procedural and other issues when the Estates General finally met in May. The kind of pamphlet propaganda that Jacques Necker himself had sponsored could only have heightened expectations in the same sense.

That, of course, is what the monarchy did not do. Perhaps the Third Estate's deputies might have better endured the many ceremonial insults they sustained in the meeting's inaugural events if, in the Estates' first plenary session, they had heard an encouraging word from Necker, their putative advocate. Instead they listened in astonishment to Necker's invitation to the three estates to begin their deliberations separately. At the same time his interminable speech also alienated such "patriotic" noble delegates as d'Antrigues by intimating that the king intended to relinquish no part of his prerogative, that he awaited advice but not orders from the Estates General only. Having thereby both alienated the goodwill of all three orders as well as pitting them procedurally against each other, the monarchy did nothing for the next three crucial weeks.[80]

The initial effect of this inactivity on the Third's delegation was to strengthen the hand of the rabidly antiaristocratic Breton delegates, like Isaac-René-Guy Le Chapelier, fresh from a polarizing conflict with the nobility over the composition of the estates in that province. It also strengthened the influence of delegates of an enlightened stamp, like the comte de Mirabeau, to whom it principally fell to plead the cause of the monarchy in the Third Estate. It was on his advice that the Third Estate refused to verify the credentials of its delegates separately—refused even to constitute itself in any way—until the clergy and nobility agreed to the verification of credentials in common. The Third's growing antiaristocratic sentiment found further fodder when, far from agreeing to any such demand, the nobility verified its own delegates' credentials and sent a haughty duc de Praslin at the head of its delegation to announce this noble gospel to the Third Estate on 13 May. "Are not the nobles all of France?" Mirabeau sarcastically asked.[81] In reaction to the nobility's initiative, the Third Estate only narrowly rejected Le Chapelier's peremptory motion to invite the two "privileged corps" to join it in a common verification and instead temporized by accepting Rabaut de Saint-Etienne's motion to accept the clergy's proposal to participate in

---

80. *AP* (5 May 1789), 8:16, 23–24. Although John Hardman in *Louis XVI* (New Haven, 1993) has recently attempted with some success to rehabilitate our view of Louis XVI's competence as a king, that attempt is least convincing for the crucial period from August 1788 and August 1789.

81. *AP* (13 May 1789), 8:36; and in general, pp. 36–47.

"conciliatory" conferences with commissioners of the other two orders. These conferences proved fruitless, what with Target and Rabaut invoking reason and equity while d'Antraigues appealed to history and the division of the orders as the best antidote to despotism. After the collapse of these conferences the noble delegates declared that if their "binding" mandates obliged them to give up their fiscal privileges, the same mandates as well as France's historic constitution committed them to the principle of deliberation by separate orders.[82]

Thus did the nobles "affirm themselves more and more in their system of aristocracy," intoned the journalist Le Hodey de Sault Chevreil on 28 May.[83] Like Le Hodey, most who spoke for the Third Estate outside its meeting place shared the deputies' antiaristocratic reactions and continued hope in the monarchy as their best hope. "Oh nobles, Nobles, how I hate you," cried the anonymous *Vespers' First Coup,* perhaps the nec plus ultra of all antiaristocratic rhetoric to appear in the period of May–June 1789. Holding out "no reform to wait for, no regeneration to hope for, so long as the nobility subsists," the author urged the Third Estate to have done with the conciliatory negotiations and to declare itself the nation's only mandatories—in the certainty, however, that "you will be supported in this by a Prince whose popularity seems to increase daily, and by a Minister whose signal protection will not fail you in that decisive moment." So while this author's diagnosis that France suffered from a noble "leprosy spread throughout the body politic" may have been radical, his cure was still the traditional one of an alliance of king and commoners.[84] More moderate pamphlets reached the same conclusion. The author of *The Awakening of a Great King,* for example, had a roused Louis XVI telling the nobles that "I know the origin and extent of my rights; I will defend them, and I will not let you crush my faithful commons." The constitution that this pamphleteer expected the united delegates to make was not even to be a mitigated monarchy. Rather, "the government of a single person ruling on behalf of the laws by the Law, ought to be the only one desired by the entire Nation, and most especially by the Commons."[85]

This quest for unity between king and people also entailed a hostility toward any constitutional balance of powers as a cover for particular privileged interests. One self-styled plebeian rhetorically asked the comte d'Antraigues whether he was "still so little advanced in politics as to believe in that childish plaything of intermediate counterweights," while the author of *Le premier coup de vêpres* pronounced the idea of "a balance of three powers in a Legislative Corps" to be a "monster in politics." Yet a third pamphleteer urged the Third Estate's assump-

82. Ibid. (28 May 1789), pp. 52–55.

83. Le Hodey, *Journal des Etats-généraux* (28 May 1789), 1:65.

84. *Le premier coup de vêpres: Avis à la chambre des communes, sur la retraite des privilégiés* (n.p., 1789), 7–9, 15–16.

85. *Le reveil d'un grand roi, 8 juin 1789* (n.p., 1789), pp. 3, 6.

tion of the title of National Assembly with the argument that no matter how small the number of citizens animated by the general interest, that number "would nonetheless form an absolute entity, together with all its prerogatives and power to organize its interests as a veritable sovereign." To such lengths did this pamphleteer take a possibly Rousseauian logic that he did not shrink from the conclusion that even if that number consisted of "a single just citizen . . . he would concentrate within himself the entire plenitude of sovereignty." Not surprisingly he regarded the king as the "supreme guardian of the public interest."[86]

Back in the Estates General, meanwhile, aristocracy remained the Third Estate delegates' chief concern, apparently leaving patriot constitutionalism to d'Antraigues and his noble reading of it, until the government finally intervened to break the procedural deadlock by demanding on 4 June that the conciliatory conferences be resumed in the presence of royal commissioners. It was only then that the Third Estate's own veterans of patriot constitutionalism, appropriately led by the Jansenist barrister Camus, found a chance to make themselves heard. Speaking, to believe Le Hodey, with "prodigious force and energy," Camus warned his fellow delegates that the king's request represented "a danger even greater than that of the awful privileges of the other two orders," because the monarchy was clearly trying its old tactic of dividing the orders the better to "renew its blows of authority" and "violate [our] liberty"; he moved to reject the royal request outright. It took all of Mirabeau's power to persuade his colleagues that the Third Estate was still strongest "united with the king" against the "resistances of private interest," and therefore to accept the king's invitation to resume the conciliatory conferences.[87] This new round of conferences ended in deadlock along the same lines as before, prompting the commons—as the Third now styled itself—to remind the king "of that natural alliance of throne and people against diverse aristocracies whose power can establish itself only on the ruins of royal authority and public felicity."[88]

That natural alliance failed the test of the following days, as royal policy drifted away from the "people" toward "diverse aristocracies," and "despotic" events did more than Camus himself could have done to make patriot constitutionalism the Third Estate's new order of the day. Letting the nobility bear the onus of rejecting Necker's proposed compromise, the commons let the conciliatory conferences run their course, whereupon, on 10 June, they revived Le

---

86. *Un plébian, à M. le comte d'Antraigues, sur son apostasie, sur le schisme de la noblesse, et sur son arrêté inconstitutionel, le 28 mai 1789* (n.p., 1789), pp. 7, 21, 27; *Le premier coup de vêpres*, pp. 19–20; and *Exposé des principes de droit public, qui démontrent que les députés du Tiers-état se sont légalement constitués comme représentant la nation; par l'auteur des Quatre mots, adressés au journaliste des Etats-généraux* (n.p., 1789), pp. 1–3, 12.

87. Le Hodey, *Journal des Etats-généraux* (28 May 1789), 1:73–74; and *AP* (28 May 1789), 8:52–55.

88. *AP* (5 May 1789), 8:16, 23–24.

Chapelier's proposal of 13 May and, on Sieyès's motion, voted to invite the two "privileged chambers" to join them for common verification and began the fateful roll call of all the delegates, clergy, nobility, and commoners alike. After crucial defections from the clergy by a handful of curés, the commons finally cut the Gordian knot on 17 June and, in a clear usurpation of sovereignty, abandoned the interim label of "commons" in favor of Sieyès's proposed title of National Assembly. Even at that late date, however, Camus alone made himself entirely clear about the antiroyal implications of what the Third Estate was doing, as opposed to Nicolas Bergasse's subterfuge that they were only defending the king's authority against "a religious, military, and judicial aristocracy" and against Mirabeau's insistence that the measure required the king's sanction.[89] That they had inherited the Parlement of Paris's long war of attrition against despotism became clearer still on the morning of 20 June, when, disbarred from their meeting place by royal troops, they repaired to an indoor tennis court, where they swore an oath not to disperse until they had "established and fortified" the constitutional rights of the nation.[90] And the assembly's break with royal despotism came with the force of a revelation during the infamous royal session three days later. But by this point even Mirabeau, who as recently as on 16 June still thought aristocracy the Assembly's chief enemy, joined Camus in a posture of defiance, and on 27 June he wondered aloud why Louis XVI, "who had the noble courage to convoke the National Assembly, would not listen to its members with at least as much favor as [he had] the judicial courts, which defended their own interests as often as the people's." Objecting to the peculiarities of royal discourse in the royal session, the Jansenist Lanjuinais observed the same day that the king had no more right to say "I wish" and "I order" than he previously had had to say "we wish, and we order."[91]

Outside the Assembly these events elicited a patriotic rhetoric competitive with the ministerial one. In language that recalled judicial Jansenism and the *Maximes du droit public françois public*, for example, an anonymous pamphlet addressed "to the three orders" urged the Third Estate to deliberate no longer and "to reclaim power without delay," not, in this instance, from the first two orders but from royal power that had become too "arbitrary and indefinite." The myth that the Third Estate was only *reclaiming* power obviously helped reconcile the habitual passivity of patriotic parlance to the degree of activity required to *seize* sovereign power from the king and to stretch judicial Jansenism to its breaking

89. For Bergasse's comment, see Le Hodey, *Journal des Etats-généraux* (15 June 1789), 1:95; for Rabaut de Saint-Etienne's, Mirabeau's, and Camus's opinions on the need for the king's sanction, see *AP* (15–16 June 1789), 8:113, 118, 121.

90. *AP* (20 June 1789), 8:138–39.

91. For Mirabeau's comments see ibid. (16 & 27 June 1789), pp. 124, 165–66; for Lanjuinais, ibid., p. 163.

point. If the Third Estate had always been as faithful to the monarchy as anti-aristocratic publicists had maintained, this pamphleteer continued in more familiar language, "that is only because it is fully persuaded that it is God who calls princes to the throne and by the people that they are elected . . . and that it is only at the request of the people that they become *his anointed*."[92]

Le Hodey also had recourse to judicial Jansenist language to react to the events of 20 and 23 June, contrasting the "silence of the hall" and the "consternation" and "sorrow written on all the [deputies'] faces" with the "imposing march, that magnificent pomp, that numerous cortège" that attended the royal session—language that could have come directly from Le Paige's *Lettre sur les lits de justice*.[93] But it took still other pamphleteers to call what happened on 23 June by its proper name. What Louis XVI attempted to do to the National Assembly, another pamphleteer had a former minister explain to Louis XV in a dialogue of the dead, was "what in your time was called a *Lit de Justice*, even though that Assembly witnessed neither justice nor a bed."[94]

If the events of May and June 1789 did not yet entirely conflate patriotic and ministerial ideologies and all that lay behind them, the events of 11–14 July did. The nobility's continued defense of the "constitutional" separation of orders after being commanded to join the Third Estate on 27 June, followed by the monarchy's concentration of royal troops around Paris and Versailles, the dismissal of Necker on 12 July and the consequent fear of a monarchist coup d'état against Paris and the National Assembly—these well-known events, featuring a despotic use of royal power in apparent *defense* of an embattled aristocracy, cemented the negative conflation of *despotism* and *aristocracy* once and for all. On the day of the storming of the Bastille on 14 July and in the National Assembly itself, the abbé Henri Grégoire set the tone, proclaiming that "a constitutional despotism is trying . . . to destroy the hopes of the nation," while "aristocrats hope to consummate their crimes with military force."[95] Discourse outside the Assembly followed suit. "It is all over with it, my dear fellow citizens, despotism has been destroyed forever," exulted the author of *Ministerial Despotism's Demise* in the wake of the storming of the Bastille. If successful, however, the attempted coup would have preceded a massacre of the people by "Aristocrats and their pusillanimous partisans."[96]

The events of the summer of 1789, then, vindicated both ministerial and

92. *Aux trois ordres assemblées et non réunis*, 2d ed. (n.p., 1789), pp. 9–15.

93. Le Hodey, *Journal des Etats-généraux* (23 June 1789), 1:198–99, 218–19; see also Le Paige, *Lettre sur les lits de justice*, pp. 1–3.

94. *Dialogue entre M. Paporet et Louis XV, ou réflexions sur la séance royale du 23 juin 1789* (n.p., 1789), p. 5.

95. *AP* (14 July 1789), 8:232.

96. *Le tombeau du despotisme ministériel, ou l'aurore du bonheur* (Paris, 1789), p. 3.

patriotic prophecies, bringing antiaristocratic and antidespotic agendas together, along with all the social and constitutional reforms that each had been urging against the other in the course of this last and most apocalyptic of the Old Regime's parlementary-royal confrontations. So, too, did the national pamphlet, in a minority in late 1788, come to prevail and constitute revolutionary ideology in 1789. It was this national synthesis that made possible if not inevitable the French Revolution's early legislative achievements: the abolition of "feudalism" and the "Old Regime" of 4–11 August 1789, the Declaration of the Rights of Man and the Citizen of 27 August 1789, and the main lineaments of the new constitution in the debates about the legislature and the royal veto of September 1789. For if on the one hand the legislation of 4–11 August laid low the Old Regime's whole world of corporate and provincial privilege and particularity, thereby vindicating the ministerial agenda, the Declaration of Rights and the Constitution of 1791 enshrined the principles of national legislative sovereignty, ministerial responsibility, and personal liberty, thereby vindicating much of patriotism's agenda.

Yet the synthesis that made possible these legislative achievements was itself possible only at the cost of some major ambiguities, not to say misunderstandings, which were bound to become apparent as the Revolution proceeded. For notwithstanding its denigration of French history, that synthesis brought together two long-term histories of France: religiously defined absolutism and religious resistance to absolutism. Nor could these have come together as they did without creating some major fault lines, the source of no small part of the Revolution's future instability.

At the center of this unstable synthesis stood a highly ambiguous notion of national sovereignty: on the one hand a unitary and indivisible notion inherited from the defense of the monarchy, which, transferred from king to National Assembly, tended to vest as much power in that body as the king in theory had ever enjoyed, as well as to construe resistance to it as an aristocratic conspiracy; and on the other hand a profoundly defensive if not anarchically frondish conception of sovereignty inherited from patriotic resistance to absolutism, which, in the absence of intermediate bodies, tended to vest it whole and entire in the soul of each individual, and as apt to detect despotism in a supposedly representative body as it had ever done in the monarchy. Already visible in the National Assembly's debate over the Declaration of Man and the Citizen, these fault lines widened in the debate over the constitution, especially on the questions of whether the new legislature should consist in two houses or one and whether the king should have an absolute veto, a suspensive veto, or no veto at all.[97] For although

97. For a fuller analysis of these cleavages, see Keith M. Baker's insightful analysis in "Fixing the French Constitution," in *Inventing the French Constitution: Essays on French Political Culture in the Eighteenth Century* (Cambridge, 1990), pp. 252–305; and Dale Van Kley, "From the Lessons of French History

the National Assembly voted in favor of a unitary and indivisible legislature of Sieyèsian specifications, with no Senate or upper house to moderate it or balance it, the Assembly also gave the king a suspensive veto over the legislature's acts, which, in the minds of its proponents, represented a way to appeal from the legislature back to the nation. Once the king had (provisionally) vetoed some measure of the legislature, it was supposed to be for the electoral nation to decide the issue by returning the same majority in the next several elections.

What is interesting about that debate from the point of view of religious origins is that it witnessed a parting of the paths between Jansenist and parlementary constitutionalism—components that for long years had been so close as to be virtually synonymous. For in that debate it was left to delegates more sympathetic to the nobility or to the parlements than to Jansenism—d'Antraigues, Adrien Duport, Mounier, or the marquis de Lally-Tollendal—to try to thwart the danger of representative despotism by means of such Montesquieuian institutional counterpoises as an upper house or constitutional court, usually in combination with an absolute royal veto. Identifiably Jansenist delegates who addressed themselves to the question, whether inside or outside of the Assembly—Camus, Grégoire, Lanjuinais, the abbé Jacques Jallet, and Etienne Polverel—stood with Protestants like Barnave and Rabaut and Rousseauians like Jean-Baptiste Crénière and Jérôme Pétion in adamantly opposing both a two-chamber legislature and an absolute veto, seeing in the suspensive royal veto an indirect "appeal to the people" and the only antidote to the danger of representative absolutism that did not court the even greater danger of royal or ministerial despotism.[98] In unmistakably Jansenist accents, Grégoire warned his fellow delegates on 4 September against both forms of this human tendency "to dominate," while Camus for his part was both the first to oppose the absolute royal veto when defended by Mirabeau on 16 June and the last to do so, again against Mirabeau, just before the vote on 9 September.[99]

That is not to say that all Jansenists were happy with all that the National Assembly had done or was soon to do. On the contrary, such embattled veterans as the abbés Mey, Maultrot, and Jabineau denounced the "despotism" of the National Assembly for what it did to the Gallican Clergy, first by divesting it of its property and then "reforming" it in the Civil Constitution of the Clergy. Yet they,

---

to Truths for All Times and All People: The Historical Origins of an Anti-Historical Declaration" in *The French Idea of Freedom: The Old Regime and the Declaration of Rights of 1789*, ed. Van Kley (Stanford, Calif., 1994), pp. 72–113.

　　98. Etienne Polverel, *Observations sur la sanction royale et sur le droit de veto* (n.p., 1790); Barère, *Le Point du jour* (8 Sept. 1789), 2:321–22; and Jacques Jallet, *Idées élémentaires sur la constitution* (Versailles, n.d.), pp. 4–5, 10.

　　99. Henri Grégoire, *Opinion de M. Grégoire, curé d'Emberville, député de Nanci, sur la sanction royale. A la séance du 4 septembre [1789]* (Versailles, 1789), pp. 5, 10; and Barère, *Le point du jour* (16 June 1789), 1A:392; and Le Hodey, *Journal des Etats-généraux* (9 Sept. 1789), 3:361–62.

too, denounced these measures in the name of the nation as mandator against the Assembly as an unfaithful mandatory, sure that the nation had given the Assembly no such mandate and that it would disavow the Civil Constitution if given a chance.[100]

Nor is this to say that, simply because and for no other reason than that this national ideological synthesis was inherently unstable, the Revolution as a whole was doomed to fail in its attempt to erect a stable constitutional monarchy or representative democracy—was doomed, in other words, to end in the Terror.[101] In order for any such result to have been virtually unavoidable the Revolution needed, among other things, a real enemy or counterrevolution armed with an ideology composed of more than the same raw materials of revolutionary ideology differently arranged. In order to take shape, in turn, that counterrevolutionary ideology would have had to invent something like the Civil Constitution of the Clergy if the Revolution had not done so in its stead. And some if not all of the content of that Civil Constitution was the culmination of a century of Jansenist efforts at ecclesiastical reform.

Clerical Jansenism at the End of the Old Regime

That effort survived both Maupeou's constitutional coup and the restored Parlement of Paris's reconciliation with the episcopacy in 1774. Indeed, the last decade or so of the Old Regime witnessed the culmination of canonistic activity on behalf of the second order of the clergy against the episcopacy by aging Jansenists like Piales, Mey, and Maultrot, joined by some younger recruits like Agier and Camus. Entirely blind after the age of fifty, Maultrot dictated a veritable summa on the subject in more than ten works in many more volumes, beginning with the *Institution divine des curés (The Divine Origin of Curés)* in 1778 and ending with *La défense des droits du second ordre (The Defense of the Rights of the Second Order)* in 1789.

If, as Préclin maintains, Maultrot began to regard priests as successors to the apostles in lesser measure than bishops, this claim represents an advance and not a strategic retreat on Maultrot's part, for he continued to hold as before that "if the Bishops have succeeded the apostles, the pastors of the second order have succeeded the seventy-two disciples." By adding the one claim to the other Maultrot fortified the position of the priest, regarding him as the bishop's equal so far as the

---

100. Henri Jabineau, *La légitimité du serment civique . . . convaincu d'erreur* (n.p., 1791), pp. 4–5; Gabriel-Nicolas Maultrot, *Vains efforts des défenseurs du serment, ou réplique à M. l'abbé B[aillet]* (Paris, 1791), pp. 24–25, 39. See also the anonymous but clearly Jansenist *Peuple françois, vous êtes trompés* (n.p., 1790), pp. 32–33.

101. I part paths here with Keith M. Baker's otherwise very compelling analysis of the debate over the veto in "Fixing the French Constitution," in *Inventing the French Revolution*, p. 305.

powers to preach, say Mass, and administer five of the seven sacraments were concerned.[102] Nor did Maultrot hesitate to give the curé the title of "judge of the faith" in all God's councils high and low, beginning with the diocesan synod; he also steadily enlarged the number of rights that the priest might exercise without episcopal interference and by virtue of his ordination alone, even holding that an interdicted priest might validly absolve penitents.[103] Without denying the superiority of the bishop in extent of jurisdiction, Maultrot above all pleaded for a radically different conception of the ecclesiastical hierarchy: one where the quality of bishop added to but did not "absorb" the quality of priest, where vertical as well as horizontal "common deliberation" and "unanimous consent" obtained, and where the example of the first and most "beautiful days of the church" still inspired respect and emulation.

In stark contrast to this governance of "humility, charity, and reason" was episcopal comportment as Maultrot perceived it in the last decade before the Revolution.[104] Far from convening the all too rare diocesan synods—ecumenical councils in miniature, in Maultrot's opinion—with the intention of profiting from the "lights" of their diocesan clergy, bishops came as "absolute monarchs" to hold their "lits de justice" assemblies, there to require "blind obedience" to their "absolute orders" by their humble and obedient "subjects." And far from respecting the dictates of natural law, to say nothing of the sacred canons, bishops treated their clerical cooperators as "absolute masters" might have treated their "domestic servants" or "slaves," behaving like episcopal "despots" animated by nothing but "pride and the desire to dominate."[105] It is this peremptory language that is most radical about the late Maultrot, fraught as it is with implications that went far beyond the domain of ecclesiastical polity. What was implicitly more conservative than in a younger Maultrot was the apparent exclusion of the laity from that domain. Gone, it seems, was the Maultrot of the *Apologie de tous les jugements*.

102. On Maultrot and his canonical thought during the 1780s see Edmond Préclin, *Les jansénistes du dix-huitième siècle et la Constitution civile du clergé: La développement du richérisme, sa propgation dans le bas clergé, 1713–1791* (Paris, 1929), pp. 336–62. For evidence that the one claim about the divine origin of priests did not simply replace the other in Maultrot's thought, see Gabriel-Nicolas Maultrot, *Les droits du second ordre, défendus contre les apologistes de la domination épiscopale, ou réfutation d'une consultation sur l'autorité législative des évêques dans leurs diocèses, publiée en 1775 en faveur de M. de Condorcet, évêque de Lisieux, contre les curés de son diocèse* (n.p., 1779), pp. 4–6.

103. Préclin, *Les jansénistes du dix-huitième siècle*, pp. 354–55.

104. Maultrot, *Les droits du second ordre, défendus contre les apologistes de la domination épiscopale*, p. 59.

105. For the reference to the lit de justice see Maultrot, *Le droit des prêtres dans le synode ou concile diocésain*, 2 vols. (n.p., 1779), 1:128. For examples of Maultrot's comparison of bishops to monarchs or absolute masters and of priests to subjects and slaves, see ibid., 1:225–26, 2:116–18, 257, 282–83. The appeal to natural law is to be found in ibid., pp. 8–9; while denunciations of episcopal despotism, domination, and "absolute wishes," as well as of the "desire to dominate" and blind obedience, are to be found on virtually every page of Maultrot's late treatises.

Maultrot's silence on the subject of the laity in the late 1770s and 1780s reflects in part the Parlement of Paris's retreat from ecclesiastical contestation at that time. No longer able to count on the support of the lay magistracy in the cause of ecclesiastical reform, Maultrot was too much the old patriot to look to a lay monarchy, either. But Maultrot's reluctance on this score was not shared by Jansenists younger than he or by clerics who had not borne the brunt of the patriotic front's battles against despotism. Although some Jansenists who shared his patriotism but not his concern for ecclesial reform could rejoice at the end of the long conflict between the magistracy and the episcopacy because patriotism would benefit, others more interested in ecclesiastical reform, like the anonymous author of *The Ecclesiastical Citizen*, clearly regretted the Parlement's new valuation of ecclesiastical property over reform and looked accordingly to the monarchy. "So the Parlement wishes that all properties be respected?" queried the author, apropos of the tithe. His answer was that the possession of the tithe by anyone other than real curés was no kind of property at all; his solution to the problem was to have the king "evoke everything having to so with the church's temporalia to his tribunal where a couple of councillors of state would suffice to regulate it." A good model for Louis XVI, he thought, was Joseph II of Austria, who had done that much and much more without sacrilegiously "touching the censer."[106]

Published in 1787, *L'ecclésiastique citoyen* presents a panoply of Jansenist ideas on ecclesiastical reform on the eve of the Revolution. What identifies *L'ecclésiastique citoyen* as a Jansenist utterance is its stated preference for Joachim Colbert's Montpellier catechism, its citation of the consultations of Camus and Maultrot, and its call for the reading of the Scriptures by the laity and women. The book's organization as a series of conversions between a parlementary president and an unsuspecting prior also recalled the model of the provincial layman's interrogations of an unwitting Jesuit in Pascal's *Provincial Letters*.[107] That Jansenist identity only underscores the radicalism of some of its proposals, even in comparison with such war horses as Maultrot.

To Maultrot's exaltation of the parish curé by virtue of his divine origin this book added a considered denigration of the regular clergy as of purely human origin and parasitic on the parish. "If monks and canons regular had ever been necessary to [the church], she would have done without them during her comeliest

106. *Lettre d'un ecclésiastique de province à M. l'évêque de Blois, au sujet des représentations adressées au roi par le clergé assemblé en 1788* (n.p., 1788), pp. 1–2; *L'ecclésiastique citoyen, ou lettres sur les moyens de rendre les personnes, les établissemens, et les biens de l'église encore plus utiles à l'état et même à la religion* (Paris, 1787), pp. vii, 240–41, 417–18.

107. *L'ecclésiastique citoyen;* for references to Bishop Colbert's *Catéchisme de Montpellier* see pp. 366, 369–70; to Camus and Maultrot, pp. 130–31; and to the reading of Scripture by the laity and the importance of literacy by women, pp. 210–11, 341–42, 368–69.

days." To Maultrot's rehabilitation of the curé as a judge in the diocesan synods this anonymous author added the material rehabilitation of the curé, entitled to the tithe at the expense of the canons and priors, who had put "all the honors and revenues on the one side, all the work and responsibility on the other." To Maultrot's occasional denunciations of the undue wealth of the episcopacy *L'ecclé-siastique citoyen* added the principle that ecclesiastical property was "always the property of the state" and "might be disposed of for the good of the state." And to Maultrot's denunciation of episcopal domination and despotism this Jansenist added some practical proposals to diminish it. Parish priests would be elected by the bishop and his council, which would itself be composed of other parish priests; grands vicaires would be chosen from among veteran parish priests, just as bishops themselves would be chosen from among grands vicaires. As its title suggests, the book went so far in places as to question the clergy's "particular" identity as the kingdom's first order with its attendant privileges and "party spirit," as opposed to the priest's first identity as a simple citizen.[108]

However radical, *L'ecclésiastique citoyen*'s agenda for church reform was neither unique nor unprecedented. The overall tendency of Jansenist ecclesial thought since the 1730s had been hostile to the church's independence as an order vis-à-vis the state in all things external, including some matters pretty spiritual. More specifically, Controller-General Machault's attempt to impose the vingt-ième tax on the clergy in 1749 had given rise to recognizably Jansenist proclamations of the nation's ownership of ecclesiastical property and the right to tax it, attaining clearest expression in the abbé Etienne Mignot's *Traité* on the subject in 1755. These statements had continued to appear in the decade or so before the Revolution, encouraged by the ministry's intermittent attempts to assert the principle of the king's suzerainty over the church's landed property in the realm.[109] Again, the trial of the Jesuits in the 1760s had given rise to plenty of Jansenist denunciations of particular privileges and "party spirit," if only in the context of the Society of Jesus. These denunciations reappeared in the wake of the papal dissolution of the Jesuits in 1773 in the form of pamphlets reproaching them for being an antipatriotic "state apart" and a "particular nation" possessed of privileges and a "blind love of their corps."[110]

One obviously novel—and not typically Jansenist—feature of this agenda for ecclesial reform after 1775 was an emphasis on the more material aspect of the

---

108. Ibid.: on regular clergy, pp. 265–66 (and in general pp. 185–86, 200–201, 327); on honors and revenues, pp. 65–66 (in general pp. 130–31, 145–76); on state ownership of ecclesiasical property, p. 321 (in general pp. 305, 313–14, 386–89); on elections of priests and bishops, pp. 309–11; on clerical identity as opposed to citizenship, pp. xvi–xxii, 313–14, 322, 335, 389.

109. For an example in the 1770s see *Réponse du pape à Monseigneur l'archévêque de Paris, qui lui avoit demandé le rappel des jésuites* (Rome, 1778), pp. 39–41; for the *foi et homage* controversy in 1785 see *Lettre d'un conseiller au parlement à M. l'évêque de Xxx* (n.p., n.d.), pp. 2–4.

clerical second order. That emphasis came in part from the movement associated with Dauphinois curé Henri Reymond, whose *Droits des curés (Rights of the Curés)*, published in 1776, resonated far outside Dauphiné itself. Educated by the Jesuits and lacking any real theological bone to pick with the upper clergy, Reymond concentrated on the deterioration of the social and economic condition of parish clergy in a period of quickened inflation and in areas like the southeast, where that clergy subsisted on the *portion congrue:* the fixed stipend paid to them by the more privileged cathedral or monastic clergy, who actually "owned" and collected the tithe.[111] This more or less autonomous movement produced a litany of grievances all its own: for instance, against the misappropriation of the tithe by the regular clergy; against the woeful inadequacy of the portion congrue; against the opulence and even existence of these "useless" benefice holders; against the regressive incidence of the *décime* or internal clerical tax; against the exclusion of curés from the diocesan bureaus that apportioned this tax; and in general against the aristocratic stranglehold on all the positions of power, wealth, and influence in the ecclesiastical hierarchy.[112]

This material agenda of reform did not remain hermetically sealed and predictably contaminated utterances of an otherwise Jansenist ilk. Whence its presence in *L'ecclésiastique citoyen,* which gave voice to such un-Jansenist concerns as the unequal apportionment of the décime, the very existence of *curés primitifs,* the inadequacy of the portion congrue, the indignity of having to collect the fees called the *casuel* for the administration of the sacraments—the poor figure, in a word, that the indigent curé was obliged to cut in the parish community.[113] That contamination was mutual, however, because the Reymondian agenda could not do without theological justification and typically found it in the Richerist theology of the curé's divine and apostolic origin. Hence the occasional appearance in pamphlets of otherwise Reymondian inspiration of more typically Jansenist concerns, like the rights of curés to be judges in diocesan synods and to appoint their own vicaires.

The contamination of Richerism by Reymond's more social agenda added the charge of aristocracy to that of the desire to dominate. The effect was to amplify the effect of the upper clergy's post-1775 entente with the Parlement by

---

110. *Lettre à un ami sur la destruction des jésuites* (n.p., 1774), pp. 10, 24; and *Seconde lettre ou commentaire du bref de Clément XIV* (n.p., 1774), pp. 143, 153–54. See also the *Réponse du roi à Monseigneur l'archévêque de Paris, qui lui avoit demandé le rappel des jésuites,* p. 41.

111. Timothy Tackett, *Priest and Parish in Eighteenth-Century France: A Social and Political Study of the Curés in a Diocese of Dauphiné* (Princeton, N.J., 1977), pp. 141–51.

112. For the full register of the curés' litany of woe on the eve of the Revolution, see Maurice Hutt's classic article, "The Curés and the Third Estate: The Ideas of Reform in the Pamphlets of the French Lower Clergy in the Period 1787–1789," *JEH* 8 (1957):74–92.

113. *L'ecclésiastique citoyen,* pp. 74, 88–89, 145–76, 390–91.

associating the cause of ecclesiastical reform with the politics of anticorporatism—and therefore with the ministry. No sooner, indeed, had the prerevolutionary crisis begun than Charles-François Le Brun's *Letter from an Englishman in Paris* singled out the clergy's behavior in the Calonne's Assembly of Notables for special abuse, accusing the clergy of self-interestedly maneuvering to protect its "immunities" in the meetings of the Assembly of Notables. It was by means of an "incredible magic," added a *Letter from a Friend on the Last Meeting of the Notables,* that the clergy had "found the secret of possessing the best benefices, positions, recompenses, and highest dignities of every kind . . . without contributing hardly anything to the State's expenses."[114]

That same association with the ministry also tended to align the cause of ecclesiastical reform with certain strands in the French Enlightenment, most notably physiocracy's valorization of the parish curé as a useful agent of agricultural reform and a Rousseauistic infatuation with the country vicar as a reservoir of naive native virtue. That alignment made for some more mutual contamination. Hence, in part, *L'ecclésiastique citoyen*'s exaltation of the "virtuous" curé as a "useful" citoyen, its denigration of monks as "useless" and even nobility as an empty "honor" apart from real social service, and its occasional kind words for "humanity," "simplicity," and a "philosophical century." If useful curés were still indigent while parasitic benefice holders were still rich, that disparity, the anonymous author hinted, was not likely to last much longer because "no benefice holder these days dares to despise a curé on the portion congrue, a hundred times more useful than he, without reaping society's contempt a hundredfold." That new "way of thinking" the author thought attributable "to philosophy," which he regarded as "above reproach on that score."[115]

If "philosophically" acceptable social service were to take precedence over hierarchical honor, it might perhaps do so over dishonor, too, including that of heresy. For prerevolutionary Jansenists also found themselves allied with some philosophes on behalf of civil toleration of Protestants. Based in part, as has been noted, in the shared experience of persecution as well as theological developments within Jansenism, Jansenist interest in this cause also continued to do double duty in the larger campaign against episcopal despotism. To urge the civil toleration for Protestants was to urge the legitimacy of Protestant marriages; and to defend these was in turn to place them under the jurisdiction of the secular prince by virtue of natural law as well as to contest the episcopacy's control of marriage by virtue of its status as a sacrament. To refute that bit of "episcopal despotism" the

114. [Charles-François Le Brun], *Lettre d'un Anglois à Paris* (London, 1787), pp. 19–23; *Lettre d'un ami, sur ce qui c'est passé à la dernière assemblée des notables* (n.p., 1787), p. 1.

115. *L'ecclésiastique citoyen,* p. 52. On curé and humanity see p. xii; on curé as citizen see pp. xvi–xvii; on curé as useful, pp. 106–7; on curé and social distinctions, pp. 114–15; on curé and philosophy, p. 123.

tireless Maultrot wrote a two-volume treatise on the Council of Trent and marriage in 1788 and a hefty *Dissertation on Matrimonial Dispensations* in 1789.[116] And like the cause of ecclesial reform, that of civil toleration for Protestants also aligned clerical Jansenists with the royal ministry, reinforcing that unlikely alliance against the Parlement. For the Parlement of Paris was reluctant to take up the issue at the cost of alienating an episcopal General Assembly that remonstrated against toleration for Protestants at the same time, in 1788, that it remonstrated in favor of the parlements.[117]

It is true that the person who first publicly raised the issue of civil toleration during the prerevolution, Robert de Saint-Vincent, was a parlementary magistrate. Yet his appeal was essentially to the king.[118] So was that of the marquis de Lafayette, who also took up the cause in the Assembly of Notables, persuading his colleagues in the second bureau to petition the king on behalf of toleration for Protestants in May 1787. By that time Calonne's place as chief minister had been taken by Brienne, a former member of that bureau, who both sponsored the idea of an edict of civil toleration and delegated the task of drafting of it to the philosophe-minister Lamoignon de Malesherbes and the barrister Target. Malesherbes's edict continued to deny Protestants the right to celebrate their "cult" in public, but it gave them a civil existence in France, allowing them to register their births, marriages, and deaths with either a secular judge or a Catholic priest acting as the state's agent. And although Jansenists like Robert de Saint-Vincent and Goislard de Montsabert were simultaneously leading the Parlement's opposition to Brienne on the fiscal and constitutional front, the same magistrates shepherded the Edict of Toleration past the hostility of many of their colleagues, whose remonstrances made the edict somewhat more restrictive than it might otherwise have been.[119]

The chief "enlightened" contribution to the pamphlet debate accompanying the edict's progress toward registration was Lamoignon de Malesherbes's two *Memoirs on Protestant Marriages*.[120] But Malesherbes's more enlightened agenda is

---

116. Gabriel-Nicolas Maultrot, *Examen des decrets du Concile de Trente et de la jurisprudence françoise sur le mariage*, 2 vols. ("En France," 1788); and *Dissertation sur les dispenses matrimoniales* (Paris, 1789).

117. *Remontrances du clergé de France au roi, sur l'édit du mois de novembre 1787, concernant les non-catholiques, arrêtés le 18 janvier 1788* (n.p., 1787); and *Remontrances du clergé, présenté au roi le 15 juin 1788* (n.p., 1788). See also Egret, "La dernière assemblée du clergé de France," pp. 10–15.

118. [Robert de Saint-Vincent], *Aux chambres assemblées: Un de messieurs, conseiller de Grand' chambre* (n.p., 1787).

119. *L'édit du roi concernant ceux qui ne font pas profession de la religion catholique;* and *Remontrances du parlement de Paris concernant les non-catholiques, arrêtés le 18 janvier 1788* in *Protestantisme et tolérance en France au XVIIIe siècle, 1685-1789*, ed. Catherine Bergeal (Carrière-sous-Poissy, 1988), pp. 176–93, 198–207.

120. Chrétien-Guillaume Lamoignon de Malesherbes, *Mémoires sur le mariage des protestants*, 2 vols. (n.p., 1785–86).

evident only by reading his two published memoirs in the light of his unpublished ones.[121] Alongside Malesherbes's memoirs in defense of the edict appeared at least seven pamphlets of Jansenist inspiration, which argued that marriage was a civil contract governed by secular natural law quite apart from its status as a Catholic sacrament and that Catholicism, properly understood, persuaded rather than forced the believer's conscience. Not Catholicism, argued Robert de Saint-Vincent, but episcopal despotism and Jesuitism had had recourse to force, impeding the Protestants' return to the Catholic fold. "Those who destroyed Port-Royal," he remembered, "are the same ones who were also the most determined persecutors of the Protestants."[122]

If some of the edict's Jansenist defenders took pains to distance themselves from Protestants as well as philosophes, it was in defensive reaction to a devout denunciation of a Protestant, Jansenist, and philosophical plot to de-Catholicize and de-monarchicalize France. "Now there without doubt is a most extraordinary alliance!" sarcastically exclaimed the anonymous but surely Jansenist author of *An Impartial Letter,* commenting on this supposed Protestant "union with Jansenism and philosophism" and denouncing in turn this "pendant of the fable of Bourg-fontaine."[123] This pamphleteer was not imagining things. For while some devout pamphlets like the anonymous *Secret Revealed* contented themselves with a Protestant-philosophe plot designed, in its words, to undermine "the true religion of monarchies"—Catholicism of course—so that the two would "fall together as soon as they cease to support each other mutually," others like the ex-Jesuit abbé Jacques-Julien Bonnaud's *Discourse To Be Read* indeed enlarged this same plot to include the Jansenists, conspicuous as these were in the debate about civil toleration.[124] The plot in question aimed at nothing less than the destruction of Bourbon throne and Catholic altar, which therefore had to stand together if they did not wish to fall together. Common enough in the 1750s and 1760s, this devout motif had all but disappeared after the 1770s only to reappear in 1787 in reaction to the Edict of Toleration for Protestants. With this exception, however, this devout motif remained curiously on the sidelines of the prerevolutionary debate going on simultaneously in 1787–88, as though the monarchy were worth defending only

121. Pierre Grosclaude, *Malesherbes témoin et interprète de son temps,* 2 vols. (Paris, 1961), 1:560–602.

122. [Robert de Saint-Vincent], *Aux chambres assemblées,* pp. 35–36. For an indication of the Jansenist contribution to the debate on this edict, see Charles O'Brien, "Jansénisme et tolérance civile à la veille de la Révolution," in *Jansénisme et Révolution,* ed. Catherine Maire, *Chroniques de Port-Royal* 39 (Paris, 1990):131–45.

123. *Lettre impartial: Sur l'édit des protestans; à M. le comte de Xxx,* pp. 35–36.

124. [Abbé Jacques-Julien Bonnaud], *Discours à lire au conseil en présence du roi, par un ministre patriote, sur le projet d'accorder l'état civil aux protestans* (n.p., 1787).

where religion was directly concerned.[125] It would soon find other religious reasons to come belatedly to the monarchy's defense in 1789.

The Clergy in the Crossfire

Meeting for the last time since its creation in 1560, the General Assembly of the Gallican Clergy of June 1788 not only dealt a blow to the ministry of Cardinal Loménie de Brienne by contributing less than a fourth of the *don gratuit* he had requested, but gratuitously intervened in the political conflict by remonstrating on behalf of the parlements against Brienne's May edicts. Contemporaries like the abbé de Véri could only rub their eyes in disbelief to see the General Assembly defend the Parlement of Paris as a stable "repository of laws" and as the only constitutional body qualified to approve the monarchy's fiscal demands in the absence of the Estates General.[126] Symptomatic of the episcopacy's exceptional political situation on the eve of the Revolution is the Montesquieuian and parlementary cast of the few pamphlet defenses of clerical property and privilege to appear in 1787–88. If some pamphleteers attacked the clergy, it was only the prelude to their attack on the magistracy, warned *A Letter to the Count of Xxx*, because the magistracy "is itself a sort of sacerdoce no less threatening to their licentiousness and passions; and they have correctly sensed that to strike down [the clergy's] constitutional privileges . . . would be imperceptibly to take them from the nobility." While acknowledging the principle of national ownership of ecclesiastical property, another pamphleteer maintained that the nation was best represented by "the sovereign courts," which no more than the nation itself could alienate that proprietary debt to the poor and to religion without breaking a national contract with God.[127]

But the defense of ecclesiastical privilege as articulated by the General Assembly was very difficult to distinguish from episcopal privilege. And it says mountains about the reputation of the episcopacy at the end of the century of *Unigenitus* that not even its eleventh-hour participation in the Parlement's patriotic passion merited for it so much as a momentary grace in public opinion. Even on the patriot and parlementary side of the debate, judicial Jansenism fell upon the General Assembly's remonstrances with its waning strength, one pamphleteer

125. One notable exception is Jean-Baptiste Duvoisin's *La France chrétienne et vraiment libre* (n.p., 1789).

126. *Remontrances du clergé de France, présentés au roi le 15 juin 1788* (n.p., 1788); or in AN: G8, Ms. 706, fols. 158–83; and Egret, "La dernière assemblée du clergé de France," pp. 13–15. On the abbé de Véri's reaction see the abbé Lavaquery's *Le cardinal de Boisgelin, 1732–1804*, 2 vols. (Paris, 1921), 1:337–39.

127. *Lettre à M. le comte de Xxx, ou considérations sur le clergé* (Rome, 1787), pp. 10–11; *Réflexions sur les immunités ecclésiastiques, considérées dans leurs rapports avec les maximes du droit public et l'intérêt national* (Paris, 1788), pp. 103–8.

faulting the bishops for failing to address the realm's post-*Unigenitus* religious malaise and another for having been inadequately patriotic and Gallican. Instead of restricting its purview to taxes and its posture to "humble remonstrances," this pamphleteer maintained, the General Assembly should have acknowledged in its remonstrances that the Estates General's authority over the king and law was even more sovereign than the ecumenical council's over the pope and doctrine.[128] As time went on and the meeting of the Estates General approached, such pamphlets in the patriotic tradition combined continuing praise of the parlements for their resistance to despotism with an acceptance of the Third Estate's claims against the Second and parish priests' claims against the episcopal First.[129]

Even worse for the clergy, however, was the fire that came from ministerial quarters. For the General Assembly's aristocratic composition and notorious niggardliness in the face of the state's impending bankruptcy intensified the already ongoing critique of the Gallican Church's misuse and internally inequitable distribution of its wealth, as well as of the church's right to it in the first place. The pamphlet attack on these closely related "abuses" invited similar attacks on others because, as events in the Estates General-turned-National Assembly were soon to show, it was not possible to take up the subjects of the clergy's use and right to its landed property without at the same time broaching that of the reform of the church as a whole. And although many of these attacks came from curés themselves, and some of these were Jansenists, just about all of them made common cause with the ministerial side.

Typical of the early ministerial attacks that functioned as part of a wider attack on the parlements are a supposed *Capuchin General Chapter's Ruling* and a series of posthumous *Lettre[s]* from Cardinal Fleury that, starting from the premise that the church's "empire" was "not of this world," excoriated the General Assembly's intervention in favor of the parlements and proposed that the church be stripped of all temporal functions. Accepting the principle of national ownership of ecclesiastical property, they also derided the whole clergy for its "gourmandism," "laziness," and "voluptuousness" and proposed to tax the church heavily.[130] As time went on and as attention shifted from the parlementary-ministerial confrontation to the coming Estates General and the reforms likely to be entertained, the reforms that such pamphlets urged grew ever more surgical, calling for the end of the clergy as a separate order, the gradual elimina-

---

128. *Observations sur les remontrances du clergé, du 15 juin 1788* (n.p., n.d.), pp. 9–10, 28–29. This pamphlet is favorably commented on by Hardy in "Mes loisirs," BN: Ms. Fr. 6687 (22 Dec. 1788), p. 183.

129. For example, *Cave tibi, popule!, ou instructions au Tiers-état sur le danger de sa position actuelle par un noble de fraîche date* (n.p., 1788), esp. pp. 34–35.

130. *Arrêté du chapitre général des Capuchins, tenu extraordinairement en juin 1788* (n.p., n.d.), pp. 10–11, 13; and *Lettre du cardinal de Fleury au conseil de Louis XVI* (n.p., 1788), pp. 9–12; *Troisième lettre du cardinal de Fleury au conseil du roi* (n.p., 1788), pp. 11, 15–16, 24–25.

tion of most if not all monks and canons, and the national expropriation of some if not all of its property. So certain did the oft-proposed elimination of the monastic clergy began to appear that even a *Regular Clergy's Cahier* that pretended to speak in its favor aspired only to ensure the survival of the displaced victims.[131] And so widespread was the acceptance of the principle of national ownership of ecclesiastical property that a few pamphleteers made bold to propose the national expropriation of all ecclesiastical property, putting an elected clergy on the state's payroll, and using the rest of the property to redeem the royal-national debt.[132]

It is worth noting, though, that even the few pamphleteers who advanced such reforms under the banner of "a century of reason and philosophy" also typically proposed to "restore [clergymen] to the origin of their first institution, and to the precepts of the Gospel."[133] However opposed they may appear, these two sets of appeals, one to enlightened progress and the other to primitive perfection, were not mutually exclusive. Nor did appeals to enlightened or utilitarian reason outnumber Jansenist-like appeals to the standard of "the comely first days of the infant Church" and its pristine polity of "gentleness" and "charity" in contrast to "haughtiness" and "despotism."[134] Polemics against the regular clergy similarly held them guilty not only for their material "uselessness" but also for the "blind submission" that they owed to their monastic superiors, thus taking a charge once lodged by Jansenists against Jesuits and enlarging it to include regulars as a whole: "Such a [monastic] subject, be he in whatever order you suppose him, will be a veritable Jesuit, and his superior in respect of him will be no less of a veritable despot."[135]

Pamphleteers also stumbled over each other in their zeal to extol and exonerate poor parish priests—those "friends of suffering humanity" or "pious solitaries who recall for us the best days of Christianity," to juxtapose enlightened and Jansenistical versions of this commonplace.[136] Relatively rare were those pamphleteers who reproached the parish priesthood for its crass ignorance and du-

---

131. *Cahier du clergé regulier* (n.p., 1789), pp. 11–12.

132. *De la différence qu'il y a entre les Etats-généraux et les assemblées nationales; ou, principes radicaux de la constitution* (Paris, 1789), pp. 30–33.

133. *Observations sur les prétendues immunités du clergé; relativement à l'impôt; suivies de l'état générale des biens du clergé de France; avec un plan de réforme soumis à la délibération des Etats-généraux par un citoyen impartial* (n.p., 1789), p. 40.

134. For reference to "comely days" see *Hommage à l'humanité: Dénonciation au gouvernement et aux Etats-généraux; sur l'abus du gouvernement temporel des évêques de France* (n.p., 1789), pp. 33–34; for a description of the marks of the polity of the pristine church and their opposites see *Projet en faveur de la religion, le 18 juillet 1789* (n.p., n.d.), pp. 8–9.

135. *Le clergé dévoilé, pour être présenté aux Etats-généraux par un citoyen patriote* (n.p., 1789), pp. 46–48.

136. *Hommage à l'humanité,* p. 25; *Le Tiers-état éclairé, ou ses droits justifiés* (n.p., 1788), pp. 12–13.

bious morals, rarer still those who, like the author of *A Word of Advice for Priests,* blamed priests in general as the "agents of the extinction" of the Christian religion. Yet even this pamphleteer did so in the name of Christianity itself. "Tremble, unworthy priests; for your condemnation will be the more terrible as your estate . . . requires a greater purity of morals than in the rest of men."[137] However prominent they became later on, finally, vulgar Voltairian or French freethinking motifs show up in prerevolutionary literature as trace elements alone.[138] That things would later not go very well for priests, that even those who accepted the French Revolution would not be to that Revolution what priests had been to Leaguer or Frondish Paris, was in 1788 or 1789 perhaps clearer at street level than it was in pamphlets. In the popular demonstrations that attended the triumphal return of the Parlement of Paris from its enforced "vacation" in September 1788, Hardy reported that "four priests were forced by the populace to kneel before the equestrian statue of Henri IV, which also happened to four good dévotes for having charitably refused to dispatch the sieur Lamoignon to all the demons."[139]

Meanwhile priests themselves continued to press a mix of theological, ecclesial, and economic reform, ranging from Jansenist pleas for an end to the Formulary of Alexander VII and participation in synods to the Dauphinois curés' call for an augmented portion congrue and a better representation in diocesan bureaus.[140] In accord with lay pamphleteers, the most radical priestly pamphlets freely acknowledged the nation's ownership of ecclesiastical property and right to undertake ecclesial reform, looking to king and nation to redistribute that property at the expense of much of the cathedral and regular clergy and to the benefit of the parish clergy and the poor. In contrast to many lay pamphleteers, however, the curés' agenda for reform tended to assume the clerical order as its cadre. Even pamphlets that urged the election of bishops did so on the assumption that they would be elected by curés and not by the lay faithful, notwithstanding the widespread definition of the church as the "assembly of all the faithful."[141] Not totally naive, the lower clergy produced a stray pamphleteer or two who dis-

137. *Le clergé dévoilé,* pp. 17–19; and *Un mot aux prêtres par un laique de la même religion que le pape Alexandre VI* (n.p., n.d), p. 4.

138. Two examples are *Chacun son mot, ou idées sur l'ordre du clergé dans l'assemblée des Etats-généraux* ("Rome," 1789); and *Les sept péchés capitaux, ou examples tirés de l'état ecclésiastique, occupant actuellement le clergé de France, par un ex-ci-devant soidisant j[ésuite], et copié litéralement par un homme qui s'amuse de tout* (Paris, 1789).

139. Hardy, "Mes loisirs," BN: Ms. Fr. 6687 (17 Sept. 1788), p. 85.

140. Two examples of these extremes are the obviously Jansenist *Avis de l'église à ses enfants* (n.p., 1789), p. 22; and the economically preoccupied *Mémoire pour les curés de France, relativement à la convocation prochaine des Etats-généraux* (Avignon, 1788).

141. *Cahier d'un Capuchin, vérifié dans l'assemblée du Tiers ordre de Saint-François* (n.p., 1789), pp. 21–27.

cerned this discrepancy between lay and clerical agendas and warned fellow curés to beware of Third Estate laypeople bearing gifts.[142]

Yet it is mainly hindsight that makes it possible, with Maurice Hutt, to discern a greater readiness among lay pamphleteers to dismantle the clergy as a separate corps than in pamphlets written by curés themselves.[143] For prerevolutionary political circumstances obliged those curés advocating structural reform to align themselves at least rhetorically with the ministry and the king against an episcopacy that, in the words of one pamphleteer, had become "the price of intrigue and the patrimony of nobility" and against the cathedral and regular clergy in the role of Montesquieuian "intermediary corps."[144] Like the Third Estate propagandists, therefore, curés too were concerned with achieving numerical parity with nobles in the upcoming Estates General, even if only within their own order. As a memoir from the curés of Angers put it, "they stood to the Church of France as the Third Estate today stands vis-à-vis the nation."[145] The same conjuncture that aligned curés with the Third Estate also obliged them to look to the ministry or the king as "first temporal minister and Bishop of all the churches of France" and to make a heroic attempt to assimilate themselves to lay commoners. "There are not two sorts of subjects in the State," lay and clerical, maintained a curé from Picardie, recalling the Jansenized Gallican maxim that the church was in the state and not the other way around. He added that if ecclesiastics had to distinguish themselves from laypeople, they would do so in terms of "greater fidelity and obedience" to the king.[146]

Although with a rhetoric that remained more antidespotic than antiaristocratic, then, delegates of the second order of the Gallican Clergy were to go to the meeting of the Estates General rhetorically on the side of the ministry and the Third Estate and at several removes from the patriotic and parlementary associations of an earlier eighteenth century. Clerical Jansenists were soon to rejoin some of their erstwhile lay Jansenist allies, however, and that under the most dramatic circumstances and with the most revolutionary consequences imaginable.

142. *Objets de réclamation à mettre sous les yeux de l'assemblée; où doit être rédigé le cahier des doléances du clergé par un citoyen inutile, et qui se lasse de l'être* (n.p., 1789), pp. 28–46.

143. Hutt, "The Curés and the Third Estate," n. 112.

144. *Avis aux curés, sur leur convocation aux Etats-généraux, et sur les objets de leurs doléances* (n.p., 1789), pp. 8–9; and *Mémoire en faveur des curés* (n.p., 1789), p. 15.

145. *Mémoire des curés du diocèse de Xxx adressée au roi, le 30 décembre 1788 relativement à la convocation des Etats-généraux* (n.p., 1788), p. 11; and *Pétition des curés* (n.p., 1789), pp. 10–11.

146. *Les cris du bas clergé, ou analyse et réfutation des prétentions et des préjués du haut clergé* (n.p., 1789), pp. 15–17; and *Lettre d'un curé de Picardie à un évêque, sur le droit des curés d'assister aux assemblées du clergé et aux Etats-généraux, et sur quelques objets interessans qui y sont relatifs* (n.p., 1789), p. 12.

Jansenists, Jansenism, and the Civil Constitution of the Clergy

Another plausible candidate for the title of last day of the Old Regime is 13 June 1789, when three curé delegates from Poitou, led by Jacques Jallet, broke ranks with the clergy as the realm's First Order and answered the Third Estate's summons to join it for the common verification of credentials. The commons gave them a delirious welcome, "all pressing around them, embracing them, and expressing concern about what might happen to them."[147] These three curés were joined by six more, led by Grégoire, on the next day, and then another ten on the following two days, giving courage to the "commons" to declare themselves the National Assembly on the seventeenth. This clerical defection from the First Estate culminated on 19 June, when a majority of about 149 delegates, most of them curés, voted to join the National Assembly and then stood by their decision despite the events of 20 and 23 June, until Louis XVI ordered the clerical and noble delegations to join the National Assembly on the twenty-seventh.[148] Although the Third Estate may well have succeeded in transforming the Estates General into the National Assembly without the defection of part of the clergy, it would have been much harder to do than it was.

What animated the defecting curés was no doubt in part the aloof and aristocratic morgue of the episcopal delegates whom they outnumbered. "Upon arriving here I was still inclined to believe that bishops were also pastors," wrote the abbé Emmanuel Barbotin to a colleague in hometown Rouvry on 30 May 1789, "but everything I see obliges me to think that they are nothing but mercenaries, almost Machiavellian politicians, who mind only their own interests and are ready to fleece—perhaps even devour—their own flocks rather than to pasture them."[149] To these social offenses the bishops added some pointedly political ones, for although some maintained their post-1775 stance of distance from the monarchy, others, notably Le Clerc de Juigné of Paris, remembered the union of throne and episcopal altar and implored Louis XVI to thwart the "philosophical" threat of the Third Estate and impose his absolute will as he later tried to do.[150] These maneuvers became known, and seemed all the more aristocratic to curés because, like the Third Estate's delegates, many had come to Versailles believing

147. Le Hodey, *Journal des Etats-généraux* (13 June 1789), 1:75; and *AP* (13 June 1789), 8:97.

148. On the meeting of the First Estate in May–June 1789 and the defection of the curés and liberal bishops to the Third, see Maurice Hutt, "The Role of the Curés in the Estates General of 1789," *JEH* 6 (1955):190–220; Ruth Necheles, "The Curés in the Estates-General of 1789," *JMH* 46 (1974):125–44; and most recently Nigel Aston, *The End of an Elite: The French Bishops and the Coming of the Revolution* (Oxford, 1992), pp. 157–81.

149. Abbé Emmanuel Barbotin, *Lettres de l'abbé Barbotin, député de l'Assemblée constituante*, ed. Alphonse Aulard (Paris, 1910). p. 9.

150. Hardman, *Louis XVI*, p. 151.

that the king and his ministers wished to effect the union of the three orders.[151] Thus Grégoire peppered his appeals to his fellow curés with as many denunciations of episcopal "aristocrats" as with the more predictable ones of "despotism" and "domination."[152]

Yet there was more to the revolt of the curés than rank resentment against episcopal aristocracy. Animating many curés as well was a less hierarchical and authoritarian vision of the church, a vision that would have undoubtedly enhanced the role of themselves and the laity, but a vision of the church as a still integral corps all the same. Grégoire again hinted at it when he reminded the curés of the Old Regime legislation that had deprived them of rights to associate, to participate in the governance of the diocese, and to preach and confess without episcopal authorization, adding that it had not been the Third Estate that had lobbied for this legislation.[153] Of those who left records of their thoughts, Grégoire alone seemed more or less aware that common verification of credentials would entail the vote by undifferentiated delegates on all matters, including the clergy's; while the curés' other chief leader, Jacques Jallet, assured his fellow delegates as late as mid-June that he and those who had followed him to the Third Estate would remain free to return to the clerical chamber as soon as it was duly constituted, there to vote on "interests peculiar to the order of the clergy."[154]

That this was not to be so, that the Gallican Church had all but ceased to exist as a separate corps and had entrusted its fate to the votes of twelve hundred mostly lay delegates, began to become clear as early as 2 July, when Mirabeau and the Rousseauian deputy Pétion de Villeneuve mercilessly refuted Archbishop Boisgelin's tearful attempt to exempt ecclesiastical concerns from common deliberation.[155] Meanwhile, the extent of popular hatred for the episcopacy declared itself in Versailles on 24 June in the physical attack on the Archbishop of Paris, who, blamed for his opposition to the union of orders and for persuading the king to hold the royal session, also bore the brunt of a whole century's accumulated hostility against Christophe de Beaumont and Vintimille Du Luc.[156] In the weeks and months that followed it became gradually apparent that that hostility was not to be restricted to the episcopacy but would eventually fall on curés as well. Parisian curés repeatedly found themselves the object of the hostile cry "a bas la

151. Hutt, "The Role of the Curés," p. 194, n. 2.

152. Henri Grégoire, *Nouvelle lettre à MM. les curés, députés aux Etats-généraux; par M. Grégoire, curé d'Embermenil, député de Lorraine* (n.p., n.d.), pp. 9–11, 19, 22, 24, 34–35, 40.

153. Ibid., pp. 24–25.

154. Ibid., pp. 4, 20, 23–24, 36–37; and [Jacques Jallet], *Pièces relatives à la démarche de MM. les curés qui ont passé dans la salle nationale le 12* [sic] *juin 1789, et les jours suivans* (Paris, 1789), p. 12.

155. *AP* (2 July 1789), pp. 182–83.

156. Barbotin, *Lettres*, pp. 23–24; and Jacques Jallet, *Journal inédit de Jallet, curé de Chérigné, député du clergé du Poitou, aux Etats-généraux de 1789*, ed. J.-J. Brethé (Fontenay-Le-Comte, 1871), pp. 102–3.

calotte" even when, as in the case of the curé of Saint-Séverin, they were trying to act as patriots.[157] In a case at once reminiscent of and ominously different from incidents provoked by the refusal of sacraments earlier in the century, Hardy described how on 29 September an angry crowd forced a traumatized curé of Saint-Jacques de la Boucherie to bury a poor journeyman carpenter after he had initially refused to do so for less than twenty-three livres. On the next day a bigger and angrier crowd laid siege to the presbytery of Etienne Parent, curé of the neighboring parish of Saint-Nicolas-des-Champs—the same Parent who had replaced the sacrament-refusing L'Ecluse in 1767—after hearing that Parent had dismissed his choir leader for having officiated in a requiem mass sung for the deceased journeyman carpenter that same morning.[158]

During the summer of 1789 Hardy also noted almost daily processions of white-robed women going from Paris's various parishes to the newly built church of Saint-Geneviève and from thence to the cathedral of Notre Dame. Reminiscent of the white-robed processions of the League, these popular processions were in part traditional and religious in form and content, their main purpose being to offer consecrated bread and bouquets of flowers to Paris's patron saint and the Virgin Mary in thanksgiving for the deliverance of 14 July and from other nameless threats. Yet piety, as Hardy was uncomfortably aware, "did not form the whole object" of these processions, which also anticipated the later revolutionary journées, notably the women's march of 5–6 October to Versailles. For they also proceeded to the beat of drums and martial music and in the company of detachments of the new National Guard. Although usually featuring such icons as the standard of the Holy Sacrament, one immense procession in September replaced the traditional relics with a wooden replica of the recently stormed Bastille; and although curés and other ecclesiastics came in time to participate in and even to lead these processions, they were conspicuously absent when the processions began in early August and behaved more like hostages than like leaders after appearing in them in September.[159] Even before the Civil Constitution of the Clergy alienated many priests from the Revolution, these processions portended that Parisian priests would not be to the French Revolution what Leaguer curés had been to the revolt of 1588, what Jansenist curés had been to the Fronde, or even what Calvinist preachers had been to the American Revolution.

But none of that prevented Jansenist curés from making their crucial contribution to the Revolution, even at that late date. For, as it happens, the two men

157. Hardy, "Mes loisirs," BN: Ms. Fr. 6687 (16 July 1789), p. 392. See also ibid. (12 July 1789), p. 385; (14 Aug. 1789), p. 435; and (7 Oct. 1789), pp. 504–5.

158. Ibid. (29–30 Sept. 1789), pp. 493–94, 497. These incidents are also cited in George Rudé, *The Crowd in the French Revolution* (Oxford, 1967), p. 66.

159. Hardy, "Mes loisirs," BN: Ms. Fr. 6687 (23 & 30 Aug. 1789), pp. 445–46, 455; (14 Sept. 1789), p. 476.

most active in engineering the curés defection to the Third Estate, Grégoire and Jallet, were both jansénisant to a degree. Grégoire was of course a man of many parts, entitled to a prominent place in any history of the French Revolution, whether cultural, intellectual, or religious. But he was also self-consciously devoted to the memory of Port-Royal and most, if not all, that it had come to stand for, even if the totality of his interests and concerns were much larger than that.[160] As for Jallet, he faithfully talked like Jansenists about things that Jansenists liked to talk about, leaving no good reason not to consider him a Jansenist. Speaking for the three curés on 13 June, Jallet typically justified their démarche with appeals to the "wish *(voeu)* of our constituents" and the "cry of our conscience," placing the onus of schism in the clerical order on the mitred heads of the bishops.[161] Thus after fifteen years of estrangement did clerical Jansenism rejoin judicial Jansenism, which in the person of Camus, then secretary of the National Assembly, appropriately received the curés' verified credentials. And thus did Jansenists help join the antiaristocratic to the antidespotic agenda, with results more revolutionary than they could have anticipated.

The role of these curés in the events of May–June 1789 inevitably invites consideration of the question of the role of Jansenists and Jansenism in the revolutionary legislation that abolished the tithe, nationalized the church's property, redrew ecclesiastical boundaries, dissolved the regular clergy, transformed the secular clergy into elected and salaried agents of the national state, and virtually cut them off from the papacy.[162] Known collectively as the Civil Consti-

---

160. The starting point for any consideration of Grégoire as a Jansenist remains Augustin Gazier's *Etudes sur l'histoire religieuse de la Révolution française d'après les documents originaux et inédits* (Paris, 1887), but Rita Hermon-Belot's introductory essay in her edition of Grégoire's *Essai sur la régénération physique, moral et politique des juifs* (Paris, 1988), goes beyond it, especially on the relations between figuratist theology and Grégoire's interest in Jewish emancipation. Other aspects of Grégoire's multifaceted career are highlighted in Ruth Necheles, *The Abbé Grégoire (1787–1831): The Odyssey of an Egalitarian* (Westport, Conn., 1971); Bernard Plongeron, *L'abbé Grégoire ou l'arch de la fraternité, 1750–1831* (Paris, 1989); and Lynn Hunt, *Politics, Culture, and Class in the French Revolution* (Berkeley, Calif., 1984), pp. 1–119.

161. [Jallet], *Pièces relatives à la démarche de MM. les curés*, p. 12.

162. The most focused scholarship on this subject, Préclin's *Les jansénistes du dix-huitième siècle et la Constitution civile du clergé*, tends to minimize the Jansenist contribution to the Civil Constitution when the book finally gets to the Revolution on pp. 463–540. This minimization is achieved, however, by means of a kind of scholarly sleight of hand. For having often employed a generous definition of Jansenism in his long discussion of the Old Regime, Préclin adopts a very narrow and technical one (essentially the parochialism of Nicolas Le Gros) at the threshold of the Revolution, making his mountainous book give birth to a most mouselike conclusion. In differing from Préclin on this subject by consistently adopting a wider characterization of Jansenism, I am essentially siding with an older body of scholarship, including Du Breuil de Saint-Germain's "Les jansénistes à la Constituante," *Revue des études historiques* (1913):163–76; and (surprisingly) Louis Blanc's *Histoire de la Révolution française*, 12 vols. (Paris, 1847–69), 4:272–93; and Jean Jaurès's *Histoire socialiste de la Révolution française*, 6 vols. (Paris, 1983–), vol. 1, pt. 1:181–214, esp. p. 203.

tution of the Clergy, these measures divided the Gallican Church into "constitu-tional" and "refractory" clergies even more hostile to each other than during the refusal-of-sacraments controversy. In the longer run, of course, it also divided the church as a whole from the Revolution and the cause of the republic, blocking any overtly Christian route to political secularization.

If the emphasis falls on individual Jansenists rather than on Jansenism, then that role was at most a modest one. Jansenists like Jean-Denis Lanjuinais and Louis-Simon Martineau, it is true, sat on the Ecclesiastical Committee that drafted the Civil Constitution, Martineau reported and defended it before the National Assembly, and others like Camus, Grégoire, Jallet, and the abbé Jean-Louis Gouttes were conspicuous enough in debates about ecclesial issues to cause Sieyès to take to task those "who seem to have seen nothing more in the Revolution than a superb occasion to exalt the theological importance of Port-Royal and to arrange for the apotheosis of Jansenisus on the tomb of his enemies."[163] With Louis Charrier de La Roche, another Jansenist deputy in the Assembly, Jansenists could have congratulated themselves that the Civil Constitution had enforced episcopal residence, instituted clerical elections, nearly nullified papal influence, suppressed uncanonical benefices, restored diocesan synods, disallowed formulas like that of Alexander VII, and, in general, "banished arbitrary government from the church of France and replaced it with the concourse of the first and second orders, without prejudice to the legitimate authority of the first or the just subordination of the second."[164] And like Charrier de La Roche, Jansenists also took the lead in publicly defending the Civil Constitution in the pamphlet debate surrounding it, including the controversial oath to it required of all clerics.

That much said, Jansenists left to their own devices would not have re-formed the church half so surgically as the National Assembly did. They would neither have abolished the church's tithe without any compensation nor nation-alized all ecclesiastical property. On the contrary, Gouttes, Grégoire, and Jallet tried valiantly but vainly to reserve a permanent landed endowment for parish curés that would have enabled them to be model "ecclesiastical citizens."[165] Nor would Jansenists have abolished all monastic orders. For a while, at least, Camus and others were able to protect such learned, educational, and charitable orders—

163. On the composition and complexion of the Ecclesiastical Committee see Pierre-Toussaint Durand de Maillane, *Histoire apologétique du Comité ecclésiastique de l'Assemblée nationale* (Paris, 1791), pp. 3, 33–34. I am indebted to my friend Rita Hermon-Belot for calling my attention to Sieyès's remark, which is in *AP* (7 May 1791), 25:648.

164. Louis Charrier de La Roche, *Questions sur les affaires présentes de l'église de France, avec des réponses propres à tranquilliser les consciences* (Paris, 1791), p. 60.

165. *AP* (10 Aug. 1789), 8:380–83; (13 Oct. 1789), 9:431–34; (11 Apr. 1790), 12:668–75; (17 June 1790), 16:240, 246. Grégoire's speech also appeared as a pamphlet entitled *Mémoire sur la dotation des curés en fonds territoriaux, lu à la séance du 11 avril 1790* (Paris, 1790).

and longtime Jansenist holdouts—as the Benedictines of Saint-Maur, the Oratory, and the hospital orders.[166] Although Jansenists would probably have abolished cathedral chapters as they then existed, they would almost surely have recomposed the episcopal council differently than with "episcopal vicars" appointed by the bishop. Maultrot would have substituted the cathedral city's parish clergy, while Lanjuinais would have preferred the diocesan synod and a small episcopal council elected by it.[167]

Although Jansenists were in general sympathetic to the principle of clerical elections, they would never have made the electorate the same departmental and district electors who chose secular administrative officers. The abbé Claude Jacquemart spoke for most if not all of his Jansenist colleagues when he urged the Assembly to allow the clergy itself to elect both bishops and curés, and to restrict the secular electors to the role of witnesses or ratifiers.[168] And because eighteenth-century Jansenists had displayed little aptitude for what Pascal had called the "geometrical spirit," they made no contribution to reducing the number of dioceses to make them congruous with the newly created administrative departments or to changing the size of parishes so that they might bear some fixed ratio to population. Had it been up to the likes of Grégoire or Jallet, the Assembly would have probably increased the number of dioceses and parishes to enhance the contact between priests and parishioners. And although Jansenists typically allowed wide latitude for the "temporal power" to reform the church on its own initiative and authority, few if any of them would have absolutely opposed the concurrent involvement of the "spiritual authority" in the work of reform, especially if the resulting church councils contained as high a proportion of curés as did the clergy's representation in the National Assembly.[169]

If, however, the role of Jansenists in the National Assembly's ecclesiastical legislation is recast as that of eighteenth-century Jansenism, then that role becomes an essential—even a central—one. For buttressing the whole edifice of reform stood five or so principles without which it would have inevitably foundered. And even if some of these principles were strictly speaking more Gallican than Jansenist, they bear witness to a Gallicanism so radicalized by contact with Jansenism in the course of the eighteenth century's *Unigenitus*-related conflicts that they may be thought of as just as Jansenist as Gallican.

166. *AP* (12 Feb. 1790), 11:575; (19 Feb. 1790), 11:647.

167. Barère, *Le point du jour* (10 June 1790), 10:425–26; and Gabriel-Nicolas Maultrot, *Vains efforts*, pp. 21–22.

168. Claude Jacquemart, *Opinion de M. l'abbé Jacquemart, député de la sénéchaussée d'Angers, sur l'élection des évêques, prononcée le 9 juin, et imprimée par l'ordre de l'Assemblée nationale* (Paris, 1790); and *Opinion . . . sur l'élection des curés, prononcée . . . le 15 juin 1790* (Paris, 1790).

169. Jansenist participation in the National Assembly's debate on the Civile Constitution is ably summarized in Yann Fauchois's "Les jansénistes et la constitution civile du clergé: Aux marges du débat, débats dans le débat," in *Jansénisme et Révolution,* ed. Maire, pp. 195–207.

The first of these principles is that the administration of the church's property lay with the clerical hierarchy but that the ownership lay with the French church as a whole. This principle of ultimate possession extended not only to temporal property—buildings, land, and income—but even to the spiritual "keys"— the church's sacraments and anathemas. Although this principle would not by itself have authorized the National Assembly to put ecclesiastical property "at the disposition of the nation," it did so in combination with a second: that the church comprised not the clerical hierarchy only but the entire "assembly of the faithful." Because the assembly of the faithful was virtually congruous with the "nation" in Catholic France, the National Assembly could feel itself more than authorized to declare church property to be the nation's, entailing the right to redistribute it as salaries for priests and bishops as well as to use it to retire the national debt. That the National Assembly should also reform the Gallican Church root and branch would seem to follow from the national state's new role as the clergy's paymaster, but it followed more directly from a third familiar principle: that the state alone possessed coercive power and therefore jurisdiction over all public, exterior, and temporal aspects of the church's mission, which for its part was purely and ethereally "spiritual." This principle enabled the National Assembly to deny that it was treading on the church's spiritual power even as it suppressed monastic orders and cathedral chapters, redrew diocesan and parish boundaries—even abrogated François I's Concordat of 1516 and instituted elections for bishops and curés. But just in case bishops and curés objected that the care of souls that they had exercised over their particular parishioners was spiritual and hence beyond the competence of the National Assembly, that Assembly was ready with a fourth principle, though it may also be thought of as a corollary of the second and third. Invoked by Jansenists during the refusal-of-sacraments controversy and urged by Richerist priests against their bishops, this principle held that while the sacrament of ordination was purely spiritual, giving its recipient an indefinite power to preach and administer the sacraments, its assignment to and exercise within a particular territory was temporal and factual, and therefore within the competence of the National Assembly to alter. And just in case anyone doubted that the mode of providing for benefices was temporal and therefore variable, as even Camus did, yet a fifth—and traditionally Jansenist—principle stood Camus's and like-minded consciences in good stead. And that principle was that the practice of the early church represented spiritual authority at its purest, and that the National Assembly was only restoring that ancient and pristine discipline after centuries of usurpation. The same principle also included the corollaries that bishops could do without papal consecration, that of the archbishop sufficing, and that the curés were successors to Christ's seventy-two disciples, and hence the equal of bishops in spiritual authority.

Indeed, this fifth principle fortified the length and breadth of the National

Assembly's ecclesiastical reform, filling any breaches inadequately covered by the others. Reinforcing the revolutionary call for a regeneration, it was a principle appealed to by Jansenist, radically Gallican, and even philosophic defenders of the Civil Constitution alike, however much they might disagree about some of the others. "Finally, we would do well to bring the clergy back to the pristine spirit of the church"–thus Joseph-Michel Pellerin, apropos of the nationalization of church property on 23 October 1789.[170] "Your Ecclesiastical Committee thus judged . . . that it could hardly do better than to adopt the maxims [of the church's] ancient discipline as the foundation of its work"–thus Louis-Simon Martineau, introducing his report to the Ecclesiastical Committee on 21 April 1790.[171] "Far from doing any damage to religion, your decrees will bring back its pristine purity; you will then find yourselves reborn as Christians of the evangelical era, Christians like the Apostles and their first disciples"–thus the jurist Jean-Baptiste Treilhard, defending these proposals on 30 May.[172] So pervasive was this language that, whatever he may have really thought, even Mirabeau found himself publicly justifying the Assembly's ecclesiastical legislation with reference to Christ's intentions as "Founder of Christianity" and the church's "pristine institutions."[173]

These principles were in turn buttressed by a plethora of precedents that in part defied the Revolution's general tendency to put French history behind it. Some of these precedents, to be sure, came from Christianity's "pristine" centuries, the Catholic counterpart to the classical precedents that furnished the Revolution with its "usable past." Figuring prominently among these were the so-called Council of Jerusalem (Acts 2:21–26), which "elected" Matthias to replace Judas as the twelfth apostle; the electoral praxis of the third-century North African church as recorded in Saint Cyprian's letters; the fifth-century Council of Chalcedon, which subordinated diocesan boundaries to the civil geography of the Empire; and Saint Augustine's comportment during the Donatist controversy, which suggested that "charity" might take liberties with canonical niceties for the avoidance of "schism." Yet medieval precedents hardly took second place to these: for example, Saint Martin's "popular" election as Bishop of Tours in the fifth century, Charlemagne's initiatives in reforming the church in the eighth century, the Concordat of Bourge's assertion of royal authority in favor of canonical

---

170. *AP* (24 Oct. 1789), 9:518–19.

171. Louis-Simon Martineau, *Rapport fait à l'Assemblée nationale au nom du comité ecclésiastique, par M. Martineau, député de la ville de Paris, sur la constitution du clergé* (Paris, 1790), pp. 6–7.

172. *AP* (30 May 1790), 15:751.

173. Honoré-Gabriel Riquetti, comte de Mirabeau, *Discours sur l'Exposition des principes de la Constitution civile du clergé, par les évêques députés à l'Assemblée nationale. Présentée à la séance du soir, du 26 novembre 1790* (Paris, 1790), pp. 13–14.

election in the fifteenth century, and the Estates General's contention in 1560 that church property belonged to the nation.[174] Not even the recent Old Regime escaped exploitation. "I suppress other examples in order to get to our own century," Treihard told the National Assembly on 31 May. "In our own days the temporal authority declared by a solemn edict in 1764 that an over-mighty religious corps would cease to exist in France," he reminded the deputies, on whom Adrien Duport had earlier urged the example of the suppression of the Jesuits in defense of the nationaliation of all ecclesiastical property and Barnave had done so to justify the suppression of all religious orders.[175]

The deputy who most eloquently deployed this erudition on behalf of the National Assembly's ecclesiastical legislation was the canonist Armand-Gaston Camus, especially in his great speeches of 31 May, 1 June, and 27 November 1790— although he regularly made himself heard on all subjects, surpassing even Mirabeau as the Assembly's most loquacious member. Opposing papal, episcopal, and grand-vicarial despotism while appealing to "the law of charity," sundry "unanimities," and the "faithful witness of the church's most glorious days," Camus sealed the Civil Constitution with the imprimatur of his Catholic Jansenist conscience, whatever his reservations about particular provisions.[176] But discourse was not notably different outside the Assembly, where such Jansenist clerics as Paul-Félix Baillet, Pierre Brugière, Louis Charrier de La Roche, Luc-François Lalande, Noël de Larrière, and Guénin de Saint-Marc in the *Nouvelles ecclésiastiques* took the lead in publicly defending the Civil Constitution of the Clergy against an emergent episcopal and devout Right.[177] In redrawing the ecclesiastical map, to believe Baillet, the National Assembly "had only performed a mechanical and purely temporal operation" that had left the church's spiritual power entirely intact. And in substituting elections for the Concordat of Bologna's formula of royal appointment and papal confirmation, the Assembly had only "exchanged an arbitrary government for a communal one, so conformed to the church's true spirit." As further evidence of this communal polity Baillet added

174. On this contention see L. Serbat, *Les assemblées du clergé de France: Origines, organisation, developpement, 1561–1615* (Paris, 1906), pp. 31–36.

175. *AP* (31 May 1790), 15:748–49; and Barère, *Le point du jour* (25 Oct. 1789), 3:436; and 16 Feb. 1790, 7:61.

176. *AP* (31 May 1790), 16:3–10. Camus expanded his speeches of 30 May and 27 November 1790 into pamphlets entitled *Opinion de M. Camus, dans la séance du 31 mai 1790, sur le plan de constitution du clergé, proposé par le comité ecclésiastique* (Paris, 1790); and *Développement de l'opinion de M. Camus, député de l'Assemblée nationale, dans la séance du samedi 22 novembre 1790, sur l'exécution des lois concernant la Constitution du clergé* (Paris, 1790). On Camus's contribution to the Civil Constitution, see also David C. Miller, "A.-G. Camus and the Civil Constitution of the Clergy," *Catholic Historical Review* 76 (July 1990):481–505.

177. See Préclin, *Les jansénistes du dix-huitième siècle*, pp. 483–89, 498–501, 519–24.

the subjection of bishops to the council of their episcopal curates, and the restoration of diocesan synods—measures together spelling the liberation of curés from the "shameful slavery to which the notorious Edict of 1695 had reduced them."[178]

But while appeals to these judicial Jansenist principles and precedents may have served to justify the National Assembly's ecclesiastical legislation, they did not account for all of its content. Even its most ardent Jansenist defenders were aware that neither Jansenism nor Gallicanism nor even the two in combination could have produced legislation so unsatisfactory to Gallican bishops, to say nothing of other Jansenists. For one of the more poignant subplots of this pamphlet debate pitted these Jansenists, not only against a revived parti dévot en route toward a new political Right, but also against an older generation of Jansenists, not excepting such monuments as Maultrot, Jabineau, and Mey. In the opinion of these veterans the National Assembly's reforms had simply gone too far, much further than the Parlement of Paris had ever gone, and had really transgressed the line that divided temporal from spiritual jurisdictions. The jurisdiction that a bishop acquired over particular parishioners by virtue of his benefice was not an exclusively external or mechanical matter, argued Maultrot, concluding that a secular assembly could not legitimately deprive fifty-three bishops of their dioceses, much less depose them if they refused to take the oath that the Assembly imposed on them on 27 November. Nor, argued these canonists, did the proposed election by lay departmental and district electors have anything to do with the patristic mode of canonical elections, which, in their opinion, consisted in the election of the clergy by the clergy in the presence of the lay faithful. So if, Maultrot pointed out, the National Assembly wished to impose these and other canonical innovations on the governance of the Gallican Church, it could hardly do so without the concurrent authority of that church.[179]

What made this intra-Jansenist debate within the debate even more poignant is that Maultrot's Jansenist opponents, though not without their own qualms about the issues in question, especially the exclusively lay elections of the clergy, could calm them by invoking the ghosts of other Jansenist worthies past, among them Jacques Duguet, Ellies Dupin—even an earlier edition of Maultrot himself. Had not Maultrot argued in defense of the clergy's second order that the sacrament of ordination alone gave its recipient a plenitude of spiritual power, meaning that its restriction to this or that territory was a purely disciplinary and more or less temporal matter? Was it not Maultrot who had stood by the Parlement of Paris's violation of ecclesiastical territoriality by dragooning cooperative priests in one parish to administer the sacraments in neighboring ones? And had not

---

178. Paul-Félix-Joseph Baillet, *La légitimité du serment civique justifiée d'erreur* (Paris, 1791), pp. 77–78, 99–100.

179. See Préclin, *Les jansénistes du dix-huitième siècle*, pp. 480–92.

Maultrot and Mey defended the Parlement when it had virtually deposed priests as "disturbers of the public peace" and sometimes even replaced them, as in the case of Jacques de L'Ecluse and the parish of Saint-Nicolas-des-Champs in 1767?[180] Pleading with Maultrot "simply to be in accord with yourself," Baillet came close to quoting Maultrot verbatim against himself when he invoked the maxim that "the legal possession of even the most spiritual things is itself temporal."[181] It was not without cause that Noël de Larrière deemed it "legitimate to oppose what he wrote in the weakness of old age with what he so solidly established forty years ago, as indeed he continued to do during many years since that time with a perseverance worthy of the highest praise."[182]

But it was not merely age that divided Maultrot and Jabineau from Baillet and Camus and others who defended the Civil Constitution, because Le Paige too accepted it, octogenarian and former fellow combatant with Maultrot in the "good cause" though he was.[183] What also in part divided the two groups were long-standing tensions between judicial and clerical or conciliar Jansenism which the Old Regime's common enemies had obscured but which the Revolution stretched to the breaking point. While Maultrot's conciliar constitutionalism made it easier for him than for Le Paige to replace the Parlement of Paris with the National Assembly when the latter assumed constituent power in 1789, Le Paige's figuratist constitutionalism made it easier for him than for Maultrot to replace the Parlement with the National Assembly when the latter imposed its temporal authority on the church in 1790. For there where figuratist constitutionalism readily transferred to the National Assembly the power over the church that it had previously attributed to the prince cum Parlement of Paris, conciliar constitutionalism now pleaded in vain for a national church council that, peopled with curés as well as with bishops, might well have reformed in a more Jansenist mode.[184] This debate thus witnessed a partial parting of the paths between varieties of judicial Jansenist constitutional-

180. For Baillet's appeal to the L'Ecluse case see his *La légitimité du serment civique justifiée d'erreur;* and for Maultrot's less than convincing attempt to deconstruct this precedent see his *Vains efforts,* pp. 27–28.

181. Baillet, *La légitimité du serment civique justifiée d'erreur,* pp. 88–89, 105–6. For Maultrot's original see his *Les droits de la puissance temporelle, défendue contre la seconde partie des Actes de l'Assemblée du clergé de 1765 concernant la religion* (Amsterdam, 1777), p. 82, which lays it down that "the legal possession [*possessoire*] of even spiritual things is a purely profane matter."

182. Noël de Larrière, *Suite du préservatif contre le schisme* (Paris, 1791), pp. 153–54.

183. Le Paige's acceptance of the Civil Constitution is evident in a manuscript note that he appended as an octogenarian in 1790 to a copy of his own *Observations sur les Actes de l'Assemblée du clergé de 1765* (n.p., n.d.), published in 1765 in BPR: CLP, Ms. 785, no. 12, p. 127.

184. This conclusion does not differ sharply from that of Préclin when remembering that La Borde's laicism was as much a part of eighteenth-century Jansenism as Le Gros's more clerical Richerism (*Les jansénistes du dix-huitième siècle,* pp. 500, 503). Nor does it diverge from that of Catherine Maire in her "L'église et la nation: Du dépôt de la vérité au dépôt des lois; la trajectoire janséniste au dix-huitième siècle," *Annales* 46 (Sept.–Oct. 1991):1198–1200.

isms, just as the debate over the veto had seen a parting of Jansenism from parlementary constitutionalism.

But new ideological combinations kept pace with the new fissures. For what was missing in both judicial and clerical Jansenism—and what was needed to make the Civil Constitution all that it became—was the radically individualist and anticorporatist bias inherited from Rousseauian and physiocratic notions of the general interest as conveyed by the ministerial side of the prerevolutionary synthesis. Physiocratic influence made itself felt in the National Assembly's Ecclesiastical Committee in the persons of Dionis Du Séjour, Dupont de Nemours, and the marquis de La Coste de Messelière, while those who best articulated the ideology from the podium of the Assembly were the likes of Duport, Mirabeau, Sieyès, and Robespierre, but especially Jacques-Guillaume Thouret and Isaac-René-Guy Le Chapelier, author of the original motion to have the Third Estate invite the others to join it as the nation.[185]

A crucial premise, for example, in the argument that led to the National Assembly's decision of 2 November to place ecclesiastical property "at the disposition of the nation" was that individuals alone possessed property by virtue of natural law, whereas corporate bodies, artificial creations of the nation, at best administered property in the interests of the nation. Principally the work of Thouret, this argument received some inadvertent but crucial help from Sieyès, who argued that, because the clerical corps might possess property just as validly as the nation, which was also a corps, the nation would have to destroy the clergy as a corps if it wished to nationalize ecclesiastical property.[186] But it was left to Le Chapelier to conclude that the legislation of 4–11 August 1789 had already destroyed the clergy as well as all other separate corps, and that the nation might therefore help itself to former ecclesiastical property. Intervening crucially after a patriotic curé had argued persuasively that the Assembly should redistribute the church's property in favor of the parish priesthood and the poor but leave its administration to a reformed clergy, Le Chapelier attacked ecclesiastical property "from a political angle" and, citing Turgot, argued that, having destroyed the orders for the "salvation of the state," the National Assembly could not now entrust the administration of property to the clergy without allowing it "to rise from its ashes in order to reconstitute itself as an order." Beware of the clergy

185. On the presence of physiocrats in the Ecclesiastical Committee see Yann Fauchois, "La Constitution civile du clergé: Intégration de l'église à l'état et laicité" (third-cycle thesis, University of Paris, 1980).

186. Sieyès delivered his speech during the first installment of the debate over the status of ecclesiastical property on 10 Aug. 1789. See *AP*, 8:389–94, where however it is wrongly attributed by the editors to the abbé de Montesquieu. Thouret's crucial contribution and its debt to physiocracy are most apparent in Barère, *Le point du jour* (24 Oct. 1789), 3:428–29.

bearing gifts, he warned, because "its gifts are more dangerous than our [fiscal] distress."[187]

Anticorporatist ideology again made its influence felt in the debate that led to the suppression of religious orders on 14 February 1790, when the Rousseauian deputy Pétion de Villeneuve told the Assembly that monks "were dangerous as corps."[188] And while radical Gallican or judicial Jansenist arguments sufficed to convince the National Assembly that it possessed the power to reform the church's "exterior" on its own authority, anticorporatist ideology was the real inspiration behind several of the Civil Constitution's most controversial provisions: the reduction of the number of dioceses to make their boundaries coincide with the new administrative departments, and the elimination of the clergy's separate role in the election of bishops and curés. When on 9 June the abbé Jacquemart tried to approximate antique canonical discipline by proposing to entrust the election of bishops to the departmental clergy aided or otherwise abetted by its administrative personnel, the reporter Martineau abandoned his own Ecclesiastical Committee to support Jacquemart's motion and the whole Assembly seemed on the verge of endorsing it. But that motion's fleeting season in the sun ended abruptly when Robespierre denounced it as "giving the clergy a particular political influence" and as "reconstituting a solitary corps," whereupon Le Chapelier rushed to Robespierre's aid in his characteristically peremptory fashion. "The will of any corps expresses the mind-set of that corps, the particular interest of that corps, and the will of the clergy will always express the mind-set and interest of that corps," Robespierre explained, announcing that, as advocate of the people, he would "conclude in favor of the people."[189] Jacquemart fared no better six days later when he ventured a similar motion apropos of the election of curés.[190]

So it happened that the Civil Constitution nationalized all ecclesiastical property, abolished nearly all religious orders, surgically reduced the number of dioceses from 135 to 82, and mixed clergymen pell-mell with laypeople as "electors" of their "moral officers." As in the secular parts of the constitution, it also happened that ideological elements having roots in the Old Regime's political divisions—and hitherto opposed as patriotic to ministerial—combined with each other in the revolutionary crucible to produce results more corrosive than any mere addition of their parts. By eliminating the clergy itself as a visibly independent corps, this ideological combination hastened the interiorization of religion

187. Barère, *Le point du jour* (3 Nov. 1789), 4:28–30; and *AP* (2 Nov. 1789), 9:639.

188. *AP* (12 Feb. 1790), 11:575–76.

189. Ibid. (9 June 1790), 16:154–56; [Abbé Thomas-Marie Royou and Galart de Montjoie et al.], eds., *L'ami du roi, des Français, de l'ordre et sur-tout de la vérité, par les continuateurs de Fréron* (Paris, 1790–91), 10 June 1790, p. 39.

190. *AP* (15 June 1790), pp. 222–24.

and the state's monopolization of public functions, a tendency long evident in judicial Jansenism by itself. In other words, it helped transform the old duality of temporal versus spiritual into that of public versus private. It also provoked the transformation of a moribund parti dévot into a religious Right that, as in the refusal-of-sacraments controversy, made its own contrary contribution to the privatization of religion.

If these features of the Civil Constitution were roadblocks in the way of some Jansenists' acceptance of it, they were roads to Golgotha for those Gallican bishops in the Assembly who desperately sought some kind of canonical compromise. It says volumes about the sincerity of their Gallicanism that their chief spokesman in the National Assembly, Boisgelin de Cucé of Aix, allowed himself to be advised by someone like Maultrot. Opening the debate on the Civil Constitution on 29 May 1790, Boisgelin voiced the predictable objections to the unilateral reduction of dioceses and parishes, the suppression of cathedral chapters, and the "alien" mode of election of bishops and curés, yet recognized the need "to reform abuses" and the exemplary value of the "spirit of the primitive church." But he pleaded above all for the permission to convoke provincial and national councils in order to "canonize"—and perhaps renegotiate—the proposed changes. The church's ministers "ought to hasten to fulfill the will of the civil power," he granted, but how, he asked, "could they fulfill it if the civil power refused them so much as the power to concur?"[191] That power is, of course, what the National Assembly steadfastly refused to give them, ironically placing all its hope in a papacy that had approved similarly drastic reforms recently imposed by Emperor Joseph II on his Austrian Habsburg dominions. And the tone of Boisgelin's *Explanation of Principles,* published later in 1790, was already less conciliar as well as conciliatory and more papal in its appeal than his earlier utterances had been.[192] As during the refusal-of-sacraments controversy but to an unprecedented power, the logic of these events was profoundly polarizing. Willy-nilly these would-be episcopal compromisers were to find themselves thrown into the camp of counter-revolution, reuniting episcopacy and royalty in adversity and helping to give that counterrevolutionary Right an ideology of which neither feudal nor absolutist interests had the making.[193]

As in the 1750s and 1760s, that ideology touted the alliance of absolutist

191. *AP* (29 May 1790), 15:724–31. Boisgelin also printed the speech as a pamphlet entitled *Discours sur le rapport du comité ecclésiastique, concernant la Constitution du clergé; prononcé dans l'Assemblée nationale* (Paris, 1790).

192. [Jean de Dieu-Raymond Boisgelin de Cucé, Archbishop of Aix], *Exposition des principes sur la Constitution civile du clergé par les évêques députés à l'Assemblée nationale* (n.p., 1790).

193. The counterrevolutionary ideology I have in mind is not that of conservatism generally, which was internally quite diverse, but of what J. M. Roberts in an illuminating article has called the Right. See his "The French Origin of the 'Right,'" in *Transactions from the Royal Historical Society* 23 (1973):27–53. Roberts also emphasizes the religious trigger in the formation of this ideology.

throne and papal altar against a conspiracy of heretics and philosophes, and it did not wait for Boisgelin or his Gallican colleagues to raise its ebenezer. Evident already in reaction to the Edict of Toleration for Protestants, this ideology may have found a convert in the Archbishop of Paris, who was popularly believed to have persuaded Louis XVI to hold the royal session by invoking the specter of a Protestant and philosophic threat to royal authority and religion in the persons of Necker and the astronomer Jean-Sylvain Bailly, the new president of the National Assembly.[194] And it soon found new reasons for outrage in the nationalization of ecclesiastical property and dissolution of religious orders, and even earlier in the debate of 22–23 August over the freedom of religious conscience that led to article 10 of the Declaration of the Rights of Man and the Citizen. In the pandemonium of that confrontation between advocates of the freedom of public worship for religious dissidents and defenders of an integrally Catholic France, the Protestant pastor Rabaut delivered a passionate paean to religious toleration, the Jansenist Camus came to Rabaut's defense, and the philosophe Mirabeau dared to employ some Voltairian irony, observing "that Protestants, inevitably damned in the next world as everyone knows, have done reasonably well for themselves in this one, without doubt by virtue of compensation due to the goodness of the Supreme Being."[195] The other two debates about religion also seemed to substantiate a Protestant, Jansenist, and philosophic nexus, as Barnave, Mirabeau, and Jansenist curés figured prominently as advocates of the nationalization of church property and the abolition of religious orders. Each of these debates prompted clerical delegates to try to persuade the National Assembly to declare Catholicism the "religion of the nation, and its cult the only established one." The National Assembly's refusal to approve this motion on 13 April 1790 provoked about three hundred deputies to sign a formal protest several days later, a protest that in many ways defined the Assembly's emerging Right.[196]

But it was above all the Civil Constitution of the Clergy that convinced this emerging Right that the Assembly aimed at nothing less than the destruction of Catholicism, as it was the Right's opposition to this supposed project that filled its ideological sails. This ideology found few spokesmen in the National Assembly

194. Hardy, "Mes loisirs," BN: Ms. Fr. 6687 (24 June 1789), p. 364.

195. This debate is conveniently reconstructed in Antoine de Baecque, Wolfgang Schmale, and Michel Vovelle, eds., *L'an 1 des droits de l'homme* (Paris, 1988), which contains Rabaut's speech, pp. 174–79, as well as Mirabeau's, pp. 166–67. But this reconstruction leaves out the sense of Camus's attempt to speak, which is clearer in the comte de Mirabeau's *Courier de Provence* (22–23 Aug. 1789), 1:9.

196. Jacques de Saint-Victor, "L'action parlementaire et les clubs contre-revolutionnaires," in *La contre-révolution*, ed. Jean Tulard, (Paris, 1990), pp. 39–51; and Timothy Tackett, "Nobles and Third Estate in the Revolutionary Dynamic of the National Assembly, 1789–1790," in *AHR* 94 (Apr. 1989):296–97. Tackett, it is true, emphasizes the "noble" contribution as much as the religious one, as he does in *Becoming a Revolutionary: The Deputies of the French National Assembly and the Emergence of a Revolutionary Culture*, 1789–1790 (Princeton, N.J., 1995).

itself, in part because, with the Assembly's transfer from Versailles to Paris, anticlerical hecklers in the galleries intimidated would-be defenders of the clergy; in part because, with the discussion of the Civil Constitution of the Clergy, most of the Right refused to deliberate or vote on religious issues on the grounds that they lay beyond the Assembly's purview. The abbé Guillaume-Gabriel Leclerc nonetheless found occasion to reiterate, with the Gallican Clergy's *Acts* of 1765, that the church possessed an "exterior jurisdiction" replete with "coaction" and the "necessary force to execute its canons," which even the "prince"—and by implication the National Assembly—had to obey; the abbé Jean-Claude Goulard, for his part, evoked the "majestic edifice" of "episcopal authority" culminating in the ultimate power of the pope, to whom "alone . . . Jesus Christ entrusted the government of the church universal with jurisdiction." Nor did Goulard neglect to remind the Assembly that the spiritual power, which the church "received from heaven," existed as well "for the glory and strengthening of the monarchy." Both also peppered their case against the Civil Constitution with denunciations of Lutherans and Calvinists, the "Presbyterianism of the Protestants," and the canonical "formula of the little church of Utrecht"—that is to say of Jansenists.[197] At this point only the philosophes remained unscathed.

But by mid-June only the abbé Jean-Siffrein Maury consistently made himself heard above the anticlerical din. Outside the Assembly the architects of rightist ideology could make themselves read if not heard. Abbé Thomas-Marie Royou's and Galart de Montjoie's daily *King's Friend*, for example, began to appear in the midst of the Assembly's discussion of the Civil Constitution and specialized in linking the cause of Catholic altar with Bourbon throne. And however much a "friend of the king" was Royou, his royalism clearly took second place to his devotion to the altar: "From the attacks on the Altar [the Revolution] proceeded to attack the Throne," for the ferment had begun with "impiety" and "insults against priests."[198] That the altar in question was first and foremost a papal one became clear when, reacting to the virtual elimination of papal influence from the new Gallican polity, the journal observed that "the pope is treated just as the king is: the head of the church, like that of the state, is stripped of all influence over the nomination of bishops . . . and the pope will henceforth be no more than the 'Bishop of Rome,' just as . . . the king will be no more than the 'executive power.'"[199]

Nor was the journal's royalism as integral as its clericalism. Although the editors tried to take issue with the doctrine of popular sovereignty, they were unable to do so except in terms of the revolutionary concept of contract itself,

---

197. *AP* (31 May 1790), 16:2–3, 10–16.
198. [Thomas-Marie Royou et al.], *L'ami du roi*, 1 (June 1790), p. 2.
199. Ibid., 15 (15 June 1790), p. 58.

maintaining that the nation could not unilaterally break its "sacred" contract with its king. It therefore fell to the clerical editor of a more clearly counterrevolutionary journal, the ex-Jesuit abbé Augustin Barruel, to explain why such contracts were indeed sacred by restating the doctrine of divine right with a great show of logical rigor. Arguing, as had Lefranc de Pompignan in defense of the clergy's *Acts* of 1765, that no amount of contracting between essentially equal human constituents would ever give anyone the right to command or others the duty to obey, Barruel concluded that nothing less than divine intervention could ever legitimate and sanctify any constitutional or governmental contract, and that "all [political] authority . . . hence comes essentially, uniquely, and immediately from God."[200] The result of this rehabilitation of divine right for Barruel was an integral royalism that no amount of subsequent conceptual backpedaling or show of "flexibility" was able to negate. "Does my theory then make the king a kind of God? So much the better, then!" defiantly exulted Barruel.[201] Yet royal right thus established by divine right remained subordinate to divine right. For among all the domains off limits to royal power in Barruel's theory, none was more taboo than that of religion. Not only might the king not foist a religion of human making on his subjects—by which Barruel clearly meant the Civil Constitution of the Clergy—but he had an obligation to protect and uphold the only true and divine one, namely Catholicism, even against all heretical comers like Calvinism. The specifically anti-Gallican—and ultramontanist—implications of this limitation Barruel simultaneously made clear in the periodical *Journal ecclésiastique* and other pamphlets against the Civil Constitution of the Clergy.[202]

Of all the heresies that a legitimate king might fear, none, of course, was more fearful than those that undermined legitimate government itself by teaching that God conferred sovereignty on the people in the first instance and only mediately via the people on governments, including kings. The villains Barruel had in mind were the same ones fingered by Lafitau in 1754, chiefly conciliarism, Calvinism, and Jansenism. Indeed, Barruel established a sort of diabolical "genealogy" of ideas that went from Jean de Paris to Jan Hus to Martin Luther to Thomas Münzer to Edmond Richer, culminating in the philosophes, the French Revolution and the casuists of the Civil Constitution of the Clergy. Behold "Germany in revolt in virtue of Luther's selfsame principles, . . . the French monarchy at war for two centuries against the children of Calvin, . . . and finally in our own day all this anarchy, all these massacres, all these conflagrations, and all these horrors in an empire that a detestable philosophy, that an indomitable heresy

200. Augustin Barruel, *Question nationale sur l'autorité et sur les droits du peuple dans le gouvernement, par M. l'abbé Barruel* (Paris, 1791), p. 72.

201. Ibid., pp. 61–62.

202. For example, Augustin Barruel's *Prône d'un bon curé, sur le serment civique exigé des évêques, des curés, des vicaires et tous les prêtres en fonctions* (Paris, 1790), p. 4.

drags down toward its ruin."[203] Barruel was later to expand this genealogy of subversive ideas into his famous theory of a full-blown plot—an updated version, in effect, of the parti dévot's Bourgfontaine plot—to explain the genesis of the French Revolution, even if by 1797 he was to valorize the role of philosophes and Freemasons to the detriment of Calvinists and Jansenists.

But the connection between rightist ideology's plot theory and the parti dévot's earlier anti-Jansenist Bourgfontaine plot is more evident in immediate reaction to the Civil Constitution, especially in the work of the comte d'Antraigues, who was by 1791 disinvesting in the Calvinist, Jansenist, and encyclopedic sources that had served him so well in his earlier *Mémoire sur les Etats-généraux*. To be sure, all three groups figured prominently in his 1791 *Denunciation to French Catholics* as well, but as the villains this time in a dastardly plot that, like that of Bourgfontaine, aimed "to topple the edifice of the religion of our fathers onto the bloody debris of the monarchy."[204] This plot's longest-term protagonists were, of course, Calvin and his "sectaries," showing up in the persons of Barnave, Necker, and Rabaut de Saint-Etienne. From the mid-eighteenth century on, however, the philosophes, led by Voltaire, had replaced Calvinists as the most dangerous plotters. For while the Calvinists still dreamed of replacing Catholicism with Calvinism, the National Assembly's many philosophes, led by Mirabeau, aimed to replace all religion with atheism. But neither Calvinists nor philosophes, it turned out, found themselves able to dispense with the "surprising" yet crucial aid of the Assembly's Jansenist contingent, led by Camus and Fréteau de Saint-Just. Although "imitating" Calvinists "they also anathematized them," enabling Jansenists to masquerade as Catholics, the better to obscure the Calvinists' and philosophes' more revolutionary designs under the verbiage of "restoring the church to its pristine purity." Conserving Catholicism's "exterior forms" and "sacerdotal garments," the Jansenists reassured an unsuspecting populace with the semblance of "a cult that their errors have destroyed."[205]

It took until toward the end of the Revolution for these elements to coalesce as rightist ideology in the mature thought of Bonald, Barruel, and de Maistre. But it hardly took that long for rightist ideology and the Civil Constitution that elicited it to bedevil the Revolution and to ensure something like a Terror. For by putting it to the conscience of the king, both the Civil Constitution and the charge that it was heretical resulted in his attempted flight and arrest in Varennes and the consequent demise of the constitutional monarchy. And in tormenting the con-

203. Ibid., pp. 79–83.
204. Emmanuel-Louis-Henri de Launay, comte d'Antraigues, *Dénonciation aux Français catholiques, des moyens employés par l'Assemblée nationale, pour détruire en France, la religion catholique* (London, 1791), pp. 5–6.
205. Ibid.: on Protestants, pp. 96–106; on philosophes and Jansenists, pp. 111–13.

science of the clergy, the Civil Constitution and the conviction that it was heretical provoked a full-scale schism between the constitutional clergy that accepted it and the refractory clergy that did not.[206] The refractory clergy then boycotted even the civic functions administered by the constitutional one, thereby contributing to the privatization of religion and the laicization of the state.[207] The same refractory clergy also lent substance to revolutionary ideology's already ample capacity to espy enemies, making constitutional and refractory clergies alike into symbols of counterrevolution and giving leave to the most virulent forms of anticlericalism available.

And so it happened that a revolution with many—indeed, too many—Christian origins became the first revolution to attempt to "dechristianize" society. Too distant and diverse to have presided overtly over the destinies of the French Revolution, those origins were nonetheless much too near for the Revolution to have entirely escaped the long shadow they cast. For even the "dechristianization" campaign and Terror of 1792–94 remained largely confined within forms bequeathed to them by the history of French Christianity. By defacing churches, changing sacral place-names, and forcing priests to abdicate or marry, the dechristianizers mainly mimed the iconoclastic gestures of sixteenth-century Calvinists— with this obvious difference, of course, that whereas Calvinists had aspired to purify revealed religion of "pagan" remnants for the greater glory of a transcendent and "majestic" God, revolutionary dechristianizers sought to purify a "natural" religion of revealed remnants for the greater good of an immanent social order. But if, as seems plausible, there exists some kind of law of the conservation of the sacred, then the price paid for the desacralization of the remaining symbols of transcendence was an ideological resacralization of a "regenerated" body politic—the nation, the *patrie,* the people—along with anathematizing or eliminating those deemed impolitic by the new secular order. And thus was the French Revolution destined to perpetrate not only the gestures of Protestant iconoclasm against counterrevolutionary symbols, but numerous Saint-Bartholomew's days against counterrevolutionary people as well.

206. On the reception of the Civil Constitution of the Clergy by the clergy and the rest of France, see above all Bernard Plongeron, *Les reguliers de Paris devant le serment constitutionel* (Paris, 1964); and Timothy Tackett, *Religion, Revolution, and Regional Culture in Eighteenth-Century France: The Ecclesiastical Oath of 1791* (Princeton, N.J., 1986).

207. On this transformation, see Yann Fauchois, "Révolution française, religion et logique de l'état," *Archives de Sciences Sociales des Religions* 66 (1988):9–24.

Conclusion

THE RECENT DEMISE OF THE SOCIAL INTERPRETATION OF the French Revolution in Marxian form as a victory of a protocapitalistic bourgeois class over a neofeudal nobility has sent many historians scurrying back to Alexis de Tocqueville's mid-nineteenth-century classic, *The Old Regime and the French Revolution,* which stressed the prerevolutionary state's leveling effect on the social hierarchy and the continuity between royal and revolutionary administrative centralization. It has also stimulated a renewed interest in politics and high culture as agents in their own right in the coming of the Revolution. Whence a quest for political and cultural continuities between the Old Regime and the Revolution in addition to the administrative and social ones that Tocqueville most emphasized. But post-Marxian revisionism has so far left the subject of religion more or less where it found it. Indeed, socialist historians from Louis Blanc to Albert Soboul paid it more mind. Nor, with the exception of François Furet, has revisionism revived interest in many of Tocqueville's contemporary historians of the Revolution, among them Edgar Quinet.[1]

Writing in exile after Louis Napoleon's coup d'état ended the short-lived French Second Republic, Quinet, like Tocqueville, set out to answer the question why the Revolution's promise of political liberty remained so largely unfulfilled at that late date. But while stressing, as Tocqueville did, the nefarious legacy of royal absolutism, Quinet put equal if not more emphasis on long-run religious factors,

---

1. François Furet, *La gauche et la Révolution au milieu du XIXe siècle: Edgar Quinet et la question du jacobinisme [1865–1870]* (Paris, 1986).

particularly the failure of the Protestant Reformation in France, from which his conception of absolutism was inseparable. Anything but a conservative, Quinet was among the few French liberal historians of the Revolution to take a positive interest in religious phenomena, regarding them as agents of modernity as well as of reaction. And although he did not inherit his mother's Protestantism, Quinet wrote a profoundly Protestant history of the French Revolution. A brief look at Quinet's *La Révolution* may therefore stand in lieu of a conclusion, if only by making this book's overall argument more salient by contrast and comparison.

If Marx tended to regard the mode of economic production and class relations as the driving motors of historical change, Quinet came close to standing Marx on his head, regarding religion as fundamental and the economy and society as epiphenomena. Most basic to Quinet's conception of the Old Regime and the Revolution was hence the long-term failure of the sixteenth-century Reformation in France: "The French, having been unable to accept the advantages of the religious revolution of the sixteenth century, were eventually led to deny them . . . and from there, how many false views did they not end by embracing."[2] For the survival of the confessional, the sacramental system, and a celibate and self-anointed priesthood likewise spelled the triumph of royal absolutism with which, in Quinet's opinion, these features of Catholicism were all too compatible. Where the victory of Protestantism in England, the Netherlands, and elsewhere liberated the laity from the priesthood and enshrined the principle of the free lay conscience via the doctrine of scriptural authority—a necessary prerequisite, Quinet thought, for the subsequent development of political freedom—Catholicism kept the French in thrall to "spiritual absolutism" and the habits of "absolute domination" for another two centuries—and quite unprepared, at a basic level, to take full advantage of the opportunity of 1789.[3]

Trying to reap the political harvest, as it were, of a philosophical century without any prior religious preparation, the French revolutionaries prematurely proclaimed the doctrine of "philosophical" toleration instead of first uprooting Catholicism root and branch as the sixteenth-century Reformation had. For it was only after having disallowed Catholicism long enough to wean their populations from the habits of spiritual subservience that Protestant countries were later able to adopt a policy of confessional toleration, whereas France, having bypassed the Reformation, fruitlessly tried to institute political liberty without a prior revolution in religious consciousness. With Catholicism, in still other words, left in possession of the workaday lay religious conscience, it was only a matter of time before the revolutionaries would fail to persevere in pursuit of a political liberty for which they were morally unprepared, and to leave it to wither on the proverbial vine.

2. Edgar Quinet, *La Révolution*, ed. Claude Lefort (Paris, 1987), p. 158.
3. Ibid., pp. 176, 180.

The chief mistake of the National Assembly's ecclesiastical legislation was hence not, in Quinet's estimation, that it "thrust its hand into the censer" and dared to reform the Gallican Church, but rather that it did not reform it radically enough. For in limiting itself to externals and permitting the priesthood, even if elected, to maintain the tyranny of the confessional, the Civil Constitution of the Clergy failed to enfranchise the laity and so to create a church significantly superior to the nonjuring or "refractory" one. At most, therefore, this constitutional church held down crucial spiritual terrain for the counterrevolution, which, in the form of the "refractory" clergy, easily reoccupied it as soon as, in 1792, the Revolution began to leave the constitutional church to twist in the wind. The Revolution was then obliged to fight a religious civil war within French borders against Catholic Vendéean peasants without a new gospel of its own to fight for. Hence, too, the Terror of 1793–94 was all the more terrible in being conceptually impotent and in formal contradiction with itself. Adhering, as had the National Assembly, to the principle of religious toleration, the Convention and its Committee of Public Safety struck all the more savagely at priests for want of a real antidote to their doctrines. And having tried to effect a political regeneration without a concomitant religious one, the French Revolution condemned itself to a terroristic sterility, leaving it for Napoleon and his Concordat to end the terror and perpetuate the sterility.

From the perspective of the preceding pages, the chief merit of Quinet's argument is to have called attention to the long-term consequences of the failure of the Reformation in France. One need not share Quinet's Whiggish association of Protestantism with political liberalism to suppose as he did that, whether or not the sixteenth-century reformers intended to enfranchise the lay religious conscience—almost certainly not—a greater *de facto* freedom in the domain of the conscience was the effect of a drastically scaled-down church and the valorization of the written word over tradition in areas where the Reformation succeeded. And however difficult their effects may be to gauge, the successful suppression of a religious revolution in the sixteenth century and another two centuries of "truth" defined as the pronouncements of legitimate hierarchical authority may well have set intangible limits to the French Revolution's experiment with political liberty, as Quinet held. While these were the consequences that Quinet himself insisted upon, it may be at least parallel to his train of thought to argue, as this book has, that the failure of the Reformation also meant the survival of a conspicuously propertied and privileged church with an episcopacy more perilously tied to the monarchy than ever before, as well as a monarchy with so positive a religious charge as to transform religious dissent into political challenge on contact or by mere proximity. The suppression of the Protestant Reformation and even some parts of the Catholic reformation in Leaguelike form moreover made that monarchy more absolute than ever before, not only in the rights it claimed over the individual conscience but in its pathological aversion to all autonomous partial or intermediate associations, whether they were Protestant synods and consistories or Catholic councils and diocesan assemblies. The extension of this aversion to national or provincial estates would have gone more or less without saying, even had they not also damned themselves by association with the same reformations.

Although Jansenism obviously represents a further remove from Quinet's ken, it may likewise be in a line with it to stress, as this book again has, that a religious reformation failed to take hold not only in the sixteenth but also in the seventeenth century in the more Catholic form of Jansenism. The result of the monarchy's suppression of this second attempted reformation was not only an augmentation of the consequences of the first—the persistence of a privileged church, the dependence of the church on the monarchy, the monarchy's reinforced religious identity, a more invasive absolutism, an intrusive censorship—but the renewal and persistence of a reformational religious controversy about grace and morals that soon extended to politics and ecclesiology and that lasted throughout the "century of lights." By the time it died down in the 1770s, this controversy had in turn repeatedly purged and demoralized the Catholic priesthood, bespattered and besmirched a sacral monarchy, dismantled the conceptual underpinnings of absolutism, polarized Gallican and ultramontanist ecclesiologies, and radicalized an Enlightenment that defined itself in far more virulently anticlerical, anti-Catholic—even anti-Christian—terms than its considerably tamer counterparts elsewhere, whether in Catholic or Protestant Europe. The devout and Jansenist sides to this religious controversy also began to shade off into something like ideological and political groupings that, entering the French Revolution as adversaries, would later divide up the spoils of French absolutism.

Yet another of the merits of Quinet's argument is to have stressed the close relations between religious and political change and hence to have put the religious question at the center of his interpretation of the French Revolution. The traumatic and dislocating effects of rapid political change without concurrent or prior changes in religious convictions are surely visible enough in our day to give point to Quinet's query, if not to make it the order of the day. It is in the details of Quinet's argument, however, especially in his treatment of the Civil Constitution of the Clergy, that this book most obviously parts paths with his. Sensing, perhaps quite profoundly, that one religion is most effectively displaced by another, Quinet faulted the National Assembly for hoping to circumvent Catholicism instead of proclaiming a new gospel as the Reformation did. But religious revolutions do not typically occur on legislative command, nor was Quinet ever entirely clear on what form a new religion could or should have taken in 1789. At one point Quinet suggested, for example, that only "another form of Christianity" could have gotten the better of the Catholicism that animated the Vendéean peasants in the West and their revolt against the Revolution in 1793.[4] Yet, aside from Protestantism, he provided no hint as to what other form that might have been, although no one knew better than Quinet that the Protestant moment had long come and gone in France. Elsewhere Quinet seemed to suggest that the only revolutionary religion worthy of a century of "philosophy"—that is, the Enlightenment—would have been the worship of "eternal reason" or some higher stage in the consciousness of transcendence. Yet Quinet found the Paris commune's cult of reason and Robespierre's cult of the supreme being to be at once idolatrous and artificial, and equally inadequate to the task at hand, and elsewhere he acknowledged that scientific reason and immanent ideology would never altogether take the place of religion rooted in a sense of transcendence.[5] That Quinet took virtually no notice of the only religiously going concern in eighteenth-century France that might have answered to his purpose, that hardly a line in eight hundred pages is devoted to Jansenism or more broadly to eighteenth-century reform Catholicism—all this may be testimony to Quinet's simplistic conflation of Catholicism with political absolutism and of absolutism in turn with the whole Old Regime, but to very little else.

Contra Quinet, the argument of this book has insisted on nothing if not the religious, indeed Catholic, origins of the undoing of absolutism and especially on the Jansenist Catholic provenance of notions of political liberty in eighteenth-century France. In playing this role, Jansenism, while remaining discernibly Catholic, transmitted a part of the Protestant monarchomach heritage to the eighteenth century as well as becoming a little more Protestant itself. It is of course true that the Jansenist moment had also come and gone in France. That the monarchy's chronic fiscal insolvency did not come to crisis point until 1789 rather than, say, in 1730, 1750, or even 1770 meant that the Revolution inherited only the ragtag remains of a movement that, for all the damage it did to sacral absolutism, itself emerged from numerous exiles, interdictions, and the Bastille very much the worse for the wear. Bona fide Jansenists in the National Assembly did not add up to a party, what party there was had blurred into ideological "patriotism," and even Jansenistical patriotism had to share the podium with Rousseauians like Robespierre and religious skeptics like Mirabeau. Whether Rousseauian or skeptical, French revolutionary disciples of the philosophes were more anti-Catholic than elsewhere; and whether Jansenist or not, French priests encountered more popular hostility than ever before.

That much said—and it is a great deal—it remains true that both the Protestant and Jansenist controversies had left profound cleavages in the religious

4. Ibid., p. 411.
5. Ibid., p. 718.

sensibility and geography of Old Regime France. During the Revolution itself, these cleavages showed up in contrasts like that between a rural Angevin West, which went to war against the Revolution under the ensign of the Sacred Heart while protecting refractory priests, and a formerly Jansenist–and still earlier Protestant–Auxerrois Southeast that wanted Catholicism and the Revolution too, and experimented with lay masses in the absence of exiled priests.[6] Left to its own devices after 1795–the Revolution's brief experience with separating church from state–the formerly constitutional church led by the abbé Grégoire elaborated a polity featuring church councils seconded by diocesan synods including lay delegates, and wanted only the Revolution's benevolent neutrality in order to bless the republic, antipapalism and all.[7] But what it got instead was a persecution that, especially after September 1797, was the equal of the Great Terror's and that fell on the formerly juring and nonjuring alike. Having thus deprived itself of any fulcrum in the French religious conscience, the Revolution, in Quinet's words, "had the knack of unleashing all religions against itself without having legally or officially proscribed any one of them."[8]

If tragedy there was, it was neither that the early Revolution dared to reform the church at all nor, as Quinet thought, that it reformed it too little, but rather that it reformed it in such a way as to divide and ultimately to alienate even that considerable body of Catholic opinion sympathetic to radical ecclesiastical reform and, potentially, to the Revolution itself. The decisive–and divisive–factor in this reform was the National Assembly's dogmatic opposition to autonomous partial associations arguably inherited from absolutism, whence its decision to promulgate the Civil Constitution of the Clergy exclusively on it own secular authority and its refusal to allow for a meeting of a national council that alone would have enabled Gallican churchmen to accept the reforms in good conscience in the face of certain papal anathemas. And although radical Gallicans or judicial Jansenists were certainly able to and did justify this initiative by secular authority, that initiative itself unquestionably came from the Mirabeaus, Le Chapeliers, and Robespierres, bearers of the torch of enlightenment all. And although obviously not Catholic, these thus played the role of executors of the absolutist will as drawn up in reaction to the sixteenth-century reformations. The result in the long run was to have doomed even the constitutional church, radicalized the Revolution against both churches, thrown most of the clergy into arms of the papacy, and ensured the triumph of the devout and ultramontanist variety of Catholicism that

6. Suzanne Desan, *Reclaiming the Sacred: Lay Religion and Popular Politics in Revolutionary France* (Ithaca, 1990); and Timothy Tackett, "The West in 1789: The Religious Factor in the Origins of the Counterrevolution," *JMH* 54 (1982):714–45.

7. Bernard Plongeron," Chrétiens-citoyens en dialogue: Les structures de l'église constitutionelle (1790–1801)," in *L'abbé Grégoire (1750–1831) ou l'arch de la fraternité* (Paris, 1989), pp. 75–78.

8. Quinet, *La Révolution,* p. 181.

Quinet so readily associated with legitimism and political reaction in his own day, not only in France but in the rest of Catholic Europe as well. Thus began an ever more sterile standoff that, in France, made perennial enemies of Catholicism and political liberalism, as neither Lamennais's attempts to liberalize Catholicism nor Victor Cousin's project of "spiritualizing" liberalism took root, and an anticlerical French Left carried on without much spiritual help from the church, while Catholicism chronically compromised itself in association with first a royalist and later a quasi-fascist right.

But only a purely institutional conception of religion would justify the conclusion that its relation to the Revolution was uniquely negative. For better or worse, as Quinet knew, religion as mediated by ideology entered into the very texture of revolutionary republicanism, making sense of many of its otherwise paradoxical traits. Quinet himself would have laid unique stress on the Catholic origins of an ideological quest for a republican community that, like Catholic unity, brooked no dissent, and to the construction of a state outside of which, like the church, there was no salvation. And to someone writing in exile against a tinhorn dictatorial regime that doted over the post-Napoleonic concordatary clergy in the wake of yet another failed revolution, it may well have seemed that such was indeed Catholicism's last and most enduring political legacy. But that was not the end of the story, nor had even Quinet's kind of Catholicism invariably sided with "order," as witnessed by Lamennais's extraordinary pilgrimage from ultramontanist royalism to Catholic republicanism around 1830. So while doing full justice to the absolutist affinities of "devout" Catholicism, this book has put equal if not entirely opposite emphasis on the Catholic as well as Protestant origins of notions of constitutional liberty, the inviolability of the conscience, the duty to disobey unjust authority, and the right to resist the majority, even if, in the Jansenist case, these rights and duties were typically justified in the very name of the authorities and majorities at issue. If, thus more catholically understood, Catholicism's ideological and political legacy seems internally contradictory rather than merely paradoxical, then so is French republican political culture itself, consisting as it has in just this bewildering balance between quest for community and individual defiance, between authority and spaces off-limits to it. That is to say that if, in an obvious sense, French republicanism put religion behind it, it did not do so without retaining the ideological stigmata of religion.

Bibliographical Note

I HAVE NOT CONCLUDED THIS STUDY WITH AN EXHAUSTIVE bibliography of the materials it has used, mainly out of consideration for space. The number of titles consulted for the last chapter alone exceeds a thousand, consisting of the entire bibliography of section 5, "The Pre-Revolutionary Debate," in Pergamon Press's bicentennial *French Revolution Research Collection*, plus the revolutionary periodicals, the *Archives parlementaires*, and the titles relating to the controversy over the Civil Constitution of the Clergy, most of these accessible in Chicago's Newberry Library and its magnificent French Revolution Collection. Besides the *Nouvelles ecclésiastiques*, Jules Flammermont's edition of the Parlement of Paris's remonstrances, and such standard memoirs and journals as those of Barbier and d'Argenson, the other printed primary sources on which this book is based consist mainly of the books and pamphlets listed chronologically in Taschereu's and Marchal's *Catalogue de l'histoire de France*, 15 vols. (Paris, 1855–59), especially vol. 2, "Histoire politique par règne," series Ld4; and vol. 5, "Détails de l'histoire ecclésiastique," series Ld38&39. The call numbers in this catalogue are of course for the Bibliothèque nationale, although many of the books and pamphlets in question may also be found in the Bibliothèque de l'Arsenal and Adrien Le Paige's library in the Bibliothèque de Port-Royal as well as in the Bibliothèque Mazarine.

The most important manuscript sources used in this study include the entire Le Paige Collection in the Bibliothèque de Port-Royal (which is being moved from 169 rue Saint-Jacques to the ruins of Port-Royal-des-Champs near Saint-Remy-les-Chevreuse); the entire Joly de Fleury Collection and Anisson-Duperron collections in the Bibliothèque nationale; Hardy's and Lefebvre de Beauvray's manuscript diaries, also in the Bibliothèque nationale; the registers and some of the trial records of the Parlement of Paris (series X) and the archives of the Paris commissioners of police (series Y), both in the Archives nationales; the pertinent portions of the Lamoignon de Malesherbes (AP 154) and the Maurepas papers (AP 257), also in the Archives nationales; and the Archives de la Bastille, especially the police reports for the 1720s and 1730s and the individual dossiers for the 1750s and early 1770s, which are housed in the Bibliothèque de l'Arsenal.

Three books on eighteenth-century French political history, all published by Cambridge University Press, appeared just as this book was going to press. They are Munro Price's *Preserving the Monarchy: The Comte de Vergennes, 1774–1787*, John Rogister's long-awaited *Louis XV and the Parlement of Paris, 1737–1754*, and Julian Swann's *Politics and the Parlement of Paris under Louis XV, 1754–1774*. As I am not entirely unfamiliar with the thinking of all three authors, and as their books treat of political history at a level considerably more microscopic than does mine, they are not likely to have altered this book's general argument significantly.

Index